FUN FAMILY

1,100 things to do with your kids
on *Long Island* **& Beyond**
Includes Over **450 FREE** *Activities*

By Linda Reid Bryce

Escapade
Publishing

Published by
Escapade Publishing, LLC, P.O. Box 361, Woodbury, NY 11797 USA
www.escapadepublishing.com
ISBN 978-0-9822391-0-0

Proofreading & Editing by Christina Heiser
Printed and bound in the United States

Attention authors: If you would like to publish a similar book in your area please
contact: **Escapade**Publishing@verizon.net or www·**Escapade**Publishing·com

This book is available in quantity discounts for bulk purchases.
For information, contact Linda Vorbach at: **Escapade**Publishing@*verizon.net*

∼

Note to our readers: Although Escapade Publishing and the author of Fun Family
*have taken reasonable care in preparing this book, we make no warranty about the
accuracy or completeness of its content, and to the maximum extent permitted,
disclaim all liability arising from its use. The information contained within these
pages has been acquired through many public sources. Since that time,
information may have been added, cancelled, corrected or altered. The events
described reflect the previous year's agenda and may be different in the coming year.
Always double-check all pertinent information before registering for or attending
events as well as visiting specific locations. In an attempt to fit as many activities as
possible within these pages, this book speaks through an abbreviated format.*

∼

ABOUT THE AUTHOR

Hi, I'm Linda Reid Bryce and I grew up in East Northport right here on Long Island. My goal in writing this book was to create an easy-to-navigate resource where you can quickly find things to do with kids on Long Island: A book that would fit in your backpack, pocketbook or glove compartment. If the kids in your life are into speed, vehicles of flight, dinosaurs, lighthouses, boats, seal watching, skate parks, go-karts, art, planetariums or animals, you can find it all here. There is even a comprehensive table of contents and index to aid in helping you on your journey as a family. My hope for your children and mine is that when they look back on their childhood they remember having had great times and adventures with their families... the kinds of memories that spark warm feelings, laughter and close ties.

> **"**This book was inspired by two distinct roles that we as parents keep finding ourselves playing. The first is Spectator. We attend events and watch our children having fun. The second is Sender. We send our children away to have fun. I kept asking myself, 'What will my children remember about the time when we were a family if these are the most common modals we live by?' In the busy world we live in, it is hard to find the time to plan new and interesting outings for our children.**"**

This resource attempts to make it easier for parents, grandparents, aunts, uncles teachers, scout leaders and anyone who interacts with children to quickly find fun on Long Island with the children in their lives. It is my dream that this book will help procure memories built on laughter, adventure, exercise, and most of all fun. My hope is for children to see life as both fascinating and jovial.

I have always loved my time growing up and living on Long Island. I attended John Glenn High School in East Northport, got my B.A. in Art Education from Hofstra University and received my M.A. in English Education at St. John's University. I also studied many areas of the visual arts at The School of Visual Arts in Manhattan, and I studied abroad at the Byram Shaw School of Drawing and Painting in London. My education helped me have a successful career as both an artist and a writer. After working in New York City as an Art Director, I moved to Sweden and worked with clients such as SAAB Cars and Scandinavian IBM. With the opening of the Eastern Bloc I became a creative consultant in Poland for the United Nations Development Project. I am a recipient of Sweden's "50 Watt Award" in the Annual Report category, have had several solo painting exhibitions in Europe, and have been an invited speaker in both the United States and Europe.

My husband Jim and I have two boys, two panda hamsters named Cupcake and Felix, a fighting fish named Fighty and a gecko named Leo.

Let Fun Flow Like A River

Linda can be reached at: Linda.ReidBryce@verizon.net
Escapade Publishing LLC, P.O. Box 361, Woodbury, NY 11797

CONTENTS

CONTENTS

CONTENTS

Family

Fun Happens

Have you ever gone on a whale watch?
A seal walk?
What about a pumpkin fling?
Ever followed a butterfly's erratic flight?
Climbed the lighthouse steps to the tiptop?
Been to a hot air balloon festival?
Driven in a go-kart race?
Canoed down a river?
Hiked through a sunken forest?

When they transition from childhood,
What do you want your children to remember
About the time when you were a family?

Discover fun within these pages and
Let Fun Flow Like A River

Town of Riverhead

Riverhead	Northville
Aquebogue	Roanoke
Baiting Hollow	Wading River
Jamesport	

Town of Brookhaven

Bellport	Medford
Blue Point	Middle Island
Brookhaven	Miller Place
Mastic, Mastic	Moriches
Beach & Shirley	Mount Sinai
Port Jefferson	Old Field
Patchogue	Poquott
Stony Brook	Port Jefferson
Belle Terre	Station
Calverton	Ridge
Centereach	Rocky Point
Center Moriches	Selden
Coram	Setauket
East Moriches	Shirley
East Patchogue	Shoreham
Eastport	Sound Beach
Farmingville	South Haven
Holbrook	South Manor
Holtsville	Speonk
Hagerman	Terryville
Lake Grove	Yaphank

Town of Huntington

East Northport	Greenlawn
Huntington	Halesite
Northport Village	Wheatley Heights
Northport	Huntington Bay
Asharoken	Huntington
Centerport	Station
Cold Spring	Lloyd Harbor
Harbor	Lloyd Neck
Dix Hills	Melville
Eaton's Neck	South Huntington
Elwood	

Town of North Hempstead

Great Neck	Great Neck
Village	Estates
Great Neck	Herricks
Chamber of	Kings Point
Commerce	Manhasset
Manhasset	Manorhaven
New Hyde Park	New Salem
Port Washington	North Hills
Saddle Rock	Roslyn
Sands Point	Roslyn Heights
Albertson	Searingtown
East Williston	Stewart Manor
Floral Park	Westbury
Flower Hill	Williston Park

Town of Southold

Greenport	Mattituck
Mattituck	Orient Point
Chamber	Peconic
Cutchogue	Southold
Laurel	

Town of Southampton

East Quogue	Rose Grove
Hampton Bays	Sagaponack
Sag Harbor	Sag Harbor
Sag Harbor	Scuttlehole
Bridgehampton	Shinnecock Hills
Flanders	Southampton
Hampton Bays	Tiana
Mecox	Tuckahoe
North Haven	Water Mill
North Sea	Westhampton
Noyack	Westhampton
Quogue	Beach
Remsenburg	

Town of Smithtown

St. James	Kings Park
Smithtown	Lake Ronkonkoma
Commack	Nesconset
Fort Salonga	Nissequogue
Hauppauge	San Remo
Head of the	
Harbor	

City of Glen Cove

Town of Oyster Bay

Bayville	Jericho
Bethpage	Laurel Hollow
Hicksville	Locust Valley
Massapequa Park	Massapequa
Plainview	Matinecock
Old Bethpage	Mill Neck
Syosset	Muttontown
Syosset	Old Bethpage
Woodbury	Old Brookville
Brookville	Oyster Bay
Centre Island	Oyster Bay Cove
Cove Neck	Plainedge
East Hills	Upper Brookville
East Norwich	Woodbury
Farmingdale	

Town of East Hampton

East Hampton	Hardscrabble
East Hampton	Springs
Montauk	Wainscott
Amagansett	
Georgica	

Town of Islip

Bay Port-Blue	Brightwaters
Point	Central Islip
Bay Shore	East Islip
East Islip	Great River
Oakdale	Islandia
Ocean Beach	Islip
Sayville	Islip Terrace
West Islip	Oakdale
Bohemia	West Islip
Brentwood	

Town of Babylon

Amityville	Deer Park
Babylon Village	East Farmingdale
Lindenhurst	North Amityville
Bay Shore	Wyandanch
Copaigue	

City of Long Beach

Town of Hempstead

Baldwin	East Meadow
Bellmore	East Rockaway
Chamber of	Hempstead
Commerce	Hewlett Harbor
Elmont	Inwood
Franklin Square	Island Park
Freeport	Lake Success
Village	Malverne
Garden City	Mineola
Levittown	New Hyde Park
Lynbrook	North Woodmere
Chamber of	Oceanside
Commerce	Old Westbury
Merrrick Chamber	Plandome
of Commerce	Roosevelt
New Hyde Park	Seaford
Village	Uniondale
Rockville Centre	Wantagh
Uniondale	Woodmere
Valley Stream	
Cedarhurst	

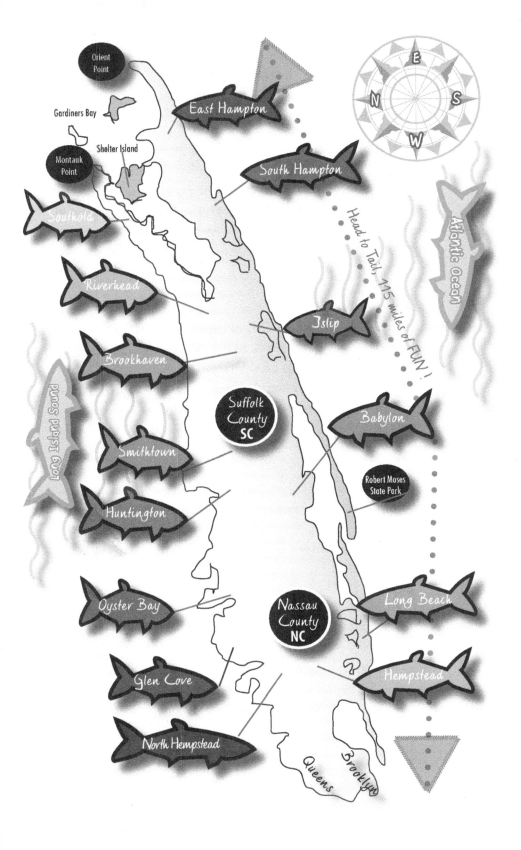

Thanks

• Thanks to the park rangers and their support staff all over Long Island. I acknowledge with deep appreciation their committed efforts and personal dedication in providing so many services for the general public. They offer well informed educational programs for our children, rescue us from emergency situations, take us on hikes, teach us about the various ecosystems on Long Island while gently reminding all of us to be proactive in protecting our environment. Their commitment to great service provides so much to the quality of our lives. They are always helpful, supportive and fun.

• The circle of angels, friends and colleagues-particularly the Balesano family, the Baranowski family, the Cach family, the Carter family, the Delle family, the Forno family, the Graceffo family, the Gurovich family, the Horn family, the Agramonte-Hynes family, the Leibowitz family, the Lewin family, the Valentine-O'Beirne family, the Parrish family, the Ryan family, the Scala family, the Schnieder family, the Taylor family, the Marino-Thompson family, the Vergis family, the White Family, the Witt family, the Yaboni family and Peter Smith, Marlena Luhr, Joy Graceffo, and Stephanie Graceffo who not only add great value to my life but generously allowed photos of their families having fun on Long Island to be used in this book.

• A very special note of appreciation to long time friend Kathy Berbig-Rus who has always been a great source of inspiration, and support throughout my life.

• My dear friend Christina Maida who has added literary value, good times and insight into myself and the editing of this book.

• My inspiring family Jim, Reid and Bryce who always surprises me while offering support, love, advice, and adding spirituality to my life.

• I want to send a big hug to Lisa Parrish who gave me the courage to write this book.

Linda Reid Bryce

This book is dedicated to
my husband Jim and my two children Reid and Bryce
whom inspired the quest for fun.

Let Fun Flow Like A River

SUGGESTIONS • COMMENTS • ERRORS

Linda.ReidBryce
@verizon.net

Thanks

Join our blog or buy a copy of **Fun Family** at:
www.**Escapade**Publishing•com

STOP — Read This First!

Icons used in this book

Whenever I want to indicate a family favorite location, I mark it with a Heart Icon.

SC The **SC** Icon marks locations governed by the The Suffolk County Department of Parks, Recreation and Conservation. *www.co.suffolk.ny.us/*

NC The **NC** Icon marks locations governed by the The Nassau County Department of Parks Recreation and Museums. *www.nassaucountyny.gov/*

NYS The **NYS** Icon refers to the New York State Department of Parks, Recreation and Historic Preservation. *http://nysparks.state.ny.us/sites/info*

Free The Free icon marks locations that offer free admission and sometimes free parking.

All information in this book is based on the previous two years events. Please check individual location web sites or call for exact and current dates, fees, and specific activities.

EMPIRE PASS

New York State Parks provides New York State residents unlimited day use & vehicle entry to most of New York's State parks and recreational facilities. The Passport provides access to 178 state parks, 55 Department of Environmental Conservation (DEC) forest preserve areas, and to boat launch sites, arboretums & park preserves.

Residents Empire Pass:
$65, valid for one year
Call: **518-474-0458**
Online Orders:
nysparks.state.ny.us/admission/empire-passport/default.aspx

GREEN KEY

Suffolk County's Green Key Card is required to access the automated golf & camping reservation system. It provides county residents with reduced fees for park activities. Green Key Cards can be purchased in person with proof of residency.

Residents Green Key:
$20, valid for three years
Non-Residents Green Key:
$35, valid for one year
The card can be purchased via phone, Mon.-Fri. 8:30 a.m.-4:30 p.m. with a credit card.
Call main office:
631-854-4949
Online Orders:
http://www.thefishingline.com/get.htm

LEISURE PASS

Nassau County's Leisure Pass provides residents with discounts to parks & locations operated by the county.

Residents Leisure Pass:
$25, valid for three years
There are Leisure Pass offices at: Cantiague Park, Christopher Morley Park, Eisenhower Park, Grant Park, Nickerson Beach Park, North Woodmere Park & Wantagh Park.
http://www.nassaucountyny.gov/agencies/Parks/leisure.html

1 **IN THIS SECTION**

Fall Events

FALL FOLLY

Let
Fun Flow
Like A
River

FALL EVENTS

SCARE CROWS, HOT CIDER, & BOLD COLORS

September

Annual Bayville Waterside Festival • *347-203-8269* • **Features Include:** 2-Day Festival, Kid's Inflatable Attractions, Music, Arts & Crafts Exhibits, Clam Eating Contest, Food Court, Clams (courtesy of the North Oyster Bay Baymen's Association), Overlooking 1 of the most scenic views of Long Island Sound **Hours:** Usually during the first weekend in Sept. **Fee: Free** admission, Free Parking & Shuttle Bus **Directions:** *I-495 Long Island Expwy., take exit 41 N., Rte. 106N. (toward Oyster Bay), cross 25A and continue toward the village, signs will direct visitors to parking areas & access to the free shuttle bus service to the waterfront* www.bayvillechamberofcommerce.com • www.theoysterfestival.org

St. James Day Street Festival • *Lake Ave., St. James, NY* • *631-584-8510* • **Features Include:** Children's Activities, Music, Dancing, Crafts, Gifts, Vendors, Food **Hours:** 10 a.m.-5 p.m., usually the last weekend in Sept. **Fee: Free Directions:** *I-495 Long Island Expwy., take exit 53 toward Bay Shore/Kings Park/Sagtikos Pkwy., merge onto Sagtikos State Pkwy., continue on Sunken Meadow Pkwy., take exit SM3E. for Jericho Tpke./NY-25 toward Smithtown, merge onto Jericho Tpke./NY-25, turn Left onto Lake Ave., activities are between Woodland & Railroad Ave.* www.stjameschamber.org

Country Fair • *Sands Willets House* • *336 Port Washington Blvd., Port Washington, NY* • **Features Include:** House circa 1735, Period Costumed Event, Face Painting, Crafts for Kids, Pony Rides, Live Sea Creatures, Petting Zoo, Fly Tying, Civil War Soldiers **Hours:** Sat.-Sun.: 10 a.m.-5 p.m. mid-Sept., **Directions:** *I-495 Long Island Expwy., to exit 36 toward Searingtown Rd., merge onto N. Service Rd., turn Right onto Searingtown Rd., continue on Port Washington Blvd., make a U-turn at Concord Rd.* www.cowneck.org

FALL FOLLY

10th Annual Chili/Chowder Contest • *Presented by Hampton Bays Chamber of Commerce* • *Boardy Barn* • *270 W. Montauk Hwy., Hampton Bays, NY* • *631-728-2211*• Features Include: Chili & Chowder Competition, Restaurants & Individuals Submissions, Fun Family, Face Painting, Children's Games **Fee:** Adults $10, Kids $3, **Hours:** Noon-4 p.m., last week in Sept. **Directions:** *I-495 Long Island Expwy., exit 67 toward Yaphank, turn Right onto Yaphank Ave., turn Left onto Country Rd. 16/Horseblock Rd. merge onto NY 27 E., exit onto Riverhead-Hampton Bays Rd., turn Right onto Montauk Hwy. W., the festival will be on the Right*

Garlic Festival • *Garden of Eve* • *4558 Sound Ave., Riverhead, NY* • *631-722-8777* • Features Include: Garlic-Inspired Foods, Crafts, Live Music, Farm Tours, Pony Rides, Organic Foods, Local Agriculture **Hour:** Sat. & Sun.: 10 a.m.-6 p.m., usually the last weekend in Sept. **Fee:** $2, Under 6: Free **Directions:** *I-495 Long Island Expwy., exit 73 Old Country Rd., Orient/Greenport/Co Hwy. 58, slight Left onto Rte. 58 Old Country Rd., turn Left onto Rte. 43 Northville Tpke., turn Right onto Sound Ave., turn Left onto Pennys Rd.* *www.gardenofevefarm.com*

Long Island Naturally - Environmental Fair • *Manor Farm* • *Manor Rd., Huntington, NY* • *516-938-6152* • Features Include: Environmental Fun/Learning, Exhibits, Games, Community Yard Sale, Demonstrations of Environment-Friendly Practices, Folk Music, Local Wildlife Safari **Hours:** 10 a.m.-5 p.m., usually the last weekend in Sept. **Fee:** **Free** Directions: *Northern State Pkwy., take exit 42 N., Deek Park Ave. N., bear Left at the fork (firehouse), 1ˢᵗ light turn Right onto Old Country Rd., Left onto Jericho Tpke., make an immediate Right onto Manor Rd. (Green Cactus on corner), make a Right turn just past the blinking light into the farm* *www.starflowerexperiences.org*

Fall Festival • *Brightwaters Farms & Nursery* • *162 Manatuck Blvd., Bay Shore, NY* • *631-665-5411* • Features Include: Live Entertainment, Unlimited Hayrides, Giant Inflatables, Trikes & Small Tractor Ride, Face Painting, Characters, Farm Animals, Pumpkin Picking, Hay Rides, Pony Rides, Little Farmers Playland, Nursery, Barn Animals, Fresh Apple Cider, Homemade Pies, Roasted Corn, Orchard Apples, Working Farm, Seasonal Family Events **Hours:** Mid Sept.-Oct. 31, Mon.-Sat.: 9 a.m.-6 p.m., Sun.: 9 a.m.-4 p.m. **Fee:** $5, Under 1 Free, downloadable discount coupon **Directions:** *Southern State Pkwy, exit 42 S., turn Right off the exit ramp onto Spur Dr. S., turn Right onto Manatuck Blvd. (at traffic light), proceed North on Manatuck Blvd. Brightwaters Farms will be on the Left .5 mi. up the road* *www.brightwatersfarms.com*

Annual Bellmore Family Street Festival • *Dellamore Parking Field* • *Bellmore, NY* • *516-679-1875* • Features Include: Character Parade, Live Entertainment, Animal Zone, Crafts, Carnival, Interactive Games For kids, Shows for Kids, Remote Control

Model Airplane Display, Car Show, Pony Rides, Petting Zoo, Kiddie Rides, Face Painting, Balloon Sculpting, Cookie Painting, Spin/Wax/Sand Art, Craft Expo, Sports Expo, Information Technology Expo, Health & Safety Expo, Military Expo, Firefighter/ Police Demonstrations, Petting Zoo, Car Show, International Foods, Rides **Hours:** Parade: Sat. & Sun.: Noon, Thurs.-Fri.: 6 p.m.–11 p.m., Sat. & Sun.: 11 a.m.–11 p.m., usually during the last weekend in Sept. **Fee:** Admission, parking, & shuttle bus: **Free**, there is a fee for the rides **Directions:** *Seaford-Oyster Bay Expwy. 135 S. to exit 2W. Sunrise Hwy. W., turn Right onto Centre Ave., turn Right onto Pettit Ave., the station will be on the Left, take the shuttle bus to the fair* *http://bellmorechamber.com*

East Northport Annual Festival • *John Walsh Park • 24 Larkfield Rd., East Northport, NY • 631-261-3573* • Features Include: Magic Show, Exhibits, Petting Zoo, Bicycle Stunt Shows, Rides, Games, Live Entertainment, Performers, Sidewalk Sale, Craft Vendors, Food **Hours:** Fri.: 6-11 p.m., Sat.: 11 a.m.-11 p.m., Sun.: 11 a.m.-6 p.m., usually during early Sept. **Fee: Free** entry **Directions:** *Northern State Pkwy., to exit 42N. toward Northport, merge onto Deer Park Ave., merge onto Jericho Tpke. E., turn Left onto Larkfield Rd., festival is on the corner of Pulaski Rd. & Larkfield Rd.* *www.eastnorthport.com/annual_events_festival.asp*

The Long Island Fair ⊗ • *Old Bethpage Village Restoration • Round Swamp Rd., Old Bethpage, NY • 516-572-8400* • Features Include: 19th Century Fair, Competitions, Vintage Baseball Games, Potato Sack Races, Interactive Farm Exhibition, Jugglers, Puppet Shows, Magicians, Wagon Rides, Contra Dancing, Traditional Music, Food, Brass Bands, Children's Flying Horse Carousel, Tour the Village, Prize Winning Plants & Farm Animals, Hobbies, Crafts, Needlework, Craft Show **Hours:** Thurs. & Fri.: 10 a.m.-5 p.m., Sat.: 10 a.m.- 6 p.m., usually during the last weekend in Sept. **Fee:** Adults $10, Kids & Seniors $5, Under 5: Free **Directions:** *I-495 Long Island Expwy., exit 48 Round Swamp Rd. toward Old Bethpage/ Farmingdale, make a Left onto Round Swamp Rd., turn Left onto Old Country Rd., make a slight Right onto Round Swamp Rd.* *www.lifair.org*

White Post Farms ⊗ • *Annual Fall Farm Festival • 250 Old Country Rd. Melville, NY • 631-351-9373* • Features Include: Hay Rides, Storytellers, Singing Chicken Show, Clowns, Game Shows, Balloon Boomer Blaster Game, Play in the Hay, Bounce-n- Slide Inflatable, Wooden Playground, Feed the Animals, Pony & Train Rides, Pumpkin Picking **Hours:** Sat. & Sun.: 10 a.m.-6 p.m., mid Sept.-last weekend in Oct. **Fee:** $14 per person **Directions:** *Northern State Pkwy., exit 40S. (Rte. 110), turn Left at 1st light onto Old Country Rd., the farm is .25 mi. on the Right* *www.whitepostfarms.com*

FALL FOLLY

Wildwood Fall Festival • *Wildwood State Park* • *Hulse Landing Rd., Wading River, NY* • *631-321-3510* • **Features Include:** Pony Rides, Wagon Rides, Inflatables, Funny Photos, Magic Show, Games, Children's Entertainment, Pie-Eating Contest, Environmental Displays, Crafts Fair, Food **Hours:** 11 a.m.-4 p.m., last weekend in Sept. **Fee: Free,** Parking: $6 **Directions:** *I-495 Long Island Expwy., to exit 68 N. on Rte. 46, to Rte. 25A E., turn Left onto Sound Ave., turn Left at traffic light onto Hulse Landing Rd., park entrance is on the Right* www.nysparks.com

Annual Auto Show • *Robert Moses State Park, Robert Moses Cswy., Fire Island, NY* • *Fire Island Lighthouse* • *Fire Island National Sea Shore & Fire Island Lighthouse Preservation Society* • *Programs & Special Events* • *631-661-4876* • *631-669-0470* •. **Features Include:** Vintage Car Display, Day on the Bay, Lantern Light Tour, Self Guided Tours, Ranger at the top to answer questions, Lighthouse Keepers Behind the Scenes Tour (every other month at 9 a.m.) **Hours:** Sat. & Sun.: 10 a.m-4 p.m., last weekend in Sept. or first weekend in Oct. **Fee:** Adults: $10, Kids: $5 **Directions:** *Southern State Pkwy. to Robert Moses Cswy., to exit 40 S., park in Field 5 & walk to the lighthouse* www.fireislandlighthouse.com

Great Neck Antiques & Antique Auto Extravaganza • *Sponsored by The Village of Great Neck Plaza & BID Business Improvement District* • *North Station Plaza, LIRR Station, Great Neck, NY* • *516-868-2751* • **Features Include:** 100 Antique Automobiles on Display, Model A's and T's, Buicks, Cadillacs, Jaguars, Bentleys, Music, Clowns, Rides, Games, Hayrides, Petting Zoo, Pony Rides, Art Show, Minstrels, Multicultural Foods **Hours:** Noon-5 p.m., mid-Sept. **Fee: Free Directions:** *I-495 Long Island Expwy., to exit 33 Community Dr./Lakeville Rd., merge onto N. Service Rd., continue on Horace Harding Blvd., turn Right onto Lakeville Rd., continue on S. Middle Neck Rd., turn Right into S. Station Plaza, the train station will be on the Left* www.pekaleshows.com • www.greatneckplaza.net

Long Island Car Show & Swap Meet • *Presented by LongIslandCars.com* • *Bar Beach Park , 802 W. Shore Rd., Port Washington, NY* • *516-767-4625* • *631-567-5898* • **Features Include:** Street Rods, Antiques, Muscle Cars, SUVs, Imports, Cars of the 50s, 60s & 70s, Custom Cars, Exotic Cars, Show Cars **Hours:** 8 a.m.-5 p.m., last weekend in Sept. or the first in Oct., **Fee:** Adults: $8, **Directions:** *I-495 Long Island Expwy. to exit 37 Willis Ave., merge onto Old Powerhouse Rd., turn Right onto Mineola Ave., turn Right onto Layton St., take the 1st Right onto Old Northern Blvd., turn Left onto W. Shore Rd., the beach will be on the Right* www.LongIslandCars.com

LABOR DAY WEEKEND

Grande Festa Italiana • *North Hempstead Beach Park* • *North Hempstead Beach Park, W. Shore Rd, Port Washington, NY* • *516-767-3123* • **Features Include:** Rides, Games,

Prizes, Live Entertainment, Gambling Casino, Craft Vendors, 1 of Long Island's oldest & Biggest Festivals, Cooking Demonstrations, Fireworks **Hours:** Wed.-Fri.: 6 p.m.-11 p.m., Sat.-Sun.: 2 p.m.-11 p.m. **Fee:** *Free* entry, Kids Ride Free on Sun. from 12:30-1:30 p.m., usually Wed.-Sun. after Labor Day **Directions:** *I-495 Long Island Expwy. to exit 37, turn Left on Roslyn Rd. follow to end (just over 1 mi.), bear Left onto W. Shore Rd. (clock tower on Right), continue for 2.4 mi., Festa & parking entrance on Right* *www.marinolodge.org/festival.html* • *http://nassaucountyny.gov/agencies/Parks*

Annual Labor Day Sand Creation Contest • *Watch Hill: 631-597-6455* • *Sailors Haven: 631 597-6183* • **Features Include:** End of Season Celebration, Creativity, Ingenuity, All Ages Welcome, this event usually takes place during Labor Day weekend **Fee:** *Free* **Directions:** *Please see Fire Island Ferries in the back of the Summer Boating section, for info about the Patchogue-to-Watch Hill ferry service.* *www.davisparkferry.com*

MEDIEVAL & RENAISSANCE

Medieval Festival ⊗ • *Sands Point Preserve* • *127 Middleneck Rd., Port Washington, NY* • *516-571-7900* • **Features Include:** Period Entertainment, Royal Court Procession, Archery Demonstrations, Madrigal Singers, Maypole Dance, Medieval-Style Puppet Show, Lords & Ladies Fashion Show, Games for Kids & Adults, each day closes with a rescue attempt to free the queen by "Storming Castelgould" **Hours:** 11 a.m.-5 p.m., usually during the 1st 2 weekends in Sept. **Fee:** Adults: $10, Kids 4-12: $5, Under 4: Free **Directions:** *I-495 Long Island Expwy. to exit 36 Searingtown Rd. N., drive for approx. 6 mi., the road becomes Port Washington Blvd. & then Middleneck Rd., entrance is on the Right 1 mi. past the stone & brick gate of the Sand Point Village Club* *www.sandspointpreserve.org*

Medieval Festival • *The Cloisters Museum & Gardens* • *99 Margaret Corbin Dr., NY, NY,* • *212 923-3700* • **Location: Fort Tryon Park in northern Manhattan** • *Festival Information: 212-795-1600* • *Information: 212-781-4051 or 212-408-0217* • **Features Include:** Royal Procession, Celtic Music, Musical Performances, Mystic Minstrels, the Living Chess Game, Children's Costume Parade, Music on Period Instruments, Magicians, Celtic Dancers, Medieval Knights Joust, Medieval Art, Hudson River Views, Medieval Customs, Medieval Market Town, Little Theatre for Children's Shows, Plays, Tournaments **Hours:** Sun.: 11:30 a.m.-6 p.m., end of Sept. **Fee:** $2 parking **Directions:** *Fort Tryon Park is North of 190th St. & South of Dyckman St., between Broadway and the river. By Train/Bus: Take the A Train to 190th St., or the M4 Madison Ave. bus uptown, By Car: Take the Henry Hudson Pkwy. to the 178th St. exit, a Free shuttle bus will run from the Columbia-Presbyterian Medical Center parking garage, at 165th St. & Fort Washington Ave. (Parking is $2)* *www.whidc.org/cloisters.html*

Renaissance Festival • *600 Rte. 17A, Sterling Forest, Tuxedo Park, NY • 845-351-5171* • Features Include: Renaissance Village, Period Entertainment, Crafts, Food, Games Hours: 10 a.m.-7 p.m., usually Aug.-Sept. Fee: Adults: $16.75, Kids 5-12: $7.50, Under 5: Free Directions: *I-495 Long Island Expwy. to exit 31 Cross Island Pkwy. S., take exit I-295 N. toward New England, George Washington Bridge, take I-95 S. to Rte. 4 W., take Rte. 17, follow signs for 17 N. (Exit 15A off NYS Thruway), continue 8 mi. to Rte. 17A, make Left into the fair grounds*   *www.renfair.com*

NAUTICAL THEMES

Fall Harvest & Seafood Festival Captree Carnival • *Captree State Park • Ocean Dr. • P.O. Box 247, Babylon, NY • 631-669-0449 • 631-581-1072 • Group Tours: 631-669-1000, ext. 223 • 631- 321-3510* • Features Include: Crab Races, Activities for Children, Boat Rides, Interactive Pirate Show, Wine Tasting Hours: 11 a.m.-5 p.m., usually during mid-Sept. Fee: Free entry Directions: *Southern State Pkwy. to exit 40 S., Robert Moses Cswy. S. to Park*   *http://nysparks.state.ny.us/parks*

Maritime Festival • *Organized by the East End Seaport Museum & Marine Foundation • Greenport, NY • 631-477-2100* • Features Include: Kayak Derby, Whale Boat Race, Clam Chowder Contest, Parade, Live Music, Land & Sea Cocktail Reception (Fri. evening), 106 Rescue Demonstration, HC-130 Hercules & the HH-60 Rescue Helicopter, Mitchell Park Family Activities Include: Captain Kid's Alley, Old-Fashioned Children's Games, Snapper Fishing Contest, Traditional Arts & Crafts Demonstrations, the Greenport Pirates, the Carousel, Saturday Night Dancing, Food Hours: vary per event, usually mid-Sept. Fee: Free entry Directions: *I-495 Long Island Expwy. to exit 73 E. County Rd. 58/Orient, Rte. 58 becomes Rte. 25, continue East on Rte. 25 approx. 25 mi. to Greenport*   *www.eastendseaport.org*

Pickle Festival • *Greenlawn-Centerport Historical Associations • John Gardiner Farm • 900 Park Ave., Greenlawn, NY • 631-754-1180* • Featuress Include: Hay Rides, Corn Maze, Face Painting, Pumpkin Picking, Chicks & Ducks, Potato Digging, Homemade Pickles, Jams, Jellies, Farm-Grown Vegetables, Baked Goods Hours: 11 a.m.–4 p.m., usually the last weekend in Sept. Fee: $2, Under 12: Free Directions: *Northern State Pkwy. to exit 42 N., take Deer Park Rd. N., cross Jericho Tpke. which becomes Park Ave., continue North approx. 1-2 mi., the farm is on the Right at the Little Plains Rd. intersection*

Annual Maritime Kite Festival • *Long Island Maritime Museum • 86 West Ave., West Sayville, NY 11796 • East End Seaport Museum & Maritime Foundation • Mitchell Park • 631-447-8679* • Features Include: Parade, Vendors, Music, Traditional Arts

& Crafts Demonstrations, Captain Kid's Alley, Old-Fashioned Games, Kayak Derby, Whaleboat Races, Peconic Radio Club, Pirate Shows, Chowder Contest, Greenport Band, Fireworks, Dancing **Hours:** vary per event, mid-Sept. **Fee:** $2 **Directions:** *I-495 Long Island Expwy., exit onto W. Main St./Middle Country Rd./NY-25 E. toward Riverhead, continue to follow W. Main St./NY-25 E., turn Right onto Main Rd./NY-25 E., continue to follow NY-25 E., turn Left onto Main St., Village of Greenport*

www.eastendseaport.org/Maritime.htm • www.limaritime.org

Estuaries Day Festival • *Alley Pond Environmental Center • 228-06 Northern Blvd., Douglaston, NY • 718-229-4000* • **Features Include:** Demonstrations, Crafts, Games, Boat/Kayak Rides, Music, Nature Walks, Educational Booths, Children's Activities, Alley Watershed Hike **Hours:** Registration Required, usually last Sat. in Sept. **Fee:** Free, donations accepted **Directions:** *I-495 Long Island Expwy. to the Cross Island Pkwy. N., exit 31 E. Northern Blvd., the center is on the Right as you come around the ramp*

www.alleypond.com

October

Lantern Light Tour • *Robert Moses State Park • Fire Island, NY • 631-661-4876 • 631-669-0470* Reservations Required • **Features Include:** Storytellers, USA Life Saving Service Stories, Fire Island Light Station Stories, Tower Tours **Hours:** 6-8 p.m., usually the 1st weekend in Oct. **Fee:** $10 per-person **Directions:** *Southern State Pkwy. to exit 40 Robert Moses Cswy. S., enter Robert Moses State Park, drive around the water tower, park in the East end of Field 5, walk on the boardwalk to the lighthouse*

http://fireislandlighthouse.com

Egyptian Festival • *St Abraam, St. Mark's Coptic Orthodox Church • 90 Woodbury Rd., Woodbury, NY • 516-367-1328* • **Features Include:** Imported Pharonic Goods, Jewelry, Handmade Crafts, Egyptian Foods & Desserts **Hours:** 11 a.m.-6 p.m., early Oct. **Directions:** *I-495 Long Island Expwy. to exit 44 N. Rte. 135, exit toward Jericho Tpke.-Woodbury, turn Left onto Avery Rd., the event will be on the corner of Avery Rd. & Woodbury Rd.* *www.stabraam.org*

Ghost Stories • *Montauk Chamber of Commerce • Montauk, NY • 631-668-2544* • **Features Include:** Storytelling Event **Hours:** usually the last weekend before Halloween **Fee:** Free **Directions:** *I-495 Long Island Expwy. to exit 70, South on County Rd. 111, take Rte. 27 E. to Montauk Point* *www.montauklighthouse.com*

Benner's Farm • *56 Gnarled Hollow Circle, Setauket, NY • 631-689-8172* • **Features Include:** 14 acre Family Farmed Homestead circa 1700s, Pumpkin Picking, Haunted Hay Rides, Farm Animals, Ride the Big Swing, Organically Self-Sufficient Living, Workshops, Festivals, Special Events **Hours:** Open during October.

FALL FOLLY

Directions: *I-495 Long Island Expwy. E., to exit 62 Nicoll's Rd. N./County Rd. 97 to end, cross Rte. 25, Rte. 347 & Stony Brook Univ., turn Right on 25A E., at the 5th light turn Right onto Old Town Rd. & follow to end, turn Right onto Gnarled Hollow Rd., the farm is the 2nd house on Right, use 3rd driveway for parking, the sign is at the 2nd driveway*   *www.bennersfarm.com*

Radio Controlled Fall Aero Show • *Sunken Meadow State Park* • *Route 25A & Sunken Meadow Pkwy., Northport, NY* • *631-321-3510* • *631-269-4333* • Features **Include:** Miniature Aircraft Demonstrations **Hours:** 10 a.m.-5 p.m., first Sun. in Oct. **Fee: Free**, Parking: $8 **Directions:** *I-495 Long Island Expwy. to exit 53 Sunken Meadow/ Sagtikas Pkwy., take to the end*   *http://nysparks.state.ny.us/parks*

Fall Harvest Festival • *Borella's Farm Stand* • *485 Edgewood Ave., St. James, NY* • *631- 862-7330* • **Features Include:** Corn Maze, Live Music, Hay Ride, U-Pick-Pumpkins from the vine, Inflatable Rides, Face Painting, Roasted Corn, Candied Apples, Cotton Candy, Popcorn, Apples, Apple Cider **Hours:** Sun.-Sat.: 8:30 a.m.-6:30 p.m., Harvest Festival: every weekend in Oct., 9 a.m.-6 p.m. **Fee:** Adults: $15, Kids $10, Under 3: Free, Parking: Free **Directions:** *I-495 Long Island Expwy. to exit 53 toward Bay Shore/Kings Park, take Sagtikos State Pkwy./Sunken Meadow Pkwy., to exit SM3E. Jericho Tpke. toward Smithtown, Jericho Tpke./NY-25, turn Left onto Edgewood Ave., the farm is on the Left*

National Public Lands Day • *Fire Island's National Seashore* • *Wilderness Visitors Center* • *120 Laurel St., Patchogue, NY* • *631-281-3010, Reservations Required* • *631-687-4765* • *631-687-4750* • **Features Include:** Participate in the International Coastal Clean-Up, Clean Up Bayside Beaches, work at sites along the seashore **Hours:** 8 a.m-1 p.m., usually mid-Oct. **Fee: Free** **Directions:** varies by location   *www.nps.gov/fiis/.../2009_WVC_CoastalCleanupDay_10-18-2009.pdf*

Festival By The Sea • *Lido Beach Town Park* • *630 Lido Blvd., Lido Beach, NY* • *516-431-6650* • **Features Include:** Entertainment, Games, Nautical Exhibits, Food **Hours:** 11 a.m.-6:30 p.m., 1st weekend in Oct. **Fee: Free** **Directions:** *Southern State Pkwy. to Meadowbrook Pkwy. S. toward Jones Beach, take exit M10 toward Point Lookout, turn Right onto Loop Pkwy., turn Right onto Lido Blvd., take to the end Lido Beach Town Park*   *www.townofhempstead.org* • *www.discoverlongisland.com*

Annual Fall Festival • *Sagtikos Manor, Montauk Hwy., P.O. Box 5344, Bay Shore, NY* • *631-661-8348* • *631-661-5169* • *631-854-0939* • **Features Include:** Haunted House circa 1692, Old-Fashioned Games, Face Painting, Baladeer, Pumpkins, Halloween-Themed Dancers, Hay Jump, Ghostly Manor Tours, "Scary Symphony Strings," Food **Hours:** 11 a.m.-4 p.m., mid-Oct. **Fee:** Adults: $10, Kids: $5 **Directions:** *Northern State Pkwy. to exit 44 Sunken Meadow Pkwy./ Sagtikos State Pkwy., take Robert Moses Cswy. S. to exit RM*

2 E. (Rte .27A) Bay Shore, turn Right onto Rte. 27A & continue East approx. .5 mi., entrance to the Sagtikos Manor will be on the Left   *www.sagtikosmanor.org*

Hallockville Fall Festival and Crafts Show • *Hallockville Museum Farm • 6038 Sound Ave., Riverhead, NY • 631-298-5292* • **Features Include:** Children's Activities, Pumpkin Picking, Hay Rides, Straw Play Area, Old-Fashioned Games, Music, Demonstrations, Craft Vendors, Home-Baked Goods, Food **Hours:** Sat.-Sun.: 10 a.m.-5 p.m., usually the 1st weekend in Oct. **Fee:** Adults: $7, Kids 6-12 & Seniors: $5, Under 5: Free **Directions:** *I-495 Long Island Expwy. to exit 73 Old Country Rd. towards Orient/Greenport/Co Hwy. 58, turn Left onto County Rte. 58/Old Country Rd., turn Left onto Rte. 43/Northville Tpke., turn Right onto Sound Ave.*   *www.hallockville.com*

Goofy Gourds & Pumpkins • *Connetquot River State Park Preserve • Sunrise Hwy., Oakdale, NY • 631-581-1072* • **Features Include:** Gourds, Pumpkins, Decorating **Hours:** 1:30-2:30 p.m., usually in mid-Oct., for children 5 yrs. & Older, register beforehand **Fee:** Adults: $3, Kids: $2, Parking: $6, Empire Pass Accepted **Directions:** *Southern State Pkwy. to exit 44 Sunrise Hwy. E., the preserve is located on the North side of Sunrise Hwy., just west of Pond Rd.*   *http://nysparks.state.ny.us/parks/info.asp?parkID=69*

Montauks Annual Fall Festival • *742 Montauk Hwy., Montauk, NY • 631-668-2428 • 631-668-2355* • **Features Include:** Wagon & Pony Rides, Pumpkin Decorating, Kids Art Contest, Live Music, Carousel Rides, Great Clam Chowder Contest, Clam Shucking, LI Wine Tasting, Montauk Madness Boat Race Drawing **Hours:** Sat.: 11 a.m.-5 p.m., Sun.: Noon-5 p.m., usually in early Oct. **Fee: Free** admission **Directions:** *I-495 Long Island Expwy. to exit 70 S., travel south on County Rd. 111, to Rte. 27 E. to Montauk Point*   *www.montaukchamber.com • www.longislandhost.com/montauk/montauk_chamber.html*

Oyster Festival • *On the Waterfront at Theodore Roosevelt Park, Oyster Bay, NY • 516-628-1625* • **Features Include:** Thrill Rides, Tall Ships, Pirates, Entertainment, Craft Vendors, Oyster Bay Waterfront, Fresh Seafood, Food Court **Hours:** Sat.-Sun.: 11 a.m.-6 p.m., usually in mid-Oct. **Fee: Free** admission **Directions:** *I-495 Long Island Expwy. to exit 41N. Rte. 106 N. toward Oyster Bay, cross 25A & continue toward Oyster Bay Village, follow signs for visitor parking areas & the free shuttle bus service to the waterfront*   *www.theoysterfestival.org*

Pumpkin Fest • *Suffolk County Farm & Education Center Cornell Cooperative Extension • 350 Yaphank Ave., Yaphank, NY • 631-852-5300* • **Features Include:** Wagon Rides, Corn Maze, Pumpkin Picking & Painting, Carnival Games, Farm Animals, Crafts, Food **Hours:** 11 a.m.-5 p.m., usually the 1st weekend in Oct. **Fee:** $10, Under 3: Free **Directions:** *I-495 Long Island Expwy. to exit 67 S. Yapank Ave., the farm entrance will be on the Right*   *www.ccesuffolk.org*

FALL FOLLY

Pumpkin Fling • *Suffolk County Farm & Education Center Cornell Cooperative Extension* • *Yaphank Ave., Yaphank, NY* • *631-852-4602* • Features Include: Catapult Contest, Pumpkin Flinging Constructions, Field Event, Adult & Youth Catagories **Hours:** 11a.m.-5 p.m., usually the 3rd or 4th week in Oct. **Fee: Free** to spectators **Directions:** *I-495 Long Island Expwy. to exit 67 S. Yapank Ave. farm entrance is on the right*
http://counties.cce.cornell.edu/suffolk/SCFprograms/PumpkinFling.htm

Rock Hall Museum Country Fair • *199 Broadway, Lawrence, NY* • *516-239-1157* • Features Include: Outdoor Festival, Colonial Cooking Demos, Blacksmith, Woodworking, Petting Zoo, Pony Rides, Crafts, Scarecrow Making, Military Re-enactments, Colonial Historian, Country Band, Vendors, Food **Hours:** 11 a.m., mid-Oct. **Fee: Free** **Directions:** *Southern State Pkwy. to the Hempstead Ave. exit, turn Right onto Hempstead Ave., turn Right onto Merrick Rd., turn Left onto Broadway, the museum will be on the Left* www.toh.li/content/rc/rockhall.html

Sagamore Hill Days Fall Family Festival ⊛ • *Sagamore Hill National Historic Site* • *12 Sagamore Hill Rd., Oyster Bay, NY* • *516-922-4788* • Features Include: Children's Entertainment, Old-Fashioned Games, Crafts, Demonstrations, Exhibits, Music, Pony Rides, Farm Animal Petting Area, Live Raptors, Food Vendors **Hours:** 11 a.m.-5 p.m., usually mid-Oct.,**Fee: Free** **Directions:** *Northern State Pkwy. to exit 35 N. or I-495 Long Island Expwy. to exit 41 N., to Rte. 106 N., drive for 6 mi. into downtown Oyster Bay, turn Right onto E. Main St. (at Nobman's Hardware Store) & travel 2 mi., turn Left onto Cove Neck Rd. & drive 1.5 mi. to Sagamore Hill*
www.nps.gov/sah

The Twilight Pumpkin Spectacular • *Nassau County Museum of Art* • *1 Museum Dr., Roslyn Harbor, NY* • *516-484-9338* • Features Includes: Meandering Pathways, Illuminated Jack O' Lanterns, Spooky Music & Sound Effects, Hand-Carved Pumpkins, Theme Arrangements **Hours:** 6 p.m.-9:30 p.m., usually the last weekend in Oct. **Fee:** Adults & Seniors $14, Kids under 12: $7, Under 6: Free, online ticket purchase, tickets are for timed entry **Directions:** *I-495 Long Island Expwy. to exit 39 Glen Cove Rd. N., turn Left onto Northern Blvd./25A, drive 1.5 blocks & turn Right onto Museum Dr.*
www.nassaumuseum.com

COLUMBUS DAY

Huntington Fall Festival • *Heckscher Park, Huntington, NY* • *631-423-6100* • Features Include: Carnival Rides, Pony Rides, Youth Talent Stage, Historical Exhibitions, Sat. Night Show, Read-a-Thon, Entertainment, Celebrity Autograph Signings, Craft Vendors, Food Court **Hours:** Fri.: 6-10 p.m., Sat. & Sun.: 11 a.m-10 p.m., Mon.: 11 a.m-5 p.m., Columbus Day weekend **Fee: Free** admission, Parking: Free at the train station, shuttle

bus service **Directions:** *Northern State Pkwy. to exit 40 (toward Huntington) Rte. 110 N., (Rte. 110/Walt Whitman Rd. becomes New York Ave.), make a Right turn onto Rte. 25A/ Main St. in Huntington Village, turn Left onto Prime Ave. the hill is located along Rte. 25A just 1 traffic light East of the intersection with Rte. 110 in Huntington Village*
www.lifallfestival.com • www.huntingtonchamber.com

November

Fall Fair • *Cold Spring Harbor Fish Hatchery & Aquarium •* **1660 Rte. 25A, Cold Spring Harbor, NY • 516-692-6768 • Features Include:** Games, Fish for Trout (children under 12 only), Fishing Gear Provided, Learn from Conservation & Environmental Groups, Food **Hours:** 10 a.m.-5 p.m., usually mid-Nov. **Fee:** Adults: $6, Kids Under 12: $4 **Directions:** *I-495 Long Island Expwy. to exit 44 N. onto Rte. 135 toward Syosset, take the exit for Jericho Tpke. E. toward Woodbury, turn Left onto S. Woods Rd., turn Right onto Cold Spring Rd., turn Right onto 25A E., the hatchery will be on the Right*
www.cshfha.org/events.html

Thanksgiving Celebration • *Old Bethpage Village Restoration •* **Round Swamp Rd., Old Bethpage, NY • 516-572-8400 • Features Include:** Fiddle Music, Children's Stories, Demonstrations, Traditional Thanksgiving Preparations, Old-Fashioned Wood Burning Stoves, Beehive Ovens, Open Hearths **Hours:** 10 a.m.-4 p.m., usually the week before Thanksgiving **Fee:** Adults: $10, Kids & Seniors $7 **Directions:** *I-495 Long Island Expwy. to exit 48 Round Swamp Rd. toward Old Bethpage/Farmingdale, make a Left onto Round Swamp Rd., turn Left onto Old Country Rd., slight Right onto Round Swamp Rd.*

Macy's Thanksgiving Day Parade Balloon Practice • *Flushing Meadows Corona Park, Queens, NY •* **718-760-6565 •** The Macy's Thanksgiving Day Parade balloons usually come to Flushing Meadows for practice in early Nov. **Hours:** call for info **Fee: Free** Directions: *Northern State Pkwy. which becomes the Grand Central Pkwy. W. to exit 9P toward Flushing Meadows Corona Park, turn Left onto New York Ave., continue onto Great Lakes Ct./Perimeter Rd., turn Right onto Perimeter Rd., the park will be on the Right*
www.flushingmeadowscoronapark.com

THANKSGIVING CELEBRATIONS

The First Thanksgiving Ⓥ **•** *Theodore Roosevelt Sanctuary & Audubon Center •* **134 Cove Rd., Oyster Bay, NY • 516-922-3200** Reservation Required • **Features Include:** Local Mattinecock Customs & Activities, Woodland Hiking, Journey Cake Making (a Native American food) **Hours:** 1 p.m., usually the weekend before Thanksgiving **Fee:** Non-Members: $3, Members: Free **Directions:** *I-495 Long Island Expwy. to exit 41 N., Rte. 106, proceed on Rte. 106 N. to the Village of Oyster Bay, turn Right onto E. Main St., proceed 1.5 mi. up E. Main St., becomes Cove Rd. (at Oyster Bay High School), look for the signs for the TR Sanctuary, parking lot on the Right* trsac@audubon.org

FALL FOLLY

Annual Native American Feast • *Garvies Point Museum & Preserve* • *50 Barry Dr., Glen Cove, NY* • *516-571-8010* • **Features Include:** Hands-On Activities, Tool Making, Face Painting, Fire-Making, Storytelling, Campfire Cooking, Hike the Nature Trails **Hours:** 10 a.m.-4 p.m., usually the weekend before Thanksgiving **Fee:** Adult $3, Kids 5-12: $2, Under 5: Free **Directions:** *Northern State Pkwy. to exit 107 N. toward Oyster Bay/Glen Cove, 107 N. becomes Pratt Blvd./Glen Cove Rd., which becomes Glen Cove Ave., turn Right onto Village Sq./Brewster St., turn Left onto Mill Hill Rd. which becomes The Place, stay straight to go onto Ellwood St., turn Left onto McLaughlin St., turn Left onto Barry Dr.* www.garviespointmuseum.com

Thanksgiving Weekend Evening Tower Tour • *Fire Island Lighthouse* • *631-661-4876* Reservations Required • **Features Include:** Experience the Fire Island Lighthouse at night **Hours:** 4 p.m., usually the Sat. after Thanksgiving **Fee:** Adult: $15 **Directions:** *Southern State Pkwy., exit 40 Robert Moses Cswy. S., toward Robert Moses State Park, get to the park, drive around the water tower, head East, park in the East end of Field 5, walk on the boardwalk to the lighthouse* www.fireislandlighthouse.com

Annual Custom Car & Bike Show • *Nassau Veterans Memorial Coliseum & Exhibition Center* • *1255 Hempstead Tpke., Uniondale, NY* • *516-794-9303* • **Features Include:** Phenomenal Cars Display, Judged Competition **Hours:** Usually Thanksgiving weekend **Directions:** *Northern State Pkwy. to exit 31A & merge onto Meadowbrook State Pkwy. S., take exit M4 W. toward Hempstead/Coliseum, merge onto Meadowbrook State Pkwy. Service Rd., continue onto Hempstead Tpke., the coliseum will be on the Right* www.nassaucoliseum.com

Macy's Thanksgiving Day Parade • *151 West 34th St., NY, NY* • *212-494-4495* • **Features Include:** Arrive between 7 & 8 a.m. to find a place along the parade route, especially if you'd like a front spot. Dress in layers & bring a warm drink in a thermos. The parade begins outside the Museum of Natural History at 77th St. & Central Park W., heads south on Central Park W., alongside Central Park, at Columbus Circle, on the southwest corner of Central Park, the parade turns onto Broadway. The balloons are not raised to full height until the parade reaches Broadway. The parade ends at the Macy's building in Herald Square (where Broadway intersects with 34th St. & the Avenue of the Americas). The Parade comes to a conclusion with a right turn onto 34th St., & a final right onto 7th Ave., where the balloons & floats are disassembled. **Public Viewing Areas:** Central Park W.: West side of street from 70th St. to Columbus Circle, East side of street from 70th to 65th Sts., Columbus Circle: West side of street, Broadway: East & W. side of avenue, between 58th & 38th Sts., 34th St.: South side of street between Broadway & 7th Ave. **Hours:** 9 a.m.-Noon, Thanksgiving morning **Fee: Free Directions:** *Begins at 77th St. & Central Park W., Ends at Macy's, Herald Square, 34th St. & 6th Ave.*

www.macys.com/campaign/parade/parade.jsp

The Evening Before the Parade the floats are blown up right outside the Museum of Natural History, providing an excellent opportunity to witness the floats getting blown up & to get a close view of the floats. **Fee:** **Free** **Directions:** *77ᵗʰ St. & Central Park W..*

U-PICK APPLES, PUMPKINS & MORE

Fall: Sept., Oct., Nov.

Apples: Sept.-Oct.

Blueberries, Peaches: July-Sept.

Broccoli, Cabbage: June-Nov.

Cauliflower: July-Nov.

Corn: July-Oct.

Cucumbers: July-Sept.

Eggplant: July-Oct.

Lettuce: June-Oct.

Peas: June-July

Peppers: July-Oct.

Potatoes: Aug.-Oct.

Pumpkins: Sept.-Oct.

Squash: June-Oct.

Tomatoes: July-Oct.

See Summer for U-Pick Locations & Information on pg. 226

www.longisland.com/ fruit_picking.php

www.pickyourown.org

SUGGESTIONS • COMMENTS • ERRORS

Linda.ReidBryce @verizon.net

Thanks

APPLE FESTIVALS

CRISP, CRUNCHY & COLORFUL

September

Annual Long Island Apple Festival · *Sherwood-Jayne Farm* · *55 Old Post Rd., East Setauket, NY* · *631-692-4664* · *Apple Pie Contest: 631-751-3730* · **Features Include:** 18th Century Farmhouse, Apple Orchard, Crisp Apples, Old-Fashioned Apple Games, Traditional Music, Hay Rides, Colonial Storytelling, Craft Demonstrations, Tours of Sherwood-Jayne House, Open-Hearth Cooking Demonstrations, Pony Rides, Apple Pie Baking Contest, Colonial-Themed Arts & Crafts **Hours:** Sun.: 11 a.m.-4:30 p.m., usually mid-Sept. **Fee:** Adults: $6, Kids 2-12 & Seniors: $4 **Directions:** *I-495 Long Island Expwy. to exit 62 N., follow sign for North Stony Brook to Nichols Rd. N., continue to the end & bear Right onto 25A E., take 25A E. through Setauket & East Setauket, turn Right onto Old Coach Rd., see red schoolhouse offices on the corner, continue to fork, turn Left onto Old Post Rd.*

www.splia.org · www.threevillagehistoricalsociety.org/calendarofevents.html

Apple Festival · *Wyckoff Farmhouse Museum: Pieter Claesen Wyckoff House* · *5816 Clarendon Rd., Canarsie, NY* · *718-629-5400* · **Features Include:** Dutch Farm House, Apple Celebration, Live Music, Fresh Pressed Apple Cider, Apple Fritters, Dance, Children's Apple Craft Workshop, House Tour **Hours:** Museum: Tues.-Sun.: 10 a.m-4 p.m., usually the last weekend in Sept. **Fee:** **Free**, **Musesum Fee:** Adults: $5, Kids: $3, Under 10: Free **Directions:** *Southern State Pkwy. to the Belt Pkwy., take exit 13 Rockaway Pkwy., turn Left on Ditmas Ave., cross Ralph Ave. the park is on the Left side of the street* *www.wyckoffassociation.org*

October

Apple Festival • *Queens County Farm Museum* • *73-50 Little Neck Pkwy., Floral Park, NY* • *718-347-3276* • Features Include: Learning Fun Apple Facts, Hay Rides, Children's Games, a Large Variety of Apples, Apple Products, Freshly Pressed Cider, the Nation's Largest Apple Cobbler Baked on Site, Cider Pressing Demonstrations, Food **Hours:** 11 a.m.–4 p.m. usually the 1st Sun. in Oct. **Fee: Free** **Directions:** *I-495 Long Island Expwy., to exit 32 Little Neck Pkwy., turn Left onto Little Neck Pkwy., drive South for 1.5 mi. to museum entrance*   *www.queensfarm.org*

Apple Festival • *Islip Grange* • *10 Broadway Ave., Sayville, NY* • *631-224-5430* • *Sponsor: Town of Islip* • Features Include: Pony Rides, Music, Demontration, Scarecrow Contests, Crafts Fair, Apple-Themed Cooking Contest, Pie Eating **Hours:** 10 a.m.-4:30 p.m., usually mid-Oct. **Fee: Free,** Directions: *I-495 Long Island Expwy., take exit 59 toward Ocean Ave./Ronkonkoma, turn Right onto Ocean Ave., continue on County Rd. 93/Lakeland Ave., turn Left onto NY-454 E./Veterans Memorial Hwy., turn Right onto Broadway Ave., Islip Grange will be on the Right*

Apple Festival • *Kissam House* • *434 Park Ave., Huntington, NY* • *631-427-7045 401* • *Sponsor: Huntington Historical Society* • Features Include: Local Apples, Games, Storytelling, Historic Craft Demonstrations, Historic Music, Baked Goods, Cider Making **Hours:** Noon-4p.m., usually mid-Oct. **Fee: Free** **Directions:** *Northern State Pkwy.to exit 40 N. Rte. 110, cross Jericho Tpke., continue N. on New York Ave., turn Right onto Main St./25A E., turn Right onto Park Ave., Kissam House will be on the Left*
    www.huntingtonhistoricalsociety.org/kissam.htm

SUGGESTIONS • COMMENTS • ERRORS

Linda.ReidBryce
@verizon.net

Thanks

CORN MAZES

CORN HUSKS, LAUGHTER & CLUE HUNTING

Mazes begin to open in mid-Sept. + some stay open through Nov.

Andrews Family Farm & Greenhouses • *1038 Sound Ave., Wading River, NY* • *631-929-5963* • Features Include: Corn Maze for the Younger Set **Hours:** 9 a.m.-5:30 p.m. **Fee:** $3 **Directions:** *I-495 Long Island Expwy. to exit 68 William Floyd Pkwy. to Wading River, take Rte. 46 William Floyd Pkwy., slight Right onto 25A, turn Left onto Sound Ave.*

Fairview Farm • *69 Horsemill Ln., • overlooking Mecox Bay, Bridgehampton, NY 11932* • *631-537-6154* • Features Include: 8-acre Corn Maze (10-ft. tall), Corn Cannon (test your aim), Pumpkin, Gourd, Squash Picking, Farm Animals, Corn Box, Long Island Raw Milk Cheese, Corn Kernel Sandbox **Hours:** Fri.: Noon-6 p.m., Sat.: 10-6 p.m., Sun.: Noon-6 p.m., 1st weekend in Sept.-1st weekend in Nov. **Fee:** Adults: $10.00, Under 12: $7.00, Under 3: Free, download discount coupon, **Directions:** *I-495 Long Island Expwy. to exit 70 to Rte. 27, go to end of 4-lane hwy., take Montauk Hwy. E./ Rte. 27 through the hamlet of Water Mill, turn Right onto Mecox Rd., travel 1.25 mi. to the 2nd stop sign & turn Left, Horsemill Ln. is about .25 mi. on the Right, park on the Left along Horsemill Ln.*   *www.cornfieldmaze.com*

F&W Schmitt Brothers • *26 Pinelawn Rd., Melville, NY* • *631-423-5693* • *271-3276* • Features Include: Haunted Mansion, Corn Maze, Night Corn Maze, Pumpkin Picking, Hay Rides, Hay Pyramid, Fire Truck Slide, Farm Animals, Pumpkin Patch Playground, Pony Rides, 30-ft. Slide, Inflatables **Hours:** Noon-5 p.m., weekends only, Night Maze: 7-11 p.m., opens the 1st weekend in Oct. **Fee:** Fri-Sun: Kids Maze: $7, Night Maze:

$11, Haunted Mansion: $16, Night Maze & Haunted Mansion: $22, download discount coupons **Directions:** *I-495 Long Island Expwy. to exit 49 N., merge onto Rte. 110, go 3 lights, turn Right onto Pinelawn Rd., the farm is on the Left*   *www.schmittfarms.com*

Annual Fall Festival • *The Garden Spot • 366 Railroad Ave., Center Moriches, NY •*
631-878-5662 • **Features Include:** Haunted House, Hay Rides, Corn Maze, Pumpkin Picking & Decorating, Petting Zoo, Costume Contest, Activities Geared for Kids 12 & under **Hours:** 10 a.m.-5 p.m., usually the 1st weekend in Oct. **Fee:** Adults: $5, Unlimited Rides Under 16 yrs: $15 **Directions:** *I-495 Long Island Expwy. to exit 69 for Wading River Rd. towards Center Moriches, turn Right onto Wading River Rd., turn Left onto Sunrise Hwy. South Service Rd., take the 3rd Right onto Railroad Ave., the festival will be on the Right*

Gramma's Flower Cottage • *2891 Montauk Hwy., Brookhaven, NY 11719* • *631-730-6264* • **Features Include:** Haunted Corn Maze, Face Painting, Pony Rides, Pumpkin Picking, Refreshment Stand, Restrooms, Activities for kids under 10 **Hours:** Mon.-Fri.: 10 a.m.-6 p.m., Sat.: 9 a.m.-6 p.m., Sun.: 10 a.m.-6 p.m., during Oct. **Fee: Free** **Directions:** *I-495 Long Island Expwy., to exit 65, turn Left at the 1st traffic light onto Horse Block Rd., turn Left at last traffic light onto Montauk Hwy.*   *www.grammasflowercottage.com*

Hank's Pumpkin Town • *240 Montauk Hwy., Water Mill, NY* • *631-726-4667* •
Features Include: 8.5-acre Corn Maze, Wagon Rides, Kiddie Playground, Tractor Train Rides, Calf Roping, Cow Milking, Giant Maze Mountain Slide, 50-ft. Tube Slide, Pedal Cart Race Track, Sand Box with Diggers, Corn Table, Corn Swing, Duck Races **Hours:** Weekends: 9:30 a.m.-6 p.m., usually open mid-Sept.-1st weekend in Nov. **Fee:** Adults: $10, Under 12: $7, Wrist Band: $10, unlimited usage **Directions:** *I-495 Long Island Expwy. to exit 68 William Floyd Pkwy. toward Shirley, turn Left onto Montauk Hwy./NY-27*

http://hankspumpkintown.com/farm

Harbes Pumpkin Fall Festival • *631-734-6441* • **Features Include:** Corn Maze, Hay Rides, You-Pick Pumpkins, Roasted Corn, Gemstone Mining, Homemade Candy Apples, Wooden Play Strucutres, Pony Rides, Live Music, Corn Toss Games, Baby Farm Animals, Picnic Tables, Farm Stand **Hours:** Mid Sept-end of Oct. Sat.-Sun.:10 a.m.-6 p.m., Oct. only Night Maze: Fri.-Sat. 7-10 pm., **Fee:** Adult: $11.95, Under 2: Free, Mattituck, Jamesport, and Riverhead have different corn maze themes

Harbes Family Farm Stand • *Sound Ave., Mattituck, NY* • *631-365-1870k* •
Features Include: 2-acre Barnyard Adventure, 2-acre Wizard of Oz Themed Corn

Maze, Bunnyville, Chick Hatchery, Bee Museum, Pig Races, Mini Train Ride, Play Area **Directions:** *I-495 Long Island Expwy. to exit 71, turn Left onto Edwards Ave., continue North (straight) for 3.8 mi., turn Right onto Sound Ave., drive East for 10 mi.*

Harbes Jamesport Location ⑤ • Features Include: 10-acre Wild West Adventure, Characters, Mini Train Ride, Rewards, Straw Fortress, Rope Maze, Trike Track, Games, Activities **Directions:** *I-495 Long Island Expwy., take exit 73, take Rte. 58 E., becomes Rte. 25, travel 6.5 mi., continue straight at the traffic circle in Riverhead*

Harbes Middle Earth Pumpkin Farm • *Riverhead, NY* • Features Include: 5-acre Middle Earth Adventure, Corn Maze, Hay Ride, Trike Track **Directions:** *I-495 Long Island Expwy. to exit 71, turn Left onto Edwards Ave., continue North (straight) for 5 mi., turn Right onto Sound Ave., continue East for 8.6 mi., the farm will be on the Left* *www.harbesfamilyfarm.com*

Kaufold's Country Florist & Farm Inc. • *724 Middle Country Rd., Ridge, NY* • *631-924-1265* • Features Include: 1.5-acre Themed Corn Maze with Scavenger Hunt, Tricycle Maze, Pony & Hay Rides, Children's Playground, Roast Corn **Hours:** 9 a.m.-5 p.m., weekends in Oct. plus Columbus Day **Fee:** $5 **Directions:** *I-495 Long Island Expwy. to exit 68 William Floyd Pkwy. toward Shirley, take the County Hwy. 46/William Floyd Pkwy. ramp to Wading River, take the ramp onto Middle Country Rd.*

Krupski's Pumpkin Farms • *38030 Main Rd., Peconic, NY* • *631-734-6847* • Features Include: Corn Maze, Actors on Weekends, Haunted Barn, You-Pick-Pumpkins from the vine, Hay Rides **Hours:** 9 a.m.-6 p.m. **Directions:** *I-495 Long Island Expwy. to the last exit, head East, the road changes names several times, travel approx. 16 mi. & the farm will be on the Right*

Seven Ponds Orchard • *65 Seven Ponds Rd., Water Mill, NY* • *631-726-8015* • Features Include: 5-acre Corn Maze, Wagon Rides, Toy Land Area, Magic Talking Apple **Hours:** 9 a.m.-6 p.m. **Directions:** *I-495 Long Island Expwy., exit 70 toward Eastport, merge onto Captain Daniel Roe Hwy./CR-11 S. Port Jefferson West Hampton Rd., merge onto 27 E., ramp on Left, turn Left onto David Whites Ln., stay straight to go onto Seven Ponds Rd./becomes Upper Ponds Rd., turn Left onto Seven Ponds Rd./Seven Ponds Town Rd. ends at Water Mill*

Stakey's Pumpkin Farm • *270 West Ln. (between Sound Ave. & Rte. 25), Aquebogue, NY* • *631-722-3467, 631-298-0880* • Features Include: 2 Themed Corn Mazes, Hay Rides, Face Painting, Pony Rides, Bounce House, Pick-Your-Own Pumpkins (18 varieties)/Gourds/Squashes off the vine, Family Picnic Area **Hours:** Sat.-Sun.: 10 a.m.-6 p.m., Mon.-Fri.: Noon-5 p.m., mid. Sept.-Oct. **Fee:** Adult: $5, Kids 3-12: $4

Directions: *I-495 Long Island Expwy., take exit 72, Rte. 25 (Riverhead/Calverton), bear Right & follow signs for Rte. 25 E. Riverhead, take Rte. 25 through downtown Riverhead, make 2ⁿᵈ Right onto Hubbard Ave., make a Left at stop sign onto Edgar Ave., take to traffic light, make a Right onto Rte. 25, then make the 1ˢᵗ Left onto West Ln. after the Modern Snack Bar restaurant, drive 1 mi. to the farm*   *www.stakeyspumpkinfarm.com*

Queens County Farm Museum • 718-347-3276 • Features Include: 3-acre "Amazing Maize Maze," Hay Rides, Feed Sheep & Goats, Farm Museum, Farm House **Hours:** 11 a.m.-4:30 p.m., corn maze open weekends only, mid Sept.-Nov.1, Night Maze until 9 p.m. **Fee:** Fall Harvest: Adults: $7, Kids 4-11: $4, Under 3: Free **Directions:** *I-495 Long Island Expwy., take exit 32 Little Neck Pkwy., turn Left onto Little Neck Pkwy., drive South for 1.5 mi. to museum entrance*   *www.queensfarm.org*

October

Bayville Scream Park • *8 Bayville Ave., Bayville, NY* • *516-624-4678* • Features **Include:** Bloodworth Mansion, Uncle Needles 3D Funhouse of Fear, Temple of Terror, Zombie Pirates, Evil in the Woods **Hours:** Fri.-Sat.: 6 p.m.-Midnight, Sun. & Weekdays: 6-10 p.m., Kids' "Not So Scary" Days, Sat., Sun. & Columbus Day: 11 a.m.-5 p.m. , Sept.-Oct. **Fee:** Single Attraction: $14.95, Combined Attraction Pricing: Check website **Directions:** *I-495 Long Island Expwy., take exit 41 N. Oyster Bay Rd./Rte.106 N., turn Left onto W. Main St., continue on W. Shore Rd., continue on Ludlam Ave., turn Left onto Bayville Ave., make a U-turn & the park will be on the Right*

www.bayvillescreampark.com

Bayville's Haunted Firehouse • *Bayville Fire Company, Inc.* • *258 Bayville Ave., Bayville, NY* • *516-628-1922* • Features **Include:** Transformed Fire House, House of the Undead, Bloodthirsty Firefighters, Local Ghouls, Strobe Lights **Hours:** Fri.: 7-11 p.m., Sat: 6-11 p.m., Halloween Night: 6-9 p.m., check the web site, hours change as Halloween approaches **Fee:** $12 **Directions:** *I-495 Long Island Expwy., take exit 41 N. Rte. 106, cross Northern Blvd./25A, turn Left onto Lexington Ave., to end, turn Left onto W. Main St., bear Right onto W. Shore Rd., the water is on your Right, go over the bridge & the road becomes Ludlam Ave., follow the signs to the free bus shuttle parking area*

www.bayvillehauntedfirehouse.com

Darkside Haunted House • *Dark Side Productions Inc.* • *Rte. 25A, Wading River, NY* • *631-369-SCAR(E) 7227* • **Features Include:** Outdoor Haunted Village, Haunted House with Fog Machines, Strobe Lights, Special Effects, not recommended for kids under 10, except the outdoor village on weekend afternoons **Hours:** Mon.-Thur.: 7-11 p.m., Fri.: 7 p.m.-Midnight, Sat.: 1 p.m.-Midnight, Sun.: 1-11 p.m., Matinees Sat.-Sun.: 1-5 p.m., during Oct. **Fee:** Haunted House $20, Outdoor Village $5 on weekend afternoons, download discount coupons online **Directions:** *I-495 Long Island Expwy., take exit 68 William Floyd Pkwy. N. to end, turn Right onto 25A E., bear Right at the fork, the house will be on the Left* *www.darksideproductions.com/main.htm*

Festival of Frights • *James Ln., East Hampton, NY* • *631-324-6850* • Features **Include:** Pumpkin Carving Workshops, Scarecrow Display, Haunted Cemetery Tour, **Hours:** Fri.-Tues. **Fee:** Haunted Cemetery Tour: $10, Workshops & Scarecrow Display: **Free** Directions: *I-495 Long Island Expwy., take exit 68, William Floyd Pkwy. toward Shirley, exit onto NY 27 E., turn Left onto Montauk Hwy./NY-27, turn Left onto Main St., take the 1st Right towards James Ln., turn Left onto James Ln., the farm will be on the Right* *www.easthamptonhistory.org*

Ghost Stories & Legends of Fire Island • *Fire Island Lighthouse* • *Fire Island Lighthouse Preservation Society* • *631-661-4876* • **Features Include:** Eerie Barrier Beach Tales, Dress Warmly, Bring Blankets & Flashlights, held on the Lighthouse Terrace **Hours:** Tower Tours: 4-6 p.m. **Fees:** **Free** Directions: *I-495 Long Island Expwy. to exit 53 toward Bay Shore/Kings Park/Sagtikos Pkwy., take the exit toward Robert Moses Pkwy., keep Left at the fork, follow signs for Southern State Pkwy., take exit 40 S. toward Robert Moses Cswy., continue straight, at the traffic circle, take the 2nd exit onto Robert Moses State Pkwy., continue to the Coast Guard Station, turn Left* *www.fireislandlighthouse.com/html/upcoming_events.html*

Halloween Boat Burning • *Maritime Museum* • *86 West Ave., P.O. Box 184, West Sayville, NY* • *631-447-8679* • *631 854-4974* • **Features Include:** Bonfire Apple Cider, Magic, Snacks **Hours:** call for date, usually in Oct. **Directions:** *Southern State Pkwy. to Heckscher State Pkwy. S., take exit 45 E. for State Hwy. 27A E., merge onto E. Main St./Rte. 27A, continue on S. Country Rd./County Rte. 85/Main St., turn Right at West Ave., continue to follow County Rte. 85/Main St., the museum will be on the Right* *www.limaritime.org*

Halloween Family Fun Day • *Long Island Museum of American Art, History & Carriages, 1099 Rte. 25A, Stony Brook, NY* • *631-751-0066* • **Features Include:** Pumpkin Decorating, Petting Zoo, Carriage Rides, Trick-or-Treating, Musical Storyteller Performance, Wear Costumes **Hours:** Noon-5 p.m., usually the weekend before Halloween **Fee:** **Free** with museum admission **Directions:** *I-495 Long Island Expwy., take exit 62 N. County Rd. 97/Nicoll's Rd. to its end, turn Left onto Rte. 25A for 1.5 mi., turn Left onto Main St. in Stony Brook, the entrance is on the Right* *http://longislandmuseum.org*

FALL FOLLY

Halloween Party • *Walt Whitman's Birthplace Historic Site & Interpretive Center* • *209 Walt Whitman Rd., Huntington Station, NY* • *631-427-5240* • Features Include: Professional Storytellers, Spooky Halloween Tales & Legends, Music, Puppet Performance, Face Painting, Wear Costumes, Raffle Baskets, Guided Tours **Hours:** 11 a.m-1 p.m., usually the Sat. before Halloween, appropriate for pre-K-6th grade **Directions:** *Northern State Pkwy., take exit 40 N. Rte. 110 toward Huntington, turn Right onto 110/Walt Whitman Rd., make a U-turn at Spruce Tree Ln., the site will be on the Right* www.waltwhitman.org

Haunted House at North Patchogue Fire Department • *North Patchogue Fire Department, 33 Davison Ave., North Patchogue, NY* • *631-475-1788 ext. 517* • Features Include: 3 Floors of Horror, House Built to Terrorize, Concession Stand, Wall of Shame for those who don't make it through, not recommended for small children **Hours:** Fri-Sat.: 6-11 p.m., Sun.: 6-10 p.m., during Oct. **Fee:** Adults: $10, Kids Under 13: $6 **Directions:** *I-495 Long Island Expwy., take exit 69 for Wading River Rd. toward Wading River/Center Moriches, turn Right onto Wading River Rd., turn Left onto South St., turn Right onto Silas Carter Rd., turn Right onto Davidson Dr., the firehouse will be on the Left* www.northpatchoguefd.com

Forest Of Fear • *600 Rte. 17A, Sterling Forest, Tuxedo Park, NY* • *845-351-5171* • *845-351-5171* • Features Include: 30-Room Haunted House, Live Actors, Animatronic Creatures, Rides, Games **Hours:** Fri.: Nightfall-Midnight, Sat.: Nightfall-1 a.m., Sun.: Nightfall-11 p.m., during Oct. **Fee:** $20 **Directions:** *I-495 Long Island Expwy. to exit 31 Cross Island Pkwy. S., take exit I-295 N. toward New England, George Washington Bridge, take I-95 S. to Rte. 4 W., take Rte. 17, follow signs for 17 N., take exit 15A off the NYS Thruway, continue 8 mi. to Rte. 17A, turn Left to Forest of Fear* www.TheForestOfFear.com

Ghost Stories at the Montauk Lighthouse • *631-668-2544* • *631-661-1876* • Features Include: Ghost Stories & Legends of Fire Island **Hours:** usually the weekend closest to Halloween **Fee: Free** Directions: *I-495 Long Island Expwy., take exit 70 S., travel South on County Rd. 111, take Rte. 27 East to Montauk Point* www.longislandhost.com/montauk/montauk_chamber.html

Ghouls & Gourds • *Brooklyn Botanic Garden* • *1000 Washington Ave. between Eastern Pkwy. & Empire Blvd., Brooklyn, NY* • *718-623-7333* • Features Include: Halloween Costume Parade (wear your costumes), Junk Instrument-Making Workshops, Create Masks, Halloween Extravaganzas, Live Performances, Meet Children's Book Authors & Illustrators, Larger-than-Life Puppets **Hours:** Noon-6 p.m., last weekend in Oct. **Fee:** $8, Under 12: Free, Students & Seniors $4 **Directions:** *I-495*

Long Island Expwy. to the Brooklyn Queens Expwy. W., exit onto Kent Ave., follow the service road (Park Ave.) alongside & then under the Expwy. for 5 blocks, turn Left onto Washington Ave. for 1.75 mi.   *www.bbg.org*

Halloween at the A-Scarium • *New York Aquarium • Wildlife Conservation Society • Surf Ave. & West 8th St., Brooklyn, NY* • *718-265-3454* • Features Include: Wear

Costumes, Learn About Monsters of the Deep, Face Painting, Games, Prizes, Arts & Crafts, Experience the Haunted Pavilion, & 3D Halloween Ride **Hours:** Noon- 4 p.m., last 2 weekends in Oct. **Fee:** Adults $13, Kids 3-12: $9 **Directions:** *Belt Pkwy W. to exit 7B Ocean Pkwy., turn Left onto Ocean Pkwy., continue on Surf Ave. to the New York Aquarium*   *www.nyaquarium.com*

Halloween Harvest in Old Brooklyn • *Wyckoff Farmhouse Museum: Pieter Claesen Wyckoff House* • *5816 Clarendon Rd., Canarsie, NY* • *718-629-5400* •

Features Include: Halloween Celebration, Colonial Brooklyn Halloween Traditions **Hours:** Museum: Tues.-Sun.: 10 a.m-4 p.m., mid-Oct. event **Fee:** Adults $5, Kids $3, Under 10 Free **Directions:** *Southern State Pkwy., exit onto the Belt Pkwy., take exit 13 Rockaway Pkwy., turn Left on Ditmas Ave., cross Ralph Ave., the park is on the Left side of the street*   *www.wyckoffassociation.org*

Annual Halloween Parade • *Main St., Montauk Point, NY• Montauk Chamber of*

Commerce • Features Include: Costume Parade **Hours:** 4 p.m. **Fee: Free** Directions: *I-495 Long Island Expwy., take exit 70 S., travel South on County Rd. 111, take Rte. 27 East to Montauk Point   www.longislandhost.com/montauk/montauk_chamber.html*

The Medford Haunted House • *41 Balsam Dr., Medford, NY* • *631-466-8096* • Features

Include: Spooktacular Haunted House, Ghouls, Goblins, Children can visit during the day through the week of Halloween **Hours:** Fri.-Sun.: after sundown, the weekend closest to Halloween **Fee: Free**, donation requested **Directions:** *I-495 Long Island Expwy. to exit 65, turn Right onto Horse Block Rd., turn Right onto Station Rd., 1st Right onto Patchogue Yaphank Rd., 1st Right onto Southaven Ave., turn Left onto Willow Ct., 1st Right onto Balsam Dr., the house will be on the Left   www.medfordhauntedhouse.com*

Mills Pond House of Horrors • *660 Rte. 25A, St. James, NY* • *631-862-6575* • Features

Include: Historic House circa 1838, 3,700-sq.-ft. Mansion, Special Effects, Live Actors, Not recommended for young children **Hours:** Fri.-Sun.: 6-10 p.m., check web site for specific dates & times, weekends through Oct. **Fee:** $15 **Directions:** *Northern State Pkwy. to end, take 347/Nesconset Hwy., take Moriches Rd. about 1.5 mi., take the 1st Right to Mill Pond Rd., pass the train tracks & continue to the Flower Field   http://stacarts.org/page/show/Halloween*

FALL FOLLY

Trick or Treat Trail & Maze • *Camp Edey* • *1500 Lakeview Ave., Bayport, NY* • *631-472-1625* • *Info.: 631-472-2927* • *Sponsor: Girl Scouts of Suffolk County* • Features **Include:** Trick-or-Treat Trail, Fun Maze, Hourly Costume Pageant, Games, Crafts, Food **Hours:** Sat.: 10 a.m.-3 p.m., Haunted Trail of Terror: 5:30-7:30 p.m. during Oct. **Fee:** Adults: Free, Kids K-4th grades: $10, Haunted Trail of Terror: $12 **Directions:** *I-495 Long Island Expwy., take exit 62 Nicoll's Rd. toward Stony Brook/Blue Point, turn Right at County Rte. 85, turn Right onto Lakeview Ave.* www.gssc.us

New York Witch Festival • *Sheraton Long Island Hotel Grand Ballroom* • *110 Vanderbilt Motor Pkwy., Smithtown, NY* • *516-827-4399* • *631-231-1100* • **Features Include:** Family Events, Entertainment, Workshops, Musical Performances, Tarot Readers, Workshops, Entertainment, Astrology, Healers, Samhain Ritual **Hours:** 9 a.m.-5 p.m., usually 3rd weekend in Oct. **Fee:** Adults $15, Under 12: Free **Directions:** *I-495 Long Island Expwy. to exit 53 Wicks Rd., take the 1st Right off service road to light, turn Right onto Vanderbilt Motor Pkwy., the hotel is on the Left*

SUGGESTIONS • COMMENTS • ERRORS
Linda.ReidBryce @verizon.net
Thanks

Bring: Binoculars for birding, comfortable shoes for walking on sand + rocks. Check the May section in Spring Events for information about the Long Island Lighthouse Challenge.

Web Resources:

www.lilighthousesociety.org/challenge_page_2008/challenge2008.htm

www.NewYorkLighthouses.com

http://www.LongIslandLighthouses.com/challengedirections.htm

Cedar Island Lighthouse • *East Hampton, NY* • *631-852-7620* • *631-207-4331* • *Camping Reservations: 631-244-7275* • *Cedar Island Lighthouse Preservation Committee, P.O. Box 440, East Hampton, NY, 631-645-5230* • In 1860 this lighthouse stood on an island 200 yds.. from shore, guiding whaling ships in & out of Sag Harbor. The hurricane of 1938 joined the lighthouse to the mainland. **Features Include:** 1839 Original Wooden Structure fragment, 35-ft. Boston Granite-Style Structure, Attached Structure is 2.5 stories, 5-ft. Wide Walkway around the Structure, View the Lighthouse from the Bluff, Walk out to the Lighthouse (approx. 45 Min. along the beach each way), Not Open for Tours, Visit the Grounds Only, Bathrooms Available in the Park, Handicap Access to the Bluff Overlook with Viewing Aids, Parking Available in Cedar Point County Park **Hours:** Grounds Open Dawn-Dusk **Fee: Free**, donations appreciated **Directions:** *Montauk Hwy. E., turn North onto Stephen Hands Path in East Hampton, turn Right onto Northwest Rd., bear Left & continue to Alewive Brook Rd., the park entrance is approx. 100 yds. down the road*

www.sagharborchamber.com • www.co.suffolk.ny.us/Home/departments/parks/Parks.aspx

East End Seaport Lighthouse • *Long Beach Bar Lighthouse* • **"Bug Light"** • *East End Seaport Museum & Marine Foundation* • P.O. Box 624, Greenport, NY • 631-477-2100 • Features Include: Museum, 1871 Victorian Structure, Flashing Light, 63-ft. above water, located between Orient Harbor & Gardiner's Bay, its beacon warned navigators rounding the Long Beach Sandbar. The lighthouse is a federal aid to navigation. During "Clean-up the Bug Light day" in the spring, young & old can spend the day helping to clean up this lighthouse. There is also a springtime cruise around the area's offshore lighthouses. For more information on these events, contact the museum. There is a bathroom in the museum. **Hours:** Summer Hours: Mon.,Wed.-Fri.: 11 a.m.-5 p.m., Sat.-Sun.: 9:30 a.m.-4:45 p.m., open mid-May-Sept., open for Tours **Fee:** Museum: $2 **Directions:** *I-495 Long Island Expwy., take exit 73 E. on Rte. 58 which becomes Rte. 25, continue East on Rte. 25 approx. 25 mi. to Greenport*   *www.eastendseaport.org*

Eaton's Neck Lighthouse • *Lighthouse Rd., Northport, NY* • *U.S. Coast Guard at Eaton's Neck* • *Information: 631-261-6959* • Features Include: LI's 2nd Oldest Lighthouse, 73-ft. Sandstone Tower circa 1799, Long Island's only remaining active Fresnel Lens, Bathroom available, Handicap Accessible grounds, visit the grounds by appointment, Gov. facility must call to tour the grounds, no tour of the lighthouse **Fee: Free** Directions: *Northern State Pkwy., take exit 42 toward Hauppauge, merge onto Deer Park Ave., turn Right onto Jericho Tpke., turn Left onto Elwood Rd. which becomes Reservoir Ave., turn Left onto Church St., becomes Ocean Ave., turn Left onto Eaton's Neck Rd. which becomes Asharoken Ave. & then becomes Eaton's Neck Rd. again, turn Right onto Lighthouse Rd. N., to the Coast Guard Station, the lighthouse is at the end of the road*
www.longislandlighthouses.com/eatonsneck.htm

Fire Island Lighthouse ♿ • *Fire Island National Seashore* • *Robert Moses State Park* • *Fire Island, NY* • *631-661-4876* • The Fire Island Lighthouse is an active aid to navigation. **Features Include:** Guided Tower Tours, Panoramic Views of the Atlantic Ocean/Great South Bay/Fire Island/Long Island/Manhattan Skyline & Empire State Building, Birds, Foxes, Deer, Self-Guided Nature Walk, Historic Exhibit Area, Gift Shop **Hours:** Grounds & Lighthouse open Year Round, Tours available **Fee:** Grounds & Museum: **Free**, Tower: Adults: $5, Kids: $3.50, Seniors: $4, Parking: $6, Empire Pass Accepted, grounds & museum Handicap Accessible Bathrooms in parking lot & in museum **Directions:** *Southern State Pkwy. to exit 40 Robert Moses Cswy. S., toward Robert Moses State Park, get to the park & drive around the water tower, head East, park in the East end of Field 5, walk on the boardwalk to the lighthouse*   *www.fireislandlighthouse.com*

Horton Point Lighthouse • *Lighthouse Rd., Southold, NY* • *631-765-5500* • Features Include: 58-ft. Cliff Mounted Lighthouse, Tours Available, Brick & Granite Structure,

Copper Dome, Green Flash Every 10 Seconds, Active Aid to Navigation, 29 Wooden-Step Tower Staircase & two 11-Step Ladders, Museum, Bathroom available in Lighthouse, Handicap Accessible grounds & museum **Hours:** Grounds: Dawn-Dusk, Museum: Summer Weekends, 11:30 a.m.-4 p.m. **Fee:** $4 **Directions:** *I-495 Long Island Expwy. to exit 73 Old Country Rd. toward Greenport, take the 2ⁿᵈ exit in the roundabout onto Old Country Rd., turn Left onto Northville Tpke., turn Right onto Sound Ave. which becomes Middle Rd., turn Left onto Young's Ave., turn Right onto Old North Rd., turn Left onto Lighthouse Rd.*   *www.longislandlighthouses.com/hortonpt.htm*

Huntington Harbor Lighthouse • *P.O. Box 2454, Halesite, NY* • *W. Shore Rd., Huntington Bay, NY* • *631-421-1985* • **Features Include:** Circa 1854, Tower Light Stands 42-ft. above high tide, 5ᵗʰ Order Fresnel Lens, present Light Flashing Every 6 Seconds, Active Aid to Navigation, Tours Available, No Handicap Access, No Bathrooms, Flat rubber-soled shoes required, Children must be older than 5, the 15 min. boat ride accommodates 24 people & runs continuously, Eaton's Neck lighthouse is nearby, there are 2 nice parks and the remains of the original lighthouse on Lloyd Neck **Hours:** 1-hr. Tours: 11 a.m.-3 p.m., May-Oct. weather permitting, Tours are conducted on a first-come-first-serve basis **Fee:** $8 for the boat ride to the lighthouse, includes tour of lighthouse **Directions:** *I-495 Long Island Expwy., Rte. 110 N., through Huntington Village, at the 3ʳᵈ traffic light past Main St./Rte. 25A, turn Left onto Mill Dam Rd., to the end, turn Right onto W. Shore Rd., follow to the town park at Gold Star Battalion Beach, pull into the far parking lot by the flag pole & meet your guide at the beach*
www.longislandlighthouses.com/huntington.htm

Montauk Point Lighthouse & Museum • *2000 Montauk Hwy., Montauk, NY* • *631-668-2544* • *Montauk Historical Society: 631-668-2544* • *Outside of the area, call: 888-685-7646* • **Features Include:** Oldest Lighthouse in New York State, Keeper's House & Tower, circa 1796, 137-step Spiral Staircase Climb, Guided Tours, Views of the Atlantic Ocean from Turtle Hill, Flashing White Light Every 5 Seconds, 110-ft. Octagonal Tower, White & Brown Sandstone Structure, Active Aid to Navigation, Picnic Tables, Small Playground, Great Birding Area, the Museum Exhibit Includes: Drawings Depicting Storms, Photos of 40-ton Whales & Shipwrecks, 25-min. Documentary, Docents Offer Historical Facts & Trivia, Interactive Display of Lighthouses around Long Island, Views of Connecticut, Rhode Island, Block Island & the meeting of tides between the Atlantic & Block Island Sound when weather is clear, tower steps cannot be climbed wearing babies in frontpacks or backpacks, Café Patio Overlooking the Water **Hours:** Mon.-Sun.: 10:30 a.m.-5 p.m. **Fees:** Adults: $6, Kids over 41-in.: $3, Kids under 41-in.: Free (no tower climb), Seniors: $5, Parking: $6 **Directions:** *I-495 Long Island Expwy., take exit 70 S., County Rd./111 S., take Rte. 27 E. to Montauk Point*
www.montauklighthouse.com

FALL FOLLY

Old Field Point Lighthouse • *Old Field Rd., Port Jefferson, NY* • *Village of Old Field Administrative Offices: 631-941-9412* • **Features Include:** 1869 Structure, VRB-25 Light Flashes Alternating Red & Green every 10 seconds, Granite Structure, Black Iron Tower, Active Aid to Navigation, No Public Access, the light is visible from Old Field Rd., but parking is prohibited anywhere on the road **Hours:** Grounds Tour only by appointment **Fee:** $2, Not Handicap Accessible, No Bathrooms **Directions:** *Northern State Pkwy. toward Hauppague, to the end, merge onto Rte. 347 East, turn Left onto Nicolls Rd., turn Right onto N. Country Rd./25A, turn Left onto Main St. which becomes Old Field Rd., turn Right onto Old Field Pl., the lighthouse is at the end of the road, it is West of the entrance to Port Jefferson Harbor* www.longislandlighthouses.com/oldfield.htm

Orient Point Lighthouse • *"The Coffee Pot,"* • *Point Rd., Orient Point, NY* • *631-207-4331* • **Features Include:** 3-Story 64-ft. Tower Circa 1899, Flashing White Light Every 5 Seconds, Active Aide to Navigation, the lighthouse helps mariners navigate through Plum Gut, which runs between the reef & Plum Island, Orient Point is the furthest point East on the North Fork of Long Island, No Tours, View from Land Only **Fee: Free**, No Bathrooms, Not Handicap Accessible **Directions:** *I-495 Long Island Expwy. toward Riverhead, take exit 73 towards Greenport/Orient Point, take the 2nd exit on the roundabout Old Country Rd., turn Left onto Northville Tpke., turn Right onto Sound Ave., which becomes Middle Rd., & later becomes Main Rd., & then Point Rd., the lighthouse is at the end of the road* www.longislandlighthouses.com/orientpt.htm

Plum Island Lighthouse • *Long Island Chapter of the US Lighthouse Society* • *631-207-4331* • **Features Include:** Circa 1869, 34-ft. Tall, No Longer Active, No Public Access, Plum Island is a restricted area for Animal Disease Research, No Bathrooms, Not Handicap Accessible, No Tours, View the Lighthouse from the Land Only **Fee: Free Directions:** *Follow the directions for the Orient Point Lighthouse* www.longislandlighthouses.com/plumisl.htm

SUGGESTIONS • COMMENTS • ERRORS

Linda.ReidBryce @verizon.net

Thanks

Canoe + Kayak season runs from mid April-mid Nov. weather permitting.

NASSAU COUNTY

The Waterfront Center • *One West End Ave., Oyster Bay, NY* • **516-922-7245** •
Features Include: Boat & Kayak Rentals, the Oyster Bay Sailing School, The Oyster
Sloop "Christeen" (historic landmark), Harbor Tours, Sailing Lessons, Sailboat Racing
& Rentals, Fishing, Sunset Sails, Private Charters, Sailing Vacations, Children's
Summer Camp, Educational Programs, & Certification Classes Hours & Fees: vary
per event Directions: *Northern State Pkwy., take exit 35 N., Rte. 106 N. at the Milleridge
Inn, drive approx. 6.5 mi., cross over Rte. 25A, make a Left onto Audrey Ave. (see the Coin
Gallery on the corner) drive 1 light & go to the 2nd stop sign, turn Right at the railroad
tracks onto Theodore Roosevelt Park, make an immediate Left onto West End Ave. (before
entrance booth), red brick building on the Left*   www.thewaterfrontcenter.org

SUFFOLK COUNTY

Amagansett Beach & Bicycle • *624 Montauk Hwy. (at Cross Hwy.), Amagansett, NY* •
631-267-6325 • Features Include: Row, Kayak, Surf or Kiteboard Lessons, Guided
Tours, Accabonac Harbor Hours & Fees: vary per event Directions: *I-495 Long Island
Expwy., take exit 68 William Floyd Pkwy./Rte. 46, take the ramp onto NY 27 E., turn Left onto
Montauk Hwy./Rte. 27, turn Left onto Main St./NY 27, Amagansett Beach & Bicycle will be on
the Right*   www.amagansettbeachco.com

Belmont Lake State Park • *625 Belmont Ave., West Babylon, NY 11704* • **631-667-
5055** • This full service park is the headquarters of the Long Island State Park Region.
Features Include: Boating, Fishing, Picnicking, Playgrounds, Handicap Accessible Boat

Rentals **Hours:** Dawn-Dusk, Year-Round **Fee:** Off Season: **Free**, April-Nov.: $8, Empire Pass Accepted **Directions:** *Southern State Pkwy., exit 37 N., merge onto Belmont Ave.*

http://nysparks.state.ny.us/parks/list.asp

Brookhaven • NYS • *567 Middle Country Rd., Brookhaven, NY • 631-929-4314 •* **Features Include:** 2,300-acre Park (The Pine Barrens), Canoeing, Boating, A Free Pine Barrens Recreation Brochure can be downloaded at: http://pb.state.ny.us/chart_ recreation_main_page.htm **Hours:** Dawn-Dusk **Fee: Free** **Directions:** *I-495 Long Island Expwy. to exit 68 William Floyd Pkwy. toward Shirley/Co Hwy. 46 N., to Wading River, merge onto County Rte. 46/William Floyd Pkwy., take the ramp onto Middle Country Rd./Rte. 25* *http://nysparks.state.ny.us/sites/info*

Bob's Canoe Rental, Inc. Ⓥ **• *Nissequogue River State Park, P.O. Box 529, Kings Park, NY 11754 • 631 269-9761 •*** **Features Include:** Canoe & Kayak Rentals, Guided Tours, Tidal River between Kings Park & Smithtown **Directions:** *I-495 Long Island Expwy. to exit 53 Sunken Meadow Pkwy. N. to exit SM3E., Rte. 25/Jericho Tpke. E., 4 mi. to Paul T. Given Park on Right, park is just past the Rte. 25 & 25A merger, diagonally across the road from the statue of the Smithtown Bull* **Directions to the Kings Park Bluff:** *I-495 Long Island Expwy. to exit 53 Sunken Meadow Pkwy. N., take exit SM4E., Pulaski Rd. E., drive 4 mi. to road's end, if you are using Mapquest, use 790 Old Dock Rd., Kings Park, NY 11754* *www.canoerentalslongisland.com*

Eagle's Neck Paddling Company • *49295 Main Rd./Rte. 25, Southold, NY • 631-765-3502 •* **Features Include:** Kayaks, Canoes, Paddling Gear, Tours, Recreational Boats, Angler Boats, Rentals, Paddling School, Sunset Tours: every night (except Mon.) 5-8 p.m., Hike & Paddle Tours: at Arshamomaque Pond, Sat.-Sun. from 8 a.m.-12:30 p.m., Kayak for Kids Tours: Gooseneck Creek, Sat. & Sun. from 8-11 a.m., Full Moon Tours: at Arshamomaque Pond, Endurance Paddle: at Gooseneck Creek, Wed., Long Island Treasure Tours: at Arshamomaque Pond: Sat. 5-8:30 p.m. **Hours & Fee:** vary, Double Keowee II or Fiberglass Individual Cockpit Doubles: 2 hr.: $40, .5-day: $50, Daily: $60, 2-Day: $100, Singles 2 hr.: $30, Half day: $45, Daily: $50, 2-Day: $75, weekly & 1-3 month leasing, 4 Paddling Areas, Maps, Including: Hallock Bay from Orient State Park, Cutchogue Harbor from Captain Marty's, New Suffolk **Directions:** *I-495 Long Island Expwy., take exit 73 E. Rte. 58 which becomes Rte. 25, continue on Rte. 25 E. to Southold (approx. 20 mi. from the end of the expwy.), Eagle's Neck is directly across from the Gulf Service Station on the Left (North) side of the road* *www.eaglesneck.com*

Glacier Bay Sports • *81-C Fort Salonga Rd., Northport, NY • 631-262-9116 •* **Fearures Include:** Introductory, Intermediate & Advanced Lessons, Tours, Located on Northport

Harbor, Singles & Double Kayak Rentals, Recreational Kayaks, Long Touring Kayaks, staff members will discuss some important points about kayaking & water safety & launch you into Northport Harbor. Kayaks can be rented from March 31-Nov. 15, Northport Harbor is not restricted by tide schedules & there is a floating dock behind the shop. **Hours:** Mon.-Fri.: 11 a.m.-6 p.m., Sat.: 10 a.m.-5 p.m, Sun.: 11 a.m.-4 p.m., **Fee:** Single: 1.5 hrs.: $25, 3 hrs.: $37, 4 hrs.: $49, Full Day: $59, Double: 1.5 hrs.: $32, 3 hrs.: $47, 4 hrs.: $59, Full Day: $67 **Directions:** *I-495 Long Island Expwy. To exit 53N Sunken Meadow Pkwy. to the last exit, Rte 25A W. toward Huntington, travel 5.5 mi. on the Right in front of Brittania Yacht Club* www.glacierbaysports.com

Main Beach Surf & Sport • *352 Montauk Hwy., Wainscott, NY* • *631-537-2716* •

Features Include: Canoe & Kayak Rentals, Surf Boards, Kiteboarding Lessons, Standup Paddleboards, Surf Camp for Kids, Lessons, Tours, Organize Beach Cleanups, Promote Athletic Events, Showcase New & Classic Extreme Sport Films, Full Moon Wine & Cheese Tours, Lobster Bakes, Sun. Morning Weekly Tours at Northwest Harbor, sign up space is limited **Hours & Fees:** vary per event **Directions:** *I-495 Long Island Expwy., take exit 68 William Floyd Pkwy. S. toward Shirley, turn Right onto NY 27 E. toward Montauk, turn Left onto Montauk Hwy./NY 27 E., the shop will be on the Right* www.mainbeach.com

Nissequogue River Canoe & Kayak Rentals • *112 Whittier Dr., Kings Park, NY* • *631-979-8244* • **Features Include:** Individual & Group Trips, all trips are Tide Dependent, the trip begins & ends at either the Nissequogue River: "River Mouth"/The Bluff, Foot of Old Dock Rd., Kings Park, NY or the "Head Waters", Paul T. Given County Park, Rtes. 25 & 25A, Smithtown, NY (opposite the Smithtown Bull) **Hours::** vary with tides **Fee:** Canoe Rental: $50 (holds family of 4), 2-Man Kayack $60 **Directions: The Nissequogue River:** *I-495 Long Island Expwy., take exit 53N. Sagtikos/Sunken Meadow Pkwy. N.* **The "Bluff:"** *Take exit SM4 E. Pulaski Rd. E. for 3 mi., Pulaski Rd. becomes Old Dock Rd., when it crosses Main St./Rte. 25A & ends at the water's edge* **The "Bull:"** *Exit SM3 E. - Jericho Tpke. E. for 4 mi., to, the Paul T. Given County Park located on the south side of Jericho Tpke. diagonally across from the Smithtown Bull statue* www.canoerentals.com

Nissequogue River State Park • *799 St. Johnland Rd., Kings Park, NY* • *631-269-4927*

• **Features Include:** Canoe & Kayak Launch, Marina, Boat Launch Sites, Boat Rentals, Bird Watching, Museum/Visitor Center, Family Events, the best time to be on the river is from 4 hrs. before high tide until 4 hrs. after. Launch a craft 2.5 hrs. before high tide, this will allow 2 hrs. to paddle up, with the current, to the headwaters at Jericho Tpke. have a half hr. for lunch, & then the current will head back downriver with the outgoing tide, back to the Nissequogue River State Park. Check the tide schedule. **Hours:** Dawn-Dusk, Year-Round

Fee: **Free** off-season, Memorial Day-Labor Day: $8, Empire Pass Accepted, **Directions:** *Sunken Meadow Pkwy., take exit SM 4, drive East on Pulaski Rd. which changes into Old Dock Rd. at the 5th traffic light, make a Right onto St. Johnland Rd., park entrance is about .5 mi. on the Left* *http://nysparks.state.ny.us/parks*

Peconic Paddler ⑤ • *89 Peconic Ave., Riverhead, NY* • *631-727-9895* • Features **Include:** Canoeing, Kayaking, Specializing in Sea Paddling & Fishing, Parking, Drop-Off **Hours:** Thurs.-Sun.: 8 a.m.-5 p.m., Season: late April-mid-Oct. **Directions:** *I-495 Long Island Expwy. to exit 71, turn Right at stop, drive 4 mi. to traffic circle, Peconic Paddler is on the traffic circle* *www.peconicpaddler.com*

Peconic River Canoe Launch • *Rte. 25, Riverhead, NY* • *631-854-4949* • This new launching site was made possible through the Peconic Estuary Improvement Project conducted by the NYS Department of Transportation. This site provides direct access for canoe/kayak enthusiasts to the Peconic River. **Directions:** *I-495 Long Island Expwy., to exit 72 Rte. 25 E., the launch is located approx. 1.3 mi. on Rte. 25 after the Tanger Outlet & Forge Rd., on the Right-hand side*

Puff-n-Putt Family Fun Center • *659 Montauk Hwy., Montauk, NY* • *631-668-4473 • 631-271-6549* • Puff-n-Putt is located on the shore of Fort Pond, an enclosed 1.5-mi. freshwater lake. **Features Include:** Sailboat, Pedal Boat, Kayak, Canoe, Row Boat Rentals, Pizza Village, 18-hole Miniature Golf Course, Video Arcade, Family Fun Center, Fort Pond located on the right side of road **Hours:** Mon.-Sat.: 9 a.m.-11 p.m., Sun.: 10 a.m.-11 p.m., Last Boat Rental: 6 p.m., Last Golf Game: 10 p.m., Memorial Day-mid-Sept., weekends only from mid-Sept.-Columbus Day, closed Columbus Day-Memorial Day **Fee:** Starting at: $18 per hr. **Directions:** *I-495 Long Island Expwy., take exit 68 for William Floyd Pkwy. S., slight Right to merge onto NY 27 E. toward Montauk, turn Left to stay on NY 27 E., turn Left onto Main St., continue onto NY 27 E./Pantigo Rd., continue to follow NY 27 E., Puff-n-Putt will be on the Left* *www.puffnputt.com*

Robert Cushman Murphy County Park • **SC** • *River Rd., Calverton/Manorville, NY* • *631-854-0971 • 631-854-4949* • Features **Include:** 60-acre Swan Pond, Fishing, Boating, Fishing is permitted on the Swan Pond with a required NYS Fisherman's License. This Swan Pond offers Large Mouth Bass, Eastern Chain Pickeral, Yellow Perch, Blue Gill, Bullhead Catfish and Pumpkinseed Sunfish. Car top boats only. Park on the side of the road. There are no services in this park. **Hours:** Year-Round **Fee:** **Free**, **Directions:** *I-495 Long Island Expwy., take exit 70 CR 111 S., turn Left onto Halsey Manor Rd., follow North, cross the Long Island Expwy. & railroad tracks, Halsey Manor Rd. becomes Connecticut Ave. once railroad tracks have been crossed, follow Connecticut*

Ave. N., make a Left turn onto River Rd. & make the next Left onto Old River Rd., follow Old River Rd. to the 1ˢᵗ entrance on the Right (North side of the road)

www.co.suffolk.ny.us/departments/parks

Sears Bellows • SC • *Sears Bellows Pond Rd., Hampton Bays, NY • Park Office: 631-852-8290 • Big Duck: 631-852-8292 • Camping Reservations: 631-244-7275 •* Sears

Bellows is situated within the Long Island Pine Barrens. **Features Include:** Rowboat Rentals, Camping (tents & trailer), Picnicking, Lifeguard Protected Swimming, Freshwater Fishing (bluegill, bass, perch & pickerel), this park is closed to certain activities during waterfowl hunting season. NYS regulations apply to all sporting activities. This is the home of the Big Duck. **Hours:** Dawn-Dusk, Year-Round **Fee: Free** off-season, mid-June-Labor Day with Green Key: $5, no Green Key: $8 **Directions:** *Northern State Pkwy., take Wantagh State Pkwy. S., exit onto Sunrise Hwy. take exit 65 N., follow Rte. 24, make a Left onto Bellows Pond Rd., the park entrance is on the Right*

www.co.suffolk.ny.us/Home/departments/parks/Parks.aspx

Shelter Island Kayak Tours • *71 Cartwright Rd., P.O. Box 360, Shelter Island, NY • 631-749-1990, 631-453-0205 •* Features Include: Guided Kayak Tours around

Coecles Harbor, Self-Guided Tours, Marsh Lands, Protected Creeks, Explore Shore Lines, Osprey & Hawks, Watch Egrets & Turtles, Observe Fish & Marine Life, Clear Waterways **Hours:** Daily Tour: 10-Noon **Fee:** Tour : $60, Kids Under 12: $30, Double Kayak: $50-2 hrs., $70-4 hrs., Single Kayak $30-2hrs, $45-4 hrs. **Directions:** *I-495 Long Island Expwy., exit 73, take Rte. 58 E., drive approx. 3 mi., merge onto Rte. 25 E., drive approx 20 mi. to Green Port, follow signs for Rte. 114 S., turn Right onto 6ᵗʰ St., drive 1 block , turn Left onto Wiggins St., to end, make a hard Right & continue turning to enter the final staging area, take the ferry to Shelter Island Heights, take Rte.114 S. 2.2 mi, just past the Shelter Island School see a hut on the same side of the road, meet there to use bathrooms & then follow a guide to Cockles Bay or take SummerField Pl., turn Right onto Grand Ave., turn Left onto Chase Ave., turn Left onto Bridge St./Ferry Rd., continue on Manwaring Rd., turn Left onto Ram Island Rd., turn Right onto N. Cartwright Rd., Jay Damuck's Shelter Island Kayak Tours is on the Right* www.kayaksi.com *North Ferry Company • 631-749-0139 • no reservations, pay onboard*

www.northferry.com/schedule.html

Southaven County Park • SC • *Victory Ave., Brookhaven, NY • 631-854-1414 • 631-924-4490 • 631-345-2449 •* The Carman's River flows through this park. **Features**

Includes: 1,356-acre Park, Canoe Launch Site, Rowboat Rentals, Hiking, Camping (tents & trailers), Picnicking, Freshwater Fishing, Hunting, Bicycle Hostel, Bridal Paths, & the LI Steamer Trains (see museums) **Hours:** Dawn-Dusk **Fee: Free Directions:** *Southern State Pkwy., exit at Sunrise Hwy., take exit 58 N., as you enter William Floyd Pkwy., turn West onto Victory Ave., follow signs to the main entrance of the park*

www.co.suffolk.ny.us/Home/departments/parks/Parks.aspx

FALL FOLLY

Sunken Meadow State Park • *Rte. 25A & Sunken Meadow Pkwy., Northport, NY* • *631-269-4333* • The park is located on the Long Island Sound, & has a wide range of plant and animal life. **Features Include:** Kayaking, Canoeing, Windsurfing, Fishing,**Hours:** Dawn-Dusk, Year-Round **Fee:** Free off season, Memorial Day-Labor Day: $10, Weekends Labor Day-Oct.: $8, Empire Pass Accepted **Directions:** *I-495 Long Island Expwy., take exit 53 Sunken Meadow/Sagtikos Pkwy. to the end*

http://nysparks.state.ny.us/parks

Theodore Roosevelt County Park • **SC** • *Montauk Hwy., Montauk, NY* • *631-852-7878* • *Camping: 631-852-7879* • **Features Include:** Canoeing, Kayaking, Check in at the Third House/Park Office, no rentals available. America's 1st cattle ranching system was located in 17th century Montauk. "Big Reed" Pond, located off East Lake Dr. is noted for its fishing opportunities/Canoeing & kayaking. There Spanish-American War Exhibit displaying photos & memorabilia from the war, Camp Wikoff, & gift shop **Hours:** Camp Wikoff is open to the public from May-Oct., Wed.-Sun:. 10 a.m.-5 p.m. **Fee:** Free off-season **Directions:** *Southern State Pkwy., follow Montauk Hwy. E. through Montauk Village, past E. Lake Dr., park sign & entrance are on North side of Montauk Hwy.*

www.co.suffolk.ny.us/Home/departments/parks/Parks.aspx

LI'S 4 LARGEST RIVERS

The Nissequogue is a tidal river. An 8-ft. rise & fall of the tide can produce rapid currents, & sometimes strong winds occur. The best time to be on the river is from 4 hrs. before high tide until 4 hrs. after. All canoe or kayak trips, therefore, should be planned with this in mind. If you are not familiar with this river, seek some advice before launching. To take maximum advantage of the current & enjoy the longest trip, launch your craft 2.5 hrs. before high tide. This will give you 2 hrs. to paddle up with the current, to the headwaters at Jericho Tpke. Once there you will have a .half hr. or so for a little lunch break, then you & the current will head back down river with the outgoing tide, back to the Nissequogue River State Park. High tide is different every day. Make sure you plan ahead.

The Peconic River provides an easy paddling, relaxing 8-mi. canoe trip which takes about 4 hrs. Much of its upper watershed remains undisturbed. This is a productive warm water fish habitat, & the only location in NYS where banded sunfish are found. The Peconic is an estuary of the Atlantic Ocean. Many species of birds inhabit the wetlands bordering the river, including Canadian Geese, American Black Ducks, Pied-Billed Grebe & Great Blue Heron. The Peconic River is 1 of few locations on Long Island where River Otters can be found.

The Connetquot River is also known as Great River. This 6-mi. long river in Islip is recognized by NYS as a Wild, Scenic & Recreational River. 1 of the nice destination spots on the river is the Bayard Cutting Arboretum. You can visit Timber Point Park and stop for lunch on the riverbank in front of Dowling College. The river's habitat is the largest contiguous area of undeveloped land in Suffolk County that encompasses an entire river watershed. It is known for its brook, brown & rainbow trout fly fishing. The upper reaches of the river including its headwaters are totally in the Connetquot River State Park Preserve or Lakeland County Park before it becomes an estuary. It starts just South of the Long Island Expwy. from springs in the Lakeland County Park in Islandia, NY where it is called Connetquot Brook. The estuary portion is South of Sunrise Hwy. in Oakdale.

The Carman's River is a fresh water river for the first 8-mi. & then becomes an estuary for the last 2. The upstream portion of the Carman's River is great for beginning paddlers, however, be cautious when planning a trip as the downstream opens quickly into the Great South Bay with conditions that are much more suited for experienced paddlers. Most of the river is specifically protected by the Central Long Island Pine Barrens. Adjoining the river is the Wertheim National Wildlife Refuge. The river is designated by NYS as a Scenic & Recreational River. Southhaven County Park encompasses upstream parts of the river & special regulations trout fishing can be accessed through them.

QUEENS

LIC Community Boathouse • *46-01 5ʰ St., Queens, NY* • 718-228-9214 • Features **Include:** Kayak from Hallets Cove in Astoria, Paddle to see a film at Socrates Sculpture Park, Manhattan Skyline & Sunsets Paddles, Tidal Currents determine the launch & return time, launching from the beach next to Socrates Sculpture Park on Vernon Blvd. at 31ˢ Ave., first-come first-served basis, all participants must be able to swim, departing from Anable Basin near 46ᵗʰ Ave. and 5ᵗʰ St. or from Hallets Cove back to the LICCB, all paddles are subject to cancellation due to bad weather or recent heavy rain, visit web site for calender of events, please check telephone hotline for possible cancellation announcements **Hours:** vary **Fee:** Free

Directions: *Northern State Pkwy. to Grand Central Pkwy., exit onto Union Tpke., turn Right onto Union Tpke., turn Right onto Queens Blvd., turn Left onto Jackson Ave./New York 25A W., turn Right onto 46ᵗʰ Ave., turn Left onto 5ᵗʰ St., the boathouse will be on the Left* www.liccb.com

SUGGESTIONS • COMMENTS • ERRORS

Linda.ReidBryce @verizon.net

Thanks

ARCHERY

ARROWS, SKILL & PRECISION

Cedar Creek Park • *3524 Merrick Rd., Seaford, NY* • *516-571-7470* • The park is on Seaman's Creek & the East Bay. • **Features Include:** 259 acres, Archery Range (25-100 yd. Lengths) **Directions:** *Northern State Pkwy., exit onto 135 S. Seaford Oyster-Bay Expwy., take exit 1 W. Merrick Rd. W. toward Freeport, merge onto Merrick Rd.*

www.nassaucountyny.gov/agencies/Parks/

American Outdoor Sports, Inc. • *2040 Broadhollow Rd., Farmingdale, NY* • *631-249-1832* • **Features Include:** Indoor Archery Range, 10, 20, 30 yd. Shooting Ranges **Hours:** Tues.-Fri.: 11 a.m.-8:30 p.m., Sat.: 11 a.m.-5:30 p.m., Sun.: 11a.m.-3:30 p.m.,**Fee:** All-Day Range Pass: $5, Guest Fee: $10 with annual registration of $10, March-May 31, Registration: $8, Guest Fee June-Aug. 31, parent supervision required for kids under 18 **Directions:** *I-495 Long Island Expwy. W., take exit 49 S. Rte. 110 S., take Rte.110 approx. 2.5 mi., American Outdoor Sports is on the Right* www.americanoutdoorsports.com

Long Island Shooting Range • *Rte. 25, Middle Country Rd., Ridge/Brookhaven, NY* • *631-924-5091* • **Features Include:** 8 Outdoor Archery Stations, Seasonal: Skeet & Trap Fields, Year-Round Facility, Newly Renovated, Accommodates Beginner & Competition Shooters, Premier East Coast Shooting Facility, Instructors Available **Hours:** Wed.-Sun.: 9 a.m.-5 p.m., Seasonal: Skeet & Trap Fields open Thurs. nights until 9 p.m. **Directions:** *Long Island Expwy. to exit 68 N. William Floyd Pkwy., go N. approx. 5 mi. to Rte. 25 E. Middle Country Rd., go E. 1 mi., the Range is on the Left, North side of Rte. 25* www.longislandshootingrange.com

Smith Point Archery Lanes • *215 East Main St., Patchogue, NY* • *631-289-3399* •

Features Include: 20 Indoor 20 yd. Stations, 25 Indoor 10-40-yd. Stations, League & Tournament **Fee:** $8, Members: $6, Yearly Membership: $49.95, Rental: $5 **Directions:** *I-495 Long Island Expwy., take exit 62 for Nicolls Rd. toward Blue Point/County Hwy. 97/Stony Brook, turn Left onto Nicolls Rd., turn Left onto County Rte. 85, continue on W. Main St., the facility will be on the Left* *www.smithpointarchery.com*

C&B Archery • *11 Commercial St., Hicksville, NY* • *516-933-2697* • Features Include:

Indoor Range, Adult & Junior Leagues, 3D & Regulation Leagues, D.E.C. Hunter Safety Courses (Bow & Guns), NFAA Certified Instruction, Shooting Techniques, Techno Hunt System, 26 Shooting Lanes, Indoor Range, 10, 15 & 20-yd. Targets, Suffolk Archers Specials, Adult Night Out, Birthday Parties, Retail Store, PAL & Boy Scouts **Hours:** Tues.-Thurs.: 11 a.m.-9 p.m., Fri.: 11 a.m.-7 p.m., Sat.: 11 a.m.-6 p.m., Sun.: 11 a.m.-4 p.m. **Fee:** Range Time 1st hr.: $9, each additional hr.: $5, Archery Affiliation Discount: $2 off the 1st hr., Shoot All Day: $20, Bow Rental: $11 per. hr. , First time basic instruction: $5 per hr., Targets: .50, Advanced Instruction: $50 per hr., Group Rates Available **Directions:** *Northern State Pkwy., take exit 36 S. Oyster Bay Rd. turn Right onto S. Oyster Bay Rd., turn Right onto Walter Ave., turn Left onto Joseph Ln., turn Right onto Field Ave., turn Left onto New South Rd., turn Right onto Commercial St.*

www.cbarchery.net

Suffolk Archers • *86 Pidgeon Hill Rd., Huntington Station, NY* • *516-873-8898*

• **Features Include:** 20-acre Archery Park, 2 Ranges, Target Course, Practice Butts from 10-80 yds. in 2 Fields, Field & Target Archery, Hunting Archery, Traditional & Compound Bows, 28 Target National Field Archery Association (NFAA) Sanctioned Field Course, 28 Knock-a-Block Target Stations, 28 Life-Size, Full Body 3D Animal Targets Including: Deer, Bear, Coyotes, Mountain Lions, Elk, Caribou, Hogs, Multi-Deer Shots, Family Tree Stand accessible without climbing, Moving 3D Deer Target, Illuminated Night Shooting, Scheduled Events Throughout The Year, 3D Events, NFAA Sanctioned Tournaments, Knock-a-Block Tournaments, 6-week Snowflake League, Traditional Bow Events, Novelty Shoots, Tournaments for All Levels **Hours:** 24 hrs., 7 days a week, 365 days a year **Fee:** Family Membership: $200 with 16 service hrs., $250 with 8 service hrs., $300 without service hours **Directions:** *I-495 Long Island Expwy., take exit 50 Bagatelle Rd. N., to "T," intersection, turn Left onto Half Hollow Rd. to 1st, Right onto Carman Rd., to next "T" intersection turn Left onto Wolf Hill Rd., to 1st, traffic light, turn Right onto Pidgeon Hill Rd.* *www.suffolkarchers.com*

HIKING & WALKING

LEAVES CRUNCH, TRAILS CLIMB & COLOR IGNITES

Make walking more fun for kids by having them wear a pedometer to count the number of steps they take while hiking or exercising (2,000 steps = about 1 mi.).

The book *Short Nature Walks On L.I.* made the following suggestions: Wear a hat, a light colored long sleeve shirt, long pants, and long socks. Stretch the tops of the socks over trouser legs to keep the ticks out, and use insect repellent. Long pants and a hat will protect you from many hazards on the trail." Be conscious of the fact that a hat will protect your hair from insects and your eyes from sweat and sun. (Rodney Albright & Priscilla Albright 2-3) If your clothes or body come in contact with poisonous plants such as poisonous sap, wash thoroughly with a special cleansing product such as "Ten-check spell." Deer ticks can get on your clothes simply by brushing against plants because they look for a warm patch of skin to borrow. It is a good idea to especially check your head, armpits and in-between your legs. It's a great idea to stay on groomed trails & avoid the problem altogether. "After a hike examine your body for ticks. If you find one attached to your skin, promptly use a fine-tipped tweezer to remove it. Grab the tick as close to the skin as possible and firmly tug. After removing a tick, watch to see if a rash develops. Not all deer ticks are infected with Lyme Disease: you can be bitten several times without having a problem. However, an untreated bite my have serious medical consequence (2-3).

NASSAU COUNTY
Bailey Arboretum • NC • *194 Bayville Rd. (& Feeks Ln.), Lattingtown, NY • 516-571-8020* • Features Include: 42-acre Estate, Nature Trail, Guided Walks,

Picnics, Concerts, Educational Programs available by appointment, Rare Shrubs, Plants, & Flower Beds **Hours:** Tues.-Sun.: 9 a.m.-4 p.m., Year-Round **Fee: Free** **Directions:** *Northern State Pkwy., take exit 35N., 106/107 N. State Hwy. toward Oyster Bay, merge onto N. Broadway Ave./Rte. 106/107, continue to follow Rte. 106/107 N., turn Right onto Jericho Oyster Bay Rd./Rte. 106, turn Left onto Brookville Rd., continue on Wolver Hollow Rd., turn Right onto Chicken Valley Rd., turn Left onto Oyster Bay Rd., turn Right onto Bayville Rd.* *www.baileyarboretum.org*

Bethpage State Park • *99 Quaker Meeting House Rd., Farmingdale, NY* • *516-249-0701* • **Features Include:** Hiking, Nature Trail, Playground, Picnic Area **Hours:** Dawn-Dusk, Year-Round **Fee: Free** entry off-season on weekdays, Parking: $8, Sun.-Sat., Memorial Day-Labor Day, Empire Pass Accepted **Directions:** *I-495 Long Island Expwy. E., take exit 44 S. Rte. 135/Seaford Oyster Bay Expwy., take exit 8 E. Powell Ave. & follow signs to the park, park in the picnic area, the trail will take you through the woods* *http://nysparks.state.ny.us*

Charles T. Church Nature Preserve • *North Shore Wildlife Sanctuary* • *Frost Mill Rd., Mill Neck, NY* • *516-671-0283* • **Features Include:** 60-acre Preserve, known as "Shu Swamp," Wooded Wetland, 2.5 mi. of Trails, Boardwalks across muddier areas **Hours:** Sat.-Thurs **Fee: Free Directions:** *Northern State Pkwy., take exit 35 N. 106/107 N., take 106 N., turn Left onto Brookville Rd., continue on Wolver Hollow Rd., turn Right onto Chicken Valley Rd., turn Left onto Oyster Bay Rd./Oyster Bay Glen Cove Rd., turn Right onto Frost Mill Rd.*

Christopher Morley Park • **NC.** *500 Searingtown Rd., Roslyn, NY* • *516-571-8113* • Christopher Morley wrote books, plays, poetry & essays & founded the Book of the Month Club. The "Knothole," a 1-room wooden cabin, & was Morley's former studio. • **Features Include:** 98-acres Park, 30 acre of Nature Trails, 1-mi. walk **Hours:** Dawn-Dusk, Year-Round, call for (Knothole) hrs. **Fee: Free Directions:** *I-495 Long Island Expwy., take exit 36N. Searingtown Rd., take Searingtown Rd. N. & look for the park entrance on the Right, it is about 200 yds. from the I-495* *www.nassaucountyny.gov/*

Cow Meadow Park & Preserve • **NC** • *South Main St., Freeport, NY* • *516-571-8685* • The park is located on Freeport Creek. **Features Include:** 171-acre Park, Hiking, Nature Trails, Marine Wetlands, Salt Marsh, Mud Flat, Tidal Creek Habitats **Hours:** Dawn-Dusk, **Fee: Free Directions:** *Southern State Pkwy., take exit 22 S. Meadowbrook Pkwy., exit at M9 W. Merrick Rd., immediate Left onto Mill Rd., turn Left onto S. Main St., the entrance is on the Left*

C.W. Post Community Arboretum • *Long Island University, 720 Northern Blvd., Brookville, NY • 516- 299-3500* • A 40-acre portion of the C.W. Post Campus is designated as an arboretum. The trail winds past the Tudor mansion that was the home of heiress Marjorie Merriweather Post. • **Features Include:** 40-acres Arboretum, 120 species of Native Trees, Nature Trails, Formal Gardens, Self-Guided Walking Trail (maps available at Hillwood Commons Information Desk or by calling 516-299-3500 **Hours:** Dawn-Dusk **Fee: Free Directions:** *I-495 Long Island Expwy., take exit 39 Glen Cove Rd., head North for 2 mi., turn Right onto Northern Blvd. E./Rte. 25A, C.W. Post is 2 mi. on the Right.*   *www.liu.edu/arboretum*

Fox Hollow Preserve • *The Nature Conservancy • White Oak Tree Rd., Laurel Hollow, NY • 631-367-3225* • **Features Include:** 26-acre Preserve, Former Farm, Bird Watching, Hiking **Hours:** Dawn-Dusk **Fee: Free**, contact the Nature Conservancy for permission (250 Lawrence Hill Rd., Cold Spring Harbor)

Garvies Point Museum & Preserve • *NC* • *50 Barry Dr., Glen Cove, NY • 516-571-8010* • **Features Include:** 62-acre Preserve, Hikes, Walks, Exhibits, Educational Programs, Guided Tours, Preserve Trail Guide available at the museum, Dinosaur Fossils have been found on the beach hike **Hours:** 10 a.m.-4 p.m. **Fee: Free** for hiking, Museum Entry: Adults: $3, Kids: $2 **Directions:** *Northern State Pkwy., exit 107 N. toward Oyster Bay/Glen Cove, take 107 N., becomes Pratt Blvd./Glen Cove Rd./Glen Cove Ave., turn Right onto Village Sq./Brewster St., turn Left onto Mill Hill Rd. which becomes The Place, stay straight to go onto Ellwood St., turn Left onto McLaughlin St., turn Left onto Barry Dr.*
www.garviespointmuseum.com

Hempstead Lake State Park • *NYS* • *Eagle Ave. & Lake Dr., West Hempstead, NY • 516-766-1029* • This is the largest lake in Nassau County. • **Features Include:** Hiking Trails, 2.5-mi. Northern Pond Hike (map available in park office), 2-mi. Walk around the Lake **Hours:** Dawn-Dusk, Year-Round **Fee: Free** off-season, April-Oct.: $8, Empire Pass Accepted **Directions:** *Southern State Pkwy., take exit 18 Eagle Ave., keep Right at the fork, follow signs for Rockville Centre/Hempstead Lake State Park, turn Right at Eagle Ave.*
www.stateparks.com/hempstead_lake.html

John F. Kennedy Memorial Wildlife Sanctuary • *Town of Oyster Bay & the NYS Department of Environmental Conservation • Ocean Pkwy., Massapequa • 516-797-4110* • The sanctuary is considered 1 of the most important refuges for waterfowl in the northeast. It is located just West of Tobay Beach. **Features Include:** 500-acre Bayside Sanctuary, Hiking Trails, Wintering Area for Waterfowl, Ducks & Wading Birds, Stopover for Hawks & Falcons, Guggenheim Pond attracts Herons, Egrets & Ibis,

Black Duck, American Bittern, Visitors must obtain a pass from the Town of Oyster Bay Parks Department, Call for application, parking pass & maps • 977 Hicksville Rd., Massapequa, NY **Office Hours:** 9 a.m.-4 p.m. **Fee: Free Directions:** *Northern State Pkwy. to exit 23 Cross Island Pkwy. toward I-495, continue on the Belt Pkwy., take exit 7B toward Ocean Pkwy, drive approx. 4-mi. East of the Jones Beach traffic circle, to the Tobay Beach parking lot, just East of parking lot 9, head West along the south border of the lot, look for the parking area provided by the sanctuary*

Massapequa Preserve • NC • *Merrick Rd. & Ocean Ave., Massapequa, NY* • *516-571-7443* • **Features Include:** 423-acre Preserve, Birding, Hiking Trails, Hike 5 mi. of the Greenbelt Hiking Trail, Lake, Sandy-Bog Area (habitat for endangered Long Island plants, including Orchids, Carnivorous Sundews & Bladderworts), Freshwater Swamps, Marsh, Stream, Pine Barrens, No Amenities in the park, Hiking maps can be downloaded through Friend of Massapequa Preserve at: www.fdale.com/FMP/FMP.htm or the Long Island Greenbelt at: www.ligreenbelt.org **Hours:** Dawn-Dusk **Fee: Free Directions:** *Seaford-Oyster Bay Expwy., exit onto Sunrise Hwy. E., on Left pass a small brick building, make the next U-turn at the traffic light & park in the parking lot across from Train Station* www.ligreenbelt.org • www.fdale.com/FMP/FMP.htm

Muttontown Preserve • NC • *Muttontown Ln., East Norwich, NY* • *516-571-8500* • **Features Include:** 550-acre Preserve, Marked Nature Trails, Self-Guiding Maps & Brochures on the Local Wildflowers, Trees, Birds, Mammals, Reptiles & Amphibians, Nature Photography, Horse Trails, Guided Hikes, Bill Paterson Nature Center, Fields, Woodlands, Ponds, Marked Nature Trails, 40-room Chelsea Mansion Estate Grounds, Wildflowers, Trees, Birds, Mammals, Reptiles, Amphibians, Educational Programs: Orienteering, Bird Watching, & Glacial Geology, Youth Groups can rent conservation camp sites **Hours:** 9 a.m.-5 p.m. **Fee: Free Directions:** *I-495 Long Island Expwy. to exit 41 N. Rte. 106 N., make a Left onto Rte. 25A Northern Blvd., make a Left onto Muttontown Ln.*
www.nassaucountyny.gov

Nassau County Museum of Art ⊛ • *1 Museum Dr., Roslyn Harbor, NY* • *516-484-9338* • **Features Include:** 200-acre Estate, Outdoor Sculpture Garden (great for walking with young children), Georgian Mansion, Hiking Trails, 2 Marked Trails approx. 1-mi. long, 6 Marked Trails approx. .5-mi. long, Trail Maps are available at the house **Hours:** Grounds Open Dawn-Dusk **Fee: Free** to hikers, donations appreciated **Directions:** *I-495 Long Island Expwy., exit 37A W., exit 39 towards Glen Cove Rd., turn Left onto Old Westbury Rd., right Glen Cove Rd. N., turn Left onto Northern Blvd./25A, turn Right onto Museum Dr.* www.nassaumuseum.com

FALL FOLLY

Planting Fields Arboretum State Historic Park ⊗ • NYS • *1395 Planting Fields Rd., Oyster Bay, NY • 516-922-9210, 9200* • Great for hiking with small children. • **Features Include:** 409-acre Arboretum, Former Gold Coast Estate & Arboretum, 6 Marked Walking/Hiking Trails, Wooded Trails, Field, Pond & Beach Trails, LI Sound, Trail Maps, Scheduled Guided Nature Walks, Picnicking, Photography, Greenhouses, Rolling Lawns, Formal Gardens, Woodland Paths, Plant Collections, Coe Hall 65 Room Mansion, Open for Tours Spring-Fall, Annual Events, Family & Children's Programs, Educational Programs **Hours:** 9 a.m.-5 p.m., May-Oct. **Fee:** $6, Empire Pass Accepted **Directions:** *I-495 Long Island Expwy., exit 41 N., take, Rte. 106 N. approx. 5-mi., make a Left onto 25A/Northern Blvd., make the 1ˢᵗ, Right onto Mill River Rd., follow signs to the arboretum*   *www.plantingfields.org*

The Roosevelt Sanctuary & Audubon Center • *134 Cove Rd., Oyster Bay, NY • 516-922-3200* • Great for hiking with small children. **Features Include:** 15-acre Sanctuary, Bird Research & Habitat Restoration Facility, 3 Hiking Trails approx 1-mi. Hike, Trail Map Available in Gift Shop, Bird Watching, Educational Programs, Special Events, Environmental Stewardship Programs for Children & Adults **Hours:** Mon.-Fri.: 9 a.m.-5 p.m. , Sat., Sun., Holidays: 10 a.m.-4 p.m., Year-Round **Fee: Free Directions:** *I-495 Long Island Expwy., exit 41 N., Rte. 106 N., to the Village of Oyster Bay, turn Right onto E. Main St., proceed 1.5 mi. to E. Main St., becomes Cove Rd. at Oyster Bay High School, see signs for the T.R. Sanctuary parking lot on the Right*   *http://ny.audubon.org/CentersEduTRoosevelt.html*

Sands Point Preserve, Nature Trails, & Habitats • NC • *127 Middleneck Rd., Port Washington, NY • 516-571-7900* • **Features Include:** 216-acre Preserve, 6 Marked Walking/Hiking Trails, Woods, Fields, Forests, Meadows, Young Woodlands, Shoreline Beach (on the LI Sound), Cliffs, Lawns, Gardens, Freshwater Pond, Trail Maps, Guided Nature Walks, Self-Guiding Literature, each natural area provides habitats for a variety of plants & animals **Hours:** 10 a.m.-5 p.m., Year-Round **Fee:** Mon.-Fri.: **Free,** Sat.-Sun.: $2 **Directions:** *I-495 Long Island Expwy., take exit 36 Searingtown Rd. N., drive for approx. 6 mi., the road becomes Port Washington Blvd. & then Middleneck Rd., the entrance is on the Right, 1-mi. past the stone & brick gate of the Sands Point Village Club*
                     www.sandspointpreserve.org/htm/info.htm

Stillwell Woods Preserve • NC • *South Woods Rd., Syosset, NY • 516-572-0200* • Stillwell Woods Preserve is part of the Nassau-Suffolk Greenbelt Trail & it offers Old Fields & Oak Barren Communities. **Features Include:** 270-acre Preserve, Hiking Trails, Bird Watching **Hours:** Dawn-Dusk **Fee: Free Directions:** *I-495 Long Island Expwy. to exit 46 N. Sunnyside Blvd. N., turn Right onto Woodbury Rd., turn Left onto Rte. 25, turn Right onto South Woods Rd., pass Syosset High School, turn Right into the soccer field, bear Right & go to the end of the field, the trailhead is in the southeastern corner*   *www.trails.com*

FUN FAMILY

Tackapausha Museum & Preserve Ⓢ • **NC** • *Washington Ave., Seaford, NY* • *516-571-7443* • **Features Include:** 84-acre Preserve, Plants & Wildlife Sanctuary, Oak Forests, Ponds & Streams, Small Mammals (raccoons, muskrats, gray squirrels & opossums), 170 Bird Species, Waterfowl, Amphibians, & 5-mi. Walk/Hike on Marked Trails **Hours:** Tues.-Sat.: 10 a.m.-4 p.m., Sun.: 1-4 p.m. **Fee:** $1-$2 **Directions:** *I-495 Long Island Expwy. to exit 44 S., Rte. 135S. Seaford-Oyster Bay Expwy., take exit 1E. Merrick Rd. E., turn Left onto Washington Ave., the museum is on the Right* *www.nassaucountyny.gov*

Tiffany Creek Preserve • **NC** • *45 Sandy Hill Rd., Oyster Bay, NY* • *516-571-8500* • **Features Include:** 197-acre Preserve, Hike/Walk, Oak Forest, Wet Meadows, Self-Guided Trails, Public Nature Trails (located in the 45-acre parcel West of Sandy Hill Road), the trail on the North side of the road leads into Tiffany Creek Preserve, a walk of about a third-mi. downhill leads to Tiffany Creek Pond **Hours:** Year-Round **Fee:** **Free** **Directions:** *I-495 Long Island Expwy., take exit 44 N., merge onto the Seaford Oyster Bay Expwy. N., toward Syosset, take exit 14 W. to merge onto Jericho Tpke./Rte. 25 W., turn Right onto Jackson Ave., turn Left to stay on Jackson Ave., continue on Berry Hill Rd., continue on Sandy Hill Rd.* *www.nassaucountyny.gov*

Valley Stream • **NYS** • *320 Fletcher Ave., Valley Stream, NY* • *516-825-4128* • **Features Include:** Children's Play Areas, Nature Trails, .5-mi. Walking Course, 15 Exercise Stations **Hours:** Dawn-Dusk **Fee:** **Free**, during the winter, Late May-early Sept.: $4 per car, Empire Pass Accepted **Directions:** *Southern State Pkwy., exit 15A, exits into the park* *http://nysparks.state.ny.us/parks/info.asp?parkID=51*

Welwyn Preserve • **NC** • *Glen Cove, Crescent Beach & New Woods Rd., NY* • *516-571-7900* • **Features Include:** 204-acre Preserve, 4 Marked Nature Trails, Education Center, Holocaust Memorial, Habitats Include: Wooded Stream Valley, Fresh Water Ponds, Swamps, Long Island Sound Shoreline, Coastal Salt Marsh **Fee:** **Free** **Directions:** *I-495 Long Island Expwy., exit 36 Searingtown Rd. N., go approx. 6-mi., the road changes to Port Washington Blvd. then Middle Neck Rd., the entrance will be on the Right*

SUFFOLK COUNTY

Bayard Cutting Arboretum Ⓢ • **NYS** • *440 Montauk Hwy., Great River, NY, P.O. Box 466, Oakdale, NY* • *631-581-1002* • This is a favorite place for small hikes with young children. There are many animal & plant specimens to see, & there's a café in the Cutting Family Manor House. **Features Include:** Hiking, Birding, Concerts, Art Exhibitions, Performances, the Connetquot River, Walking Paths, Land & Aquatic Birds, Foxes, Raccoons & other Small Wildlife, Educational Classes, & Historical House

Tours (on Sun. afternoons at 2 p.m.), the Cutting Family Manor House is decorated by local garden clubs during the month of Dec. **Hours:** Tues.-Sun.: 10 a.m.-5 p.m. **Fee: Free** during the winter, Parking: $6 April-Oct., Empire Pass Accepted **Directions:** *I-495 Long Island Expwy., take exit 56, Rte. 111 Islip Ave., head East on Montalk Hwy., the Arboretum will be on the Right side of street*

www.bayardcuttingarboretum.com • http://nysparks.state.ny.us/sites/info

Blydenburgh Hiking Club • SC • *Smithtown, Veteran's Memorial Hwy., Smithtown, NY • Tours & Programs: 631-360-0753 •* Features Include: 627-acre Park, the club often leads Hikes through the park. For a hike schedule contact the Greenbelt Trails Conference web site. Hikes are planned for Families, Singles, & at night on the Greenbelt Trail. Hikes range from 3-12 mi. There are forested hills & valleys at the headwaters of the Nissequogue River & casual walks through the Blydenburgh Farm & New Mill Historic District which features a grist mill. The Long Island Greenbelt Trail Conference has headquarters in one of the historic district's **Hours:** Dawn-Dusk, Year-Round **Fee: Free** off-season, Memorial Day-Labor Day: $8, Green Key Holders: $3 **Directions:** *Northern State Pkwy., to end, slight Right onto Rte. 347/454, the main (southern) entrance to the park is on 347, to get to the Historic District go to the North side of the park, take Rte. 347, turn Left onto Brookside Dr. N., at next light turn Left onto New Mill Rd., follow to the park entrance at end, walk in to the Right, see the Weld House/ Blydenburgh Farmhouse* *www.hike-ligreenbelt.com/page/page/1007314.htm*

Brookhaven • NYS • *567 Middle Country Rd., Brookhaven, NY • 631-929-4314 •* **Features Include:** 2,300-acre Park (also known as the Pine Barrens), Walking, Hiking, 1 area for hiking is at the SW corner of Shoreham-Wading River HS lot, NY 25A, .25 mi. East of William. Floyd Pkwy. The Brookhaven Trail heads South & connects with the White-Blazed Paumanok Path. A Free Pine Barrens Recreation brochure can be downloaded at: http:// pb.state.ny.us/chart_recreation_main_page.htm **Hours:** Dawn-Dusk **Fee: Free Directions:** *I-495 Long Island Expwy., take exit 68 for William Floyd Pkwy. toward Shirley/Co Hwy. 46N, to Wading River, merge onto County Rte. 46/William Floyd Pkwy., take the ramp onto Middle Country Rd./Rte. 25* *http://nysparks.state.ny.us/sites/info*

Caleb Smith Park & Preserve • NYS • *581 West Jericho Tpke., Smithtown, NY • 631-265-1054 •* **Features Include:** 543-acre Park, Birding, Nature Trails, Museum/Visitor Center, Gift Shop, Recreation Programs, Family Events have included: Animal Olympics, South Side Saunter & Buzz Says the Bee **Hours:** 8 a.m.-Dusk, Year-Round, Closed Mon.: April-Sept., Closed Mon.-Tues.: Oct.-March **Fee: Free Directions:** *I-495 Long Island Expwy., exit 53 N. Sunken Meadow Pkwy. N., take exit SM 3 E. to Smithtown, take Jericho Tpke./Rte. 25 E., drive approx. 3-mi. to the park* *http://nysparks.state.ny.us*

Camp Hero • NYS • *50 South Fairview Ave., Montauk, NY • 631-668-3781* • This park is a National Historic Site, former military base & a world class fishing destination. **Features Include:** 415-acre Park, Beach (Atlantic Ocean), Bird Watching, Bridle Path, Hiking, Wooded Areas, Historic Military Installation, Maritime Forests, Freshwater Wetlands, Ocean Views, Bluffs Rising above the Beach **Hours:** Year-Round, Dawn-Dusk **Fee: Free** off-season, Empire Pass Accepted **Directions:** *I-495 Long Island Expwy., exit 68 for William Floyd Pkwy./Co. Hwy. 46 S. toward Shirley, turn Left onto Rte. 27 E. Sunrise Hwy., turn Right at Camp Hero State Park Rd., turn Left to stay on Camp Hero State Park Rd.* *http://nysparks.state.ny.us/parks/info.asp?parkID=82*

Cathedral Pines County Park • SC • *Yaphank-Middle Island Rd., South of Rte. 25, Middle Island, NY• 631-852-5500 • Campground: 631-852-5502* • Features Include: 320-acre Park on the Carman's River, Hiking, Camping, Mountain Biking, Bridle Paths, Picnicking & Nature Photography. Adjacent to Cathedral Pines Park is Prosser Pines Nature Preserve, which features white pines planted in 1812. Prosser Pines is a popular site for hikers & photographers. **Hours:** Dawn-Dusk, Year Round **Fee: Free** off-season, $5 with Green Key, $10 without Green Key Memorial Day-Labor Day **Directions:** *I-495 Long Island Expwy., take exit 68 N. William. Floyd Pkwy., turn Left onto Longwood Rd. to end, turn Left, the entrance is immediately on the Right* *http://www.co.suffolk.ny.us/departments/parks*

Cedar Point County Park • SC • *East Hampton, NY • 631-852-7620 • Camping Reservations: 631-244-7275* • Cedar Point was settled in 1651, & became a busy shipping port for farm goods, fish & timber from Sag Harbor. **Features Include:** 607-acre Park, Views of Gardiner's Bay, Hiking, Nature Trails, Picnicking, Lighthouse, Playground, Bicycling, The Cedar Point General Store & Snack Bar (631-324-7147) are operated by Kaelin's. They offer Sat. night family movies on the lawn behind the store & free use of recreational equipment. **Hours:** Dawn-Dusk **Fee: Free Directions:** *Montauk Hwy. East to Stephen Hands Path in E. Hampton, turn North & continue to Old Northwest Rd., turn Right onto Northwest Rd., bear Left and continue to Alewive Brook Rd., the park entrance is 100 yds. down the road* *www.co.suffolk.ny.us/Home/departments/parks*

Cold Spring Harbor • NYS • *25 Lloyd Harbor Rd., Huntington, NY • 631-423-1770* • The park serves as the northern trailhead of the Nassau/Suffolk Greenbelt Trail & extends to Bethpage State Park & the South shore of Nassau County. **Features Include:** 40-acre Park, Birding, Hiking, Hilly Terrain, Views of Cold Spring Harbor, Hardwood Forest (large Oak Specimens that measure 3-ft. in diameter), Wild Mountain Laurel thickets, in the historic village of Cold Spring Harbor, the parking field is on Main St. close to the village's waterfront, restaurants, & shopping area **Hours:** Dawn-Dusk **Fee:**

Free Directions: *I-495 Long Island Expwy., take 135 N. Seafood-Oyster Bay Expwy., to Jericho Tpke. E., turn Left onto Woodbury Rd. N., turn Left onto Rte. 108 & follow to end, turn Left & make an immediate Right onto Rte. 25A E., drive .5 mi. to parking field & trailhead is on Right*   *http://nysparks.state.ny.us/parks/info*

Connetquot River Park & Preserve • NYS • *P.O. Box 505, Oakdale, NY* • *631-581-*

1005 • The park maintains 3,473-acres of land & water for the protection & propagation of game birds, fish & animals **Features Include:** 50-mi. of Hiking trails, Nature Photography, Bridle Path, Deer, Waterfowl, Rare Nesting Birds, Osprey, Rare Plants, Trailing Arbutus, Pyxie Moss **Hours:** 6 a.m.-Dusk, closed Mon. Year-Round, closed Mon.-Tues. Oct.-March, **Fee:** $8, Empire Pass Accepted **Directions:** *Southern State Pkwy., take exit 44 Sunrise Hwy. E., the Preserve is located on the North side of Sunrise Hwy., just west of Pond Rd.*

       http://nysparks.state.ny.us/parks/info.asp?parkID=69

Dwarf Pines Plains Preserve • SC • *West Hampton, NY* • *631-444-0270* • Features

Include: The Dwarf Pine Plain community is a rare ecosystem that exists in only a few locations in the world. 3 existing communities are: the New Jersey Dwarf Pine Plains, the Shawangunk Mountains Dwarf Pine Plains (Catskill Region) & the Long Island Dwarf Pine Plains. Each is dominated by pitch pines & scrub oak, trees that rarely exceed 3-6 ft. in height due to poor soil conditions, extreme heat in the summer, & harsh, cold winters. This rare ecosystem supports some uncommon wildlife species such as: the Black-Throated Green Warbler Breeds, American Kestrels & Marsh Hawks. Nocturnal birds include: Owls, Northern Saw-Whet, Long-Eared Owls, Nighthawks & Whippoorwills. Visitors are asked to respect this globally rare ecological community. There is a new .7 mi. trail that takes about 20 min. to walk. **Directions:** *Rte. 27 to County Rd. 31 S. toward West Hampton, the trail head is located about .15 of a mi. off of the exit on the East side of County Rd. 31, turn Left into the SCWA complex*

       www.co.suffolk.ny.us/departments/parks/Dwarf Pines Plains Preserve.aspx

Gardiner County Park • SC • *Montauk Hwy., West Bay Shore, NY* • *631-854-0935* •

631-581-1005• Administration: 631-854-4949 • The Gardiner family was Suffolk's 1st non-native landowners. **Features Include:** 231-acre Park, Nature Trails, Fitness Trail, Hiking, Great South Bay, Sagtikos Manor Estate, Restrooms **Hours:** Dawn-Dusk, Open Seasonally **Fee: Free** Directions: *I-495 Long Island Expwy., take exit 53 toward Bay Shore/Kings Park/Sagtikos Pkwy. S., take exit 40 S. toward Robert Moses Cswy., take exit RM2E. for state Hwy. 27 E. Montauk Hwy., the park is about 1.5 mi. East of the Robert Moses Cswy.*   *www.co.suffolk.ny.us/Home/departments/parks/Parks.aspx*

Heckscher Park • NYS • *Heckscher Pkwy., Field 1, East Islip, NY* • *631-581-2100* •

Reservations: 800-456-2267 • **Features Include:** 20 mi. of Nature Trails, Hiking,

Bicycling, Great South Bay Beach Playgrounds, Picnic Areas & Tables, Recreation Programs, many deer can be observed at dusk **Hours:** Year Round, 7 a.m.-Dusk **Fee:** **Free** off-season, Memorial Day-Labor Day: $10, Labor Day-Oct.: $8. weekends only, Empire Pass Accepted **Directions:** *Southern State Pkwy. East, it ends in the park*

Hither Hills • NYS • *50 South Fairview Ave., Montauk, NY • 631-668-2554 • Reservations: 800-456-2267* • Features Include: Hiking, Nature Trail, Walking Dunes, Ocean Beach, Bridle Path, Food, Playground, "Walking Dunes" of Napeague Harbor (on the eastern boundary of the park), Russian Olive/Oak/Shade/Pine Trees, Summer Programs, Recreation Program, Family Movies, Folk & Line Dancing, Children's Theatre, Magic Shows, Environmental Interpretation Programs **Hours:** Dawn-Dusk, Year-Round **Fee: Free** off-season, Memorial Day-Labor Day: $10, Weekends only until Oct. $8, Empire Pass Accepted **Directions:** *I-495 Long Island Expwy., take exit 68, William Floyd Pkwy. S., take Sunrise Hwy. Rte. 27 E., turn Left onto 27 E., Right turn onto Birch Dr./Oak Ln., Right onto Birch St./Birch Dr., turn Left onto Old Montauk Hwy.* *http://nysparks.state.ny.us/parks/*

Indian Island County Park • SC • *Riverhead, Cross River Dr. (Rte. 105), Riverhead, NY • 631-852-3232* • The "Island" at Indian Island County Park is now connected to the mainland by a causeway composed entirely of white sand. The park is located at the estuarine mouth of the Peconic River. **Features Include:** 275-acre Park, Short Hikes, Longest Hike is 3 mi., Best Picnicking in Suffolk County, views of Flanders Bay, Playground, Picnic Tables & Grills, Restrooms, off-season Restrooms open by Maintenance Building, Camping (reservations required), there is a check-in-station & hiking maps in the office **Hours:** Year-Round **Fee: Free** off-season, Green Key: $3, non-residents: $8 Memorial Day-Labor Day **Directions:** *I-495 Long Island Expwy., take exit 71, Right turn onto Rte. 24 at end of exit ramp, follow Rte. 24 S. through the Riverhead Traffic Circle, continue on Rte. 24 & make a Left turn at the next traffic light onto Rte. 105, follow Rte. 105 to the entrance on Right* *www.co.suffolk.ny.us/Home/departments/parks/Parks.aspx*

Lakeland County Park • SC • *Johnson Ave., Islandia, NY • 631-853-2727 • Administration: 631-854-4949* • Features Include: Nature Trail, Boardwalk (over the headwaters of the Connetquot River), Picnic Area, Gazebo, Wetland Vegetation, Waterfowl Fish, Handicap-Accessible Facility, designed for the disabled & their families **Hours:** Office/Restrooms Open Memorial Day-Labor Day **Directions:** *I-495 Long Island Expwy. to exit 58 S. Nicholls Rd., turn Left at Johnson Ave., the park entrance is .5 mi. on the Right* *www.co.suffolk.ny.us/Home/departments/parks/*

Nissequogue River Park • NYS • *799 St. Johnland Rd., Kings Park, NY • 631-269-4927* • The Greenbelt Trail parallels the Nissequogue River & provides scenic views of the river & the Long Island Sound from the top of the bluffs. **Features Include:** Hiking, Walking,

Bird Watching, Museum/Visitor Center, Nature Trail, Guided Tours, Family events have included: Long Island Sound Saunter, Nature Hide-n-Seek, Salt Marsh Exploration, Family Evening Walks, Family Nature Walks, Habitats Include: Tidal & Fresh Water Wetlands, Hardwood Forests, Shore Birds, Reptiles & Amphibians **Hours:** Dawn-Dusk, Year-Round Fee: **Free** off-season, Memorial Day-Labor Day: $8, Empire Pass Accepted **Directions:** *Sunken Meadow Pkwy., take exit SM 4, drive East on Pulaski Rd. which changes into Old Dock Rd. at the 5th traffic light, make a Right onto St. Johnland Rd., park entrance is about .5 mi. on the Left*   *http://nysparks.state.ny.us/parks*

Orient Point Beach Park • NYS • Rte. 25, Orient Point, NY • 631-323-2440 • Orient Beach State Park was named by Travel.msn.com as a 2007 Top 10 Family Beach in the US **Features Include:** 45,000 ft. on Gardiner's Bay, Beach, Showers, Food, Hiking, Biking, Fishing, Walk the Nature Trails, Picnic Tables, Pavilions, Playground, Playing Fields, Recreation Programs, Environmental Tours, Bike Rentals, Rare Maritime Forest, Wood Deck (overlooking Gardiner's Bay), Party Pavilions **Hours:** Dawn-Dusk, Year-Round **Fee: Free** off season, Memorial Day-Labor Day: $10, weekends only until Oct.: $8, Empire Pass Accepted **Directions:** *I-495 Long Island Expwy., take exit 73 for Old Country Rd. toward Orient/Greenport/Co. Hwy. 58, slight Left onto County Rte. 58/Old Country Rd./Rte. 58, at Roanoke Ave., take the 2nd exit & stay on County Rte. 58/Old Country Rd./Rte. 58, slight Left at Main Rd./Middle Country Rd./Rte. 25, continue to follow Main Rd./Rte. 25, turn Left at Love Ln., turn Right at County Rte. 48/Rte. 48, continue to follow County Rte. 48, continue on Main Rd./Rte. 25 E. to the park*   *http://nysparks.state.ny.us/sites/info*

Pine Barrens Trails Information Center • SC • County Rd. 111, Manorville, NY • 631-852-3449 • This facility was established to provide the public with an environmental interpretation of the Pine Barrens. **Features Include:** Hiking, Environmental Education, Visitor Center, Pine Barrens Coastal Plain Ponds Exhibits, a short, interpretive "Blueberry Loop" trail is routed on the grounds of the center to introduce visitors to a Pine Barrens experience. Also on the grounds is El's Trail, a .75-mi. accessible trail (trail chair available). There is a children's "Pine Barrens Touch Museum" in the Information Center. **Hours:** Fri.-Mon., May-Oct. **Directions:** *Long Island Expwy., take exit 70, head North on County Rd. 111, follow .25 mi. to visitor center on Right*
                    www.co.suffolk.ny.us/Home/departments/parks/Parks.aspx

Robert Cushman Murphy County Park • SC • River Rd., Calverton/Manorville, NY • 631-854-4949 • Features Include: 60-acre Swan Pond, Hiking, Bird Watching, Biological Research Center, Fishing, Boating, Hunting **Hours:** Year-Round **Fee: Free Directions:** *I-495 Long Island Expwy. to exit 70 CR 111 S., turn Left onto Halsey Manor Rd., follow North across the Long Island Expwy. & railroad tracks, Halsey Manor Rd. becomes Connecticut Ave. once railroad tracks have been crossed, follow Connecticut Ave. N., make a Left turn* *onto River Rd. & make the next Left onto Old River Rd., follow Old River Rd. to the 1ˢᵗ entrance on the Right (North side of the road)*

www.co.suffolk.ny.us/departments/parks

Sailors Haven ⑨ • *Sailors Haven Ranger Station, Patchogue, NY 11772 • 631-597-6183* • **Features Include:** Hike the Sunken Forest **Hours:** mid-May-mid-Oct. **Fee: Free Directions:** *Southern State Pkwy., take the exit for Sunrise Hwy. Service Rd., take NY 27 E., take exit 52A toward Suffolk Co. 83/N. Ocean Ave./Patchogue, merge onto Sunrise Hwy. S. Service Rd., turn Right onto Co. Rd. 83/N. Ocean Ave., follow N. Ocean Ave., or take the Fire Island Ferry* *www.fireislandferries.com • 631-665-8885*

St. John's Pond Preserve • *1660 Rte. 25A (Cold Spring Fish Hatchery & Aquarium entrance), Cold Spring Harbor • 631-367-3225* • **Features Include:** 14-acre Preserve, Marked Trails, Opossums, Red Foxes, Flying Squirrels, Turtles, Frogs, Marsh, Pond, Woodland, the Cold Spring Harbor Fish Hatchery admission booth will provide the key to enter the preserve **Hours:** 10 a.m.-5 p.m., contact the Nature Conservancy-Long Island Chapter: 250 Lawrence Hill Rd., Cold Spring Harbor **Directions:** *Northern State Pkwy., exit onto 135 N. Seaford-Oyster Bay Expwy. towards Woodbury, take Jericho Tpke. E., turn Left onto Woodbury Rd., turn Left onto Rte. 108, turn Left into Northern Blvd., the hatchery will be on the Left* *www.co.suffolk.ny.us/Home/departments/parks/Parks.aspx*

Sears Bellows • **SC** • *Sears Bellows Pond Rd., Hampton Bays, NY* • *Park Office: 631-852-8290* • *Big Duck: 631-852-8292* • *Camping Reservations: 631-244-7275* • Sears Bellows is situated within the Long Island Pine Barrens & is the home of the Big Duck **Features Include:** Hiking, Extensive Trail System, Camping, Picnicking, Swimming, Freshwater Fishing, Rowboat Rentals **Hours:** Dawn-Dusk, Year-Round **Fee: Free** off-season, mid-June-Labor Day with Green Key: $5, No Green Key: $8 **Directions:** *Northern State Pkwy., take exit onto Wantagh State Pkwy. S., take exit onto Sunrise Hwy., take exit 65 N., follow road (Rte. 24), make a Left onto Bellows Pond Rd., the park entrance is on the Right* *http://www.co.suffolk.ny.us*

Shadmoor • **NYS** • *50 South Fairview Ave., Montauk, NY* • *631-668-3781* • **Features Includes:** 99-acre Park, 2,400-ft. of Ocean Beach, Biking, Hiking Trails, and Elevated Platforms for Bird Watching, Shade Bushes, Bluffs, Freshwater Black Cherry Trees, there are 2 concrete bunkers built during World War II & once equipped with artillery guns to protect the coast from enemy invasion **Hours:** Year-Round, Dawn-Dusk **Fee: Free** parking **Directions:** *I-495 Long Island Expwy., take exit 68 for William Floyd Pkwy./Co. Hwy. 46 S. toward Shirley, merge onto William Floyd Pkwy., take the ramp onto Rte. 27 E., turn Left at Main St./Rte. 27, turn Right, park is .5 mi. East of the village on the Right, at the southwest corner of Rte. 27 & Seaside Ave.* *http://nysparks.state.ny.us/sites/info*

Southaven County Park • **SC** • *Victory Ave., Brookhaven* • *631-854-1414* • Features **Include:** 1,356-acre Pine-Oak Forest, 2.3-mi. Marked Nature Trail, 5 mi. of Unblazed Hiking Trails, Picnicking, Freshwater Fishing, Rowboat Rentals, Boating, Canoeing, Hunting, Bicycle Hostel, Camping, Bridle Paths, the LI Steamer Trains (Miniature Steam Engine Train Ride), The Carman's River flows through this park, the park is the headquarters for the Long Island Equestrian Center **Hours:** Spring weekends only **Fee: Free Directions:** *Southern State Pkwy., exit at Sunrise Hwy., take exit 58 N., as you enter William Floyd Pkwy., prepare to turn West onto Victory Ave., follow signs to the main entrance of park*

www.co.suffolk.ny.us/Home/departments/parks/Parks.aspx

Sunken Meadow Park • **NYS** • *Rte. 25A & Sunken Meadow Parkway, Northport, NY* • *631-269-4333* • The park is located on the Long Island Sound. Habitats Include: Glacier-Formed Bluffs (at the West end of the shoreline), Brackish Creek, Marshes (from the tidal flats), & Heavily-Wooded Rolling Hills. **Features Include:** 6 mi. of Hiking Trails, Marked Trails, Northern Starting Point of the Suffolk County Greenbelt Trail, Biking, 3 mi. of Beach, Picnicking, Picnic Tables, Playground, Swimming, a .75-mi. Boardwalk, Showers, Children's Summer Theatre Programs: Sat. at 2 p.m., Recreation Programs, Hiking Maps are available in the Park Office at Field 1, by the beach & boardwalk **Hours:** Dawn-Dusk, Year-Round **Fee: Free** off-season, Memorial Day-Labor Day: $10, weekends only until Oct.: $8, Empire Pass Accepted **Directions:** *I-495 Long Island Expwy., take exit 53 Sunken Meadow/Sagtikos Pkwy. to the end, park office is at Field 1*

http://nysparks.state.ny.us/parks

Theodore Roosevelt County Park • **SC** • *Montauk Hwy., Montauk, NY 11954* • *631-852-7878* • *Camping: 631-852-7879* • America's 1st cattle ranching system was located in 17th century Montauk. **Features Include:** Self-Guided Nature Trail (brochure available), Hiking, Biking, Picnicking, Gift Shop, Museum, check in at the Third House Park Office, Spanish-American War Exhibit, Camp Wikoff **Hours:** Museum: May-Oct., Wed.-Sun.: 10 a.m.-5 p.m. **Fee: Free** off-season **Directions:** *Southern State Pkwy., follow Montauk Hwy. E. through Montauk Village past East Lake Dr., park sign & entrance is on North side of Montauk Hwy.* *www.co.suffolk.ny.us/Home/departments/parks/Parks.aspx*

Trail View • **NYS** • *25 Lloyd Harbor Rd., Huntington, NY* • *631-423-1770* • Trail View is a link along the Nassau/Suffolk Greenbelt Trail that extends from Cold Spring Harbor State Park on the North shore of Suffolk County to Bethpage State Park, & eventually to the South shore of Nassau County. **Features Include:** 400-acre Park, Hiking, Nature Trails, Bird Watching (on the Atlantic flyway during the spring & fall bird migrations), Hardwood Forests, Marshes, Succession Fields (elevations from 60-300 ft. above sea level) **Hours:** Dawn-Dusk, Year-Round **Fee: Free Directions:** *Northern State Pkwy., to*

*the Seaford Oyster Bay Expwy. (135) N., take Jericho Tpke. (25) E., pass 2 traffic lights,
parking will be on the Left side of the road*

www.longislandexchange.com/parks/trailview-statepark.html

**Wildwood · NYS · P.O. Box 518, North Wading River Rd. Wading River, NY ·
631-929-4314, Reservations: 800-456-2267** · **Features Include:** 600 acres of
Undeveloped Hardwood Forest, Nature Trails, High Bluffs, View of Long Island
Sound, Beach, Showers, Playground, Biking, Fishing, Food, Picnic Tables, Recreation
Programs **Hours:** Dawn-Dusk, Year-Round **Fee: Free** off-season, Memorial Day-Labor
Day: $10, weekends only until Oct.: $8, Empire Pass Accepted **Directions:** *I-495 Long
Island Expwy., take exit 68, head North on Rte. 46, take Rte. 25A E., turn Left onto Sound
Ave., turn Left at traffic light onto Hulse Landing Rd., park entrance is on the Right*

Hike LI hosts hiking programs during the school year ·   *www.hike-li.org/stps*

Long Island Greenbelt Trail sponsors monthly hikes ·   *www.ligreenbelt.org*

Southampton Trails Preservation Society sponsors trail hikes by the Mashashimuet
Park, Sag Harbor throughout the year · E-mail for more info · 631-725-4287
www.hike-li.org/stps · southamptontrailspreservationsociety@hotmail.com

East Hampton Trails Preservation Society sponsors trail hikes by the Red Dirt Road in
Amagansett, NY · 631-324-8662   *www.ehtps.org*

SUGGESTIONS · COMMENTS · ERRORS

Linda.ReidBryce
@verizon.net

Thanks

CYCLING

PEDALS, SUNSHINE & ICE CREAM

Young Children-Getting Started: Riding on traffic-free bike paths such as the 3-mi. loop in Caumsett Park insures safety while allows you to adjust to distance riding.

Planning Road Rides: Plan road rides for early weekend mornings, when car traffic is lightest.

Review Bike Safety Rules:
- Ride on the right side in the direction of traffic
- Use hand signals when turning.
- Obey traffic signals & stop signs.
- When riding in a group, keep to the right in single file, with adequate distance between riders.
- Make sure each bicycle has reliable brakes, a bell or horn, a headlight, rear & side reflectors for night riding, & a headlight for night riding.
- Wear a protective helmet & bright clothing.

(Short Bike Rides On Long Island, Phil Angelillo, xii)

NASSAU COUNTY

Bay Park • NC • *First Ave., East Rockaway, NY • 516-571-7245* • Features Include: 96-acre Park, East Rockaway Channel & Hewlett Bay, Bicycle & Running Paths, Picnic Area, Playground, Spray Pool, Dock **Hours:** Parts of the park are open Year-Round **Fee: Free** Directions: *Southern State Pkwy., take exit 17 Hempstead Ave. S., take Hempstead Ave. to fork (Ocean Ave.), take Left fork (Ocean Ave.) through Lynbrook & E. Rockaway to Main St. (follow park signs), make a Left onto Front St., make a Right onto Althouse Ave., make a Left onto First Ave., & follow to the park www.nassaucountyny.gov*

Bethpage Bikeway • *Bethpage State Park* • **NYS** • *99 Quaker Meeting House Rd., Farmingdale, NY • 516-249-0701* • **Features Include:** 14-mi. Round-Trip Bethpage Bikeway, which connects Bethpage State Park with Merrick Rd. in Massapequa, Bikeway Path Runs South through the Park, Scenic Paved Path, Views of the Polo Field & Golf Course. There are a few parkway exits & busy street crossings along the way, but all crossings are clearly marked. The only major road crossing is at Sunrise Hwy., near the southern end of the trail, but there is a stoplight & crossing lane. **Start Point:** The trail leaves the park, parallels Bethpage State Pkwy. crossing Southern State Pkwy., enters the Massapequa Preserve **Hours:** Dawn-Dusk **Fee:** **Free**, Empire Pass Accepted during season **Directions:** *Northern Trailhead: I-495 Long Island Expwy., take Rte. 135 Seaford-Syosset Expwy. S., follow Rte.135 to the Bethpage State Park exit, at the end of the ramp make a Left, cross over Rte. 135, the entrance to the park will be on the Left, follow signs to the picnic area, just past the booth, park on your Left, the trailhead is at the far Left side of the parking lot   http://nysparks.state.ny.us*

Four rides from this park compiled by exploreli.com:

1. Brookhaven • **NYS** • *567 Middle Country Rd., Brookhaven, NY • 631-929-4314* • **Features Include:** 2,300-acre Park (also known as the Pine Barrens), Bicycling, Road Touring, Mountain Biking **Start Point:** 1 area for hiking is at the SW corner of Shoreham-Wading River HS lot, NY 25A, .25 mi. East of William. Floyd Pkwy. The Brookhaven Trail heads South & Connects with the White-Blazed Paumanok Path. **Directions:** *I-495 Long Island Expwy., take exit 68 for William Floyd Pkwy. toward Shirley/Co. Hwy. 46N to Wading River, merge onto County Rte. 46/William Floyd Pkwy., take the ramp onto Middle Country Rd./Rte. 25   http://nysparks.state.ny.us/sites/info* A Free Pine Barrens Recreation brochure can be downloaded at: *http://pb.state.ny.us/chart_recreation_main_page.htm.*

2. Central Suffolk Bikeway • **Features Include:** 80-mi. Ride & marked street Rte. **Start Point:** Bethpage State Park, & runs along Quaker Meeting House Rd., Bethpage Rd. & Main St. to the Farmingdale LIRR station, it then follows the railroad line into Riverhead. LIRR bike boarding passes are available for $5 (a 1-time fee).

3. Nassau-Suffolk Greenbelt Mountain Bike Trail • **Features Include:** 8-mi. Ride, Off-Road National Recreation Trail, Unpaved Portions, Marked for Mountain Bikes (helmets required), Challenging Hills, At Stillwell Woods, bikers can opt for a 4-mi. loop with some difficult terrain. **Start Point:** Bethpage State Park picnic area, head North to Stillwell Woods in Syosset.

4. Bethpage Multiuse Path • **Features Include:** 9.5-mi. Ride, Good for Beginners, Paved Route, Runs the Length of Bethpage Pkwy., **Start Point:** Bethpage State Park picnic area parking lot, cuts through Massapequa Preserve to Merrick Rd. Bethpage Mountain Bike Trail • **Features Include:** 4-mi. Ride, Off-Road, Marked Loop Trail through Pine Forest, has a Varied Terrain & 2 Challenging Hills. **Start Point:** Bethpage State Park picnic area parking lot, & look for white triangles on trees for starting point South of the gatehouse.

Jones Beach • *Ellen Farrant Memorial Bikeway* • **Features Include:** 4.5-mi. Ride, Multipurpose Path, Path Parallels the Pkwy. to Jones Beach State Park **Start Point:** Cedar Creek Park, South of Merrick Rd., East of Wantagh Pkwy., the path follows the Pkwy. & terminates near the Jones Beach Amphitheater   *www.exploreli.com*

Hempstead Lake State Park • *NYS* • *Eagle Ave. & Lake Dr., West Hempstead, NY* • *516-766-1029* • This is the largest lake in Nassau County. • **Features Include:** Biking, Picnic Areas, & Pavilion, Ponds **Hours:** Dawn-Dusk, Year-Round, Empire Pass Accepted **Directions:** *Southern State Pkwy., take exit 18 Eagle Ave., keep Right at the fork, follow signs for Rockville Centre/Hempstead Lake State Park, turn Right onto Eagle Ave.*   *www.stateparks.com*

Grant Park • *NC* • *1625 Broadway, Hewlett, NY* • *516-571-7821* • **Features Include:** 35-acre Park, Bicycling, 2 Playgrounds, Spray Pool Area, Lake, Paths **Directions:** *Southern State Pkwy., take exit 15S. for Corona Ave. S., turn Right onto N. Corona Ave., turn slight Left toward Rockaway Pkwy., then slight Right at Rockaway Pkwy., turn Right to stay on Rockaway Ave., turn Right onto Broadway*   *www.nassaucountyny.gov*

Massapequa Preserve • *NC* • *Merrick Rd. and Ocean Ave., Massapequa, NY* • *516-571-7443* • **Features Include:** 423-acre Preserve, 4.5 mi. of the Bethpage Bikeway, Birding, Hiking, there are No Amenities in the park, Maps Available **Hours:** Dawn-Dusk **Fee: Free Directions:** *Seaford-Oyster Bay Expwy., exit onto Sunrise Hwy. E., on Left pass a small brick building, make the next U-turn at the traffic light, & park in the parking lot, across from the train station*   *www.fdale.com/FMP/FMP.htm*

Stillwell Woods Preserve • *NC* • *South Woods Rd., Syosset, NY* • *516-572-0200* • Stillwell Woods Preserve is part of the Nassau-Suffolk Greenbelt Trail. **Features Include:** 270-acre Preserve, Bicycle Trails, Mountain Bike Trails, Bird Watching, Equestrian Trails **Directions:** *I-495 Long Island Expwy. to exit 46N. Sunnyside Blvd. N., turn Right onto Woodbury Rd., turn Left onto Rte. 25, turn Right onto South Woods Rd., pass Syosset High School, turn Right into the soccer field, bear Right & go to the end of the field, the trailhead is in the southeastern corner*
       www.trails.com • http://thebicycleplanet.com/page.cfm?PageID=393

Wantagh Park • *NC* • *Kings Rd. & Canal Pl., Wantagh, NY* • *516-571-7460* • **Features Include:** 111-acre Park, Biking Paths, 2-mi. Fitness Trail with 20 stations, Playground, Picnic Areas with Barbeques & Shelters, Marina **Hours:** Dawn-Dusk **Fee: Free**, Non-residents Memorial Day-Labor Day: $5 **Directions:** *Southern State Pkwy., take exit 27 S. (Wantagh Pkwy.), take the exit for Sunrise Hwy. E., make a Right onto Wantagh Ave., to end, make a Right onto Merrick Rd., at 1ˢᵗ light make a Left into the park*
       www.nassaucountyny.gov/agencies/Parks/WhereToGo/active/wantagh.html

Westbury-Bayville Loop • **Features Include:** 30-mi. Ride, Hilly Terrain, Unmarked Street Route: **Start Point:** Take Post Ave. to Westbury Village North, take Wheatley Rd., cross Rte. 25A, take Wolver Hollow Rd., head East on Chicken Valley Rd. to the Planting Fields Arboretum, continue on Shore Rd. to Oak Neck Beach in Bayville, on the return loop take Bayville Ave., to Piping Rock Rd., to Wheatley Rd. & Post Rd.

www.exploreli.com

SUFFOLK COUNTY

Belmont Lake Park • **NYS** • *625 Belmont Ave., West Babylon, NY* • *631-667-5055* •
This full service park is the headquarters of the Long Island State Park Region. **Features Include:** Biking, Picnicking, Playgrounds **Hours:** Dawn-Dusk, Year-Round **Fee: Free** off-season, April-Nov.: $8, Empire Pass Accepted **Directions:** *Southern State Pkwy., exit 37 N., merge onto Belmont Ave.* *http://nysparks.state.ny.us*

Brookhaven • **NYS** • *567 Middle Country Rd., Brookhaven, NY* • *631-929-4314* •
Features Include: 2,300-acre Park (also known as the Pine Barrens), Bicycling Road Touring, Mountain Biking **Hours:** Dawn-Dusk **Fee: Free Directions:** *I-495 Long Island Expwy., take exit 68 for William Floyd Pkwy. toward Shirley/Co. Hwy. 46N., to Wading River, merge onto County Rte. 46/William Floyd Pkwy., take the ramp onto Middle Country Rd./Rte. 25* *http://nysparks.state.ny.us/sites/info*

Cathedral Pines County Park • **SC** • *Yaphank-Middle Island Rd., Middle Island, NY* •
631-852-5502 • **Features Include:** 6-mi. Ride, Optional Hill Climbs = 7.5-mile Ride, Relatively Flat, Wooded, Single-Track, Off-Road Route, Multi-Ability Level Trail, Advanced Hill Climbs for Experienced Riders **Hours:** Dawn-Dusk, Year-Round **Fee: Free** off-season, With Green Key: $5, Without Green Key Memorial Day-Labor Day: $10 **Directions:** *I-495 Long Island Expwy., take exit 68 N. for William Floyd Pkwy., turn Left onto Longwood Rd., to end, turn Left, the entrance is immediately to the Right* *www.co.suffolk.ny.us/departments/parks*

Caumsett State Historic Park ⚇ • **NYS** • *25 Lloyd Harbor Rd., Huntington, NY* • *631-423-1770* • The park is situated on a peninsula extending into the Long Island Sound. **Features Include:** 3-mi. Loop for Biking, No Car Traffic except park personnel **Hours:** Dawn-Dusk, Year-Round **Fee: Free** off-season, April-Nov., Empire Pass Accepted, Handicap Accessible **Directions:** *I-495 Long Island Expwy., exit Rte. 110 N. becomes New York Ave., turn Left onto Main St. 25A W., turn Right onto West Neck Rd. N., the park entrance is on the Left* *http://nysparks.state.ny.us/parks/info.asp?parkID=68*

Eastport Trail • **Features Include:** 8.5-mi. Ride, Flat, Single-Track, Off-Road Trail, Loops through Wooded Areas, Helmets & Eye Protection Required, Free Permit Required from the State Department of Environmental Conservation: 631-444-0273, **Start Point:** Rte. 51 & Rte.111 in Eastport   *www.exploreli.com*

Cold Spring Harbor-Sagamore Hill • **Features Include:** 36-mi. Ride, Hilly, Unmarked Street Route **Start Point:** Cold Spring Harbor, follow Rte. 25A into Oyster Bay, take Oyster Bay Cove Rd. N. to the Theodore Roosevelt grave, turn onto Cove Neck Rd., follow to Sagamore Hill, return by retracing the route   *www.exploreli.com*

Heckscher State Park • *Heckscher Pkwy., Field 1, East Islip, NY* • *631-581-2100* • *Reservations: 800-456-2267* • **Features Include:** 20 mi. of Nature Trails, Hiking, Bicycling, Swimming on the Great South Bay Beach, Pool Complex with Showers, Playgrounds, Fishing, Picnic Areas & Tables, Boat Launch Ramp, Playing Fields, Food, Recreation Programs **Hours:** 7 a.m.-Dusk, Year-Round, 7 days a week **Fee: Free** off-season, Memorial Day-Labor Day: $10, Weekends Only until Oct.: $8, Empire Pass Accepted **Directions:** *Take Southern State Pkwy. E., it ends in the park*
                        http://nysparks.state.ny.us/parks/info.asp?parkID=153

Heckscher Park-Central Islip • **Features Include:** 10-mi. Ride, Flat Bikeway **Start Point:** Heckscher State Park, ride North for 5 mi. along the Connetquot River into Central Islip, then join the Central Suffolk bike path   *www.exploreli.com*

Huntington-Lloyd Neck • **Features Include:** 16-mi. Ride, Hilly, Scenic, Paved, Unmarked Route **Start Point:** Woodbury Rd. North toward Huntington Village, cross Main St., becomes West Neck Rd., follow through Lloyd Harbor to Caumsett State Historic Park & Target Rock National Wildlife Refuge, in Caumsett there is a 2 mi., Off-Road-Route (helmet required) leads to a pond & the Long Island Sound   *www.exploreli.com*

Kings Park Hike & Bike Trail • **Features Include:** 1.4-mi. Ride, Hilly Trail, Good for Beginners, Short, Scenic Ride **Start Point:** Downtown Kings Park, follow the old railroad spur from Old Dock Rd., just East of Church St. to St. Johnland Rd., the trail runs through the grounds of the former Kings Park Psychiatric Center & into the Nissequogue River State Park   *www.exploreli.com*

Nissequogue-Stony Brook-Old Field • **Features Include:** 28-mi. Ride, Hilly Terrain, Ride through Historic Stony Brook **Start Point:** Moriches Rd. to Head of the Harbor, take Harbor Rd. into Stony Brook, route turns North, ride through Setauket & the Old

Field estate area to the lighthouse, return on Pond Path S. to Nissequogue River Rd., & back toward Smithtown   *www.exploreli.com*

North Fork • **Features Include:** 40-mi. Ride, Round-Trip, Flat Terrain, Marked Bikeway through Wine Country **Start Point:** Rte. 48 E. Mattituck, pass Southold Beach, join Rte. 25 at Greenport, continue to Orient Beach State Park, return via bikeway to Greenport, then follow truck Rte. 25 to Rte. 25 W.   *www.exploreli.com*

Orient Point • **NYS** • *Rte. 25, Orient Point, NY* • *631-323-2440* • Orient Beach State Park & Beach **Features Include:** 45,000 ft. of frontage on Gardiner's Bay, Biking, Bike Rentals, Beach, Food, Picnic Tables, Playground, Recreation Programs, Environmental Tours **Hours:** Dawn-Dusk, Year-Round **Fee: Free** off-season, Memorial Day-Labor Day: $10, Weekends only until Oct.: $8, Empire Pass Accepted **Directions:** *I-495 Long Island Expwy., take exit 73 for Old Country Rd. toward Orient/Greenport/Co. Hwy. 58, slight Left onto County Rte. 58/Old Country Rd./Rte. 58, at Roanoke Ave., take the 2nd exit & stay on County Rte. 58/Old Country Rd./Rte. 58, slight Left at Main Rd./Middle Country Rd./Rte. 25, continue to follow Main Rd./Rte. 25 , turn Left at Love Ln. , turn Right at County Rte. 48/Rte. 48, continue to follow County Rte. 48, continue on Main Rd./Rte. 25 E. to the park*
http://nysparks.state.ny.us/sites/info

Rocky Point Mountain Bike Trail • **Features Include:** 13-mi. Ride, Marked Trail, runs through the Natural Resources Management Area in the Pine Barrens, Bikers pass typical barrens vegetation, Helmets & Eye Protection Required, Free Permit Required (good for 3 yrs.), call for permit: 631-444-0273   *www.exploreli.com*

South Fork • **Features Include:** 60-mile Ride, Mostly Flat Terrain, Some Hills, Saltwater Marshes, Freshwater Ponds **Start Point:** From Rte. 24 E. in Riverhead, through Hubbard County Park, to Montauk Hwy., cross the Shinnecock Canal into Southampton, follow Rte. 38 along the Peconic Bay into Sag Harbor, take Rte. 114 SE into East Hampton, ride near the ocean through Hither Hills Park to the Montauk Lighthouse   *www.exploreli.com*

Shadmoor • *NYS* • *50 South Fairview Ave., Montauk, NY* • *631-668-3781* • **Features Includes:** 99-acre Park, 2,400-ft. of Ocean Beach, Biking, there are 2 concrete bunkers, that were built during World War II & once equipped with artillery guns to protect the coast from enemy invasion **Hours:** Year-Round **Fee: Free** parking **Directions:** *Rte. 27 Sunrise Hwy. E. to Montauk Village, the park is .5 mi. East of the village on the Right, at the southwest corner of Rte. 27 & Seaside Ave.*
www.tripadvisor.com/Attraction_Review-g48194-d532149-Reviews-Shadmoor_ State_Park-Montauk_New_York.html

Shelter Island • **Features Include:** 25-mile Ride, Ferry Ride Required, Moderate to Easy, Street Route **Start Point:** Following Rte. 114 across the island to the South ferry dock in North Haven, a marked on-street route along Rte. 114 leads to East Hampton   *www.exploreli.com*

Southaven County Park • **SC** • *Victory Ave., Brookhaven, NY* • *631-854-1414* • *631-924-4490* • *631-345-2449* • The Carman's River flows through this park. **Features Includes:** 1,356-acre Pine-Oak Forested Park, Bicycle Hostel, Picnicking, the LI Steamer Trains (see museums) **Hours:** Spring Weekends Only **Fee: Free Directions:** *Southern State Pkwy., exit at Sunrise Hwy., take exit 58 N., as you enter William Floyd Pkwy., turn West onto Victory Ave., follow signs to the main entrance of the park* *www.co.suffolk.ny.us/Home/departments/parks/Parks.aspx*

Sunken Meadow Park • **NYS** • *Rte. 25A & Sunken Meadow Pkwy., Northport, NY* • *631-269-4333* • The park is located on the Long Island Sound & has a wide range of plant & animal life. **Features Include:** 3 mi. of Beach, Biking, Picnicking & Picnic Tables, Playground **Fee: Free** off-season, Memorial Day-Labor Day: $10, Weekends only until Oct.: $8, Empire Pass Accepted **Directions:** I-495 Long Island Expwy., take exit 53 Sunken Meadow/Sagtikos Pkwy. to the end   *http://nysparks.state.ny.us/parks*

Theodore Roosevelt County Park • **SC** • *Montauk Hwy., Montauk, NY* • *631-852-7878* • America's *1st* cattle ranching system was located in 17th century Montauk. **Features Include:** Biking, Picnicking, Outer Beach Access, Spanish-American War Exhibit **Hours:** Camp Wikoff is open to the public from May-Oct. Wed.-Sun.: 10 a.m. -5 p.m. **Fee: Free** off-season **Directions:** *Southern State Pkwy., follow Montauk Hwy. East through Montauk Village, past East Lake Dr., park sign & entrance is on N. side of Montauk Hwy.* *www.co.suffolk.ny.us/Home/departments/parks/Parks.aspx*

Trail View • **NYS** • *25 Lloyd Harbor Rd., Huntington, NY* • *631-423-1770* • Trail View is a link along the Nassau/Suffolk Greenbelt Trail that extends from Cold Spring Harbor State Park on the North shore to the south shore of Nassau County. **Features Include:** 400-acre Park, Hiking, Bicycling, Hilly Terrain, Elevations Ranging from 60-300-ft. above Sea Level **Hours:** Dawn-Dusk, Year-Round **Fee: Free Directions:** *Northern State Pkwy., to Rte. 135 Seaford-Oyster Bay Expwy. N., take Jericho Tpke. (25) E., pass 2 traffic lights, parking will be on the Left side of the road* *www.longislandexchange.com/parks/trailview-statepark.html*

Wildwood • **NYS** • *P.O. Box 518, North Wading River Rd., Wading River, NY* • *631-929-4314* • *Reservations: 800-456-2267* • **Features Include:** 600-acre Park, Biking, Beach, Playground, Picnic Tables **Hours:** Dawn-Dusk, Year-Round **Fee: Free** off-season, Memorial Day-Labor Day: $10, Weekends only until Oct.: $8, Empire Pass

Accepted **Directions:** *I-495 Long Island Expwy., take exit 68, head North on Rte. 46, take Rte. 25A E., turn Left onto Sound Ave., turn Left at traffic light onto Hulse Landing Rd., the park entrance is on the Right*   *http://nysparks.state.ny.us/sites/info*

CYCLING CLUBS ON LONG ISLAND

Bike Around Long Island • *631-499-3953* • **Features Include:** Most of their trips are on Long Island, although sometimes they drive to other places & combine bike riding with other tourist activities. Ride schedule can be found on their web site. **Fee: Free**

bikearoundlongisland.com

Climb • *Concerned Long Island Mountain Bicyclists* • *P.O. Box 203, Woodbury* • *631-271-6527* • **Features Include:** Mountain Bicyclist Club Rides on & off Long Island, Workshops, **Beginner Rides:** 9 a.m., 1st Sat. of the month at Bethpage State Park, meet at picnic area parking lot, 9 a.m., 3rd Sun. of the month at Cathedral Pines County Park **Fee:** Annually: $15, Family: $25   *climbonline.org*

East End Cycling Team • *10 Bell St., Bellport* • *631-286-1829* • **Features Include:** Competitive Team, Low-Key Atmosphere, Long Island Racing, 3 Skill Levels (Beginner-Expert), Free Children's Races (ages 3 to 11), Year-Round Weekend & Weekday Rides **Fee:** Membership: $20, newsletter & team uniforms available for an extra fee   *krebcycle.com*

Gbsc/Carl Hart Bicycle Racing Team • *298 Bayville Ave., Bayville* • *516-628-2590* • **Features Include:** Weekend Training Rides, Average Pace is 20-23 mph, 35-mi. minimum, call for races on Long Island **Fee:** $10 per year *bicyclelongisland.org/gbsc*

Huntington Bicycle Club • *Greenlawn* • *631-220-9517* • **Features Include:** Beginners-Advanced Rides, Weekends & Holidays, April-Nov., 12-100-mi. Rides **Fee:** Annually: $20, Family: $25   *huntingtonbicycleclub.org*

Long Island Bicycle Club, Westbury • *516-489- 3958* • **Features Include:** Standard rides: 9:30 a.m., Sat., Sun., Mon. & Holidays, March-Nov. from Westbury High School on Post Rd.: Away Weekend Trips: April, Memorial Day & Labor Day. **Fee:** Annually: $20, Each Additional Family Member: $5   *libike.org*

Massapequa Park Bicycle Club • *P.O. Box 231, Massapequa* • *516-581-3819* • **Features Include:** Recreational Rides for All Levels, on Sat., Sun. & Holidays, Non-members Invited, Racing & Multisports, Winter Mountain Biking, Aug. Hamptons Tour, Rides from 25-100-mi., **Fee:** Annually: $20, Family: $25 *massparkbikeclub.org*

FALL FOLLY

Paumonok Bicycling Of Long Island • *19 Julia Circle, East Setauket* • Features **Include:** Federation of Long Island's Bicycling Clubs, Represents 5,000 Bicyclists, Promotes Better Bicycling Conditions **Fee: Free** for members   *bicyclelongisland.org*

Shoreham Bmx Parents Association • *Track: 631-821-5569,* available on race days only or leave message • **Features Include:** Bicycle Racing for Girls/Women & Boys/ Men, All Ages, Racing Sun. from April-June & Sept.-Nov., Summer Racing on Tues. July & Aug. **Fee:** $8 per race, Annual membership required: $45, National Bicycle League

shorehambmx.org

Suffolk Bicycle Riders Association • *P.O. Box 404, St. James, NY* • Features Include: Long Island Bicycle Club, approx. 700 Members, Beginner/Advanced Rides, Day Trips, Safety & Maintenance Classes **Fee:** Annually: $20, Family: $25   *sbraweb.org*

SUGGESTIONS • COMMENTS • ERRORS

Linda.ReidBryce
@verizon.net

Thanks

Paintball Long Island • *Granny Rd., Coram, NY* • *800-352-4007* • *800-FLAG.007* •
Features Include: 88-acre Outdoor Complex, 26 Individual Paintball Fields, Active
Playing Fields for Competitions, Special Events, Big Game, Tournaments, Airsoft
Games, Parties, Reservations are sometimes required 2 weeks in advance, 12-17 need
parental consent (forms available at the office & on the web site) **Hours:** Sat.-Sun.:
8:30 a.m.-4 p.m., open daily for pre-paid bookings of 20 or more **Fee:** Field Paint: $8
for 100 rounds, $30 for 500, Camouflage Rental Outfit: $7, the $49.99 package, per
person, includes: 500 Paintballs, High Quality Semi-Automatic Paintgun, Initial Co2
air fill (20 oz.), Goggles & Mask System, & a 6-hr. outdoor session. For players with
their own equipment, all day air will be substituted for rental equipment. **Directions:**
I-495 Long Island Expwy., take exit 64 toward Patchogue/Port Jefferson, merge onto
Waverly Ave. S., turn Left onto Medford Rd./Rte.112, Rte. 112 becomes Granny Rd.
www.playpaintball.com • www.cousinspaintball.com

Wild West Target Paintball • *Five Towns Mini Golf* • *570 Rockaway Tpke., Law-*
rence, NY • *516-239-1743* • **Features Include:** Wild West Scene Loaded with Targets,
Shooting Range, 10 Paintball Targets, Outdoor Interactive Game Area **Hours:** Winter:
Mon.-Fri.: Noon-7 p.m., Sat.-Sun.: 11 a.m-7 p.m., Spring: Mon.-Fri.: Noon-9 p.m., Sat.:
11 a.m-10 p.m., Sun.: 11 a.m-7 p.m. **Fee:** 50-Shoots $6, 100-Shoots: $10, 150 Shots: $14
Directions: *I-495 Long Island Expwy., Cross Island Pkwy. S., Southern State Pkwy. W.,*
exit onto Peninsula Blvd. S., turn Right onto Rockaway Tpke.
www.5townsminigolfbatting.com

MORE FUN

BAKING FUN, SEASONED WITH SWEETNESS

The Edible Painted Cookie
Suggested Supplies: Use any pre-made cookie dough. Place a small amount of flour on a cutting board & have the children use their fingers to press the dough flat enough to use cookie cutters. Bake the cookies according to the directions (never let them brown). Once they are cool they can be painted.

Paint/Icing

3 cup Confectioner's Sugar	1/4 cup Water or Milk
1 tsp. Vanilla Extract	1 tbs. Melted Butter optional
Food Coloring	

Paint Brushes (buy a cheap, 10 pack of paint brushes with plastic handles & vinyl bristles. These can go into the dishwasher & be re-used for painting with icing.

Mix the sugar, vanilla & butter together. Add liquid as needed until it reaches the consistency of heavy cream. The mixture should be watery enough to drip off a paint brush, but not so watery that it runs right through the brush. Divide the icing into 3 small containers (lidded plastic is best), & add food coloring to each.

Place 1 or 2 paint brushes in each container & tell the children to return the brush to the appropriate color container before taking another color. This keeps all the colors clean. Have them paint the cookie with one color then let them drip a 2nd & 3rd color creating dots & streaks to make faces and patterns. Fill small Dixie cups with chocolate chips, sprinkles & red-hots for more decorating fun. Place the cookies on a flat tray to dry. They dry in about 15-20 min.

Due to the high sugar content, this type of icing can keep for weeks in the refrigerator. Store in lidded plastic containers. Icing will thicken so it will need to be stirred & may need a little more liquid to get the right consistency.

IN THIS SECTION

Winter Events

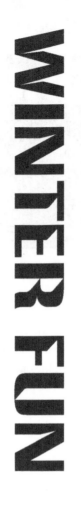

WINTER FUN

Let
Fun Flow
Like A
River

December

Village of Bayville's Winter Festival • *Ransom Beach* • *Presented by the Bayville Chamber of Commerce* • *347-203-8269* • *516-624-6160* • Features Include: Ice Carving Exhibition, Magician, Carriage Rides, Tree Lighting Ceremony, Refreshments, "Breakfast with Santa", Petting Zoo, Matt the Music Man, Photos With Santa, Music, Tree Lighting, Boy Scouts Holiday Wreaths, Girl Scouts Holiday Caroling **Hours:** Usually the 1st weekend in Dec. **Fee: Free** Directions: *Northern State Pkwy., take exit 35 N. 106/107 toward Oyster Bay, continue on 106 N., turn Left onto W. Main St., which becomes W. Shore Rd., drive over the Bayville Bridge & continue on Ludlam Ave., turn Left onto Bayville Ave.* *www.bayvillechamberofcommerce.com/contact.html*

Annual Village of Port Jefferson Charles Dickens Festival • *Presented by the Greater Port Jefferson Northern Brookhaven Arts Council* • *Festival Information: 631-802-2160* • *63-473 5220* • Features Include: Cultural Programs, Victorian Lantern Lighting, Children's Holiday Crafts, Dickens Reading Marathon, Puppet Show, Various Musical, Theatrical & Dance Performances, Exhibitions, Ice Skating at the Port Jefferson Village Center, Annual Cookie Walk, Christmas Fair, Storytellers, Wood Carvers Exhibit & Demonstration, Model Train Exhibition, Clinics, Choir, the Story of St. Nicholas (explains his feast day celebrated around the world in early Dec.), Animals of Victorian England, Annual Ball featuring mimicry of 19th century high society, Children's Maritime Open House Tours, Horse & Carriage Rides, Old-Fashioned Trolley Ride, *A Christmas Carol* Radio Show, Magic Show,

Annual Victorian Tea, Family Puzzle Hunt, Mr. Pip's Pesky Pursuit (print out a questionnaire online & follow the directions, participants can interview the street characters during the festival by asking their names & what they do in town), Hours: 2 days & 3 nights, usually the last weekend in Nov. or 1st weekend in Dec. Fee: All programs are **Free** & open to the public unless otherwise indicated, check the web site for specifics **Directions:** *I-495 Long Island Expwy., take exit 64 N. Rte. 112 to the end (approx. 9 mi.), Rte. 112 becomes Rte. 25A at the Nesconset Hwy. intersection, turn Right at the yellow blinking light, pass E. Main St. (1st right), enter Port Jefferson Village* *www.pjvillagecenter.com • www.gpjac.org*

Baldwin Chamber of Commerce Holiday Festival • *Baldwin LIRR Station • 516-223-8080* • Features Include: Santa Arrives on a Fire Truck, Local Musicians & Dance Performaces, "Reindeer" Rides for the Kids, Christmas, Hanukkah & Kwanzaa Programs **Hours:** 4 p.m.-6 p.m., usually the 1st weekend in Dec. **Fee: Free Directions:** *Southern State Pkwy., take exit 20 S. Grand Ave., merge onto Baldwin Rd., continue on Grand Ave., turn Right onto Brooklyn Ave., the train station will be on the Left* *www.baldwinchamber.com*

Candle Light Walk • Old Bethpage Village Restoration • NC • *1303 Round Swamp Rd., Bethpage, NY • 516-572-8401 • 516-572-8400* • Features Include: A 19th Century Holiday Experience Lit by Candlelight, Magic Lantern Show, Caroling, Bonfire, Period Storytelling, Period Costumes (worn by all guides) & Hot Cider, the Village is Open & Decorated for the Holidays **Hours:** 5 p.m.-9:30 p.m., usually for 2 weeks in Dec. **Fee:** Adults: $10, Kids 5-12 & Seniors: $7, Under 5: Free **Directions:** *I-495 Long Island Expwy., take exit 48 Round Swamp Rd. toward Old Bethpage/Farmingdale, make a Left onto Round Swamp Rd., turn Left onto Old Country Rd., slight Right at Round Swamp Rd., the village will be on the Left* *www.nassaucountyny.gov/agencies/Parks*

Christmas at the Montauk Lighthouse • *Presented by The Montauk Historical Society • 2000 Montauk Hwy., Montauk, NY • 631-668-2544* • Features Include: Lighthouse Illuminated with Thousands of White Lights, Live Music, Free Hot Cider, Cookies & Candy Canes, Santa Will Arrive **Hours:** 4:30-7 p.m., usually the Sat. of Thanksgiving weekend, call for the time schedule **Fee: Free Directions:** *I-495 Long Island Expwy., take exit 70 S., travel South on County Rd. 111, take Rte. 27 E. to Montauk Point* *www.montauklighthouse.com*

Patchogue Boat Parade of Lights • *Patchogue River • Presented by the Patchogue Chamber of Commerce • 631-475-0121* • Features Include: Private &

WINTER FUN

Commercial Boats Decorated for the Holidays, Patchogue River Procession, Grucci Grand Illumination Fireworks Display, Elaborately Decorated Boats, Judged Competition, Santa Arrives by Boats **Hours:** Check the events page on the Chamber of Commerce's web site **Hours:** 6 p.m., usually in early Dec. **Fee: Free Directions:** *I-495 Long Island Expwy., take exit 62, Nicolls Rd. toward Stony Brook, take Nicolls Rd. S., turn Left onto County Rte. 85, turn Right at Atlantic Ave., turn Left at County Rte. 65/Weeks St., turn Left onto River Ave., turn Right onto River View Ct.* www.patchoguechamber.com

Celebrate Kwanzaa! • Long Island Children's Museum • 11 Davis Ave., Garden City, NY • 516-224-5800 • Features Include: Enjoy the traditions & the meaning behind this week-long holiday, Kwanzaa Craft Projects for kids 5 & up **Hours:** Call for the exact date in Dec. **Fee:** Adults & Kids: $9, Under 1 & Members: Free, approx. membership fee for a family of 4 is $85 **Directions:** *Northern State Pkwy., take the Meadowbrook Pkwy. S., take exit M4 (Nassau Coliseum), bear Right (before Hempstead Tpke.) nto Charles Lindbergh Blvd., go to the 1st traffic light (Nassau Coliseum on your Left, Nassau Community College on your Right) proceed through this traffic light & continue on to LICM on the Right side of the road* www.licm.org

The Festival of Lights • The Long Island Children's Museum • 11 Davis Ave., Garden City, NY • 516-224-5800 • Features Include: Kids 5 & up will learn about the traditions of Hanukkah **Hours:** Call for exact date & time **Fee:** Adults: $9, Under 1 & Members: Free, membership for a family of 4 is approx. $85 **Directions:** *Northern State Pkwy., take the Meadowbrook Pkwy. S. to exit M4 (Nassau Coliseum), bear Right (before Hempstead Tpke.) onto Charles Lindbergh Blvd., go to the 1st traffic light (Nassau Coliseum on your Left, Nassau Community College on your Right) proceed through this traffic light & continue on to LICM on the Right side of the road* www.licm.org

Seal Walk • Cupsogue Beach County Park Coastal Research & Education Society of Long Island • West Hampton Beach, NY • 631-244-3352 • Features Include: Seal Walk, 2-hr. Naturalist-Led Walk, Observe, Photograph, Seals in the Wild **Hours:** Times & days vary, call for specifics or check the web site, Dec.-March **Fee: Free**, $5 suggested donation **Directions:** *I-495 Long Island Expwy., take exit 68 S. William Floyd Pkwy. toward Shirley, slight Right to merge onto NY-27 E. toward Montauk, take exit 63 S. for County Rd. 31 S. toward Westhampton Beach, merge onto County Rd. 31/Old Riverhead Rd./Riverhead Rd., continue onto Oak St., at the traffic circle, take the 2nd exit onto Potunk Ln., turn Left onto Main St., slight Right onto Beach Ln., turn Left onto Dune Rd., look for Cupsogue Beach County Park* cresli.org

Holiday Lights & Boat Parade • Freeport, NY • 516-223-8840 • Teachers Center: 516-377-2314, ext. 10 • Features Include: Weekend Event, Nautical Mile of Lights

Parade, Best Decorated Boat Contest, Free Boat Rides, Santa Arrives at the Recreation Center, Winter Wonderland Display, Gingerbread Houses, Model Trains, Dozens of Decorated Trees in the Recreation Center, Freeport Ice Skating Academy Annual Holiday Show Synchronized Skating Teams, Individual Skater Performances, Tree Decorating Event, Children's Activities (in the main parking lot from 2-5 p.m.), Kids Eat Free at Participating Restaurants **Hours:** Boat Parade: Fri. at 6 p.m., Street Parade: Sun. at 5 p.m., 1st weekend in Dec. **Fee: Free Directions:** *Northern State Pkwy., take I-135 Seaford Oyster Bay Expwy. S., take exit 2W. State Hwy. 27 W., merge onto 27 W., make a Left onto N. Grove St./ Guy Lombardo Ave.* *www.freeportchamberofcommerce.com*

Holiday Celebration at Old Westbury Gardens • *Westbury House • 71 Old Westbury Rd., P.O. Box 430, Old Westbury, NY* • 516-333-0048 • Features Include:

Historic Westbury House Decorated for the Holidays, Visit Santa, Holiday Gift Shop, Musical Performances, Hot Cider & Cookies, Children's Crafts, First Night (New Year's Eve Celebration which includes family & cultural events), Tree Lighting, Holiday Tea **Hours:** 10 a.m.-4 p.m. This 2-week event usually begins the 1st weekend in Dec. **Fee:** Adults: $8, Kids 2-12 & Seniors: $5, Members: Free **Directions:** *Northern State Pkwy., take exit 32 Post Ave., bear Left at end of exit ramp, turn Left onto Post Ave. heading North, turn Left onto Jericho Tpke./Rte. 25, turn Right at the 1st light onto Old Westbury Rd., the garden's gate is on the Right* *www.oldwestburygardens.org*

Annual Holiday Festival • *Stony Brook Village Center • The Ward Melville Heritage Organization hosts this Annual Holiday Festival • 111 Main St. on the Harbor, Stony Brook, NY* • Features Include: The Promenade Of Trees (with more than 80

decorated trees), Santa Arrives at 2 p.m. by Horse Drawn Carriage, Carolers, Live Music, Tree Lighting (at 5:30 p.m.), Music, **Hours:** early Dec. **Fee: Free Directions:** *I-495 Long Island Expwy., take exit 53 Sagtikos State Pkwy. N., continue on Sunken Meadow Pkwy. N., take exit SM3E. for State Hwy. 25 E./Jericho Tpke. toward Smithtown, merge onto Jericho Tpke./Rte. 25, turn Left at N. Country Rd./Rte. 25A, follow N. Country Rd./Rte. 25A, continue on County Rte. 68/Main St./N. Main St., the Village Center will be on the Right* *www.stonybrookvillage.com • www.stonybrook.com*

Musical Christmas at Sagtikos Manor • *Montauk Hwy. • P.O. Box 5344, Bay Shore, NY • Suffolk County Parks* • 631-661-8348 • 631-661-5169 • 631-854-0939 • Features Include: Manor House (circa 1692) Tour, Observe Dutch

Colonial Christmas Customs, Period Christmas Music, Caroling, American Revolutionary & Victorian Eras, Clothing from the Civil War to the 1950s, Holiday Refreshments **Hours:** 11 a.m.-3 p.m., mid-Dec., Reservations Required **Fee:** Advanced purchase: Adults: $15, Kids: $5, $20 at the door **Directions:** *Southern State Pkwy., take*

exit 40 Robert Moses Cswy. S., take exit RM 2E. (Rte. 27A) Bay Shore, turn Right onto
Rte. 27A & continue East approx. .5 mi., the entrance to will be on the Left

www.sagtikosmanor.org

Solstice First Light & Lantern Festival • *The Children's Museum of the East End* • **376**
Sag Harbor Tpke., Bridgehampton, NY • **631-537-8250** • Features Include: Winter
Solstice, Celebrate the Shortest Day of the Year **Hours:** 3 p.m., late Dec., **Fee:** Adults: $9,
Kids under 1 & Members: Free, membership for a family of 4 is approx. $85 **Directions:**
I-495 Long Island Expwy., take exit 68 S. William Floyd Pkwy./Co. Hwy. 46 S. toward Shirley, merge
onto County Rte. 46/William Floyd Pkwy., take the ramp onto Rte. 27 E., turn Left at Rte. 27, make
a U-turn, turn Right at Stephen Hands Path, turn Left at Rte. 114/Sag Harbor Rd./Sag Harbor East
Hampton Tpke./Sag Harbor Tpke. *www.cmee.org*

Victorian Christmas Open House • *Hallockville Museum Farm* • **6038 Sound Ave.,**
Riverhead, NY • **631-298-5292** • Features Include: Celebrate Victorian Era Christmas
Traditions, Free Cider & Hot Chocolate, Goodies Served in the Homestead Kitchen **Hours:**
Sun.: 11 a.m.-4 p.m., usually the first Sun. in Dec. **Fee:** Adults: $7, Kids 6-12: $5, Under
6: Free, Families: $18 **Directions:** *I-495 Long Island Expwy., take exit 73, Old Country Rd.*
toward Orient/Greenport/Co. Hwy. 58, stay on Old Country Rd., at Roanoke Ave., take the 2nd
exit & stay on County Rte. 58/Old Country Rd./Rte. 58, turn Left at County Rte. 43/Northville
Tpke., continue straight to stay on County Rte. 43/Northville Tpke., turn Right onto Sound Ave.,
the farm will be on the Left *www.hallockville.com*

Winter Open House • *The Long Island Museum of American Art, History &*
Carriages • *1200 Rte. 25A Stony Brook, NY* • **631-751-0066** • Features Include:
Local Students Perform Holiday Songs **Hours:** Noon-5 p.m., usually the 1st weekend in
Dec. Fee: **Free** museum admission **Directions:** *I-495 Long Island Expwy., take exit 62,*
proceed North on Nicolls Rd., take it to the end, turn Left onto Rte. 25A drive 1.5 mi. to
the intersection of 25A & Main St. in Stony Brook, turn Left

www.longislandmuseum.org

Bayville Winter Wonderland • *8 Bayville Ave., Bayville, NY* • **516-628-8697** •
Features Include: Santa's Toy Factory Funhouse, Captain Bay's Yo Ho Holiday
Light Show, Skating, Bayville Holiday Express Train Ride, Meet Santa, Arcade, Rock
Climbing **Fee:** Daytime: $10 per person, Night: $12 per person, Blizzard Bay's Artic
Skating Adventure: $8 per person, Bradley Bay's Indoor Rock Climbing Challenge:
$6.75 **Hours:** Weekends: Noon-9 or 10 p.m., Weekdays: 5 p.m.-10 p.m., check web site
for exact hours & days the facility is open **Directions:** *Northern State Pkwy, take exit 35 N.*
106/107 State Hwy., take 106 N., turn Left onto W. Main St. which becomes W. Shore Rd., drive
over the Bayville Bridge, continue on Ludlam Ave., turn Left onto Bayville Ave., make a U-turn,
the wonderland will be on your Right *www.bayvillewinterwonderland.com*

Cold Spring Harbor Victorian Christmas • *Village of Cold Spring Harbor* • *631-367-6060* • **Features Include:** Historic Village of Cold Spring Harbor, Victorian Christmas Themes, Violin Concert on Sundays, Horse Drawn Buggy Rides **Hours:** Noon-5 p.m., every weekend in Dec. **Fee:** Free **Directions:** *Southern State Pkwy., take exit 28A Seaford- Oyster Bay Pkwy. 135 N., take exit 14 E. Jericho Tpke., turn Left onto Woodbury Rd., turn Left onto Harbor Rd./108, turn Left onto Lawrence Hill Rd., turn Right onto Harbor Rd./ Rte. 25A East, the harbor will be on the Left side of the village of Cold Spring Harbor*

Free December - Saturday Films For Children & Families • *Guild Hall of East Hampton/ John Drew Theater* • *158 Main St., East Hampton, NY* • *631-324-0806* • **Box Office: 631-324-4050•** **Directions:** *Southern State Pkwy., take exit 40 Robert Moses Cswy. S., take exit RM1E. towards Rte. 27 E./Montauk, turn Right onto Sunrise Hwy., take the Left ramp and merge onto NY 27 E., turn Left onto NY 27/Montauk Hwy., turn Left onto Main St./NY 27*   *www.guildhall.org*

Gingerbread University • *3225 Sound Ave., Baiting Hollow, NY* • *631-727-7309* • **Features Include:** 4,000-sq.-ft. Red Barn, Decorate Gingerbread Houses/Cookies & Ornaments, Gingerbreadology Diplomas, Candyland Walk, Meet Santa, Cookie Factory, Retail Store **Hours:** Fri.: 5-8 p.m., Sat.-Sun.: Noon-6 p.m. **Fee:** $2-$3 a person, Decorate Gingerbread House: $27, Decorate a Gingerbread Ornament: $10 **Directions:** *1-495 Long Island Expwy., take exit 73 Old Country Rd. toward Orient/Greenport/Co. Hwy. 58, stay on Old Country Rd. Hwy. 58, take the Roanoke Ave. exit, turn Left onto Sound Ave., Gingerbread University will be on the Left*   *www.gingerbreaduniversity.com*

Holiday Gift Event • *Maritime Museum* • *P.O. Box 184, 86 West Ave., West Sayville, NY* • *631-447-8679* • **Features Include:** Art Exhibition, Stationery, Note Cards, Toys, Wine & Cheese, Poinsettias & Holiday Decorations in the Flower & Garden Shop, Winter Lecture Series **Hours:** Mon-Sat.: 10 a.m.-4 p.m., Sun.: Noon-4 p.m. **Fee:** Free **Directions:** *Southern State Pkwy., to Heckscher State Pkwy S., take exit 45 E. for State Hwy 27A E., merge onto E. Main St./Rte. 27A, continue on S. Country Rd./County Rte. 85/Main St., turn Right at West Ave., continue to follow County Rte. 85/Main St., the museum will be on the Right*   *www.limaritime.org*

Holiday Tree Lighting • *Orient Point, State Park, Rte. 25, Orient, NY* • *631-323-2440* • **Features Include:** Family Oriented Event, Holiday Songs (sung by the local elementary school), Santa Lights the Holiday Tree **Hours:** 6:30 p.m., usually the first Fri. in Dec. **Fee:** Free **Directions:** *I-495 Long Island Expwy. E. to the end, take Rte. 25 E. to the park*   *http://nysparks.state.ny.us/sites/info*

Saint Nicholas Day • *Wyckoff Farmhouse Museum: Pieter Claesen Wyckoff House* • *5816 Clarendon Rd., Brooklyn, NY* • *718-629-5400* • **Features Include:** St.

WINTER FUN

Nicholas Arrives on Horseback, Chocolate Coins for the Children, Stories Read by St. Nicholas, Feed Santa's Horses, Review the Naughty & Nice List **Hours:** Tues.-Sun.: 10 a.m.-4 p.m., Tours Tues.-Fri.: 1-3 p.m., Tours Sat.-Sun.: 11 a.m., 1 p.m., 3 p.m., usually the 1st weekend in Dec. **Fee:** Adults: $5, Kids Under 10: Free, Students & Seniors: $3 **Directions:** *Southern State Pkwy., Belt Pkwy. W. toward Brooklyn, take exit 14 for Pennsylvania Ave., turn Right onto Granville Payne Ave./Pennsylvania Ave., turn Left onto Flatlands Ave., turn Right onto E. 80th St., turn Right onto Ralph Ave., turn Left onto Clarendon Rd., the farm museum is on the Left*   *www.wyckoffassociation.org*

The Magical Banquet & Holiday Decorations at Coe Hall • *Planting Fields Arboretum State Historic Park* • *1395 Planting Fields Rd., Oyster Bay, NY* • *516-922-9200* • **Hours:** Noon-3 p.m., every weekend in Dec. **Directions:** *I-495 Long Island Expwy., take exit 41 N., take Rte. 106 N. toward Oyster Bay, turn Left onto 25A Northern Blvd., make 1st Right onto Mill River Rd., follow the green & white signs to the Arboretum on Planting Fields Rd.*   *http://www.plantingfields.org/Calenda2/events.htm*

NEW YORK CITY

Tropical Butterflies Alive In Winter • *The Butterfly Conservatory* • *American Museum of Natural History* • *Central Park West at 79th St., NY, NY* • *212-769-5100* • **Features Include:** Walk among Butterflies, See Hatching Butterflies, Observe while they Eat/Fly & Land, Learn about Butterfly Camouflage. "The butterfly vivarium is a custom-fabricated temporary shell structure that sits within one of the Museum's galleries. The vivarium is approximately 1,315 Sq. ft. Butterflies are contained within the adult flight area which is approximately 62-ft. long, 20-ft. wide, and 13-ft. high (amnh.org). **Hours:** 10 a.m.-5:45 p.m., vivarium open mid-Oct-mid-May **Fee:** Adults: $24, Kids: $14, Students: $18, Members: Free, 5-10 hr. Parking: $35 **Directions:** *I-495 Long Island Expwy., drive through the Queens Midtown Tunnel, drive East on 34th St., turn Right on 8th Ave., at Broadway/Columbus Circle, take the 3rd exit onto Central Park West, museum will be on the Left, parking is available under the museum, the entrance is on 81st St. between Central Park West & Columbus Ave.*
                    www.amnh.org/exhibitions/butterflies/highlights/architecture.php

Holiday Display: Winter Plants of Interest • *Brooklyn Botanic Garden* • *900 Washington Ave., Brooklyn, NY* • *718-623-7200* • **Features Include:** Indoor Holiday Display, Seasonal Horticulture/Art & Science **Hours:** Dec.-Feb.: Tues.-Fri.: 8 a.m.-6 p.m., Weekends & Holidays: 10 a.m.-6 p.m., closed Mon., Nov.-March: Tues.-Fri.: 8 a.m.-4:30 p.m., Weekends & Holidays: 10 a.m.-4:30 p.m., closed Mon., Wheelchair Accessible Gardens **Fee:** Adults: $8, Students: $4, Under 12: Free **Directions:** *I-495 Long Island Expwy. W., take the BQE W., exit onto Kent Ave., follow the service road (Park Ave.) alongside & then under the expwy. for 5 blocks, turn Left onto Washington Ave., drive for 1.75 mi.*   *www.bbg.org*

Chase Away the Winter Blues • *Brooklyn Botanic Garden* • *1000 Washington Ave.* •
Brooklyn, NY • *718-623-7333* • **Features Include:** An hr.-long outdoor narrated winter-time guided tour held rain, snow or shine **Hours:** Tues.-Fri.: 8 a.m.-4:30 p.m., Sat.-Sun.: 10 a.m.-4:30 p.m., closed Mon.:Nov.-March **Fee:** Adults: $8, Under 12: Free, Students & Seniors: $4 **Directions:** *I-495 Long Island Expwy., to the BQE Brooklyn Queens Expwy. W., exit onto Kent Ave., follow the service road (Park Ave.) alongside & then under the expwy. for 5 blocks, Left onto Washington Ave. for 1.75 mi.* *www.bbg.org*

Christmas at The Cloisters Museum & Gardens • *99 Margaret Corbin Dr., Fort Tryon*
Park, NY, NY • *212-923-3700* • **Features Include:** Holly, Ivy & Plants of the Medieval Feast of Christmastide, Arches of Apples, Hazelnuts, Rosehips & Ivy Decorate Doorways, Wheat/Bay & Nuts Wreath, Medieval Holiday Music Performances **Hours:** Tues.-Sun.: 9:30 a.m.-4:45 p.m., closed Mon.: Nov.-Feb. **Fee:** Free, donation appreciated **Directions:** *Nothern State Pkwy. W., becomes Grand Central Pkwy., go over the Triborough Bridge, take FDR Drive south-bound/downtown, take the 96th St. exit, turn Left onto York Ave., turn Right on 86th St., turn Left onto Fifth Ave. & enter Museum parking garage at 80th St.* *www.metmuseum.org*

Annual Christmas Tree ⊚ • *Metropolitan Museum of Art* • *1000 Fifth Ave. at 82nd*
St., NY, NY • *212-535-7710* • *212-570-3828* • **Features Include:** 20-ft. Blue Spruce Decorated with 18th Century Neapolitan Angels & Cherubs, Neapolitan Baroque Crèche Display, 18th Century Spanish Choir Screen from the Cathedral of Valladolid, Location: Medieval Sculpture Hall **Hours:** Tues.-Thurs.: 9:30 a.m.-5:30 p.m., Fri.-Sat.: 9:30 a.m.–9 p.m., Sun.: 9:30 a.m.–5:30 p.m., Closed: Mon. **Fee:** Free, Recommended Donation: Adults: $20, Under 12: Free, Students: $10, Seniors: $15 **Directions:** *From Penn Station: Take the M4 bus to 83rd St. & Madison Ave., or take the C local train to 81st St. & transfer to the M79 cross town bus across Central Park to Fifth Ave.* *www.metmuseum.org*

Annual Holiday Train Show • *The New York Botanical Garden* • *200th St. &*
Kazimiroff Blvd., Bronx, NY • *718-817-8700* • **Features Include:** Model Train Exhibit, 140 Replicas of New York Landmarks Made from Plant Parts, Bridges one can Walk Under, Trains Pass Overhead, Family Garden, Children's Garden **Hours:** Sat.: 9:30 a.m.-6:15 p.m. Sun.: 10 a.m.-5 p.m., available weekdays: 4:30 p.m.-5:15 p.m., mid-Nov.-mid-Jan., tickets required & timed in 15 min. intervals, Ticket Purchase: 718-817-8716 **Fee:** Adults: $20, Kids 2-12: $10, Students: $18 **Directions:** *Northern State Pkwy., take the Cross Island Pkwy. N. to the Throgs Neck Bridge, take I-95 New England Thrwy. N., take exit 8C Pelham Pkwy. W., cross Bronx River Pkwy. (Pelham Pkwy. turns into Fordham Rd. after 2 mi.), turn Right onto Kazimiroff Blvd. & continue to the garden, entrance on the Right* *www.nybg.org*

WINTER FUN

Wild In Winter • *Bronx Zoo* • *Wildlife Conservation Society* • *2300 Southern Blvd., Bronx, NY* • *718-367-1010* • **Features Include:** Horse Drawn Wagon Rides, Marshmallow Roasting, Reindeer, Caroling, Storytelling, Craft Workshops **Hours:** 11:30 a.m.-3:30 p.m., weekends through Dec., & every day in Jan. **Fee:** Adults: $15, Kids 3-12: $11, Seniors: $13 **Directions:** *I-495 Long Island Expwy., take exit 31N. Cross Island Pkwy., take exit 33 & merge onto I-295 N. toward New England, exit onto I-95 S., take exit 4B toward Bronx River Pkwy./Rosedale Ave, take the Cross Bronx Expwy., turn Right onto Rosedale Ave., turn left onto E. Tremont Ave., turn Right onto Southern Blvd., the zoo will be on the Right, or take the Whitestone Bridge to Hutchinson River Pkwy. N. to Pelham Pkwy. W. follow Pelham Pkwy. W. for 2 mi. & turn Left on Boston Rd. (after passing under the subway), turn Right at light, the zoo's entrance (Gate B) is located directly after the underpass* *www.bronxzoo.com*

SANTA SIGHTINGS

Breakfast with Santa • *The LI Marriott* • *101 James Doolittle Blvd., Uniondale, NY* • *516-794-3800* • **Hours:** 9:30-11 a.m. advance reservations required, 1ˢᵗ weekend in Dec. **Fee:** contact the Marriott **Directions:** *Northern State Pkwy., take exit 31A Meadowbrook State Pkwy. S., take exit M4 State Hwy. 24 W., Hempstead Tpke., turn Right onto Hotel Dr./James Doolittle Blvd., the hotel will be on the Left* *www.marriott.com*

Breakfast With Santa • *Atlantis Marine World* • *431 East Main St., Riverhead, NY* • *631-208-9200, ext. 426* • **Features Include:** Family Breakfast, Santa & the Atlantis Mascots, Reservations Required **Hours:** 2 seatings: 10 a.m. & 11:45 a.m., mid-Dec. **Fee:** Contact Atlantis, pricing varies **Directions:** *I-495 Long Island Expwy., take exit 71 Rte. 24, turn Right onto Rte. 94/24 E., drive to the traffic circle, turn Right onto Peconic Ave., turn Right onto Main St., Atlantis Marine World is on the South side of the street, follow the signs for free parking* *www.atlantismarineworld.com*

Flying Santa at the Fire Island Lighthouse • **Features Include:** Hear the historic story of the real Flying Santa from former Lighthouse Keeper Gottfried Mahler & his wife Marilyn. **Hours:** 11:30 a.m., 1ˢᵗ weekend in Dec. **Fee: Free** **Directions:** *Southern State Pkwy., exit 40 Robert Moses Cswy. S. toward Robert Moses State Park, get to the park, drive around the water tower, head East, park in the east End of Field 5, walk on the boardwalk to the lighthouse* *www.fireislandlighthouse.com*

Santa Comes to Greenport • *The Railroad Museum of Long Island in Greenport (adjacent to the LIRR Station)* • *440 4ᵗʰ St., Greenport, NY* • *631-477-0439* • **Features Include:** Santa arrives on the Noon train & departs on the 3 train **Hours:** The

museum is open from 11:30 a.m.-3:30 p.m., usually the *1st* weekend in Dec. **Fee: Free**
Directions: *I-495 Long Island Expwy., take exit 73, Old Country Rd./County Rte. 58 E., drive to the Rte. 25 intersection, take Rte. 25 E./Main Rd., follow Rte. 25 E. to the Village of Green-port (approx. 23 mi. East of the end of I-495), Main Rd. becomes Front St. in Greenport, turn Right onto 4th St. & drive 2 blocks to the railroad tracks, the museum will be on the Left*

www.rmli.us/Welcome.htm

Santa Comes to Town Parade • *Brookwood Hall, 50 Irish Ln., East Islip, NY 11730* • *Town Hall West (401 Building), 401 Main St., Islip, NY* • *co-sponsored by the Islip Chamber of Commerce & the Town of Islip* • *631-581-2720* • **Features Include:** The parade begins at Brookwood Hall on Irish Ln. & ends at Town Hall West on Main St. in Islip. Santa arrives in a horse-drawn carriage. There is a craft show. **Hours:** Parade: 2 p.m., Event: 10 a.m.-4:30 p.m., 1st Sat. in Dec. **Fee: Free Directions:** *Southern State Pkwy., take exit 43 S. for Islip Ave./ Rte. 111 S. to end, make Right onto Main St., Islip Town Hall is on the Right, Town Hall West is located on Montauk Hwy., .25 mi. W. of Town Hall, the parade begins at Brookwood Hall, Montauk Hwy. & Irish Ln., East Islip & ends at Town Hall West, 401 Main St., Islip*

http://silverstarcs.com • www.islipchamberofcommerce.com

BROOKLYN

Winter Park Events • *Prospect Park Alliance* • *95 Prospect Park West, Brooklyn, NY* • *718-965-8951* • *718-965-8999* • **Features Include:** Indoor (Wollman Rink) & Outdoor Skating, Musical Events (associated with skating), Nature Crafts, Winter Bird Counting Hike, Early American Crafts & Games, Nature Crafts **Hours:** vary by event **Fee:** vary by event, Free parking Year-Round for park visitors **Directions:** *I-495 Long Island Expwy., take the Brooklyn-Queens Expwy., exit at Tillary St., turn onto Flatbush Ave., (the Brooklyn Public Library will be on your Left & the Park on your Right), pass the zoo & Lefferts Historic House on the Right, make a Right at the traffic light onto Ocean Ave., at the next major intersection (Ocean & Parkside Ave.), turn Right into the park, take Park Dr. to the flashing light, make a Left into the Wollman Rink parking lot, follow signs to the Audubon Center, a 5 min. walk from the parking lot* www.prospectpark.org/calendar

CUT YOUR OWN CHRISTMAS TREE

Most tree farms open the day after Thanksgiving + remain open until December's end.

Baiting Hollow Nurseries • *830 Sound Ave., Calverton, NY* • *631-929-6439* • **Hours:** vary, call for hours **Directions:** *I-495 Long Island Expwy., take exit 68 William Flloyd Pkwy. toward Shirley, take Rte. 25A, turn Left onto Sound Ave.*

Dart's Christmas Tree Farm • *2355 Main Bayview Rd., Southold, NY* • *631-765-4148* • **Hours:** 9 a.m.-5 p.m. **Fee:** Check web site for coupons **Directions:** *I-495 Long Island Expwy., take exit 73 Old Country Rd. toward Orient/Greenport, turn Left onto Old Country Rd./*

Rte. 58 at Roanoke Ave., take the 2nd exit & stay on Old Country Rd./Rte. 58, turn Left onto Main Rd./Rte. 25, continue to follow Main Rd./Rte. 25, turn Right onto Corwin Ln., turn Right onto Main Bayview Rd., the farm will be on the Left   www.dartstreefarm.com

Lewin Farm • *Sound Ave., Wading River, NY* • **631-929-4327** • Features Include: 4-12-ft. Christmas Trees **Hours:** Opens the weekend after Thanksgiving **Directions:** *I-495 Long Island Expwy., to exit 68 for William Floyd Pkwy. toward Shirley/Co. Hwy. 46, take the William Floyd Pkwy./Co. Hwy. 46 N., turn Right onto Rte. 25A, turn Left onto Sound Ave., the farm will be on the Left*

Matt's Christmas Tree Farm • *309 Weeks Ave., Manorville, NY* • **631-874-6260** • Features Include: 10,000 Trees ranging from 2-14-ft., Trailer Rides, Candy Canes, the farm supplies bow saws & netting, loading & tying assistance **Hours:** 8 a.m.-4:30 p.m. **Directions:** *I-495 Long Island Expwy., take exit 68 S. onto William Floyd Pkwy., turn Left at the 2nd light onto Moriches-Mid Island Rd., continue for 2.25 mi. to Weeks Ave., make a Left onto Weeks Ave. & go approx. .5 mi. to Matt's Christmas Tree Farm on the Right side of the road*   www.mattschristmastreefarm.com

Shamrock Christmas Tree Farm • *Main Rd., Mattituck, NY* • **631-298-4619** • **631-298-4118** • Features Include: Cut Your Own Tree, Train Rides, Antique Sleigh Display, Free Hot Chocolate, Popcorn, Santa Visits (on weekends with purchase) **Hours:** 9 a.m.-5 p.m., Santa Visits: Sat.-Sun.: Noon-5 p.m., opens the weekend after Thanksgiving **Directions:** *I-495 Long Island Expwy., take exit 73, turn Right onto Old Country Rd., pass Tanger Mall on the Right, Old Country Rd. becomes Main Rd./Rte. 25, see the farm's sign on the Left immediately after Elijah's Ln., turn Left at the farm entrance*

HOLIDAY LIGHT SHOWS

Brookhaven BriteNites • *Town of Brookhaven Holtsville Ecology Site* • *249 Buckley Rd., Holtsville, NY* • **631-758-9536** • **631-758-9664** • Features Include: Drive-Through Light Show, 1.2-mi. Trail, Illuminated Light Displays **Hours:** 5:30-9:30 p.m., last week in Nov.-New Years **Fee:** $12 per car load, see web site for coupon **Directions:** *I-495 Long Island Expwy., take exit 62 Nicolls Rd., turn Right onto Waverly Ave., turn Left onto Blue Point Rd., turn Right onto Canine Rd., turn Right onto Buckley Rd.*   www.patchoguechamber.com

Holiday Light Show • *Camp Edey* • *1500 Lakeview Ave., Bayport, NY* • **631-472-1625** • *Sponsored by: Girl Scouts of Suffolk County* • Features Include: Drive through a Wooded Trail, Light Displays, Holiday Vignetts, 3D Firework Glasses, 87.9 FM Holiday Light Show Radio Station **Hours:** 5-9 p.m., month of Dec. **Fee:** $12 per car **Directions:** *I-495 Long Island Expwy., take exit 62 Nicolls Rd. toward Stony Brook/Blue Point, turn Right at County Rte. 85, turn Right onto Lakeview Ave.*   www.gssc.us

Holiday Safari • *47 Awixa Ave., Bay Shore, NY* • Features Include: 3 acres of Displays for All Winter Holidays **Hours:** 5-9 p.m., last 2 weeks in Dec. **Fee: Free** **Directions:** *I-495 Long Island Expwy., take exit 53 Sagtikos Pkwy., take the exit toward Bay Shore/ Bay Shore Rd., merge onto Bay Shore Rd./Rte. 57 becomes Howells Rd., turn Right onto 3rd Ave., turn Left onto Main St., turn Right onto Awixa Ave.*

Santa's Corner • *166th St. & 23rd Ave., Bayside, NY* • Features Include: Numerous Houses Wrapped in Lights, Lawn Ornaments, this neighborhood has been known to have some of the best all-around displays in NY **Fee: Free** **Directions:** *I-495 Long Island Expwy., take exit 28 Francis Lewis Blvd./Oceania St., merge onto Horace Harding Expwy., turn Right onto Francis Lewis Blvd., turn Right onto 166th St.*

Winter Garden Holiday Lights • *World Financial Center* • *NY, NY* • Features Include: 100,000 lights adorn the palm trees in the Winter Garden, making this 1 of New York's more unique light displays **Hours:** 7-11 p.m. every day through the 2nd weekend in Jan. **Fee: Free** **Directions:** *I-495 Long Island Expwy., take the Queens Midtown Tunnel, turn Right onto 34th St., turn Left onto 12th Ave., continue straight onto 11th Ave., continue on West St., turn Right at Liberty St., turn Right at S. End Ave., the Winter Garden will be on the Right. By train: take the LIRR to Penn Station, take the 3 train to the Chambers St. Station*

Grand Central Kaleidoscope Light Show • *Grand Central Station Main Concourse* • *East 42nd St., NY, NY* • Features Include: Every half-hr. the Sky Ceiling in Grand Central's main concourse is illuminated by a multitude of lights as holiday music plays. There are also special holiday shops set up in the terminal. **Hours:** 11 a.m.-9 p.m., Dec.-Jan. 1, **Fee: Free** **Directions:** *I-495 Long Island Expwy., take the Queens Midtown Tunnel, merge onto 37th St., turn Right onto 3rd Ave., turn Left onto 42nd St. By train: take the LIRR to Penn Station, take the 4,5,6 or 7 to Grand Central Station*

Fantasy of Lights • *Lighthouse Point Park, Lighthouse Rd., New Haven, CT* • **Features Include:** Drive through Lighthouse Point Park, Enchanted Fantasyland, Enormous Holiday Light Displays, Ice Tunnel **Hours:** Sun.-Thurs.: 5 -9 p.m., Fri. & Sat.: 5-10 p.m, open every night including holidays, Nov.-Dec. **Fee:** Car Load: $10, Mini-Bus: $25, Bus: $50 **Directions:** *I-495 Long Island Expwy., take exit 31 Cross Island Pkwy. to I-295 N. toward New England, follow signs for I-95/695, take I-95 N., take exit 50 for Woodward Ave., at the 2nd light turn Right onto Townsend Ave., continue to the 2nd traffic light approx. 2 mi., turn Right onto Lighthouse Rd., & the event is at the end of the road in Lighthouse Point Park* http://newhavengoodwill.easterseals.com

WINTER FUN

January

Seal Walk • *Cupsogue Beach County Park Coastal Research & Education Society of Long Island* • *West Hampton Beach, NY* • *631-244-3352* • Features Include: Seal Walk, 2-hr. Naturalist-Led Walk, Observe, Photograph, Seals in the Wild, Bring Binoculars & Dress Warmly **Hours:** times & days vary, call for specifics or check the web site, Dec.-March **Fee: Free**, $5 suggested donation **Directions:** *I-495 Long Island Expwy. to exit 68 S. William Floyd Pkwy. toward Shirley, merge onto NY-27 E. toward Montauk, take exit 63S. for County Rd. 31 S. toward Westhampton Beach, merge onto County Rd. 31/Old Riverhead Rd./Riverhead Rd., continue onto Oak St., at the traffic circle take the 2nd exit onto Potunk Ln., turn Left onto Main St., turn Right onto Beach Ln., turn Left onto Dune Rd., look for the Cupsogue Beach County Park*   *cresli.org*

Family New Year's Eve Event • *Cradle Of Aviation Museum* • *"Museum Row"* • *Charles Lindbergh Blvd.* • *1 Davis Ave., Garden City, NY* • *516-572-4111* • Features **Include:** Interactive Family Entertainment, Teen Center, IMAX Short Films, Admission to the Cradle of Aviation Museum Exhibits & the Nassau County Firefighters Museum, Local School Performers, Live Performances throughout the Night, Children's Games, Family Shows, All Museum Exhibits Available, Buffet Dinner, Special Midnight Countdown to a Laser Light Show programmed to music **Hours:** 7 p.m.–Midnight **Fee:** Museum Members: $30, Non-members: $35, Under 3: Free **Directions:** *Northern State Pkwy., to the Meadowbrook Pkwy., take exit M4, follow signs to Museum Row onto Charles Lindbergh Blvd., stay on Charles Lindbergh Blvd. to the 2nd traffic light & turn Right into the parking lot*   *www.cradleofaviation.org*

Family New Year's Eve Party • *Bayville Winter Wonderland* • *8 Bayville Ave., Bayville, NY* • *516-628-8697* • **Features Include:** Santa's Toy Factory Funhouse, Captain Bay's Yo Ho Holiday Light Show, Bayville Holiday Express Train Ride, Meet Holiday Characters, Party Favors, Champagne for Adults, Sparkling Cider for the Kids, Appetizers, Entrees, Desserts, menus vary per party **Hours:** Lunch Party: 1-4 p.m., Dinner Party: 6-8 p.m., Family New Year's Eve Ice Cream Party: 12:30-2 p.m., Dinner Party: 5:30-7 p.m., Adult Party: 9 p.m.-Midnight, check web site for exact hours & prices **Fee:** Shipwreck Tavern: $24.95 per person, Kids Under 12: $14.95 **Directions:** *Northern State Pkwy., take exit 35 N. 106/107 State Hwy., take 106 N., turn Left onto W. Main St. which becomes W. Shore Rd., drive over the Bayville Bridge, continue on Ludlam Ave., turn Left onto Bayville Ave., make a U-turn, the wonderland will be on the Right*   *www.bayvillewinterwonderland.com*

Children's New Year's Eve Event • *Children's Museum of the East End* • *376 Sag Harbor Tpke., Bridgehampton, NY* • *631-537-8250* • Features Include: Countdown to Noon, Watch the Ball Drop from CMEE "Square" (in the Museum's permanent exhibit),

Celebratory Confetti, Sparkling Juice, Holiday Noisemaker Craft (10 a.m.) **Hours:** 11 a.m.–1 p.m. **Fee:** Members: Free, Non-members: $7 **Directions:** *I-495 Long Island Expwy., take exit 68 S. William Floyd Pkwy./Co. Hwy. 46 S. toward Shirley, merge onto County Rte. 46/ William Floyd Pkwy., turn Left onto Rte. 27 E., make a U-turn, turn Right onto Stephen Hands Path, turn Left onto Rte. 114/Sag Harbor Tpke.*

Winter Fest Weekend • *Hicks Nurseries, 100 Jericho Tpke., Westbury, NY* • *516-334-0066* • **Features Include:** Fun Activities, Magic Show, Garden & Craft Projects for kids under 12, Cooking Demonstrations, Nature Programs presented by the Theodore Roosevelt Sanctuary & Audubon Center **Hours:** 9 a.m.-4 p.m., usually the last weekend in Jan. **Fee: Free** **Directions:** *Northern State Pkwy., take exit 32, follow sign to Old Westbury N., turn Left onto Post Ave., Left on Jericho Tpke., Hicks Nurseries is on the Left* *www.hicksnurseries.com*

MARTIN LUTHER KING JR. DAY

Dr. Martin Luther King Jr. Celebration • *African American Museum* • *110 North Franklin St., Hempstead, NY* • *516-572-0730* • **Features Include:** Multimedia Exhibit, Photography, Theatrical Performance, Historic Documents & Documentaries **Hours:** Call for specific celebration events & Times, Tues.-Sat.: 10 a.m.-5 p.m. **Fee: Free** **Directions:** *Northern State Pkwy., take the Meadowbrook Pkwy. S., take exit 31 A Jones Beach, take the W. Old Country Rd. exit, take M1 W. toward Mineola, turn Right onto Old Country Rd., turn Left onto Clinton Rd. which becomes Clinton St., turn Right onto Fulton Ave./Hempstead Tpke., turn Right onto N. Franklin St.* *www.aamoflongisland.org*

Dreaming with Dr. Martin Luther King Jr. • *Long Island Children's Museum* • *11 Davis Ave., Garden City, NY* • *516-224-5800* • **Features Include:** Workshops, Explore Dr. King's Life & Messages **Hours:** Wed.-Sun.: 10 a.m.-5 p.m., Closed: Mon., call for specific event times **Fee:** Adults: $9, Members & Kids under 1: Free, Membership for a family of 4 is approx. $85 **Directions:** *Northern State Pkwy., take the Meadowbrook Pkwy. S. to exit M4 (Nassau Coliseum), bear Right (before Hempstead Tpke.) onto Charles Lindbergh Blvd., go to the 1st traffic light (Nassau Coliseum on the Left, Nassau Community College on the Right) proceed through this traffic light & continue on to LICM on the Right side of the road* *www.licm.org*

Martin Luther King Jr. Day Parade • *5th Ave., NY, NY* • *212-397-8222* • *Parade Organized by NYC & Company, 810 7th Ave., NY, NY* • **Features Include:** Floats, Marching Bands, Musicians, Civil Rights Activists, Veterans, Boy Scouts. The Parade begins on 5th Ave. at 61st St., & continues North along Fifth Ave. to 86th St. Before the parade there is a **Free** memorial event at New York's Convention Center. The pre-parade memorial event includes speeches, dancers, & an interfaith service. **Hours:** Parade begins at 1 p.m. This event

takes place on Martin Luther King Day. **Fee:** **Free** **Directions:** *Penn Station, take the E. train to 5th Ave. & 53rd St. & walk up 5th to 61st St., or take the C train to 59th St./Columbus Circle & 8th Ave. & walk to 5th Ave.*

www.ehow.com/how_2065032_join-new-yorks-martin-luther.html - 56k

February

Family Winter Carnival Week • Long Island Wine Country Winter Festival • 631-477-8493 • Sponsored by Long Island Wine Council, Long Island Convention & Visitors Bureau & Sports Commission & the East End Arts Council • Features **Include:** Family Week: Kids Concerts, Cooking Classes for Kids, Kids Carnival with Toys/Music/Food, Book Readings, Kids Photo Contest, Dance Performances & Lessons, Concerts, Mid-Winter Picnic, Women's Weekend/Girl's Getaway: Discounts at Spas, Film Screening, Art Exhibit & Sample the Best Food & Wine on the Twin Forks, Valentine's Day & Romance: Your Name Carved into a Vineyard Fence Post, Sample Fine Chocolates with Local Dessert Wines **Hours:** During the month of Feb., check the web site for locations, event times & dates **Fee:** Festival Passport: $30 good for a couple or family with children under 18 **Directions:** *I-495 Long Island Expwy., take exit 73 Old Country Rd. toward Greenport, make a Left onto Main Rd./25A*
www.liwines.com/default.ihtml?page=winterfestival • www.winecountryfilmfest.com

Ward Melville Heritage Organization, Educational & Cultural Center • Stony Brook Village Center • 111 Main St., Stony Brook, NY • 631-751-2244 • 631-689-5888 • The center hosts many children's events during the month of Feb. **Activities Have Included:** Hot Cocoa Children's Series, getting to know each other through puppets, Meet & Greet Winter Animals: Storytelling & Craft Activities, Groundhog Day: Storytelling & Craft Activities, Valentine's Day: Storytelling & Craft Activities, Say Hello to George & Abe, Craft Activities, Adieu to your New Friends: Puppet Show, Chinese New Year Celebration: Drumming, Dancers & a 9-ft. Lion, Lion Dance Performance, Drum Ensemble & Spotlight Dance Academy, some events require reservations **Hours:** Call or check the web site for specific dates & times **Fee:** varies, some events are **Free** **Directions:** *I-495 Long Island Expwy., take exit 53 Sagtikos State Pkwy. N., continue on Sunken Meadow Pkwy. N., take exit SM3E. for State Hwy. 25 E./Jericho Tpke. toward Smithtown, merge onto Jericho Tpke., turn Left onto N. Country Rd./Rte. 25A, follow N. Country Rd./Rte. 25A, continue on County Rte. 68/Main St. N., the Village Center will be on the Right*
www.wmho.org • www.stonybrookvillage.com • www.stonybrook.com

Winter Seals & Waterbirds Audubon EcoCruise • New York Water Taxi • South St. Seaport, Battery Park, NY • 212-742-1969 • Features Include: Wildlife Cruise, Explore Waterways & Shores of New York Harbor, Gulls, Ducks, Geese, Loons, Grebes, Cormorants, Harbor Seals, Outdoor Deck, Heated Cabin, Meet at South St. Seaport, Bring Binoculars & Warm Winter Clothing **Hours:** Feb. event **Fee:** Adults: $35, Kids: $25 **Directions:** *LIRR to*

Penn Station, take the 2,3,A,or C train, to Fulton St. station, walk 6 blocks East on Fulton St. to South St.

CHINESE NEW YEAR

Chinese New Year Celebrations typically begin the last weekend in Jan. or the first weekend in Feb. Traditional Celebrations include: Turning Over a New Leaf, Sweeping of the Grounds, Kitchen God, Family Celebration, Lai-See, Everybody's Birthday, Lantern Festival, Chinese Zodiac, + the Twelve Animal Signs.

Annual Lunar New Year Parade • *Flushing, NY* • **Features Include:** Dragon Dancers, Steel Drummers, Fireworks. About 4,000 people march each year. The best place to watch is at the Flushing Library (Main St. & Kissena Blvd.) & at the parade's end. Most people watch on Main St. The Chinese performers in the parade end the procession with a celebration at the Flushing Mall including Chinese Food & Folk Performances. The Flushing Mall is located at 133-31 39th Ave., 2 blocks west of Main St. Flushing is home to 1 of the largest Chinese & East Asian populations in New York City, rivaling Manhattan's Chinatown. The Korean community & other East Asian groups also participate in the parade. Parade Route: Starts at Union St. & 37th Ave. & ends at Main St. & 39th Ave. **Hours:** 11a.m.-1 p.m. **Fee: Free**
Directions: *I-495 Long Island Expwy., take exit 23 toward Main St., stay straight to go onto Horace Harding Expwy. N., turn Right onto Main St., the Flushing Library is at 6005 Main St., 718-359-8332*

www.2chambers.com/flushing.htm • www.flushingchamber.com/history.html
queens.about.com/cs/neighborhoods/p/2004_chinesenew.htm

Chinese New Year Celebration • *Ward Melville Heritage Organization Educational & Cultural Center* • *Stony Brook Village Center* • *111 Main St., Stony Brook, NY* • *631-751-2244* • *Reservations Required: 631-689-5888* • *Presented by The Ward Melville Heritage Organization* • **Features Include:** Chinese New Year Celebration, Drumming, Dancers, 9-ft. Lion, Lion Dance Performance, Drum Ensemble **Hours:** Call for specific times **Directions:** *I-495 Long Island Expwy., take exit 53 Sagtikos State Pkwy. N., continue on Sunken Meadow Pkwy. N., take exit SM3E. for State Hwy. 25 E./Jericho Tpke. toward Smithtown, merge onto Jericho Tpke./Rte. 25, turn Left at N. Country Rd./Rte. 25A, follow N. Country Rd./Rte. 25A, continue on County Rte. 68/Main St./N. Main St., the Village Center will be on the Right*
www.wmho.org • www.stonybrookvillage.com • www.stonybrook.com

Chinatown Independence Day Festival • *Columbus Park & Chinatown (Canal, Mott, Bayard & Pell Sts., & the Bowery), NY, NY* • *Better Chinatown Society: 917-660-2402* • *212-754-6500* • **Features Include:** Chinatown's Biggest Parade & Festival, New Year's Day Firecracker Ceremony, Cultural Festival Performances, Parade features Cultural Performers & Organizations from China, Korea, Japan, Vietnam, Taiwan,

WINTER FUN

Malaysia & Singapore **Hours:** 11:30-3:30 p.m., mid-Feb. **Fee: Free Directions:** *LIRR to Penn Station, walk to 34th St./Herald Sq. station, take the D train toward Coney Island & Stillwell Ave., get off at Grand St., walk West on Grand St. to Mott St. or walk West on Grand St., make a Left onto Mulberry St., Columbus Park is on the corner of Bayard St. & Mulberry St.* www.betterchinatown.com

Korean Lunar New Year Celebration • *Korea Village's Open Center* • *150-24 Northern Blvd. at 150th St., Flushing, NY* • *718-353-8969* • Features Include:
Explore the Korea Village's Open Centers cultural space, Korean Food, Games, Dancing, Martial Arts, Music, Karaoke Contest **Hours:** Check the web site **Fee: Free Directions:** *I-495 Long Island Expwy., take exit 27N. merge onto the Clearview Expwy. N., take exit 5 toward Northern Blvd., merge onto 206th St., turn Left onto Northern Blvd., make a U-turn at a 150th St., the Korea Village's Open Center will be on the Right* queens.about.com/cs/neighborhoods/p/2004_chinesenew.htm

Lunar New Year Celebration • *Flushing Town Hall* •*137-35 Northern Blvd. at Linden Pl., Flushing, NY* • *718-463-7700* • Features Include: Traditional Drumming
& Music Events, a month-long Exhibit of Traditional Hand Puppets from Taiwan **Hours:** call for the schedule of events, weekends during Feb. **Fee: Free Directions:** *I-495 Long Island Expwy., take exit 27N., merge onto the Clearview Expwy. N., take exit 5 toward Northern Blvd., merge onto 206th St., turn Left onto Northern Blvd., Flushing Town Hall will be on the Right* www.flushingtownhall.org

SUGGESTIONS • COMMENTS • ERRORS

Linda.ReidBryce @verizon.net

Thanks

WINTER PINS

CRISP WINTER DAYS, FALLING PINS, & LAUGHTER

Bowling

Make it more fun to bowl. Have the bumpers put up to encourage confidence by reducing gutter balls. Many alleys provide a ball slide for toddler use. Call ahead for open bowling hours to avoid crowded bowling leagues. Keep a family bowling book + record the scores after each bowling outing. Lighten up, encourage laughter + Let fun flow like a river.

NASSAU COUNTY

AMF Syosset Lanes • *111 Eileen Way, Syosset, NY* • *516-921-7575* • **Hours:** Mon.-Tues.: 9 a.m.-Noon, Wed.: Noon-Midnight, Thurs.: 9 a.m.-Midnight, Fri.-Sat.: 9 a.m.-1 a.m., Sun.: 9 a.m.-Noon **Fee:** Weekdays: $4, Night & Weekend Bowling: $5.25, Shoe Rentals: $4.35 **Directions:** *Northern State Pkwy., take Rte. 135 Seaford-Oyster Bay Expwy. N. toward Syosset, take exit 14 W. for Jericho Tpke./25 W., AMF Syosset Lanes will be on the Left*

www.amf.com/syossetlanes/centerHomepage.htm

AMF Sheridan Lanes • *199 E. Jericho Tpke., Mineola, NY* • *516-741-3444* • **Hours:** Mon.-Thurs.: 9 a.m.-Midnight, Fri.: 9 a.m.-1 a.m., Sat.: 9 a.m.-2 a.m., Sun.: 9 a.m.-Midnight **Fee:** Night & Weekend Bowling: $5.25, Shoe Rental: $4.35 **Directions:** *Northern State Pkwy. W., take exit 31A for Meadowbrook State Pkwy., turn Right onto Glen Cove Rd., turn Left onto Jericho Tpke./Rte. 25, make a U-turn at Sheridan Blvd., Sheridan Lanes will be on the Right*

www.amf.com/sheridanlanesny/centerHomepage.htm

AMF Garden City Lanes • *987 Stewart Ave., Garden City, NY* • *516-222-0808* • **Hours:** Mon.-Thurs.: 8 a.m.-Midnight, Fri.: 8 a.m.-2 a.m., Sat.: 9 a.m.-2 a.m., Sun.: 9 a.m.-Midnight **Fee:** Weekdays: $4, Night & Weekend Bowling: $5.25, Shoe Rental: Adults: $4.35, Kids: $3.25 **Directions:** *Northern State Pkwy., take exit 31A to merge onto Meadowbrook*

WINTER FUN

State Pkwy. S., take exit M3 W. toward Stewart Ave., turn Right onto Merchants Concourse, turn Right onto Stewart Ave., AMF Garden City Lanes will be on the Right

www.amf.com/gardencitylanes/centerHomepage.htm

AMF East Meadow Lanes • *1840 Front St., East Meadow, NY • 516-794-1111* • Hours:

Mon.: 11 a.m.-1 a.m., Tues.-Wed.: 9 a.m.-1 a.m., Thurs.: 11 a.m.-1 a.m., Fri.-Sat.: 9 a.m.-2 a.m., Sun.: 9 a.m.-1 a.m. **Fee:** Weekdays: $4, Night & Weekend Bowling: $5.25, Shoe Rental: Adults: $4.35, Kids: $3.25 **Directions:** *Northern State Pkwy., exit onto Wantagh State Pkwy. S., take exit W3 W. for State Hwy. 24 W. toward Hempstead, turn Right onto Hempstead Tpke., turn Left onto Front St., the AMF East Meadow Lanes will be on the Left*

www.amf.com/eastmeadowlanes/centerHomepage.htm

AMF Wantagh Lanes • *1300 Wantagh Ave., Wantagh, NY • 516-781-1460* • Hours:

Mon.-Thurs.: 9 a.m.-Midnight, Fri.-Sat.: 9 a.m.-1 a.m., Sun.: 9 a.m.-Midnight **Fee:** Weekdays: $4, Night & Weekend Bowling: $5.25, Shoe Rental: Adults: $4.35, Kids: $3.25 **Directions:** *Southern State Pkwy. W., take exit 28 S. toward Wantagh, take Wantagh Ave. to the AMF Wantagh Lanes which will be on the Right*

www.amf.com/wantaghlanes/centerHomepage.htm

AMF Plainview Lanes • *500 Old Bethpage Rd., Plainview, NY • 516-433-9595* • Hours:

Mon.: 11 a.m.-11 p.m., Tues.-Wed.: 9 a.m.-Midnight, Thurs.: 2 p.m.-Midnight, Fri.-Sat.: 9 a.m.-1 a.m., Sun.: 9 a.m.-10 p.m. **Fee:** Weekdays: $4, Night & Weekend Bowling: $5.25, Shoe Rental: Adults: $4.35, Kids: $3.25 **Directions:** *I-495 Long Island Expwy., turn Left at Round Swamp Rd., turn Right onto Haypath Rd., turn Right onto Sweet Hollow Rd./Old Bethpage Rd., AMF Plainview Lanes will be on the Right*

www.amf.com/plainviewlanes/centerHomepage.htm

Baldwin Bowling Center • *2407 Grand Ave., Baldwin, NY • 516-223-8980* •

Features Include: Cosmic Glow Bowl, Live DJ, Glow-In-The-Dark Giveaways **Hours:** Sun.-Wed.: 9 a.m.-1 a.m., Thurs.-Sat.: 9 a.m.-4 a.m. **Fee:** Weekdays: $5, Night & Weekend Bowling: $5.75, Sun.: $2.50, Thurs.: $17 unlimited bowl for 5 hrs., Shoe Rental: $4 **Directions:** *Southern State Pkwy. W., take 20 S. towards Grand Ave., merge onto Baldwin Rd., take Grand Ave., the Baldwin Bowling Center will be on the Left*

www.baldwinbowl.com

Dave & Busters • *1504 Old Country Rd., Westbury, NY • 516-542-8501* • Features

Include: Over 200 Games, Billiards-railed table, Shuffleboard, Power Hour, Winner's Circle (redeem your tickets for toys & high tech gadgets) **Hours:** Mon.-Wed., Sun.: 11:30 a.m.-11 p.m., Thurs.: 11:30 a.m.12 a.m., Fri.-Sat.: 11:30 a.m.-2 a.m. **Fee:** Power Hour: $10 for 60 min. video game play, Half Price Wed.: Open-Close **Bowling Fee:** Day Time: $15., After 5 p.m.: $29, Weekend Bowling: $25 per hr., fees are for the lane, not per person, half-off game Wed., Shoe Rental: $2.95 **Directions:** *Northern State Pkwy. to exit 32 for Post Ave. toward Westbury, turn Left onto Post Ave., turn Right onto Old Country Rd., Dave & Busters will be on the Left*

www.daveandbusters.com

Herrill Lanes Inc. • *465 Herricks Rd., New Hyde Park, NY* • **516-741-8022** • Features

Include: 36 Lanes, League Bowlers Playroom, Computer Scoring, Pro Shop, Coffee Shop, Chatterbox Lounge, Rock'N Bowl with Sat. Evening Cosmic Lighting **Hours:** Mon.-Fri.: 9 a.m.-Midnight, Sat.: 9 a.m.-Midnight, Sun: 8:30 a.m.-Midnight **Fee:** Weekdays: Adults: $4, Kids: 3.50, Weekends: Adults: $5, Kids: $4.50, Sat. Night: $5.75, Show Rental: $3.75, ATM on premises, Cash Only, Wheelchair Accessible **Directions:** *Northern State Pkwy. W., take exit 31 Glen Cove Rd., turn Right onto Glen Cove Rd., turn Right onto Hillside Ave./Rte. 25B, turn Left onto Herricks Rd., Herrill Lanes Inc. will be on the Right* *www.herrilllanes.com*

Rockville Centre Lanes Inc. • *100 Maple Ave., Rockville Centre, NY* • **516-678-3010**

• **Features Include:** Cosmic Bowling, Leagues, Family Packs, Mommy & Me, Youth Programs **Hours:** Weekdays: 9 a.m.-Midnight, Weekends: 9 a.m.-2 a.m. **Fee:** Dollar Days: Mon.-Fri.: $1 from 3-6 p.m., Two Fer Tues.: $2 9:30 p.m., Weekdays: Adults: $5.25, Kids: $4, Seniors: $3.75, Night & Weekend Bowling: $5.75, Shoe Rental: $3.75 **Directions:** *Southern State Pkwy. W., take exit 19S. to Peninsula Blvd., turn Left onto Lakeview Ave., turn Right onto Morris Ave., turn Right onto Maple Ave., Rockville Centre Lanes Inc. will be on the Right* *www.rvclanes.net*

San-Dee Lanes Of Malverne • *342 Hempstead Ave., Malverne, NY* • **516-599-1134**

• **Hours:** Winter: open 7 days a week, Summer: open 6 days a week (closed Sun.) **Fee:** Weekdays: Adults: $5, Kids: $4.25, Night & Weekend Bowling: $5.50, Shoe Rental: $3.25 **Directions:** *Southern State Pkwy., take exit 17 S. Hempstead Ave. toward Malverne, travel 1 block to a forked intersection with a traffic light, bear Right at the fork & drive 2 blocks in the town of Malverne, make a Left onto Francis St., San-Dee Lanes Of Malverne will be on the Left, park in the municipal parking lot* *www.san-deelanes.com*

Strike • *1350 Union Tpke., New Hyde Park, NY* • **516-354-1222** • Features Include:

Bowling, Arcade, Billiards, Restaurant, DJ Booth, Glow-in-the-Dark Bowling, Big Screen Video, Lane-Side Food & Beverage Service, Sports Bar, Children's Birthday Parties **Hours:** Thurs.: 4 p.m.-Midnight, Fri.: 2 p.m.-2 a.m., Sat.: 11 a.m.-2 a.m., Sun.: 11 a.m.-11 p.m., must be 21 & over after 9 p.m., hours change seasonally **Fee:** Adults: $34.95, up to 8 people on the lane, Thurs.: $16 per person, Thurs. Night unlimited bowling, Shoe Rental: $4.50 **Directions:** *Northern State Pkwy., take exit 25 S. Lakeville Rd., toward New Hyde Park, turn Left onto Union Tpke.* *www.bowlmor.com*

South Levittown Lanes • *56 Tanners Ln., Levittown, NY* • *516-731-5700* • Features Include: Junior League Program, Rock-n-Glow Bowling, Karaoke Night, Ladies Night Hours: Mon.: Noon-11:30 p.m.,Tues., Thurs., Sun.: 9 a.m.-11:30 p.m., Sat.-Sun.: 9 a.m.-3 a.m. Fee: Per Game: $3.50, or Lane Rental: $14 per hr., Shoe Rental: $4, Fri.: $18 Unlimited Bowling, 11 p.m.-2 a.m. Directions: *Southern State Pkwy. W., take exit 28 N. Wantagh Ave., turn Right onto Wantagh Ave., turn Left onto Hempstead Tpke., turn Left onto Cotton Ln., 3rd light turn Left onto Tanners Ln., South Levittown Lanes will be on the Left (directly across from Loew's Theater Sign)* www.kpsearch.com/df/bowling/all-southnew.asp

Westbury Bowl • *4000 Brush Hollow Rd., Westbury, NY* • *516-333-7444* • Features Include: Children & Adult Parties, Snack Bar, Cocktail Lounge, Billiards Hours: Sun.-Thurs.: 9 a.m.-1 a.m., Fri. & Sat.: 9 a.m.-4 a.m., Rock-N-Glow: Fri. & Sat.: 10 p.m. Fee: $1.50-$4.75, Shoe Rental: $2.50 Directions: *Northern State Pkwy., take exit 34 Brush Hollow Rd. toward Westbury, turn Right onto Brush Hollow Rd., Westbury Bowl will be on the Right* www.westburybowling.com

SUFFOLK COUNTY

AMF Commack Vets Lanes • *2183 Jericho Tpke., Commack, NY* • *631-499-7722* • *7723* • *7745* • Features Include: Xtreme Bowling, Leagues, Birthday Parties Hours: Mon.: 9:30 a.m.-Midnight, Tues.: 9 a.m.-11 p.m., Wed.: 9 a.m.-Midnight, Thurs.: 9:30 a.m.-1 a.m., Fri.: 9 a.m.-1 a.m., Sat.: 9 a.m.-2 a.m., Sun.: 9 a.m.-Midnight Fee: Weekdays: $3.75, Night & Weekend Bowling: Adults: $5, Kids: $4.35, Shoe Rental: $3.25 Directions: *Northern State Pkwy N., take exit 28 N. for Jericho Tpke. W./Rte. 25, AMF Commack Lanes is on the Right* www.amf.com/commackvetslanes/centerHomepage.htm

AMF 300 Long Island • *895 Walt Whitman Rd., Melville, NY* • *631-271-1180* • Features Include: State-Of-The-Art Bowling Alley & Sound System, 49 Lanes, 9 Private Lanes, Plush Lounge, Lane-Side Seating, Meeting Rooms, Birthday Parties Hours: 3 p.m.-closing Fee: Weekdays: $4, Weeknights: $5, Weekend Bowling: $7, Shoe Rental: $4.50 Directions: *Northern State Pkwy., take the Rte. 110 exit North, AMF 300 Long Island will be on the Left*

AMF Babylon Lanes • *430 Sunrise Hwy., West Babylon, NY* • *631-661-6600* • Hours: Mon.-Thurs.: 9 a.m.-Midnight, Fri.-Sat.: 9 a.m.-2 a.m., Sun.: 10 a.m.-Midnight Fee: Weekdays: $3.75, Sun.-Tues.: $1.99 after 9 p.m., Wed.-Thurs.: $5 after 9 p.m., Weekend Bowling: $6, Shoe Rental: $4.35 Directions: *Southern State Pkwy., take exit 33 for Rte.109 E. toward Babylon, take Rte. 27 E. Sunrise Hwy., AMF Babylon Lanes will be on the Right* www.amf.com/babylonlanes/centerHomepage.htm

AMF Smithtown Lanes • *200 Landing Ave., Smithtown, NY* • *631-265-0121* •

Features Include: Xtreme Bowling. Leagues, Birthday Parties **Hours:** Mon. & Thurs.: Noon-Midnight, Tues.-Wed.: 9 a.m.-Midnight, Fri.-Sat.: 9 a.m.-1 a.m., Sun.: 9 a.m.-Midnight **Fee:** Weekdays: $3.75, Weeknights: $5, Weeknights after 9 p.m.: $3.75, Sat.: 9 a.m.-Noon: $5, Noon-8 p.m.: $5.50, 8 p.m.-Close: $5, Sun.: 9 a.m.-Noon: $2.50, Dollar Mania Sun.: 9 p.m.-Midnight $1 games, Shoe Rental: $4.35 **Directions:** *Northern State Pkwy. E., take exit 45 N., Sunken Meadow Pkwy. N., take exit SM3 E. for Jericho Tpke./25 E. toward Smithtown, take Jericho Tpke E., turn Left at Landing Ave., AMF Smithtown Lanes will be on the Left* *www.amf.com/smithtownlanes/centerHomepage.htm*

AMF Bay Shore Lanes • *1840 Sunrise Hwy., Bay Shore, NY* • *631-666-7600* • Fee:

Weekdays: $3.75, Weeknights: $5, Weekend Bowling: $5 before 9 p.m., $6 after 9 p.m., Shoe Rentals: $4.35 **Directions:** *Southern State Pkwy. E., take exit 40 for Robert Moses Cswy. S., take exit RM1 E. toward Montauk, take the Sunrise Hwy. Service Rd. S. (27 E.), take the Left ramp onto Rte. 27 E., take exit 44 toward Brentwood Rd., merge onto Sunrise Hwy. S. Service Rd., AMF Bay Shore Lanes will be on the Right*

AMF Centereach Lanes • *40 Horseblock Rd., Centereach, NY* • *631-588-2118* •

Features Include: Xtreme Bowling, Adventure of Lights, Great Music, Wild Bowling Challenges **Hours:** Mon.: Noon-11 p.m., Tues.: 9 a.m.-11 p.m., Wed.: 11 a.m.-11 p.m., Thurs.: 9 a.m.-Midnight, Fri.-Sat.: 9 a.m.-1 a.m., Sun.: 9 a.m.-11 p.m. **Fee:** Weekdays: $3.75, Weeknights: $5, Weeknights after 9 p.m.: $3.75, Weekends: $5, $5.50 after 9 p.m., Shoe Rental: $4.35 **Directions:** *Northern State Pkwy. to the end, take Rte. 347, turn Right onto Jericho Tpke., turn Right onto Horseblock Rd., AMF Centereach Lanes will be on the Right* *www.amf.com/centereachlanes/centerHomepage.htm*

AMF Sayville Lanes • *5660 Sunrise Hwy., Sayville, NY* • *631-567-8900* • Hours:

Mon.: Noon-Midnight, Tues.-Thurs.: 9 a.m.-Midnight, Fri.-Sat.: 9 a.m.-2 a.m., Sun.: 9 a.m.-Midnight **Fee:** $3.75, $5 after 5:00 p.m., $3.75 after 9:00 p.m., Sun.-Mon. after 9:00 p.m.: $1 per game with $5 entrance fee, Shoe Rental: $4.35 **Directions:** *I-495 Long Island Expwy., take exit 57 toward Patchogue, take Express Dr. S./L.I.E. Service Rd., turn Right onto Rte. 454, turn Right onto Lincoln Ave., turn Left onto S. Sunrise Hwy. Service Rd., AMF Sayville Lanes will be on the Right* *www.amf.com/sayvillelanes/centerHomepage.htm*

AMF Shirley Lanes • *On The Green, Shirley, NY* • *631-399-1800* • Hours: Mon.

& Thurs.: Noon-Midnight, Tues.: 10 a.m.-Midnight, Wed.: 10 a.m.-Midnight, Fri.: Noon-2 a.m., Sat.: 9 a.m-2 a.m., Sun.: 9 a.m.-Noon **Fee:** Weekdays: $3.50, Weeknights: $4.75, Weekend Bowling: $4.75, Shoe Rental: $4.35 **Directions:** *I-495 Long Island Expwy., take exit 68 William Floyd Pkwy./Rte. 46 toward Shirley, turn Right onto Essex*

Circle, turn Left onto Merrick Rd., turn Left at Roberts Rd. W.
www.amf.com/shirleylanes/centerHomepage.htm • www.amfbowling.com.au

Dave & Busters • *261 Airport Plaza Blvd., Farmingdale, NY* • **631-249-0708** •
Features Include: Over 200 Games, Billiards Table, Shuffleboard, Power Hour, Winner's
Circle (redeem your tickets for toys & high tech gadgets) **Hours:** Mon.-Wed., Sun.: 11:30
a.m.-11 p.m., Thurs.: 11:30 a.m.12 a.m., Fri.-Sat.: 11:30 a.m.-2 a.m. **Fee:** Power Hour:
$10 for 60 min. video game play, Half Price Wed.: Open-Close **Bowling Fee:** Day Time:
$15 hr. , After 5 p.m.: $29 hr., Weekend Bowling: $25 per hr., fees are for the lane, not
per person, half-off game Wed., Shoe rental: $2.95 **Directions:** *I-495 Long Island Expwy.,
take exit 49 S., turn Right onto Broadhollow Rd./Rte. 110 S., turn Left onto Conklin St., turn
Right onto Fairchild Loop, turn Right onto Airport Plaza Blvd. www.daveandbusters.com*

Deer Park Bowl • *849 Long Island Ave., Deer Park, NY* • **631-667-7750** • Hours:
Mon.-Fri.: 10 a.m.-Midnight, Sat.: 10 a.m.-1 a.m., Sun.: 9 a.m.-11 p.m. **Fee:** Weekdays:
$5, Adults $4.75, Kids: $3.50, Seniors: $4.50, Weeknights & Weekends: $5.50 after 6:00
p.m., Sat.-Sun.: $30 lane rental, 9 p.m.-Midnight, Shoe Rental: $4 **Directions:** *I-495
Long Island Expwy., take exit 51 toward Babylon, turn Right onto Deer Park Ave./Rte.
231, turn Left onto Long Island Ave., Deer Park Bowl will be on the Left*
www.deerparkbowl.com

East Islip Lanes Inc. • *117 E. Main St., East Islip, NY* • **631-581-6200** •
Features Include: Rock-n-Bowl, Parties, Youth Fun, Leagues, Super Saver Sun. **Fee:**
Adults: $3.75, Kids: $3.45, Sat.: $2.75 per game from 5-7 p.m., Sun.: 99¢ From 8:30-
11:30 a.m., Quartermania Tues. & Thurs.: 25¢ games from 9:30 a.m.-12:30 p.m.,
SuperSaver Sun.: $8.95 unlimited bowling for 2 hrs. 8:30 a.m.-Noon, Shoe Rental: $3.15
Directions: *Southern State Pkwy., Heckscher State Pkwy. S., take exit 45 W. toward E.
Islip/State Hwy. 27A W., merge onto Harwood Ave., turn Right onto E. Main St./Rte. 27A,
East Islip Lanes will be on the Right* *www.eilanes.com*

Farmingdale Lanes LLC • *99 Conklin St., Farmingdale, NY* • **516-249-4300** • Features
Include: Nickelodeon Bowling Club, Teen Party League, Cosmic Bowl, Parties **Hours:**
$20 Unlimited Bowling: Sat. 9:30 a.m.-12:30 p.m., Sun.-Thurs.: 9 a.m.-1 a.m., Fri.-
Sat.: 9 a.m.-2 a.m. **Fee:** Bowling: $3, 2-for-Tues.: $2 games, Shoe Rental: $2 **Directions:**
*Northern State Pkwy., take exit 36 A, take 135 Seaford-Oyster Bay Expwy., take exit 7 E. for
Hempstead Tpke./24 E. toward Farmingdale, merge onto Hempstead Tpke., Farmingdale
Lanes will be on the Left* *www.farmingdalelanes.com*

Larkfield Lanes Bowling Center • *332 Larkfield Rd., East Northport, NY* • **631-
368-8788** • Fee: Weekdays: $3.75, Weeknights: $4.50, Weekends: $4.95, Sun. after 5

p.m.: $4.50,Shoe Rental: $3.50 **Directions:** *Northern State Pkwy., take exit 42 toward Northport, merge onto Deer Park Ave. N., turn Right onto Jericho Tpke. E., turn Left onto Elwood Rd., turn Right onto Clay Pitts Rd., turn Left onto Larkfield Rd., Larkfield Lanes Bowling Center will be on the Left*

Patchogue Bowling Center • *138 West Ave., Patchogue, NY* • *631-475-5164* • Hour: Mon.: 10 a.m.-11 p.m., Tues.-Thurs.: Noon-11 p.m., Fri.: Noon-Midnight, Sat.: 11 a.m.-Midnight, Sun.: 11 a.m.-11 p.m. **Fee:** Weekdays: $4, Weeknights: $4.50, Weekends: $5, Sun. is Family Day, $2 games from 9 a.m.-Noon, Join Kids Bowl Free: visit the web site

Directions: *I-495 Long Island Expwy., exit 61 Patchogue Holbrook Rd. S., cross Sunrise & Montauk Hwys., road changes name from Waverly Ave. to Clare Rose Blvd., to West Ave., cross over railroad tracks, Patchogue Bowling is on the corner of Division & West Ave. & across from the train station*　　　　　　　　　　*www.bowllongisland.com*

Port Jeff Bowl Inc. • *6 Chereb Ln., Port Jefferson Station, NY* • *631-473-3300* • Features Include: Parties, Tournaments, Leagues, Family Fun Pack (1 lane up to 6 people for 1 hr. includes 12-in. Pizza Hut Pizza, pitcher of soda, shoe rental), Live Music **Hours:** Mon.-Sun.: 9 a.m.-Midnight **Fee:** Weekdays 10 a.m.-5 p.m.: Adults: $4.25, Kids: $4, Sat.-Sun.: $5.50, Family Fun Pack: $39, Summer Special: Shoe Rental: $1, Bowling: $1 from 3-6 p.m., Shoe Rental: $3.50, visit web site for Discount Coupons **Directions:** *Northern State Pkwy. E. to the end, take Rte. 347, turn Left onto Nesconset Rd./Rte. 347, turn Left onto Patchogue Rd./Rte. 112, turn Left onto Chereb Ln./Dr., Port Jeff Bowl will be on the Left www.portjeffbowl.com*

SUGGESTIONS • COMMENTS • ERRORS

Linda.ReidBryce @verizon.net

Thanks

• **More** • **Fun** • **Family** • **& To Buy This Book** •

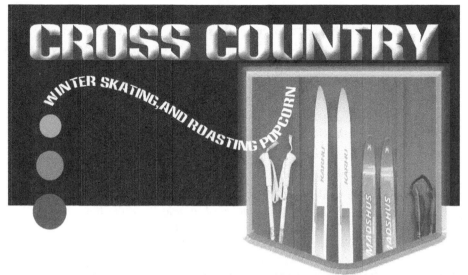

CROSS-COUNTRY SKIING & SNOWSHOEING

The parks listed below offer Cross-Country Skiing + Snowshoeing after a sizable snowfall. These are all self-guided situations. It is expected that participants arrive with their own gear. Gear can be rented at some ski rental shops. It is a great idea to carry a cell phone, compass, trail map, + wear a backpack containing water + snacks. Clothing should include: hat, insulated gloves, gator, ski goggles, insulated pants, + a jacket. *Let fun flow like a river*

Bethpage State Park ✇ • *99 Quaker Meeting House Rd., Farmingdale, NY* • *516-249-0701* • **Features Include:** Cross-Country Skiing is available on both the Blue & Yellow Golf Courses. The Yellow Course is right near the golf-start booth & tennis bubble. The Club House is open for hot chocolate & coffee. **Hours:** Dawn-Dusk, Year-Round **Fee: Free** entry off-season weekdays, Parking: $8 on weekends, Memorial Day-Labor Day, Empire Pass Accepted **Directions:** *I-495 Long Island Expwy. E., take exit 44S. Seaford Oyster Bay Expwy. (Rte. 135), take exit 8 E., turn Left onto Powell Ave., follow signs to the park (near the clubhouse)* *http://nysparks.state.ny.us*

Hempstead Lake State Park • *Eagle Ave. & Lake Dr., West Hempstead, NY* • *516-766-1029* • This is the largest lake in Nassau County. • **Features Include:** Cut your own trails or follow a previous skier's trail. Bathrooms open in Field 2. **Hours:** Dawn-Dusk, Year-Round **Fee: Free** off-season, April-Oct.: $8, Empire Pass Accepted **Directions:** *Southern State Pkwy., take exit 18 Eagle Ave., keep Right at the fork, follow signs for Rockville Centre/Hempstead Lake State Park, turn Right onto Eagle Ave.* *www.stateparks.com*

Muttontown Preserve • **NC** • *Muttontown Ln., East Norwich, NY* • *516-571-8500* • *571-7608* • **Features Include:** 550-acre Winter Wonderland, Marked Hiking Trails, Trail

Map (outside the Bill Paterson Nature Center), rangers recommend lost individuals to find a fence & follow it until they find an opening. The sun is usually to the South. Carrying a cell phone is an excellent idea. **Hours:** 9 a.m.-5 p.m. **Fee: Free**, there is an open bathroom at the nature center **Directions:** *I-495 Long Island Expwy., take exit 41 N. Rte. 106 N., make a Left onto Rte. 25A Northern Blvd., make a Left onto Muttontown Ln.*

www.nassaucountyny.gov

North Woodmere Park • NC • *750 Hungry Harbor Rd., Valley Stream, NY • 516-571-7800 • 7801* • Features Include: 150-acre Park Surrounded by Water, Cross-Country Skiing, Bathroom in the Museum, No Trail Map Available **Hours:** Dawn-Dusk **Fee: Free** off-season, Non-residents: $5 Memorial Day-Labor Day **Directions:** *Belt Pkwy. to Rockaway Blvd., take Rockaway Blvd., make a Left onto Peninsula Blvd., make a Left onto Branch Blvd., follow it around to the Right, the park entrance is on the Left*

www.nassaucountyny.gov/agencies/Parks

Valley Stream State Park • *320 Fletcher Ave., Valley Stream, NY • 516-825-4128* •

Features Include: Trail Map (at the Park Office), Restroom (open at Field 1) **Hours:** Dawn-Dusk **Fee: Free** off-season, Empire Pass Accepted **Directions:** *Southern State Pkwy., exit 15 A exits into the park*   *http://nysparks.state.ny.us/parks/info.asp?parkID=51*

SUFFOLK COUNTY

Belmont Lake State Park • *625 Belmont Ave., West Babylon, NY • 631-667-5055* •

Features Include: Cross-Country Skiing-available on the Horse Trails, walk to the lake & the trail starts on the South side, goes under the pkwy., & is approx. a 2-mi. run, Restrooms are open **Hours:** Dawn-Dusk, Year-Round **Fee: Free** off-season, April-Nov.: $8, Empire Pass Accepted **Directions:** *Southern State Pkwy., exit 37 N., merge onto Belmont Ave.*   *http://nysparks.state.ny.us/parks/*

Caleb Smith State Park Preserve ⊘ • *581 West Jericho Tpke., Smithtown, NY • 631-265-1054* • Features Include: 543-acre Park, Cross-Country Skiing & Snowshoeing (weather permitting), the Novice Trail is 1.25-mi. long & the marker is a green diamond with an arrow. The Advanced Trail is 1-mi. long & the marker is a red diamond with an arrow. Completing both trails is a nice 2.25-mi. loop. Please check in at the park office (Green Building/Museum) & sign in. When leaving sign out at the park office, so the rangers will know who may be lost or hurt. Bathrooms are open. **Hours:** 8 a.m.-4 p.m., can't go out after 3 p.m., Year-Round, Closed Mon.: April-Sept., Closed Mon.-Tues.: Oct.-March **Fee: Free** off-season, Memorial Day-Labor Day: $10, Weekends only until Oct. : $8 **Directions:** *I-495 Long Island Expwy., take exit 53 N. Sunken Meadow Pkwy. N., take exit SM 3 E. to Smithtown, take Jericho Tpke./Rte. 25 E., drive approx. 3 mi. to the park, entrance on Left*   *http://nysparks.state.ny.us/parks/info.asp?parkID=160*

WINTER FUN

Caumsett State Historic Park • **NYS** • *25 Lloyd Harbor Rd., Huntington, NY* • *631-423-1770* • Features Include: Cross-Country Skiing & Snowshoeing. A Hiking & Bridle trail map is available at the kiosk next to the flag pole at the front entrance. The Bathrooms are open. **Hours:** Dawn-Dusk, Year-Round **Fee: Free** off-season, April-Nov., Empire Passport Accepted, Handicap Accessible **Directions:** *I-495 Long Island Expwy., exit Rte. 110 N. which becomes New York Ave., turn Left onto Main St. 25A W., turn Right onto West Neck Rd. N., the park entrance is on the Left*
http://nysparks.state.ny.us/parks/info.asp?parkID=68

Cold Spring Harbor • **NYS** • *25 Lloyd Harbor Rd., Huntington, NY* • *631-423-1770* • Features Include: 40-acre Park, Cross Country Skiing, Snowshoeing **Hours:** Dawn-Dusk **Fee: Free** **Directions:** *I-495 Long Island Expwy., take 135 N. Seaford-Oyster Bay Expwy. to Jericho Tpke. E., turn Left onto Woodbury Rd. N., turn Left onto Rte. 108 & follow to end, turn Left & make an immediate Right onto Rte. 25A E., drive 1.5 mi. to parking field, the trailhead is on the Right* *http://nysparks.state.ny.us/parks/info*

Connetquot River State Park Preserve • *Box 505, Oakdale, NY* • *631-581-1005* • Features Include: 4 Cross-Country Skiing & Snowshoeing Trails, Trail Map (in the little booth at the entrance), the Green Trail is 3.9 mi., the Blue Trail is 8.4 mi., the Yellow Trail is 1 mi., the Red Trail is 3.3 mi. (available only when a lot of snow has fallen due to the number of exposed tree roots), Restrooms are open **Hours:** 7:30 a.m.-4:30 p.m., closed Mon. & Tues. **Fee:** $6 parking, Free with the Empire Pass **Directions:** *Southern State Pkwy., take exit 44 Sunrise Hwy. E., the preserve is located on the North side of Sunrise Hwy., just west of Pond Rd.*
http://nysparks.state.ny.us/parks/info.asp?parkID=69

Heckscher State Park • *Heckscher Pkwy., East Islip, NY* • *631-581-2100* • Features Include: Cross-Country Skiing on open fields, trails available after a significant snowfall, Trail Map (available in the park office), Restrooms open at Fields 1 & 6 **Hours:** 7 a.m.-Dusk **Fee: Free** off-season, Empire Pass Accepted **Directions:** *Southern State Pkwy. E., it ends in the park* *http://nysparks.state.ny.us/parks/info.asp?parkID=153*

Hither Hills State Park • *50 South Fairview Ave., Montauk, NY* • *631-668-2554* • Features Include: Cross-Country Skiing, No Marked Trails, Skiers Cut their Own Trails, Follow in another Skier's Trail **Hours:** Year-Round, Dawn-Dusk **Fee: Free** off-season, Memorial Day-Labor Day: $10, Weekends only until Oct.: $8, Empire Pass Accepted **Directions:** *I-495 Long Island Expwy., take exit 68 William Floyd Pkwy. S., take Sunrise Hwy. Rte. 27 E., turn Left onto 27 E., Right turn onto Birch Dr./Oak Ln., Right onto Birch St./Birch Dr., turn Left onto Old Montauk Hwy.* http://nysparks.state.ny.us/parks/

FUN FAMILY

Nissequogue River State Park • *799 St. Johnland Rd., Kings Park, NY* • *631-269-4927* • **Features Include:** Snowshoeing, Cross-Country Skiing, Marked Trails, Orange Skier Graphic Signage Markers, Restrooms are open in the Museum/Visitor Center **Hours:** Dawn-Dusk **Fee:** **Free** off-season, Empire Pass Accepted **Directions:** *Sunken Meadow Pkwy., take exit SM 4, drive East on Pulaski Rd. which becomes Old Dock Rd. at the 5th traffic light, make a Right onto St. Johnland Rd., the park entrance is about .5 mi. on the Left*　　　*http://nysparks.state.ny.us/parks*

Sunken Meadow State Park • *Rte. 25A & Sunken Meadow Pkwy., Northport, NY* • *631-269-4333* • **Features Include:** Cross-Country Skiing (permitted anywhere in the park), No Marked Ski Trails, 6 mi. of Hiking Trails to Follow, Restrooms are open **Hours:** Dawn-Dusk, Year-Round **Fee:** **Free** off-season,Memorial Day-Labor Day: $8, Empire Pass Accepted **Directions:** *I-495 Long Island Expwy., take exit 53 Sunken Meadow/ Sagtikos Pkwy. to the end*　　　*http://nysparks.state.ny.us/parks*

Wildwood State Park • *P.O. Box 518, North Wading River Rd., Wading River, NY* • *631 929-4314* • **Features Include:** 600-acre Park, 11.5 mi. of Marked Trails, Cross-Country Skiing (start at the kiosk), the trail markers are square disks, 4 Trails: Yellow/Red/Orange & Blue, Restrooms are open **Hours:** Dawn-Dusk, Year-Round **Fee:** **Free** off-season, Memorial Day-Labor Day: $10, Weekends only until Oct: $8, Empire Pass Accepted **Directions:** *I-495 Long Island Expwy., take exit 68, head N. on Rte. 46, take Rte. 25A E., turn Left onto Sound Ave., turn Left at the traffic light onto Hulse Landing Rd., the park entrance is on the Right*　　　*http://nysparks.state.ny.us/sites/info*

SUGGESTIONS • COMMENTS • ERRORS
Linda.ReidBryce@verizon.net
Thanks

ICE SKATING

Dressing in layers allows for the removal or adding of clothing as bodies heat + cool from activity. It is often more comfortable to wear a hat, scarf, gloves, + a sweater than a bulky coat. Wear socks that have no seams, they are less likely to cause an irritation where the skate boot + sock seam meet. Call or check individual web sites for skate times + pricing, which tend to vary from season-to-season.

NASSAU COUNTY

Town of Oyster Bay Ice Center · *Indoor Ice Rink* · *Operated by the Town of Oyster Bay* · *1001 Stewart Ave., Bethpage, NY* · *516-433-7465* · **Features Include:** NHL Regulation Facility, Lessons, Open Skate Times, Skate Rentals **Hours:** Mon.-Thurs.: 4-6 p.m., Fri.: 4-6 p.m., 7-9 p.m., Sat.: 1-3 p.m., 4-6 p.m., 7-9 p.m., 10-Midnight, Sun.: 1-3 p.m., 4-6 p.m., Nov.-Feb. **Fee:** Adults: $4, Kids 5-17: $3, Under 4: Free, Seniors: $1, Skate Rental: $3 **Directions:** *Northern State Pkwy., take the I-135 exit N., to exit 9, make a Right at the end of the ramp, bear Right at the fork onto Cherry Ave., pass Bethpage HS, the road ends at Stewart Ave., cross over into the parking lot*

Cantiague Park · *Indoor & Outdoor Ice Rinks* · **NC** · *1 West John St., Hicksville, NY* · *516-571-7058* · **Features Include:** Indoor Ice Skating Rink, Outdoor Ice Skating Rink, Recreational Skate Sessions, Hockey Team Ice Time, Skate Lessons, Snack Bar, Bleacher Seating, Skate Rentals, Ice Rental (approx fee: $325 per hour for proprietary groups & $295 for nonprofits) **Hours:** change monthly, call for session times **Fee:** With Leisure Pass: Adults: $7, Under 5: Free, Without Leisure Pass: Adults: $14, Kids: $10 **Directions:** *I-495 Long Island Expwy., take exit 41S. (Broadway), take the fork for 106/107 to West John St., turn Right onto West John St., the park entrance is on the Right* www.longislandgolfnews.com/Course20description/cantiague.htm

Christopher Morley Park · *Outdoor Ice Rink* · **NC** · *500 Searingtown Rd., Roslyn, NY* · *516-571-8113* · **Features Include:** Outdoor Ice Skating Rink, Recreational Skate Times, Hockey Teams, Group & Private Lessons, Skate Rentals, Snack Bar, Fireplace **Hours:** Mon.-Wed.: 10:30 a.m.-12:30 p.m., 1:15-3:15 p.m., 4-6 p.m., weekend hours vary, early Dec.-mid-March **Fees:** With Leisure Pass: Adult: $5.50, Kids: $3.50, Without Leisure Pass: Adults: $12, Kids: $8, Skate Rental: $4 **Directions:** *I-495 Long Island Expwy., take exit 36 N. Searingtown Rd. N., the park entrance is on the Right & the rink is at the far end of the park, the entrance to the rink is below the clock tower, follow the ramp down to the cashier*

www.nassaucounty.gov/agencies/Parks/WheretoGo/active/morley.html

Grant Park · *Outdoor Ice Rink* · **NC** · *1625 Broadway, Hewlett, NY* · *516-571-7821* · **Features Include:** Open Skate Times, Skating Lessons, Groups Ice Charters, Hockey Game Rentals, Private Rentals **Hours:** Mon.-Sun.: 10 a.m.-Noon, 12:45-2:45 p.m., 3:30-5:30 p.m., Fri.: 8:30-10:30 p.m. **Fee:** With Leisure Pass: Adult: $7, Kids & Seniors: $5, Disabled, Volunteer Firefighter, Ambulance Corp., Auxiliary Police, Veterans: $4, Without Leisure Pass: Adults: $14, Kids: $10, Skate Rentals: $5, early Dec.-mid-March **Directions:** *Southern State Pkwy. to exit 19S. Peninsula Blvd., continue through Rockville Centre & Lynbrook, turn Left onto Rockaway Ave., the sign is on the Left, follow the road around to the traffic light on Broadway, go past the light onto Sheridan Ave., the park entrance will be on the Right just past the police station, turn slight Right into Rockaway Pkwy., then slight Right at Rockaway Pkwy., turn Right to stay on Rockaway Ave., turn Right onto Broadway*   *www.nassaucountyny.gov*

Hempstead Lake State Park · *Outdoor Ice Rink* · *Eagle Ave. & Lake Dr., West Hempstead, NY* · *516-766-1029* · **Features Include:** Ice Skating occurs only when it is cold enough for the lake to freeze. Signs are posted to indicate skating areas. This is the largest lake in Nassau County. **Hours:** Any time is skate time, weather permitting, Dawn-Dusk, Empire Pass Accepted **Fee:** **Free** **Directions:** *Southern State Pkwy., take exit 18 Eagle Ave., keep Right at the fork, follow signs for Rockville Centre/Hempstead Lake State Park, turn Right onto Eagle Ave.*

www.stateparks.com/hempstead_lake.html

Iceland Skating Rink · *Indoor Ice Rink* · *3345 Hillside Ave., New Hyde Park, NY* · *516-746-1100* · **Features Include:** Family Skate Sessions, Lessons, Teen Night every Fri. (8:30 p.m. with DJ) **Hours:** Session times change weekly, call for the schedule **Fee:** Adults & Kids: $7, Under 6: $6, Skate Rentals: $4 **Directions:** *I-495 Long Island Expwy., take exit 36 Searintown Rd., take the service road, make a Left at the light onto Searingtown Rd., continue for 2 mi., turn Left onto Herricks Rd., go to the 2nd traffic light, make a Right onto Hillside Ave., the rink is a half block up on the Right*

Long Beach Ice Arena · *Indoor Ice Rink* · *150 West Bay Dr., Long Beach, NY*· *516-431-6500* · **Features Include:** Public Skating, Ice Hockey, Figure Skating Arena, Recreational In-House Children's League, Apple Core Youth Travel Hockey, Freestyle Training Sessions, International Coaches & On & Off Ice Training Options, Roller Hockey **Hours:** Session times change monthly, call for current schedule **Fee:** Adults: $8, Kids Under 12: $6, Skate Rentals: $4 **Directions:** *Northern State Pkwy., to the Meadowbrook Pkwy. S., take exit M10 Loop Pkwy. to the end, turn Right onto Lido Blvd., when entering Long Beach, Lido Blvd. becomes Park Ave., pass the intersection of Long Beach Rd., make a Right onto Magnolia Blvd., when the road ends make a Right into the parking lot*

www.thearenaoflongbeachny.com

Marjorie R. Post-Massapequa Community Park · *Outdoor Ice Rink* · *451 Unqua Rd., Massapequa, NY* · *516-797-7990* · **Features Include:** There are limited skate sessions when weather permits. **Hours:** Closed Mon. & Tues., Wed.: 3:30-5:30 p.m., Fri.: 1-3 p.m., 4-6 p.m., 7-9 p.m., Sat. & Sun.: 10 p.m.-Midnight, Sat. 7-9 p.m., late Nov.-Feb. **Fee:** Adults: $4, Kids Under 17: $3, Under 4: Free, Seniors: $1, Skate Rental: $3 **Directions:** *I-135 Seaford-Oyster Bay Expwy., exit onto Merrick Rd. E., pass Massapequa HS, turn Left onto Unqua Rd., next light make a Left into the park, turn Right at the next stop sign, follow the road all the way back, the rink is near the tennis courts*

Newbridge Arena · *Indoor Ice Rink* · *2600 Newbridge Rd., Bellmore, NY* · *516-783- 6181* · **Features Include:** Public Skating, Holiday Sessions, Birthday Parties, Spring & Summer Youth Leagues, House Leagues, Adult Leagues, doors open 30 min. prior to start time **Hours:** Fri.: 9:45-11 a.m., 1:45-3:45 p.m., 4-6 p.m., 8:30-10:30 p.m., Sat.- Sun.: Noon-2 p.m., 2:30-4:30 p.m., Mon.: 4-6 p.m., Thurs.: 8-10 a.m. **Fee:** Town of Hempstead Resident: Adults: $7.50, Kids: $6.50, Town of Hempstead Park District Resident: $5.50, Skate Rental: $3.25-$3.75 **Directions:** *Southern State Pkwy., take exit 27 S., Wantagh State Pkwy. S., take exit W6 W. for Merrick Rd. toward Bellmore, turn Right onto Merrick Rd., turn Left onto Newbridge Rd.*   *www.newbridgearena.com*

Parkwood Ice Skating Rink · *Indoor Ice Rink* · *65 Arrandale Ave., Great Neck, NY*· *516-487-2975* · **Features Include:** Public Skating, Full Sized Rink, Hockey, Speed & Figure Skating, Food Service, Skate Shop **Hours:** Tues. & Thurs.: 10 a.m.-Noon, 12:30-2:30 p.m., Wed.: 10 a.m.-Noon, 12:30-2:20 p.m., 2:45-4:45 p.m., 8:30-10 p.m., Fri.: 3:30-5:30 p.m., 8-10 p.m., Sat.: 2:30-4:30 p.m., Sun.: 10 a.m.-Noon, 2-4 p.m., 8:15- 10 p.m. (18 & over) **Fee:** Adults: $7, Kids & Seniors: $5, Guests: Adult $10, Kids: $6, Skate Rental: $3.50, current park card required for admission **Directions:** *I-495 Long Island Expwy., take exit 33, make a Left onto Lakeville Rd. (after crossing Northern Blvd., it becomes Middle Neck Rd.), drive through the village of Great Neck, when the barrier* *between the lanes disappears, turn Left onto Arrandale Rd., make the 1ˢᵗ Right onto Wood Rd., the rink is on the Left side of the road* www.greatneckpark.org

Port Washington Skating Center · *Indoor Ice Rink* · *70 Seaview Blvd., Port Washington, NY* · *516-484-6800* · Features Include: Open Skate Times, Competition for kids Ages 5-13, Skate Lessons, Tot Classes, Hockey Leagues, Camp **Hours:** Mon.-Fri.: Noon-2:30 p.m., Sat.-Sun.: 2:15-3:45 p.m. **Fee:** $7, Skate Rental: $4 **Directions:** *I-495 Long Island Expwy., take exit 37 Mineola Ave. N., turn Right onto Old Northern Blvd., turn Left onto W. Shore Rd., turn Left onto Seaview Blvd.*

Syosset-Woodbury Community Park · *Outdoor Ice Rink* · *7800 Jericho Tpke., Woodbury, NY* · *516-677-5990* · *516-677-5992* · Features Include: Family Skate Sessions, Lessons, Leagues, Rentals, Fireplace, Snack Bar **Hours:** Closed: Mon. & Tues., Wed.: 3:30-5:30 p.m., Fri.: 4-6 p.m., 7-9 p.m., Sat. & Sun.: 10 a.m.-Noon, 1-3 p.m., Sat.: 7-9 p.m., **Fee:** Adults: $4, Kids 5-17: $3, Under 4: Free, Seniors: $1, Skate Rental: $3 **Directions:** *I-495 Long Island Expwy., take exit 44, I-135 N. Seaford-Oyster Bay Expwy., take exit 14 E. Jericho Tpke. E. toward Woodbury, the park is on the Right side of the road*

United Skates of America Roller Skating Center · *Indoor Ice Rink* · *1276 Hicksville Rd., Seaford, NY* · *516-795-5474* · Features Include: Ice Skating, Roller Skating, Birthday Parties **Hours:** Session times vary, call for current times, open Year-Round, **Fee:** Adults: $9, Kids: $8, Skate Rental: $4 **Directions:** *Southern State Pkwy., take exit 29 Rte. 107 Hicksville Rd., continue for 1 mi., the arena will be on the Right side of the road* www.unitedskates.com

SUFFOLK COUNTY

The Arches at Tanger Outlet · *Outdoor Ice Rink* · *455 Commack Rd., Deer Park, NY* · *631-940-8167* · Features Include: Oval Rink encircles a 50-ft. tree in the complex's center court **Hours:** Tues., Thurs., Fri.: 2-9:30 p.m., Sat.: 11 a.m.-9:30 p.m., Sun.: 11 a.m.-7 p.m., Mon. & Wed.: 2-7 p.m. **Fee:** $10, Under 5: Free, Skate Rental: $4 **Directions:** *I-495 Long Island Expwy. to the Sagtikos State Pkwy., take exit S3, Pine Aire Dr., drive .5 mi., turn Left onto Corbin Ave. heading South, drive .5 mi., turn Right onto Grand Blvd. heading West, drive approx. .5 mi., the Arches will be on the Right side of the street* tangeroutlet.com

Dix Hills Ice Rink · *Indoor Ice Rink* · *575 Vanderbilt Pkwy., Dix Hills, NY* · *631-462-5883* · Features Include: Full-Sized Rink, Figure Skating, Ice Hockey, Figure Skating Instruction, Food Service **Hours:** Mon.-Fri.: 10 a.m.-Noon, Mon. & Fri.: 12:15-2:15 p.m., Thurs. & Fri.: 3:45-5:45 p.m., Fri.: 8-10:15 p.m., Wed. 9-10 p.m., Sat.-Sun.: 11:30-1:30 p.m., 1:45-3:35 p.m. **Fee:** With Rec. Card: Adult: $8, Kids: $5, Without Rec. Card:

WINTER FUN

Adult: $10 Kids: $8, 50¢ higher on weekends **Directions:** *I-495 Long Island Expwy., take the Commack Rd. N. exit, make a Left onto Vanderbuilt Pkwy., the park will be on the Right*   *www.skateny.com/dixhills*

Hidden Pond Park Skating Rink · *Indoor Ice Rink* · *660 Terry Rd., Hauppauge, NY* · *631-232-3222* · *631 436-6020* · Features Include: Open Skate Times, Friday Night Rock Skate, Birthday Parties, Super Session, Rock-n-Roll Session, Adult Hockey Tournaments, Day Camps, Preschool **Hours:** Mon.: 12:30-2:30 p.m., Tues-Thurs.: 4-5:45 p.m., Fri.: 8:15-10:15 p.m., Sat.-Sun.: 11 a.m.-3 p.m., Open Year-Round **Fee:** Weekdays: Adults: $10, Kids: $8, Skate Rental: $5, Night Prices: $11 all, Weekends: Adults: $10.50, Kids: $8.50, Skate Rental: $5 **Directions:** *I-495 Long Island Expwy., take exit 58 toward Nesconset/Old Nichols Rd., turn Left onto Nichols Rd., turn Left onto Terry Rd.*
www.therinx.com

Superior Ice Rink · Indoor Ice Rink · *270 Indian Head Rd., Kings Park, NY* · *631-269-3900* · Features Include: Ice Skating, Ice Hockey, 12 Game Sessions Year-Round, Adult League, Youth Leagues **Hours:** Tues.: 10 a.m.-Noon, Wed.: 12:30-2:30 p.m., 4-6 p.m., Fri.: 8:30-10:30 p.m. with DJ, Sat.-Sun.: 1-3 p.m. **Fee:** Adults: $9, Kids Under 11: $7, Skate Rentals $4 **Directions:** *I-495 Long Island Expwy., take exit 53 N. Sagtikos/Sunken Meadow Pkwy. N., take exit SM3A Indian Head Rd., at the light turn Left onto Indian Head Rd., the rink is 2 mi. on the Left*   *www.superioricerink.com*

Rinks at Port Jefferson · *Outdoor Ice Rink* · *101-A East Broadway, Port Jefferson, NY* · *631-403-4357* · Features Include: Family Skate Sessions, Watch the Port Jefferson Ferry come & go as you skate **Hours:** Sun.-Thurs.: 10-11:30 a.m., 12:30-2 p.m., 2:30-4 p.m., 4:30-6 p.m., 9 a.m.-10 p.m., Fri.-Sat.: 9 a.m.-11 p.m. **Fee:** Adult: $9.50, Kids: $7, Skate Rental: $5 **Directions:** *I-495 Long Island Expwy., take exit 64 N., head North on Rte. 112 to end approx. 9 mi., Rte. 112 becomes Rte. 25A at Nesconset Hwy. intersection, turn Right at the blinking yellow light, pass East Main St. (1st Right), the rink will be on the Left side next to the Danford Inn*

NEW YORK CITY

Chelsea Piers Sky Rink · *61 Chelsea Piers, NY, NY* · *212-336-6200* · *212-336-6100* · Features Include: Twin Indoor Ice Skating Rinks, Public Skating, Skate Lessons, Figure Skating Lessons, Camp, Parties, Adult & Youth Hockey **Hours:** Mon.: 1:30-5:20 p.m., Tues.: 3-5:20 p.m., Thurs.: 3-5:20 p.m., Fri. 1:30-5:20 p.m.., Sat.-Sun. 1-3:50 p.m., Open Year-Round **Fee:** Adult: $13, Kids: $10.50, Skate Rental: $7.50, Helmet Rental: $4 **Directions:** *I-495 Long Island Expwy. to the Queens Midtown Tunnel, continue South to 23rd St., turn Right onto 23rd St. W. to the Hudson River, turn Right onto 11th Ave., turn Left onto 24th St., turn Left at the light onto W. Side Hwy., & turn Right at the next traffic light into the entrance of Chelsea Piers, between 17th St. & 23rd St.*
www.chelseapiers.com

Lasker Rink • *Outdoor Ice Rink* • *Central Park* • *212-534-7639* • *917-492-3856* • **Features Include:** Outdoor Rink, Public Skate, Lessons, Skate Rentals, Lockers **Hours:** Mon., Wed. & Thurs.: 10 a.m.-3:45 p.m., Tues: 10 a.m.-3:30 p.m., 8-10 p.m., Fri: 10 a.m.-5:15 p.m., 7 p.m.-11 p.m., Sat: 1 p.m.-11 p.m., Sun: 12:30 p.m.-4:30 p.m., late Oct.-March **Fee:** Adult: $6.25, Kids: $3.50, Seniors: $2.25, Skate Rentals: $5.50, Locker: $3.25 **Directions:** *mid-park between 106th St. & 108th St., enter the Park at 110th St.& Lenox Ave.*

BROOKLYN

Prospect Park Alliance • *Indoor & Outdoor Ice Rink* • *95 Prospect Park West, Brooklyn, NY* • *718-965-8951* • *718-965-8999* • Features Include: Indoor Wollman Rink, Outdoor Rink, Musical Skating Events, Open Skate Times, Skating School, Ice Hockey, Winter's Night Skating **Hours:** Mon.-Tues.: 10 a.m.-2:30 p.m., Wed.-Thurs.: 10 a.m.-10 p.m., Fri.-Sat.: 10 a.m.-11 p.m., Sun.: 10 a.m.-9 p.m., Nov.1-Apr.1 **Fee:** Mon.-Fri.: Adults: $10, Kids: $5.25, Seniors: $4.75, Sat.-Sun.: Adults: $14.75, Kids: $5.75, Seniors: $8.25, Skate Rentals: $6.25, Spectator Fee: $5, Parking: Free **Directions:** *I-495 Long Island Expwy., take the Brooklyn-Queens Expwy., exit at Tillary St., turn onto Flatbush Ave., (the Brooklyn Public Library will be on your Left & the Park on your Right), pass the zoo & Lefferts Historic House on the Right, make a Right at the traffic light onto Ocean Ave., at the next major intersection (Ocean Ave. & Parkside Ave.), turn Right into the park, take Park Dr. to the flashing light, make a Left into the Wollman Rink parking lot, follow signs to the Audubon Center, a 5 min. walk from the parking lot* www.prospectpark.org

Linda.ReidBryce @verizon.net

Thanks

Lazer Tag is a fun adventurous game allowing for running, hiding + shooting opponents for points. Players attempt to score points by engaging targets, typically with a hand-held infrared-emitting targeting device. There is usually a base spot in the room which also delivers points + is easier to hit than a moving target. Lazer tag combines the games of Hide + Seek, + Tag. Wearing black or dark colored clothing makes it is harder for the opposing team to spot in the dark. Most lazer tag places will allow groups as small as 4 to play in between birthday parties. They will group teams together with others who arrive to play during in-between times.

Let Fun Flow Like A River

Fun Station USA · *40 Rocklyn Ave., Lynbrook, NY* · *516-599-7757* · Features **Include:** Lazer Tag, Indoor Park, Kiddie Rides, Bumper Cars, Playport Maze, Bowling, Red Baron & Safari Jeep, Animated Stage Show, Food Court **Hours:** Sun.-Thurs.: 11 a.m.-9 p.m., Fri.-Sun: 11 a.m.-11 p.m. **Fee:** Lazer Tag: $5 per person, 4 Game Tokens: $1, Bowling: $2, Action Token: $1, Pay-One-Price Rides: Weekdays: $5.95-$7.95, Weekends: $7.95-$10.95 **Directions:** *Southern State Pkwy., take exit 19 S. Peninsula Blvd., make a Left onto Ocean Ave., 1ˢᵗ light make a Right onto Merrick Rd., 1ˢᵗ Left onto Rocklyn Ave., see sign for Fun Station* *www.funstationfun.com*

Fun Zone · *229 Rte. 110, Farmingdale, NY* · *631-847-0100* · Features **Include:** Lazer Tag, Indoor-Outdoor Family Amusement Center, Outdoor Thrill Rides, Rock Climbing Wall, Kiddie Rides, Bowling, Carousel, Jungle Climb, Bumper Cars, over 100 Games, Open Year-Round, Rides & Attractions are for all ages **Hours:** Mon.-Thurs.: 11 a.m.-10 p.m., Fri.: 11 a.m.-Midnight, Sat.: 10 a.m.-Midnight, Sun.: 10 a.m.-10 p.m. Lazer Tag is offered after 4 p.m. during the week **Fees:** Lazer Tag: $7 per person, 4 Game Tokens: $1, Action Token: $1, Pay-One-Price Rides: $8.95-$13.95 **Directions:** *I-495 Long Island Expwy., take Rte. 110 exit South* *www.funzoneamusements.com*

FUN FAMILY

Laser Kingdom · *544 Middle Country Rd., Coram, NY* · *631-698-0414* ·
Features Include: Public Sessions 7 days a week, Lazer Tag Amusement Center
Arena, Arcade Games, Teen Night on Fri. **Hours:** Mon.-Fri.: Noon-8 p.m., Sat.-Sun.: 10
a.m.-8 p.m., Games start on the half-hr. **Fees:** 2 Games: Mon.-Thurs.: $5, Fri.-Sun.: $8
Directions: *I-495 Long Island Expwy., take exit 63 North Ocean Ave., merge onto
Expwy. Dr. S./I-495 Service Rd., turn Left onto N. Ocean Ave., turn Right onto Middle
Country Rd.* www.laserkingdoms.com

Laser Kingdom · *133 Milbar Blvd., Farmingdale, NY*· *631-694-6148* ·
Features Include: Lazer Tag Amusement Center Arena, Arcade Games **Hours:** Mon.-
Fri.: Noon-8 p.m., Weekends: 10 a.m.-8 p.m., Open Public Sessions 7 days a week,
games start on the half-hr. **Fees:** 2 Games: Mon.-Thur.: $5, Fri.-Sun.: $8 **Directions:**
*I-495 Long Island Expwy., take exit 49 S. Rte.110 towards Amityville, turn Left onto
Milbar Blvd.* www.laserkingdoms.com

LazerLand · *54 Vanderbilt Motor Pkwy., Commack, NY* · *631-543-8300* ·
Feature Include: Lazer Tag, Dodgeball, Arcade Games, Special Events, Parties **Hours:**
Tues.-Thurs.: 4-9 p.m., Fri.: 4-11:30 p.m., Sat.: 11 a.m.-11:30 p.m., Sun.: 11 a.m.-6 p.m.,
Dodgeball: Fri.-Sat.: 7:30-11 p.m. **Fee:** Open Play: $10 per half hr., $20 per hr.,
Dodgeball/Lazer Tag Package: $20 **Directions:** *I-495 Long Island Expwy., take exit 53,
bear Right onto Wicks Rd., turn Left onto Wicks Rd., at the 1ˢ traffic light turn Left onto
Vanderbilt Motor Pkwy., Lazerland will be on the Right* www.lazerlandofli.com

Q-Zar · *151 Voice Rd., Carle Place, NY* · *516-877-7200* · Features Include:
Indoor Lazer Tag Games & Contests, Star Wars-Type Maze, Glowing Walls, Games of
Increasing Skill & Strategy, Special Effects, Schizophrenic Lighting & Electronic-
Techno Sound, Deactivating the Opposing Team's Headquarters, Parties **Hours:** Mon.-
Thur. & Sun.: 10 a.m.-10 p.m., Fri.-Sat.: 10 a.m.-1 a.m. **Fee:** $7 a session **Directions:** *I-495
Long Island Expwy., take exit 39 S., Glen Cove Rd., travel through 8 traffic lights, turn Right
onto Voice Rd., turn Right into the parking lot* www.qzarny.com

SUGGESTIONS · COMMENTS · ERRORS
Linda.ReidBryce
@verizon.net
Thanks

WINTER FUN

SEAL WATCH

WARM SWEATERS, BINOCULARS, & HOT CIDER

Seals can be seen off the shores of Long Island between Dec. + May. Whether walking on a beach or viewing from a boat, part or all of the time will be spent outside. Dress warmly + wear a hat, gloves, gator + scarf. Bring binoculars to see these beautiful creatures swim + play with each other. As the weather warms + more boats enter the water fewer seals can be seen as they tend to stay away from the boats. Bring a camera to record the excited expressions on children's faces.

Let Fun Flow Like A River

Cresli Seal Walks · *Coastal Research and Education Society of Long Island Inc.*· *150 Idle Hour Blvd., Oakdale, NY* · *Department of Earth & Marine Sciences, Dowling College* · *Reservations Required: 631-244-3352* · Features Include: Seal walks take place between Dec. & May at Cupsogue Beach County Park & Montauk Point State Park. Types of seals that can be viewed include Grey Seals, Harbor Seals, Hooded Seals, & Ringed Seals. **Hours:** vary according to the weather **Fee:** Adults: $5, Kids Under 13: $3 **Directions: Cupsogue Beach County Park:** *I-495 Long Island Expwy., take exit 68 for William Floyd Pkwy./Co. Hwy. 46 S. toward Shirely, take the ramp onto Rte. 27 E., take exit 63 S. for Co. Hwy. 31 S. toward Westhampton Beach, merge onto County Rte. 31/Old Riverhead Rd./ Riverhead Rd., continue on Oak St., at the traffic circle, take the 2nd exit onto Potunk Ln., turn Right onto Stevens Ln., turn Left onto Jessup Ln., turn Right onto County Rte. 89/Dune Rd., follow Dune Rd. to the park* **Directions: Montauk Point State Park:** *I-495 Long Island Expwy., take exit 68 William Flloyd Pkwy. S. toward Shirley, turn Left onto Rte. 27 E. Sunrise Hwy., take Rte. 27 E. to the park* www.cresli.org/cresli/seals/sealwalk.html

Seals of Long Island ⓢ • *Hempstead Bay Long Island Recreation & Amusements Boating & Cruises • Captain Lou's Fleet • 28A Woodcleft Ave., Freeport, NY • 631-369-9840 • Riverhead Foundation for Marine Research & Preservation* • **Features Include:** Join Riverhead Foundation to view winter harbor

seal populations throughout Hempstead Bay. The most common seals in these waters are Harbor Seals, Grey Seals, Hood Seals, & Harp Seals. The cruise from Freeport offers a heated cabin & snack bar on board. Bringing a lunch snack is permitted providing all is cleaned up. The members of the Riverhead Foundation for Marine Research & Preservation are available for questions & they bring many artifacts children will find fasinating, including seal skin samples. They also teach people how to see the seals. **Hours:** Fri.-Sun.: 12:30-3:30 p.m., (2-12 hr. cruises available), Reservations Required **Fee:** Adults: $24, Kids: $19, Seniors: $21 **Directions:** *Northern State Pkwy., take Meadowbrook Pkwy. S., exit 27 W., or 135 Seaford-Oyster Bay Expwy. S., exit onto Sunrise Hwy. W., drive through Bellmore, Merrick & pass the Meadowbrook Pkwy. turn Left onto Henry St., the Freeport RR station will be on the Right (becomes S. Main St, turn Right onto Atlantic Ave., turn Left onto Guy Lombardo Ave., turn Right onto Front St., turn Left onto Woodcleft Ave., Captain Lou's Fleet (28A Woodcleft Ave.) Will be on the Left* www.captloufleet.com • www.riverheadfoundation.org

Montauk Point State Park • *50 South Fairview Ave., Montauk, NY • 631-668-3781* • **Features Include:** Walk along the beach & spend time watching the seals sun themselves on the rocks off-shore. The view is unique because when the water is calm, visitors can clearly see the "race" of converging tides from the Atlantic & Block Island Sound. Montauk Point State Park is a heavily wooded area on the eastern tip of Long Island & the historic Montauk Lighthouse is there. **Fee: Free** off-season, Empire Passport Accepted **Directions:** *I-495 Long Island Expwy., take exit 68 William Flloyd Pkwy. S. toward Shirley, turn Left onto Rte. 27 E. Sunrise Hwy., take Rte. 27 E. to the park* http://nysparks.state.ny.us/sites/info

Linda.ReidBryce
@verizon.net
Thanks

It is essential to to keep kids warm while they sled. Dress them with insulated gloves, insulated pants, boots + a hat. Bring a thermos of hot chocolate or hot cider to warm them up. Build happy memories + Let fun flow like a river.

NASSAU COUNTY

Bethpage State Park • NYS • *99 Quaker Meeting House Rd., Farmingdale, NY • 516-249-0701* • Features Include: The park opens both the Red & Green courses for public sledding when weather permits. **Hours:** Dawn-Dusk, Year-Round **Fee:** Weekdays: **Free** off-season, Weekends: $8 parking only, Memorial Day-Labor Day: Sun.-Sat.: $8 Parking, Empire Pass Accepted, Sledding: $5 **Directions:** *I-495 Long Island Expwy. E., take exit 44S. Seaford-Oyster Bay Expwy. (Rte. 135) South, take exit 8 East Powell Ave. http://nysparks.state.ny.us*

Cedar Creek Park • *3524 Merrick Rd., Seaford, NY • 516-571-7470* • Features Include: The park is on Seaman's Creek & the East Bay. The sled hills are steep & a favorite among youngsters. **Hours:** Dawn-Dusk, Year-Round **Fee: Free** Directions: *Northern State Pkwy., exit onto 135 S. Seaford Oyster-Bay Expwy., take exit 1 W. Merrick Rd. W. toward Freeport, merge onto Merrick Rd.* *www.nassaucountyny.gov/agencies/Parks/*

Christopher Morley Park • NC • *500 Searingtown Rd., Roslyn, NY • 516-571-8113* • Although people sled on the hill here, the Parks Department does not encourage it on the hill because of the presence of plantings & the boat basin below. **Hours:** Dawn-Dusk, Year-Round **Fee: Free** Directions: *I-495 Long Island Expwy., take exit 36N., Searingtown Rd., take Searingtown Rd. N. & look for the park entrance on the Right (about 200 yds. from the LIE)* *www.nassaucountyny.gov*

Eisenhower Park • NC • *1899 Hempstead Tpke., East Meadow, NY • 516-572-0348, 572-0290, 572-0327, 542-0015 • Eisenhower Recreation Center: 303-692-5650 •*
Features Include: Great for Young Children, Wide & Long Sled Hill, Gentle Downgrade **Hours:** Dawn-Dusk, Year-Round **Fee: Free**, Non-residents: $5 Memorial Day-Labor Day **Directions:** *Northern State Pkwy., take the Meadowbrook Pkwy. S., take exit M3 E. Stewart Ave., make a Right onto Stewart Ave., continue to the park, the Sled Hill is located by parking Field No. 1, off Merrick Ave.*

www.nassaucountyny.gov/agencies/Parks/WhereToGo/active/eisenhower.html

Grant Park • NC • *1625 Broadway, Hewlett, NY • 516-571-7821* • Features Include:
35-acre Park, Multi-Age Sledding Opportunities **Hours:** Dawn-Dusk **Fee: Free Directions:** *Southern State Pkwy., take exit 15S. for Corona Ave. S., turn Right onto N. Corona Ave., turn slight Left toward Rockaway Pkwy., then slight Right at Rockaway Pkwy., turn Right to stay on Rockaway Ave., turn Right onto Broadway, use the hill behind the baseball field*

www.nassaucountyny.gov

Newbridge Rd. Park • *Bellmore, NY • 516-783-2500* • Features Include: Short &
Steep Sled Hill, round hill allows for Sledding in any direction, approx. 2 stories High, 50-ft. Long Run to Flat Ground, Indoor Ice Skating Rink (just across the way, **Hours:** Dawn-Dusk **Fee: Free**, **Directions:** *Southern State Pkwy., take exit 27 S. Wantaugh State Pkwy., take exit W6 W. Merrick Rd. toward Bellmore, turn Right onto Merrick Rd., turn Left onto Newbridge Rd.*

SUFFOLK COUNTY

Calmset Park • NYS • *25 Lloyd Harbor Rd., Huntington, NY • 631-423-1770* • Features
Include: There is sledding in the park across from the parking lot. **Hours:** Open Year-Round **Fee: Free** off-season, April-Nov., Empire Passport Accepted, hrs. of operation change throughout the year, call for details, Handicap Accessible **Directions:** *I-495 Long Island Expwy., exit Rte. 110 N. which becomes New York Ave., turn Left onto Main St. 25A W., turn Right onto West Neck Rd. N., the park entrance is on the Left*

http://nysparks.state.ny.us/parks

Heckscher Museum & Park • *Private • 2 Prime Ave., Huntington, NY • 516-351-3250 • 631-581-2100* • Features Include: Long Narrow Hill, Hill begins behind the
Old First Presbyterian Church on Main St., leads into Heckscher Park, 4-Trees at top create natural lanes for riders **Hours:** Dawn-Dusk **Fee: Free Directions:** *Northern State Pkwy., take exit 40 (toward Huntington) Rte. 110 N., (Rte.-110/Walt Whitman Rd. becomes New York Ave.), turn Right onto Rte. 25A/Main St. in Huntington Village, turn Left onto Prime Ave., the hill is located along Rte. 25A just 1 traffic light East of the intersection with Rte. 110 in Huntington Village*

WINTER FUN

Koster Park • *45 Magerus St., Huntington Station, NY* • Features Include: Great spot for little ones **Hours:** Dawn-Dusk **Fee: Free** Directions: *Northern State Pkwy., take exit 40 (toward Huntington) 110 N., turn Right onto Jericho Tpke. E., turn Right onto Engelke Ave., turn Left onto Reynolds Rd. which ends at the park*

Montauk Downs • **NYS** • *50 South Fairview Ave., Montauk, NY* • *631-668-5000* • *668-3781* • There is sleigh riding available on the golf course. Great for little ones **Hours:** Dawn-Dusk **Fee: Free** off-season, Empire Pass Accepted **Directions:** *I-495 Long Island Expwy., take exit 68 for William Floyd Pkwy./Co. Hwy 46 S. toward Shirley, merge onto County Rte. 46/William Floyd Pkwy., turn Left at Rte. 27 Sunrise Hwy., turn Left at S. Fox St., turn Right at S. Forest St., turn Left at S. Fulton Dr., turn Right at S. Fairview Ave.*

http://nysparks.state.ny.us/sites/info

Wildwood • **NYS** • *P.O. Box 518, North Wading River Rd., Wading River, NY* • *631 929-4314* • Features Include: There is a small sleigh riding hill off the parking lot. **Hours:** Dawn-Dusk, Year-Round **Fee: Free** off-season, Memorial Day-Labor Day: $10, Weekends only until Oct.: $8, Empire Pass Accepted **Directions:** *I-495 Long Island Expwy., take exit 68, head North on Rte. 46, take Rte. 25A E., turn Left onto Sound Ave., turn Left at traffic light onto Hulse Landing Rd., the park entrance is on the Right*

http://nysparks.state.ny.us/sites/info

Nissequogue River State Park • *799 St. Johnland Rd., Kings Park, NY* • *631-269-4927* • Features Include: People like to sled on Old Dock Rd. Rangers are concerned because children can slide out onto the road. Parents tend to stand at the bottom as a precautionary measure. **Hours:** Dawn-Dusk, Year-Round **Fee: Free** off-season, Memorial Day-Labor Day: $8, Empire Pass Accepted **Directions:** *Sunken Meadow Pkwy., take exit SM 4, drive East on Pulaski Rd. which changes into Old Dock Rd. at the 5th traffic light, turn Right onto St. Johnland Rd., the park entrance is about .5 mi. on the Left*

http://nysparks.state.ny.us/parks

SUGGESTIONS • COMMENTS • ERRORS

Linda.ReidBryce
@verizon.net

Thanks

Children are intrigued by a live show. Small theatres will sometimes provide seating recommendations when informed that the tickets are for small children. Sometimes young children have trouble remaining seated for an entire performance so give them a chance to run in the lobby or walk in the back of the theatre + then be seated. It is important not to disturb the performance for other viewers. When children get restless during the performance it's helpful to take another walk. Bring a camera, + a pen because many children's performances include an autograph signing after the show. The actors are usually very happy to pose with the children. Showtimes + performances schedules change seasonally. Call or visit individual theatre web sites for precise information. Let Fun Flow Like A River

The Airport Playhouse • *218 Knickerbocker Ave., Bohemia, NY • 631-589-7588 •*
Show Times: Sat: 1 p.m., Fri & Sat.: 8 p.m. **Fee:** $12-$22 **Directions:** *I-495 Long Island Expwy. to exit 57 toward Patchogue/Vets Hwy., merge onto Express Dr. S./Long Island Expwy. Service Rd., turn Right onto Rte. 454, turn Right onto Knickerbocker Ave., the theatre will be on the Right* www.airportplayhouse.com

Arena Players Second Stage ⑨ • *294 Rte. 109, East Farmingdale, NY • 516-293-0674 •* **Features Include:** Throughout the performance children are randomly selected from the audience to participate in various portions of the show. **Show Times:** Sat. & Sun.: 1 p.m., Evening Shows Fri & Sat.: 8:30 p.m. **Fee:** $9 **Directions:** *I-495 Long Island Expwy., take exit 44 S. for 135 S. Seaford-Oyster Bay Expwy. toward Seaford, take exit 7E. for 24 E. Hempstead Tpke. E. toward Farmingdale, turn Right onto Rte.109/Fulton St., the theatre will be on the Right* www.arenaplayers.org

Authors' Playhouse Community Theatre • *34 West Main St., Bay Shore, NY • 631-666-7529, • 917-679-2984 •* Features Include: Professional-quality community

theatre performs popular classical & original plays. **Show Times:** Sun.: matinee 2-5 p.m., Fri.-Sat.: 8-11 p.m. **Fee:** $10-$15 **Directions:** *I-495 Long Island Expwy., take exit 53, take the Right fork toward Sagtikos State Pkwy. S., take exit 40 & 41 S. toward Bay Shore/Bay Shore Rd., merge onto Bay Shore Rd./County Rte. 57, follow to County Rte. 57, at the traffic circle, take the 1ˢᵗ exit & stay on County Rte. 57, turn Right onto E. Main St./ Rte. 27A, the theatre will be on the Left* www.AuthorsPlayhouse.org

BayWay Arts Center ☺ • **265 East Main St., East Islip, NY • 631-581-2700 •** **Features Include:** After each performance the children can meet the actors in the lobby & collect autographs in their Playbills. Bring a camera for this segment. Very cute! **Show Times:** Sat.: 2, 7 or 8 p.m. **Fee:** Adults: $25, Kids: $14, Students: $18, Seniors: $23 **Directions:** *I-495 Long Island Expwy., take the Sagtikos Pkwy. S., exit onto Southern State Pkwy. E., take exit 45 W., Rte. 27A toward East Islip, turn Left at the stop sign at the end of the exit ramp, turn Right onto East Main St., turn Right at the 2ⁿᵈ traffic light into the parking lot* www.broadhollow.org

Bridgehampton Chamber Music Associates • 2429 Montauk Hwy., Bridgehampton, NY • 212-741-9073 • 631-537-3507 • Features Include: Summer Performances, Special Events **Directions:** *I-495 Long Island Expwy. to exit 68 for William Floyd Pkwy./Co. Hwy. 46 S. toward Shirley, take the ramp onto Rte. 27 E., turn Left onto Rte. 27, the theatre will be the Right* www.bcmf.org

Broadhollow Theatre • 700 Hempstead Tpke., Elmont, NY • 516-775-4420 • Show Times: Sat.: 2:30 & 8 p.m. **Fee:** Adults: $25, Kids: $14, Students: $18, Seniors: $22 **Directions:** *I-495 Long Island Expwy., take the Cross Island Pkwy. S., take exit 26B E., Hempstead Ave. (becomes Hempstead Tpke. at the Nassau County border), the Broadhollow Theatre is in the Elmont Memorial Public Library, East of Home Depot shopping center on Hempstead Tpke.* www.broadhollow.org

Center Stage • at Molloy College • Broadhollow Theatre Company • 1000 Hempstead Ave., Rockville Centre, NY • Main Box Office: 631 581-2700 • (office: 8 Laurel Ave., Ste. 2, East Islip, NY • 631-581-5119) • Features Include: 8 Productions Yearly **Show Times:** 2 & 8 p.m., some Wed.: 8 p.m., Fri.: 3 & 8 p.m., Sat.: 3 p.m., some Sun.: 7 p.m. **Fee:** $20-$22 **Directions:** *Southern State Pkwy., take exit 20 S. toward Grand Ave., merge onto Baldwin Rd., continue on Grand Ave., turn Right onto Georgia St., continue on Beech St., turn Left at Hempstead Ave., turn Right into the Molloy College parking lot* www.broadhollow.org

Creative Ministries ☺ • **931 Montauk Hwy., P.O. Box 388, Oakdale, NY • 631-218-2810** • **Features Include:** After each performance the children can meet the actors in the lobby & collect autographs in their Playbills. Bring a camera for this segment. Very cute! **Show Times:** Sat. & Sun.: 2 p.m., Fri., Sat. & Sun. 8 p.m. **Box Office Hours:** Mon.-Fri.: 10 a.m.-7 p.m., Sat.: 10 a.m.-7 p.m., Sun.: 11 a.m.-2: p.m. **Fee:** Kids Matinee: $9, Evening Performances: $22, Students & Seniors: $20 **Directions:** *Northern State Pkwy., take 135 S., take Sunrise Hwy. E. (Rte. 27), take exit 47A (Oakdale-Bohemia Rd.), at the light make a Right onto Oakdale-Bohemia Rd., drive over the railroad track, make a Left onto Montauk Hwy., next light make a Left into the shopping center, Creative Ministries is located in the corner of the strip* http://www.cmpac.com

Goat on a Boat Puppet Theatre ✆ • *East Union St. off Rte. 114* • *P.O. Box 327, Sag Harbor, NY* • *631-725-4193* • Goat On A Boat is among only 50 established puppet theatres listed by the Puppeteers of America (the only national organization of puppeteers, www.puppeteeers.org). **Features Include:** Puppet Shows, Costumed Characters, Puppet Club, Puppet Play Groups, Tot Art, Talent Show, Dance Party, Outdoor Puppet Festival, call or check the web site for performance schedule & playgroups **Show Times:** Sat.: 11 a.m. & 3 p.m. **Fee:** Adults & Kids: $10, Under 3: $5 **Directions:** *I-495 Long Island Expwy., take exit 68 William Floyd Pkwy./Co. Hwy. 46 S. toward Shirley, merge onto County Rte. 46/William Floyd Pkwy., take the ramp onto Rte. 27 E., turn Left onto Rte. 27, slight Left onto Bridgehampton Sag Harbor Tpke./County Rte. 79/Sag Harbor Tpke., continue to follow County Rte. 79, continue on Main St., turn Right onto Union St., turn Right onto Division St./Rte. 114, the church will be on the Left (theatre is behind the Christ Episcopal Church in the parish hall, on the lower level)*
www.goatonaboat.org/puppet-theatre-calendar.shtml • www.puppeteeers.org

Hampton Theatre Company • *Quogue Community Hall* • *126 Jessup Ave., Quogue, NY* • *P.O. Box 734, Westhampton Beach, NY* • *631-653-8955* • **Features Include:** Theatre Troop, Performances from Sept.-June, Historic Quogue Community Hall **Show Times:** Thurs.: 8 p.m., Fri. & Sat.: 2:30 p.m. **Fee:** Adults: $22, Under 21: $10, Seniors: $20 (except Sat.) **Directions:** *I-495 Long Island Expwy., take exit 68 for William Floyd Pkwy. 46 S. toward Shirley, take the ramp onto Rte. 27 E., take exit 63S. for County Hwy. 31 S. toward Westhampton Beach, merge onto County Rte. 31/Old Riverhead Rd./ Riverhead Rd., turn Left at County Rte. 8, turn Right at Jessup Ave., the theatre will be on the Left* www.hamptontheatre.org

Hamptons Shakespeare Festival • *P.O. Box 63, Amagansett, NY* • *631-267-0105* • **Features Include:** Children's Performances, Camp Shakespeare, Children's Workshops, Playwrights Reading Series, Internship Program, Artist Discussions, Shake It Up! (an in-school artist residency), *Romeo & Juliet, Taming of the Shrew,* the Hamptons Shakespeare Festival performs in 2 locations: Theodore Roosevelt County Park in Montauk & Agawam Park in Southampton **Fee: Free** outdoor theatre **Directions: Theodore Roosevelt County Park in Montauk, NY:** *I-495 Long Island Expwy., take exit 70, turn Right onto County Rd. 111 S., follow 111 until it ends, bear Left onto Rte. 27 Montauk Hwy. E., it becomes a local road through different villages, eventually coming to Montauk, proceed on Rte. 27 3-mi. East of Montauk, Theodore Roosevelt County Park is on the Left directly after a bend to the Left. If you see a horse ranch, you have gone too far. If you see a lighthouse, you have really gone too far.*

Directions: Agawam Park in Southampton, NY: *I-495 Long Island Expwy. to exit 70, turn Right onto County Rd 111 S., follow Rte. 27 E., it becomes a local road into Southampton, make a Right onto North Sea Rd., take it into the Village of Southampton, veer Right onto Windmill Ln., Windmill Ln. ends at Agawam Park*   *www.hamptons-shakespeare.org*

Jeanne Rimsky Theater *at Landmark on Main St. • 232 Main St., Port Washington, NY • Box Office • 516-767-6444 •* Features Include: Performances have included: Concerts, Family Specials, Theatrical Children's Series Performances Show Times: Sat.-Sun.: 2 p.m. Fee: vary per event Directions: *I-495 Long Island Expwy., take exit 36 toward Searringtown Rd., turn Left onto Searringtown Rd. N. Which becomes Port Washington Blvd. after crossing Northern Blvd., turn Left onto Main St., the theatre will be on the Left, look for the blue canopy*   *www.landmarkonmainstreet.org*

John W. Engeman Theater ⑳ • *250 Main St., Northport, NY • 631-261-2900 • 631-261-2963 •* Features Include: Professional Theatre, Beautiful Harbor-Side Village of Northport Show Times: Sat.: Noon & 3 p.m. Fee: Children's Theatre: Adults & Kids: $15, Adults Performances: $60 Directions: *Northern State Pkwy., take exit 42 N. toward Northport, take Deer Park Ave., turn Right onto Jericho Tpke., turn Left onto Elwood Rd. which becomes Reservoir Ave., turn Left onto Church St., turn Left onto Main St., the theatre will be on the Left*   *www.johnwengemantheater.com*

Nassau Community College Theatre & Events for kids • *1 Education Dr., Garden City, NY •* 516-572-7153 • *Box Office:* 516-572-7676 • Children's Performances Have Included: African Folk-Tales, Juggling, Children's Opera Show Times: vary Fee: Classics for Kids Series: $1.50 Directions: *Northern State Pkwy., take exit 31A Meadowbrook Pkwy. S., take exit M3 W. Stewart Ave., turn Right onto Merchants Concourse to Endo Dr., turn Right onto Miller Ave., turn Left onto East Rd., turn Left on to Education Dr.*   *www.ncc.edu*

North Fork Community Theatre • *12700 Old Sound Ave., P.O. Box 86, Mattituck, NY • 631-298-4500 • 631-298-6328 •* Features Include: The theatre produces 4-5 shows yearly. Show Times: Thurs., Fri., Sat.: 8 p.m., Sun.: 2 p.m. Fee: $15 Directions: *I-495 Long Island Expwy., take exit 73 toward Greenport, merge onto Old Country Rd., take the 2nd exit in the roundabout to stay on Old Country Rd., turn Left onto Northville Tpke., turn Right onto Sound Ave., turn Right onto Old Sound Ave.*
     http://nfct.com/main.html • online ticket purchase: www.BrownPaperTickets.com

The Capital One Bank Theatre at Westbury • *960 Brush Hollow Rd., Westbury, NY •* 516-334-0800• *Box Office:* 516-334-0800 • 631-298-NFCT • *Group Sales:* 516-333-2101 • Features Include: Plays, Musicals, Music Concerts, Kid-Friendly Productions Show Times: 2:30 & 8 p.m. Fee: varies per performance Directions: *Northern State Pkwy., take exit 34 Brush Hollow Rd. toward Westbury, turn Right onto Brush Hollow Rd., the theatre will be on the Right*   *www.livenation.com*

FUN FAMILY

Patchogue Theatre for the Performing Arts • *71 E. Main St., Patchogue, NY •*
631-207-1313 • **Features Include:** A Full Season of Children & Family Programs, Comedy, Classical Music Performances **Matinees Times:** 12:30 & 3 p.m. **Fee:** Children's Shows: $10, Comedy & Musical Performances: $7-$60 **Directions:** *I-495 Long Island Expwy., take exit 62 for Nicolls Rd. toward Stony Brook, turn Left onto Nicolls Rd. S., turn Left at County Rte. 85, becomes West Main St.*

patchoguetheatre.com

Plaza Theatrical Productions • *222 Pettit Ave., Bellmore, NY • Box Office: 516-599-6870* • **Features Include:** Traveling Theatre Company performs at both the Bellmore Theatre & the Milleridge Cottage, Plaza Theatricals (resident production company of The Showplace at the Bellmore Movies), Newly Renovated Vaudeville House, State of the Art Lighting & Sound, Handicap Accessible, Refreshments **Show Times:** 11 a.m., 4 p.m., 8 p.m. **Fee:** Matinee: $10 (includes soda & popcorn), Afternoon & Evening Performance: $25 **Directions:** *Northern State Pkwy., take the Meadowbrook Pkwy. S., to Sunrise Hwy. E., turn Left onto Bedford Ave. N., pass under the railroad tressel, make 1ˢᵗ Left onto Pettit Ave., the theatre is 1 block on the Right, across from the Bellmore Train Station, On weekends, parking is available in the train station parking lot*

The Milleridge Cottage • *585 N. Broadway, Jericho, NY •* **Show Times:** Wed.: Noon lunch & 1:15 p.m. performance **Fee:** $43.50 per person includes 3-course meal **Directions:** *I-495 Long Island Expwy., take exit 41 N. or Northern State Pkwy., take exit 35 N., the Milleridge will be on the Right side of the street .5 mi. up*

www.plazatheatrical.com

Staller Center for the Arts • *Stony Brook University • 2031 Staller Center, Stony Brook, NY • Ticket Office: 631-632-7230 • The Performing Arts Center at SUNY Stony Brook* • **Features Include:** Children's Shows, Cultural Arts Performances Include: Dance, Music & Theatre, Staller hosts a Summer Film Festival **Show Times:** Children's shows are typically on Sat. or Sun. at: 3 or 4 p.m. **Fee: Children's Shows:** $12 **Directions:** *I-495 Long Island Expwy., take exit 62. Nicolls Rd. N. toward Stony Brook, take Nicolls Rd. N. approx. 9 mi., (pass Suffolk Community College, Rte. 25 Jericho Tpke., & Rte. 347), after crossing Rte. 347 (the 2ⁿᵈ major intersection), pass 2 traffic lights, go past the 1ˢᵗ Stony Brook entrance (South Campus entrance), at the 2ⁿᵈ entrance (Main Campus/ West Campus entrance), make a Left at the Stony Brook sign, follow signs to the Visitors' Parking Garage to the Left, park in the garage & walk around the Fine Arts Loop to the Staller Center* *www.stallercenter.com*

Studio Theatre ⊛ • *141 South Welwood Ave., Lindenhurst, NY • (Mailing Address: 265 East Main St., Ste. 162, East Islip, NY) • 631-581-2700* • **Features Include:** A Full Season of Children's Performances, Full Season of Adult Performances. After each performance the children can meet the actors in the lobby & collect autographs in their

Playbills. Bring a camera for this segment. Very cute! Perfect for ages 2-5 **Show Times:** Sat.: 2 p.m. **Fee:** $8 **Directions:** *Northern State Pkwy., take exit 33 for Wantagh State Pkwy. S., take exit W5 E. for State Hwy 27 E. toward Montauk, merge onto Rte. 27, exit onto N. Wellwood Ave. toward Lindenhurst, the theatre is on the Left on the 2nd floor* *www.broadhollow.org • www.theatermania.com*

OPENING SOON---**Suffolk Theatre** • *Performing Arts Center* • *11 West Main St., Riverhead, NY* • *631-208-0003* • **Features Include:** Children's, Music Dance, Adult Performances, Art Deco Theatre circa 1933, Historic Renovation **Directions:** *I-495 Long Island Expwy., take exit 71 toward Hampton Bays, turn Right onto County Rte. 94/ Edwards Ave. (follow signs for Rte. 24/Hampton Bays/Montauk/Riverhead), at the traffic circle take the 2nd exit onto Center/County Rte. 94A, turn Right onto W. Main St. (Rte. 25), the theatre will be on the Right* *www.suffolktheatre.com*

Theatre Three ⑤ • *412 Main St., P.O. Box 512, Port Jefferson, NY* • *Box Office: 631-928-9100* • **Features Include:** A full Season of Children's Performances, Friday Night Face-Off event takes place on Theatre Three's 2nd stage at Griswold's Café. This is interactive competitive improvisational comedy. **Box Office Hours:** Mon.-Sat.: 10 a.m.-5 p.m. **Show Times:** matinee times vary **Fee:** $12 **Directions:** *Northern State Pkwy., to the end, Veterans Memorial Hwy. (Rte. 347) East toward Port Jefferson (left-hand fork at 347/454) to Rte. 112 (approximately 17 mi.), turn Left onto Rte. 112 N., cross the railroad tracks, go down the hill, & the theatre is on the Left* *www.theatrethree.com*

Tilles Center • **Long Island University** • *C.W. Post Campus - School of Visual & Performing Arts* • *720 Northern Blvd., Brookville, NY* • *516-299-3100* • *516-299-3108* • **Features Include:** Family Shows, Classical Jazz, Dance, Opera, World & Pop Music **Show Times:** vary by show **Fee:** $30-50 **Directions:** *I-495 Long Island Expwy., take exit 39 toward Glen Cove, turn Right onto Northern Blvd. (Rte. 25A), the university will be on the Right* *www.tillescenter.org*

West Hampton Beach Performing Arts Center • *76 Main St., West Hampton, NY* • *Box Office: 631-288-1500* • **Features Include:** Family Friendly Performances, Shows, International Cinema, Special Events, Performing Arts Camp **Children's Performance Times:** 11 a.m., 1 p.m. **Fee:** Children's Performances/Cinema: Adults: $10, Children: $7, Members: $3, General Theatre Performances: $15-25 **Directions:** *I-495 Long Island Expwy., take exit 68 William Floyd Pkwy. S. toward Shirley, take the ramp onto Rte. 27 E., take exit 61 toward Co. Hwy. 51 N. toward Riverhead, follow signs for Eastport, turn Right onto County Rte. 55/Eastport Manor Rd., turn Left onto Main St./ County Rte. 80, make a slight Right at S. Country Rd., the theatre will be on the Left* www.whbpac.org

YMCA Boulton Center for the Performing Arts • *37 West Main St., Bay Shore, NY* • *631-969-1101* • *Tickets: 866-811-4111* • **Features Include:** Musical Performances such as: Jazz, Hip Hop, Funk, & various Ethnic musical performances, in 2008 they had the Russian Circus **Box Office Hours:** Wed.-Sat.: Noon-4 p.m. **Show Times:** Matinee: 2 p.m. **Fee:** Adults: $8, Kids: $5 **Directions:** *Southern State Pkwy., take the 5th Ave. S. exit to Montauk Hwy., drive 2.2 mi., the theatre is on the North side of Montauk Hwy., between 4th and 5th Ave., park in the rear of the building*

www.boultoncenter.org

NEW YORK CITY

Marionette Theater • *Central Park* • *212-988-9093* • **Features Include:** The Swedish Cottage Marionette Theater presents puppet shows for children **Hours:** Tues. Thurs., Fri.: 10:30 a.m. & Noon, Wed.: 10:30 a.m., Noon, 2:30 p.m., Sat.-Sun.: 1:00 p.m. Open Year-Round, Reservations Required **Fee:** Adults: $8, Kids: $5 **Directions:** *Penn Station, take the: B/C subway to 72nd St., enter the park at W. 79th St. & walk to the Swedish Cottage*

www.centralpark.com/pages/activities/marionette-theater.html

NYC Ballet • **Ballet for Young People** • *David H. Koch Theater* • *W. 63rd St. & Columbus Ave., NY, NY* • *212-870-4074* • **Features Include:** Artists of the New York City Ballet, Introduction for Children to Choreography & Music, Family Performances, Programs, Workshops, 45 min.-1 hr. in length., themes, exact times, & program topics vary throughout the year **Times:** Sat.: 11 a.m. **Fee:** $8-12 per person **Directions:** *From Penn Station, take the 1 train toward 242nd St. - Van Cortlandt Park, exit at the 66th St. - Lincoln Center station*

www.nycballet.com/nycb/content/kids.aspx?ID=3926

New Victory Theatre ⓥ • *c/o The New 42nd St.* • *229 West 42nd St., 10th fl., NY, NY* • *646-223-3082* • *212-239-6200* • **Features Include:** Family Theatre, Seasonal Family Shows, Kids Club Membership (visit working rehearsals), Lower Lobby Free Extras (1 hr. before & a half hr. after the show), Exhibits, Activities, Displays, "Talk-Back" Performances (cast question & answer sessions from the stage edge after the show), Family Workshops, Puppet Basics, Story & Character Development Games, Poetry Slam, Tapping Feet, Circus Skills, Latin Beat, Improv, Juggling & Physical Comedy, Job Training & Employment (high school & college students), Education Programs, VicTeens & Youth Corps (11-18 yrs.), Behind the Curtain (technical aspects of theatre) **Show Times:** Thur., Fri.: 7 p.m., Sat.: 2 p.m., 4 p.m., Sun.: Noon, 5 p.m. **Fee:** On Stage: $40, Worst Seats: $12, school discount tickets are as low as $2, call: 646-223-3095 **Directions:** *From Penn Station, take the 1 train toward 242nd St. - Van Cortlandt Park, exit at the Times Sq. - 42nd St. station*

www.newvictory.org

Public Theatre • *425 Lafayette St., NY, NY* • *Box Office: 212-260-2400 (Sun.-Mon.: 1-6 pm, Tues.-Sat.: 1-7:30 p.m.)* • *General Information: 212-539-8500* • *Ticket Sales: 212-967-7555* • *Member Hotline: 212-539-8650* • *Delacorte Info*

WINTER FUN

Line: 212-539-8750 Joes Pub, Shakespeare In The Park • **Features Include:** The nation's foremost theatrical producer of Shakespeare & new work, dedicated to making theater accessible & relevant to all people **Productions have included:** New Plays, Musicals & Innovative Stagings of the Classics, the theatre was founded by Joseph Papp 1st as the Shakespeare Workshop & has become one of the nation's outstanding cultural institutions **Show Times & Fee:** vary **Directions:** *Penn Station, take the R train toward 95th St. - Bay Ridge, exit at the 8th St - New York University station*   *www.publictheater.org*

NEW JERSEY

Medieval Times •*149 Polito Ave., Lyndhurst, NJ* • *888-WE-JOUST* • *888-935-6878* • *201-933-2220* • **Features Include:** Faux 11th Century Castle, Knights Joust & Perform Feats of Horsemanship, Rescue a Princess, Dinner Theatre, Medieval Dinner, Costumed Wait Staff, Medieval Style Dining (no silverware), bring a pack of wipes to clean hands **Show Times & Fee:** vary seasonally, there are many online discounts **Directions:** *I-495, Midtown Tunnel, Left at 34th St. downtown, Right into Lincoln Tunnel to New Jersey, merge Right onto 495 W. as you enter New Jersey, merge onto Rte. 3W., exit at Ridge Rd. toward Park Ave., Left onto Ridge Rd., Left onto Rte. 17/Rutherford Ave., Right onto Polito Ave.*   *www.medievaltimes.com*

SUGGESTIONS • COMMENTS • ERRORS

Linda.ReidBryce @verizon.net

Thanks

Snowman Building Tips

Suggested Supplies: Spray Bottle of Water for spraying + smoothing the snowman, Food Coloring to create special effects such as: blood, beauty mark, polka dots, stripes, Buckets for packing + moving snow, Shovels for moving + shaping snow, Dixie Cups + Paint Brushes for painting enhancements with watered-down food coloring, Camera for the memories, *Let Fun Flow Like A River*

Eyes: Coal, Raisins, Rocks, Large Buttons, Sunglasses
Nose: Carrots, Celery Stalk, Banana, Candy Cane
Mouth: Coal, Red M&M's, Red Grapes, Small Buttons, Curved Stick, Red Hots, Cranberries
Hats: Knit Hat (less likely to blow away)
Hair: Old Plant, Tangled Yarn, Shredded T-Shirt
Buttons For the Snowman's Chest: Small Plastic Animals, Big Buttons, Small Figures
Other Accessories: Boots, Old Shoes, Scarf, Shirt, Mittens, Gloves, Broom & Shovel

Start by building a solid base. Instead of rolling a snowball, try using a shovel & push a large quantity of snow into a pile & then shape it into a rounded base using your hands. Spray it with a water spray & rub the snow to get a better finish. The 2nd & 3rd snowballs could be made in the same way & then lifted with 2 shovels into place. Pack some extra snow between the layers to make the layers stick together. Place sticks down the center if the sections are having trouble standing up.

Add arms, legs & other accessories. Try finding bent sticks. Adding joints makes the snowman look more animated. Place boots at the bottom to imply legs or sticks & boots making the snowman appear to be seated. Create more animation by adding a shirt, cape, scarf & sunglasses.

Consider making a snow family. For added humor & creative fun, why not create family of crashed sleigh riders with just their face, arms & legs sticking out of the snow. Tell a story with a snow family being chased by a crocodile with a big mouth coming out of the snow & paint the crocodile with green food coloring.

Snow Ice
How to make a delicious Snow Ice
Suggested Supplies: Lots of Fresh New Fallen Snow. Flavoring Options: Chocolate, Strawberry Syrup, Maple Syrup, or Condensed Juice. Added Enhancements: Chocolate Chips, Sprinkles, * Whipped Cream topping. For Mom + Dad Only: Bailey's, Amaretto, or other cordials make a great snow ice.

Give each child a large plastic bowl, a spatula or a large spoon. Wearing boots & jackets, walk into the yard to a spot where no one has walked. Carefully remove the top layer of snow. Have them place the clean under snow into their bowls being careful not to go down to the grass.

Have them mix their snow ice at the kitchen table with teaspoons in hand. When finished, they can place their creation in a special dessert bowl & top with whipped cream.

A Hot Chocolate Snow Walk
Suggested Supplies: Back-Packers Mini Stove ($29 item), any Small Pot for boiling water, Instant Hot Chocolate Mix, Dry Matches, Hot Paper Cups + Spoon

Plan a short hike the day after a snow. Wear boots & dress warmly, bring a small backpack & choose a nice location near a sitting rock. Have the children find a place where no one has walked. Carefully remove the top layer of snow, place the clean under snow into the pot being careful not to go down to the grass, heat the snow until it melts. Have each of them pour their instant hot chocolate mix into their cup, add the melted snow, now hot water & stir. Yum! It tastes so much better with snow.

Smores Indoors
Roasting Marshmallows is a fun process that should be supervised by an adult at all times. It is important to review fire safety with children before they begin.

Fire Safety Reminders: If anyone makes a burning torch their marshmallow roasting privileges will be evoked. Never point a hot stick at another person. If a marshmallow catches on fire, quickly blow it out. Wear cotton clothing because man-made fabrics melt when a spark lands on them. No bare feet. When finished roasting, hand your stick to an adult to check that it is not smoldering.

Fireplace Smores
Ingredients & Supplies: Tray with Marshmallows, Broken Chocolate Bars, Graham Crackers, Tin Foil, 3-ft. long roasting sticks

Line the floor within the fireplace with tin foil. Review open fire precautions with the children. Have the children use roasting sticks that are approx. 3-ft. long & approx. .25-in. thick. When the timbers have cooled the next day, roll up the foil & toss. This approach prevents food remnants from landing in the fireplace which would require a much bigger clean-up.

Table Top Smores

Ingredients & Supplies: Tray with Marshmallows, Broken Chocolate Bars, + Graham Crackers, Fondue Forks, the Base from a Fondue Pot + Sterno.

Have the children sit at the table & roast their marshmallow using fondue folks.

Movie Night with a Living Room Picnic

Suggested Supplies: Choose a movie. Then fill a basket with plates, folks, napkins & whatever else is needed. Let the children choose the placement of the picnic blanket & set the picnic "table." This is a great photo opportunity.

Variations on a Theme: A Chinese Picnic complete with tea, chopsticks & fortune cookies can be especially fun. Any meat cooked on a stick with dipping sauce is a welcomed change. English muffin pizzas & sliced apples with caramel dip are also fun & special treats.

SUGGESTIONS • COMMENTS • ERRORS

Linda.ReidBryce
@verizon.net

Thanks

3 IN THIS SECTION

Spring Events

SPRING BLISS

Let
Fun Flow
Like A
River

March

Winter Seal Walk • *Theodore Roosevelt Nature Center at Jones Beach* • *516-679-7254* • **Features Include:** Seals in the Wild, View from Fishing Piers, Meet at the Nature Center **Hours:** 1:30 p.m., during mid-March, call for specific times **Fee:** Adults: $3, Kids: $2, Under 3: Free **Directions:** *Northern State Pkwy., take the Meadowbrook Pkwy. S., pass the toll booths, go over the bridge, exit to the Right after the bridge onto Bay Dr. Pkwy., the Nature Center is the first bldg. on Left, make a U-turn .25 mi. down to get to the center*

Seal Walk • *Cupsogue Beach County Park Coastal Research & Education Society of Long Island* • *West Hampton Beach, NY* • *631-244-3352* • Features Include: Seal Walk, 2-Hour Naturalist-Led Walk, Observe, Photograph, Seals in the Wild **Hours:** Times & Days vary, call for specifics or check the web site, Dec.-March **Fee: Free**, $5 suggested donation **Directions:** *I-495 Long Island Expwy., take exit 68 S. William Floyd Pkwy. toward Shirley, slight Right to merge onto NY-27 E. toward Montauk, take exit 63S. for County Rd. 31 S. toward Westhampton Beach, merge onto County Rd. 31/Old Riverhead Rd./Riverhead Rd., continue onto Oak St., at the traffic circle, take the 2nd exit onto Potunk Ln., turn Left onto Main St., slight Right onto Beach Ln., turn Left onto Dune Rd., look for Cupsogue Beach County Park* cresli.org

Festival of One Act Plays • *Theatre Three* • *412 Main St., P.O. Box 512, Port Jefferson, NY* • *631-928-9100* • **Features Include:** Theatre Three selects 5-6 original works to premiere at The Ronald F. Peierls Theatre on their 2nd stage. Over the past 9 yrs. they have received more than 2,000 submissions from across the world. **Hours:** Box Office:

10 a.m-5 p.m. **Fee:** varies according to seating **Directions:** *Northern State Pkwy., take to the end, Veterans Memorial Hwy./347 E. toward Port Jefferson (Left fork at 347/454) to Rte. 112 drive approx. 17 mi., turn Left onto Rte. 112 N., cross the railroad tracks, go down the hill & the theatre is on the Left* www.theatrethree.com

Annual Early Spring Art & Craft Festival • *Stony Brook University Sports Complex Arena* • *Gym Rd. (Nichols Rd. main entrance), Stony Brook, NY* • Features Include: Celebrate Spring Events, Art Exhibits, Craft Exhibits **Hours:** 10 a.m.-5 p.m., last weekend in March **Fee:** Adults: $5, Under 12: Free **Directions:** *I-495 Long Island Expwy., take exit 62N. Nichols Rd./Rte. 97, take Nichols Rd. N. for 9 mi., pass the main entrance on Left, at the next light turn Left into the north entrance, at the top of the hill turn Right, go past the football stadium and make the first Left onto Gym Rd., take Gym Rd. to the Sports Complex parking lot* www.sunysb.edu

Maple Sugaring Day • *Benner's Farm* • *56 Gnarled Hollow Rd., Setauket, NY* • *631-689-8172* • *631-689-8172* • Features Include: Benner's Farm circa 1700s, Get a Sense of Past Centuries Farm Life, Organic Farm Since the 1970s, Maple Sugar Demonstrations, Family Garden, Fields of Strawberries, a Variety of Farm Animals for Self-Sufficient living, Workshops, Festivals, Events throughout the Year **Hours:** Weekends: 12-4 p.m., **Fee:** Adults: $6, Kids: $5 **Directions:** *I-495 Long Island Expwy., take exit 62 Nicoll's Rd. N./County Rd. 97, follow Nicoll's to the end, (cross Rte. 25, Rte. 347 and Stony Brook Univ.), turn Right onto 25A E., go 5 traffic lights, at the 5th light (Apple Savings Bank on corner) turn Right onto Old Town Rd., take Old Town Rd. to the end, turn Right onto Gnarled Hollow Rd., the farm is the 2nd house on the Right, turn into the 3rd driveway for parking, if there is no parking in lot, park along the street* www.bennersfarm.com

Spring Festival ⓑ • *Old Bethpage Village Restoration* • **NC** • *1303 Round Swamp Rd., Bethpage, NY* • *516-572-8400* • *572-8401* • Features Include: 209-acre Park, Living History Museum, Mid-19th-Cent. Long Island Village, Homes, Farms, Businesses, Educational Programs, Old Time Baseball Games, the Noon Inn Serves Pretzels & Root Beer, See: Chickens, Cows, Sheep, Oxen, Pigs at the Powel Farm **Hours:** 10 a.m.-5 p.m. **Fee:** Adults: $4, Kids: $3, Seniors: $2 **Directions:** *I-495 Long Island Expwy., take exit 48 Round Swamp Rd. toward Old Bethpage/Farmingdale, make a Left onto Round Swamp Rd., turn Left onto Old Country Rd., slight Right at Round Swamp Rd.* www.oldbethpage.org

ST. PATRICKS DAY

Huntington's Annual St. Patricks Day Parade • Start Time: 2 p.m. **Parade Path:** Formation at the Big H, heads North along New York Ave., then turns West onto Main St. & ends at St. Patrick's Church **Fee:** *Free* www.huntingtonhibernians.com

Ward Melville Heritage Organization Educational & Cultural Center • *Stony Brook, NY* • *Reservations Required: 631-689-5888* • Features Include: Entertainment, Irish

FUN FAMILY

Soda Bread Competition, Irish Dance, Interactive Dance Participation, Craft Activitiy for Children, Irish Soda Bread & Tea, Boutique **Fee:** Adults: $13, Under 10: $10, Seniors: $12 **Directions:** *I-495 Long Island Expwy., take exit 62 County Rd. 97 N., to the end, turn Left onto 25A, see "Historic Stony Brook" sign, 1.5 mi. to Main St., turn Right .25 mi. into Stony Brook Village Center & WMHO Educational & Cultural Center parking*

www.wmho.org/WMHOEventCalendar.asp

Bayport/Blue Point's Annual St. Patrick's Day Parade • **Start Time:** 11:30 a.m. **Parade Path:** From Snedecor Ave. to Blue Point Ave. along Montauk Hwy., usually entertains 25,000 onlookers **Fee: Free**

www.sayville.com/news.asp

Bay Shore/Brightwater's Annual St. Patrick's Day Parade • **Features Include:** Bagpipe Bands, Fire Department Bands, Brass Bands, Horses, Antique Cars, Floats, Clowns **Start Time:** Noon **Parade Path:** Starts at Saxon Ave. & travels West onto Main St. (Montauk Hwy.) 1.6 mi. to St. Patrick's Church, 9 N. Clinton Ave., Bay Shore & viewing stand **Fee: Free**

www.saintpatricksdayparade.com/bay_shore/index.htm

Rockville Centre's Annual St. Patrick's Day Parade • *265 Sunrise Hwy., Ste. 1-350, Rockville Centre, NY* • **Start Time:** Noon **Parade Path.:** Sunrise Hwy. in Rockville Centre, Franklin Ave. & Old Country Rd. **Fee: Free**

www.rvcchamber.org

Garden City/Mineola's Annual St. Patrick's Day Parade • This is the oldest St. Patrick's Day parade on Long Island. **Start Time:** Noon **Parade Rte.:** Formation at 9th St. & Kellum Ave., follows Franklin Ave. & Old Country Rd. **Fee: Free**

www.gcnews.com

Patchogue's St. Patrick's Day Parade • *631-475-0121* Patchogue Chamber of Commerce • **Start Time:** 11 a.m. **Parade Path:** Main St., Patchogue **Fee: Free**

www.patchoguechamber.com

Glen Cove's St. Patrick's Day Parade • **Start Time:** 1 p.m. **Parade Path:** Forms at the Finley Middle School, Forest Ave. S. of Dosoris Ln., follows Brewster St., to School St., to Glen St., follows Glen St. to the end, parade ends at St. Patrick's Church, which is located at the corner of Glen St. & Pearsall Ave. **Parking:** Glen Cove Parking Garage on Brewster St., Free staging area shuttle bus, or St. Patrick's Church parking lot, or multilevel parking garages behind School St. & Glen St. viewing areas, the garages on the North side of School St. may be entered from Brewster St. & the garages on the South side can be entered from Glen St., both parking areas give easy access to the School St. & Glen St. viewing areas **Fee: Free** parking

www.glencoveirish.org

Hampton Bay's St. Patrick's Day Parade • *72 Ponquogue Ave., Hampton Bays, NY* • **Start Time:** 11 a.m. **Parade Path:** Formation at The Hampton Bays Elementary School, 72 Ponquogue Ave. **Fee: Free**

www.kjoy.com/pages/6311701.php

SPRING BLISS

Montauk's Annual St. Patrick's Day Parade • *Main St., Montauk, NY* • Features Include: Prizes offered for best floats: 1st place: $500, 2nd place: $250, 3rd place: $100 Start Time: 12:30 p.m. **Parade Path:** The parade begins at the firehouse across from the LIRR station & continues through town on Main St. **Fee: Free**

www.montaukfriendsoferin.com/parade.htm

Westhampton Beach's St. Patrick's Day Parade • *Westhampton Beach, NY* • *631-560-6392* • **Features Include:** Awards for Floats, Classic Cars, Vintage British Tank, Horses, Fire Dept., Scouts **Fee: Free**   *www.whbstpats.com*

Rocky Point's Annual St. Patrick's Day Parade • *631 744 - 2502* • Start Time: 1 p.m. **Parade Path:** Formation at the intersection of Harrison Ave. & Rte. 25A in Miller Pl. & continues along Rte. 25A to Broadway in Rocky Point **Fee: Free**

saintpatricksdayparade.com/rocky_point/index.htm

EASTER EGG EVENTS

Easter Egg Spectacular • *White Post Farm* • *250 Old Country Rd., Melville, NY* • *631-351-9373* • **Features Include**: Indoor Animal Farm, Beautiful Tribute to Spring Decorations, Meet the Easter Bunny, Craft Station, Create-A-Cookie Crafts, Super-Sized Easter Egg Decorating including Goose, Australian Emu & African Ostrich, Indoor Pony Rides & Train Rides, Indoor Playground, Giant Indoor Sandbox Area, Singing Chicken Show, Outdoor Playground, Giant Pirate Ship Playground, Children's Wooden Village, Farm Market, Download Discount Coupons **Hours:** Fri.-Sun.: 10 a.m.-5 p.m. **Fee:** Adults & Kids: $7, Pony Rides: $5, Feed Cones: $1, Train Ride: $2, Mining: $6.50 **Directions:** *Northern State Pkwy., take exit 40 S. Rte. 110 S., turn Left onto Old Country Rd., .25 mi. on the Right*   *www.whitepostfarms.com*

Spring Egg Hunt • *Belmont Lake State Park* • *North Babylon, NY* • *631-321-3510* • **Features Include:** Egg Hunt, Age Groups: 4 & Under, 5-6 yrs., 7-9 yrs., Live Animals, Temporary Tattoos, Pony Rides, Giveaways **Hours**: Noon, the weekend before Easter **Fee: Free** Directions: *Southern State Pkwy. to exit 38, brings you into the park*

Spring Egg Hunt • *Sponsor: Natural Heritage Trust* • *Orient Beach State Park* • *Orient, NY* • *631-323-2440* • **Features Include:** Egg Hunt, Prizes, Refreshments, Open to All Ages **Hours:** Starts at 1 p.m., the weekend before Easter **Fee: Free** Directions: *I-495 Long Island Expwy., exit onto W. Main St./Middle Country Rd./NY-25 E. toward Riverhead, follow W. Main St./NY-25 E., turn Right onto Main Rd./NY-25 E., follow NY-25 E., turn Left at Main St./NY-25 E., turn Right onto Main Rd./NY-25 E., slight Right onto N. Rd., N. Rd. turns slightly Right & becomes State Pkwy., the park will be on the Left*

Annual Easter Parade & Easter Bonnet Festival • *5th Ave. from 49th to 57th Sts., NY, NY* • **Activities Include:** This is an International People Watching Event, See Elegant & Outrageous Outfits, Costumed Pets, Outfits Accented with Live Animals, Civil War Period Costumes, High Fashion Costumes, Easter Bonnets to the New York City Extreme, "Paraders" Wander along 5th Ave. from 49th to 57th Sts., 5th Ave. is closed to traffic between theses points. The area around St. Patrick's Cathedral is the ideal place to see the parade. **Hours:** 10 a.m.-4 p.m., Easter Sun. **Fee: Free Directions:** *LIRR to Penn Station, walk up 5th Ave. to 51st St., or take the E. train to 5th Ave. & 53rd St., or take the C to 50th St. & 8th Ave.*

http://gonyc.about.com/cs/holidays/a/easter.htm

Eggstreme Weekend at the Bronx Zoo • *2300 Southern Blvd., Bronx, NY* • *718-367-1010* • **Activities Include:** Meet Bunny Mascot Bella, Crafts, Egg Races, Egg Hunt **Hours:** Sat.-Sun.: 10 a.m.-4:30 p.m., mid-March event **Fee:** Adults: $15, Kids 3-12: $11, Seniors: $13, Eggstreme Activities are included with the cost of zoo admission **Directions:** *I-495 Long Island Expwy., take exit 31N. Cross Island Pkwy., take exit 33 & merge onto I-295 N. toward New England, exit onto I-95 S. take exit 4B toward Bronx River Pkwy./Rosedale Ave., take the Cross Bronx Expwy., turn Right onto Rosedale Ave., turn Left onto E. Tremont Ave., turn Right onto Southern Blvd., the zoo will be on the Right. Or take the Whitestone Bridge to Hutchinson River Pkwy. N. to Pelham Pkwy. W., follow Pelham Pkwy. W. for 2 mi. & turn Left on Boston Rd. (just after passing under the train). turn Right at light, the zoo's Bronx River entrance (Gate B) is located directly ahead after the underpass*

www.bronxzoo.com

Annual Easter Bonnet Competition • *The Minskoff Theatre* • *200 W. 45th St., NY, NY* • *212-869-0550* • *Order Tickets: 212-840-0770, ext. 268* • **Activities Include:** Parade of Bonnets (hand-crafted by the cast & crews of dozens of participating productions), Presented in Song, Dance, Comedic Sketches, Proceeds Benefit Broadway, Off-Broadway & Touring Theatre Companies **Hours:** Usually the weekend before Easter Sun. **Fee:** $20-$350 **Directions:** *LIRR to Penn Station, take the 3 train toward 148th St., get off at Time Square-42nd St., walk to 45th St.*

www.minskofftheatre.com

Easter Egg Hunt • *Brightwaters Farms & Nursery* • *162 Manatuck Blvd., Bay Shore, NY* • *631-665-5411* • **Features Include:** Go Inside the Heated Greenhouse **Hours:** 10 a.m.-4 p.m., 2 weekends before Easter **Fee:** $5 per child, download a discount coupon **Directions:** *Southern State Pkwy., take exit 42 S., turn Right off the exit ramp onto Spur Dr. S., take Spur Drive S., turn Right onto Manatuck Blvd.(at traffic light), proceed North on Manatuck Blvd. Brightwaters Farms will be on the Left .5 mi. up the road*

www.brightwatersfarms.com

April

Spring Family Freshwater Fishing Festival • *Belmont Lake State Park* • *631-321-3510* • *I Fish NY: 631-444-0283* • **Features Include:** Freshwater Fishing, Outdoor Education, Children's Raffle Prizes, Spring Fling Casting Contest, Fly Fishing Instructions, Temporary Tattoos, Educational Seminars, Open Fishing, Demonstrations, Cleaning of Catch, Free Bait & Looner Fishing Rods, Outdoor Exhibits from Local Fishing Clubs, No Angler's License Needed to Participate **Hours:** 10 a.m.-4 p.m., 2nd weekend in April **Fee: Free**, $6 parking fee or Empire Pass Accepted **Directions:** *Southern State Pkwy. to exit 38, exits into the park*

Benner's Farm, Baby Barn Yard Weekend • *56 Gnarled Hollow Rd., Setauket, NY* • *631-689-8172* • *631-689-8172* • This farm dates back to the 1700s. **Hours:** Weekends: 12-4 p.m. **Fee:** Adult: $6, Kids: $5 **Directions:** *I-495 Long Island Expwy., take exit 62, Nicoll's Rd. N./Co. Rd. 97, follow Nicoll's Rd. to the end (cross Rte. 25, Rte. 347 & Stony Brook Univ.), turn Right on Rte. 25A E., at the 5th light turn Right onto Old Town Rd., drive 2.5 blocks to the end, turn Right onto Gnarled Hollow Rd., farm is on the Right, use the 3rd driveway for parking, if there is no parking in lot park along the street* www.bennersfarm.com

Lighthouse Tract Trek • *Fire Island Lighthouse* • *Fire Island National Seashore* • *Robert Moses State Park* • *Fire Island, NY* • *Reservations Required: 631-661-4876* • The Fire Island Lighthouse is located within the Fire Island National Seashore & is an active aid to navigation. **Features Include:** Guided Walk around Historic Surrounding area of the Lighthouse **Hours:** Grounds & Lighthouse are open Year-Round, Tours **Fee: Free** grounds & museum, Tower: Adults: $5, Kids: $3.50, Seniors: $4, Parking: $6 (in state park), Empire Pass Accepted, Handicap Accessible grounds & museum, Bathrooms in parking lot & museum **Directions:** *Southern State Pkwy., exit 40 Robert Moses Cswy. S., toward Robert Moses State Park, get to the park drive around the water tower, head East, park in the East end of Field 5, walk on the boardwalk to the lighthouse* www.fireislandlighthouse.com

MoCCA Art Festival • *Puck Building 594 Broadway, Ste. 401* • *NY, NY* • *212-254-3511* • **Features Include:** Comics Books, Cartoonists Art Show **Hours:** Sat.-Sun.: mid.-April **Fee:** Adults: $5, Under 13: Free **Directions:** *LIRR to Penn Station, B or D train to Broadway/Laffayette St. station, the museum is between Houston St. & Prince St.* www.moccany.com

EARTH DAY

Annual Earth Day Celebration • *Indian Island County Park & Country Club* • *Cross River Dr., Rte. 105, Riverhead NY* • *631-845-4949* • **Features Include:** Interactive Exhibits, Nature Walks, Beach Grass Planting, Live Entertainment, Trail Clean-Ups,

Marine Life Exhibits, Activities for Kids, Face Painting, Wildlife Demonstrations, Kayak Demonstrations **Hours:** 10 a.m.-4 p.m., last weekend in April **Fee: Free Directions:** *I-495 Long Island Expwy., exit onto W. Main St./Middle Country Rd./25 E. toward Riverhead, continue to follow W./Main St./25 E., turn Right onto Hubbard Ave., turn Right onto Indian Point Rd., take the the 3rd Left onto Dredging Pond Rd.*

Eco-Friendly Fun • *The Nassau County Museum of Art, 1 Museum Dr., Roslyn Harbor, NY* • *516-484-9338* • *Registration Required* • Features Include: Family Workshop for Ages 6 & Up, Guided Nature Trail Tour, Finding Ideas/Materials & Inspiration, Hands-On Workshop, Eco-Friendly Art Making, Collage, Rubbings, Printmaking, Using Natural/Found & Recycled Materials **Hours:** 10 a.m.-12:30 p.m., last weekend in April **Fee:** Adults & Kids: $35, Additional Kids: $10, Members: $25, fee includes materials, Parking: $2 weekends only **Directions:** *I-495 Long Island Expwy., take exit 39 Glen Cove Rd. N., turn Left onto Northern Blvd./25A, drive 1.5 blocks & turn Right onto Museum Dr.*

www.nassaumuseum.org • click on Events/Lectures & Trips

Earthstock Festival • *Stony Brook University* • *100 Nicolls Rd., Stony Brook, NY* • *Festival Programing: 631-632-7320, Southampton Events: 631-632-5132* • Features Include: Campus-Wide Public Event, Environmental Art, Environmental Sculpture, Environmental Dance, Environmental Music, Rubber Duck Races, Ice Cream Social, Green Drinks, Environmental Organization Exhibits, Earth-Friendly Message, Student Research Exhibits, Blue Ocean Institute Exhibit, Local Schools Celebrate on the Academic Mall, Environmental History/Population & Cultural Issues **Hours:** Sat.: 11 a.m-3 p.m. **Fee: Free Directions:** *Northern State Pkwy. to exit 45 toward Sunken Meadow Pkwy. N., merge onto Sagtikos Pkwy., continue onto Sunken Meadow Pkwy., take exit SM3E. for 25 E./Jericho Tpke. toward Smithtown, turn Right onto Jericho Tpke./NY-25 E., continue to follow NY-25 E., turn Left onto 25A E./Nissequogue River Rd./River Rd., follow 25A E. onto Long Hill Rd./Stony Brook Rd., turn Left onto South Dr., turn Left onto County Rd. 97 N./Nicolls Rd., the University will be on the Right*

www.stonybrook.edu • *www.stonybrook.edu/sb/earthstock*

Coastal Clean-Up Volunteer Day • *The Theodore Roosevelt Wildlife Sanctuary & Audubon Center & the Town of Oyster Bay coastal clean-up in celebration of Earth Day* • *West End Ave., Oyster Bay, NY* • *516-624-6202* • *516-922-3200* • Features Include: Kids & Parents, Beach Clean-Up, Bring Work Gloves, Volunteer Opportunity **Hours:** Starts at 9 a.m., rain or shine, last Sat. in April **Fee: Free Directions:** *Northern State Pkwy., exit onto N. Broadway 106/107 N., slight Right onto106 N., turn Left onto W. Main St., turn Right onto Bayside Ave., take the 3rd Left onto Westend Ave.*

www.oysterbaytown.com

Earth Day Celebration • *Long Island Children's Museum* • *1 Davis Ave., Garden City, NY* • *516-224-5800* • **Features Include:** Fun Activities, Learn Ways to Keep the Earth Clean, Create Crafts from Recyclables, Celebrate Our Beautiful Planet, All Ages Welcome **Hours:** Noon-4 p.m. **Fee: Free** with museum admission **Directions:** *Northern State Pkwy., take the Meadowbrook Pkwy. S. to exit M4 (Nassau Coliseum), bear Right (before Hempstead Tpke.) onto Charles Lindbergh Blvd., go to the 1ˢᵗ traffic light (Nassau Coliseum on your left, Nassau Community College on your Right, proceed through this traffic light & continue on to LICM on the Right side of the road* www.licm.org

Earth Day • *Vanderbilt Museum* • *180 Little Neck Rd., Centerport, NY* • *631-854-5555* • **Features Include:** Family Day, Earth Month Coloring Contest, Poster Competition, Hands-On Touch Tables, Natural History Specimens, Planetarium Shows, Arts & Crafts Workshops, there will be a small fee for planetarium shows & mansion tours **Fee: Free** to all contest entrants & their families (entrants must bring their coloring books to Family Day for free admission) **Directions:** *Northern State Pkwy., take exit 42N., drive North on Deer Park Ave., bear Left at the fork (at traffic light), onto Park Ave., at the 3ʳᵈ light, turn Right onto Broadway, drive 4-5 mi. to Rte. 25A, Cross 25A (to left of Centerport Automotive), & you are on Little Neck Rd., the museum is 1.5 mi. on the Right* www.vanderbiltmuseum.org

NATIONAL PARK WEEK

National Park Week-Junior Ranger Day ⊛ • *Fire Island Lighthouse* • *Robert Moses State Park* • *Fire Island ,NY* • *631-661-4876* • **Features Include:** Ranger-led Program, Kids 7 & Up, Completion of the Junior Ranger Booklet Earns Kids a Patch **Hours:** 11 a.m.-4 p.m., late April event **Fee: Free Directions:** *Southern State Pkwy., take exit 40 Robert Moses Cswy. S. toward Robert Moses State Park, get to the park & drive around the water tower, head East, park in the East end of Field 5, walk on the boardwalk to the lighthouse* http://fireislandlighthouse.com

NATIONAL ASTRONOMY DAY

Astronomy Day • *Vanderbilt Museum* • *180 Little Neck Rd., Centerport, NY* • *631-854-5579* • *631-854-5555* • **Features Include:** Family Day, Planetarium Astronomy Shows, Model Rocketry Demonstrations, Safe Sun Viewing through Solar Telescopes, Planetarium Astronomy Shows, Sky Talks, Children's Games, Craft Projects, Astronomy & Space Storytelling, Telescope Demonstrations, Night Sky Observing with Telescopes, 15 Telescopes Focused on Specific Stars, Live Sky Talk, Laser Show, Camera Concepts, the Astronomical Society of Long Island, LI Advanced Rocketry Society **Hours:** 11 a.m.-Midnight **Fee: Free** to all contest entrants & their families **Directions:** *Northern State Pkwy., take exit 42N., drive North on Deer Park Ave., bear Left at the fork (at traffic light), onto Park Ave., at the 3ʳᵈ light, turn Right onto Broadway, drive 4-5 mi. to Rte. 25A, cross 25A (to left of Centerport Automotive), & you are on Little Neck Rd., the museum is 1.5 mi. on the Right* www.vanderbiltmuseum.org

May

Mayday Festival • *Benner's Farm* • *56 Gnarled Hollow Rd., Setauket, NY* • *631-689-8172* • *631 689-8172* • **Features Include:** This Historic 1700s Farm offers a Special Kids Day Programs during the month of May. **Hours:** Weekends: Noon-4 p.m. **Fee:** Adults: $6, Kids: $5 **Directions:** *I-495 Long Island Expwy., take exit 62 Nicoll's Rd. N./County Rd. 97, follow Nicoll's to the end, (cross Rte. 25 & Rte. 347 & Stony Brook Univ.), turn Right onto 25A E., go 5 traffic lights, at the 5th light (Apple Savings Bank on corner) turn Right onto Old Town Rd., take Old Town Rd. to the end, turn Right onto Gnarled Hollow Rd., the farm is the 2nd house on the Right, turn into the 3rd driveway for parking, if there is no parking in lot park along the street*   *www.bennersfarm.com*

Annual Tulip Festival • *Heckscher Park, Huntington, NY* • *631-351-3099* • *Presented by the Town of Huntington in cooperation with various community agencies* • **Features Include:** Hands-On Children's Activity Booths, Family Performances on the Chapin Rainbow Stage, Art Exhibitions, Lectures, Demonstrations, Refreshments, Face Painting, Crafts, Planting Activities, Music, Dance, Books, Shows, Photo Contest, Sales Booths, Over 20,000 Tulips **Hours:** 11 a.m.-4 p.m., *1st* Sat. in May **Fee:** **Free** **Directions:** *I-495 Long Island Expwy., exit Rte. 110 N. toward Huntington Village, turn Right onto Rte. 25A East, to next traffic signal at Prime Ave., park is in the NE Corner*

http://town.huntington.ny.us

Annual Sheep-to-Shawl Festival ☺ • *Kissam House & Barn* • *434 Park Ave., Huntington, NY* • *Presented by the Huntington Historical Society* • *516-427-7045* • **Features Include:** Old-Fashioned Fun, Children's Games, Sheep Shearing Demonstrations, Blacksmithing Demonstrations, Folk Music Society Performances, Petting Zoo, Spinning, Weaving, Crafts, Games, Scavenger Hunt, Food, Music **Hours:** 11 a.m.-4 p.m., *1st* weekend in May **Fee:** Adults: $2, Kids: 75¢ **Directions:** *I-495 Long Island Expwy. to exit Rte. 110 N. toward Huntington Village, turn Right onto Rte. 25A E.*

Festival Of Cultures • *Sponsored by Green Meadow Farms* • *7350 Little Neck Pkwy., Floral Park, NY* • *718-470-0224* • *800-336-6233* • This event takes place at several Long Island locations during April & May. **Features Include:** Outdoor Program, First-Hand Experience with Wildlife, Gain Understanding of Many Cultures, Dance with Native Americans/Spanish Americans/West Africans, Watch the Birds of Prey Soar through the Sky **Hours:** opens May **Directions:** *Northern State Pkwy. to the Grand Central Pkwy., take exit 24 Little Neck Pkwy., turn Left onto Little Neck Pkwy.*

www.visitgreenmeadowsfarm.com

The Long Island Lighthouse Challenge • **Features Include:** The challenge is to visit the following lighthouses in 2 days: Fire Island, Montauk Point, Cedar Island, East End Seaport, Long Beach Bar, Orient Point, Plum Island, Horton Point, Old Field Point, Eaton's Neck & Huntington Harbor. It is helpful to bring a large Hagstrom Road Map & a copy of *Long Island's Lighthouses: Past and Present*. Directions tips for the challenge can be found on the web site. Check out the Lighthouse section in this book for locations, driving directions & phone numbers of the various lighthouses. **Hours:** Challenge Weekend: 8 a.m.-6 p.m., mid-May, please check the web site & print out what you will need. It is a great day. Finish the Maryland Challenge in Sept. & the New Jersey Challenge in Oct. Present proof of completion of all 3 Challenges at your last stop during the New Jersey event to receive a Triple Crown Award! **Fee: Free**

www.lilighthousesociety.org

39*th* **Annual Heritage Fair** • *Park Ave. & Ireland Pl., Amityville Village, NY* • *631-598-1486* • *631-264-1866* • *Sponsored By the Amityville Historical Society* • *631-598-1486* • **Hours:** mid-May **Features Include:** Historic Trolley Tours, Raffle Prizes, White Elephant Sale, Food & Beverage Tents **Hours:** 10 a.m.-5 p.m. **Fee: Free** **Directions:** *Southern State Pkwy., exit onto Broadway/NY-110 S., turn Right onto Ireland Pl.*

www.amityvillehistoricalsociety.com

Nautical Festival • *Long Island Maritime Museum* • *86 West Ave., West Sayville, NY* • *631-447-8679* • Features Include: Vintage & New Boats, Regattas, Antique & Classic Engines **Hours:** Sat.-Sun.: 10 a.m.-4 p.m., mid-May **Fee:** Adults: $4, Kids: $2 **Directions:** *I-495 Long Island Expwy., take exit 59 South-Ocean/Lakeland Ave., bear Left at the fork where Ocean & Lakeland divide, follow Lakeland into the village of Sayville, about 6 mi., turn Right onto Main St. (Montauk Hwy./Rte. 27A/CR85), follow Main St. West through Sayville about 1 mi., 2 blocks past the West Sayville Fire Department turn Left onto West Ave., turn Left onto West Ave., going South about .25 mi., the entrance to the Museum is on the Right* *www.limaritime.org*

HORSES

Fun Family Day • *Belmont Park Race Track* • *2150 Hempstead Tpke., Elmont, NY* • *718-641-4700* • **Features Include:** Belmont Backyard & Picnic Area, Games, Pony Rides, Petting Zoo, Face Painting, Giant Inflatables, Special Weekly Activities, Past Themes: Speedway Challenge, Crazy Maze, Mime Shows, Mini Golf Course, Weekly Theme Inflatables **Hours:** 1*st* Sun. in May-last Sun. in July **Fee:** All Family Fun Day activities are **Free**, Pony Rides: $1 donation, General Admission: $2, Under 13: Free **Directions:** *Northern State Pkwy., take NY-135 Seaford-Oyster Bay Expwy. S., take exit 4W. Southern State Pkwy. W., take exit 26B Cross Island Pkwy., exit onto Hempstead Tpke./NY-24, the track will be on the Left* *www.nyra.com*

MEMORIAL DAY

Annual Jones Beach Air Show Ⓥ • *Jones Beach State Park* • *South of Wantagh, NY* • *516-785-1600* • Features Include: US Navy Blue Angels Jet Team, Civilian & Military Aerobatic Performers, Show Tips: Arrive Early, Wear Beach Attire, Bring Warm Clothes (in case of temperature changes), Glasses, Sunscreen, Beach Towels, Chairs, check the web site for last minute news items & updates **Hours:** 10 a.m.-3 p.m., last 2 weekends in May **Fee:** Empire Pass Accepted **Directions:** *Northern State Pkwy., to the Meadowbrook Pkwy. S. or Wantagh Pkwy. S. to the park* 　　　　　　*www.jonesbeachairshow.com*

Craft As Art Festival • *Nassau County Museum of Art* • *1 Museum Dr., Roslyn Harbor, NY* • *516-484-9338* • *516-484-9337* • Features Includes: National Craft Displays, Entertainment, Craft Demonstrations, Shearing of Live Alpacas, Exotic & Natural Foods **Hours:** Sat.: 11 a.m.-6 p.m., Sun.: 10 a.m.-6 p.m., mid-May **Directions:** *I-495 Long Island Expwy., take exit 39 Glen Cove Rd. N., turn Left onto Northern Blvd./25A, drive 1.5 blocks & turn Right onto Museum Dr.*

　　　　　　　　　　www.nassaumuseum.com • *www.craftatlincoln.org*

Concert Series at Coe Hall • *Planting Fields Arboretum* • *Oyster Bay, NY* • *516-922-9210* • *516-922-8600* • *516-922-9210* • Features Include: Tudor-Style Manor House, Limited Seating, Museum, Chamber Music **Hours:** vary per performance **Fee:** Per Ticket: $35, Parking: $6, May-Oct., Empire Pass Accepted **Directions:** *Northern State Pkwy., take the exit toward N. Broadway/107 N., turn Right onto N. Broadway/107 N., follow 107 N., turn Right at Wheatley Rd., slight Left at Brookville Rd., continue onto Wolver Hollow Rd., turn Right at Chicken Valley Rd., take the 3rd Right onto Planting Fields Rd.* 　　*www.plantingfields.org*

Bird Walk • *Fire Island Lighthouse* • *Reservations Required: 631-661-4876* • Features Include: Guided Birdwalk around the Lighthouse, Light Keepers Behind the Scenes Tour, Follow a Lighthouse Keeper on his/her Rounds, Top-To-Bottom Tour, from the Beacon in the Lantern Room of the Lighthouse to the Auxiliary Generator in the Basement of the Keeper's Quarters **Hours:** Open Year Round, meet at the Keepers Quarters, May event **Fee: Free Directions:** *Southern State Pkwy., exit 40 Robert Moses Cswy. S., towards Robert Moses State Park, get to the park, drive around the water tower, head East, park in the East end of Field 5, walk on the boardwalk to the lighthouse www.fireislandlighthouse.com*

U-PICK STRAWBERRIES, ASPARAGUS & MORE

Spring: April, May, June
Strawberries: May-June
Asparagus: May

See Summer for U-Pick locations & Information on page: 226

www.longisland.com/fruit_picking.php

www.pickyourown.org

Adventure Land • *2245 Rte. 110 Farmingdale, NY* • *631-694-6868* • *Birthday Party Info: 631-694-6300, 516-694-6868* • **Features Include:** 7 Thrill Rides: Hurricane Coaster, Pirate Ship, Silvers Twister, Bumper Cars, Haunted House, 9 Family Rides, 4 Water Rides, 10 Kiddie Rides, over 300 Video & Other Games, Restaurant, Gift Shops **Hours:** March-Oct.: opens at Noon on weekends, July & Aug.: Weekdays at 11 a.m., June: Some weekdays: 10 a.m. **Fees:** P.O.P bracelet (unlimited rides) 48-in. & over: $21.99, Under 48-in.: $19.99, Individual Tickets: $1 each (most rides are 3-5 tickets), Birthday Parties **Directions:** *I-495 Long Island Expwy., take the Rte. 110 S. exit, the park will be on the Left*   www.adventureland.us

Bayville Adventure Park • *8 Bayville Ave., Bayville, NY* • *516-624-7433* Features Include: 5-acre Pirate-Themed Amusement Park, High-Wire Rope Course, Low-Speed Bumper Boats, 19-hole Miniature Golf Course, Rock Climbing, Super Slides, Arcade, Inflatables, Skating Adventure, Lost Adventure Maze, Train Ride **Hours:** Mon.-Thurs.: 11a.m.-10 p.m., Fri.-Sat.: 10 a.m.-11 p.m., Sun.: 10 a.m.-10 p.m., open as long as weather permits **Fee:** Unlimited Usage Ticket: $39.50, 3 Attraction Usage: $23.50, 5 Attraction Usage: $28.50, 6 Attraction usage: $31.50, Single Attraction Usage: ranges from $5-$10 **Directions:** *I-495 Long Island Expwy., take exit 41 N., State Hwy. 106/107 N., follow Rte. 106 N., turn Left onto W. Main St., becomes W. Shore Rd., go over the Bayville Bridge, & continue on Ludlam Ave., turn Left onto Bayville Ave., make a U-turn continue to #8*

www.bayvilleadventurepark.com

Boomers Family Fun Park • *655 Long Island Ave., Medford, NY* • *631- 475-1771* • **Features Include:** Cartoon Theme Park, Indoor Carousel, Kiddie Swing, Restaurant,

Animated Show, 70 Redemption & Ride Games, Outdoor Mini Golf (18 holes), 6 Outdoor Kiddie Rides, Bumper Boats, 7 Outdoor Batting Cages, Go-Karts, Outdoor Facilities open weather permitting **Hours:** 11 a.m., close time varies **Fees:** Per Game Token: 25¢, Go-Karts: $5, Mini Golf: $4.25 per game, Batting Cages: $2, Rides: $3.25, Bumper Boats: $4.50, Pay-One-Price: $15.95 **Directions:** *I-495 Long Island Expwy., take exit 64, get on the S. Service Rd., the park is .5 mi. on the Right side of the road* www.boomersparks.com

Chuck E Cheese • **Features Include:** Indoor Complex, Mini-Kiddie Rides (ages 2-11), Ball Crawl, Video Games, Skee Ball, Air Hockey, Restaurant, Handicap Accessible **Hours:** Sun.-Thur.: 10 a.m.-10 p.m., Fri.-Sat.: 10 a.m.-11 p.m. **Fees:** Games & Rides: 25¢ each **Directions:** contact individual locations
155 Sunrise Highway, West Islip, NY • 631-376-1800
11 Hanover Pl., Hicksville, NY • 516-433-3343
2115 Jericho Tpke., Commack, NY • 631-864-5434
62 Fulton Ave., Hempstead, NY • 516-483-3166
121 Sunrise Hwy., Patchogue, NY • 631-654-9373

www.chuckecheese.com

The County Fair Entertainment Park ☻ • *3351 Rte. 112, Medford, NY* • *631-732-0579* • **Features Include:** Mini-Golf (1 of the most elaborate & beautiful golf courses in the country), Driving Range, Batting Cages, Go-Kart Track, Go-Kart Racing Features Include: Realistic Racing Environment, Huge Figure-8 Race Track, Single & Double Go-Karts **Hours:** March-Nov. weather permitting **Fee:** Mini Golf: $6.50 per person per game, Go-Karts: Kids: $5.50, Adult: $6 per ride, Height Requirement: 55-in. tall to Drive Intermediate, 60-in. tall to drive Adult Car, Under 55-in. tall must drive w/licensed driver Free **Directions:** *I-495 Long Island Expwy., take exit 64 N. 1 mi., go to the crossroads of Granny & Horseblock* www.countryfairpark.com

Dave & Busters • **Features Include:** Dining & Entertainment Complex, Video Games, Bowling, Video Cafe & Bar with 8 flat screen TVs & 3 giant screen projectors **Hours:** Mon.-Wed., Sun.: 11:30 a.m.-11 p.m., Thurs.: 11:30 a.m.12 a.m., Fri.-Sat.: 11:30 a.m.-2 a.m.
261 Airport Plaza Blvd., Farmingdale, NY• 631-249-0708
Mall at the Source Old Country Rd., Westbury, NY • 516-542-8501
1856 Veterans Memorial Hwy., Islandia, NY • 631-582-6615

www.daveandbusters.com

Fun4All • *200 Wilson St., Port Jefferson Station, NY* • *631-331-9000* • **Features Include:** Indoor Entertainment Area, Slides & Towers, Rock Wall Climb, Basketball Court, Ball Pits & Tunnels, Preschool Play Areas, Quiet Area, Huge Sand Room, Game

Room, Snack Bar, Birthday Parties **Hours:** 10 a.m.-8 p.m. daily **Fees:** Kids 2-12: $7.99 unlimited play, Adults: Free, weekly admission specials **Directions:** *I-495 Long Island Expwy., take exit 64 Rte. 112 N. to Port Jefferson Station, pass the intersection of 347, make a Left onto Wilson St., 1 block past the RR Tracks*   *www.fun4all-ny.com*

Fun Station USA • *40 Rocklyn Ave., Lynbrook, NY* • *516-599-7757* • Features Include: Indoor Park, Kiddie Rides, Bumper Cars, Lazer Tag, Playport Maze, Bowling, Red Baron & Safari Jeep, Animated Stage Show, Food Court **Hours:** Sun.-Thur.: 11: a.m.-9 p.m., Fri.-Sat.: 11 a.m.-11 p.m. **Fee:** $1 for 4 game tokens, Bowling: $2, Attraction Tokens: $1, Pay-One-Price Rides: $5.95-$7.95 weekdays, $7.95-$10.95 weekends **Directions:** *Southern State Pkwy., take exit 19 S. Peninsula Blvd., make a Left onto Ocean Ave., 1ˢᵗ light turn Right onto Merrick Rd., 1ˢᵗ Left onto Rocklyn Ave., see sign for Fun Station*

www.funstationfun.com

Nathan's & Fun Zone • *229 Rte. 110, Farmingdale, NY* • *631-847-0100* • Features **Include:** Indoor-Outdoor Family Amusement Center, Outdoor Thrill Rides, Lazer Tag, Rock Climbing Wall, Kiddie Rides, Bowling, Carousel, Jungle Climb, Bumper Cars, over 100 Games, Rides & Attractions are for all ages **Hours:** Mon.-Thur.: 11 a.m.-10 p.m., Fri.: 11:00 a.m.-Midnight, Sat.: 10 a.m.-Midnight, Sun.: 10 a.m.-10 p.m., open Year-Round rain or shine **Fees:** Tokens: $1 for 4 game tokens, Action Token: $1 each, Pay-One-Price Rides: $8.95-$13.95 **Directions:** *I-495 Long Island Expwy., take the Rte. 110 exit S. or Southern State Pkwy., take exit 32 N., .13 mi. on the Right*   www.funzoneamusements.com

NY Party Zone • *1270 Broad Hollow Rd., Farmingdale, NY* • *516-694-0079* • *888- 538-7586* • Features Include: Open Play on Fridays, Inflatable Rides & Slides, Interactive Obstacle Course, Crazy Cow Soft Mechanical Bull Ride, 28-ft. Inflatable Volcano **Hours & Fee:** Open Play Times: Fri.: $10 from 11 a.m-2 p.m., Fri. Night: $15 from 5:30-8:30 p.m., Sat.: $15 from 8-11 p.m., Mon.- Fri.: Start Times from 10 a.m.- Noon & 1-3 p.m. **Directions:** *Northern State Pkwy., take exit 40 S. to Rte. 110, the NY Party Zone will be on the Right*   www.nypartyzone.com

Port Jefferson Raceway • *1075 Portion Rd., Ste. 20, Farmingville, NY* • *631- 696- 7721* • Features Include: Indoor Race Tracks, Smart Kids Race Free Program **Hours:** Tues.-Fri.: 1-10 p.m., Sat.: 11 a.m.-9 p.m., Sun.: 11 a.m.-6 p.m. **Directions:** *I-495 Long Island Expwy., take exit 62 Nichols Rd., take Nichols Rd. N. approx. .5 mi., take the Portion Rd. exit (heading West on Portion), the store is on the Right-hand side in the Tiffany Plaza about .5 mi. down Portion Rd.*   *www.portjeffraceway.com*

NEW YORK CITY
Victorian Gardens Amusement Park • *Central Park, NY* • *212-982-2229* • Features **Include:** Unique Handcrafted Rides, Face Painting, Balloon Sculpting, Interactive

Games & Activities, Live Entertainment every weekend & holiday, Hand-Spun Cotton Candy, Fresh-Popped Caramel Corn, check the web site for the entertainment schedule which is jammed packed, Rides are specifically geared toward 2-12 yr. olds & can also accommodate adult sizes **Hours:** Mon.-Thurs.: 11 a.m.-7 p.m., Fri.: 11 a.m.-8 p.m., Sat.: 10 a.m.-9 p.m., Sun./Holidays: 10 a.m.-8 p.m., May-Sept. **Fee:** Unlimited Rides: $18.50 **Directions:** *LIRR to Penn Station, located in Central Park at Wollman Rink* *www.victoriangardensnyc.com*

WESTCHESTER

Playland Amusement Park • *Playland Pkwy., Rye, NY* • **914-874-5005** • Playland has provided family fun since 1928 & is a National Historic Landmark. Often referred to as "Rye Playland," it is America's only government-owned & operated amusement park. **Features Include:** 50 Rides & Attractions, Free Entertainment, Big Band Dance Concerts, Beach, Pool, Boardwalk, Pier on Long Island Sound, Lake Boating, Picnic Area, Mini Golf, Indoor Ice Skating, Fire Works during July & Aug. **Hours:** May-Sept., Tues.-Sun.: hrs. vary, June-Aug. Sat.: 1 p.m.-Midnight, Sun.: 1-10:30 p.m. **Fee:** Unlimited Rides: $30, Unlimited Kiddyland: $20, Unlimited Season Pass: $80, Ride Sampler: $15.50 **Directions:** *Northern State Pkwy. W., take the Cross Island Pkwy. N., cross the Throgs Neck Bridge, merge onto I-95 N. to Playland Pkwy. to exit 19, follow to the park* *www.ryeplayland.org*

NEW JERSEY

Six Flags • *Jackson, NJ* • *Group Reservations: 732-928-2000, ext. 2076* • Six Flags includes 3 parks in Jackson, New Jersey, Great Adventure, Hurricane Harbor & Wild Safari. **Great Adventure Features Include**: 14 Thrill Rides, 12 Family Rides, 25 Kid Rides **Hurricane Harbor Features Include:** 1 of America's Largest Water Parks, 45-acre Tropical Island Paradise Theme Park, 5 Thrill Rides, 4 Family Rides, Kid Ride Area **Wild Safari Features Include:** 350-acre 1,200 Animal Wildlife Preserve, 4.5-mi. Auto Trail, Animals Walk up to Your Car, Hands-On Adventure with Creatures at the Wild Safari Exploration Station, Educational Shows, Interactive Science Exhibits, Touch Creatures, Air-Conditioned Bus Tour (purchased at Georgia's Guest Relations in the Exploration Station) **Hours:** May-Aug. Great Adventure: 10:30 a.m.-10 p.m., Wild Safari: 9 a.m.-4 p.m., March/April/Sept./Oct. Great Adventure: 10:30 a.m.-8 p.m., Wild Safari: 9 a.m.-4 p.m., hrs. vary, check the web site for specific dates **Fee:** Adults: $49.99, Under 54-in.: $29.99, Under 2: Free, Safari Upgrade: $10, Online Discount Ticket: Adult: $34.99, Play Pass: $69 unlimited visits, just Wild Safari: $19 **Directions:** *I-495 Long Island Expwy. W., take exit 31 Cross Island Pkwy. N., take exit 31N. toward Whitestone Bridge, I-295 N. via exit 33 toward Bronx/New England/ GWB, I-295 N. becomes I-95 S. Cross Bronx Expwy., keep Right to take I-95 S. toward George Washington Bridge/Lower Level/Last NY exit (crossing into New Jersey), keep Left to take I-95 Express Ln. S./New Jersey Tpke. S. to exit 7A, proceed on I-195 E. to exit 16A, then 1 mi. West on Rte. 537 to Six Flags* *www.sixflags.com/greatAdventure/index.aspx*

PENNSYLVANIA

Dutch Wonderland Family Entertainment Complex • *2249 Lincoln Hwy E., Lancaster, PA* •

Dutch Wonderland's web site offers puzzles & games that kids can do at their leisure. **Features Include:** Amusement park offers Rides, Royal Entertainment & Strolling Entertainment throughtout the park, Water Rides, Mini Golf **Hours:** June- Aug.: 10 a.m.- 8:30 p.m. (check web site) **Fee:** Tickets ages 3-59: $29.95 **Directions:** *I-495 Long Island Expwy. W., Cross Island Pkwy. N., take exit 31N. toward Whitestone Bridge, take I-295 N. via exit 33 toward Bronx/New England, I-295 N. becomes I-95 S./Cross Bronx Expwy., keep Right to take I-95 S. toward George Washington Bridge/Lower Level/Last NY exit (crossing into New Jersey), keep Left to take I-95 Express Lane S./New Jersey Tpke. S. toward I-80/Garden State Pkwy./Paterson, take I-95 S./New Jersey Tpke. S. toward US-46/Newark, merge onto I-78 W. toward US-1/Newark Airport/US-222, keep Left to take I-78 Express Lane W. toward Garden State Pkwy./Clinton, I-78 Express Lane W. becomes I-78 W. (crossing into PA), merge onto US-222 S. via exit 54A, merge onto US-222 S. toward Sinking Springs, merge onto US-222 S. toward Lancaster/Lebanon, merge onto US-30 E. via the exit on the Left toward Coatesville*

www.dutchwonderland.com

HOBBY/AMUSEMENTS

The Brothers Grim Games & Collectables • *1244 Middle Country Rd., Selden, NY* • *631-698-2805* •

Events have included: Battletech Events, Shadowrun Events, Warhammer Fantasy Tournaments, Yu-Gi-Oh Tournaments, Warhammer League Nights, Magic the Gathering Tournaments **Hours:** Mon.-Tues.: 2-10 p.m., Wed.: 2 p.m.-Midnight, Thurs.-Fri.: 2 p.m.-1 a.m., Sat.: 10 a.m.-1 a.m, Sun.: 10 a.m.-10 p.m. **Fee:** varies per event **Directions:** *event locations vary*

www.catalystdemos.com • www.brgrim.com/large.html

Central Operating Lines Ltd. Model Railroad Club • *Ronkonkoma, NY* • *631-737-4634* •

Features Include: Model Railroad Club (formed in 1976) invites non-members to come visit, see their layout & meet members any Friday evening from 7-11 p.m.

www.trainweb.org

Nick Ziroli Plans • *29 Edgar Dr., Smithtown, NY* • *631-467-4765* • Features Include:

"Ziroli Plan" designs are world renowned for their scale authenticity & excellent flying characteristics. Attend a Ziroli event & see these exquisite birds in action. It is also interesting to meet the builders & discuss your favorite designs. Aircraft Questions/Information: Planes@ziroliplans.com • *www.ziroliplans.com*

SUGGESTIONS • COMMENTS • ERRORS

Linda.ReidBryce @verizon.net

Thanks

BATTING CAGES Have more fun playing ball.

Safety: Injuries can result from using batting cages. ABC Service & Technical Help offered the following precautions:

1. Enter the cage. Read the sign that explains: how to start the game, when balls will pitch & when the game is over.

2. Be aware. Pitching machines will throw both balls & strikes.

3. Batters should wear a helmet with a face cover, & sneakers not cleats.

4. Only the batter should be in the batting cage, & the cage door closed.

5. Be aware. If balls are thrown out of the strike zone something is wrong with the machine.

6. Children should be at least 6 yrs. old to enter a batting cage.

7. Batters should be over 16 yrs. to enter a cage throwing balls at speeds of 70-75 mph.

8. Never take practice swings outside the cage unless there is a designated area.

www.battingcages.com/techweb/safety.htm

Batter Up Batting Range • *130 Hicksville Rd., Bethpage, NY* • *516-731-2020* • Features **Include:** Batting Cages: Hardball & Softball, Arcade Games, Snack Bar **Hours:** 9 a.m.-10:30 p.m. **Fee:** 9 Pitches: $1.25, 30 min.: $30, off-peak hrs. only **Directions:** *I-495 Long Island Expwy., exit 44 S., Rte. 135 Seaford-Oyster Bay Expwy., take exit 7W. Hempstead Tpke., go 3 lights, turn Left onto Hicksville Rd., turn Left into the parking lot, for Batter Up & Bethpage Miniature Golf*   *www.batterupli.com*

Boomers Family Fun Park • *655 Long Island Ave., Medford, NY* • *631- 475-1771* • **Features Include:** Outdoor Batting Cages **Hours:** 11 a.m.-close, time varies **Fees:** Batting

Cages: $2, Pay-One-Price: $15.95, for a full overview of this location, see Amusement Parks
Directions: *I-495 Long Island Expwy., take exit 64, take the S. Service Rd. .5 mi., the park will be on the Right side of the road*   *www.boomersparks.com*

The County Fair Entertainment Park • *3351 Rte. 112, Medford, NY • 631-732-0579* • **Features Include:** 9 Stall Batting Cages, Baseball Slow Pitch, Medium Pitch & Fast Pitch, Speeds Range from 30-90 mph, Men's Softball Arc, Women's Modified (windmill) Fast Pitch, Bats & Helmets Provided **Hours:** 11 a.m.-6 p.m., April: 11 a.m.-9 p.m., open March-Nov. weather permitting **Fee:** 10 Pitches: $1, 30-min. Cage Rental: $12, 1-hr. Cage Rental: $20, Cage Rental: $35, Team Cage Rentals: $30.00 **Directions:** *I-495 Long Island Expwy., take exit 64, N. 1 mi., the crossroads are Granny & Horseblock*

www.countryfairpark.com

Eisenhower Park • *East Meadow off Merrick Ave.* • *516-572-0407* • **Features Include:** 9 Stall Outdoor Batting Cages, Baseballs or Softball Speeds of 40-45, 60-65 & 80-85 mph, 2 Mini Golf Courses **Hours:** 11 a.m.-6 p.m., stays open later as weather warms, March-Nov. **Fee:** 25 Pitches: $3 **Directions:** *Northern State Pkwy., exit onto Meadowbrook Pkwy. S., take exit 24 Hempstead Tpke. E., turn Left into the main entrance at East Meadow Ave., see sign for mini golf & batting cages, park in Field 5*

www.co.nassau.ny.us/golf.html

Five Towns Mini Golf • *570 Rockaway Tpke., Lawrence, NY* • *516-239-1743* • **Features Include:** 11 Batting Cages, 6 Baseball Machines, 4 Softball Cages, Wiffle Ball Pitch Cage, 18-hole Mini Golf, Weekly Sweepstakes, Baseball Trivia for Prizes, Outdoor Interactive Game Area **Winter Hours:** Mon.-Fri.: Noon-7 p.m., Sat.-Sun.: 11 a.m-7 p.m. **Spring Hours:** Mon.-Fri.: Noon-9 p.m., Sat.: 11 a.m-10 p.m., Sun.: 11a.m-7 p.m., open March-Oct. **Fee:** Tokens: 10 pitches for $2, Buy 10 tokens get 2 free, Cage Rental: 150 pitches for $24, Wiffle Ball Pitch Cage: 16 pitches for $2, Family Flex Pack: 10 Batting Tokens & 4 Games of Miniature Golf for $38, Print Web Coupon **Directions:** *South, Southern State Pkwy., exit onto Peninsula Blvd. S., turn Right onto Rockaway Tpke.*   *www.5townsminigolfbatting.com*

SUGGESTIONS • COMMENTS • ERRORS

Linda.ReidBryce
@verizon.net

Thanks

"Long Island is one of the best places on the east coast for Bird Watching, especially for migratory birds. It is located on a major flyway, and it has a wide variety of habitats that appeal to diverse species. Although there are wide seasonal variations in visiting populations, the best time for seeing them is in the spring. That's when the birds are in their best plumage for breeding, and foliage has not yet reached full summer density" (pg.1 *Short Nature Walks LI*).

Here are recommendations for bird watching supplies. Also check the Hiking/Walking section for a broader set of options. Back Pack Items: Binoculars, a small spiral notebook, pencil to write + draw bird pictures, find + identify bird feathers, Water, Snack, Small First Aid Kit, Compass, Spotting Scope, Cell Phone, Print Out of "Long Island Seasonal Birds to look for" from *www.libirding.com/LI_Birds/Welcome.html* or bring a book on birding

Long Island Rare Bird Alert • *212-979-3070* • This recorded message is updated weekly, & offers information about the birds recently reported in the local regions. This information is also reported on the RBA's web site: *http://www.nybirds.org/RecordsRBA.htm*

South Shore Audubon Society sponsors bird walks once a month. *www.ssaudubon.org*

NASSAU COUNTY *www.nassaucountyny.gov*
John F. Kennedy Memorial Wildlife Sanctuary • *Ocean Pkwy., Massapequa, NY* • *516-797-4110* • This sanctuary is considered 1 of the most important refuges for waterfowl in the northeast. It is located just West of Tobay Beach. **Features Include:** 500-acre Bayside Sanctuary, Wintering Area for 50 Species of Waterfowl, Habitat for

SPRING BLISS

Several Species of Ducks & Wading Birds, Location for Hawks & Falcons, Guggenheim Pond Attracts Herons, Egrets & Ibis, Black Duck & American Bittern, visitors must obtain a pass from the Town of Oyster Bay Parks Department at 977 Hicksville Rd., Massapequa, NY • 516-797-4110 • **Office Hours:** 9 a.m.-4 p.m. **Fee: Free Directions:** *Northern State Pkwy., take exit 31A Meadowbrook Pkwy. S., take Ocean Pkwy. E., drive approx. 4 mi. East of the Jones Beach traffic circle to the Tobay Beach parking lot, just East of parking lot 9, head West along the south border of the lot, look for the parking area provided by the sanctuary*

Massapequa Preserve • NC • *Merrick Rd. & Ocean Ave., Massapequa, NY • 516-571-7443* • **Features Include:** 423-acre Preserve, 4.5 mi. of the Bethpage Bikeway, Birding, Hiking, Jogging/Walking, Rollerblading, Photography, 5 mi. of the Greenbelt Hiking Trail, Lake, Sandy-Bog Area (provides habitat for many rare & endangered Long Island plants, including Orchids, Carnivorous Sundews & Bladderworts), Freshwater Swamps, Marsh, Stream, Pine Barrens, No Amenities in the park, Maps available **Hours:** Dawn-Dusk **Fee: Free Directions:** *I-495 Long Island Expwy., take exit 44 S. for the Seaford-Oyster Bay Expwy., exit onto Sunrise Hwy. E., pass a small brick bldg. on the Left, make the next U-turn at the traffic light, park in the parking lot across from the train station* The Greenbelt Trail Conference & Friends of Massapequa Preserve: *www.fdale.com/FMP/FMP.htm*

Muttontown Preserve • NC • *Muttontown Ln., East Norwich, NY • 516-571-8500* • **Features Include:** 550-acre Preserve, Marked Nature Trails, Self-Guided Maps, Brochures for Observing Local Birds/Mammals/Reptiles/Amphibians/Wildflowers/Trees, Nature Photography, Horse Trails, Guided Hikes, Bill Paterson Nature Center Fields, Woodlands, Ponds, Estate Grounds, the 40-room Chelsea Mansion is located on the northern end of the Muttontown Preserve & is listed on the National Register of Historic Places, Educational Programs (Orienteering, Bird Watching & Glacial Geology), Youth Groups can rent conservation campsites **Hours:** 9 a.m.-5 p.m. **Fee: Free Directions:** *I-495 Long Island Expwy., take exit 41 N. Rte. 106 N., make a Left onto Rte. 25A Northern Blvd., make a Left onto Muttontown Ln.*

Tackapausha Museum & Preserve • *Washington Ave., Seaford, NY • 516-571-7443* • **Features Include:** 84-acre Preserve, Plant & Wildlife Sanctuary, Oak Forests, Ponds & Streams, Small Mammals (raccoons, muskrats, gray squirrels & opossum), 170 Bird Species, Waterfowl, Amphibians, 5-mi. Walk/Hike on Marked Trails **Hours:** Tues.-Sat.: 10 a.m.-4 p.m., Sun.: 1-4 p.m. **Fee:** $1-$2 **Directions:** *I-495 Long Island Expwy., take exit 44 S., Rte. 135S. Seaford-Oyster Bay Expwy., take exit 1E. Merrick Rd. E., turn Left onto Washington Ave., the museum is on the Right* *http://www.nassaucountyny.gov/agencies/Parks/WhereToGo/preserves/south_shore_preserve/Tackapausha_Pres.html*

FUN FAMILY

The Roosevelt Sanctuary & Audubon Center • *134 Cove Rd., Oyster Bay, NY • 516-922-3200* •

Bird research & habitat restoration are important parts of the center's focus. **Features Include:** 12-acre Sanctuary, Hiking, Bird Watching, Educational Programs, there are weekend Environmental Stewardship programs for children & adults throughout the year **Hours:** Year-Round, Mon.-Fri.: 9 a.m.-5 p.m., Sat., Sun. & Holidays: 10 a.m.-4 p.m. **Fee: Free Directions:** *I-495 Long Island Expwy., exit 41 N., Rte. 106 N. to the Village of Oyster Bay, turn Right onto E. Main St., proceed 1.5 mi. to E. Main St., becomes Cove Rd. at Oyster Bay High School, see signs for the T.R. Sanctuary parking lot on the Right* *http://ny.audubon.org/CentersEduTRoosevelt.html*

Stillwell Woods Preserve • *South Woods Rd., Syosset, NY • 516-572-0200* •

Stillwell Woods Preserve is part of the Nassau-Suffolk Greenbelt Trail & offers Old Fields & Oak Barren Communities. **Features Include:** 270-acre Preserve, Bird Watching, Equestrian Trails, Hiking Trails, Bicycle Trails, Mountain Bike Trails **Directions:** *I-495 Long Island Expwy., take exit 46 N. Sunnyside Blvd. N., turn Right onto Woodbury Rd., turn Left onto Jericho Tpke./Rte. 25, turn Right onto South Woods Rd., pass Syosset High School, turn Right into the soccer field, bear Right & go to the end of the field, the trailhead is in the southeastern corner*

SUFFOLK COUNTY

Dwarf Pines Plains Preserve • SC • *West Hampton, NY • 631-444-0270* •

The Dwarf Pine Plain community is a rare ecosystem that exists in 3 world communities: the New Jersey Dwarf Pine Plains, the Shawangunk Mountains Dwarf Pine Plains (Catskill Region) & the Long Island Dwarf Pine Plains. The Dwarf Pine Plains are dominated by pitch pines & scrub oak, trees that rarely exceed 3-6 ft. in height mostly due to poor soil conditions, extreme summer heat, & harsh, cold winters. This rare ecosystem supports some uncommon wildlife species such as: the Black-Throated Green Warbler Breeds, American Kestrels & Marsh Hawks, nocturnal birds such as Owls, Northern Saw-Whet & Long-Eared Owls, Nighthawks & Whippoorwills. Visitors are asked to respect this globally rare ecological community. There is a new .6-mi. trail for hiking which takes about 20 min. to walk. **Directions:** *Southern State Pkwy., exit onto Sunrise Hwy., Service Rd., take the ramp onto Rte. 27E. to County Rd. 31 S. toward West Hampton, the trail head is located about .2 mi. off of the exit on the East side of County Rd. 31, turn Left into the SCWA complex* *www.co.suffolk.ny.us/departments/parks/Dwarf Pines Plains Preserve.aspx*

STATE PARKS

Bayard Cutting Arboretum • *440 Montauk Hwy., Great River, NY, Box 466, Oakdale, NY • 631-581-1002* •

This is a great place for small hikes with young children. There are many animal & plant specimens to see & a café in the Cutting Family Manor House. **Features Include:** Hiking, Birding, Concerts, Art Exhibitions, Performances, the

Connetquot River, Walking Paths, Land & Aquatic Birds, Foxes, Raccoons & other Small Wildlife, Educational Classes, Historical House Tours (on Sun. afternoons at 2 p.m.), the Cutting Family Manor House is decorated by local garden clubs during the month of Dec. **Hours**: Tues.-Sun.: 10 a.m.-5 p.m. **Fee:** Free, Parking: Free during the winter, Parking April-Oct.: $6, Empire Pass Accepted **Directions:** *I-495 Long Island Expwy., take exit 56, Rte. 111 Islip Ave., head East on Montalk Hwy., the Arboretum will be on the Right side of street* www.bayardcuttingarboretum.com,

Caleb Smith State Park Preserve • *581 West Jericho Tpke., Smithtown, NY* • *631-265-1054* • **Features Include:** 543-ace Park, Birding, Nature Trails, Museum/Visitor Center, Gift Shop, Recreation Programs, Oak-Pine Habitats, Scattered Wetlands, Family Events have included: Animal Olympics, South Side Saunter, Buzz Says the Bee, and Wet-n-Wild **Hours:** 8 a.m.-Dusk, Year-Round, Closed Mon.: April-Sept., Closed Mon. & Tues.: Oct.-March **Fee:** Free **Directions:** *I-495 Long Island Expwy., exit 53 N. Sunken Meadow Pkwy. N., take exit SM 3 E. to Smithtown, take Jericho Tpke./Rte. 25 E., drive approx. 3 mi. to the park*

Camp Hero • *50 South Fairview Ave., Montauk, NY* • *631-668-3781* • The park boasts some of the best surf fishing locations in the world. This is a National Historic Site & former military base. **Features Include:** 415-acre Park, Beach (Atlantic Ocean), Bird Watching, Bridle Path, Hiking, Wooded Areas, Historic Military Installation, Maritime Forests, Freshwater Wetlands, Ocean Views, Bluffs Rising above the Beach **Hours:** Year-Round, Dawn-Dusk, 7 days a week **Fee:** Free, parking fee during the summer months, Empire Pass Accepted **Directions:** *I-495 Long Island Expwy., exit 68 for William Floyd Pkwy./Co. Hwy. 46 S. toward Shirley, turn Left onto Rte. 27 E./Sunrise Hwy., turn Right onto Camp Hero State Park Rd., turn Left to stay on Camp Hero State Park Rd.*

Cold Spring Harbor • *25 Lloyd Harbor Rd., Huntington, NY* • *631-423-1770* • The park serves as the northern trailhead of the Nassau Suffolk Greenbelt Trail & extends to Bethpage State Park & eventually the south shore of Nassau County. **Features Include:** 40-acre Park, Birding (spring & fall migrations of Songbirds, many Great Horned Owls & Red-Tailed Hawks), Hiking, Habitats Include: Hilly Terrain, Views of the Cold Spring Harbor, Hardwood Forest (large Oak Specimens that measure 3 ft. in diameter), Wild Mountain Laurel thickets. The park is in the historic village of Cold Spring Harbor. The parking field is on Main St., close to the village's waterfront, restaurants & shopping area. **Hours:** Dawn-Dusk **Fee:** Free **Directions:** *I-495 Long Island Expwy., take 135 N. Seafood-Oyster Bay Expwy. to Jericho Tpke. E., turn Left onto Woodbury Rd. N., turn Left onto Rte. 108 & follow to end, turn Left & immediately Right onto Rte. 25A E., drive 1.5 mi. to parking field & trailhead is on Right*

Connetquot River State Park Preserve • *Box 505, Oakdale, NY* • *631-581-1005* •
Features Include: 50 mi. of Hiking Trails, 3,473 acres of land & water for the protection & propagation of Game Birds, Fish, Animals, Deer & Waterfowl, Rare Nesting Birds, Osprey, Rare Plants, Nature Photography, Nature Trails, Bridle Path **Hours:** Dawn-Dusk, Year-Round Fee: **Free** Directions: *Southern State Pkwy., take exit 44 Sunrise Hwy. E., the Preserve is located on the North side of Sunrise Hwy., just West of Pond Rd.*

Montauk Point Lighthouse & Museum • *2000 Montauk Hwy., Montauk, NY* •
Montauk Historical Society: 631-668-2544 • 888-685-7646 • Montauk Point is the easternmost point on Long Island. **Features Include:** Great Birding Site, check the Long Island area rare bird alert before making the trip. Pack: binoculars & spotting scope **Hours:** Mon.-Sun. :10:30 a.m.-5 p.m. **Fee:** Adults: $6, Kids over 41-in.: $3, Under 41-in.: Free (no tower climb), Seniors: $5, Parking: $6 **Directions:** *I-495 Long Island Expwy., take exit 70 S., County Rd./111 S., take Rte. 27 E. to Montauk Point*

www.montauklighthouse.com

Nissequogue River State Park & Marina • *799 St. Johnland Rd., Kings Park, NY* • *631 269-4927* • **Features Include:** Bird Watching, Interpretive Signs, Tidal & Fresh Water Wetlands, Hardwood Forests, Shore Bird Habitats, Reptiles, Amphibians, Guided Tours, Group Tours by reservation, Museum/Visitor Center, Nature Trail. A section of the park has been designated as a State Bird Conservation Area. The Greenbelt Trail for walking & hiking parallels the Nissequogue River & provides scenic views of the river & the Long Island Sound from the top of the bluffs. There are family events throughout the year such as: Long Island Sound Saunter, Nature Hide-n-Seek, Salt Marsh Exploration, Family Evening Walk, Family Nature Walk & Family Adventures. **Hours:** Dawn-Dusk, Year-Round **Fee:** $2 per child for programs **Directions:** *Northern State Pkwy., take exit 45 Sunken Meadow Pkwy. N., take exit SM4, head East on Pulaski/ Old Dock Rd., at the 5th traffic light make a Right onto St. Johnland Rd., the park entrance is about .5 mi. on the Left*

Shadmoor • *50 South Fairview Ave., Montauk, NY* • *631-668-3781* • **Features Includes:** 99-acre Park, 2,400 ft. of Ocean Beach, Elevated Platforms for Bird Watching, Biking, Hiking Trails, Shade Bushes, Bluffs, Freshwater Black Cherry Trees, Clusters of the Rare & Federally-Endangered Sand Plain Gerardia Plant, there are 2 concrete bunkers built during World War II & once equipped with artillery guns to protect the coast from enemy invasion **Hours:** Dawn-Dusk, Year-Round **Fee: Free** parking **Directions:** *Southern State Pkwy., exit onto Rte. 27E. Sunrise Hwy. E. to Montauk Village, the park is .5 mi. East of the village on the Right, at the southwest corner of Rte. 27 & Seaside Ave.*

www.tripadvisor.com/Attraction_Review-g48194-d532149-Reviews-Shadmoor_ State_Park-Montauk_New_York.html

SPRING BLISS

Trail View State Park • *631-423-1770* • *Contact Information: 25 Lloyd Harbor Rd., Huntington, NY* • **Features Include:** 400-acre Park, Year-Round Bird Watching (especially during the spring & fall bird migrations because it lies on the Atlantic flyway). This is a 7.4-mi. linear park that serves as a link along the Nassau-Suffolk Greenbelt Trail that extends from Cold Spring Harbor State Park on the north shore of Suffolk County to Bethpage State Park, & eventually to the south shore of Nassau County. The park offers a variety of habitats & undeveloped natural resources such as Hardwood Forests, Marshes & Fields with elevations ranging from 60-300 ft. above sea level. **Hours:** Dawn-Dusk, Year-Round **Fee:** Free **Directions:** *I-495 Long Island Expwy., take exit 49N. Rte. 110N., make a Left onto Rte. 25 Jericho Tpke. W., pass the Woodbury Rd. intersection, approx. .25 mi. on Right, park in the dirt lot on the Right*

BROOKLYN

West Pond Trail • *Jamaica Bay Wildlife Refuge* • *Gateway NRA, Floyd Bennett Field, Queens, NY* • *718-318-4340* • **Features Include:** 2-mi. Loop, .5-mile Terrapan Trail Spur, 300 Bird Species with Warbler Migration (April/May), Shorebirds (July/Aug.), Raptor Migration (Sept.-Nov.), Winter Waterfowl (March-early April), Nesting Terrapins (June/July), Interpretive Signs, Bird & Bat Nesting Boxes, Osprey Nesting Platforms, Benches for Resting, hikers must carry a visitors pass which can be obtained at the Visitors Center. The trailhead is located at the Visitors Center. Hike the wide gravel trail to the Left. The trail ends back at the Visitors Center. No bikes or pets allowed in this refuge. Educational walks & workshops are periodically offered. **Hours:** 8:30 a.m.-5 p.m., Year-Round **Fee:** Free **Directions:** *Northern State Pkwy., or Southern State Pkwy., to the Belt Pkwy., take exit 17S. Cross Bay Blvd. for Gateway National Recreation Area, drive approx. 3.5 mi., turn Right for the visitors center & trailhead*

http://www.nyharborparks.org/visit/jaba.html

Huntington Audubon Society: *www.huntingtonaudubon.org*
Sponsors many field trips throughout the year.
Brooklyn Bird Club: *www.brooklynbirdclub.org/jamaica.htm*
Queens County Bird Club: *www.qcbc.all.at/*
Alley Pond Environmental Center (APEC): 228-06 Northern Boulevard, Douglaston, NY
New York State Bird Watching Clubs:
www.birdingguide.com/clubs/new_york.html
Long Island Green Belt Trail:
www.hike-ligreenbelt.com/page/page/1007314.htm
Trail Info:
www.trails.com/tcatalog_trail.aspx?trailid=HGN195-043

CAMPING

SLEEPING BAGS, FLASHLIGHTS, & SMORES

Camping Tips:

Reserve your site ahead of time. Many Long Island campsites allow reservations up to 180 days in advance. The most popular ones such as Hither Hills get filled up fast.

Camping Buddies: Everyone should be assigned a camp buddy. No one should go off without their camp buddy. Wear a whistle & pocket compass.

Dress Appropriately: Check the weather conditions ahead of time. Dressing in layers offers the most adjustability for shifting weather throughout the day. For example, wear a T-shirt, sweat shirt & poncho & as the day wears on, remove & add layers.

Tent Placement: Locate the flattest surface area to build the tent. Small loose leaves & pine needles can provide a nice cushion under the tent. Have the children pick out any sticks or rocks because these could damage the tent & cause discomfort while sleeping.

Leave No Trace: Leaving no trace is a Boy Scout motto. When departing the campsite, pick up anything that doesn't belong to nature & take it out with you.

(Pg.7 Aaron Starmer, Catherine Wells & Timothy Starmer, *The Best Tent Camping*)

NASSAU COUNTY

Battle Row Campground • NC • *Claremont Rd., Old Bethpage, NY • 516-572-8690* •

Features Include: 44 acres of Campground & Dense Woods, 64 campsites ranging in length from 40-45 ft., Half Equipped with Water & 30-amp/125-volt Electric Hookups, 12 Designated Tent Sites, 2 Dump Station Facilities, 2 Comfort Stations, Wheelchair Accessible, Reservations Required **Fee:** Tent: $12 (Leisure Pass), $18 (w/o Leisure Pass), RV: $20 (Leisure Pass), $26 (w/o Leisure Pass) **Directions:** *I-495 Long Island Expwy.,* *take exit 49 S. Broadhollow Rd./Rte.110 toward Amityville, turn Right onto Bethpage-Spagnoli Rd., follow Spagnoli Rd., turn Left onto Winding Rd., turn Right onto Round Swamp Rd.*

Nickerson Beach Park • *880 Lido Blvd., Lido Beach, NY* • *516-571-7700* • Features **Include:** 121-acre Park, .75 mi. on the Atlantic Ocean, Campground (Reservations Required: 516-571-7701), Cabana Area, Fun Zone Area, Playground, 2 Basketball Courts, 2 Tennis Courts, 9 Beach Volleyball Courts (for leagues & individuals), Baseball Field, 2 Pools, Skate Park Skateboard Facility (7 ramps of varying difficulty & 2 railings), Picnic Tables & Grills, Dog Run (size sensitive), "Nathan's at Nickerson" Restaurant (open Labor Day-Oct.), Seasonal Movie Nights, Concerts **Hours:** Dawn-Dusk **Fee: Free** off-season, $8 per day for Nassau County Leisure Pass, $20 for non-residents **Directions:** *Meadowbrook Pkwy., take exit M10 Loop Pkwy., take to the end, bear Right onto Lido Blvd., continue for 2 lights, make a Left into the park*

SUFFOLK COUNTY

A Suffolk County's Green Key or a Tourist Key Card (631-854-4949) is required to make camping reservations in Suffolk County. See page 14 for full information regarding this card.

Blydenburgh County Park • *Smithtown Veteran's Memorial Hwy., Smithtown, NY* • *631-854-3713* • *Camping Reservations: 631-244-7275* • *Camping: 631-854-3712* • **Features Include:** 627-acre Park, 50 Tent & Trailer Camp Sites, Shower Facilities, 15 Sites Available for Group Camping, Hiking, Picnicking, Freshwater Fishing, Rowboat Rentals, Playground, Dog Run, Historic Trust Area, Horseback Riding, Extensive Bridle Path System & Practice Ring, Forested Hills, Valleys, Headwaters of the Nissequogue River, Rowing, Fishing, Stump Pond, Blydenburgh Farm & New Mill Historic District, Grist Mill, Trailer Parking (New Mill Rd. entrance), Horseback Riding (permits required), freshwater fishing for pumpkinseed sunfish, large-mouth bass, perch & bluegill is permitted at Stump Pond between Dawn & Dusk. New York State freshwater fishing laws apply. Rowboat Rentals: mid-May-Labor Day. Use the southern Veteran's Memorial Hwy. entrance for these activities. The Long Island Greenbelt Trail Conference (whose headquarters are located in 1 of the historic district houses) often leads hikes through the park. For a hike schedule, contact the Greenbelt Trails Conference Office: 631-360-0753, Reservations for camping can be made 180 days in advance. **Hours:** 7 days a week, May-Oct. **Fee:**$15-$25 per night **Directions:** *Northern State Pkwy. to the Eastern end, stay straight for 454/Veterans Memorial Hwy., the main entrance will be on the Left opposite the H. Lee Dennison County Center in Smithtown, the northern entrance can be reached by following Rte. 347 to Brooksite Dr. N., turn Left onto New Mill Rd., follow to the park entrance at end*

Cathedral Pines County Park • *Yaphank-Middle Island Rd. South of Rte. 25, Middle Island, NY* • *631-852-5500* • *Campground: 631-852-5502* • Features Include: 320-

acre Park, Carmans River, 400 Camp Sites, Campsites for Individuals, Youth Group Camping, Club Camping (10 or more units) & Family Camping, 10 Sites with Water & Electric Hookups, Hiking, Mountain Biking, Bridle Paths, Nature Photography, Picnic Sites, George Broome Memorial Activity Building, Prosser Pines Nature Preserve which features white pines adjacent to Cathedral Pines Park & is a popular site for hikers & photographers **Hours:** May-Oct. **Fee:** $15-$25 per night **Directions:** *I-495 Long Island Expwy., take exit 68 N. William Floyd Pkwy., turn Left onto Longwood Rd. to end, turn Left, the entrance is immediately on the Right*

Cedar Point County Park • *5 Cedar Point Rd., East Hampton, NY* • *631-852-7620* • *Camping Reservations: 631-244-7275* • Cedar Point was settled in 1651 & was a busy shipping port for farm goods, fish & timber from Sag Harbor. **Features Include:** 607-acre Park, Views of Gardiner's Bay, 190 Camp Sites for Tents & Trailers, Youth Group & Club Camping with Permit, Hiking, Nature Trails, Picnicking, Lighthouse, Playground, Rowboat Rentals, Bicycling, Saltwater Fishing, Scuba Diving, Fishing, Surfcasting for Bass & Bluefish, Hunting, Vehicle Access to the Outer Beach (with permit only), licensed Hunting for Waterfowl (in season), General Store, Snack Bar: 631-324-7147, the Cedar Point General Store & Snack Bar are operated by Kaelins. They offer Sat. night family movies on the lawn behind the store & Free use of recreational equipment. **Fee:** $15-25 per night **Directions:** *I-495 Long Island Expwy., take exit 68 for William Floyd Pkwy./County Hwy. 46 toward Shirley, take the ramp onto NY-27 E. Montauk Hwy. E., turn Left onto NY-27, make a U-turn, to Stephen Hands Path in E. Hampton, turn North & continue to Old Northwest Rd., turn Right onto Northwest Rd., bear Left & continue to Alewive Brook Rd., the park entrance is 100 yds. down the road*

Cupsogue Beach County Park • *Dune Rd., Westhampton, NY* • *631-852-8111* • During the summer season there is lifeguard-supervised swimming & sunbathing on white sand beaches. Cupsogue Beach offers some of the best saltwater bass fishing on Long Island. **Features Include:** 296-acre Barrier Beach Park, Outer Beach Camping for 20 Self Contained Trailers, No Tent Camping, Swimming, Fishing, Scuba Diving, Outer Beach Access, Food Concession (www.thebeachhuts.com), First Aid Center, Restrooms, Showers, Changing Rooms, Special Events (in season), campers & recreational vehicles are permitted along the access road running parallel to the outer beach. Diving is permitted at slack tide on the bay side of the park only. Water depth is approx. 12 ft. **Fee:** $15-25 per night, Green Key Card or Tourist Key Card Required **Directions:** *I-495 Long Island Expwy., take exit 68 William Floyd Pkwy./Co. Hwy. 46 S. toward Shirley, take the ramp onto Rte. 27 E., take exit 63 S. Co. Hwy. 31 S. toward Westhampton Beach, merge onto County Rte. 31/Old Riverhead Rd./Riverhead Rd., continue on Oak St., at the traffic circle take the 2nd exit onto Potunk Ln., turn Right onto Stevens Ln., turn Left onto Jessup Ln., turn Right onto County Rte. 89/Dune Rd., follow Dune Rd. to the park*

Indian Island County Park • *Riverhead, Cross River Dr. (Rte. 105), Riverhead, NY* • *631-852-3232* • *Camping Reservations: 631-244-7275* • The "island" at Indian Island County Park is now connected to the mainland by a causeway composed entirely of white sand. It is located at the estuarine mouth of the Peconic River. **Features Include:** 275-acre Park, 100 Camp Sites for Tents & Trailers (reservations required), 37 Premium Sites with Water & Electric Hookup, Hiking, Finest Picnicking in Suffolk County, Views of Flanders Bay, Picnic Tables & Grills, Restrooms, Shower Facilities, Fishing, Activity Field, Playground **Hours:** 7 days a week, April-Oct., off-season camping available for self contained campers only **Fee:** $15-25 per night **Directions:** *I-495 Long Island Expwy., take exit 71, Right turn onto Rte. 24 at end of exit ramp, follow Rte. 24 S. through the Riverhead traffic circle, continue on Rte. 24 & make a Left turn at the next traffic light onto Rte. 105, follow Rte. 105 to the entrance on Right just past the golf course*

Meschutt Beach County Park • *Canal Rd. & Old North Hwy., Hampton Bays, NY* • *631-852-8205* • **Features Include:** 10 Self-Contained Trailer & Camper Sites, No Tents Permitted, No Beach Camping, Windsurfing, Sailing Area, Supervised Bathing Area, Great Peconic Bay, Playground, Picnicking, Food Concession with Dining Area, Restrooms, Showers, Special Events in season, The Beach Hut Raw Bar & Grill • 631-728-2988 • serves breakfast, lunch & dinner & they offer seafood specialties, & live entertainment **Hours:** Dawn-Dusk **Fee:** $15-25 per night **Directions:** *I-495 Long Island Expwy., take exit 68 for William Floyd Pkwy./Co. Hwy. 46 S. toward Shirley, merge onto County Rte. 46/William Floyd Pkwy., take Rte. 27 E. Sunrise Hwy., take exit 66 (1ˢᵗ exit on East side of the Shinnecock Canal), proceed straight through intersection, turn Right at the stop sign, make the 1ˢᵗ Left, park entrance on the Right*   www.thebeachhuts.com

Sears Bellows • *Sears Bellows Pond Rd., Hampton Bays, NY* • *Park Office: 631-852-8290* • *Big Duck: 631-852-8292* • *Camping Reservations: 631-244-7275* • **Features Include:** 30 Tent & 40 Trailer Camping Sites, All Trailer Sites have Water Spigots, 2 Group Camping Areas, Youth Group & Club Camping Areas Available by Permit, Long Island Pine Barrens, Hiking (extensive trail system), Picnicking, Lifeguard-Protected Swimming, Freshwater Fishing (bluegill, bass, perch & pickerel), Rowboat Rentals, Hunting, Horseback Riding (permit required). This is the home of Long Island's famous *Big Duck*. This park is closed to certain activities during waterfowl hunting season. NYS regulations apply to all sporting activities. **Hours:** Dawn-Dusk, check in & out time for campers is 4 p.m. **Fee:** $15-25 per night, Green Key Card or Tourist Key Card Required **Directions:** *Northern State Pkwy., exit onto Wantagh State Pkwy. S., exit onto Sunrise Hwy., take exit 65 N., follow Rte. 24, make a Left onto Bellows Pond Rd., the park entrance is on the Right*

FUN FAMILY

Shinnecock East County Park • *Dune Rd., Southampton, NY* • *631-852-8290* • This undeveloped barrier beach park borders the Shinnecock Inlet where it meets the Atlantic Ocean. **Features Include:** Ocean & Bay Beaches, Outer Beach Camping for self-contained vehicles only (103 campsites), No Tent Camping, Saltwater Fishing (striped bass), Off-Road Recreational Vehicle Use, Off-Road Recreational Vehicles May Drive on the Outer (Ocean) Beach, permits are given to self-contained campers with a valid Suffolk County Parks Green Key Card. A small parking lot is available for Green Key cardholders who do not have an Outer Beach Recreational Vehicle Permit. Vehicles with Suffolk County Parks Outer Beach Recreational Vehicle Permit must park on the beach. Reservations for camping can be made 180 days in advance. **Fee:** $15-25 per night **Directions:** *Southern State Pkwy., exit at Sunrise Hwy., exit at Montauk Hwy., turn South on Halsey Neck Ln., make a Right turn onto Dune Rd. heading West to the park entrance*

Smith Point County Park • *Fire Island, Shirley, NY* • *631-852-1313* • *Camping Reservations: 631-244-7275* • **Features Include:** Suffolk County's Largest Oceanfront Park, 221 Tent & Trailer Camp Sites, All Sites Have Water, Premium Sites Have Sewer & Electric Hookups, Outer Beach Access, Off-Season Club Camping Available, Outer Beach Camping for 75 Self Contained Trailers & Campers, No Outer Beach Tent Camping, Swimming, Lifeguards, Scuba Diving, Surfing, White Sand Beach, Atlantic Surf, Saltwater Fishing, Food Concession, Playground, Showers, Restaurant, Special Events (in season), reservations are required for all campground sites. Outer beach camping is available on a first-come basis (beach conditions permitting). Off-road vehicles must have a permit & may drive on the western portion of the outer beach. There is marked, protective fencing around the nest sites of endangered shorebirds inhabiting the ocean & bay beaches. The Raw Bar & Grill serves breakfast, lunch, dinner, they offer seafood specialties, live entertainment & a beautiful setting. Beach Hut: 631-728-2988, www.thebeachhuts.com. Special events are scheduled throughout the summer months at Smith Point County Park. **Fee:** $15-25 per night, Green Key Card or Tourist Key Card Required **Directions:** *I-495 Long Island Expwy., take exit 68 William Floyd Pkwy. S. to the end*

Southaven County Park • *Victory Ave., Brookhaven, NY* • *631-854-1414* • *631-924-4490* • *631-345-2449* • The Carman's River flows through this park. **Features Includes:** 1,356-acre Pine-Oak Forested Park, 104 Tent & Trailer Camp Sites, Water Available at Each Site, Hiking, Picnicking, Freshwater Fishing, Rowboat Rentals, Boating, Canoeing, Hunting, Bicycle Hostel, Bridle Paths, the LI Steamer Trains (see museums), Showers Available **Fee:** $15-25 per night **Directions:** *Southern State Pkwy., exit at Sunrise Hwy., take exit 58 N., as you enter William Floyd Pkwy. turn West onto Victory Ave., follow signs to the main entrance of the park*

Theodore Roosevelt County Park • *Montauk Hwy., Montauk, NY* • *631-852-7878* • *Camping: 631-852-7879* • America's 1st cattle ranching system began in 17th century

Montauk. **Features Include:** Canoeing & Kayaking on "Big Reed" Pond (located off East Lake Dr.), No Canoe or Kayak Rentals Available, Outer Beach Access, Camping for Self Contained Campers Only, No Tent Camping Available, Horseback Riding, Hiking, Self-Guided Nature Trail Brochure Available, Biking, Picnicking, Fishing, Hunting, Spanish-American War Exhibit displaying photos & memorabilia from the war **Hours:** Camp Wikoff is open to the public from May-Oct. (Wed.-Sun.: 10 a.m.-5 p.m.), campers should check in at the Third House Park Office **Directions:** *Southern State Pkwy., follow Montauk Hwy. E. through Montauk Village, past East Lake Dr., park sign & entrance are on North side of Montauk Hwy.*

West Hills County Park • *Sweet Hollow Rd., Melville, NY* • *Park Office: 631-854-4423* • *Stables: 631-351-9168* • *Starflower Experiences: 516-938-6152* • *Sweet Hollow Hall: 631-854-4422* • Features Include: Youth Group Camping Only, Tent Campsites, Lean-Tos Campsites, Shelter Campsites, Hiking, Picnicking, Playground, Bridle Paths, Dog Run, Horseback Riding Facility, Nature Trails, Historic Walt Whitman Trail to Jayne's Hill (Long Island's highest peak, at an elevation of 400 ft.), West Hills flora & fauna include wild Mountain Laurel, Moccasin Flower, several Fern Species, Salamanders, Turtles, Chipmunks, Squirrels & Red Foxes **Directions:** *I-495 Long Island Expwy., exit 48 N. to High Hold Dr., entrance is on the Right. For picnics & horseback riding, use exit 49 N. to Rte. 110 North, from Rte. 110 N., turn Left onto Old Country Rd., turn Right onto Sweet Hollow Rd. For hiking, take Sweet Hollow Rd. & turn Right into the North entrance.*

STATE PARKS

Heckscher State Park • *Heckscher Pkwy., Field 1, E. Islip, NY* • *631-581-2100* • *Reservations: 800-456-2267* • *Camping Information: 631-581-4433* • Features Include: 69 Camp Sites (Tent/Trailer), 20 mi. of Nature Trails, Hiking, Bicycling, Cross-Country Skiing, Swimming on the Great South Bay Beach, Pool Complex/Showers, Playgrounds, Fishing, Picnic Areas & Tables, Boat Launch Ramp, Playing Fields, Food, Recreation Programs, Pavilions (by Permit Only), only vehicles under 11-ft. high can come into the campgrounds **Hours:** 7 a.m.-Dusk, Year-Round **Fee:** $18 per night, Empire Pass Accepted **Directions:** *Southern State Pkwy. E., the Pkwy. ends in the park*

Hither Hills • *50 S. Fairview Ave., Montauk, NY* • *631-668-2554* • *Reservations: 800-456-2267* • Named 1 of the Top 100 Campgrounds in the nation in 2007. **Features Include:** 168 Ocean Front Camp Sites, 6 People per site, 2 Tents or 1 Trailer & 1 Tent (per site), 40-acre Fresh Water Lake, 2-mi. Ocean Beach, No Fiores During High Season, Walking Dunes, Big & Small Game Hunting, Biking, Bridle Path, Food, 10-acre Picnic Area/Fireplaces/Tables, Playing Fields, Showers, Cross-Country Skiing, Camper Recreation, Dumping Stations, Fishing, Hiking, Nature Trail, Playground,

Horseshoe Courts, Volleyball, Tetherball, Recreation Programs, Year-Round & Night Fishing with a fishing permit. The unique "walking dunes" of Napeague Harbor are located on the eastern boundary of the park, which also has woodlands filled with Russian Olive, Oak, Shade & Pine Trees. Organized recreation program in high season includes Family Movies, Folk & Line Dancing, Children's Summer Theatre, Magic Shows & various Environmental Interpretation Programs. No fires permitted during the high season. In the low season fires must be in a metal container 6 in. off the ground. Campsite Availability: early April-mid-Nov., Empire Pass Accepted **Hours:** Campers must check in before 9 p.m., Quiet Time is 10 p.m.-8 a.m., Year-Round **Fee:** $32 per night, $224 per week, rate varies by date, fees & taxes apply **Directions:** *I-495 Long Island Expwy., take exit 68, William Floyd Pkwy. S., take Sunrise Hwy. Rte. 27 E., turn Left onto 27 E., Right turn onto Birch Dr./Oak Ln., turn Right onto Birch St./Birch Dr., turn Left onto Old Montauk Hwy.*

Wildwood • *P.O. Box 518, North Wading River Rd., Wading River, NY • 631-929-4314 • Reservations: 800-456-2267* • **Features Include:** 600-acre Park, Campsites, Tent/Trailer Sites, Picnic Table in every site, Dump Stations, Firewood is For Sale at the Park, Bring Your Own Barbeque or Metal Fire Container, Recycling Newspaper & Cardboard, Beach, Showers, Playground, Bluff Overlooking the Long Island Sound, Biking, Nature Trails, Food Consession, Camper Recreation, Fishing, 12 mi. of marked Hiking Trails, Picnic Tables, Recreation Programs **Hours:** April-Columbus Day weekend, Dawn-Dusk, Year-Round **Fee:** Empire Pass Accepted **Directions:** *I-495 Long Island Expwy., take exit 68, head N. on Rte. 46, take Rte. 25A E., turn Left onto Sound Ave., turn Left at traffic light onto Hulse Landing Rd., the park entrance is on the Right*

NEW JERSEY

Liberty Harbor Marina & RV Park • *11 Luis Munoz Marin Blvd., Jersey City, NJ • 201-386-7500 • 800-646-2066* • **Features Include:** 50 sites (water & electric), Visitor Maps, View of New York Skyline, Weekend Events & Guest Performers at the Sandbar Nightclub, New York City Bus Tours , 24-hr. Security, On-Site Manager, Restaurant & Bar, Path Trains to NYC, 5 blocks up Marin Blvd., Light Rail 1 block away, Ferry Service to NYC, Pets on Leashes Welcome, No Open Fires, Dump Station, Full Restrooms & Hot Showers, Laundry Room, Handicap Accessible, the nightclub operates until 2:30 a.m. & music can be overheard in the RV Parking Area **Hours:** variable & posted, Checkout Time: Noon, Quiet Hours: 11 p.m.-8 a.m. **Fee:** Rates & Reservations available upon request **Directions:** *New Jersey Tpke. to exit 14 C, pay toll & take the 2nd exit ramp toward "Jersey City/Christopher Columbus" exit, at the bottom of the ramp make 3 Lefts in a row, 1st under the tpke., 2nd is wide to the traffic light, the 3rd Left onto Grand St., go approx. 8 city blocks, turn Right onto Luis Munoz Marin Blvd., go to the end, the office is on the Right*

www.libertyharborrv.com

SPRING BLISS

Linda.ReidBryce
@verizon.net

Thanks

FUN FAMILY

CAMPING & EQUIPMENT CHECKLIST

Except for the large & bulky items on this list, keep a plastic storage container full of the essentials for car camping, so they are always ready to go. Make a last-minute check of the inventory, & resupply anything that's low or missing.

O Cooking utensils
O Bottle opener
O Small waterproof/spillproof containers of: salt, pepper, spices, sugar, cooking oil & maple syrup
O Can opener
O Plastic or tin cups
O Dish soap, bath soap, sponge & towel
O Flatware
O Frying pan
O Fuel for stove
O Matches in waterproof container
O Plates
O Pocketknife
O Pot with lid
O Spatula
O Stove

O Tin foil
O Wooden spoon

O Food: Pack less by planing meals & packing specific quantities for those meals

O **Miscellaneous:** Camp chair, Candles, Cooler, Deck of cards, Fire starter, Flashlight with fresh batteries, Bad-weather clothing, Maps (road, topographic, trails, etc.), Paper towels, Plastic zip-top bags, Sunglasses, Toilet Paper, Trowel (for burying solid waste), Water bottle, Wool blanket, Whistles & Compass to easily find children when separated

First Aid Kit Buy a prepackaged kit & put it in a waterproof bag.
Make A First Aid Kit Including: Sunscreen, Insect repellent, Ace bandage or Spenco joint wrap, Band-Aids, Neosporin antibiotic ointment, Betadine or Hydrogen Peroxide Antiseptic/disinfectant, Asprin, Benadryl, Butterfly Closure bandages, Epineprine in a pre-filled syringe (for people known to have allergic reactions), Gauze Roll, Gauze compress pads, Matches & pocket lighter, Moleskin/Spenco "Second Skin," Waterproof First-Aid Tape, Whistle for signaling rescuers

Sleeping Gear: Pillow, Sleeping bag, Inflatable or Insulated mattress, Tent with Ground tarp & Rain fly

Optional: GPS, Cell phone, Barbecue grill, Binoculars, Fishing rod & tackle, Hatchet, Lantern, Books about birds, plants & wildlife identification
(Pg.5,6 & 177, Aaron Starmer, Catherine Wells & Timothy Starmer, *The Best Tent Camping, New York State*)

FAMILY EXERCISE

SUNNY SKIES, SNEAKERS & ADRENALINE

SUGGESTIONS:

• Make walking more fun for kids by having them wear a pedometer to count the number of steps they take while hiking or excercising (2,000 steps equals about 1 mi.).

• Carry a water bottle.

• Stretch out before beginning any exercise.

• Take your pulse as you go.

• If feeling faint sit down, put head between knees + wait for the feeling to pass.

• Wearing a running sneaker with good support will better protect feet + ankles.

• Take a family walk after meals, limit television/video games/computer to less than 2 hrs. per day, shoot some hoops, select fitness-oriented gifts with your child's skills + interests in mind, visit farms + pick your own fruits + vegetables, plan cycling trips, go swimming, play water tag, water volleyball, play soccer, kick a ball around, go hiking, jump rope + practice rhythms + tricks, enter a "bike-a-thon" or "fun run" + train for it, use a hula hoop + see how long you can keep it going, schedule regular times for activity throughout the week, play hopscotch + organize a family tournament, take a pet for a walk or jog, + walk or run on a local track.

This information is based on suggestions made by Shape Up America www.shapeup.org

FITNESS STATIONS

Christopher Morley Park • NC • 500 Searingtown Rd., Roslyn, NY • 516-571-8113
• Christopher Morley wrote books, plays, poetry & essays & founded the Book of the Month Club. • **Features Include:** 98-acre Park, 30 acres of Nature Trails, Fitness Trail includes: Jogging/Walking Trail & 20 Fitness Stations. Flat .25-mi. Warm-Up, Cool-Down Trail, .5-mi. Flat Trail, 1-mi. Hill Trail **Hours:** Dawn-Dusk **Fee:** Free **Directions:** *I-495 Long Island Expwy., take exit 36N., Searingtown Rd., take Searingtown Rd. N. & look for the park entrance on the Right (about 200 yds. from I-495)*
www.nassaucountyny.gov/agencies/Parks/WheretoGo/active/morley.html

Eisenhower Park • NC • *1899 Hempstead Tpke., East Meadow, NY • 516-572-0348, 572-0290, 572-0327, 542-0015 • Eisenhower Recreation Center: 303-692-5650* • This is the largest park in Nassau County. • **Features Include:** 930-acre Park, 2-mi. Fitness Trail with 20 fitness stations offering a variety of exercises, including stretching, pull-ups, sit-ups & balance walking. The 1ˢᵗ station is located near the field house & playground by Parking Field No. 2 (near Hempstead Tpke.). The trail winds North past the Aquatic Center & Lakeside Theatre & then heads South back toward the starting point. **Hours:** Dawn-Dusk **Fee: Free**, Non-residents: $5, Memorial Day-Labor Day **Directions:** *Northern State Pkwy., Meadow Brook Pkwy. S., exit M3 E. Stewart Ave., make a Right onto Stewart Ave., continue to the park*   www.nassaucountyny.gov

Valley Stream • NYS • *320 Fletcher Ave., Valley Stream, NY • 516-825-4128* • **Features Include:** Nature Trails, .5-mi. Walking Course with 15 Exercise Stations **Hours:** Dawn-Dusk **Fee:** $4 per car from late May-early Sept., Empire Pass Accepted **Directions:** *Southern State Pkwy., take exit 15A, exits into the park*
                    http://nysparks.state.ny.us/parks/info.asp?parkID=51

Wantagh Park • NC • *Kings Rd. & Canal Pl., Wantagh, NY • 516-571-7460* • **Features Include:** 111-acre Park on Flat Creek & East Bay, 1 & 2-mi. Jogging/Walking/Biking Paths, 2-mi. Fitness Trail with 20 Stations **Hours:** Dawn-Dusk **Fee: Free**, Non-residents: $5, Memorial Day-Labor Day **Directions:** *Southern State Pkwy., take exit 27 S. (Wantagh Pkwy.), take the exit for Sunrise Hwy. E., make a Right onto Wantagh Ave., to end, make a Right onto Merrick Rd., at the 1ˢᵗ light make a Left into the park*
            www.nassaucountyny.gov/agencies/Parks/WhereToGo/active/wantagh.html

SUFFOLK COUNTY

Caumsett State Historic Park • NYS • *25 Lloyd Harbor Rd., Huntington, NY • 631-423-1770* • The park is situated on a peninsula extending into the Long Island Sound. **Features Include:** 10 Fitness Stations, Walking, Jogging, Hiking, Handicap Accessibile **Hours:** Year-Round, Dawn-Dusk **Fee: Free** off-season, April-Nov.: $8, Empire Pass Accepted **Directions:** *I-495 Long Island Expwy., exit Rte. 110 N. which becomes New York Ave., turn Left onto Main St. 25A W., turn Right onto West Neck Rd. N., the park entrance is on the Left*   http://nysparks.state.ny.us/parks/info.asp?parkID=68

Gardiner County Park • SC • *Montauk Hwy., W. Bay Shore, NY • 631-854-0935 • 631-581-1005 • Administration: 631-854-4949* • The Gardiner family was Suffolk's 1ˢᵗ non-native landowners. **Features Include:** 231-acre Nature Park, Great South Bay, Fitness Trails, Nature Trails, Hiking, Sagtikos Manor Estate, Restrooms **Hours:** Dawn-Dusk, Open Seasonally **Fee: Free** **Directions:** *I-495 Long Island Expwy., take exit 53 toward Bay*

Shore/Kings Park/Sagtikos Pkwy. S., take exit 40 S. toward Robert Moses Cswy., take exit RM2E. for State Hwy. 27 E. Montauk Hwy., the park is about .5 mi. East of the Robert Moses Cswy.
                    www.co.suffolk.ny.us/Home/departments/parks/Parks.aspx

JOGGING TRAILS, WALKS & SKATES

Bay Park • NC • *First Ave., E. Rockaway, NY • 516-571-7245* • Bay Park borders the East Rockaway Channel & Hewlett Bay. **Features Include:** Bicycle & Running Paths, Outdoor Roller Rink **Hours:** Parts of the park are open Year-Round **Fee: Free Directions:** *Southern State Pkwy., take exit 17 Hempstead Ave. S., take Hempstead Ave., take the Left fork (Ocean Ave.) through Lynbrook & E. Rockaway to Main St. (follow park signs), make a Left onto Front St., make a Right onto Althouse Ave., make a Left onto First & follow to the park*   *www.nassaucountyny.gov*

Cedar Creek Park • *3524 Merrick Rd., Seaford, NY • 516-571-7470* • Features **Include:** 259 acres, Seaman's Creek, the East Bay, 2 Family Jogging/Walking Paths (1.5 & 1 mi.), Archery Range (25-100 yd. Lengths), Roller Rink **Fee: Free** off-season, Leisure Pass Required **Directions:** *Northern State Pkwy., exit onto 135 S. Seaford-Oyster Bay Expwy., take exit 1 W. Merrick Rd. W. toward Freeport, merge onto Merrick Rd.*
                    www.nassaucountyny.gov/agencies/Parks/

Cow Meadow Park & Preserve • NC • *South Main St., Freeport, NY • 516-571-8685* • Features Include: 171-acre Park, Freeport Creek, Hiking, 1-mi. Jogging Course, Nature Trails (150 acres of Long Island's Marine Wetlands, including Salt Marsh, Mud Flat & Tidal Creek Habitats) **Hours:** Dawn-Dusk **Fee: Free Directions:** *Southern State Pkwy., take exit 22 S. Meadowbrook Pkwy., exit onto M9 W. Merrick Rd., immediate Left onto Mill Rd., turn Left onto S. Main St., the entrance is on the Left*

Grant Park • NC • *1625 Broadway, Hewlett, NY • 516-571-7821* • Features Include: 35-acre Park, Jogging/Walking Paths, Bicycling Paths, Roller Rink **Hours:** Dawn-Dusk **Fee: Free Directions:** *Southern State Pkwy., take exit 15S. for Corona Ave S., turn Right onto N. Corona Ave., turn slight Left toward Rockaway Pkwy., then slight Right at Rockaway Pkwy., turn Right to stay on Rockaway Ave., turn Right onto Broadway*
                    www.nassaucountyny.gov

Hempstead Harbor Park • NC • *West Shore Rd., Port Washington, NY• 516-327-3110* • Features Include: 60-acre Park, .5-mi. Beach on the Harbor, .5-mi. Promenade **Hours:** 11 a.m.-Dusk **Fee: Free** off-season, Leisure Pass Required, Non-residents: $20, Memorial Day-Labor Day **Directions:** *Northern State Pkwy., take exit 29, Roslyn Rd. N. to West Shore Rd.*
                    www.nassaucountyny.gov/agencies/Parks/WhereToGo/active/hempstead.html

Inwood Park • NC • Bayview Ave., Inwood, NY • 516-571-7894 • The park is surrounded by water. • **Features Include:** 16-acre Park, Jogging/Walking Path, Outdoor Lighted Roller Rink **Directions:** *Southern State Pkwy., take exit 19 S., Peninsula Blvd. S. to end, make a Left on Rockerway Tpke. (large intersection), make a Right onto Burnside Ave., curves to the Left & becomes Sheridan Blvd., take Sheridan to Bayview Ave. & turn Right, continue down Bayview Ave. into the park*

www.nycgovparks.org/parks/inwoodhillpark

Massapequa Preserve • NC • Merrick Rd. & Ocean Ave., Massapequa, NY • 516-571-7443 • Features Include: 423-acre Preserve, 4.5 mi. of the Bethpage Bikeway, Jogging/Walking, Rollerblading, 5 mi. of the Greenbelt Hiking Trail, No Amenities in the Park, Maps available **Hours:** Dawn-Dusk **Fee: Free Directions:** *Seaford-Oyster Bay Expwy., exit onto Sunrise Hwy. E., pass a small brick bldg. on Left, make the next U-turn at the traffic light, park in the parking lot, across from Train Station*

www.fdale.com/FMP/FMP.htm • www.hike-ligreenbelt.com/page/page/1007314.htm

The Greenbelt Trail Conference & Friends of Massapequa Preserve:

www.fdale.com/FMP/FMP.htm

Planting Fields Arboretum • NYS • 1395 Planting Fields Rd., Oyster Bay, NY • 516-922-9210, 9200 • This is a former Gold Coast Estate & Arboretum. • **Features Include:** 409-acre Arboretum, Hiking, Walking **Hours:** 9 a.m.-5p.m., May-Oct. **Fee:** $6, Empire Pass Accepted **Directions:** *I-495 Long Island Expwy., exit 41 N., take Rte. 106 N. approx. 5 mi, make a Left onto 25 A / Northern Blvd., make the 1st Right onto Mill River Rd., follow signs to the arboretum* *www.plantingfields.org*

Rev. Arthur Mackey Sr. Park • NC • Lakeside Dr. & Washington Rd., Roosevelt, NY • 516-571-8692 • Features Include: 27-acre Park, Walk/Jog around the Lake **Hour:** Dawn-Dusk **Fee: Free Directions:** *Southern State Pkwy., take exit 23/Meadowbrook Rd. S. (not Meadowbrook Pkwy.), make a Right onto Washington Ave., take over the pkwy., make a Right onto Lakeside Dr. (across from C.P center), enter the park on the Right*

www.nassaucountyny.gov/agencies/Parks/WheretoGo/active/mackey.html

Sands Point Preserve Nature, Trails & Habitats • NC • 127 Middle Neck Rd., Port Washington, NY • 516-571-7900 • Features Include: 216-acre Preserve, 6 Marked Walking/Hiking Trails, Woods, Fields, Forests, Meadows, Young Woodlands, Shoreline Beach (on the LI sound), Cliffs, Lawns, Gardens, Freshwater Pond, Trail Maps, Guided Nature Walks & Self-Guiding Literature, each natural area provides habitats for a variety of plants & animals **Hours:** Year-Round, 10 a.m.-5 p.m. **Fee:** Weekends: $2 **Directions:** *I-495 Long Island Expwy., take exit 36 Searingtown Rd. N., drive for approx. 6 mi., the road becomes Port Washington Blvd. & then Middle Neck Rd., enterance is on the Right, 1 mi. past the stone & brick gate of the Sand Point Village Club*

www.sandspointpreserve.org/htm/info.htm

Whitney Pond Park • **NC** • *Northern Blvd. & Community Dr., Manhasset, NY* • *516-571-8110* • **Features Include:** 24-acre Park, Walking Trails **Hours:** Dawn-Dusk **Fee:** **Free** **Directions:** *I-495 Long Island Expwy., take exit 33 Community Dr. N., make the turn onto Community Dr. N., the park is on the Right, just after the police precinct*

Island Rock Climbing Corp. ⌖ • *60 Skyline Dr., Plainview, NY* • *516-822-7625* • **Features Include:** Over 9,000 sq.-ft. Climbing Area, 25-ft. Rappel Tower, 2 Crack Climbs, Separate Lead Wall, Bouldering Cave, State-of-the-Art Indoor Rock Climbing Facility, Seamless Climbing Surface, Lessons, Rentals, Birthday Parties, 6 yrs. & up **Hours:** Mon.-Fri.: Noon-10 p.m., Sat.-Sun.: Noon-6 p.m. **Fee:** Student Quick Start Package: $45, includes lesson, day pass, harness, shoe rental, Day Pass: $14, Harness Rental: $4, Shoe Rental: $4, Adult Quick Start Package: $45, Day Pass: $16, Harness Rental: $5, Shoe Rental: $5

Directions: *I-495 to exit 46 toward Sunnyside Blvd./Plainview, merge onto Executive Dr., turn Right at Commercial St., turn Left at Skyline Dr.*

www.islandrock.net

SUGGESTIONS • COMMENTS • ERRORS

Linda.ReidBryce@verizon.net

Thanks

FISHING

GLOW LURES, SUNSETS, & CASTING LINE

Make Fishing More Fun

Check the tide schedules. Children under 16 don't need a fishing license to fish.

STARTER KIT

Spin Cast reels are easy to use & generally trouble-free. Choose a fishing rod that is light-weight & flexible, yet rugged enough to survive hard use. A beginner's rod should bend freely when shaken. Select a premium grade fishing line with a clear flexible line rated to break between 8 & 12 lbs. Performs admirably.

A 275-yd. spool is plenty.

1.5-in. diameter bobbers

.12-.5 oz. sinkers

2 packs of 6-10 size hooks

BAIT: worms, night crawlers, crickets, grasshoppers

• Have children catch bait the day before in preparation for their 1ˢᵗ fishing experience.
• If after a few minutes of fishing you don't catch anything, move the bobber deeper at about 1-ft. intervals. • Cast to different places + test each new depth. If you still haven't caught anything after adjusting the bobber to 6-ft. remove it + try fishing on the bottom. When bottom fishing, hold the line between your fingers to feel bites. • Keep the line taught, prop your rod in a forked stick + watch for the rod tip to jiggle, indicating a bite. • The best places to fish are small uncrowded waters close to home. • Try in the shallows around docks, rocky spots, weedy shore lines, places where trees overhang the water or where submerged trees, bushes or other shade is found.

www.bwca.cc/activities/fishing/kidsfishing.html

Let Fun Flow Like A River

NYS FISHERMAN'S LICEN

Everyone must have a valid fishing license in their possession
while fishing, except persons under 16 yrs. of age,
when fishing on licensed fishing preserves, or on Free Fishing Days.
Free Fishing takes place the last full weekend in June. Anyone can fish NY
State waters without a fishing license. There are always *free fishing events*
sponsored by the NYS Dept. of Environmental Conservation between April
& Oct. (such as family fishing clinics) where participants can learn about fish
identification, fishing equipment & techniques, fisheries management, angling
ethics & aquatic ecology. Each of DEC's 9 regions can sponsor up to 4 free
fishing events per yr. Most free fishing events occur April-Oct.
Fee: 1-day Fishing License: $5, 7-day License: $10, Annual License: $15
• *518-402-8845* • *www.takemefishing.org* • *www.dec.ny.gov* •

NY State Tide generator • *www.saltwatertides.com/dynamic.dir/newyorksites.html*

NASSAU COUNTY

Bay Park • **NC** • *First Ave., E. Rockaway, NY* • *516-571-7245* • **Features Include:** 96-acre Park, Fishing Dock, Sail Boat Launch, 3 Slip Boat Launch, E. Rockaway Channel & Hewlett Bay **Hours:** Parts of the park are Open Year-Round **Fee: Free Directions:** *Southern State Pkwy., take exit 17 Hempstead Ave. S., take Hempstead Ave., take the Left fork (Ocean Ave.) through Lynbrook & E. Rockaway to Main St. (follow park signs), make a Left onto Front St., make a Right onto Althouse Ave., make a Left onto First & follow to the park*   *www.nassaucountyny.gov*

Captain Lou Fleet • *28A Woodcleft Ave., Freeport, NY* • *631-369-9840* • **Features Include:** 2 Large Motor Yachts, Fishing Events, Party Cruises **Hours** & **Fees:** vary **Directions:** *Northern State Pkwy., take Meadowbrook Pkwy. S. exit 27W., or 135 Seaford-Oyster Bay Expwy. S., exit onto Sunrise Hwy. W., drive through Bellmore, Merrick & pass the Meadowbrook Pkwy., turn Left onto Henry St., the Freeport RR station will be on the Right (becomes S. Main St.), turn Right onto Atlantic Ave., turn Left onto Guy Lombardo Ave., turn Right onto Front St., turn Left onto Woodcleft Ave., Captain Lou Fleet (28A Woodclift Ave.) will be on the Left*   *www.captloufleet.com*

Cow Meadow Park & Preserve • **NC** • *South Main St., Freeport, NY* • *516-571-8685* • The park is located on Freeport Creek. **Features Include:** 171-acre Park, Marina with 30 Boat Slips (608-0514), Fishing Pier, 150 acre Marine Wetlands, Salt Marsh, Mud Flat & Tidal Creek Habitats **Hours:** Dawn-Dusk **Fee: Free Directions:** *Southern State Pkwy., take exit 22 S. Meadowbrook Pkwy., exit at M9 W. Merrick Rd., immediate turn Left onto Mill Rd., turn Left onto South Main St., the entrance is on the Left*   *www.nassaucountyny.gov/agencies/Parks*

Gilgo State Park • **NYS** • *Ocean Pkwy., Babylon, NY* • *631-669-0449* • Access to the park is via 4-wheel drive only & requires a permit. The park is a carry-in, carry-out facility. • **Features Include:** Beach, Surf Fishing, Fall Stripe Bass Migration, Blue Fish, Barrier Beach, Atlantic Ocean, Great South Bay **Hours:** Dawn-Dusk, Year-Round **Fee:** **Free** off-season, Memorial Day-Labor Day: $10, Weekends only until Oct.: $8, Empire Pass Accepted **Directions:** *Meadowbrook or Wantagh Pkwy. S. to Ocean Pkwy. E. (or Robert Moses Cswy. S.) to Ocean Pkwy. W.* *http://nysparks.state.ny.us/sites/info*

Grant Park • **NC** • *1625 Broadway, Hewlett, NY* • *516-571-7821* • Features Include: 35-acre Park, Fishing in the Lake **Hours:** Dawn-Dusk **Fee:** **Free** Directions: *Southern State Pkwy., take exit 15S. for Corona Ave S., turn Right onto N. Corona Ave., turn slight Left toward Rockaway Pkwy., then slight Right at Rockaway Pkwy., turn Right to stay on Rockaway Ave., turn Right onto Broadway* *www.nassaucountyny.gov*

Hempstead Harbor Park • **NC** • *West Shore Rd., Port Washington, NY* • *516-571-7930* • **Features Include:** 60-acre Park, Fishing Pier **Hours:** 11 a.m.-Dusk (Life Guard) **Fee:** **Free** off-season, Resident: $15, Non-Resident: $20, NC permit Memorial Day-Labor Day: $40 **Directions:** *Northern State Pkwy., take exit 29, Roslyn Rd. N., to West Shore Rd.* *www.nassaucountyny.gov*

Hempstead Lake State Park • **NYS** • *Eagle Ave. & Lake Dr., W. Hempstead, NY* • *516-766-1029* • This is the largest lake in Nassau County. • **Features Include:** 3 Ponds for Fishing (Hempstead Lake is catch & release only), Fish McDonald Pond & South Pond for: Trout, Large Mouth Bass, Chain Pickerel, Black Crappe, Perch, Tiger Muskies, Carp & Sunfish, Ice Fishing, Boat Launch Site for Car Top Boats **Hours:** Dawn-Dusk, Year-Round **Fee:** **Free** off-season, April-Oct.: $8, Empire Pass Accepted **Directions:** *Southern State Pkwy., take exit 18 Eagle Ave., keep Right at the fork, follow signs for Rockville Centre/Hempstead Lake State Park, turn Right at Eagle Ave.* *www.stateparks.com/hempstead_lake.html*

Inwood Park • **NC** • *Bayview Ave., Inwood, NY* • *516-571-7894* • The park is surrounded by water. • **Features Include:** 16-acre Park, Launch Ramp, Saltwater Fishing & Crabbing, Water Slide (Nassau residents: annual fee), Scuba Diving (with permit) **Hours:** Dawn-Dusk **Fee:** Leisure Pass Required, Non-Residents Memorial Day-Labor Day: $20 **Directions:** *Southern State Pkwy., take exit 19 S., Peninsula Blvd. S. to end, make a Left on Rockerway Tpke. (large intersection), make a Right onto Burnside Ave., curves to the Left & becomes Sheridan Blvd., take Sheridan to Bayview Ave. & turn Right, continue down Bayview into the park* *www.nycgovparks.org/parks/inwoodhillpark*

Jones Beach State Park • **NYS** • *1 Ocean Pkwy., Wantagh, NY* • *516-785-1600* • Features Include: 6.5 mi. of Ocean Beach, Surf Fishing, Boat Basin, Marina, Family Events have included: Fishing Clinics **Hours:** Dawn-Dusk, Year-Round **Fee:** **Free** off-season,

Memorial Day-Labor Day: $10, Weekends Only until Oct.: $8, Empire Pass Accepted
Directions: *Northern State Pkwy., take the Meadowbrook Pkwy. S. or Wantagh Pkwy. S. to the park*   *www.jonesbeach.com*

Massapequa Preserve • NC • *Merrick Rd. & Ocean Ave., Massapequa, NY • 516-571-7443* • Features Include: 423-acre Preserve, Fresh Water Fishing, Lake, Freshwater Swamps, Marsh, Stream, No Amenities in the Park, Maps available **Directions:** *Seaford-Oyster Bay Expwy., exit onto Sunrise Hwy. E., pass a small brick bldg. on the Left, make the next U-turn at the traffic light, & park in the parking lot across from train station*
www.fdale.com/FMP/FMP.htm

North Woodmere Parks • NC • *750 Hungry Harbor Rd., Valley Stream, NY • 516-571-7800, 7801* • Features Include: 150-acre Park Surrounded by Water, Fishing & Crabbing **Hours:** Dawn-Dusk **Fee:** *Free*, Non-Residents Memorial Day-Labor Day: $5 **Directions:** *Belt Pkwy. to Rockaway Blvd., take Rockaway Blvd. (Tpke.), make Left onto Peninsula Blvd., make a Left onto Branch Blvd., follow it around to the Right, the park entrance is on the Left*   *www.nassaucountyny.gov/agencies/Parks*

Wantagh Park • NC • *Kings Rd. & Canal Pl., Wantagh, NY • 516-571-7460* • Features Include: Boating, Marina, Launch Ramp, 111-acre Park, Flat Creek & East Bay, Fishing Pier **Hours:** Dawn-Dusk **Fee:** *Free*, Non-Residents Memorial Day-Labor Day: $5 **Directions:** *Southern State Pkwy., take exit 27 S. Wantagh Pkwy., take the exit for Sunrise Hwy. E., make a Right onto Wantagh Ave., to end, make a Right onto Merrick Rd., at first light make a Left into the park*
www.nassaucountyny.gov/agencies/Parks/WhereToGo/active/wantagh.html

The Waterfront Center • *One West End Ave., Oyster Bay, NY • 516-922-7245* • The Waterfront Center is a not-for-profit organization focused on educating children & adults about the marine environment. **Features Include:** Fishing on the Long Island Sound, Boat & Kayak Rentals, Sailboat or Sea Kayak Rentals, Private Charters, Educational Programs, Certification Classes **Directions:** *Northern State Pkwy., take exit 35 N., 106/7 N. veer onto Rte. 106 N. at the Millerage Inn, drive approx. 6.5 mi., cross over Rte. 25A, make a Left onto Audrey Ave. (see the Coin Gallery on the corner) go 1 light & go to the 2nd stop sign, turn Right at the railroad tracks onto Theodore Roosevelt Park, make an immediate Left onto West End Ave. (before entrance booth), red brick bldg. on the Left*   *www.thewaterfrontcenter.org*

SUFFOLK COUNTY
Belmont Lake State Park • *625 Belmont Ave., West Babylon, NY • 631-667-5055*
• This full service park is the headquarters of the Long Island State Park Region. **Features Include:** Fishing, Row & Paddle Boat Rentals, Handicap Accessible **Hours:** Dawn-Dusk,

Year-Round **Fee: Free** off-season, April-Nov.: $8, Empire Pass Accepted **Directions:** *Southern State Pkwy., exit 37 N., merge onto Belmont Ave.* *http://nysparks.state.ny.us*

Blydenburgh County Park • SC • Veteran's Memorial Hwy., Smithtown, NY • 631-854-3713 • **Features Include:** 627-acre Park, Freshwater Fishing, Rowboat Rentals, Freshwater Fishing for Pumpkinseed Sunfish, Large-Mouth Bass, Perch & Bluegill is permitted at Stump Pond, NYS Freshwater Fishing Laws apply **Hours:** Dawn-Dusk, Year-Round **Fee: Free** off-season, Memorial Day-Labor Day: $8, Green Key Holders: $3, Rowboat Rentals: mid-May-Labor Day **Directions:** *Northern State Pkwy. to end, slight Right onto Rte. 347/454 the main entrance to the park is on the North side of Veterans Memorial Hwy., opposite the H. Lee Dennison County Center in Smithtown*

www.co.suffolk.ny.us/departments/parks/

Caleb Smith State Park Preserve • 581 W. Jericho Tpke., Smithtown, NY • 631-265-1054 • **Features Include:** 543-ace Park, Nissequogue River, Fly Fishing, Oak-Pine Habitats, Scattered Wetlands Family Events have included: Animal Olympics, South Side Saunter, Buzz Says the Bee, Wet-n-Wild. **Hours:** 8 a.m.-Dusk, Year-Round, Closed Mon.: April-Sept., Closed Mon.-Tues.: Oct.-March **Fee: Free** off-season, Memorial Day-Labor Day: $10, Weekends only until Oct.: $8 **Directions:** *I-495 Long Island Expwy., exit 53 N. Sunken Meadow Pkwy. N., take exit SM 3 E. to Smithtown, take Jericho Tpke./Rte. 25 E., drive approx. 3 mi. to the park* *http://nysparks.state.ny.us/parks*

Camp Hero • State Park • 50 South Fairview Ave., Montauk, NY • 631-668-3781 • The park boasts some of the best surf fishing locations in the world. **Features Include:** 415-acre Park, Atlantic Ocean Beach, Fishing, Maritime Forests, Freshwater Wetlands, Ocean Views **Hours:** Mon.-Sun., Dawn-Dusk **Fee: Free** off-season, Empire Pass Accepted **Directions:** *I-495 Long Island Expwy., exit 68 for William Floyd Pkwy./Co. Hwy. 46 S. toward Shirley, turn Left onto Rte. 27 E. Sunrise Hwy., turn Right at Camp Hero State Park Rd., turn Left to stay on Camp Hero State Park Rd.*

http://nysparks.state.ny.us/parks/info.asp?parkID=82

Captree State Park • 1 Rescue Rd., Babylon, NY • 631-669-0449 • Captree State Park lies at the eastern tip of Jones Beach Island in the heart of the fishing grounds. **Features Include:** Boat Basin, Charter Boats available for Fishing, Scuba Diving, Sightseeing Excursion, Boat Launch, Fishing, Marina, Family Events have included: Aug.-Snapper Derby, Sept.-Fall Harvest & Seafood Festival, Oct.-I Fish New York Salt Water Clinic, & South Shore Fishing Classic **Fee: Free** off-season, Memorial Day-Labor Day: $10, Weekends Only until Oct.: $8, Empire Pass Accepted **Directions:** *Southern State Pkwy., exit 40 Robert Moses Cswy. S. to park*

www.nysparks.com/parks/info.asp?parkID=151

SPRING BLISS

Caumsett State Historic Park • NYS • *25 Lloyd Harbor Rd., Huntington, NY • 631-423-1770* • The park is situated on a peninsula extending into the Long Island Sound. **Features Include:** Fishing, Scuba Diving (by permit), Rock Shoreline, Salt Marsh **Hours:** Dawn-Dusk, Year-Round **Fee: Free** off-season, April-Nov., Empire Passport Accepted, Handicap Accessibile **Directions:** *I-495 Long Island Expwy., exit Rte. 110 N. which becomes New York Ave., turn Left onto Main St. 25A W., turn Right onto West Neck Rd. N., the park entrance is on the Left* http://nysparks.state.ny.us/parks

Cedar Point County Park • SC • *5 Cedar Point Rd., East Hampton, NY • 631-852-7620 • Camping Reservations: 631-244-7275* • Cedar Point was settled in 1651 & became a busy shipping port for farm goods, fish & timber from Sag Harbor. **Features Include:** Rowboat Rentals, Saltwater Fishing, Scuba Diving, 607-acre Park, Views of Gardiner's Bay, Fishing, Surfcasting for Bass & Bluefish, Lighthouse, Vehicle Access to the Outer Beach (with permit only), General Store & Snack Bar: 631-324-7147 **Hours:** Dawn-Dusk **Fee: Free Directions:** *I-495 Long Island Expwy., take exit 68 William Floyd Pkwy. S. toward Shirley, turn Right onto NY-27 E. toward Montauk, turn Left onto County Rd. 113/Stephen Hands Path, follow County Rd. 113, continue onto Old Northwest Rd., turn Right onto NW Rd., turn Left onto Alewife Brook Rd., take the 1st Right onto Cedar Point Rd.* www.co.suffolk.ny.us/Home/departments/parks/Parks.aspx

Connetquot River State Park Preserve • *Box 505, Oakdale, NY • 631-581-1005* • The park maintains 3,473 acres of land & water for the protection & propagation of game birds. **Features Include:** Trout Fishing, Fish Hatchery, Deep Water Pond, Waterfowl, Rare Nesting Birds, Osprey **Hours:** 6 a.m.-Dusk, Open Year-Round, closed Mon.-Tues.: Oct.-March **Fee:** $8, Empire Pass Accepted **Directions:** *Southern State Pkwy., take exit 44 Sunrise Hwy. E., the preserve is located on the North side of Sunrise Hwy., just West of Pond Rd.* http://nysparks.state.ny.us/parks

Cupsogue Beach County Park • SC • *Dune Rd., Westhampton, NY • 631-852-8111* • Cupsogue Beach offers some of the best saltwater bass fishing on Long Island. **Features Include:** 296-acre Barrier Beach Park, Fishing, Swimming, Scuba Diving, Camping, Outer Beach Access, Food Concession (www.thebeachhuts.com), First Aid Center, Restrooms, Showers, Changing Rooms **Hours:** 8:30 a.m.-4:30 p.m., Open Year-Round **Fee: Free** off-season, With Green Key: $5, Without Green Key: $10, Memorial Day-Labor Day **Directions:** *I-495 Long Island Expwy., take exit 68 for William Floyd Pkwy./Co. Hwy. 46 S. toward Shirley, take the ramp onto Rte. 27 E., take exit 63 S. for Co. Hwy. 31 S. toward Westhampton Beach, merge onto County Rte. 31/Old Riverhead Rd./ Riverhead Rd., continue on Oak St., at the traffic circle take the 2nd exit onto Potunk Ln., turn Right onto Stevens Ln., turn Left onto Jessup Ln., turn Right onto County Rte. 89/Dune Rd., follow Dune Rd. to the park*

www.co.suffolk.ny.us/Home/departments/parks/Parks.aspx

FUN FAMILY

Heckscher State Park • *Heckscher Pkwy., Field 1, E. Islip, NY* • *631-581-2100* • *Reservations: 800-456-2267* • Features Include: Great South Bay Beach, Fishing, Boat Launch Ramp, Picnic Areas & Tables, Playing Fields, Food Hours: Year-Round, 7 days a week, 7 a.m.-Dusk Fee: Free off-season, Memorial Day-Labor Day: $10, Weekends Only until Oct.: $8, Empire Pass Accepted Directions: *Southern State Pkwy. E., it ends in the park* *http://nysparks.state.ny.us/parks*

Hither Hills • **NYS** • *50 South Fairview Ave., Montauk, NY* • *631-668-2554* • *Reservations: 800-456-2267* • Features Include: 40-acre Fresh Water Lake, Year-Round Fishing, Night Fishing, Ocean Beach, Hiking, Nature Trail, 168-site Campground on the Ocean, Playground, Food, Picnic Area, Fireplaces & Tables, Showers, Fishing Permit Required Hours: Year-Round, Dawn-Dusk, 7 days a week Fee: Free off-season, Memorial Day-Labor Day: $10, Weekends Only until Oct.: $8, Empire Pass Accepted Directions: *I-495 Long Island Expwy., take exit 68, William Floyd Pkwy. S., take Sunrise Hwy. Rte. 27 E., turn Left onto 27 E., Right turn onto Birch Dr./Oak Ln., Right onto Birch St./Birch Dr., turn Left onto Old Montauk Hwy.* *http://nysparks.state.ny.us/parks*

Indian Island County Park • **SC** • *Cross River Dr. (Rte. 105), Riverhead, NY* • *631-852-3232* • *Camping Reservations: 631-244-7275* • Indian Island County Park is located at the estuarine mouth of the Peconic River. Features Include: 275-acre Park, Views of Flanders Bay, Fishing, Finest Picnicking in Suffolk County, Picnic Tables & Grills, Playground, Restrooms, Shower Facilities Hours: Year-Round Fee: Free off-season, Green Key: $3, Non-Residents Memorial Day-Labor Day: $8 Directions: *I-495 Long Island Expwy., take exit 71, Right turn onto Rte. 24 at end of exit ramp, follow Rte. 24 South through the Riverhead traffic circle, continue on Rte. 24 & make a Left turn at the next traffic light onto Rte. 105, follow Rte. 105 to the entrance on Right* *www.co.suffolk.ny.us/Home/departments/parks/Parks.aspx*

Lakeland County Park • **SC** • *Johnson Ave., Islandia, NY* • *631-853-2727* • *Administration: 631-854-4949* • Features Include: Fishing, Nature Trail, Boardwalk (over the headwaters of the Connetquot River), Wetland Vegetation, Waterfowl, Picnic Area, Gazebo Hours: Office/Restrooms Open Memorial Day-Labor Day, Handicap Accessible Directions: *I-495 Long Island Expwy. to exit 58 S. Nichols Rd., turn Left at Johnson Ave., the park entrance is .5 mi. on the Right* *www.co.suffolk.ny.us/Home/departments/parks/Parks.aspx*

Lake Ronkonkoma County Park • **SC** • *Lake Shore Rd., Lake Ronkonkoma, NY* • *631-854-9699* • Features Include: Fishing Area, Fishing Pier Picnic Area, Handicap Accessible Directions: *I-495 Long Island Expwy., take exit 60 toward Lake Ronkonkoma/Sayville/Ronkonkoma Ave., merge onto Express Dr. S./Long Island Expwy. Service Rd., turn Left at Ronkonkoma Ave., turn Left at County Rte. 16/Portion Rd., continue to follow County*

Rte. 16, turn Right at School House Rd., turn Left at Edward Ct.
www.co.suffolk.ny.us/departments/parks/Lake Ronkonkoma County Park.aspx

Nissequogue River State Park • *799 St. Johnland Rd., Kings Park, NY • 631-269-4927*
• Features Include: Fishing, Marina, Boat Launch Sites, Boat Rentals, Bird Watching, Canoe & Kayak Launch, Tidal & Fresh Water Wetlands, Reptiles, Amphibians, Hiking, Walking, Museum/Visitor Center **Hours:** Dawn-Dusk, Year- Round **Fee: Free** off-season, Memorial Day-Labor Day: $8, Empire Pass Accepted **Directions:** *Sunken Meadow Pkwy., take exit SM 4, drive East on Pulaski Rd. which becomes Old Dock Rd. at the 5th traffic light, make a Right onto St. Johnland Rd., park entrance is about .5 mi. on the Left* http://nysparks.state.ny.us/parks

Orient Point • NYS • *Rte. 25, Orient Point, NY • 631-323-2440* • Features Include: 45,000 ft. of frontage on Gardiner's Bay, Fishing, Beach, Nature Trails, Picnic Tables, Playground, Environmental Tours, Bike Rentals, Rare Maritime Forest, Wood Deck (overlooking Gardiner's Bay) **Hours:** Dawn-Dusk, Year-Round **Fee: Free** off-season, Memorial Day-Labor Day: $10, Weekends Only until Oct.: $8, Empire Pass Accepted **Directions:** *I-495 Long Island Expwy., take exit 73 Old Country Rd. toward Orient/Greenport/ Co. Hwy. 58, slight Left onto County Rte. 58/Old Country Rd./Rte. 58, at Roanoke Ave., take the 2nd exit & stay on County Rte. 58/Old Country Rd./Rte. 58, slight Left at Main Rd./Middle Country Rd./Rte. 25, continue to follow Main Rd./Rte. 25 , turn Left onto Love Ln., turn Right onto County Rte. 48/Rte. 48, continue to follow County Rte. 48, continue on Main Rd./Rte. 25 E. to the Park* http://nysparks.state.ny.us/sites/info

Robert Cushman Murphy County Park • SC • *River Rd., Calverton/Manorville, NY • 631-854-4949* • Features Include: 60-acre Park, Fishing on Swan Pond, Large Mouth Bass, Eastern Chain Pickeral, Yellow Perch, Blue Gill, Bullhead Catfish, Pumpkinseed Sunfish, Boating, Hiking, Hunting, NYS Fisherman's License Required, there are No Facilities in this park **Hours:** Year-Round **Fee: Free Directions:** *I-495 Long Island Expwy., take exit 70 CR 111 S., turn Left onto Halsey Manor Rd., follow North across the Long Island Expwy. & railroad tracks, Halsey Manor Rd. becomes Connecticut Ave. once railroad tracks have been crossed, follow Connecticut Ave. N., make a Left turn onto River Rd. & make the next Left onto Old River Rd., follow Old River Rd. to the 1st entrance on the Right (North side of the road.)* http://www.co.suffolk.ny.us/departments/parks/

Robert Moses State Park • *Fire Island National Seashore • Box 247, Babylon, NY • 631-669-0470* • Features Include: 5 mi. of Ocean Beach, Surf-Fishing, Pier Fishing, Marina, Boat Basin (accommodates 40 boats), Swimming, Surfing **Hours:** Dawn-Dusk, Year-Round **Fee: Free** off-season Memorial Day-Labor Day: $10, Weekends Only until Oct.: $8, Empire Pass Accepted **Directions:** *Southern State Pkwy. to Robert Moses Cswy., take exit 40 S., the park is at the western end of Fire Island* http://nysparks.state.ny.us/parks

Scotty's Marina & Fishing Station • *72 Bayside Dr., Point Lookout, NY* • *516-432-4665* • **Features Include:** 15 fiberglass 16-ft. Carolina Skiffs, 6 Horsepower Motors, Charters, Bait, Tackle, Marina, Gas, Diesel, Snack Shop **Fees:** Full Day: $65, Half-Day: $45, No Motor: $30, Deposit: $25, Over 61: half-price Wed.-Thurs. **Directions:** *Southern State Pkwy., take exit 22S. toward Jones Beach, merge onto Meadowbrook State Pkwy. S., exit onto Loop Pkwy., turn Left onto Loop Pkwy., turn Left at Lido Blvd., turn Left onto Parkside Ave., Parkside Ave. turns Right & becomes Bayside Dr., the marina will be on the Right* www.scottysmarina.com

Sears Bellows • SC • *Sears Bellows Pond Rd., Hampton Bays, NY* • *Park Office: 631-852-8290* • *Big Duck: 631-852-8292* • *Camping Reservations: 631-244-7275* • **Features Include:** Freshwater Fishing, Bluegill, Bass, Perch, Pickerel, Rowboat Rentals **Hours:** Dawn-Dusk, This park is closed to certain activities during waterfowl hunting season. NYS regulations apply to all sporting activities. This is the home of the *Big Duck* (see museums). **Hours:** Dawn-Dusk, Year-Round **Fee: Free** off-season, mid-June-Labor Day with Green Key: $5, No Green Key: $8 **Directions:** *Northern State Pkwy., exit onto Wantagh State Pkwy. S., exit onto Sunrise Hwy., take exit 65 N., follow Rd. (Rte. 24), make a Left onto Bellows Pond Rd., the park entrance is on the Right* http://www.co.suffolk.ny.us/Home/departments/parks/Parks.aspx

Shadmoor • NYS • *50 S. Fairview Ave., Montauk, NY* • *631-668-3781* • **Features Include:** 99-acre Park, 2,400 ft. of Ocean Beach, Saltwater Fishing **Hours:** Year-Round **Fee: Free** parking **Directions:** *I-495 Long Island Expwy., take exit 68 for William Floyd Pkwy./Co. Hwy. 46 S. toward Shirley, merge onto William Floyd Pkwy., take the ramp onto Rte. 27 E. Sunrise Hwy. E. to Montauk Village, the Park is 1.5 mi. E. of the village on the Right, at the southwest corner of Rte. 27 & Seaside Ave.* http://nysparks.state.ny.us/sites/info

Shinnecock East County Park • SC • *Dune Rd., Southampton, NY* • *631-852-8290* • This undeveloped barrier beach park borders the Shinnecock Inlet where it meets the Atlantic Ocean. **Features Include:** Ocean & Bay Beaches, Saltwater Fishing, Striped Bass, Off-Road Recreational Vehicles may drive on the outer ocean beach. Permits are given to self-contained campers with a valid Suffolk County Parks Green Key Card. No tent camping is permitted. A small parking lot is available for Green Key cardholders who do not have an Outer Beach Recreational Vehicle Permit. Vehicles with Suffolk County Parks Outer Beach Recreational Vehicle Permits must park on the beach. **Hours:** Dawn-Dusk, Year-Round **Fee: Free** off-season, Mid-June-Labor Day with Green Key: $5, No Green Key: $8 **Directions:** *Southern State Pkwy., exit at Sunrise Hwy., exit at Montauk Hwy., turn South on Halsey Neck Ln., turn Right onto Dune Rd. W. to the park entrance* www.co.suffolk.ny.us/Home/departments/parks/Parks.aspx

Smith Point County Park • SC • *Fire Island, NY* • *631-852-1313* • *Camping Reservations: 631-244-7275* • Smith Point is Suffolk County's largest oceanfront

park. **Features Include:** Atlantic Surf, Saltwater Fishing, Outer Beach Access, Swimming, Lifeguards, Playground, Food Concession, Showers, Restaurant, Off-Road Vehicles with a permit may drive on the western portion of the outer beach. The Raw Bar & Grill serves breakfast, lunch & dinner, offering seafood specialties & live entertainment. Beach Hut: 631-728-2988, *www.thebeachhuts.com* **Hours:** Sat.-Wed.: 8:30 a.m.-6 p.m., Thurs. & Fri. 8:30 a.m.-9 p.m. **Fee: Free** off-season, With Green Key: $5, Memorial Day-Sept.: $10 **Directions:** *I-495 Long Island Expwy., exit 68 S. William Floyd Pkwy. to end, which terminates at Fire Island*
www.co.suffolk.ny.us/Home/departments/parks/Parks.aspx

Southaven County Park • SC • *Victory Ave., Brookhaven, NY • 631-854-1414 • 631-924-4490 • 631-345-2449 •* **Features Includes:** 1,356-acre Pine-Oak Forested Park, Carman's River, Freshwater Fishing, Rowboat Rentals, Boating, Canoeing, Hunting, Hiking, Camping (tents & trailers), Picnicking, Bicycle Hostel, the LI Steamer Trains (see museums) **Hours:** Spring Weekends Only **Fee: Free Directions:** *Southern State Pkwy., exit at Sunrise Hwy., take exit 58 N., as you enter William Floyd Pkwy. turn West onto Victory Ave., follow signs to the main entrance of the park* www.co.suffolk.ny.us/

Sunken Meadow State Park • *Rte. 25A & Sunken Meadow Pkwy., Northport, NY • 631-269-4333 •* **Features Include:** 3-mi. Beach, Long Island Sound, Fishing, Picnicking, Picnic Tables, Swimming, Nature Trails, Playground **Fee: Free** off-season, Memorial Day-Labor Day: $10, Weekends Only until Oct.: $8, Empire Pass Accepted **Directions:** *I-495 Long Island Expwy., take exit 53 Sunken Meadow/Sagtikos Pkwy. to the end* http://nysparks.state.ny.us/parks

Theodore Roosevelt County Park • SC • *Montauk Hwy., Montauk, NY • 631-852-7878 • Camping: 631-852-7879 •.* **Features Include:** "Big Reed" Pond, Fishing, Hunting, Canoeing, Kayaking, Outer Beach Access, Nature Trail, Picnicking, No Rentals Available-Bring Your Own Canoe or Kayak **Hours:** Dawn-Dusk, Museum: Wed.-Sun. 10 a.m.-5 p.m., May-Oct. **Fee: Free** off-season **Directions:** *Southern State Pkwy., follow Montauk Hwy. East through Montauk Village, past East Lake Dr., park sign & entrance are on North side of Montauk Hwy.* www.co.suffolk.ny.us

Wildwood • State Park • *P.O. Box 518, North Wading River Rd., Wading River, NY • 631-929-4314 • Reservations: 800 456-2267 •* **Features Include:** 600-acre Park, Fishing, Hiking, Beach, Nature Trails, Playground, Picnic Tables, Recreation Programs, Camping: April-Columbus Day Weekend **Hours:** Dawn-Dusk, Year-Round **Fee: Free** off-season, Memorial Day-Labor Day: $10, Weekends Only until Oct.: $8, Empire Pass Accepted **Directions:** *I-495 Long Island Expwy., take exit 68 N./Rte. 46, take Rte. 25A E., turn Left onto Sound Ave., turn Left at traffic light onto Hulse Landing Rd., the park entrance is on the Right* http://nysparks.state.ny.us/sites/info

Boomers Family Fun Park • *Outdoor Track* • *655 Long Island Ave., Medford, NY* • *631-475-1771* • **Features Include:** Cartoon Theme Park, Go-Karts, Indoor Carousel, Kiddie Swing, Restaurant, Animated Show, 70 Redemption & Ride Games, Outdoor Mini-Golf (18 holes), 6 Outdoor Kiddie Rides, Bumper Boats, 7 Outdoor Batting Cages, Outdoor Facilities open weather permitting **Hours:** 11 a.m., close time varies **Fees:** Go-Karts: $5, Game Token: 25¢, Mini-Golf: $4.25, Batting Cages: $2, Rides: $3.25, Bumper Boats: $4.50, Pay-One-Price: $15.95 **Directions:** *I-495 Long Island Expwy., take exit 64, take the S. Service Rd., .5 mi., Boomers will be on the Right side of the road* www.boomersparks.com

The County Fair Entertainment Park • *Outdoor Track* • *3351 Rte. 112, Medford, NY* • *631-732-0579* • **Features Include:** Go-Kart Racing, Realistic Racing Environment, Huge Figure-8 Race Track, Single & Double Go-Karts Available, Miniature Golf, Driving Range, Batting Cages **Hours:** Open March-Nov., weather permitting **Fee:** Go-Karts: $6 per ride, Under 55-in. tall: Free, Height Requirement: 55-in. tall to Drive Intermediate, 60-in. tall to drive Adult Car, Under 55-in. tall must drive with a licensed driver, Mini-Golf: $6.50 per person per game, Kids: $5.50 **Directions:** *I-495 Long Island Expwy., take exit 64 N. 1 mi., take 3351 Rte. 112, the crossroads are Granny & Horseblock* www.countryfairpark.com

Karts Indoor Raceway • *Indoor Track* • *701 Union Pkwy. Ronkonkoma, NY* • *631-737-5278* • *800-718-KART (5278)* • **Features Includes:** 27,000 sq ft., 2 Tracks (designed by racing professionals), 4-point Safety Belts, Remote Controlled, Radio-Controlled Emergency Shut-Off & Pit Speed Reduction, Pit Lane Speed allows the customers to enter & exit the charge rail grid safely, Electric Race Karts (boast 4 different speeds with the push of a button), FUN for the inexperienced or the pro go-kart driver, State-of-the-Art Timing System. Height Requirement: 54-in. For the Junior Race Track, 20-in. for the Mini Racecar on the "Microtrack Raceway," 6 drivers in each race, Game Room, "The Pit-Stop" Snack Bar, Parties: Kids & Corporations, Racing Leagues, Roller Ball (mini bowling) **Racing Hours:** Mon.-Thurs.: 11 a.m.-10 p.m., Fri.-Sat.: 11 a.m.-12 a.m., Sun.: 11 a.m.-8 p.m. **Fees:** $7, 5 Race Pkg.: $30, Junior Race Track: $4 per race, 5 Race Package: $17, Road Test+Race: $10 (must pass to compete in the fast races) **Directions:** *I-495 Long Island Expwy., take exit 59 Ocean Ave. S., drive on Lakeland Ave S. for 1 mi., take the Right fork for Ocean Ave., turn Left onto Union Pkwy., Karts Indoor Raceway is on the Left corner of Ocean Ave. & Union Pkwy.*   *www.karts1.com*

Riverhead Raceway • *Outdoor Track* • *1797 Old Country Rd., Riverhead, NY* • *Race Day Hotline: 631-727-0010* • *631-842-7223* Features Include: Monster Trucks, Super Pro Trucks, Legends, Late Models, Modifieds, NASCAR Stock Cars **Hours:** May: admission tickets available at racetrack on day of race only, Sat.: gates open at 3 p.m., show starts at 5 p.m., Sun.: gates open at Noon, group rates available **Fee:** Kids 6-12: $5, Under 5: Free **Directions:** *I-495 Long Island Expwy., take the last exit 73, head East on County Rd. 58, the raceway will be on the Right approx. .5 mi. beyond the last exit just past Tanger II*   *www.riverheadraceway.com*

Tickey Action Park • *Outdoor Track* • *formerly Castle Golf Amusements* • *1878 Middle Country Rd., Centereach, NY* • *631- 471-1267* • Features Include: Go-Karts, Mini Golf, Video & Redemption Games, Birthday Parties **Fees:** Go-Karts: $4 per ride, Kids 10 & Above, Tokens: 4 for $1, Handicap Accessible **Directions:** *I-495 Long Island Expwy., take exit 62 Nicolls Rd. toward Stony Brook, merge onto Middle Country Rd./25*   *www.tikiactionpark.com*

TETHER-CAR RACE TRACK

"In California, during the late 1930's, a hobby known as Tether Car Racing began. The idea was to power a miniature racecar with a gas engine, attach it to a center post using a wire or cord as a tether and go as fast as you can. Many of the early cars were home made."   *www.TetherCar.com*

NASSAU COUNTY

Cedar Creek Park • *3524 Merrick Rd., Seaford, NY* • *516-571-7470* • The park is on Seaman's Creek & the East Bay. • **Features Include:** 259 Acres, Tether-Car Race Track (available by permit) **Directions:** *Northern State Pkwy., exit onto 135S. Seaford-Oyster Bay Expwy., take exit 1 W. Merrick Rd. W. toward Freeport, merge onto Merrick Rd.*
www.nassaucountyny.gov/agencies/Parks/

KITE FLYING TIPS

- Delta Kites are bigger & easier to fly.
- Parafoil Kites & Sled Kites are based on modern parachute technology. They launch easily & fly steadily at a high angle & there is nothing to assemble, lose or break!
- Diamond Kites are stable & reliable flyers.
- Butterfly, Bird & Bug Kites are extremely easy to fly when the winds are steady.
- Easy flying kites can range from $15-$25.
- Tangle-resistant 500 ft. of 50 pound kite line makes flying easier.
- Hammer a tent stake into the ground as an anchor & tie the kite line to it.
- Most schools & beaches have large open fields suitable for off-season use.
- Basically any beach, park or field with a wide open area & no power lines are favorable.
www.breezechasers.com/bc-kids.htm

NASSAU COUNTY

Eisenhower Park • NC • *1899 Hempstead Tpke., East Meadow, NY •* *516-572-0348, 572-0290, 572-0327* **•** **Features Include:** Park in Field 6A. There is a big open field area. **Hours:** Dawn-Dusk **Fee: Free**, Non-Residents Memorial Day-Labor: $5 **Directions:** *Northern State Pkwy., Meadow Brook Pkwy. S., exit M3 E. Stewart Ave., make a Right onto Stewart Ave. continue to the park* *www.nassaucountyny.gov*

Hempstead Harbor Park • NC • *West Shore Rd., Port Washington, NY •* *516-571-7930* **•** **Features Include:** Fly kites on the beach. **Directions:** *Northern State Pkwy., take exit 29, Roslyn Rd. N., to West Shore Rd.* *www.nassaucountyny.gov*

Wantagh Park • NC • *Kings Rd. & Canal Pl., Wantagh, NY • 516-571-7460 •* Features Include: Use the picnic area or game fields. **Hours:** Dawn-Dusk **Fee:** **Free**, Non-Residents Memorial Day-Labor Day: $5 **Directions:** *Southern State Pkwy., take exit 27 S. Wantagh Pkwy., take the exit for Sunrise Hwy. E., make a Right onto Wantagh Ave., to end, make a Right onto Merrick Rd., at 1st light make a Left into the park*

www.nassaucountyny.gov/agencies/Parks/WhereToGo/active/wantagh.html

SUFFOLK COUNTY

Blydenburgh County Park • SC • *Smithtown Veteran's Memorial Hwy., Smithtown, NY • 631-854-3713 •* **Features Include:** Fly kites in the field near the dog run. **Hours:** Dawn-Dusk, Year-Round **Fee:** **Free** off-season, Green Key Holders: $3, No Green Key: $8, Memorial Day-Labor Day **Directions:** *Northern State Pkwy. to the eastern end, turn Right onto Rte. 347/454, the main (southern) entrance to the park is on the North side of Veterans Memorial Hwy., opposite the H. Lee Dennison County Center in Smithtown, the northern entrance can be reached by following Rte. 347 to Brooksite Dr. N., turn Left onto New Mill Rd., follow to the park entrance at end*

www.co.suffolk.ny.us/departments/parks/Blydenburgh County Park.aspx

Caumsett State Historic Park • NYS • *25 Lloyd Harbor Rd., Huntington, NY • 631-423-1770 •* The park is situated on a peninsula extending into the Long Island Sound. **Features Include:** Kite Flying, Bridle Paths, Walking, Jogging, Biking, Gardens, Fishing, Nature Trails **Hours:** Dawn-Dusk **Fee:** **Free** off-season, April-Nov., Empire Passport Accepted, Handicap Accessible **Directions:** *I-495 Long Island Expwy., exit Rte. 110 N. which becomes New York Ave., turn Left onto Main St. 25A W., turn Right onto West Neck Rd. N., the park entrance is on the Left*

http://nysparks.state.ny.us/parks/info.asp?parkID=68

Heckscher State Park • *Heckscher Pkwy., Field 1, East Islip, NY • 631-581-2100 •* **Features Include:** Kite Flying at Field 6 **Hours:** Year-Round, 7 days a week, 7 a.m.-Dusk **Fee:** **Free** off-season, Memorial Day-Labor Day: $10, Weekends Only until Oct.: $8, Empire Pass Accepted **Directions:** *Southern State Pkwy. E., the pkwy. ends in the park, park in Field 6* *http://nysparks.state.ny.us/parks/info.asp?parkID=153*

Hither Hills • NYS • *50 S. Fairview Ave., Montauk, NY • 631-668-2554 • Reservations: 800-456-2267 •* There are big open fields great for kite flying on the beach or near the picnic area. **Hours:** Year-Round, Dawn-Dusk, 7 days a week **Fee:** **Free** off-season, Memorial Day-Labor Day: $10, Weekends Only until Oct.: $8, Empire Pass Accepted **Directions:** *I-495 Long Island Expwy., take exit 68, William Floyd Pkwy. S., take Sunrise Hwy./Rte. 27 E., turn Left onto 27 E., Right turn onto Birch Dr./Oak Ln., turn Right onto Birch St./Birch Dr., turn Left onto Old Montauk Hwy.* *http://nysparks.state.ny.us/parks/info.asp?parkId=48*

Robert Moses State Park • *Fire Island National Seashore • Box 247, Babylon, NY • 631-669-0470 •* **Features Include:** Kite Flying at Field 5, 5 mi. of Ocean Beach, Picnic

Tables, Lighthouse at Field 5 **Hours:** Year-Round, Dawn-Dusk **Fee: Free** off-season, Memorial Day-Labor Day: $10, Weekends Only until Oct.: $8, Empire Pass accepted **Directions:** *Southern State Pkwy. to Robert Moses Cswy., take exit 40 S., the park is at the western end of Fire Island*   *http://nysparks.state.ny.us/parks*

Smith Point County Park • SC • *Fire Island, Shirley, NY* • *631-852-1313* • Features

Include: Fly kites in the field across from the campgrounds building. Park in the East section of the parking lot & walk out to the beach. **Hours:** Dawn-Dusk **Hours:** Sat.-Wed.: 8:30 a.m.-6 p.m., Thurs. & Fri.: 8:30 a.m.-9 p.m. **Fee: Free** off-season, With Green Key: $5, Memorial Day-Sept.: $10 **Directions:** *I-495 Long Island Expwy., take exit 68 William Floyd Pkwy. S. to the end*

Southaven Country • SC • *Victory Ave., Brookhaven, NY* • *631-854-1415* • Features

Include: Ball fields are available for kite flying when not in use by teams. **Hours:** Spring Weekends Only **Fee: Free Directions:** *Southern State Pkwy., exit at Sunrise Hwy., take exit 58 N., as you enter William Floyd Pkwy. turn West onto Victory Ave., follow signs to the main entrance of the park*
                    www.co.suffolk.ny.us/Home/departments/parks/Parks.aspx

Theodore Roosevelt County Park • SC • Montauk Hwy., Montauk, NY • 631-852-7878

• **Features Include:** Fly kites in the picnic area. Go to the 3rd house just before the ranch. **Hours:** Camp Wikoff is open to the public from May-Oct., Wed.-Sun.: 10 a.m. -5 p.m. **Fee: Free** off-season **Directions:** *Southern State Pkwy., follow Montauk Hwy. E. through Montauk Village, past East Lake Dr., park sign & entrance are on North side of Montauk Hwy., pull into the driveway, turn Left onto the dirt road*
                    www.co.suffolk.ny.us/Home/departments/parks/Parks.aspx

Wildwood • NYS • *P.O. Box 518, North Wading River Rd., Wading River, NY* • *631-929-4314* • Features Include:

The baseball field is great for kite flying when not in use by teams. **Hours:** Dawn-Dusk, Year-Round **Fee: Free** off-season, Memorial Day-Labor Day: $10, Weekends Only until Oct.: $8, Empire Pass Accepted **Directions:** *I-495 Long Island Expwy., take exit 68, head N. on Rte. 46, take Rte. 25A E., turn Left onto Sound Ave., turn Left at traffic light onto Hulse Landing Rd., the park entrance is on the Right, park in the lower parking field near the picnic area*   *http://nysparks.state.ny.us/sites/info*

SUGGESTIONS • COMMENTS • ERRORS

Linda.ReidBryce
@verizon.net

Thanks

AIR SHOWS

Tip: Air Shows are outdoor events that take place on open fields. Appropriate dress is strongly advised. Most air shows occur between June + Oct.

American Air Power Museum • *Republic Airport, 1230 New Hwy., • Hangar 3, E. Farmingdale, NY • 631-293-6398 • Office of Public Affairs: 212-843-8010 • Educational Tours: 212-843-8010 •* Features Include: Museum Tours (given by WWII Veterans), Planes, Stories, Historic Understanding, Flight Demonstrations (on certain days), Flight Experiences **Hours:** Thurs.-Sun.: 10:30 a.m.-4 p.m., (squadron of vintage aircraft operate weather permitting) **Fee:** Adults: $10, Kids 5-13: $5, Seniors: $8 **Directions:** *I-495 Long Island Expwy., take exit 49 S. Amityville, to Rte. 110 S., make a Left on Conklin St., make a Right onto New Hwy., the Museum sign is on Hangar 3*   *www.americanairpowermuseum.com*

Bayport Aerodrome Society Museum • *P.O. Box 728, Vitamin Dr. off Church St., Bayport, NY • 631-472-2393 • Cartwright Loop, Bayport, NY • Rus Faller: 631-732-6509 • Bob Fritts: 516-322-2509 •* Features Include: 24-Hangar Complex, Antique & Experimental Aircraft, Local Aviation History Exhibits, Aerodrome Tours, Living Museum, Sport Aviation, Military Trainers, Vintage Airplanes, Flight Demonstrations Every Weekend & some Wednesdays, Membership Organization, anyone can join & volunteer to assist in projects at the Aerodrome, Past Events Include: May-Hornpoint Flyout, June-Sentimental Journey Flyout, Aug.-Antique Airplane Clubs Annual Fly **Hours:** Sat.-Sun.: Noon-4 p.m., March-Dec. weather permitting, Reservations for tours required **Fee: Free** **Directions:** *Sunrise Hwy., take exit 51, take Nicolls Rd./Rte. 97 S., at 1ˢᵗ traffic light* *turn Right onto Church St., turn Left onto Vitamin Dr., turn Left into the Bayport Aerodrome parking lot*   *www.bayportaerodrome.org*

Grand Old Air Show • Brookhaven Calabro Airport • *Shirley, NY* • 516-742-0490 • Features

Include: All Day Events, WWI Dog Fights, Open Cockpit Bi-Planes, WWII Fighters, the Famous Geico Skytypers, Antique Cars, Helicopter Rides, WWII WarBirds & Bi-Plane Antics, the Brookhaven Airport was constructed during WWII to provide logistical support for U.S. Army Air Corps operations **Hours:** 11 a.m.-4 p.m. **Fee:** Adults: $10, Kids 6-12: $5, Under 6: Free, Cash Only **Directions:** *I-495 Long Island Expwy., take exit 68 S. William Floyd Pkwy./Smith Point Park, turn Left onto the Sunrise Hwy. service road, continue East, Air Show entrance on Left*   *www.thegrandoldairshow.com*

Internet Air Show Experience • *Red Bull Air Race* • Racing action every Sunday evening •

Features Include: International Online Race, Follow Race Progress on the Internet **Hours:** Sun.: 6 p.m. **Fee: Free**   *www.redbullusa.com/redbullairrace*

Bethpage Federal Credit Union New York Air Show at Jones Beach • *Jones Beach State Park, Wantagh, NY* • *General Airshow Info: 631-321-3510* • Features Include: US

Navy Blue Angels, US Army Golden Knights, USAF-F22 Raptor, NY Air National Guard Search & Rescue, American Airpower Museum War Birds, Geico Skytypers, Warbirds **Hours:** 10 a.m.-3 p.m., arrive early, once the beach is full it will be closed, Memorial Day Weekend **Fee: Free** event entry, Vehicle Use: $8 **Directions:** *Northern State Pkwy. W. or the Southern State Pkwy. W. to Wantagh Pkwy. S. to State Park*   *www.jonesbeachairshow.com/events.html*

Cole Palen's Old Rhinebeck Aerodrome • *P.O. Box 229, Rhinebeck, NY* • 845-752-3200

• **Special Event Weekends Have Included:** Aeronca Aviators Club Regional Fly-In, The Ninety-Nines Inc., International Organization of Women Pilots, Flivvers Model T Club, Police, Firefighters & EMS Weekend, Rock'n Rod Car Club **Hours:** Gates Open: 10 a.m., Air Show: 2-4 p.m., Museum: 10 a.m.–5 p.m., Fathers Day Weekend-mid-Oct. **Fees:** Adults: $20, Kids 6-12: $10, Teens & Seniors: $15, Parking: Free **Directions:** *I-495 Long Island Expwy., take exit 31 N. Cross Island Pkwy. N., take exit 33, merge onto I-295 N. toward New England, merge onto I-95 S., continue on I-80 W. (signs for I-80 W./Garden State Pkwy./Paterson), slight Right at I-380 N. (signs for Scranton/I-380 N.), merge onto I-81 N., take the exit onto I-690 W. toward Baldwinsville, take exit 1 for I-90 W., take exit 42 for State Hwy. 14 toward Lyons/Geneva, turn Left onto Rte. 14, turn Left onto the ramp to I-90 E., keep Right at the fork, follow signs for Albany/I-90 E. & merge onto I-90 E., New York State Thrwy., take exit 19 to Rte. 209 N., follow signs to Kingston-Rhinecliff Bridge, cross over the Hudson River, at the 2nd traffic light turn Right onto Rte. 9G South, next traffic light, turn Left onto Rte. 9 N. for .5 mi., turn Right onto Stone Church Rd. for 1.5 mi., turn Left on Norton Rd.*   *www.oldrhinebeck.org*

SPRING BLISS

Vintage Air Show • *Wheeler Sack Army Airfield, Fort Drum, NY* • 315-772-6011 • Features **Include:** World-Class Facility, 10th Mountain Division's Aviation Brigade, Combat Team Aircraft, Parachute Demonstration, Hang Glider Performance, Aerial Acrobatics, Aeronautic Displays, Concert, Fireworks Display (to kick off the celebration), 10,000-ft. Runway, Multiple Hangars, Control Tower, Rapid Deployment Facility, Learn How Soldiers Train & Fight, Historic Equipment, Entertaining Performers **Hours:** Gates Open: 8 a.m., Air Show: 11 a.m.–3:30 p.m., Concert: 6 p.m., followed by a Fireworks Display, June **Fee:** Air Show: **Free** event as part of their open house, there are no charges to park or enter the air show, Parking: on the airfield within .25-.5 mi. of the actual show area **Directions:** *I-81, take exit 48 E., drive 5 mi. on State Hwy. 342, turn Left, go onto Rte. 11 N. toward Evans Mills, drive 5 mi., turn Right, go onto Rte. 26 E., drive 4 mi., the airfield will be on the Left, follow the signs to the airfield*

ww.drum.army.mil/airshow

Greater Binghamtom Airshow • *Greater Binghamton Airport* • *Broome County Department of Aviation* • *2534 Airport Rd., Box 16, Johnson City, NY* • *607-763-4471* • **Features Include:** Air Aerobatics, Supersonic Military Fighters, Mega 'G' Maneuvers of World Class Civilian Performers, US Navy F/A 18C Hornet Demonstration Team, US Navy Legacy Flight (F/A 18C & Corsair), USAF F-16 Viper East Demonstration Team, USAF Heritage Flight (F-16, F-86 & P-51) (Tentative), US Army Black Daggers Parachute Team, US Coast Guard HH-65C Dauphin Search & Rescue Demonstration, Iron Eagle Airshows, Firebirds Aerobatic Team, Rob Holland Ultimate Airshows MX-2, Dr. Smoke Airshows, Kevin Russo Airshows SNJ Texan, F4U Corsair, P-40 Warhawk & P-51 Mustang, Mid-Atlantic Air Museum B-25J Mitchell "Briefing Time" **Hours:** 10 a.m.-4:30 p.m., during June **Fee:** Adults: $10, Kids 7-16: $7, Under 7: Free **Directions:** *I-495 Long Island Expwy., take exit 31 for Cross Island Pkwy. N., take exit 33 I-295 N. toward New England, merge onto I-95 S., continue on I-80 W. (signs for I-80 W./Garden State Pkwy./Paterson), slight Right at I-380 N. (signs for Scranton/I-380 N.), merge onto I-81 N., take exit 6 for US-11 toward State Hwy. 12/Chenango Bridge, turn Right onto Front St./Upper Front St./US-11 (signs for Chenango Bridge/Norwich), continue to follow Front St., Broome County Government Aviation Greater Binghamton Airport Ea Link Field: Aircraft Rescue & Fire Fighting Binghamton, NY*

www.binghamtonairport.com/aviation/AviationBCAS.php

AERODROME FIELDS

An aerodrome is basically a miniature airport for precision-crafted model planes. The planes are controlled with a handheld radio transmitter from a nearby base. Toy planes can weigh up to .55 pounds with speeds up to 100-mph. These planes look + fly like real planes + also utilize the same techniques + controls. There are fun fly-ins with timed competitions held monthly at Cedar Creek Park. The Island Fly Club has offered workshops at the Cradle of Aviation Museum in Garden City, teaching 10-16-yr.-olds to build + fly models. They recommened starting with a 2-channel glider. A 2-channel Glider (rudder+elevator) polyhedral glider is the easiest way to learn to fly. The piece O ' Cake from Dynaflite is a good way to go, if powered planes are of interest.

www.geistware.com/rcmodeling/nonpower/index.htm

FUN FAMILY

Cedar Creek Park • *3524 Merrick Rd., Seaford, NY* • *516-571-7470* • The park is on Seaman's Creek & the East Bay. • **Features Include:** 259 acres, Regulation Size Aerodrome Field Designed for Radio-Controlled Model Airplanes, Playground **Hours:** Dawn-Dusk **Fee: Free**, except during summer months **Directions:** *Northern State Pkwy., exit onto 135 S. Seaford Oyster-Bay Expwy., take exit 1 W. Merrick Rd. W. toward Freeport, Merge onto Merrick Rd.*   *www.nassaucountyny.gov/agencies/Parks*

Hempstead Harbor Park • *West Shore Rd., Port Washington, NY* • *516-327-3110* • **Features Include:** 60 acres, Aerodrome for Model Planes (permit), .5-mi. Beach on Harbor, Reservations Required, Open-Air Shelter with Picnic Tables & Grills, Playground **Hours:** 11 a.m.-Dusk **Fee: Free** off-season, Leisure Pass Required, Non-Residents Memorial Day-Labor Day: $20 **Directions:** *Northern State Pkwy., take exit 29, Roslyn Rd. N., to West Shore Rd.*   *www.nassaucountyny.gov/agencies/Parks/*

The National Soaring Museum • *Harris Hill, 51 Soaring Hill Dr., Elmira, NY* • *607-734-3128* • **Features Include:** Aviation Museum, Motorless Flight History, Gliders, Computerized Flight Simulators, Dedicated to Soaring Flight, Educational Programs, Special Exhibits & Events, News, Photos **Hours:** 10 a.m.-5 p.m., 7 days a week **Fee:** Adult: $6.50, Seniors: $5.50, Kids 5-17: $4, Under 4: Free, Family Discounts, Members: Free, AAA discount available **Directions:** *I-495 Long Island Expwy., exit 31N. for Cross Island Pkwy., exit 33 to merge onto I-295 N. toward New England, Merge onto I-95 S., merge onto I-95 S., continue on I-80 W. (signs for I-80 W./Garden State Pkwy./Paterson), slight Right at I-380 N. (signs for Scranton/I-380 N.), merge onto I-81 N., slight Left at Rte.17 W. (signs for Oswego/State Hwy. 17 W./Elmira), continue on PA-17 W., continue on Rte. 17 W./Southern Tier Expwy. W., continue on I-86 W., take exit 50 for Kahler Rd./Co. Hwy. 63, turn Left at Kahler Rd S., turn Left at Horseheads Big Flats Rd./Main St., continue to follow Horseheads Big Flats Rd., turn Right at Harris Hill Rd., turn Right to stay on Harris Hill Rd., turn Right to stay on Harris Hill Rd., turn Left at Soaring Hill Dr,. the museum is on the Right*   *www.soaringmuseum.org*

SOARING SOCIETY

International Scale Soaring Society • The ISSA sponsors a variety of scale R/C events & facilitates sharing information on building & flying techniques for Scale Gliders through this web site & its members. Their membership spans 6 countries.   *www.soaringissa.org*

The Vintage Sailplane Association, *V.S.A.* • *4673 Sapphire Dr., Hoffman Estates, IL* • The association promotes the acquisition, restoration & flying of vintage sailplanes.

www.vintagesailplane.org

Western New York Sailplane & Electrical Flyers • *716-896-6393* •

www.a1com.net/pay/wnysef/contacts.html

National Soaring Association • *P.O. Box 2100, Hobbs, NM* • *575-392-1177* • The Soaring Society promotes the development of other soaring groups, such as the National Soaring Museum, 1-26 Association, Vintage Sailplane Association, how to start a soaring club & suggested club bylaws. *www.ssa.org/myhome.asp?mbr=3891870379*

Academy of Model Aeronotics • *5161 E. Memorial Dr., Muncie, IN* • *800-435-9262* •

http://www.modelaircraft.org

WEATHER SITES

National Weather Service: Good comprehensive site that offers weather information, current radar images, marine forecasts & more interesting information.

www.weather.gov/view/national.php?thumbs=on

AccuWeather.com: Good site with a nice 4-day forecast including wind speed & direction.

http://www.accuweather.com

Intellicast Wind Forecast: This site offers projected wind direction & speed for WNY at various times over a period of days. This is 1 of the most accurate wind forecast sites around. Note that the wind speeds on the map are in KNOTS. See the scale at the top of the map to convert to MPH. *www.intellicast.com*

Institute of Global Environment & Society: Contains a lot of global weather information.

http://grads.iges.org

Explanation of Charts: This link explains how to read the charts in the previous 3 links.

http://wxmaps.org/pix/meteogramkey.html

SUGGESTIONS • COMMENTS • ERRORS

Linda.ReidBryce
@verizon.net

Thanks

Letterboxing is an outdoor quest that combines navigational skills + rubber stamp artistry in the form of a Treasure Hunt. Letterboxers hide small, weatherproof boxes in publicly-accessible places such as parks + beaches. Clues for finding boxes are posted on several web sites. There are approx. 20,000 letterboxes hidden in North America. A letterbox usually contains a Log Book, a Hand-Carved Rubber Stamp + an Ink Pad. Treasure Hunters carry a log book, + each time they find a letterbox they use the letterbox stamp to make an imprint in their book, to leave an imprint of their personal stamp on the letterbox's Log Book. Sometimes there is treasure to be had. It is customary to leave a piece of treasure when taking a piece.

To get started, the following is needed: "Trail Name," Rubber Stamp, Pen, Small Sketch Book, Ink Pad or Brush Markers, a Compass & Clues.

1. **A Trail Name** is a person or family's letterboxing identity. Most letterboxers choose a name that means something special to them. Trail Name Examples: Cindy & Leo, The Knights Clan, Quest Seekers

2. **The Rubber Stamp** image usually means something personal to the person or family. It could be a hand-carved or store-bought stamp. This is a person/family's "personal stamp" & will be used to make an imprint in the log book contained in each letterbox that is found. Each family member can make/buy their own stamp or a team stamp can be chosen.

3. **The Pen** or pencil is used to add the person or family's trail name & date next to

their stamp imprint in the log book. It is fun to add a personal comment about the experience of finding the letterbox.

4. **The Sketch Book** is person or family's "Personal Log Book" where they place stamp imprints using the stamps in the letterboxes that they find. The best imprints are made by using a smooth finish acid-free medium or heavy-weight paper. Scrapbookers like to carry plain index cards for imprints, then later cut them out & add them to their scrapbook.

5. **Carry an Ink Pad**. Archival ink pads are the best because they dry instantly, are waterproof & have a raised foam pad. Alcohol, based pads are also very good. To be more expressive, purchase a set of Marvy Brush Markers. These non-toxic, odorless ,watercolor markers have large brush points and the color stays wet longer than other markers, making them suitable for inking in multiple colors.

6. **Compass** Most letterbox clues reference magnetic compass bearings. Purchasing a $12 baseplate compass, such as the Suunto A-10 will suffice.

www.thecompassstore.com

7. **Locate some clues** to letterboxes nearby. Select a letterbox that you'd like to find, read the clues carefully & try to locate & print out a trail map of the area you'll be hiking. Here are two web sites which list letterbox locations:

www.letterboxing.org • www.atlasquest.com

Important things to remember when Letterboxing

Respect & Safety. Respect the environment & the letterbox that someone has created & your personal safety.

Respect for the environment. Letterboxing is an environmentally-friendly activity. Try to cause as little impact as possible on the environment involved in hunting for letterboxes. Letterboxes are always hidden in publicly-accessible areas, yet out of sight of casual visitors. It is never necessary to dig, remove native vegetation, disturb natural rock formations or interfere with animal habitats. Leave No Trace by removing any litter.

Respect the contents of each letterbox & the efforts of the creator of the letterbox. Letterboxes cost about $5 to make, but a lot of time & effort are put into creating & placing them.

The hazards of letterboxing include: poison ivy & creatures like snakes or spiders who like the same crevices & cavities where letterboxes are typically hidden.

To be safe, use a stick to poke into crevices before removing a letterbox, work with a partner, let others know where you are going & carry a cell phone.

When you find a letterbox don't give away the location. Make sure no one sees it being retrieved. This prevents non-letterboxers from finding & not understanding or respecting the letterbox. Once the letterbox is found, move away from the hiding spot before opening it. If someone asks what you're doing, invent a good answer. Once finished with the letterbox, carefully seal any plastic bags & the letterbox container. Replace the box as you would hope to find it: completely hidden from view, with contents protected from moisture. Moisture is the biggest threat to letterboxes. If a letterbox is found damaged, please notify its owner. It's a good idea to be helpful by replacing damaged zip lock bags with new ones you are carrying or notify the box owner if the box itself is damaged or no longer well-sealed.

When you can't find a letterbox it could be missing or simply difficult to find. This can be disappointing. Focus on the fun time had through hiking, hunting & picknicing.

A letterbox container is always watertight, can be a plastic food storage container, or an old film canister. Sometimes the containers are very small, or disguised as rocks or some other natural feature.

Creating a letterbox is exciting, but find a few 1st so you can understand the format, then have fun creating one. Happy Hunting!

This information is based on the recommendations of Letterboxing North America. To read more about this visit the web site: www.letterboxing.org

SUGGESTIONS • COMMENTS • ERRORS

Linda.ReidBryce
@verizon.net

Thanks

NASSAU COUNTY

Bay Park • NC • *First Ave., E. Rockaway, NY •* **516-571-7245 •** **516-571-7245** Features **Include:** 96-acre Park, Outdoor Roller Rink, Bicycle & Running Paths, Picnic Area, Bocce Court, Horseshoe Pit, Playground, Spray Pool **Hours:** Parts of the park are open Year-Round **Directions:** *Southern State Pkwy. to exit 17/Hempstead Ave. S., take Hempstead Ave. to fork (Ocean Ave.), take Left fork Ocean Ave. through Lynbrook & E. Rockaway to Main St., follow park signs, make a Left onto Front St., make a Right onto Althouse Ave., make a Left onto First & follow to the park* www.nassaucountyny.gov

Cedar Creek Park • *3524 Merrick Rd., Seaford, NY •* **516-571-7470 •** The park is on Seaman's Creek & the East Bay. **• Features Include:** 259 acres, Roller Rink, Playground, 2 Family Jogging/Walking Paths (1.5 & 1 mi.) **Directions:** *Northern State Pkwy., exit onto 135S. Seaford Oyster-Bay Expwy., take exit 1 W. Merrick Rd. W. toward Freeport, merge onto Merrick Rd.* www.nassaucountyny.gov/agencies/Parks/

Grant Park • NC. *1625 Broadway, Hewlett, NY •* **516-571-7821 •** Features Include: 35-acre Park, Roller Rink, Ice Skating Rink, 2 Playgrounds, Spray Pool Area, Jogging/ Walking Paths, Bicycling Paths **Directions:** *Southern State Pkwy., take exit 15S. for Corona Ave. S., turn Right onto N. Corona Ave., turn slight Left toward Rockaway Pkwy., then slight Right at Rockaway Pkwy., turn Right to stay on Rockaway Ave., turn Right onto Broadway* www.nassaucountyny.gov

Hot Skates Indoor Roller Skating Rink · *114 Merrick Rd., Lynbrook, NY ·* **516-593-1424 ·** Features Include: Public Skating, Roller Hockey, Birthday Parties, Camp

Programs **Hours:** Fri.: 4:30-6:30 p.m., no age restriction, 7-9:30 p.m. strictly for ages 10-14, Sat.: 12:30-2:30 p.m., 3-5:30 p.m., 7-9:30 p.m., Sun.: 12:30-2:30 p.m., 3-5:30 p.m., no age restriction Sat. or Sun., Open Year-Round **Fee:** Day Session: $10, Evening Session: $11, Rentals: $2.50 **Directions:** *Southern State Pkwy., take exit 17 S. Hempstead Ave. toward Malvern, travel to intersection with a fork, take the Left fork for Ocean Ave., drive 1.5 mi. to Merrick Rd., turn Right onto Merrick Rd., the rink will be the 2nd Bldg. on the Left*   *www.hotskates.com*

Inwood Park • **NC** • *Bayview Ave., Inwood, NY* • *516-571-7894* • Features Include: 16-acre Park, Outdoor Lighted Roller Rink, Playground, Water Slide, Jogging/Walking Path, Launch Ramp Picnic Area **Fee:** Nassau Residents: annual fee **Directions:** *Southern State Pkwy., take exit 19 S., Peninsula Blvd. S. to end, make a Left on Rockerway Tpke. (large intersection), make a Right onto Burnside Ave., curves to the Left & becomes Sheridan Blvd., take Sheridan to Bayview Ave. & turn Right, continue down Bayview into the park*   *www.nycgovparks.org/parks/inwoodhillpark*

Massapequa Preserve • **NC** • *Merrick Rd. & Ocean Ave., Massapequa, NY* • *516-571-7443* • **Features Include:** 423-acre Preserve, Rollerblading, 4.5 mi. of the Bethpage Bikeway, Jogging/Walking, 5 mi. of the Greenbelt Hiking Trail, Lake, No Amenities in the Park, Maps available **Directions:** *Seaford-Oyster Bay Expwy., exit onto Sunrise Hwy. E., pass a small brick bldg. on Left, make the next U-turn at the traffic light & park in the parking lot, across from train station.*   *www.fdale.com/FMP/FMP.htm*

United Skates of America Roller Skating Center • *1276 Hicksville Rd., Seaford, NY* • *516-795-5474* • *5473* • **Features Include:** Roller Skating, Ice Skating, Birthday Parties, Lessons, Adult Night 18 & over, Glow Crazy Public Skating, Hip Hop & R&B Skate, Scout Programs **Hours:** Mon.: 4-6 p.m., 6-8 p.m., 8-11 p.m., Tues.: 5-7 p.m., Thurs.: 4-6 p.m., Fri.: 4-6 p.m., 6:30-9 p.m., 9-close time varies, Sat.: 10 a.m.-Noon, 12:30-3 p.m., 3:30-6 p.m., 6:30-9 p.m., 9-close time varies, Sun.: 9:15-11:30 a.m., Noon-2:30 p.m., 3-5:30 p.m., 6-close time varies **Fee:** Adults: $9, Kids: $8, Skate Rental: $4 **Directions:** *Southern State Pkwy., take exit 28A N., merge onto NY 135 N. toward Syosset, take exit 5 for NY 107/Hicksville toward Massapequa, turn Right onto Hicksville Rd./NY 107 S., the rink will be on the Left*
www.usa-skating.com • *www.www.unitedskates.com/seaford*

NEW YORK CITY
The Roller Rinks At Chelsea Piers • *62 Chelsea Piers, NY, NY* • *212-336-6100* •
Features Include: Outdoor Roller Rinks, Lessons, In-Line Skate Rental **Hours:** vary seasonally **Fee:** Adults: $13, Kids: $10.50, Rental: $7.50, Helmit: $4 **Directions:** *I-495 Long Island Expwy., go through the Queens Midtown Tunnel, continue South to 23rd St., turn Right onto 23rd St. W. to the Hudson River, turn Right onto 11th Ave., turn Left onto 24th St., turn Left at the light onto W. Side Hwy., turn Right at the next traffic light into the entrance of Chelsea Piers between 17th St. & 23rd St.*   *www.chelseapiers.com*

SKATE PARKS

EXTREME SPEED, SKATEBOARDS & FUN

A Skate Park is a recreational environment for skateboarders, rollerbladers + BMX Riders to ride + develop technique.   **Skate Park Locator** • *http://www.skateboardpark.com*

NASSAU COUNTY

Long Beach Skate Park • *City of Long Beach Recreational Center* • *426 National Blvd., Long Beach, NY* • *516-431-2024* • Features Include: Newly Renovated, Pyramid with a Downrail, 4-ft. Mini Ramp, Small Rounded Rail, Higher Square Rail, Flat Beds, Boxes, Decks & Transitions, Drop in Ramp, 1 Quarter Pipe, Long Beach Residents Only **Safety Requirements Include:** Helmets, Knee Pads, Elbow Pads, Wrist Guards **Directions:** *Northern State Pkwy., take the Meadowbrook Pkwy. S. to exit M10 Lido-Long Beach Loop Pkwy., take Loop to end, turn Right onto Lido Blvd. W. which becomes E. Park Ave., continue into downtown Long Beach, pass the LIRR Station on the Right, turn Right onto National Blvd.*   *www.longbeachny.org*

Nickerson Beach Park • NC • *880 Lido Blvd., Lido Beach, NY* • *516-571-7700* • Features Include: 121-acre Park, .75 mi. on the Atlantic Ocean, Skate Park Skateboard Facility, 7 Ramps, Varying Difficulty, 2 Railings, Picnic Tables & Grills **Safety Requirements Include:** Helmets, Knee Pads, Elbow Pads, Wrist Guards **Hours:** Dawn-Dusk **Fee:** Nassau County Residents: $8 per day, Non-residents: $20, Leisure Pass: $40 **Directions:** *Meadowbrook Pkwy., take exit M10 the Loop Pkwy., take to the end, bear Right onto Lido Blvd., continue for 2 lights, make a Left into the park*
www.nassaucountyny.gov/agencies/Parks/WheretoGo/active/nickerson.html

SUFFOLK COUNTY

Block Island Skate Park • *Ballobrian Park* • *Block Island, NY* • Features Include: Small Skate Park **Directions:** *See Ferries for directions to Block Island, Ballobrian Park on the West side of the road*

East Hampton Skate Park • *16 Abrahams Path, E. Hampton, NY* • *631-329 8756* • Features Include: Outdoor Park, 6-ft. Half Pipe, Several Quarter Pipes, Several Roll-Ins, Fun Boxes with Grinding Ledges, Rails on the Boxes **Directions:** *I-495 Long Island Expwy., take exit 68 to merge onto William Floyd Pkwy. S. toward Shirley, slight Right to merge onto NY-27 E. toward Montauk, turn Left to stay on NY-27 E., turn Left at Main St., turn Left to stay on Main St., turn Left onto Pantigo Rd., continue onto N. Main St., turn Left onto 3 Mile Harbor Rd./County Rd. 40, turn Right onto Abrahams Path, the park will be on the Right*

Greenport • *West Side Moores Ln., Greenport, NY* • *516-477-1217* • Features Include: 7,000-sq.-ft. Street Course, 40-in. Wide Spine Ramp, 40-in. Wide Vert Ramp **Directions:** *I-495 Long Island Expwy., exit onto W. Main St./Middle Country Rd./NY-25 E. toward Riverhead, continue to follow W. Main St./NY-25 E., turn Right at Main Rd./NY-25 E., continue to follow NY-25 E., turn Left at Moores Ln., continue onto Moores Ln.*

www.teampain.com

Hampton Bays Skate Park • *Red Creek Park* • *102 Old Riverhead Rd., Hampton Bays, NY* • *631-728-8585* • Features Include: Street Course, Vert Walls, Half Pipes, Above-Ground Bowl, Helmet, Elbow & Knee Pads Required, Participants must sign a waiver, parents must sign for anyone under 18 yrs. **Fee:** Residents: **Free**, Non-Residents: $10 **Directions:** *I-495 Long Island Expwy., take exit 68 S. William Floyd Pkwy. toward Shirley, merge onto NY-27 E. toward Montauk, exit onto Riverhead-Hampton Bays Rd., turn Right onto Old Riverhead Rd., turn Left into park*

In Line 1 Sports Center • *23 Rte. 25A, Mt. Sinai, NY* • Features Include: Indoor Skate Park, Skate Park Contest, Summer Camp, Lessons **Hours:** Mon.-Fri.: 3-9 p.m., Sat.-Sun.: 10 a.m.-9 p.m. **Fee:** Members: $10, Non-Members: $20, Membership: $30, 30-min. Lesson: $30, 1-hr. Lesson: $60 **Directions:** *I-495 Long Island Expwy., take exit 64 toward NY-112/Port Jefferson/Patchogue, merge onto Waverly Ave., turn Left at Medford Ave./NY-112 N., continue to follow NY-112 N., turn Right at County Rd. 83/Patchogue-Mt. Sinai Rd., turn Left at New York 25A W., the park will be on the Right*

www.inline1.com

Montauk Skate Park • *Essex St., Montauk, NY* • *631-324-2417* • Features Include: Transition-Orientated Concrete Skate Park, 9-ft. Deep Pool, Huge Area with Half-Pipe, Bowl Sections, Table Tops, 5-ft. / 9-ft. Kidney, 9-in. of Vert in the Deep End with Pool Coping all the way around, Snake Run is 5-ft. deep with bowl corners, Str8 Banks & Metal Coping on the Trannies, Small 3-Sided Pyramid with a Ledge Tucked, Mellow Hips, Flatbars & Ledges scattered around, Bicycles are not permitted **Safety Requirements Include:** Helmets, Knee Pads, Elbow Pads, Wrist Guards **Safety Requirements Include:** Helmets, Knee Pads, Elbow Pads, Wrist Guards **Hours:** 9 a.m.-Dusk **Fee:** Town Residents: *Free*, Non-Town Residents: $10 per day **Directions:** *I-495 Long Island Expwy., take exit 68 William Floyd Pkwy. toward Shirley, merge onto NY-27 E. toward Montauk, turn Left to stay on NY-27 E. Sunrise Hwy., to end, take Rte. 27A E. Montauk Hwy., go through the town of Montauk, turn Left at the Mobil station onto Essex St., the park is on the Left next to some tennis courts*

Oil City Skate Park • *3565 Maple Ct., Oceanside, NY* • **516-442-0703** • Features Include: Indoor Skate Park, Lessons, Clinic, BMX Competitions, Bodega Oil Slick Challenge, Bikes allowed on Wed-Thurs., Birthday Parties **Hours:** Mon.: 4-6 p.m., 6-8 p.m., 8-11 p.m. BMX only, Tues.-Thurs.: 3-5 p.m., 5-7 p.m., 7-9 p.m., 9-11 p.m., Fri.: 3-5 p.m., 5-7 p.m., 9-11 p.m., 11 p.m.-1 a.m., Sat.-Sun.: 11 a.m.-11 p.m. **Fee:** Session: $12, Additional Session: $7 **Directions:** *Northern State Pkwy., exit onto Meadowbrook Pkwy., take Meadowbrook Pkwy. S. to the Loop Pkwy., take Loop Pkwy. to the end, turn Right onto Lido Blvd. & go approx. 3 mi. to Long Beach Rd. turn Right onto Long Beach Rd. & go 2.4 mi. to Daly Blvd., turn Left onto Daly Blvd & take to the end, turn Right onto Hampton Rd., turn Right onto Maple Ct.* www.oilcitysk8.com

Skate Park of Huntington • *Huntington, NY* • Features Include: 6-ft. Mini, Banks, Ledges, Rails Roll in Spine Pyrimad, Quarter Pipes, Euro Gap **Fee:** *Free* **Directions**: *Northern Pkwy., take exit 40N. for Rte. 110 N. toward Huntington, follow Rte. 110 N., turn Right onto Broadway, the park is on the corner of Broadway & Cuban Rd. next to the Tri-Village Baseball Fields*

Stowsky Skate Park • *101 Palaski St., Riverhead, NY* • **631-727-5744** • **Features Include:** Wood, 2 Levels, Mini Ramp, Spin Fun **Directions:** *I-495 Long Island Expwy., exit onto W. Main St/Middle Country Rd./NY-25 E. toward Riverhead, follow W. Main St./NY-25 E., sharp Left onto Osborne Ave., turn Right onto Pulaski St., the park will be on the Right*

Tanner Park Skate Park • *Amityville, NY* • **Directions:** *Southern State Pkwy., take exit 32S. for Rte.110 S. toward Amityville, slight Right toward Broadway/NY-110 S., turn Right onto Broadway/Rte. 110 S., turn Left onto E. Merrick Rd./New York 27A E., continue to follow New York 27A E., turn Right onto Baylawn Ave., continue to Tanner Park*

QUEENS

Forest Park Skate Park • *Department of Parks & Recreation* • *Forest Park* • *Woodhaven Blvd. & Myrtle Ave., Queens, NY* • **718-846-2731** • **718-235-0815**

• Located at the Greenhouse basketball courts. • **Features Include:** Skateboarders, Inline Skaters, Launch Ramp, Grinding Rail, Quarter Pipe, Table Top, Wedge, Grinding Ledge. Requirements Include: Signed Liability Waiver Form, Helmets, Knee Pads, Elbow Pads must be worn, Kids Under 18 yrs. must also wear Wrist Guards, the skate park is under renovation & equipment availability may be limited. Call before visiting to check on the installation status. **Hours:** Tues.-Sat.: 3-8 p.m., June 14-late Sept. **Fee: Free Directions:** *I-495 Long Island Expwy., take exit 31 N. for Cross Island Pkwy S. toward Kennedy Airport, take exit 29 E. to merge onto Grand Central Pkwy. W. toward Triboro Bridge, exit onto Union Tpke., slight Left to stay on Union Tpke., turn Right at Woodhaven Blvd., the park entrance is just past Myrtle Ave. at the Greenhouse basketball courts*

http://www.nycgovparks.org/sub_things_to_do/facilities/skate_parks/forest_park.
html • www.skatecity.com/nyc/where/queens.html

Rockaway Skate Park • *Rockaway Beach & Boardwalk* • *Shore Front Pkwy. at 91ˢᵗ St., just off the boardwalk* • *718-318-4000* • **Features Include:** 10 Ramps, 4 Grinding Rails **Safety Requirements Include:** Helmets, Knee Pads, Elbow Pads, Wrist Guards **Spring Hours:** mid-March-May 31, Mon.-Fri.: 3 p.m.-5:30 p.m., Sat.-Sun.: 10:30 a.m.-5 p.m. **Summer & Fall Hours:** June-Veterans Day (Nov.), Mon.-Sun.: 10:30 a.m.-6:30 p.m. **Directions:** *Southern State Pkwy., continue onto Belt Pkwy., take exit 17 S., merge onto Cross Bay Blvd., continue onto Cross Bay Bridge, slight Left toward Rockaway Fwy., turn Left at Rockaway Fwy., take the 1ˢᵗ Left onto Beach 94ᵗʰ St., continue onto Cross Bay Bridge/Cross Bay Veterans Memorial Bridge, take the Cross Bay Bridge to Shore Front Pkwy., turn Left onto Shore Front Pkwy., drive 3 blocks to 91ˢᵗ St. By Subway take the A train to Broad Channel, transfer to the S train, take it 1 stop to Beach 90/Holland St.*

TREASURE HUNTING

White's of Long Island Inc. • *240 Rte. 112, Patchogue, NY •* **631-447-6910/2788 •**
Features Include: Serving Treasure Hunters, Treasure Talk for Beginners, Club Membership, Club Beach Treasure Hunts for Families: Planted Treasure & Tokens/ Refreshments/Prizes, Fantastic In-Store Demonstrations, Coffee & Iced Tea Served, Best-Use Areas, Ongoing Advice & Treasure Identification, Permits, Experienced Treasure Hunter Informartion, Beach Best for Kids, Target Identification Techniques, 104 Museum Metal Detectors Dating Back to WWII **Hours:** Tues.-Sat.: 10 a.m.-5 p.m., Fri.: 10 a.m.-7 p.m. **Fee:** Equipment Purchase: $179-$300 **Directions:** *I-495 Long Island Expwy., take exit 64 S. for Rte. 112, cross over Sunrise Hwy., travel .12 mi. S. of Sunrise Hwy., 3 doors S. of Burger King, on the same side of the street www.treasuresunlimited-ny.com*

NY State Tide generator • *www.saltwatertides.com/dynamic.dir/newyorksites.html*

also see Letterboxing, p 190

SUGGESTIONS • COMMENTS • ERRORS

Linda.ReidBryce
@verizon.net

Thanks

4 **IN THIS SECTION**

SUMMER FUN

Let
Fun Flow
Like A
River

ANNUAL EVENTS

SAND, SPLASHING & WAFFLE CONES

June

Belmont Stakes • *Belmont Park Race Track* • *2150 Hempstead Tpke., Elmont, NY* • *718-641-4700* • **Features Include:** The Belmont Stakes is an annual race for 3-yr.-old horses. **Hours:** June event **Fee:** Adults: $2, Kids under 12: Free **Directions:** *Northern State Pkwy., take NY 135 Seaford-Oyster Bay Expwy. S., take exit 4W. Southern State Pkwy. W., take exit 26B Cross Island Pkwy., exit onto Hempstead Tpke./NY 24, the track will be on the Left*   *www.nyra.com*

Krupski's Pumpkin Farms • *38030 Main Rd., Peconic, NY* • *631-734-6847* • **Features Include:** You-Pick Peas & Sugar Snap Peas in June & early July, Farm Fresh Produce at All Times, School Tours Welcome **Hours:** 9 a.m.-6 p.m. daily, June-Nov. **Directions:** *I-495 Long Island Expwy. to the last exit, head East, the road changes names several times, travel approx. 16 mi. & the farm will be on the Right*

Massapequa Community Festival • *Massapequa Railroad Station, Parking Lot M-5* • *Presented by the Massapequa Chamber of Commerce* • *516-541-1443* • **Features Include:** Food, Rides, Entertainment, Vendors on Sun. **Hours:** Late May, 4 Days, Fri.: 6-11 p.m., Sat.: 1-11 p.m. (Opening Ceremonies at 1 p.m.), Sun.: 1-11 p.m., Mon.: 1-11 p.m., mid-June **Fee: Free Directions:** *I-495 Long Island Expwy., take exit 31S. for Cross Island Pkwy. S., take exit 25A on the Left for Southern State Pkwy. E., take exit 29 for NY 107/Hicksville toward Massapequa, turn Right onto Hicksville Rd./NY 107 S., turn Left at Veterans Blvd., the LIRR will be on the Right*   *www.massapequachamber.com*

Montauk's Annual Harbor Festival • *West Lake Dr., Montauk, NY* • *Sponsored by the Montauk Chamber of Commerce* • *631-668-2355* • *631-668-2428* • **Features**

Include: Celebrating Montauk Harbor, Food, Inflatable Rides, Carnival Games, Face Painting, Clam Shucking Contest, Best Baked Clam, Hot Dog Eating Contests, Fish Filleting Contest, Dunking Tank, Live Music, Retail Booths **Hours:** 12-6 p.m., mid-June **Directions:** *I-495 Long Island Expwy., take exit 68 for William Floyd Pkwy./Co. Hwy. 46 S. toward Shirley, merge onto County Rte. 46/William Floyd Pkwy., turn Left at Rte. 27 Sunrise Hwy., turn Left at S. Fox St., turn Right at S. Forest St., turn Left at S. Fulton Dr., turn Right at S. Fairview Ave.*

www.montaukchamber.com

Mattituck Annual Strawberry Festival • *Hosted by the Mattituck Lions Club •*
Herricks Ln., Mattituck, NY • 631-298-2222 • Features Include: Strawberries Prepared in Traditional & Surprising Ways, Live Music, Ongoing Arts & Crafts, Treasure Hunts, Crowning of the Strawberry Queen, Fireworks, Rides **Hours:** Fri.-Sun.: mid-June **Fee:** Adults: $5, Kids under 18: $3, Unlimited Rides Bracelet: $25 **Directions:** *I-495 Long Island Expwy., take exit 68 N. William Floyd Pkwy., go approx. 7 mi., turn Right onto Rte. 25A E., follow approx. 3 mi., turn Left onto Sound Ave. E., follow approx. 13 mi., turn Right onto Herricks Ln., the parking field will be on the Left*

mattituckstrawberryfestival.org • www.mattitucklionsclub.org

Strawberry Fair at Benner's Farm • *56 Gnarled Hollow Rd., Setauket, NY •*
631-689-8172 • 631-689-8172 • This farm dates back to the 1700s. **Features Include:** Fields of Strawberries, Hay Rides, Old-Fashioned Games, Farm, Gardens, Fields, Woods, Farm History Stories, Learn How People Lived on Long Island Before Electricity, Tractors, Tools, Vegetables & Herbs, Sheering Sheep, Collect Eggs from Hens, Swing from a 300-yr. old-Oak Tree, Wagon Rides **Hours:** Sat.-Sun.: Noon- 4 p.m., mid-June **Fee:** Adults: $6, Kids: $5 **Directions:** *I-495 Long Island Expwy., take exit 62, Nicoll's Rd. N./County Rd. 97, follow Nicoll's Rd. to the end (cross Rte. 25, Rte. 347 & Stony Brook Univ.), turn Right on Rte. 25A E., at the 5th light turn Right onto Old Town Rd., drive 2.5 blocks to the end, turn Right onto Gnarled Hollow Rd., farm is on the Right, use the 3rd driveway for parking, if there is no parking in lot park along the street* www.bennersfarm.com

Polo Matches • *Bethpage State Park •* 516 249-0701 • Features Include: Weekly Polo Matches **Hours:** Sun.: 3 p.m., June-Aug. Fee: **Free** Directions: *I-495 Long Island Expwy. E., take exit 44S., Seaford-Oyster Bay Expwy./Rte. 135 S., exit onto Powell Ave., take exit 8, drive E. to park, look for the polo fields signage.*

RVC Street Fair & Car Show • *111 North Oceanside Rd., Rockville Centre, NY •*
631-563-8551 • 516-766-0666 • Features Include: Shows, Children's Activities, Games, Car Show, Arts & Crafts Competition, Food Court **Hours:** 10 a.m-5 p.m., last weekend in June **Fee: Free** Directions: *Southern State Pkwy., exit onto Wantagh State Pkwy. S., take exit W5 W. for NY 27 W. Sunrise Hwy., turn Left onto N. Long Beach Rd., turn Right onto Lincoln Ave. the fair is between North & South Village Ave., & between Sunrise Hwy. & Lincoln Ave.* http://preferredpromotions.com • www.rvcchamber.org

Annual Arts Festival By The Sea • *Main St., Bay Shore, NY* • *631-665-7003* • Features **Include:** Pony Rides, Petting Zoo, Live Music, Food **Hours:** 11 a.m.-6 p.m., mid-June event **Fee: Free Directions:** *Southern State Pkwy., exit onto Robert Moses State Pkwy., take exit RM2E. 27A E. toward Bay Shore, turn Right onto 27A E. on Main St.*
http://bayshorecommerce.com

Annual Green Fest • *Port Jefferson, NY* • *631-473-1414* • *631-473-0420* • Features **Include:** Green-Themed Event, Energy Efficiency, Heating & Cooling, Solar Topics, Environmental Issues, Building Materials **Hours:** Noon-5 p.m., mid-June **Fee: Free Directions:** *Northern State Pkwy., take exit 45 Sunken Meadow Pkwy. N., take exit SM3E. for NY-25 E./Jericho Tpke. toward Smithtown, turn right onto Jericho Tpke./25 E., turn Left at 25A E./Nissequogue River Rd./River Rd., follow 25A E., turn Right onto N. Country Rd./25A E., becomes E. Broadway, the fair is in The Village Center & Harbor Front Park* *www.portjeff.com*

Kings Park Day Fair • *Main St. & Indian Head Rd.* • *Kings Park, NY* • *631-846-1459* • **Features Include:** Clowns, Rides, Pony Rides, Petting Zoo, Morning Bike Rally, Crafts, Raffles, Martial Arts Demonstrations, DJs, Bands, Dance Performances **Hours:** 10 a.m.-4 p.m., mid-June **Fee: Free Directions:** *Sunken Meadow Pkwy. N., take exit SM4E. Pulaski Rd., turn Right at 2nd light onto Main St./Rte. 25A, pass 1 traffic light, see the library parking lot on the Left across from the fire house*
www.kingsparkli.com

Smithtown Festival Day • *Main St./Rte.25A, Smithtown, NY* • *631-979-8069* • Features **Include:** Family Entertainment, Pony Rides, Giant Inflatable Rides, Free Balloons, Music, Theatrical Performances, Puppet Shows, Martial Arts Demonstrations, Robotics Exhibit, Raffles, Emergency Vehicles Display, Farm Machinery & Old Cars Show, Restaurants will move Tables & Chairs Outside **Hours:** 9 a.m.-5 p.m., 1st weekend in June **Fee: Free Directions:** *Northern State Pkwy., take exit 45 toward Sunken Meadow Park N., take exit SM3E. for NY-25 E./Jericho Tpke. toward Smithtown, turn Right onto Jericho Tpke./NY-25 E., continue to follow NY-25 E., Main St./Rte. 25/25A is closed to traffic from Rte. 111 west to Maple Ave.* *www.smithtownchamber.org*

Manhasset Street Fair • *Plandome Rd., Manhasset, NY* • **Features Include:** Climbing Wall, Live Music, Crafts **Hours:** 10:30 a.m.-4 p.m., 1st Sat. in June **Fee: Free Directions:** *I-495 Long Island Expwy., take exit 36 toward Searingtown Rd./Shelter Rock Rd., turn Right onto Searingtown Rd., turn Left onto 25A W./Northern Blvd., turn Right onto Plandome Rd., the fair is on Plandome Rd. between Bayview Ave. & Colonial Pkwy.*
www.manhassetny.org

Belmont Street Fair • *7th St., Garden City, NY* • *516-746-7724* • Features Include: Parade, Hat Contest, Live Music, Clowns, Street Performers, Nassau County Police

Pipe Band, Irish Dancers, The parade begins at 7 p.m. & travels from 9th St. & Franklin Ave. S. toward 7th St. before winding its way onto Hilton Ave. & concludes at the Village Gazebo **Hours:** Fri-Sun., early June event **Fee: Free Directions:** *Northern State Pkwy., take exit 31A toward Jones Beach, merge onto Meadowbrook State Pkwy. S., take exit M1 W. for Old Country Rd. W. toward Mineola, turn Right onto Old Country Rd., turn Left onto Glen Cove Rd., continue onto Clinton Rd., turn Right onto Stewart Ave., turn Left onto Hilton Ave.*

Theodore Roosevelt Nature Center • *Jones Beach State Park P.O. Box 1000., Wantagh, NY • Reservations Required: 516-679-7254 •*

Horseshoe Crab Walk • Features Include: Educational Walk, Explore Horseshoe Crabs which are known as "Living Fossils," Wear Water Shoes **Hours:** 10:30-Noon, a Sun. in June **Fee:** $4 per person,

Sunset Stroll Family Adventures • Features Include: Sunset Hike, Jones Beach Inlet, Color Observation, Bring a Cameras **Hours:** 7 p.m.-8:30 p.m., a Fri. in June **Fee:** $4 per person

Wildlife Protectors! Tiny Tots • **Hours:** 10:30-11:30 a.m & 1:30-2:30 p.m., a Tues. in mid-June **Fee:** Kids: 3-5: $4 **Directions:** *Northern State Pkwy., exit onto Meadowbrook Pkwy. S. or Wantagh Pkwy. S. to the park http://nysparks.state.ny.us/environment/nature-centers*

Connetquot River State Park Preserve • *Reservations Required: 631-581-1072•*

House Tours Family Adventures • Features Include: South Side Sportsmen's Club Main House Tour **Hours:** 1-3:30 p.m., a Sun. in early-June **Fee:** Adults: $4, Kids: $3

Cute Little Quail Family Adventures • Features Include: Visit Baby Quail, Discovery Talk **Hours:** A Sat. in mid-June, 2-3:30 p.m. **Fee:** Adults: $4, Kids: $3

Moonlit Hike Family Adventures • Features Include: Moonlit Trails Walk **Hours:** A Sat. in mid-June, 7:30-9:30 p.m. **Fee:** Adults: $4, Kids: $3

Creepy Crawlies Fun for Kids • Features Include: Learn About Not-So-Creepy Backyard Crawlies **Hours:** A Sat. in mid-June, 9:30-11 a.m. **Fee:** Kids: $3

Firefly Fun Family Adventures • Features Include: Indoor Activities, Short Outdoor Walk, Find Fireflies **Hours:** A Sat. in mid-June, 7:30-9p.m., **Fee:** Adults: $4, Kids: $3

Nurturing Dads Fun for Kids • Features Include: Discover Animal Kingdoms, Dads Care for Babies, Crafts for Dad **Hours:** A Sat. in mid-June, 9:30-11 a.m. **Fee:** Kids: $3

Directions: *Southern State Pkwy., take exit 44 Sunrise Hwy. E., the preserve is located on the North side of Sunrise Hwy., just West of Pond Rd.*

http://nysparks.state.ny.us/environment/nature-centers

Organic Food Co-Op • *Restoration Farm • Old Bethpage Village Restoration • 1303 Round Swamp Rd., Old Bethpage, NY • Co-Op Info: 631-383-1050 • 516-572-8401*

• Harvests vary from week to week & season to season. **Features Include:** Vegetables, Pick-Your-Own Herbs & Flowers, Raspberries, Strawberries & Blackberries Share Option, applications are available on the web site or at the Old Bethpage Village

Restoration desk **Hours:** Sat.: Noon-2 p.m., late June-Oct., pick-up in the parking lot

Fee: Full Share: $850, Half Share: $425, Berry Share: $40 **Directions:** *I-495 Long Island Expwy., take exit 48 Round Swamp Rd. toward Old Bethpage/Farmingdale, make a Left onto Round Swamp Rd., turn Left onto Old Country Rd., make a slight Right onto Round Swamp Rd.* *www.restorationfarm.com*

July

1890s Fair • *380 Nicolls Rd., Stony Brook, NY* • *631-751-0297* • Features Include: Family Fun, Victorian Melodrama, Kid's Games, Old-Fashioned Musical Entertainment, Food, Vendors **Hours:** Sat.-Sun.: 11 a.m.-6 p.m., 1st weekend in July **Fee:** $5 donation, Kids under 12: Free **Directions:** *I-495 Long Island Expwy., take exit 58 Old Nichols Rd./ Nesconset, merge onto Expwy. Dr. S., turn Left onto Nicolls Rd./Old Nichols Rd.*

Fun Family Day • *Belmont Park Race Track* • *2150 Hempstead Tpke., Elmont, NY* • *718-641-4700* • **Features Include:** Games, Pony Rides, Petting Zoo, Face Painting, Giant Inflatables, Special Weekly Activities & Themes such as: Circus Variety Shows, Speedway Challenge, Football Toss, Crazy Maze, Mime Shows, Mini Golf Course, Weekly Theme Inflatables **Hours:** Sundays: 1st Sun. in May-last Sun. in July **Fee:** Free Family Fun Day activities, Pony Rides: $1 donation, General Admission: $2, Kids under 12: Free **Directions:** *Northern State Pkwy., take NY 135 Seaford-Oyster Bay Expwy. S., take exit 4W. Southern State Pkwy. W., take exit 26B Cross Island Pkwy., exit onto Hempstead Tpke./NY-24, the track will be on the Left, Belmont backyard & picnic area* *www.nyra.com*

Annual Hamptons Greek Festival • *Greek Orthodox Church* • *111 St. Andrews Rd., Southampton, NY* • *631-283-6169* • **Features Include:** Family-Oriented Greek Festival, Entertainment, Food, Traditional Greek Dance Performances, Authentic Costumes, Children's Games, Flea Market **Hours:** Thurs.-Sat.: 4-11 p.m., Sun.: Noon-9 p.m., mid-July **Fee:** Free **Directions:** *I-495 Long Island Expwy., take exit 68 William Floyd Pkwy. toward Shirley, turn Right to merge onto NY-27 E. toward Montauk, turn Left onto St. Andrews Rd., the church will be on the Right, the Greek Orthodox Church is easily accessible from Sunrise & Montauk Hwy. in Southampton* *www.kimisishamptons.ny.goarch.org/festival*

Annual Hicksville Chamber of Commerce Street Fair • *Jerusalem Ave. & Rte. 107/ Broadway, Hicksville, NY* • *516-931-7170* • **Features Include:** Rides, Balloon Animals, Clothing/Jewelry/Arts & Crafts Vendors, Caricaturists, Face Painting, Ice Cream, Foods, "Showmobile" Musical Performances, Radio Stations KJOY &WMJC **Hours:** Sun.: 11 a.m-6 p.m., mid-July **Fee:** Free rides free for kids under13 **Directions:** *Northern State Pkwy., exit onto N. Broadway/NY 107 S.* *www.hicksvillechamber.com/event_fair.html*

Annual Thunderbird American Indian Pow Wow. *Queens County Farm Museum•*
73-50 Little Neck Pkwy., Floral Park, NY • 718-347-3276 • Features Include:
Mid-Summer Pow Wow Performances, New York City's Oldest & Largest Pow Wow,
Intertribal Native American Dance Competitions, Over 40 Indian Nations, Native
American Art, Crafts, Jewelry, Foods **Hours:** Check the web site for performance times,
last weekend in July **Fee:** Adults: $9, Adult Weekend Pass: $15, Kids Under 12: $4, Kids
Weekend Pass: $5 **Directions:** *I-495 Long Island Expwy., take exit 32 Little Neck Pkwy.,
turn Left onto Little Neck Pkwy., drive south for 1.5 mi. To the museum entrance*

www.queensfarm.org

Sag Harbor Energy Fair • *Sag Harbor Whaling & Historical Museum, 200 Main
St., Sag Harbor, NY • 631-725-0770* • Features Include: Interactive Public Event,
Products & Services, Cleaner Renewable Sources of Energy, Reduce a "Carbon
Footprint, Wasted Energy Issues, New Environmentally-Friendly Products, Other
Fuel Sources for Vehicle & Home, Tap into Wind, Solar & Geothermal Energy Reduce
Oil Dependence **Hours:** Sat.: 10 a.m.-5 p.m., Sun.: Noon-5 p.m., Sun. Greenhouse
Tour: Noon -2 p.m., mid-July **Fee: Free**, Sun. Green House Tour: $20 **Directions:** *I-495
Long Island Expwy., take exit 68 William Floyd Pkwy. S. toward Shirley, turn Right to
merge onto NY-27 E. toward Montauk, turn Left at Montauk Hwy./27 E., turn Left onto
Bridgehampton Sag Harbor Tpke., continue onto Main St., the museum will be on the
Left, at the corner of Garden St.* *www.sagharborwhalingmuseum.org*

Children's Summer Theatre • *Belmont Lake State Park • 625 Belmont Ave., Babylon,
NY • 631 667-5055 • Theatre Schedule: 631-321-3510* • **Hours:** Call for schedule
Fee: Free **Directions:** *Southern State Pkwy. to E. Islip, take the exit toward Belmont Ave.,
turn Right onto Belmont Ave., turn Left onto Amsterdam Ave.*

http://nysparks.state.ny.us/parks/info.asp

Whale Watching • *The Okeanos Ocean Research Foundation Inc. • Viking Starship,
Viking Dock, W. Lake Dr., Montauk, NY • 631-668-5700* • The Okeanos Ocean
Research Foundation is a non-profit research & educational organization. • **Features
Include:** Public Viewing of Great Whales, Finback, Minke & Humpback Whales,
Dolphins, Porpoises, Seabirds, Sea Turtles, Eastern Long Island, Lectures on Whales
& Marine Life, Crew Members will Answer Questions, 140-ft. Viking Starship (whale
watch/research vessel), Galley Gift Shop, Large Heated Cabin Seats 220 Passengers,
Observation Sun-Deck seats 100, Television/Video System, Public Address System for
easy listening to a Naturalist's Lecture **Hours:** 7-days a week, 4-8 hr. trip **Fee:** Adult:
$36, Kids Under 13: $13, Seniors: $18 **Directions:** *I-495 Long Island Expwy., take exit 68
William Floyd Pkwy. toward Shirley, turn Right to merge onto NY-27 E. toward Montauk, turn*

Left to stay on NY-27 E., turn Left onto Main St., continue onto NY-27 E./Pantigo Rd., continue to follow NY-27 E., turn Left at County Rd. 77/W. Lake Dr., the boat leaves the Viking dock in Montauk www.webscope.com/li/whale.html

Summer Afternoon Music, Demonstrations & Storytellers • *Sagamore Hill National Historic Site • 20 Sagamore Hill Rd., Oyster Bay, NY • 516-922-4447 •* ** Features **Include: Summer Children's Events, Estate circa 1884, 23-room Victorian Mansion (Roosevelt's "Summer White House" from 1901-1909), Old Orchard Museum, Exhibits & Audio Visual Programs, Summer Concert Series **Hours:** Sat. & Sun. Events: 2-4 p.m., open daily from 9:30 a.m.-5 p.m. **Fee:** Ages 16-62: $1 **Free** under 16 yrs. **Directions:** *Northern State Pkwy. to exit 35N. or the Long Island Expwy. to exit 41N., take Rte. 106 N. for 4 mi., turn Right/East on Rte. 25A & travel 2.5 mi., at the 3rd traffic light turn Left onto Cove Rd. N. for 1.7 mi., turn Right onto Cove Neck Rd. N., 1.5 mi. to Sagamore Hill*
www.nps.gov/sahi

Summer Sundays Tours ⓥ • ***BNL Science Museum (formerly Exhibit Center Science Museum) Brookhaven National Laboratory, Upton, NY • Public Affairs Office: 631-344-2345 • 631-344-4495 • 631-344-2651 •*** Brookhaven National Lab is under contract to the US Department of Energy & the recipient of 6 Nobel prizes. **Features Include:** 5,265-acre Lab, Science Learning Center, Interactive Exhibits & Programs, Basic Scientific Principles Demonstrations, Utilizes the Inquiry Method of Teaching, Whiz Bang Science Show, Camp Upton Historical Collection, the 2003 Nobel Prize Chemistry Exhibit, Physics, Chemistry, Biology, Mathematics, Medicine, Atmospheric Science, Oceanography & Energy Technology **Hours:** Summer Sun. Tour: July & Aug., 10 a.m.-3 p.m. **Fee: Free**, 16 yrs. & over must bring a photo ID **Directions:** *I-495 Long Island Expwy., take exit 68 William Floyd Pkwy. N., 1.5 mi. to BNL's gate on the Right at 2nd light*
www.bnl.gov/education • www.bnl.gov/slc

Summer Movie & Concert Nights • *Eisenhower Park • East Meadow, NY • 516-572-0200 •* **Hours:** Movies begin at Dusk on weekend nights on the Great Screen at the Harry Chapin Lakeside, check the Eisenhower Parks Events Calendar for Show Schedules **Fee: Free** **Directions:** *Northern State Pkwy., Meadow Brook Pkwy. S., exit M3 E. Stewart Ave., make a Right onto Stewart Ave. continue to the park, Park in Field 6 or 6A* www.tpwd.state.tx.us/newsmedia/calendar/?calpage=s0047

Colonial Kids: A History Club • *East Hampton Marine Museum • 301 Bluff Rd., Amagansett, NY • 631-267-6544 • Registration Information: 631-324-6850 •* Features **Include:** Explore the past through Art, Science, Cooking, Music & Crafts at all of their historic sites **Hours:** 2nd Sat. of each month, June-Sept. **Directions:** *I-495 Long Island*

Expwy., take exit 68 to merge onto William Floyd Pkwy. toward Shirley, slight Right to merge onto NY-27 E. toward Montauk, turn Left to stay on NY-27 E., turn Left onto Main St., continue onto NY-27 E./Pantigo Rd., continue to follow NY-27 E., turn Right onto Hand Ln., turn Right onto Bluff Rd., the museum will be on the Left

www.easthamptonhistory.org/pages/marine.html

Junior Lighthouse Keepers Program ⑤ • *Fire Island National Seashore, Programs & Special Events • Reservations Required: 631-687-4765 • 631 661-4876* • **Features Include:** Events for Children 7-14, Climb to the Top of the Lighthouse, Presentation on the US Life Saving Service, Nature Hike, Seining for Marine Life in the Great South Bay, Nautical Crafts, application available online **Hours:** Wed.: 10 a.m.-Noon on the terrace of the lighthouse, July-Aug., for 6 weeks **Fee: Free**

www.fireislandlighthouse.com

Some of the Junior Ranger Programs locations:

Fire Island Lighthouse • 631-661-4876, open Year-Round

Sailors Haven • 631-597-6183, open mid-May-mid-Oct.

Watch Hill • 631-597-6455, open mid-May-mid-Oct.

Fire Island Wilderness • 631-281-3010, open May-Dec., open weekends-April

William Floyd Estate • 631-399-2030, open Memorial Day-early Oct.

Junior Ranger Program ⑤ • *National Parks Foundation* • There are currently over 290 Junior Ranger Programs within the National Park Service. Children ages 8-12 can pick up a free Jr. Ranger Acticity book at a National Parks Visitors Center. **Features Include:** Hands-On Activities Booklet, Parents & Kids Explore the Parks, Interview Rangers, Complete Games, Answer Questions about the Park & the National Park Service, Complete the Activities, Receive an Official Junior Ranger Badge or Patch, the Visitor Center will check children's booklets, kids will be sworn in as Junior Rangers, each Junior Ranger will receive a certificate, & Junior Ranger badge/patch, Locations: Wilderness, Watch Hill & Sailors Haven Visitors Center, **Fee: Free**
http://staging.nationalparks.org/who-we-help/youth-engagement/?fa=junior-ranger

Web Ranger Program This is the National Park Service's online Junior Ranger program for kids. Learn about the National Parks, Play Games, Complete the Activities, Earn a Junior Ranger Patch *www.nationalparks.org/npf-at-work/our-programs/web-ranger*

Junior Ranger Path to Discovery Program ⑤ **Features Include:** Rangers Present Programs Each Week, Learn about National Parks, Kids Receive a Booklet, Hands-On Activities, Families Explore the Parks **Locations:** Wilderness, Watch Hill & Sailors Haven Visitors Center. For children 8-12. Get more information at any visitors center information desk. **Hours:** Fri.: 2 p.m., July & Aug. **Fee:** **Free** **Directions:** See Ferries on Pg. 243 www.nps.gov/fiis/forkids/beajuniorranger.htm

FIREWORKS DISPLAYS

Sag Harbor Fireworks • *Presented by the Sag Harbor Yacht Club, 27 Bay St., Sag Harbor, NY* • *631-725-0567 Off the Breakwater at Dark* • *631-725-0567* • Viewable along the waterfront. *www.sagharboryc.com*

East Hampton Fireworks • *Off Main Beach* • *104 Ocean Ave., East Hampton, NY* • *at 9:00 p.m.* • *East Hampton Chamber of Commerce* • *631-324-0362* •

www.easthamptonchamber.com

Fireworks Display • *Eisenhower Park* • *East Meadow, NY* • *516-572-0200* • There is always a 4th of July fireworks display by the Grucci Family before the 4th of July on the lawn of the Lakeside Theatre. Park in Field 6 or 6A. **Hours:** Check Eisenhower Parks events calendar online for time specifics **Fee:** **Free** **Directions:** *Northern State Pkwy., Meadowbrook Pkwy. S., exit M3 E. Stewart Ave., make a Right onto Stewart Ave. continue to the park, view from the Harry Chapin Lakeside Theatre* *www.tpwd.state.tx.us/newsmedia/calendar/?calpage=s0047*

Shelter Island Fireworks • *Off Crescent Beach* • *For more information, call the Shelter Island Chamber of Commerce* • *631-749-0399* • *Greenport-Shelter Island Ferry: 631-749-0139* • Hours: 9 p.m. Fee: **Free** Directions: *I-495 Long Island Expwy., take exit 73 Rte. 58 E., merge onto Rte. 25 E., drive 20 mi. to Greenport, watch for signs for Rte. 114 S., turn Right onto 6th St., turn Left on Wiggins St. to end, turn Right & continue turning Right to enter the final staging area, the ferry line diverts away from the ferry around a loop, & back in line facing the ferry dock & passenger terminal. There are no reservations. Traffic boards in first-come order. Vehicles & bicycles pay on board. The ferry only accepts cash &checks. Greenport-Shelter Island Ferry, continue straight onto Summerfield Pl., turn Right onto Grand Ave., take the 2nd Right onto Waverly Pl., take the 2nd Left onto Spring Garden Ave., turn Right onto Prospect Ave., turn Right onto Scudder Ln., Crescent Beach* *www.shelter-island.org* • *www.northferry.com*

Amagansett Fireworks • *Presented by the Devon Yacht Club* • *Devon Yacht Club, Devon Rd., Amagansett, NY* • *631-267-6340* • Hours: 9 p.m. Fee: **Free** Directions: *I-495 Long Island Expwy., take exit 68, merge onto William Floyd Pkwy. toward Shirley, turn Right to merge onto NY-27 E. toward Montauk, turn Left to stay on NY-27 E., turn Left at Main St., continue to Pantigo Rd., continue to follow NY-27 E., turn Left at Abrahams Landing Rd.* *www.devonyc.com*

4th of July North Fork Fireworks & Fireman's Carnival • *Moores Ln. off Rte. 25, Greenport, NY, the Greenport Polo Grounds* • *631-477-9801* • *631-477-2505* •

Features Include: Carnival Rides, Games, Food Consessions, Fireworks Display by First Assistant Fire Chief **Hours:** 10 p.m. **Directions:** *I-495 Long Island Expwy., exit onto W. Main St./Middle Country Rd./NY-25 E. toward Riverhead, follow W. Main St./ NY-25 E., turn Right onto Main Rd./NY-25 E., turn Left onto Moores Ln. off Rte. 25*

www.northforkphoto.com

Montauk Fireworks • *Umbrella Beach* • *Presented by the Montauk Chamber of Commerce* • **631-668-2428** • Hours: 9 p.m. Fee: **Free** Directions: *I-495 Long Island Expwy., take exit 68 for William Floyd Pkwy./Co. Hwy. 46 S. toward Shirley, merge onto County Rte. 46/William Floyd Pkwy., turn Left at Rte. 27 Sunrise Hwy., turn Left at S. Fox St., turn Right at S. Forest St., turn Left at S. Fulton Dr., turn Right at S. Fairview Ave.*

www.montaukchamber.com

Boys & Girls Club Fundraiser & Fireworks • *Off Three Mile Harbor, East Hampton, NY* • *For more information, call 631-324-4433* • Hours: 9 p.m. Fee: **Free** Directions: *I-495 Long Island Expwy., take exit 68 to merge onto Suffolk County 46 S./William Floyd Pkwy. toward Shirley, turn Right to merge onto NY-27 E. toward Montauk, drive 27.9 mi, turn Left to stay on NY-27 E., 10.6 mi., turn Left at Main St., turn Left at Pantigo Rd., continue onto N. Main St., turn Left after 3 mi. Harbor Rd./County Rd. 40, the harbor will be on the Left*

www.bgca.org

Macy's July 4th Fireworks Show • *Along FDR Drive* • *Macy's Fireworks Hotline: 212-494-4495* • **Features Include:** 120,000 brilliant bursts of pyrotechnic color. Fireworks will be launched from the East River between 10th St. & 23rd St. & from a location near South St. Seaport. **Hours:** Begins at 7 p.m. with the 1st firework set to explode into color over the East River at approximately 9:20 p.m. **Fee: Free** **Locations Include:**

• Anyplace in Manhattan, Brooklyn or Queens with a view of the East River.

• **FDR Drive** is closed to traffic for public fireworks viewing from Houston to 42nd St. from 7-10 p.m., bring chairs or a blanket to spread out (there are no bathrooms).

• **South St. Seaport** Fulton & South St., Pier 17, New York, NY, 212-732-7678

• **Roosevelt Island** offers guaranteed seatings, with chairs provided for all ticket-holders, a food court & pre-fireworks entertainment (including music & face-painting). Tickets are $20 & available online (no tickets will be sold on the day of the event). You can take the Roosevelt Island tramway from 2nd Ave. between 59th & 60th St. or the F train to Roosevelt Island (take the Queens-bound F one stop from 63rd St./Lexington Ave.).

• **Empire State Building** Watch the Macy's Fireworks from the top of the Empire State Building. Only 150 tickets are sold, so book in advance. 2 types of tickets are offered: For $100 per person, you can get access to both the 86th & 102nd floors, For $75 per person, you can view the fireworks from the 86th floor Observatory with 99 other exclusive ticket-holders. 212-736-3100 or 877-NYC-VIEW for tickets.

SUMMER FUN

• **The Circle Line's July 4**[th] **Cruise** You'll get a close-up look at Lady Liberty, then anchor for an awesome view of the fireworks from the river. A DJ will provide entertainment, & a cash bar & buffet dinner will be offered. The ship departs at 5:30 p.m. from the South St. Seaport at Pier 16 & returns at 11 p.m. Tickets are $75. Call 212-269-5755 or 866-9CLINE1 for reservations or more information.

• **Liberty State Park** offers views of the fireworks. From the North Cove Marina, directly in front of the World Financial Center, you can take the Water Taxi to the Liberty Landing Marina located in Liberty State Park.

• **Long Island City** hosts an annual Fireworks Festival featuring music, food, games & a view of the Macy's Fireworks display. The Festival takes place at Gantry Plaza State Park on the Long Island City waterfront.

4th **of July** • *Old Bethpage Village Restoration* • *NC* • *1303 Round Swamp Rd., Bethpage, NY* • *516-572-8400* • **Features Include:** 19th Century American Village, Parade, Patriotic Speeches, Musket Firing, Period Music, Childrens Games, All-Star Baseball Game **Hours:** 10:30 a.m-3 p.m. **Fee:** Adults: $7, Kids: $5 **Directions:** *I-495 Long Island Expwy., take exit 48 Round Swamp Rd. toward Old Bethpage/Farmingdale, make a Left onto Round Swamp Rd., turn Left Old Country Rd., slight Right at Round Swamp Rd.*
www.nassaucountyny.gov/agencies/Parks

August

Renaissance Festival ⊛ • *600 Rte. 17A, Sterling Forest, Tuxedo Park, NY* • *845-351-5171* • **Features Include:** Renaissance Village, Period Entertainment, Crafts, Food, Games **Hours:** 10 a.m.-7 p.m., Aug.-Sept. **Fee:** Adults: $16.75, Kids 5-12: $7.50, Under 5: Free **Directions:** *I-495 Long Island Expwy., take exit 31 Cross Island Pkwy. S., take exit I-295 N. toward New England, George Washington Bridge, take I-95 S. to Rte 4 W., take Rte. 17, follow signs for 17 N. (Exit 15A off NYS Thrwy.), continue 8 mi. to Rte. 17A, make Left into the fair grounds* *www.renfair.com*

Radio-Controlled Model Airplane Demonstration & Show • *Cedar Creek Park* • *3524 Merrick Rd., Seaford, NY* • *516-571-7470* • **Features Include:** Aerodrome Field Designed for Radio-Controlled Model Airplanes, Model-Aircraft Shows, An "Academy of Aeronautics" membership card is required for a permit, call: 516-571-7470 or go to www.modelaircraft.org/documents.aspx **Directions:** *Northern State Pkwy., exit onto 135 S. Seaford Oyster-Bay Expwy., take exit 1 Merrick Rd. W. toward Freeport, merge onto Merrick Rd.* *www.nassaucountyny.gov/agencies/Parks*

Metro NY Balloon & Music Festival ⊛ • *Brookhaven Calabro Airport* • *135 Dawn Dr., Shirley, NY* • *516-794-4444* • *516-428-9327* • *516-775-0435* • **Features Include:** 50 Hot Air Balloons, Extreme Sports Expo, Skydiving Teams, the Human Balloon Feat,

Music Acts, Home Improvement Pavilion, Carnival, Bilingual Big Top Circus, Monster Truck Rally, Automotive & Motorcycle Showcases Arts & Crafts Gallery, BMX, Skate & Moto-Cross, Firework Shows By the Grucci Family, Food Court & Kiosks **Hours:** Fri.-Sun., check the festival's web site for up-to-date information, early-Aug. **Fee:** Adults: $20, Kids: $12, Handicap Accessible **Directions:** *I-495 Long Island Expwy. E., take exit 68 to merge onto William Floyd Pkwy. toward Shirley, turn Left onto Dawn Dr., the airport will be on the Left* *www.fredbrabbit.com*

Tiny's Birthday Party ꙮ • Cold Spring Harbor Fish Hatchery & Aquarium • 1660 Rte. 25A, Cold Spring Harbor, NY • 516-692-6768 •

Features Include: Famous Snapping Turtle Tiny's Hatch Day, Turtle & Tortoise Pageant, Celebrate Tiny's Birthday, Guess His Weight, Refreshments, Learn about the Hatching Process of Turtles, Enter Your Turtles or Tortoises in the Annual Pageant, Pre-Registration & Entry Form required **Hours:** 10 a.m.-5 p.m., mid-Aug. **Fee:** Adults: $6, Kids under 12: $4 **Directions:** *I-495 Long Island Expwy., take exit 44N. onto Rte. 135 toward Syosset, take the exit for Jericho Tpke. E. toward Woodbury, turn Left onto S. Woods Rd., turn Right onto Cold Spring Rd., turn Right onto 25A E., the hatchery will be on the Right* *www.cshfha.org/events.html*

Hampton Classic Horse Show • 240 Snake Hollow Rd., Bridgehampton, NY • 631- 537-5446 • 631-537-3177 • 508-698-6810 •

Features Include: 65-acre Show Ground, ASPCA Animal Behavior Clinic, Finals of the Long Island Horse Show, Children's Hunter Classic, Adult Amateur Hunters, Cavalor Open Jumper, Wölffer Estate Equitation Championship, Jumping Derby Welcome Stake, Jumper Speed Derby, Grand Prix Qualifier, Kids Day, Amateur Owner Jumper Classic, Carolex Show Jumping Derby, Hermès Hunter Classic, Grand Prix & World Cup™ Qualifier **Hours:** 8:30 a.m.-5 p.m. daily, last week in Aug. **Fee:** $10 per person, Free under 6 yrs., or $20 car load, kids Free Sat. **Directions:** *I-495 Long Island Expwy., take exit 68 William Floyd Pkwy. toward Shirley, turn Left onto Montauk Hwy./NY-27 E., turn Left onto Snake Hollow Rd.* *www.hamptonclassic.com*

Dinausaur State Park Day ꙮ • Dinosaur Park • Dinosaur State Park, 400 West St., Rocky Hill, CT• 860-529-8423 • FDPA Phone: 860-257-7601 •

Features Include: Meet Dilly the Dilophosaurus, Games, Prizes, Experiments, Arts & Crafts, Face Painting, Food, Animal Shows, Entertainment, Nature Trails, Display Gardens, Arboretum, Indoor & Outdoor Park, Cast a Dino Track, See Dinausaur State Park in the Museum section>Natural History>Connecticut for a full description **Hours:** Sat.: 9 a.m.-4:30 p.m., mid-Aug. **Fee:** Free outdoor activities, Mining: Adults: $5, Kids 6-12: $2, Under 5: Free **Directions:** *I-495 Long Island Expwy., take exit 31 Cross Island Pkwy., take Exit 33 & merge onto I-295 Throgs Neck Bridge/ Bronx/New England, slight Right onto I-695 N. New Haven, merge onto I-95 N., take exit 48 on the Left & merge onto I-91 N. toward Hartford, take exit 23 West St.* *www.dinosaurstatepark.org*

Medieval Times • *The Long Island Science Center* • *11 W. Main St., Riverhead NY* • *631-208-8000* • **Features Include:** Medieval Science, Check out the Castle, Use Pulleys, Use a Hand Pump to Move Water, Make a Cart to Haul Hay, Experiment With Catapults **Hours:** Mid-Aug., Mon.-Fri.: 10 a.m.-2 p.m., Sun.: 11 a.m.-4 p.m., Summer Schedule: July-Aug., Wed.-Sun.: 11 a.m.-4 p.m. **Fee:** Adults: $2, Kids: $5 **Directions:** *I-495 Long Island Expwy., take exit 72 25E. & follow signs to Riverhead, enter the town of Riverhead, pass the Suffolk County Historical Society on the Left, at the 3rd traffic light make a Right, immediately make another right into the bank parking lot, bear Left pass the drive-thru & turn Right into the parking lot adjacent to the museum, museum entrance faces the parking lot on the West side of the building* www.lisciencecenter.org

Seafood Festival • *Maritime Museum,* • *86 West Ave., West Sayville, NY* • *631-447-8679* • **Features Include:** Pirate Show, National & Regional Acts, Crafts, Seafood, Musicians, Indoor & Outdoor Museum Exhibits, 150 Nautical Art Vendors, Educational Groups, Seafood Pavilion, Year-Round Educational Tours **Hours:** Sat.-Sun.: 10 a.m.-7 p.m., Sun.: Noon-4 p.m., end of Aug. **Directions:** *I-495 Long Island Expwy., take exit 53 toward Bay Shore/Kings Park/Sagtikos State Pkwy., merge onto Sagtikos Pkwy., take the exit onto Southern State Pkwy., exit onto S. Country Rd./E. Main St./27A E., continue to follow S. Country Rd., continue on Main St., turn Right at West Ave., the museum will be on the Left* www.limaritime.org

Snapper Derby • *Captree State Park* • *1 Rescue Rd., Babylon, NY* • **631-321-3510** • **631 669-0449** • *Captree Boatman's Association:* **631-669-6464** • **Features Include**: Children's Fishing Tournament, Heaviest Snapper Prizes, Age Categories: 7 & under/8-12/13-16 **Hours:** 8 a.m.-4 p.m., mid-Aug. **Fee:** Empire Passport Accepted **Directions:** *Southern State Pkwy., take exit 40 Robert Moses Cswy. S. to the park* http://222.nysparks.com/events/event.aspx?e=1350.0

Annual Outdoor Movie Night & Festival • *Love Ln., Mattituck, NY* • **631-298-4646** • **Features Include:** Fast Cars, Hot Rod Car Show, Outdoor Movie Night, Love Lane will be Closed to Cars, Shops & Restaurants Open Late, Classic Film Chosen to Entertain Families, Seating is available on a first-come first-served basis, bring lawn chairs **Hours:** Car Show: 5 p.m., movie begins at dusk, Sat. in mid-Aug. **Fee: Free Directions:** *I-495 Long Island Expwy., exit onto W. Main St./Middle Country Rd./NY-25 Riverhead, W. Main St./NY-25 E., turn Right onto Main Rd./NY-25 E., turn Left onto Sound Ave., take the 1st Right onto Love Ln.* www.mattituckchamber.org • www.northfork.org/events.html

The Vladimir Nielsen Piano Festival • *64 Laurel Trail, Sag Harbor, NY* • *Reservations Required:* **631-899-4074** • **Features Include:** Concert Series, Highly Talented International Piano Students ages 11-21, Concert Gala & Clam Bake **Hours:** 5 p.m. **Fee:** Concert: $15 per person, Free children & students, Concert Gala & Clam Bake: $75 per person **Directions:** *I-495 Long Island Expwy., take exit 68 William Floyd Pkwy. toward Shirley, turn Right to merge onto NY-27 E toward Montauk, turn Left onto N. Rd./County Rd. 39, continue onto Sandy Hollow Rd., turn Left at N. Sea Rd., turn Right onto Noyack Rd., at the traffic circle, take the 1st exit onto County Rd. 38/Noyack Rd., turn Right onto Long Beach Ln., turn Left onto Hillover Ln., turn Right onto Laurel Trail, estate will be on the Left*   *www.nielsenfest.com*

Sag Harbor Community Band · *1 Bay St., Long Wharf at Bay St., Sag Harbor, NY ·*

631-725-5858 · **Features Include:** Evening Concert Series, Bring Beach Chair, Concerts take place in front of the American Legion Building **Hours:** 8-9 p.m., July-Aug. **Fee:** *Free* **Directions:** *I-495 Long Island Expwy., take exit 68 William Floyd Pkwy. toward Shirley, turn Right to merge onto NY-27 E. toward Montauk, turn Left at Montauk Hwy./27 E., turn Left at Bridgehampton Sag Harbor Tpke., continue on Main St., turn Right at Bay St.*

Sag Harbor Summer Concert Series · *Marine Park · Bay St. in Sag Harbor, NY ·*

Features Include: Evening Concert Series, Bring a Blanket, Beach Chairs & Picnic Dinner, Concerts sponsored by the Sag Harbor Chamber of Commerce **Hours:** 7:30 p.m., Thurs. in Aug. **Fee:** *Free* **Directions:** *I-495 Long Island Expwy., take exit 68 William Floyd Pkwy. toward Shirley, turn Right to merge onto NY-27 E. toward Montauk, turn Left at Montauk Hwy./NY-27 E., turn Left at Bridgehampton Sag Harbor Tpke., continue onto Main St., turn Right at Bay St.*   *http://sagharborchamber.com*

Whale Watching · Viking Starship · *Viking Fleet · Montauk, Dock West Lake Dr.,*

Montauk Harbor, NY · 631-668-5700 · The Okeanos Ocean Research Foundation is a non-profit research organization which offers opportunities to the public to view the great whales as they feed in the waters off eastern Long Island. **Features Include:** Finbacks, Minke & Humpback Whales, Dolphins, Porpoises, Seabirds, Sea Turtles, Fish, Naturalist Lecture on Whales & Marine Life, Crew Members Answer Questions, Sightings are Not Guaranteed, but the foundation has had good success with past sightings, Comfortable 140-ft. Fast Steel Vessel, Galley, Gift Shop, Large Heated Cabin Seating over 220 Passengers, Observation Sun-Deck seating for over 100 Passengers, Television, Video System, Public Address System **Hours:** 7 days a week, 4-8 hr. trip **Fee:** Adults: $30, Kids Under 13: $15, Seniors: $27 **Directions:** *I-495 Long Island Expwy., take exit 70 toward Manorville/ Rte. 111 S., take 27 E. Sunrise Hwy. to Montauk, turn Left at the Plaza Circle in town toward the Montauk Harbor area, keep going straight, located on the Right side of the street after the stop sign, 462 West Lake Dr., look for a round white building*   *www.vikingfleet.com*

Whale Watching · *Coastal Research and Education Society of Long Island, Inc.*

(CRESLI) · *150 Idle Hour Blvd., Oakdale, NY · Attn: Dept. of Earth & Marine Sciences, Dowling College · 631-244-3352 ·* **Features Include:** Montauk Great South Channel Whale Watch, Single Day Whale Watching, 75% Success in Finding

Cetaceans, Humpback Whales, Atlantic White-Sided Dolphins, Fin Whales, Minke Whales **Hours & Fees:** Call for info, **Open:** Tues.-Sun., mid-Aug. **Directions:** *I-495 Long Island Expwy., take exit 70 toward Manorville/Rte. 111 S., take 27 E. Sunrise Hwy. to Montauk, turn Left at the Plaza Circle in town toward the Montauk Harbor area, keep going straight, located on the Right side of the street after the stop sign, 462 West Lake Dr., look for a round white building* www.cresli.org • www.vikingfleet.com

NASSAU COUNTY

Bar Beach • *North Hempstead of, Town Parks & Recreation Dept., Bar Beach Park* • *802 W. Shore Rd., Port Washington, NY* • *516-767-4625* • Directions: *I-495 Long Island Expwy., take exit 37 Willis Ave., merge onto Old Powerhouse Rd., turn Right onto Mineola Ave., turn Right onto Layton St., take the 1st Right onto Old Northern Blvd., turn Left onto W. Shore Rd., the beach will be on the Right*

Hempstead Harbor Park • **NC** • *W. Shore Rd., Port Washington, NY* • **516-869-6311** • **Features Include:** 60-acre Park, .5-mi. Harbor Beach, Basketball Court, Handball/ Paddleball Courts, .5-mi. Promenade, Picnic Area, Open-Air Shelter with Picnic Tables & Grills (reservations required), Fishing Pier, Playground, Aerodrome for Model Planes (permit), Volleyball/Badminton (nets on beach) **Hours:** 11 a.m.-Dusk (Lifeguard) **Fee:** Free off-season, Resident: $15, Non-Resident: $20, NC permit Memorial Day-Labor Day: $40 **Directions:** *Northern State Pkwy. take exit 29, Roslyn Rd. N. to W. Shore Rd.*   *www.nassaucountyny.gov*

Nickerson Beach Park • **NC** • *880 Lido Blvd., Lido Beach, NY* • *516-571-7700* • **Features Include:** 121-acre Park, .75-mi. Atlantic Ocean Frontage, Cabana Area, Fun Zone Area, Playground, 2 Basketball Courts, 2 Tennis Courts, 9 Beach Volleyball Courts (for leagues & individuals), Baseball Field, 2 Pools, Skate Park, Skateboard Facility (7 ramps of varying difficulty & 2 railings), Picnic Tables & Grills, Dog Run (size sensitive), Campground (reservations required: 516-571-7701), "Nathan's at Nickerson" Restaurant (open Labor Day-Oct.), seasonal Movie Nights, & Concerts **Hours:** Dawn-Dusk **Fee:** Free off-season, Leisure Pass: $40 or $8 per day for Nassau County residents, Non-residents:

$20 **Directions:** *Meadowbrook Pkwy., take exit M10 Loop Pkwy., take to the end, bear Right onto Lido Blvd., continue for 2 lights, make a Left into the park*
www.nassaucountyny.gov/agencies/Parks/WheretoGo/active/nickerson.html

Sands Point Preserve • NC • *127 Middle Neck Rd., Port Washington, NY* • *516-571-7900* • **Features Include:** 216-acre Preserve, 6 Marked Walking/Hiking Trails, Woods, Fields, Forests, Meadows, Young Woodlands, Shoreline Beach (on the LI sound), Cliffs, Lawns, Gardens, Freshwater Pond, Trail Maps, Guided Nature Walks & Self-Guiding Literature, each natural area provides habitats for a variety of plants & animals **Hours:** 10 a.m.-5 p.m., Year-Round **Fee: Free** weekdays, Weekends: $2 **Directions:** *I-495 Long Island Expwy., take exit 36 Searingtown Rd. N., drive for approx. 6 mi., the road becomes Port Washington Blvd. & then Middle Neck Rd., entrance is on the Right 1 mi. past the stone & brick gate of the Sands Point Village Club*
info@sandspointpreserve.org , www.sandspointpreserve.org/htm/info.htm

Jones Beach State Park • NYS • *1 Ocean Pkwy., Wantagh, NY* • *516-785-1600* • Jones Beach is considered a world-class swimming destination. • **Features Include:** 6.5 mi. of Ocean Beach, Surf Bathing, Still Water Bathing (on .5-mi. bay beach), Beach Volleyball, 2-mi. Boardwalk, Deck Games, Mini Golf, Surf Fishing, Boat Basin, Marina, Golf, Picnic Tables, Playground, Recreation Programs, Showers, Food, Gift Shop, Museum/Visitor Center, Performing Arts Theatre, Birding (in undeveloped areas that are home to a variety of migratory birds & native plants). The park is also home to the Theodore Roosevelt Nature Center, which includes environmental displays about the seashore, educational tours & programming for all ages, & a "Castles in the Sand" photo collection (at the East Bathhouse) which depicts the development of the Long Island State Park & Parkway Systems. Family events may include: Fishing Clinics **Hours:** Dawn-Dusk, Year-Round **Fee: Free** off-season, Memorial Day-Labor Day: $10, Weekends Only until Oct.: $8, Empire Pass Accepted **Directions:** *Northern State Pkwy., exit onto Meadowbrook Pkwy. S. or Wantagh Pkwy. S. to the Park* *www.jonesbeach.com*

SUFFOLK COUNTY

Camp Hero • NYS • *50 South Fairview Ave., Montauk, NY* • *631-668-3781* • This is a National Historic Site & former military base. **Features Include:** 415-acre Park, Atlantic Ocean Beach, Biking, Bird Watching, Bridle Path, Fishing, Hiking, Wooded Areas, Historic Military Installation, Maritime Forests, Freshwater Wetlands, Ocean Views, Bluffs Rising above the Beach **Hours:** Dawn-Dusk **Fee: Free** off-season, Memorial Day-Labor Day: $10, Weekends Only until Oct.: $8, Empire Pass Accepted **Directions:** *I-495 Long Island Expwy., exit 68 for William Floyd Pkwy./Co. Hwy. 46S. toward Shirley, turn Left*

onto Rte. 27 E. Sunrise Hwy., turn Right at Camp Hero State Park Rd., turn Left to stay on Camp Hero State Park Rd. *http://nysparks.state.ny.us*

Cedar Point County Park • SC • *East Hampton, NY* • *631-852-7620* • *Camping Reservations: 631-244-7275* • **Features Include:** 607-acre Park, Views of Gardiner's Bay, Surfcast Fishing, Hiking, Nature Trails, Picnicking, Lighthouse, Camping, Playground, Rowboat Rentals, Bicycling, Saltwater Fishing, Scuba Diving, Hunting, Vehicle Access to the Outer Beach (with permit only), Licensed Hunting for Waterfowl (in season), General Store & Snack Bar: 631-324-7147, Sat. Night Family Movies on the Lawn behind the Store & Free Use of Recreational Equipment **Hours:** Dawn-Dusk **Fee: Free Directions:** *Montauk Hwy. E. to Stephen Hands Path in East Hampton, turn North & continue to Old Northwest Rd., turn Right on to Northwest Rd., bear Left and continue to Alewive Brook Rd., the park entrance is 100 yds. down the road*

www.co.suffolk.ny.us/Home/departments/parks/Parks.aspx

Cupsogue Beach County Park • SC • *Dune Rd., Westhampton, NY* • *631-852-8111* •
During the summer season there is lifeguard-supervised swimming & sunbathing on white sand beaches. Cupsogue Beach offers some of the best saltwater bass fishing on Long Island. **Features Include:** 296-acre Barrier Beach Park, Swimming, Fishing, Scuba Diving, Camping, Outer Beach Access, Food Concession (www.thebeachhuts.com), First Aid Center, Restrooms, Showers, Changing Rooms, Special Events in season, Campers & recreational vehicles are permitted along the access road running parallel to the outer beach, Diving is permitted at slack tide on the bay side of the park only **Hours:** 8:30 a.m.-4:30 p.m., Year-Round **Fee: Free** off-season, With Green Key: $5, Without Green Key: $10, Memorial Day-Labor Day **Directions:** *I-495 Long Island Expwy., take exit 68 for William Floyd Pkwy. S. toward Shirley, take the ramp onto Rte. 27 E., take exit 63 S. for Co. Hwy. 31 S. toward Westhampton Beach, merge onto County Rte. 31/Old Riverhead Rd., continue on Oak St., at the traffic circle, take the 2nd exit onto Potunk Ln., turn Right onto Stevens Ln., turn Left onto Jessup Ln., turn Right onto County Rte. 89/Dune Rd., follow Dune Rd. to the park*

www.co.suffolk.ny.us/Home/departments/parks/Parks.aspx

Fire Island National Seashore • *631-661-4876* • **Features Include:** Programs & Special Events, Lighthouse, Nature Hikes, Swimming, Picnicing, Cycling **Hour & Fee:** vary per location, see Fire Island Ferry service information in the boating section **Directions:** *Southern State Pkwy., exit 40 Robert Moses Cswy. S., toward Robert Moses State Park, get to the park & drive around the water tower, head East, park in the East end of Field 5, walk on the boardwalk to the lighthouse*

Sailors Haven • 631-597-6183 • Open mid-May-mid-Oct.

Watch Hill • 631-597-6455 • Open mid-May to mid-Oct-

Fire Island Wilderness • 631-281-3010 • Open Dec.-May, weekends-April

William Floyd Estate • 631-399-2030 • Open Memorial Day-early Oct.

GilGo State Park • **NYS** • *Ocean Pkwy., Babylon, NY* • *631-669-0449* • Features **Include**: South Shore Barrier Beach with Atlantic Ocean & Great South Bay Frontage, Beach, Surf Fishing (Fall Stripe Bass Migration & Blue Fish), Scenic Views, Protected Area for Piping Plover & Sea Beach Amaranth, Educational Programs about Habitat Management, 4-wheel Drive Access Only, Permit Required, Carry-in-Carry-Out Facility **Hours:** Dawn-Dusk, Year-Round **Fee:** **Free** off-season, Memorial Day-Labor Day: $10, Weekends Only until Oct.: $8, Empire Pass Accepted **Directions:** Wantagh Pkwy. S. to Robert Moses Cswy. S., take Ocean Pkwy. W.

http://nysparks.state.ny.us/sites/info

Heckscher State Park • *Heckscher Pkwy., Field 1, East Islip, NY* • *631-581-2100* • *Reservations: 800-456-2267* • **Features Include:** 20 mi. of Nature Trails, Hiking, Bicycling, Swimming on the Great South Bay Beach, Pool Complex, Showers, Play Grounds, Fishing, Picnic Areas & Tables, Boat Launch Ramp, Playing Fields, Food, Recreation Programs, Pavilions **Hours:** Year-Round, 7 days a week, 7 a.m.-Dusk **Fee:** **Free** off-season, Memorial Day-Labor Day: $10, Weekends Only Until Oct.: $8, Empire Pass Accepted **Directions:** *Southern State Pkwy. E., it ends in the park*

http://nysparks.state.ny.us/parks/info.asp?parkID=153

Hither Hills • **NYS** • *50 South Fairview Ave., Montauk, NY* • *631-668-2554* • *Reservations: 800-456-2267* • **Features Include:** Ocean Beach, 40-acre Fresh Water Lake, Walking Dunes, Biking, Hiking, Nature Trail, Playground, Horseshoe Courts, Volleyball, Tetherball, Food, Picnic Area, Fireplaces, Tables, Playing Field(s), Showers, Fishing, Recreation Programs, Year-Round Fishing, "Walking Dunes" of Napeague Harbor, Organized recreation program in high season includes: Family Movies, Folk & Line Dancing, Children's Summer Theatre, Magic Shows, Environmental Interpretation Programs **Hours:** Year-Round, Dawn-Dusk, 7 days a week **Fee:** **Free** off-season, Memorial Day-Labor Day: $10, Weekends Only until Oct.: $8, Empire Pass Accepted **Directions:** *I-495 Long Island Expwy., take exit 68, William Floyd Pkwy. S., take Sunrise Hwy. Rte. 27 E., turn Left onto 27 E., Right turn onto Birch Dr./Oak Ln., Right onto Birch St./Birch Dr., turn Left onto Old Montauk Hwy.*

http://nysparks.state.ny.us/parks/info.asp?parkId=48

Lake Ronkonkoma Beach • *Shore Rd., Lake Ronkonkoma, NY* • *631-451-6100* • *Rec Center: 299 Rosevale Ave., Ronkonkoma, NY* • Lake Ronkonkoma was once a resort town, until the area experienced a population explosion in the mid-1900s. The was considered the most sacred lake by the Indians. **Features Include:** 100-ft. Deep Lake, Largest

Lake on Long Island **Fee: Free** for Brookhaven residents, Non-Residents: $20 **Directions:** *I-495 Long Island Expwy., take exit 59 toward Ocean Ave./Ronkonkoma, turn Left onto Ocean Ave., continue onto Rosevale Ave., the Rec Center will be on the Right*

Orient Point • NYS • *Rte. 25, Orient Point, NY • 631-323-2440* • Top 10 Family Beach in the US **Features Include:** 45,000 ft. of frontage on Gardiner's Bay, Beach, Showers, Food, Hiking, Biking, Fishing, Walk the Nature Trails, Picnic Tables, Pavilions, Playground, Playing Fields, Recreation Programs, Environmental Tours, Bike Rentals, Rare Maritime Forest (with Red Cedar, Black-Jack Oak Trees & Prickly-Pear Cactus), Wood Deck (overlooking Gardiner's Bay), Pavilions (party pavilions by reservation) **Hours:** Year-Round, 7 days a week, 7 a.m.-Dusk **Fee: Free** off-season, Memorial Day-Labor Day: $10, Weekends Only until Oct.: $8, Empire Pass Accepted **Directions:** *I-495 Long Island Expwy., take exit 73 for Old Country Rd. toward Orient, slight Left onto County Rte. 58/Old Country Rd., slight Left at Main Rd./Rte. 25, continue to follow Main Rd./Rte. 25, turn Left onto Love Ln., turn Right onto County Rte. 48, continue on Main Rd./Rte. 25 E. to the park*   *http://nysparks.state.ny.us/sites/info*

Robert Moses State Park • *Fire Island National Seashore* • Box 247, Babylon, NY • 631-669-0470 • **Features Include:** 5 mi. of Ocean Beach, Swimming, Surfing, Surf Fishing (fishermen can also fish from the piers), Marina, Boat Basin (accommodates 40 boats), Picnic Areas, Picnic Tables, 18-hole Pitch & Putt Golf Course, Food, Playground (Field 5), Lighthouse (Field 5), Recreation Programs **Hours:** Year-Round, 7 days a week, 7 a.m.-Dusk **Fee: Free** off-season, Memorial Day-Labor Day: $10, Weekends Only Until Oct.: $8, Empire Pass Accepted **Directions:** *Southern State Pkwy. to Robert Moses Cswy., take exit 40 S., the park is at the western end of Fire Island*
http://nysparks.state.ny.us/parks

Sears Bellows • SC • *Sears Bellows Pond Rd., Hampton Bays, NY • Park Office: 631-852-8290 • Big Duck: 631-852-8292* • Sears Bellows is situated within the Long Island Pine Barrens. **Features Include:** Lifeguard-Protected Swimming, Freshwater Fishing (Bluegill, Bass, Perch & Pickerel), Rowboat Rentals, Hiking (extensive trail system), Picnicking **Hours:** Dawn-Dusk, Year-Round **Fee: Free** off-season, mid-June-Labor Day with Green Key: $5, No Green Key: $8, this is the home of the Big Duck **Directions:** *Northern State Pkwy., exit onto Wantagh State Pkwy. S., take exit onto Sunrise Hwy., take exit 65 N., follow Rte. 24, make a Left onto Bellows Pond Rd., the park entrance is on the Right*
http://www.co.suffolk.ny.us/Home/departments/parks/Parks.aspx

Shadmoor • NYS • *50 South Fairview Ave., Montauk, NY • 631-668-3781* • **Features Include:** 99-acre Park, 2,400 ft. of Ocean Beach, Biking, Saltwater Fishing, Hiking Trails,

Elevated Platforms for Birdwatching. Habitats Include: Shadbushes, Bluffs, Freshwater Black Cherry Trees, Clusters of the Rare & Federally-Endangered Sand Plain Gerardia Plant. 2 concrete bunkers remain in the park that were built during WWII & once equipped with artillery guns to protect the coast from enemy invasion. **Fee: Free** off-season, Memorial Day-Labor Day: $10, Weekends Only Until Oct.: $8, Empire Pass Accepted **Directions**: *I-495 Long Island Expwy., take exit 68 for William Floyd Pkwy./ Co. Hwy. 46 S. toward Shirley, merge onto County Rte. 46 William Floyd Pkwy., take the ramp onto Rte. 27 E., turn Left at Main St./Rte. 27, turn Right, the park is 1.5 mi. East of the village on the Right, at the southwest corner of Rte. 27 & Seaside Ave.*

http://nysparks.state.ny.us/sites/info

Shinnecock East County Park • SC • *Dune Rd., Southampton, NY • 631-852-8290 •* This undeveloped barrier beach park borders the Shinnecock Inlet where it meets the Atlantic Ocean. **Features Include:** Ocean & Bay Beaches, Saltwater Fishing (Striped Bass), & Off-Road Recreational Vehicle Use. Off-road recreational vehicles may drive on the outer (ocean) beach. A small parking lot is available for Green Key cardholders who do not have an Outer Beach Recreational Vehicle Permit. **Hours:** Dawn-Dusk, Year-Round **Fee: Free** off-season, mid-June-Labor Day with Green Key: $5, No Green Key: $8 **Directions:** *Southern State Pkwy., exit at Sunrise Hwy., exit at Montauk Hwy., turn South on Halsey Neck Ln., make a Right turn onto Dune Rd. heading West to the park entrance*   *www.co.suffolk.ny.us/*

Smith Point County Park • SC • *Fire Island, Shirley, NY • 631-852-1313 • Camping Reservations: 631-244-7275 •* Smith Point is Suffolk County's largest ocean front park. **Features Include:** Swimming, Lifeguards, Scuba Diving, Surfing, White Sand Beach, Atlantic Surf, Saltwater Fishing, Food Concession, Playground, Showers, Restaurant, & Special Events in season. There is marked, protective fencing around the nest sites of endangered shorebirds inhabiting the ocean & bay beaches. The Raw Bar & Grill serves breakfast, lunch & dinner. They offer seafood specialties, live entertainment & a beautiful setting. Beach Hut: 631-728-2988, www.thebeachhuts.com **Hours:** Sat.-Wed.: 8:30 a.m.-6 p.m., Thurs. & Fri.: 8:30 a.m.-9 p.m. **Fee: Free** off-season, With Green Key: $5, Memorial Day-Sept.: $10 **Directions:** *I-495 Long Island Expwy., exit 68 S. William Floyd Pkwy. to end, which terminates at Fire Island*

www.co.suffolk.ny.us/Home/departments/parks/Parks.aspx

Sunken Meadow • NYS • *Rte. 25A & Sunken Meadow Pkwy., Northport, NY • 631-269-4333 •* The park is located on the Long Island Sound. **Features Include:** 3 mi. of Beach, Swimming, .75-mi. Boardwalk, Showers, Kayaking, Canoeing, Windsurfing, Fishing, Picnicking & Picnic Tables, Playground, Play Fields, Food, Hiking Nature

Trails, 27 holes of Golf, Driving Range, Putting Green, Children's Summer Theatre Programs: Sat. at 2 p.m., there are also Recreation Programs **Fee: Free** off-season, Memorial Day-Labor Day: $10, Weekends Only until Oct.: $8, Empire Pass Accepted **Directions:** *I-495 Long Island Expwy., take exit 53 Sunken Meadow/Sagtikos Pkwy. to the end* http://nysparks.state.ny.us/parks

Wildwood • NYS • *P.O. Box 518, N. Wading River Road, Wading River, NY • 631-929-4314 • Reservations: 800-456-2267* •

Wildwood State Park comprises 600 acres of undeveloped Hardwood Forest terminating on the high bluff overlooking the Long Island Sound. **Features Include:** 600-acre Park, Beach, Showers, Playground, Biking, Nature Trails, Food, Fishing, Hiking, Picnic Tables, Recreation Programs **Hours:** Dawn-Dusk, Year-Round **Fee: Free** off-season, Memorial Day-Labor Day: $10, Weekends Only Until Oct.: $8, Empire Pass Accepted **Directions:** *I-495 Long Island Expwy., take exit 68, head N. on Rte. 46, take Rte. 25A E., turn Left onto Sound Ave., turn Left at traffic light onto Hulse Landing Rd., the park entrance is on the Right* http://nysparks.state.ny.us/sites/info

BOARDWALKS

Charles T. Church Nature Preserve • *North Shore Wildlife Sanctuary • Frost Mill Rd., Mill Neck, NY • 516-671-0283* •

Features Include: 60-acre Preserve, known as "Shu Swamp," Wooded Wetland fed by the Beaver Brook system, 2.5 mi. of Trails, with Boardwalks across muddier areas **Hours:** Sat.-Thurs. **Directions:** *Northern State Pkwy., exit 35 N. State Hwy. 106/107 N., to 106 N., Left at Brookville Rd., continue on Wolver Hollow Rd., Right at Chicken Valley Rd., Left onto Oyster Bay Rd., Oyster Bay Glen Cove Rd., Right at Frost Mill Rd., turn Left at Frost Mill Rd.*

Hempstead Harbor Park • NC • *W. Shore Rd., Port Washington, NY • 516-571-7930* •

Features Include: 60-acre Park, .5-mi. Promenade, .5-mi. Harbor Beach, Volleyball/Badminton (nets on beach), *See Hempstead Harbor Park in the Beach section for complete information.*

Jones Beach • NYS • *1 Ocean Pkwy., Wantagh, NY • 516-785-1600* •

Features Include: Beach Volleyball, *See Jones Beach in the Beach section for complete information*

Lakeland County Park • SC • *Johnson Ave., Islandia, NY • 631-853-2727 • Administration: 631-854-4949* •

Features Include: Boardwalk (over the head-waters of the Connetquot River), Wetland Vegetation, Waterfowl, Picnic Area, Gazebo, Fishing, Nature Trail, Lakeland Park is a handicap accessible facility designed for the disabled & their families **Hours:** Office/Restrooms Open Memorial Day-Labor Day

Directions: *I-495 Long Island Expwy. to exit 58 S. Nichols Rd., turn Left at Johnson Ave., the park entrance is.5 mi. on the Right*

www.co.suffolk.ny.us/Home/departments/parks/Parks.aspx

Mashomack Preserve • *TNC The Nature Conservancy* • *Shelter Island, NY* • Feartures **Include:** 2,000-acre Preserve, Tidal Creek, 2-mi. boardwalk, Views of Gardiner's Bay, Plum Pond Overlook, Bass Creek, Log Cabin Creek, Trail House, 12 mi. of trails **Hours:** Year-Round, Closed: Tues., July-Aug.: open 7 days a week, 9 a.m.-5 p.m., Oct.-March: 9 a.m.-4 p.m., Visitors Center open Summer & Weekends Only **Fee: Free Directions:** *North Ferry Service out of Greenport, follow NY 114 S. 3 mi. to the entrance, all hikes share a common start near the Trail House Visitors Center*

Smiths Point Ranger Station • **SC** • *1450 Montauk Hwy., Mastic, NY* • *631-281-3010* • *631-852-1313* • *Camping Reservations: 631-244-7275* • Features Include: Boardwalk, *see Smiths Point in the Beach section for complete information*

Sunken Meadow State Park • *Rte. 25A & Sunken Meadow Pkwy., Northport, NY* • *631-269-4333* • **Features Include:** .75-mi. Boardwalk on the Long Island Sound, *see Sunken Meadow State Park in the Beach section for complete information*

SUGGESTIONS • COMMENTS • ERRORS

Linda.ReidBryce
@verizon.net

Thanks

NASSAU COUNTY

Christopher Morley Park • NC • *500 Searingtown Rd., Roslyn, NY •* 516-571-8113 • **Features Include:** Volleyball Courts, Horseshoes, Shuffleboard, 2 Paddle-Tennis Courts, 4 Lighted Handball/Paddleball Courts, 98-acre Park, 30 acres of Nature Trails, Playground, Picnic Areas with Barbecue Equipment **Hours:** Dawn-Dusk **Fee:** *Free* **Directions:** *I-495 Long Island Expwy., take exit 36N., Searingtown Rd., take Searingtown Rd. N. & look for the park entrance on the Right, approx. 200 yds. from I-495*

www.nassaucountyny.gov/agencies/Parks/WheretoGo/active/morley.html

Hempstead Harbor Park • NC • *W. Shore Rd., Port Washington, NY, 11050 •* 516-869-6311 • **Features Include:** Volleyball/Badminton Nets on the Beach, 60-acre Park, Basketball Court, Handball/Paddleball Courts, .5-mi. Promenade, Picnic Area, Open-Air Shelter with Picnic Tables & Grills, Playground **Hours:** 11 a.m.-Dusk **Fee:** *Free* off-season, Leisure Pass Required, Non-Residents Memorial Day-Labor Day: $20 **Directions:** *Northern State Pkwy., take exit 29, Roslyn Rd. N., to W. Shore Rd.*

www.nassaucountyny.gov/agencies/Parks/WhereToGo/active/hempstead.html

Jones Beach State Park • NYS • *1 Ocean Pkwy., Wantagh, NY •* 516-785-1600 • **Features Include:** Beach Volleyball, 6.5 mi. of Ocean Beach, 2-mi. Boardwalk, Deck Games, Miniature Golf, Picnic Tables, Playground, Showers, Food **Hours:** Year-Round, Dawn-Dusk **Fee:** *Free* off-season, Memorial Day-Labor Day: $10, Weekends Only Until Oct.: $8, Empire Pass Accepted **Directions:** *Meadowbrook Pkwy. S. or Wantagh Pkwy. S. to the park, park in Field 4* *www.jonesbeach.com*

SUMMER FUN

Nickerson Beach Park • NC • 880 Lido Blvd., Lido Beach, NY • 516-571-7700 •
Features Include: 9 Beach Volleyball Courts, Leagues, Individuals Play, 121-acre Park, .75 mi. on the Atlantic Ocean, Picnic Tables & Grills, "Nathan's at Nickerson" **Hours:** Dawn-Dusk, Restaurant open Labor Day-Oct. **Fee:** Leisure Pass accepted, or Nassau County Residents: $8 per day, Non-residents: $20 **Directions:** *Meadowbrook Pkwy., take exit M10 to the Loop Pkwy., take to the end, bear Right onto Lido Blvd., continue for 2 lights, turn Left into the park*   *www.nassaucountyny.gov*

Riverside Blvd. Beach • 1 Riverside Blvd., Long Beach, NY • Features Include: Tournaments, Prizes, a Beach Badge is required **Directions:** *Southern State Pkwy. to Meadowbrook Pkwy. S., take Loop Pkwy., turn Right at end onto Lido Blvd. (changes to Park Ave.), turn Left onto Riverside Blvd., Free parking*   *www.eevb.net/lbeach.htm*

Valley Stream • NYS • 320 Fletcher Ave., Valley Stream, NY • 516-825-4128 •
Features Include: Volleyball, Basketball, Bocce Ball Courts, Horseshoes, Picnic Areas with Tables, Fireplaces & Grills, Children's Play Area **Fee:** $4 per car from late May -early Sept., Empire Pass Accepted **Directions:** *Southern State Pkwy, take exit 15A, exits into the park*   *http://nysparks.state.ny.us/parks/info.asp?parkID=51*

SUFFOLK COUNTY

Hither Hills • NYS • 50 South Fairview Ave., Montauk, NY • 631-668-2554 •
Reservations: 800-456-2267 • Features Include: Volleyball, Tetherball, Nature Trail, Horseshoe Courts, Playground, Ocean Beach, Food, Picnic Area, Fireplaces, Tables, **Hours:** Year-Round, Dawn-Dusk **Fee: Free**, off-season, Memorial Day-Labor Day: $10, Weekends Only until Oct.: $8, Empire Pass Accepted **Directions:** *I-495 Long Island Expwy., take exit 68, William Floyd Pkwy. S., take Sunrise Hwy. Rte. 27 E., turn Left onto 27 E., turn Right onto Birch Dr./Oak Ln., Right onto Birch St./Birch Dr., turn Left onto Old Montauk Hwy.*

Robert Moses State Park • Fire Island National Seashore • Box 247, Babylon, NY •
631-669-0470 • Features Include: Beach Volleyball **Hours:** Year-Round, 7 days a week, 7 a.m.-Dusk **Fee: Free** off-season, Memorial Day-Labor Day: $10, Weekends Only until Oct.: $8, Empire Pass Accepted **Directions:** *Southern State Pkwy. to Robert Moses Cswy., take exit 40 S., the park is at the western end of Fire Island, Park in Field 2, the volleyball courts are located East of Parking Field 2*   *http://nysparks.state.ny.us/parks*

Long Island Volleyball Association • 4271 Oak Beach, Oak Beach, NY • 631-422-5555 • Features Include: Leagues, Tournaments, Clinics, Beach BBQs
www.longislandvolleyball.com
Volleyball in the Park • Sea Cliff, NY • 516-759-0955 • Features Include: Tournaments, Teams & Registraion Information   *volleyballinthepark.com*

U-PICK BERRIES, SQUASH & MORE

Summer: June, July, Aug.

Beans: June-Sept.

Blueberries, Peaches: July-Sept.

Broccoli, Cabbage: June-Nov.

Cauliflower: July-Nov.

Melons: July-Aug.

Pears, Plums,

Raspberries: Aug.-Sept.

Strawberries: May-June

Corn: July-Oct.

Cucumbers: July-Sept.

Eggplant: July-Oct.

Lettuce: June-Oct.

Peas: June-July

Peppers: July-Oct.

Potatoes: Aug.-Oct.

Squash: June-Oct.

Tomatoes: July-Oct.

www.longisland.com/
fruit_picking.php

www.pickyourown.org

Baiting Hollow Nursery • *830 Sound Ave., Calverton, NY* • *631-929-6439* • Features: Vegetables, Fruit, Christmas Trees **Hours:** July-Dec. **Fee:** varies **Directions:** *I-495 Long Island Expwy., exit 68N. to Rte. 25A, East on Sound Ave., corner of Sound Ave. & Fresh Pond Ave.*

Borella's Farm Stand • *485 Edgewood Ave., St. James, NY* • *631- 862-7330* • **Hours:** Sun.-Sat.: 8:30 a.m.-6:30 p.m., June-Dec. **Fee:** varies **Directions:** *I-495 Long Island Expwy., take exit 53 toward Bay Shore/Kings Park/Sagtikos Pkwy., take Sagtikos State Pkwy., Sunken Meadow Pkwy., take exit SM3E. Jericho Tpke., toward Smithtown, Jericho Tpke./NY-25, turn Left onto Edgewood Ave., the farm is on the Left*

Davis Peach Farm • *Hulse Landing Rd.(North of Rte 25A), Wading River, NY* • *631-929-1115* • **Features Include:** Fruit, Vegetables, Hot Dog Stand **Hours:** 9 a.m.-5 p.m. **Fee:** $1.30 per pound, no dogs or strollers **Directions:** *I-495 Long Island Expwy., take exit 68N. Rte. 46 William Floyd Pkwy. to Rte. 25A E., turn Left onto Sound Ave., turn Left at traffic light onto Hulse Landing Rd.* *http://davispeachfarm.com/directions.html*

Elwood Pumpkin Farm • *1500 Jericho Tpke., Huntington, NY* • *631-368-8626* • **Features Include:** Fruit, Vegetables **Hours:** Sat.-Sun.: 10 a.m.-5 p.m. **Fee:** varies, Cash Only **Directions:** *Northern State Pkwy., take exit 42, take Deer Park Ave. N., turn Left on Jericho Tpke., across from Warner Rd.*

Fort Salonga Farm • *30 Meadow Glen Rd., Northport, NY* • *631-269-9666* • **Features Include:** Fruit, Vegetables, Peck Bag Holds 10 lbs. of Apples **Fee:** Adults: $10, Kids Under 12: Free, Raspberries: $4 per pint **Directions:** *I-495 Long Island Expwy., take exit 53 Sagtikos Pkwy. N./Sunken Meadow Pkwy. N., Sunken Meadow Pkwy. N., take exit SM4 W. Pulaski/E. Northport Rd., drive for .5 mi., make a Right onto Meadow Glen Rd., the farm is 1 mi. down on the Left side* *www.fortsalongafarm.com*

Fritz Lewin Farms • *1989 Sound Ave., Baiting Hollow, NY* • *631-727-3346* • **Features Include:** Pumpkins, Peas, String Beans, Peppers, Tomatoes, Cranberries, Beans, Pumpkins, Plums, Nectarines, Apples, Broad Beans, Corn (sweet), Eggplant, Summer Squash, Winter Squash, Strawberries, Tomatoes **Hours:** 8 a.m.-4 p.m., 7 days a week, June-Nov. **Fee:** Cash Only **Directions:** *I-495 Long Island Expwy., take exit 71, make Left onto Edwards Ave., drive 4 mi., make a Left onto Sound Ave., the farm is .25 mi. down on the Left side, look for a big red barn*

Lewin Farms • *812 Sound Ave., Wading River, NY* • *631-929-4327* • **Features Include:** Strawberries, Peaches, Tomatoes, Peppers, Eggplant, Apples, Pumpkins, Cut Your Own Christmas Trees **Hours:** 9 a.m.–5 p.m., closed Tues., May-Dec. **Directions:** *I-495 Long Island Expwy., exit 68N. William Floyd Pkwy. to end, turn Right onto 25A E. for 3 mi., turn Left on Sound Ave., .5 mi. on Right* *www.Lewinfarms.com*

Milk Pail Farm & Orchard • *1346 Montauk Hwy., Water Mill, NY* • *631-537-2565* • **Features Include:** Pumpkins (on Mecox Rd. East), Apple varieties include: Golden & Red Delicious, Cameo, Jonagold, Empire, Mutsu, Stayman, Idared, No Restrooms Available **Hours:** Mon.-Sat.: 9:30 a.m.-5:30 p.m., Sun.: 10 a.m.-5:30 p.m., Closed Tues., Jan.-April **Fee:** 20 lb. bag, half bushel: $26, minimum pick is a half bushel **Directions:** *I-495 Long Island Expwy., exit 68 for William Floyd Pkwy./Co. Hwy. 46 S. toward Shirley, merge onto County Rte. 46/William Floyd Pkwy., take the ramp onto Rte.27 E., turn Left onto Rte. 27, turn Right onto Mecox Rd., go 1.25 mi., make a Left at the "T" & follow the signs, make a Right onto Horsemill Ln.* *www.milk-pail.com*

FUN FAMILY

Rottkamp's Fox Hollow Farm Stand • *2287 Sound Ave., Riverhead, NY* • *631-727-1786* • **Features Include:** Vegetable, Fruit, Pumpkins **Hours:** June-Oct.: 9 a.m.-5:30 p.m., closed on Wed. **Directions:** *I-495 Long Island Expwy., exit 71N., turn Right onto Sound Ave., .5 mi. on Right*

Seven Ponds Orchard • *65 Seven Ponds Rd., Water Mill, NY* • *631-726-8015* • **Features Include:** Pumpkins, Raspberries, Apples (small trees, easy picking for children), Blackberries **Hours:** 9 a.m.-6 p.m., July-Nov. **Fee:** $4, Apples: $1.25 per lb. **Directions:** *I-495 Long Island Expwy., exit 70 toward Eastport, merge onto Captain Daniel Roe Hwy./ CR-11 S. Port Jefferson Westhampton Rd., merge onto 27 E. ramp on Left, turn Left onto David Whites Ln., stay straight to go onto Seven Ponds Rd. (becomes Upper Ponds Rd.), turn Left onto Seven Ponds Rd./Seven Ponds Town Rd., ends at Water Mill*

Wickham Fruit Farms • *28700 Main Rd., Cutchogue, NY* • *631-734-6441* • **Features Include:** Strawberries, Raspberries, Cherries, Blueberries, Apples, Peaches, Pumpkins Farm circa 1661, Peconic Bay, Live Working Beehive, Old Historic Cider Press **Hours:** Mon-Thurs.: 9 a.m.-5 p.m., Fri.-Sat.: 9 a.m.-6 p.m., Closed Sun. **Fee:** Entry Fee: $1 per person, $20 per quarter bushel **Directions:** *I-495 Long Island Expwy., take exit 73 (last exit), continue on Rte. 58 E. (which becomes Rte. 25) for 14 mi. (no turns), Wickham's Fruit Farm is on the Right-hand side after the red light in Cutchogue*

www.wickhamsfruitfarm.com

Woodside Farms • *116 Manor Ln., Jamesport, NY* • *631-369-2500* • **Hours:** July-Feb., daily, 9 a.m.-6 p.m. apple picking on weekends only **Fee:** $14 a peck **Directions:** *I-495 Long Island Expwy., take exit 73, follow Rte. 25 E. to Jamesport, 8 mi., turn Left on Manor Ln, .25 mi. on Right*

Liberty View Farm • *340 Crescent Ave., Highland NY* • *845-399-9545* • **Features Include:** 11-acre Organic Apple Orchard, U-Pick Cortland & Empire Apples, Certified Naturally Grown, Working Farm, Goats, Turkeys, Chicken Coop, Family Vegetable Gardens, Long Islander & farmer: Billiam van Roestenberg, Voted one of America's Top Ten Apple Picking Farm" by *Travel & Leisure Magazine* American Express in 2009, May Apple Blossom Festival, Drum Festival **Hours:** Wed.-Sun.: 9 a.m-5 p.m., Apple Picking: Sept.-Oct. **Fee:** Lease an apple tree: $50 for the season **Directions:** *I-495 Long Island Expwy., Cross Isl. Pkwy. N., to the Throgs Neck Bridge, to the Cross Bronx Expwy., to the George Washington Bridge upper level to Palisades Pkwy. N. off the bridge, to I-87 NYS Thruway, take exit 18 New Paultz, turn Right at end of ramp onto NY-299 E./Main, drive 1.2 mi., turn Right onto County Rd. 22, drive 2.7 mi., turn Left onto Maple Ave., drive .1 mi., take the first Left onto Crescent Ave., the Tree farm will be on the left*

www.libertyviewfarm.biz

BOATING

SUN SWEPT FACES, GENTLE BREEZES

PADDLE & ROW BOATS SUFFOLK COUNTY

Belmont Lake • NYS • *625 Belmont Ave., West Babylon, NY • 631-667-5055* • This full service park is the headquarters of the Long Island State Park Region. **Features Include:** Row & Paddle Boat Rentals, Fishing, Handicap Accessible **Hours:** Boats available: May-Sept., Dawn-Dusk, Year-Round **Fee:** Boat Rental: $10 per hr., $10 deposit, Empire Pass Accepted **Directions:** *Southern State Pkwy., exit 37 N., merge onto Belmont Ave.*

http://nysparks.state.ny.us/parks

Blydenburgh County Park • SC • *Smithtown, Veteran's Memorial Hwy., Smithtown, NY • 631-854-3713* • There are forested hills & valleys at the headwaters of the Nissequogue River, rowing & fishing on Stump Pond, casual walks through the Blydenburgh Farm & New Mill Historic District which features a grist mill. **Features Include:** 627-acre Park, Freshwater Fishing, Rowboat Rentals, New York State Freshwater Fishing Laws Apply **Hours:** Dawn-Dusk, Year-Round, Rowboat Rentals: 7 a.m.-3 p.m., mid-May-Labor Day **Fee:** Boat Rental: 1st hr.: $6, 2nd hr.: $4, Deposit: $10, Park Entry: Free **Directions:** *Northern State Pkwy., to end, stay straight for 454/ Veterans Memorial Hwy. the main southern entrance to the park will be on the Left, opposite the H. Lee Dennison County Center in Smithtown* *www.co.suffolk.ny.us/departments/parks*

Cedar Point County Park • SC • *5 Cedar Point Rd., East Hampton, NY • 631-852-7620 • Camping Reservations: 631-244-7275* • Cedar Point was settled in 1651 & became a busy shipping port for farm goods, fish & timber from Sag Harbor. **Features Include:** 607-acre Park, Rowboat Rentals, Saltwater Fishing, Scuba Diving,

FUN FAMILY

Views of Gardiner's Bay, Lighthouse, Vehicle Access to the Outer Beach (with permit only), General Store & Snack Bar: 631-324-7147 **Directions:** *I-495 Long Island Expwy., take exit 68 William Floyd Pkwy. S. toward Shirley, turn Right onto NY-27 E. toward Montauk, turn Left onto County Rd. 113/Stephen Hands Path, follow County Rd. 113, continue onto Old Northwest Rd., turn Right onto NW Rd., turn Left onto Alewife Brook Rd., take the 1ˢᵗ Right onto Cedar Point Rd.*   *www.co.suffolk.ny.us/Home/departments/parks/Parks.aspx*

Puff'n Putt Family Fun Center • 659 Montauk Hwy., Montauk, NY • 631-668-4473
• 631-271-6549 • Puff'n Putt is located on the shore of Fort Pond, an enclosed 1.5 mi. long freshwater lake. **Features Include:** Sailboat, Pedal Boat, Kayak, Canoe, & Row Boat Rentals, Paddle in Fort Pond, Video Arcade, 18-hole Mini Golf Course, Family Fun Center, Pizza Village **Hours:** Mon.-Sat.: 9 a.m.-11 p.m., Sun.: 10 a.m.-11 p.m., Memorial Day-mid-Sept., weekends only from mid-Sept.-Columbus Day, closed Columbus Day-Memorial Day, Last Boat Rental: 6 p.m., Last Golf Game: 10 p.m. **Fees:** starting at $18 per hr. **Directions:** *I-495 Long Island Expwy., take exit 68 for William Floyd Pkwy. S., slight Right to merge onto NY-27 E. toward Montauk, turn Left to stay on NY-27 E., turn Left onto Main St., continue onto NY-27 E./Pantigo Rd., continue to follow NY-27 E., Puff'n Putt will be on the Left*   *www.puffnputt.com*

Sears Bellows • SC• Sears Bellows Pond Rd., Hampton Bays, NY • Park Office: 631-852-8290 • Big Duck: 631-852-8292 • Camping Reservations: 631-244-7275 •
Features Include: Rowboat Rentals, Freshwater Fishing, New York State regulations apply to all sporting activities. This is the home of the Big Duck. **Hours:** Dawn-Dusk **Directions:** *Northern State Pkwy., exit onto Wantagh State Pkwy. S., exit onto Sunrise Hwy., take exit 65 N., follow Rte. 24, turn Left onto Bellows Pond Rd., the park entrance is on the Right*   *http://www.co.suffolk.ny.us/Home/departments/parks*

Southaven County Park • SC • Victory Ave., Brookhaven, NY • 631-854-1414 • 631-924-4490 • 631-345-2449 •
The Carman's River flows through this park. **Features Includes:** 1,356-acre Park, Rowboat Rentals, Canoe Launch Site, Boating, Canoeing, Hiking, Camping (tents & trailers), Picnicking, Freshwater Fishing, Bicycle Hostel, & the LI Steamer Trains (see museums) **Hours:** Mon.-Fri.: 8 a.m.-2:30 p.m., Sat.-Sun.: 8 a.m.-4:30 p.m.,Dawn-Dusk, Spring Boat Rentals: Weekends Only **Fee: Free** entry, Row Boat Rental: *1ˢᵗ* hr.: $6., Additional hrs.: $4 **Directions:** *Southern State Pkwy., exit at Sunrise Hwy., take exit 58 N., as you enter William Floyd Pkwy., turn West onto Victory Ave., follow signs to the main entrance of the park.*
www.co.suffolk.ny.us/Home/departments/parks/Parks.aspx

BROOKLYN
Prospect Park Alliance • 95 Prospect Park West, Brooklyn, NY • 718-965-8951 •
718-965-8999 • Features Include: Peddle Boats on the Lake, Children's Carousel,

Lefferts Historical House, Prospect Park Zoo, Nature Trails, Audubon Center Café, Electric Boat Tours, Wollman Ice Skating Rink, Grand Army Plaza, Brooklyn Museum, Vanderbuilt Playground **Hours & Fee:** vary by event **Free** parking Year-Round for park visitors **Directions:** *I-495 Long Island Expwy., take the Brooklyn-Queens Expwy., exit at Tillary St., turn onto Flatbush Ave., (the Brooklyn Public Library will be on your Left & the park on your Right), pass the Zoo & Lefferts Historic House on the Right, make a Right at the traffic light onto Ocean Ave., at the next major intersection (Ocean & Parkside Ave.), turn Right into the park. take Park Dr. to the flashing light, make a Left into the Wollman Rink parking lot, follow signs to the Audubon Center, a 5 min. walk from the parking lot* www.prospectpark.org

CANOES & KAYAKS See Fall Section

CRUISES & TOURS NASSAU COUNTY

Captain Lou Fleet • *28A Woodcleft Ave., Freeport, NY* • *631-369-9840* • Features Include: 2 Large Motor Yachts, Fishing Events, Party Cruises **Hours & Fees:** vary **Directions:** *Northern State Pkwy., take Meadowbrook Pkwy. S. exit 27W., or 135 Seaford-Oyster Bay Expwy. S., exit onto Sunrise Hwy. W., drive through Bellmore, Merrick & pass the Meadowbrook Pkwy., turn Left onto Henry St. the Freeport RR station will be on the Right (becomes S. Main St.), turn Right onto Atlantic Ave., turn Left onto Guy Lombardo Ave., turn Right onto Front St., turn Left onto Woodcleft Ave., Captain Lou Fleet (28A Woodclift Ave.) will be on the Left* www.captloufleet.com

RV Garloo • *Research Vessel* • *Captain Hank Garvin* • *93 North Middletown Rd., Pearl River, Captree, NY* • *845-735-5550* • Features Include: Daily Local Trips, "Mini Cruise Ship" Sightseeing Tours, Vineyard & Nantucket Tour, Bi-Island Tour, Fall Foliage Tours, 5 Double Occupancy Cabins, Family-Style Meals prepared by a chef, Dining Room Table, Entertainment Center, 32-in. Flat Screen TV **Hours & Fees:** vary per event **Directions:** *I-495 Long Island Expwy., take exit 38S. onto the Meadowbrook Pkwy. S., cross over the Meadowbrook Bridge, it becomes Ocean Hwy., this is Jones Beach, follow the road East around the water needle to the road's end, approx. 10 mi., enter the Captree Boat Basin parking lot, go to the Right side of the parking lot to berth #5* www.garlooent.com

The Waterfront Center • *1 West End Ave., Oyster Bay, NY* • *516-922-7245* • The Waterfront Center is a not-for-profit organization focused on educating children & adults about the marine environment. **Features Include:** Sunset Sails, Private Charters, Harbor Tours, Sailing Vacations to the British Virgin Islands, the Oyster Bay Sailing School, the Oyster Sloop "Christeen," (historic landmark), Sailboat & Kayak Rentals, Sailing Lessons, Sailboat Racing, Certification Classes **Hours:** vary **Fees:** 30-ft. Islander/6 passenger: $250 for 2 hr., $400 for 4 hrs., $650 for 8 hrs, 31 ft. Tahiti ketch./6 passenger: $250 for 2 hrs., $325 for 3 hrs., $400 8 hrs., $650 for 8 hrs. **Directions:** *Northern State Pkwy., take exit 35 N., 106/7*

N., veer onto Rte. 106 N. at the Milleridge Inn, drive approx. 6.5 mi., cross over Rte. 25A, make a Left onto Audrey Ave. (see the Coin Gallery on the corner) go 1 light & go to the 2ⁿᵈ stop sign, Right at the railroad tracks onto Theodore Roosevelt Park, make an immediate Left onto West End Ave. (before entrance booth) red brick bldg. on the Left   www.thewaterfrontcenter.org

CRUISES & TOURS SUFFOLK COUNTY

Captree State Park • **1 Rescue Rd., Babylon, NY** • **631-669-0449** • Captree State Park lies at the eastern tip of Jones Beach Island in the heart of the fishing grounds. Captree is noted for fishing & picnicking. **Features Include:** Charter Boats Available for Fishing, Scuba Diving, Sightseeing, Excursion, Boat Basin, Boat Launch, Fishing, Marina, Family Events have included: Aug.: Snapper Derby, Sept.: Fall Harvest & Seafood Festival, Oct.: I Fish New York Salt Water Clinic & South Shore Fishing Classic **Hours:** Year-Round **Fee:** Empire Pass Accepted **Directions:** *Southern State Pkwy., exit 40 Robert Moses Cswy. S. to park*   *www.nysparks.com/parks*

Eagle's Neck Paddling Company • **49295 Rte. 26, Southold, NY** • **631-765-3502** • **631) 765-3502** • **Features Include:** Tours, Full Moon Tours, Endurance Paddle, Treasure Tours, Rentals, Recreational Boats, Angler Boats, Paddling School **Hours:** Kayak-4-Kids Tours, Gooseneck Creek: Sat.-Sun. from 8-11 a.m., Nightly Sunset Tours: 5-8 p.m., Hike & Paddle Tours, Arshamomaque Pond: Sat.-Sun. 8 a.m.-12:30 p.m. **Directions:** *I-495 Long Island Expwy., exit onto W. Main St./Middle Country Rd./NY-25 E. toward Riverhead, follow W. Main St./NY-25 E., turn Right at Main Rd./NY-25 E., the paddling company will be on the Left*   *www.eaglesneck.com*

East End Seaport Museum & Marine Foundation • **Third St.** • **P.O. Box 624** • **Greenport, NY** • **631-477-2100** • Greenport is a Deep Water Port. **Features Include:** Sail the "Mary E.," 75-ft. Sailing Schooner from 1906, Sail Around Greenport Harbor, Springtime Cruise of Lighthouses **Directions:** *I-495 Long Island Expwy., take exit 73 County Rd. 58/Orient E. on Rte. 58 which becomes Rte. 25, continue East on Rte. 25 approx. 25 mi. to Greenport, 8 mi. West of Orient Point*   *www.eastendseaport.org*

Main Beach Surf & Sport • Georgica Pond • **352 Montauk Hwy., Wainscott, NY** • **631-537-2716** • **Features Include:** Tours, Mini Lessons, Full Moon Paddling Tours, Camp for Kids ages 8-15, Kayak Fishing Trips & Instruction, Main Beach Tours, Adventures & Expeditions, Main Beach Paddling Club **Fee: Shop Rentals Full Day:** Softops: $40, Epoxy Surfboards: $50, Bodyboards: $25, Wetsuits: $30, Standup Paddleboards: $100, Kayak: $85, Double Kayak; $90 **Georgica Pond Rentals** Half Day Rentals: Canoe: $70, Kayak: $55, Double Kayak: $70, Full Day Rentals: Canoe: $90, Kayak: $85, Double Kayak: $90, Stand-Up Paddleboards: $100 **Directions:** *I-495 Long Island Expwy., take exit 68 William Floyd Pkwy. toward Shirley, turn Right onto NY-27 E. toward Montauk, turn Left onto Montauk Hwy/NY-27 E., Main Beach Surf & Sport will be on the Left*   *www.mainbeach.com*

Sag Harbor Sailing School • *51 Pine Neck Ave., Sag Harbor, NY* • *631-725-5100* • **Features Include:** Sunset Cruises, Day Sailing, Overnight Charters, Reservations Recommended for boat rentals & charters **Hours & Fees:** Sunset Cruise: $2, 5-7:30 p.m. **Directions:** *See Sag Harbor Sailing School in the Lessons section for information & driving directions*   *www.sailsagharbor.com*

Wetlands Discovery Cruises • *Ward Melville Herritage Organization* • *Shore Rd. off Main St., Stony Brook, NY* • *Reservations Recommended: 631-751-2244* • Features Include: 90-min. cruises from Stony Brook Harbor into the surrounding Wetlands aboard the 35-Passenger Pontoon Boat, Guides are Naturalists from the SUNY Stony Brook's Marine Sciences Research Center, Educational Group Cruises available **Hours:** May-Oct. 31: 90-min. cruises **Fee:** Adults: $25, Kids Under 6: $15, Seniors: $22 **Directions:** *I-495 Long Island Expwy., take exit 42 Northern Pkwy. E. toward Hauppauge, take exit 45 Sunken Meadow Pkwy./Sagtikos Pkwy. N., continue onto Sunken Meadow Pkwy., take exit SM3E. onto NY-25 E./Jericho Tpke. toward Smithtown, turn Right onto Jericho Tpke./NY-25 E., follow NY-25 E., turn Left onto New York 25A E./Nissequogue River Rd., follow New York 25A E., continue onto N. Country Rd./Main St., follow Main St., at the traffic circle, take the 2nd exit onto Shore Rd., look for Wetland Discovery Cruise signs across from the Three Village Inn Restaurant on Stony Brook Harbor*   *www.wmho.org*

Whale & Sea Bird Cruises • *Coastal Research & Education Society of Long Island (CRESLI)* • *150 Idle Hour Blvd., Oakdale NY* • *631-244-3352* • Features Include: Offshore Cruises, Bald Eagle Cruises, Whale Watch Cruises, Pelagic Bird Cruises, Great South Channel & other Offshore Bird & Whale Cruises, Day Cruises, Overnight Cruises, Whales, Sea Turtles, Pelagic Birds **Hours & Fees:** vary per event, reservations must be made online **Directions:** *Locations vary per trip, check the web site for specifics*   *www.cresli.org*

NEW YORK CITY

New York Water Taxi • *South St. Seaport, Battery Park, NY* • *212-742-1969* • **Features Include:** Cruises & Tours, Charter Boats **Hours:** vary per event **Fee:** Adults: $25, Kids: $15 **Directions:** *LIRR to Penn Station, take the 2,3,4,5,A or C train to Fulton St. Station, walk 6 blocks East on Fulton St. to South St.*   *www.nywatertaxi.com*

LESSONS NASSAU COUNTY

Oyster Bay Sailing School • *1 West End Ave., Oyster Bay, NY* • *516-624-7900* • Boat Rentals Include: Beginners & Advanced Lessons, Junior Sailing Program, Adult Sailing & Certificate Programs, Handicap Accessible **Fees:** Juniors: start at $300, 2-hr. Sailing Lesson, 1 Adult & 1 Kid: $60 per person **Directions:** *I-495 Long Island Expwy., take the exit toward 106/107 N., bear Right onto 106 N., turn Left onto W. Main St., turn Right onto Bayside Ave., take the 3rd Left onto Westend Ave., the school will be on the Left*   *www.oysterbaysailing.com*

Port Sailing School • *86 Orchard Beach Blvd., Port Washington, NY • 516-767-SAIL*

• **Features Include:** Fleet of 9 Sailboats, Launch & Chaseboat, Sailing Lessons, Teens & Tweens Sailing Program, Charter Vacation, Take a Course With Your Kids, Charters, Safe Boating Course, Sail a 23-ft. Sailboat-3-Day Course, Sailboat Racing Clinic **Fee:** Sail Boat Clinic: $40 per session, 3-day Course: $600, get 1 free when you get 4 people to enroll **Directions:** *I-495 Long Island Expwy., take exit 36 toward Searingtown Rd./ Shelter Rock Rd., turn Right onto Searingtown Rd., becomes Port Washington Blvd., turn Left onto Main St., take the 2nd Right onto Shore Rd., take the 2nd Left onto Manorhaven Blvd., turn Left onto Linwood Rd. S., turn Right onto Orchard Beach Blvd., the school will be on the Left* www.portsailing.com

LESSONS SUFFOLK COUNTY

Eagle's Neck Paddling Company • *49295 Rte. 26, Southold, NY • 631-765-3502 • 631-765-3502* • **Features Include:** Lessons, *See Cruises & Tours for more information & driving directions* www.eaglesneck.com

Glacier Bay Sports • *81-C Fort Salonga Rd., Northport, NY • 631-262-9116* • Features

Include: Lessons, Tours, Rentals, Northport Harbor Paddling **Fees:** vary **Directions:** *I-495 Long Island Expwy., take exit 53N. Sunken Meadow Pkwy. to the last exit, Rte. 25A W. toward Huntington, travel 5.5 mi. Glacier Bay Sports is on the Right in front of Brittania Yacht Club* www.glacierbaysports.com

Long Island Yacht Sales • *41 Degnon Blvd., Bay Shore, NY • 631-665-5144* • Features

Include: 19 45-ft. Sailboats, Sailing lessons through Atlantic Sailing School **Fees:** Boat Rental: $125 per day for boats up to 25 ft., $175-$1,900 per weekend, $375-$4,400 per week, captains extra **Directions**: *Southern State Pkwy., take the exit toward Spur Dr. S., turn Left at Spur Dr. S., turn Right at Brentwood Rd., turn Left at E. Main St./New York 27A E., turn Right at Degnon Blvd., boat rentals will be on the Left* www.longislandyachtsales.com

Main Beach Surf & Sport • Georgica Pond • *352 Montauk Hwy., Wainscott, NY • 631-*

537-2716 • **Features Include:** Mini Lessons, Full Moon Paddling Tours, Camp for Kids 8-15, Main Beach Paddling Club, *see Main Beach Surf & Sport in the Cruises & Tours section for complete information* www.mainbeach.com

Sag Harbor Sailing School • *51 Pine Neck Ave., Sag Harbor, NY • 631-725-5100*

• **Features Include:** Beginner & Advanced Lessons, Certification Classes, Rentals, Charters, Fly Fishing on Noyack Bay, Day Sailing, Overnight Charters, Reservations Recommended for boat rentals & charters **Hours & Fees:** 9 a.m-11 a.m.: Private instruction on 23-ft. keelboats: $75 per hr. or $100 per hr. for 2 students, 9:30 a.m.-4:40 p.m.: Adult/beginner lessons: $450, mid-June-Aug. **Directions:** *I-495 Long Island Expwy.,* *take exit 70, turn Right at Mobil station, follow County Rd.(CR) 111 to end, follow Rt 27E. toward the town of Southampton, turn Left onto CR38, merge with Noyac Rd. & follow it until you pass Mill Creek Marina on Left (approx. 12 min.), turn Left on Pineneck Ave. (.25 mi. past Mill Creek Marina), Sag Harbor Sailing will be .25 mi. on Left*   *www.sailsagharbor.com*

Silly Lily Fishing Station • *99 Adelaide Ave., East Moriches, NY* • *631-878-0247* •
Features Include: Sailing Lessons, Boat Rentals, Sailboat Rentals, Kayak Rentals, Full Service Marina, Launch Ramp, Dockspace, Boat Repairs, Supplies, Storage **Boat Rentals Include**: 24 Fiberglass 16-ft. Skiffs; six 14- 20-ft. Sailboats (lessons & kayaks also available)
Directions: *I-495 Long Island Expwy., take exit 69 Wading River Rd. toward Wading River/ Center Moriches, turn Right at Wading River Rd., turn Right onto Church Rd./Railroad Ave., take the 3rd Left onto County Rd. 80 E./Main St., continue to follow County Rd. 80 E., turn Right onto Adelaide Ave., the fishing station will be on the Right*   *www.sillylily.com*

Uihlein's Marina & Boat Rental • *444 West Lake Dr., Montauk, NY* • *631-668-3799*
• **Features Include:** Beginners & Advanced Water Skiing Lessons, Kayaking Lessons, Parasailing Instruction, Instruction & PADI Certification Courses (Professional Association of Diving Instructors) **Hours:** 7 days a week **Fee: Free** water ski lessons with boat rentals
Directions: *I-495 Long Island Expwy., take exit 68 William Floyd Pkwy. S. toward Shirley, turn Right onto NY-27 E. toward Montauk, turn Left to stay on NY-27 E., turn Left onto Main St., continue onto NY-27 E./Pantigo Rd., continue to follow NY-27 E., turn Left onto W. Lake Dr., the marina will be on the Right*   *www.hamptonsweb.com/uihleins/index2.htm*

RENTALS NASSAU COUNTY

Haven Marina • *12-20 Matinecock Ave., Port Washington, NY* • *516-883-0937*
• **Boat Rentals Include:** Four 19-ft. Rhodes Sailboats, 6 Canoes **Fee:** Sailboats: $100 per day, Deposit: $100, Canoes: $10 per hr., 2 People: $15, 3 People: $20 **Directions:** *I-495 Long Island Expwy., take exit 36 toward Searingtown Rd./Shelter Rock Rd., turn Right onto Searingtown Rd., becomes Port Washington Blvd., turn Left onto Main St., turn Right to stay on Main St., take the 2nd Right onto Shore Rd., take the 1st Left onto Manhasset Ave., slight Left onto Sintsink Dr.*

Old Harbour Marina • *2479 Adler Ct., Seaford, NY* • *516-785-0358* • Features
Include: 5 Fiberglass 16-ft. Skiffs, Handicap Accessible **Fees:** $60 per day, $35 without motor, Weekday Discounts: for those over 64 **Directions:** *Southern State Pkwy., take exit 28A S. for 135 S./Seaford, take exit onto E. Merrick Rd., turn Right onto S. Seamans Neck Rd., take the 3rd Left onto Atlantic View Ave., take the 1st Right onto Archer St., Archer St. turns Left & becomes Adler Pl., the marina will be on the Left*

Strong's Marine • *Orchard Beach Blvd., Port Washington, NY* • *516-304-5376* •
Features Include: 17-21-ft. Boats, Boat Club, Seasonal Rentals, Dual Consoles, Center Consoles,

Walkarounds **Fees:** $275-$395 per day **Directions:** *I-495 Long Island Expwy., take exit 36 N. Searingtown Rd., crossing over Northern Blvd./25A, becomes Port Washington Blvd., turn Left onto Main St., go 7 lights, turn Right onto Shore Rd., turn Left onto Manorhaven Blvd., turn Left onto Orchard Beach Rd., turn Right onto Orchard Beach Blvd.*

www.strongsmarine.com

Port Sailing School • *86 Orchard Beach Blvd., Port Washington, NY* • *516-767-SAIL* • **Features Include:** Fleet of 9 Sailboats, Launch & Chaseboat, Charter Vacation **Fee:** Sonar 23: $150, Members: $120 for 4 hrs., J 24: $275, Members: $250 for Full Day Rental, *see Port Sailing School in the Lessons section for information & driving directions* *www.portsailing.com*

The Waterfront Center • *1 W. End Ave., Oyster Bay, NY* • *516-922-7245* • **Features Include:** Sailboat & Sea Kayak Rental **Hours & Fees:** 23-ft. Sonar: $35 per hr., Rhodes 19 or Pixel: $25 per hr., Sunfish: $20 per hr., Kayak: $20 per hr., *See the Waterfront Center in the Cruises & Tours section for information & driving directions* *www.thewaterfrontcenter.org*

RENTALS SUFFOLK COUNTY

Colonial Shores • *83 W. Tiana Rd., Hampton Bays, NY* • *631-728-0011* • **Features Include:** Bait, Tackle, Boat Rental Includes: 4 Wood 14-ft., 16-ft. Skiffs, Paddleboats, 2 Aqua Cycles **Fees:** $75 per day, $40 per half day, $25 without motor **Directions:** *I-495 Long Island Expwy., take exit 68 William Floyd Pkwy. S. toward Shirley, turn Right onto NY-27 E. toward Montauk, exit onto Riverhead-Hampton Bays Rd., turn Right at County Rd. 80 W., turn Left at W. Tiana Rd.* *www.webscope.com/hotels/colonial*

Dinghy Shop at South Bay Sailing Center • *334 S. Bayview Ave., Amityville NY* • *631-264-0005* • **Boat Rentals Include:** Kayaks, Sunfish, Fun Sailing Boats **Fees:** Full day, half day, groups, deposit & charge card required **Hours:** Wed. evening Kayak Tours: 6 a.m.-Dusk, June 27-Aug. 29, Full Moon Kayak Tours: Reservations Required, hrs. vary **Directions:** *Southern State Pkwy., take exit 32 S. for Rte.110 S. toward Amityville, turn Right onto County Line Rd., turn Right onto Broadway/NY 110 S., turn Left onto E. Merrick Rd./ NY-27A E., turn Right onto S. Bayview Ave., turn Left onto Ave. S./Bayview Ave S., the center will be on the Left* *www.dinghyshop.com*

Eagle's Neck Paddling Company • *49295 Rte. 26, Southold, NY* • *631-765-3502* • *631-765-3502* • **Features Include:** Recreational Boats, Angler Boats, Tours, Rentals **Fee:** Double Keowee or Fiberglass Individual Cockpit Doubles: $40 for 2 hrs., $5 for half day, $60 for full day, $100 for 2 day, Singles: $30 for 2 hrs., $45 for half-day, $50 for full day, $75 for 2-days, *See Eagle's Neck Paddling Company in the Cruises & Tours section for complete information. www.eaglesneck.com*

Main Beach Surf & Sport • Georgica Pond • *352 Montauk Hwy., Wainscott, NY •* *631-537-2716* • **Features Include:** Rentals, Main Beach Paddling Club **Full Day Shop Rentals:** Softops: $40, Epoxy Surfboards: $50, Bodyboards: $25, Wetsuits: $30, Stand-Up Paddleboards: $100, Kayak: $55, Double Kayaks: $70 **Georgica Pond Rentals** Half Day Rentals: Canoe: $70, Kayak: $55, Double Kayak: $70, Full Day Rentals: Canoe: $90, Kayak: $85, Double Kayak: $90, Stand-Up Paddleboards: $100, *See Main Beach Surf & Sport in the Cruises & Tours section for complete information*   *www.mainbeach.com*

Nissequogue River • NYS • *799 St. Johnland Rd., Kings Park, NY • 631-269-4927* • This North Shore park has a State Bird Conservation Area. The Greenbelt Trail parallels the Nissequogue River & provides scenic views. **Features Include:** Canoe & Kayak Launch, Marina, Boat Launch Sites, Boat Rentals, Fishing, Museum/Visitor Center, Family Events may include: Long Island Sound Saunter, Nature Hide-n-Seek, Salt Marsh Exploration, Family Evening Walks, & Family Nature Walks, Habitats Include: Tidal & Fresh Water Wetlands, Hardwood Forests, Shore Birds, Reptiles & Amphibians **Hours:** Year-Round, Dawn-Dusk **Directions:** *Sunken Meadow Pkwy., take exit SM 4, drive East on Pulaski Rd. which changes into Old Dock Rd. at the 5th traffic light, turn Right onto St. Johnland Rd., park entrance is about .5 mi. on the Left*
                   http://nysparks.state.ny.us/parks

Puff'n Putt Family Fun Center • *659 Montauk Hwy., Montauk, NY •* *631-668-4473 • 631-271-6549* • **Features Include:** Family Fun Center Sailboat/Pedal Boat/ Kayak/Canoe & Row Boat Rentals, Paddle in Fort Pond **Fees:** start at $18 per hr., *see Puff in Putt Family Fun Center in the Paddle & Row Boats section for information driving directions*   *www.puffnputt.com*

Sag Harbor Sailing School • *Sag Harbor Yacht Yard, Sag Harbor, NY • 631-725-5100 or toll free 877-725-5200* • **Features Include:** Full & Half Day Rentals, Sailing Lessons **Boat Rentals Include:** 21 & 23-ft. Sloops Day Sailers, 28-ft. Islander, 34-ft. Catalina Bareboat Charters **Hours:** Half Day Rentals: 9 a.m.-12:30 p.m. or 2-5:30 p.m., Full Day Rentals: 9 a.m.-5 p.m. **Fees:** 21-ft. Sloop: Full Day: $175, Half Day: $140 on Weekdays, Full Day: $225, Half Day: $175 on Weekends, 23-ft. Sloop: Full Day: $200, Half Day: $175 on Weekdays, Full Day: $240, Half Day: $200 on Weekends, $300 security for rentals, 34-ft. Sloop: Full Day: $450, Full Week: $2,800, $1,000 security deposit, *see Sag Harbor Sailing School in the Lessons section for information driving directions*
                   www.yachtworld.com\sailsagharbor

Scotty's Marina & Fishing Station · *72 Bayside Dr., Point Lookout, NY* ·

516-432-4665 · **Features Include:** 15-ft. Fiberglass, 16-ft. Carolina Skiffs, 6 Horsepower Motors, Marina, Gas, Diesel, Snack Shop **Fees:** Full Day: $65, Half Day: $45, $30 without motor, $25 deposit, Half-Price Wed.-Thurs. those over 61 **Directions:** *Southern State Pkwy., take exit 22S. toward Jones Beach, merge onto Meadowbrook State Pkwy. S., exit onto Loop Pkwy., turn Left onto Loop Pkwy., turn Left at Lido Blvd., turn Left onto Parkside Ave., Parkside Ave. turns Right & becomes Bayside Dr., the marina will be on the Right* www.scottysmarina.com

Shinnecock Bay Fishing Station & Marina · *22 Shinnecock Rd., Hampton Bays, NY* · *631-728-6116* · **Features Include:** 18-ft. Fiberglass 15-ft. Skiffs, Bait, Tackle, Restaurant, Bar **Fees:** Full Day: $90, Half Day: $65, $20 per Hr., $50 without motor, 10% Discount for those over 59, Handicap Accessible **Directions:** *I-495 Long Island Expwy., take exit 71 for Rte. 24 S. toward Hampton Bays/Calverton, take exit 65 S. off Sunrise Hwy. make a Left at the Hampton Bays Diner, at 2nd traffic light turn Right onto Ponquogue Ave. to end, turn Left, the fishing station will be on the Right* www.shinnecockfishingstation.com

Silly Lily Fishing Station · *99 Adelaide Ave., East Moriches, NY* · *631-878-0247*

· **Features Include:** Boats Rentals, Sailboats Rentals, Kayaks Rentals **Boat rentals Include:** 24 Fiberglass 16-ft. Skiffs, Six 14-20-ft. Sail Boats, *see Silly Lily Fishing Station in the Lessons section for complete information* www.sillylily.com

Strong's Marine · *2400 Camp Mineola Rd., Mattituck, NY* · *631-298-4770* ·

Features Include: Seasonal Rentals, 17-21-ft. Boats, Dual Consoles, Center Consoles, Walkarounds, Boat Club **Fees:** $275-$395 per day **Directions: Flanders:** *631-727-1028* · *I-495 Long Island Expwy., take exit 73, follow signs to Rte. 58 & Orient Point, drive East, make a Right onto 105 (Flower Center on Right), travel to Rte. 24 & turn Left, Strong's Marine is located on the Left, just before Peconic Health & Racquet*

Mattituck: *631-298-4770* · *I-495 Long Island Expwy., take exit 73 Rte. 58 E., take Rte. 58 for 12 mi. to Mattituck, it changes to Rte. 25 after Riverhead, look for the Hess Station on your Right, & then Handy Pantry shortly afterwards, take a Right at the corner of Handy Pantry onto New Suffolk Ave., take the 1st Right onto Ole Jule Ln., follow signs to Strong's Marine at 2400 Camp Mineola Rd.* www.strongsmarine.com

Uihlein's Marina & Boat Rental · *444 West Lake Dr., Montauk, NY* · *631-668-3799*

· **Features Include: Boat Rentals Include:** Four 16-ft. Fishing Skiffs, Two 23-31-ft. Cabin Cruisers, 21-ft. Makos, Eight 17-19-ft. Bowriders, 20-23-ft. Wellcrafts, 23-ft. Walkaround Cutty Pro Line, 19-ft. Sea Rays, One 39-ft. Sea Ray, Six 19-23-ft. Center Consoles, 4 Rhino Ryders, Kayaks, Canoes, Paddle Boats, Eight 1-3 person Jet Skis, Parasailing, Scuba Diving, Dive Trips: Wrecks & Reefs, Block Island, Rhode Island &

Montauk • Instruction & PADI Certification Courses • Equipment Rentals, Full-Service Marina, Tanks Filled & Serviced **Hours:** 7 days a week, Motel Year-Round **Fees:** 16-ft. Skiff: $150 per day, 39-ft. Sea Ray: $1,200 per day, Center Consoles & Bow Riders: $125 per hr. or $450 per day, Rhino Ryder: $65 per hr., $100 for 2 hrs., $150 for 4 hrs. Jet Ski: $70 per half hr., $120 per hr., 10% Discount for those over 65, weekly & seasonal rentals, $500-$2,000 deposit, *see Uihlein's Marina & Boat Rental in the Lessons section for driving directions*   *www.hamptonsweb.com/uihleins/index2.htm*

Windswept Marina & Restaurant • *215 Atlantic Ave., East Moriches, NY* • *631-874-1028* • *631-878-2100* • **Features Include:** Boat Rentals, Palm Beach 21-ft. (with or without T-Top) boats, 150HP Yamaha 4 Strokes, Marine Store, Launch Ramps, 120 Slips, 10 Transient Slips, Winter Storage (outdoor, wet & dry), Gas, Repairs, Showers, Ice, Restaurant, Bait & Tackle **Directions:** *I-495 Long Island Expwy., take exit 69 for Wading River Rd. toward Wading River/Center Moriches, turn Right onto Wading River Rd., turn Right onto Church Rd./Railroad Ave., take the 3rd Left onto County Rd. 80 E./ Main St., continue to follow County Rd. 80 E., turn Right onto Atlantic Ave., the marina will be on the Left*   *windsweptmarina@optonline.net*

MARINAS, SLIPS, BASINS & LAUNCH SITES
NASSAU COUNTY

Bay Park • **NC** •*First Ave., East Rockaway, NY* • *516-571-7245* • Bay Park border's the East Rockaway Channel & Hewlett Bay. **Features Include:** Sail Boat Launch, 3 Slip Boat Launch **Hours:** Parts of the park are open Year-Round **Directions:** *Southern State Pkwy. to Exit 17/Hempstead Ave. South, take Hempstead Ave. to fork (Ocean Ave.), take Left fork onto Ocean Ave. through Lynbrook & E. Rockaway to Main St., follow park signs, make a Left onto Front St., make a Right onto Althouse Ave., make a Left onto First Ave. & follow to the park*   *www.nassaucountyny.gov*

Cow Meadow Park & Preserve • NC • *South Main St., Freeport, NY* • *516-571-8685* • *Boat Slips: 516-608-0514* • The park is located on Freeport Creek. **Features Include:** 171-acre Park, Marina, 30 Boat Slips, Fishing Pier, 150 acres of Long Island's Marine Wetlands including Salt Marsh, Mud Flat & Tidal Creek Habitats **Directions:** *Southern State Pkwy., take exit 22 S. Meadowbrook Pkwy., exit at M9 W. Merrick Rd., immediate turn Left onto Mill Rd., turn Left onto South Main St., the entrance is on the Left*
www.nassaucountyny.gov/agencies/Parks

Haven Marina • *12-20 Matinecock Ave., Port Washington, NY* • *516-883-0937* • **Features Include:** Marina, *see Haven Marina in the Rentals section for information & driving directions*   *www.havenharbour.com*

Hempstead Lake State Park • **NYS** • *Eagle Ave. & Lake Dr., West Hempstead, NY* • *516-766-1029* • This is the largest lake in Nassau County. • **Features Include:** Boat Launch Site for Car Top Boats, 3 Fishing Ponds **Hours:** Year-Round, Dawn-Dusk **Fee:** Empire Pass Accepted **Directions:** *Southern State Pkwy., take exit 18 Eagle Ave., keep Right at the fork, follow signs for Rockville Centre/Hempstead Lake State Park, turn Right at Eagle Ave.*   *www.stateparks.com/hempstead_lake.html*

Inwood Park • **NC** • *Bayview Ave., Inwood, NY* • **516-571-7894** • The park is surrounded by water. • **Features Include:** Launch Ramp, Saltwater Fishing & Crabbing, Water Slide, Scuba Diving Permit Required **Directions:** *Southern State Pkwy., take exit 19 S., Peninsula Blvd. S. to end, make a Left on Rockerway Tpke. (large intersection), make a Right onto Burnside Ave., curves to the Left & becomes Sheridan Blvd., take Sheridan to Bayview Ave. & turn Right, continue down Bayview into the park*

www.nycgovparks.org/parks/inwoodhillpark

Jones Beach State Park • **NYS** • *1 Ocean Pkwy., Wantagh, NY* • **516-785-1600** • **Features Include:** Boat Basin, Marina, Surf Fishing **Hours:** Year-Round **Fee:** Empire Pass Accepted **Directions:** *Northern State Pkwy., take the Meadowbrook Pkwy. S. or Wantagh Pkwy. S. to the park*   www.jonesbeach.com

Wantagh Park • **NC** • *Kings Rd. & Canal Pl., Wantagh, NY* • **516-571-7460** • **Features Include:** Marina, Launch Ramp, Boating, 111-acre Park, Flat Creek & East Bay, Fishing Pier **Directions:** *Southern State Pkwy., take exit 27 S. Wantagh Pkwy., take the exit for Sunrise Hwy. E., make a Right onto Wantagh Ave., to end, make a Right onto Merrick Rd., at 1st light make a Left into the park*   *www.nassaucountyny.gov*

MARINAS, SLIPS, BASINS & LAUNCH SITES
SUFFOLK COUNTY

Captree • **NYS** • *1 Rescue Rd., Babylon, NY* • **631-669-0449** • **Features Include:** Boat Basin, Boat Launch, Fishing, Marina **Hours:** Year-Round **Fee:** *See Captree in the Cruises & Tours section for information & driving directions*

Heckscher State Park • *Heckscher Pkwy., Field 1, East Islip, NY* • **631-581-2100** • **Reservations: 800-456-2267** • **Features Include:** Boat Launch Ramp, Great South Bay Beach, Fishing, only vehicles under 11 ft. can come into the campgrounds **Hours:** Year-Round, 7 days a week, 7 a.m.-Dusk **Fee:** Empire Pass Accepted **Directions:** *Southern State Pkwy. East, it ends in the park*

http://nysparks.state.ny.us/parks/info.asp?parkID=153

Nissequogue River State Park • *799 St. Johnland Rd., Kings Park, NY* • **631-269-4927** • **Features Include:** Canoe & Kayak Launch, Marina, Boat Launch Sites **Hours:**

Year-Round, Dawn-Dusk, *see Nissequogue River State Park in the Rentals section for information & driving directions* http://nysparks.state.ny.us/parks

Ralph's Fishing Station • *250 Harbor Beach Rd., Mt. Sinai, NY* • *631-473-6655* • **Features Include:** Mt. Sinai Harbor, Boat Launch, Mooring **Hours:** Launch operates daily from May 15th-Oct. 15th, Weekdays: 7 a.m.-9 p.m., Weekends: 6 a.m.-Midnight **Fee:** Transient Mooring: 18-29 ft:.Weekdays: $30 per day, Weekends: $40 per day, Weekly: $150 per week, 30-38 ft.: $200 per week, 38 ft. & up: $2 per ft., Launch service provided to & from mooring, May 15-Oct. 15 **Fee:** In-Season - May-Nov. 15, Daily: $2 per ft., Weekly: Electric $5 per day, per outlet **Directions:** *I-495 Long Island Expwy., take exit 63, turn Left off exit onto Rte. 83 N., N. Ocean Ave., follow Rte. 83 to its end, turn Right onto Rte. 25A E., turn Left at 1st light onto Echo Ave., turn Left at 1st light on Pipe Stave Hollow Rd., follow Pipe Stave Hollow Rd. to stop sign, go across N. Country Rd. & continue going straight, turn Left at stop sign onto Harbor Beach Rd., go through beach parking lot, the last building before the fishing pier* www.ralphsmarina.com

Robert Moses • **NYS** • *Fire Island National Seashore* • *Box 247, Babylon, NY* • *631-669-0470* • **Features Include:** Marina, Boat Basin accommodates 40 boats, 5 mi. of Ocean Beach **Hours:** Dawn-Dusk, Year-Round **Fee:** Empire Pass Accepted **Directions:** *Southern State Pkwy. to Robert Moses Cswy., take exit 40 S., the park is at the western end of Fire Island* http://nysparks.state.ny.us/parks

Scotty's Marina & Fishing Station • *72 Bayside Dr., Point Lookout, NY* • *516-432-4665* • **Features Include:** Marina, Gas, Diesel, Snack Shop **Fees:** *See Scotty's Marina in the Cruises & Tours section for information & driving directions* www.scottysmarina.com

Shinnecock Canal County Marina • **SC**• *Shinnecock Canal, Hampton Bays, NY* • *631-852-8291* • *631-854-4952* • **Features Include:** Fuel Dock, Sewage Pump Out Station, Electric & Water Hookups, Restrooms/Showers, 50 Vessels Capacity. Visiting yachts, passing through the Shinnecock Canal or cruising the Peconic Bay may berth at this marina for stays limited to 2 weeks, which includes 3 weekends. Reservations for transient: 631-852-8291 (In-Season) **Directions:** *Southern State Pkwy., exit at Sunrise Hwy. E., take exit 66 Old North Hwy., follow to the marina, on the Left side of the road* www.co.suffolk.ny.us/Home/departments/parks/Parks.aspx

Shinnecock Bay Fishing Station & Marina • *22 Shinnecock Rd., Hampton Bays, NY* • *631-728-6116* • **Features Include:** Marina, Bait, Tackle, Restaurant, Bar, Handicap Accessible, *See Shinnecock Bay Fishing Station & Marina in the Rentals section for information & driving directions* www.shinnecockfishingstation.com

FUN FAMILY

Silly Lily Fishing Station • *99 Adelaide Ave., East Moriches, NY* • *631-878-0247* •

Features Include: Full Service Marina, Launch Ramp, Dockspace, Boat Repairs, Supplies, Storage, *see Silly Lily Fishing Station in the Lessons section for information & driving directions* *www.sillylily.com*

Timber Point County Marina • SC• *River Rd. & Great River Rd., Great River, NY* •

Reservations: 631-854-0938 • 631-854-4952 • Features Include: Marina, 153 Slips & Transient Slips, Fuel Dock, Sewage Pump Out Station, Electric & Water Hookups, Restrooms, Situated on the Great South Bay **Directions:** *Southern State Pkwy., take Montauk Hwy. E., turn South at the traffic light onto Great River Rd., to end, head into the Timber Point Golf Course entrance, marina is located within the golf course complex* *www.co.suffolk.ny.us/Home/departments/parks/Parks.aspx*

Uihlein's Marina & Boat Rental • *444 West Lake Dr., Montauk, NY* • *631-668-3799* •

Features Include: Full-Service Marina, Year-Round Motel, Tanks Filled & Serviced **Hours:** 7 days a week, *See Uihlein's Marina & Boat Rental in the Rentals section for complete information* *www.hamptonsweb.com/uihleins/index2.htm*

Windswept Marina & Restaurant • *215 Atlantic Ave., East Moriches, NY* •

631-878-2100 • Features Include: 120 Slips, 10 Transient Slips, Winter Storage (outdoor, wet & dry), Gas, Repairs, Showers, Ice, Marine Store, Launch Ramps, Boat Rentals, Restaurant, Bait & Tackle, *See Windswept Marina and Restaurant in the Rentals section for complete information*

FERRIES SUFFOLK COUNTY

Shelter Island • North Ferry Company • *P.O. Box 589, Shelter Island Heights* • *Rte. 114, Shelter Island Heights, NY* • *631-749-0139* • Features Include: Departs from

Greenport, Operates 365 Days, No Reservations, Traffic is boarded on a first come first-serve-basis. The ride takes approx. 15 min. **Hours:** Summer Schedule: Mon. mornings until Labor Day: *1ˢᵗ* Departure from Shelter Island: 5:10 a.m., from Greenport: 5:25 a.m., Last boat on Fri. & Sat. nights from Shelter Island: 12:45 a.m., from Greenport: 1 a.m., through Labor Day Weekend **Fee:** Car & Driver Round Trip: $9-13, Additional Passengers: $2, Vehicles & Bicycles pay on board, cash & checks only **Directions:** *I-495 Long Island Expwy., to the last exit, exit 73, take Suffolk County Rte. 58 E., 3.5 mi., County Rd. 58 will merge into Rte. 25 E., continue on Rte. 25 E. for about 20 mi. to Greenport, watch for signs marked "To Rte. 114 South," these signs will direct you to turn Right onto 6ᵗʰ St., drive 1 block & make your next Left onto Wiggins St. ("To 114 S."), to end, turn Right & continues turning Right to enter the final staging area, the ferry line takes you away from the ferry, around a loop, & back in line facing the ferry dock & passenger terminal* *www.northferry.com*

Bridgeport • Cross South Ferry • *2 Ferry St., P.O. Box 33, New London, CT • 631-323-2525* • Port Jefferson & Bridgeport, 102 West Broadway Port Jefferson, NY, 631-473-0286, 888-443-3779, Bridgeport & Port Jefferson Steamboat Company, CT, 631-473-0286, 203-335-2040 **Features Include:** Departs from Port Jefferson, Sag Harbor & Shelter Island, Snack Bar, Cocktail Steamboat Lounge **Fee:** Car & Driver: $47, Adult Round Trip: $24, Kids Under 12: $10 Round Trip, Bicycles: $4 **Directions:** *I-495 Long Island Expwy., take exit 63 County Rd. 83 N., turn Left on Rte. 112 to Port Jefferson Village, follow signs in Port Jefferson Village to East Main St. & Ferry Dock on Port Jefferson Harbor, the Bridgeport terminal is located on Water St. Dock 1 block from the municipal bus terminal* *www.longislandferry.com • www.bpiferry.com*

Block Island • *Montauk Ferry • Viking Fleet • 462 West Lake Dr., Montauk, NY • 631-668-5700 Reservations Required* • **Features Include:** Departs from Montauk, Destinations: Mystic & New London CT, Point Judith, Providence & Newport Rhode Island, Ferry, Fishing Trip Services, Snack Bar **Hours:** Memorial Day Weekend-Columbus Day, 1-hr. ferry ride, no cars permitted **Fee:** Montauk-Block Island: Adults: $70 round trip, Kids: $40 round trip, Kids Under 5: Free, Bicycles: $10, Parking: $5 per day **Directions:** *I-495 Long Island Expwy. E., take exit 70 for Rte. 27 E. to Montauk, drive into the center of town, there is only 1 Left turn by the gazebo, turn Left & pass the Bank of New York, a tall red bldg., pass movie theatre, fire house, continue taking Edgemere Rd. into Montaulk Harbor, look for the Viking Fleet sign & flag pole, just before Gosman's Dock Restaurant on the Right* *www.blockisland.com • www.montaukferry.com*

FERRIES TO FIRE ISLAND

Davis Park • Watch Hill & Fire Island Seashore • *Davis Park Ferry Co. Inc. • 80 Brightwood St., Patchogue, NY • 631-475-1665* • **Features Include:** Departs from Patchogue, No Vehicles on board, Sunset Bay Cruise **Hours:** 20-min. ride, March- Sept., check web site for departure times **Fee:** Adults: $16 round trip, Kids: $10.50 round trip, Dogs: $5.25 round trip, special ferry fares: on Thurs. July 4th-Labor Day, Tues. is Family Day: Kids ride half price with 1 parent round trip ticket, Wed. Ladies Day: $14 round trip tickets, Thurs. Teenage Day: $14 round trip tickets **Directions:** *I-495 Long Island Expwy., take exit 63 S., drive 5 mi. to the bay, make the last Right onto Madden Ln., then a quick Right & a quick Left, turns into Brightwood St., the ferry is 2 blocks from S. Ocean Ave. www.davisparkferry.com*

Saltaire • Ocean Beach • Atlantique • Kismet • Dunewood • Fair Harbor • Seaview • Ocean Bay Park • *Fire Island Ferries • 99 Maple Ave., Bay Shore, NY • 631-665-3600 • 631-665-8885* • **Features Include:** Departs from Bay Shore, No vehicles, 30 min. each way, Private Charters **Hours:** Peak Service: May-Sept., Limited Year-Round Service **Fee:** Adult: $17 round trip, Kids: $7.50 round trip, cash only **Directions:** *I-495 Long*

Island Expwy., take exit 53 Sagtikos Pkwy. S., take the Southern State Pkwy. E., take exit 42 S. 5th Ave., turn Left at stop sign, turn Right onto 5th Ave. S., go to 1st traffic light after LIRR tracks, turn Left onto Union Blvd., turn Right at 3rd light onto 4th St., becomes Maple Ave. after 2nd set of traffic lights, 1st terminal on Left is Main Terminal/Ocean Beach, Seaview/ Ocean Bay Park Terminal is on the Right side of Maple Ave. www.fireislandferries.com

Sayville to • Fire Island Pines • Cherry Grove • Fire Island Pines • Sailor's Haven/ Sunken Forest • Water Island • *Sayville Ferry Service* • *41 River Rd., Sayville, NY* • *631-589-0810* • **Features Include:** Departs from Sayville **Sailors Haven**: Marina, Nature Walks, Education Programs, Exhibit, Lifeguards, Visitors Center, Picnic Area, Barbecues, Snack Bar, Gift Shop, Restrooms, Showers, Handicap Accessible **Sunken Forest**: Guided Tour of the Sunken Forest, Bay-to-Dune Nature Trail, Two Trails: 30 min. each way or 20 min. each way, No Vehicles **Hours:** April-Nov., check web site for departure schedule **Fee:** Cherry Grove & Fire Island Pines: $14 adult round trip, Kids Under 12: $6.50 round trip, Dogs: $4 round trip, Sunken Forest: Adults: $12 round trip, Kids Under 11: $7 round trip, Water Island: Adults: $22 round trip, Kids Under 12: $11 round trip, Dogs: $4 round trip **Directions:** *I-495 Long Island Expwy., take exit 53 toward Bay Shore/Kings Park/Sagtikos State Pkwy., merge onto Service Rd., take the ramp to Bay Shore, merge onto Sagtikos Pkwy., take the exit onto Southern State Pkwy., take the exit toward Timberpoint Rd., turn Right at Timberpoint Rd., continue onto River Rd., destination will be on the Left* www.sayvilleferry.com

FERRIES NEW YORK CITY

Governors Island Ferry • *Governors Island Preservation & Education Corp.* • *10 South St., NY, NY* • *Ferry Information: 212-440-2200* • *800-782-8369* • The island reopened to the public in June 2010. **Features Include**: 1 mi. of Car-Free Cycling, Parade Grounds, Concerts, Friday Morning Summer Programs, Meet National Park Rangers, People dressed as Union Soldiers, Confederate Prisoners, Middle Country Ladies from 1863, Fort Jay, Castle Williams, Summer Weekends-Children's Museum of the Arts Free Art Island Outpost, the ferries leave from Battery Maritime Building at the corner of South St. & Whitehall St., check web site for the current events schedule **Hours:** Fri.: 10 a.m.-5 p.m., programs run from 10:15 a.m.-1 p.m., Sat.-Sun.: 10 a.m.- 7 p.m., weekend programs run from 11 a.m.-3 p.m., Ferry Schedule: Fri.: 10-11 a.m., 12:15 p.m., 1:15 p.m., 5:15 p.m., Sat.-Sun.: on the hr., June-mid Oct. **Fee: Free** ferry ride, some events have fees **Directions**: *LIRR to Penn Station, take the 1 train to South Ferry Station, or 4, 5 to Bowling Green, or R, W to Whitehall St., parking is prohibited at the Governors Island Ferry building, there is a garage across from the Battery Maritime Building that you can park in for a fee* **By Car:** *Take the FDR Dr. to exit 1, South Ferry, exit & stay in the Left lane, turn Left around the (Left) U-turn at the end of the street in* *front of the Staten Island Ferry terminal, the Battery Maritime Building is the historic ferry terminal just to the northeast of the Staten Island Ferry Terminal, the Governors Island Ferry departs from the northernmost slip of the Battery Maritime Building*

www.govisland.com

Circle Line Downtown • *Pier 16, South St. Seaport, NY* • *866-925-4631* • Features **Include:** Shark Speedboat Thrill Ride, Hidden Harbor Tour, Statue of Liberty, Brooklyn Bridge & Park, Red Hook, Kill Van Tugboat Companies, Oil Docks, Marine Repair Facilities, Robbins Reef Lighthouse, the Busiest Maritime Port on the East Coast **Hours**: Tour runs June-Sept. **Fee:** Adults: $29, Kids Over 4: $17, fees vary per event **Directions**: *LIRR to Penn Station, take the 2,3,4,5,A,or C train to Fulton St. station, walk 6 blocks East on Fulton St. to South St.*   *www.circlelinedowntown.com*

CONNETICUIT

Cross Sound Ferry Services, Inc. • *Orient Point Ferry Dock* • *41270 Main Rd. (Rte. 25) Orient, NY* • *2 Ferry St., P.O. Box 33, New London, CT* • *631-323-2525, 860-443-5281* • Features **Include:** Transport between Orient Point Long Island & New London CT, Block Island, For People & Cars, Year-Round Sea-Jet Service **Hours**: trip takes approx.an hr. & 45 min., Reservations Recommended **Hours**: very per season **Fee:** Adults: $14, Kids: $6, Auto & Driver: $47, Bicycles: $4, rates & departure times vary per season, check web site **Directions:** *I-495 Long Island Expwy., take exit 71, turn Left at end of exit ramp onto Edwards Ave., follow 3.8 mi., turn Right onto Sound Ave., follow approx. 34 mi. (Sound Ave. becomes Rte. 48 which then becomes Rte. 25), the ferry is located at end of Rte. 25*   *www.longislandferry.com*

SUGGESTIONS • COMMENTS • ERRORS

Linda.ReidBryce
@verizon.net

Thanks

NASSAU COUNTY

Bayville Adventure Park • *8 Bayville Ave., Bayville, NY* • 516-624-7433 • **Features Include:** 5-acre Pirate-Themed Amusement Park, 19-hole Mini Golf Course, High-Wire Rope Course, Low-Speed Bumper Boats, Rock Climbing, Super Slides, Arcade **Hours:** Open Weather Permiting, Mon.-Thurs.: 11 a.m.-10 p.m., Fri.:-Sat. 10 a.m.-11 p.m., Sun.: 10 a.m.-10 p.m. **Directions:** *I-495 Long Island Expwy., take exit 41 N., State Hwy. 106/107 N., follow Rte. 106 N., turn Left onto W. Main St., becomes W. Shore Rd., go over the Bayville Bridge, & continue on Ludlam Ave., turn Left onto Bayville Ave., make a U-turn, continue to #8* *www.bayvilleadventurepark.com*

Cantiague Park ⑨ • **NC** • *1 West John St., Hicksville, NY* • *516-571-7082* • *Administration: 516-571-7058* • **Features Include:** 18-Hole Mini Golf Course, Driving Range, 9-hole Golf Course, par-30 Golf Course **Hours:** Mon.-Sun.: 8 a.m.-10 p.m., April-Nov., weather permitting **Fee:** Mini Golf: Adults: $7, Kids: $4, Driving Range: $7 for 60 ball bucket, $5 for 40 ball bucket **Directions:** *I-495 Long Island Expwy., take exit 41 S. (Broadway), take the 106/107 fork, turn Right onto W. John St., Cantiague Park entrance is on the Right* *www.longislandgolfnews.com/Course%20descriptions/cantiague.htm*

Crows Nest Mini Golf • *262 Woodcleft Ave., Freeport, NY* • 516- 223-0497 • **Features Include:** Mini Golf Course, Pips Ice Cream is next door **Hours:** Mon.-Thurs.: Noon-10 p.m., Fri.: Noon-11 p.m., Sat.: 11 a.m.-11 p.m., Sun.: 11 a.m.-10 p.m. **Fee:** Adults: $8.50, Kids: $7.50 **Directions:** *Northern State Pkwy., take Meadowbrook Pkwy. S. exit 27W., or 135 Seaford-Oyster Bay Expwy. S., exit onto Sunrise Hwy. W., drive through Bellmore, Merrick & pass the Meadowbrook Pkwy. turn Left onto Henry St. the Freeport RR station will be on the Right (becomes S. Main St.), turn Right onto Atlantic Ave., turn Left onto Guy Lombardo Ave., turn Right onto Front St., turn Left onto Woodcleft Ave.*

Eisenhower Park • NC ⊛ • *1899 Hempstead Tpke., E. Meadow, NY* • *516-572-0348,*
572-0290, 572-0327, 542-0015 • *Eisenhower Recreation Center: 303-692-5650* •
Features Include: 930-acre Park, Two 18-hole Mini Golf Courses with waterfalls, 2
Gazeboes, Picnic Tables Hours: Mon.-Thurs.: 10:30 a.m.-4 p.m. (last round), Fri.-Sat.:
11 a.m.-9 p.m., Sun.: 10:30 a.m.-6 p.m. Fees: Adults: $7, Kids & Seniors: $4 Directions:
Northern State Pkwy., Meadow Brook Pkwy. S., take exit 24 Hempstead Tpke. E., turn Left into
the main entrance at E. Meadow Ave., see sign for Mini Golf & Batting Cages, park in Field 5
www.nassaucountyny.gov/agencies/Parks/WhereToGo/active/eisenhower.html

Five Towns Mini Golf • *570 Rockaway Tpke., Lawrence, NY* • *516-239-1743* •
Features Include: 18-hole Mini Golf, Outdoor Interactive Game Area, Batting Cages
Hours: Winter Hours: Mon.-Fri.: Noon-7 p.m., Sat.-Sun.: 11 a.m-7 p.m., Spring Hours:
Mon.-Fri.: Noon-9 p.m., Sat.: 11 a.m-10 p.m., Sun.: 11 a.m-7 p.m. Fee: Adults: $7, Kids
Under 54 in.: $5, Family Flex Pack: $38 for 10 Batting Tokens & 4 Games of Mini Golf, print
out coupon on web site Directions: *Southern State Pkwy., exit onto Peninsula Blvd. S., turn*
Right onto Rockaway Tpke.   *www.5townsminigilfbatting.com*

Jones Beach State Park ⊛ • NYS • *1 Ocean Pkwy., Wantagh, NY* • *516-785-1600*
• Features Include: 18-Hole Mini Golf Corse, Par 3 Pitch & Putt Course adjacent to
the boardwalk & Atlantic Ocean Hours: April-Nov., call for hours Fee: $3, Empire
Pass Accepted Directions: *Northern State Pkwy., take the Meadowbrook Pkwy. S. or*
Wantagh Pkwy. S. to the park, park in Field 4   *www.jonesbeach.com*

Power Putter Miniature Golf • A.K.A. M&M Batter Up • *130 Hicksville Rd., Bethpage,*
NY • *516-731-2020* • Features Include: Family Oriented 18-hole Course, Batting
Cages, Hardball & Softball, Arcade Games, Snack Bar Hours: 9 a.m.-10:30 p.m. Fee:
$6 per person Directions: *I-495 Long Island Expwy., take exit 44 135 S. Seaford-Oyster Bay*
Expwy., take exit 7 W. Hempstead Tpke., pass 3 lights, turn Left onto Hicksville Rd./Rte. 107,
Power Putter Miniature Golf will be on the Left   *www.batterupli.com*

SUFFOLK COUNTY

Boomers Family Fun Park • *655 Long Island Ave., Medford, NY* • *631- 475-1771* •
Features Include: 18-hole Mini Golf Course, 7 Outdoor Batting Cages, Cartoon Themed
Park, Indoor Carousel, Kiddie Swing, Restaurant, Animated Show, Redemption & Ride
Games, Outdoor Kiddie Rides, Bumper Boats, Go-Karts, Outdoor Facilities open weather
permitting Hours: 11 a.m.-close time varies Fees: Game Token: 25¢ each, Go-Karts: $5,
Mini Golf: $4.25 per game, Batting Cages: $2, Rides: $3.25, Bumper Boats: $4.50, Pay-
One-Price: $15.95 Directions: *I-495 Long Island Expwy., exit 64, get on the S. Service Rd., .5*
mi., Boomers is on the Right side of the road   *www.boomersparks.com*

Calverton Links • *149 Edwards Ave., Calverton, NY* • *631-369-5200* • Features Include:
18-hole Mini Golf Course, Lighted & Covered Driving Range, Birthday Parties **Hours:** 6 a.m.-6 p.m. **Fee:** Adult: $8, Kids: $6, Driving Range: 50 Balls: $5, 100 Balls: $9, 150 Balls: $12 **Directions:** *I-495 Long Island Expwy., take exit 71 toward Calverton, turn Left on Edwards Ave. Rte. 24W., Calverton Links will be on the Left* www.calvertonlinks.com

Cedar Beach Pitch & Putt • *Ocean Pkwy. between Cedar Beach & Overlook Beach, Babylon, NY* • *631-321-4562 or 631-893-2100* • Features Include: 18-Hole Course,
Par 3 Course, Concession Stand **Hours:** 7 a.m.-6 p.m., April-Nov. **Fee:** Town Residents: $5, Seniors: $3 (weekdays) **Directions:** *Northern State Pkwy., take exit 31 A Meadowbrook Pkwy., at the traffic circle take the 1st exit for Ocean Pkwy., continue straight onto Ocean Pkwy.*

The County Fair Entertainment Park ⌘ • *3351 Rte. 112, Medford, NY* •
631-732-0579 • Features Include: Two 18-hole Courses, Waterfalls, Fountains, Flowers, Beautiful Views, Driving Range, Picnic Area, Batting Cages, Go-Kart Track **Hours:** 11 a.m.-6 p.m., April: 11 a.m.-9 p.m., March-Nov., weather permitting **Fee:** Mini Golf: Adults: $6.50, Kids Under 12: $5.50, Under 5 & Seniors: Free, Driving Range: 40 Balls: $5, 80 Balls: $8, 120 Balls: $10, Club Rental: $2 **Directions:** *I-495 Long Island Expwy., take exit 64, N., drive 1 mi., 3351 Rte. 112 will be on the Right, crossroads are Granny & Horseblock* www.countryfairpark.com

Drossos Tick Tock Miniature Golf • *69125 Main Rd./Rte. 25, P.O. Box 70, Greenport, NY* • *631-477-1339* • Features Include: 18-hole Course, Village Setting, Gardens,
Windmill, Waterfalls, Game Room, Snack Bar, Old-Fashioned Custard **Hours:** 10:30 a.m.-10:30 p.m., April-Oct. **Fee:** Adults: $6, Kids Under 10: $4 **Directions:** *I-495 Long Island Expwy., exit onto W. Main St./Middle Country Rd./NY-25 E. toward Riverhead, continue to follow W. Main St./NY-25 E., turn Right at Main Rd./NY-25 E., mini golf will be on the Left* www.drossosmotel.com

Golden Bear Golf Center *at Sky Drive* • *1024 Broad Hollow Rd., Farmingdale, NY* •
631-694-4666 • Features Include: 18-hole Mini Golf Course, Snack Bar **Hours:** Mon.-Sun.: 7 a.m.-11 p.m. **Fee:** Adults: $7, Kids: $6 **Direction:** *I-495 Long Island Expwy., exit onto Rte.110/Broad Hollow Rd. S.*

Heartland Golf Park • *1200 Long Island Ave., Brentwood, NY* • *631-667-7400* •
Features Include:18-holes, Mountain with Waterfalls **Hours:** 6:30 a.m.-Midnight, Year-Round **Hours:** vary **Fee:** $6 **Directions:** *I-495 Long Island Expwy., take exit 53 toward Sagtikos State Pkwy./Bay Shore, take exit S3 Pine Aire Dr. toward Brentwood, turn Left onto Pine Aire Dr., turn Right onto Grant Ave., take the 1st Right onto Long Island Ave.* www.hole-ycow.com

SUMMER FUN

Island Green Golf Center • *495 Middle Country Rd., Selden, NY* • *631-732-4442* • **Features Include:** 19-holes Mini Golf Course Featuring Local Landmarks **Hours:** 9 a.m.-9 p.m., until late March, weather permiting, open 24 hrs. in Summer **Fee:** Adults: $6, Kids Under 13: $4, Seniors: $5, Family of 4 Early-Bird Special: $18 **Hours:** Mon.-Fri.: 7 a.m.-11 p.m., Sat., Sun.: 7 a.m.-10 p.m. **Directions:** *I-495 Long Island Expwy., take exit 64 toward NY112/Port Jefferson/Patchogue, merge onto Waverly Ave., turn Left onto Medford Ave./NY112 N., continue to follow NY112 N., turn Left at Middle Country Rd., mini golf will be on the Right* www.islandgreengolf.com

Oakdale Golf Center • *4180 Sunrise Hwy., Oakdale, NY* • *631-244-8570* • Features Include: 18-hole Course, Waterfalls **Hours:** Mon.-Fri.: 9 a.m.-11 p.m., Sat.: 8 a.m.-11 p.m., Sun.: 8 a.m.-10 p.m. **Fee:** Adults: $5, Kids Under 12: $4 **Directions:** *Northern State Pkwy., take exit 33 Wantagh Pkwy. S. Southern State Pkwy. E., exit onto Sunrise Hwy. Service Rd., take the ramp onto NY-27 E., mini golf will be on the Right*

Puff'n Putt Family Fun Center • *6659 Montauk Hwy., Montauk, NY* • *631-668-4473* • *631-271-6549* • Puff'n Putt is located on the shore of Fort Pond in Montauk. **Features Include:** Mini Golf, Video Arcade, Paddleboats, Sail Boats, Kayaks, Canoes & Row Boat Rentals **Hours:** Mon.-Sat.: 9 a.m.-11 p.m., Sun.: 10 a.m.-11 p.m. **Fee:** $5 per person **Directions:** *I-495 Long Island Expwy., take exit 68 William Floyd Pkwy. S. toward Shirley, take the ramp onto Rte. 27 E., turn Left at Rte. 27, turn Left onto Main St./Rte. 27, continue to follow Rte. 27* www.puffnputt.com

Robert Moses State Park • *Fire Island National Seashore* • *Box 247, Babylon, NY* • *631-669-0470* • **Features Include:** 18-hole Pitch & Putt Golf Course, Food, Playground, Picnic Areas, Picnic Tables, Lighthouse, Recreation Programs **Hours:** April-Oct.: Hrs. vary **Fee:** $11 per person, Empire Pass Accepted **Directions:** *Southern State Pkwy. to Robert Moses Cswy., take exit 40 S., mini golf is located at Field 5* http://nysparks.state.ny.us/parks

Skydrive • *1024 Broadhollow Rd./Rte. 110, Farmingdale NY* • *631-694-4666* • **Features Include:** Mini Golf, Driving Range, Café **Hours:** Mon.-Sun.: 9:30 a.m.-11 p.m. **Fee:** Adult: $7, Kids: $6, Driving Range: 45 Balls: $6, 90 Balls: $10, 135 Balls: $13 **Directions:** *I-495 Long Island Expwy., exit onto Rte. 110 S., mini golf is across from Republic Airport* www.skydrivegolfcenter.com

Village Green Miniature Golf • *974 Portion Rd., Lake Ronkonkoma, NY* • *631-732-8681* • **Features Include:** 2 Courses, Wizard of Oz Course with Music, Route 66 Course, Water Wars, Jumpshot Basketball, Spiderzone, Space Shuttle Slide, Bounce House, Kids Town Adventure Playland, Coin Operated Rides, Gem Stone Mining, Group Packages, Parties

FUN FAMILY

Hours: Mon.-Thurs.: Noon-10 p.m., Fri.: Noon-Midnight, Sat.:10 a.m.-12 p.m., Sun. :10 a.m.-10 p.m. **Fees:** Unlimited Play-Kids Course: $6 or $8, $7.50 or Unlimited Play-Adult Course: $9.50, Kiddie Rides: 50¢, Bounce House: $3, Jumpshoot Basketball: $5, Spider Zone: $3, Gem Stone Mining: $5, Inclusive Packages, Downloadable Coupons **Directions:** *I-495 Long Island Expwy., take exit 62 Nicolls Rd. Blue Point/Stony Brook Expwy. Dr. S., take ramp onto Nicholls Rd. N. towards Stony Brook, take ramp onto Portions Rd., mini golf is on the Left, located .5 mi. West of Nicolls Rd., (Rte. 97) on Portion Rd. in Lake Ronkonkoma, look for the giant hot air balloon!* www.villagegreenminigolf.com

QUEENS

Pitch & Putt/Mini Golf • *100 Flushing Meadows Park, Flushing, NY* • *718-271-8182* • **Features Include:** 18 Beautifully Landscaped Holes, Streams, Waterfalls, Lit for Night Time **Hours:** Winter Hours: 8 a.m.-3:30 p.m. May **Fee:** Mini Golf: Adults: $7.50, Kids Under 12: $6, Weekdays: Adults: $13.50, Juniors $7, Seniors: $10.50, Weekday Nights: Adults: $16, Kids Under 12: $8, Seniors: $11.50, Weekend Daytime Rate: $14.75 all golfers, Weekend Night: $17.25, Club Rental: $2, Parking: Free **Directions:** *Long Island Expwy. W. to exit 22B College Pt. Blvd. N., turn Right onto College Point Blvd., drive approx. 5 lights & make a Left onto Avery Ave., pass stop sign & Home Depot, entrance is on the corner, make a Right & proceed to stop sign, parking lot will be on the Right, walk over the bridge & the clubhouse is a 1 story white brick bldg.* www.golfnyc.com

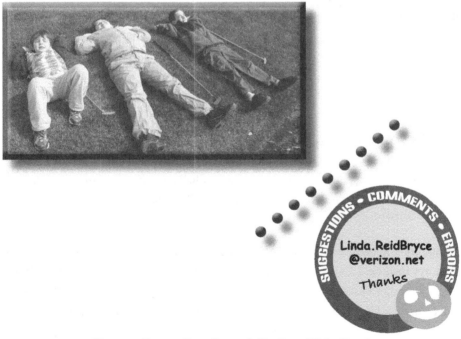

Linda.ReidBryce
@verizon.net
Thanks

SUGGESTIONS • COMMENTS • ERRORS

Napeague • NYS • *1803 Montauk Hwy., East Hampton, NY • 631-668-5000 •*
Napeague Park is located on a very narrow, low-lying strip between the Atlantic Ocean
& Gardiners Bay on the South Fork, Napeague Bay is a World-Renown Kiteboarding
destination because of its flat waters & wind. Napeague is a great spot for beginners
& advanced riders. **Features Include:** 1,364-acre Park, Surfing, Kiteboarding, Fishing
Directions: *I-495 Long Island Expwy., take exit 68 William Floyd Pkwy. S. toward
Shirley, take the ramp onto Rte. 27 E., turn Left onto Rte. 27, turn Left onto Main St./Rte.
27, continue to follow Rte. 27* *http://www.co.suffolk.ny.us/*

Robert Moses NYS • *Fire Island National Seashore •* **Box 247, Babylon, NY •** *631-
669-0470 •* **Features Include:** 5 mi. of Ocean Beach, Surfing, Swimming, Surf Fishing
(fishermen can also fish from the piers), Marina, Boat Basin (accommodates 40 boats),
Picnic Areas, Picnic Tables, 18-Hole Pitch & Putt Golf Course, Food, Playground
(Field 5), Lighthouse (Field 5), Recreation Programs **Fee: Free** off-season, Memorial
Day-Labor Day: $10, Weekends Only until Oct.: $8, Empire Pass Accepted **Directions:**
*Southern State Pkwy. to Robert Moses Cswy., take exit 40 S., the park is at the western end
of Fire Island* *http://nysparks.state.ny.us/parks*

Smith Point County Park • SC • *Fire Island, Shirley, NY • 631-852-1313 • Camping
Reservations: 631-244-7275 •* Smith Point is Suffolk County's largest ocean front
park. **Features Include:** Surfing, Swimming, Lifeguards, Scuba Diving, White Sand
Beach, Atlantic Surf, Outer Beach Access, Food Concession, Playground, Showers,
Restaurant: The Raw Bar & Grill serves breakfast, lunch & dinner. The Beach Hut:

FUN FAMILY

631-728-2988, www.thebeachhuts.com, Special Events in-season. Off-Road Vehicles, with permit only may drive on the western portion of the outer beach. There is marked protective fencing around the nest sites of endangered shorebirds inhabiting the ocean and bay beaches. **Hours:** Sat.-Wed.: 8:30 a.m.-6 p.m., Thurs. & Fri.: 8:30 a.m.-9 p.m. **Fee:** Free off-season, With Green Key: $5, Memorial Day-Sept.: $10 **Directions:** *I-495 Long Island Expwy., exit 68 S. William Floyd Pkwy. to end, terminates at Fire Island* www.co.suffolk.ny.us/Home/departments/parks/Parks.aspx

KITESURFING

Kitesurfing or kiteboarding uses wind power to pull a rider through the water on a small kiteboard which is similar to a wakeboard. There are 2 styles of kiteboarding, Free-Style + Wakestyle, each requiring a different board + performance kite. The rider uses foot-straps + the power of a large controllable kite to propel across the water.

Cosmic Kites Kiteboarding • *74 West Park Ave., Long Beach, NY* • *800-963-2142* • *516-882-5232* • *Lessons: 800-963-2142 or help@cosmickites.com* • Features Include: Year-Round Lessons, **Hours:** Mon.-Fri.: 10 a.m.-6 p.m., Sat.-Sun.: By Appointment only **Directions:** *Southern State Pkwy W., take exit 22S. Meadowbrook State Pkwy S. toward Jones Beach, exit onto Loop Pkwy., continue onto Lido Blvd., continue onto E. Park Ave., make a U-turn onto National Blvd.* www.cosmickites.com

Main Beach Surf & Sport • *411 Montauk Hwy., Wainscott, NY* • *631-537-2716* • **Features Include:** Kids as young as 7 are old enough to practice basic surf techniques (such as timing & choosing a wave), surfing etiquette, & ocean safety rules. Main Beach Surf & Sport offers 90-min. Private Lessons, Half Day Group Lessons & Full Days Lessons. **Directions:** *I-495 Long Island Expwy., take exit 68, Rte. 27 E. toward Montauk, turn Left onto Montauk Hwy./NY-27 E.*

SUGGESTIONS • COMMENTS • ERRORS

Linda.ReidBryce@verizon.net

Thanks

NASSAU COUNTY

Cantiague Park · NC · *1 West John St., Hicksville, NY* · 516-571-7061 · 516-572-0248
• **Features Include:** Outdoor Olympic-Sized Pool Complex, 2 Water Slides, Diving Pool, Kiddie Pool, Training Pool, Interactive Water-Play Area, Lockers, Showers, Refreshment Area, Shuffleboard Courts, Bocce Court, Chess & Checker Table Boards, Playground, Picnic Areas **Hours:** Mon.-Sun.: 10 a.m.-6 p.m., June-Labor Day **Fees:** Adult Residents: $7, Kid Residents 4-17: $5, Senior: $3, Disabled, Volunteer Firefighter, Ambulance Corps, Auxiliary Police, Veterans, Adult Non-Residents: $20, Kid/Guests Non-Residents: $15, Family Membership: $225, Individual & Senior Membership: $90, Leisure Pass is required for residents to receive the resident rate **Directions:** *I-495 Long Island Expwy., take exit 41 S. Broadway, turn Right onto West John St., Cantiague Park entrance is on the Right*
www.longislandgolfnews.com/Course%20descriptions/cantiague.htm

Christopher Morley Park · NC · *500 Searingtown Rd., Roslyn, NY* · 516-571-8113 ·
Golf Information: 516-571-8120 · **Features Include:** 98-acre Park, Outdoor Swimming Complex, Olympic-Sized Pool, Diving Tank with Boards, Kiddie Pool, Lockers, Showers, Playground, Horseshoes, Shuffleboard, Picnic Areas with Barbecue Equipment **Hours:** Mon.-Sun.: 10 a.m.-6 p.m., June-Labor Day **Fee:** Adult Resident: $5, Kids 4-17: $3, Senior, Disabled, Volunteer Firefighter, Ambulance Corps, Auxiliary Police, Veterans, Adult Non-Residents: $10, Kids/Guests Non-Residents: $6, Seasonal Family Membership: $225, Seasonal Individual: $90, Seasonal Senior Membership: $50, Leisure Pass required **Directions:** *I-495 Long Island Expwy., take exit 36N., Searingtown Rd., take Searingtown Rd. N. & look for the park entrance on the Right about 200 yds. from I-495*
www.nassaucountyny.gov/agencies/Parks/WheretoGo/active/morley.html

FUN FAMILY

Eisenhower Park · NC · *1899 Hempstead Tpke., East Meadow, NY · Eisenhower Recreation Center: 303-692-5650* · Features Include: Outdoor Pool, Indoor Complex, World-Class Aquatic Center, Swimming Lessons, 50-meter Pool (68 meters long, with 3 movable bulkheads), 25-meter Diving Well, Competition Diving Towers, Platforms & Springboards **Hours:** Outdoor Pool: Mon.-Sun.: Open Swim from 1 p.m.-6 p.m. **Fee:** Outdoor Pool: Adults: $3.50, Kids 2-17: **Free** for 2010 season, Leisure Pass required, **Directions:** *Northern State Pkwy., Meadow Brook Pkwy. S., exit M3 E. Stewart Ave., make a Right onto Stewart Ave., continue to the park*
www.nassaucountyny.gov/agencies/Parks/WhereToGo/active/eisenhower.html

Jones Beach State Park · *1 Ocean Pkwy., Wantagh, NY · 516-785-1600* · Jones beach is a world-class swimming destination. · **Features Include:** Outdoor Swimming Pools, 2-mi. Boardwalk, Deck Games, Mini Golf, Picnic Tables, Playground, Recreation Programs, Showers, Food, Gift Shop, Museum/Visitor Center, 6.5 mi. of Ocean Beach **Hours:** Outdoor Pool: Mon.-Fri.: 10 a.m.-7 p.m., Sat.-Sun.: 9 a.m.-8 p.m., Pool Open: late June-early Sept., Park Open Year-Round, Dawn-Dusk **Fee:** Outdoor Pool: Adults: $3, Kids: $1, Park Entry: Memorial Day-Labor Day: $10, Weekends Only until Oct.: $8, Empire Pass Accepted, Free off-season **Directions:** *Northern State Pkwy., exit onto Meadowbrook Pkwy. S. or Wantagh Pkwy. S. to the park, park in Field 3 for the West Bath House* *http://nysparks.state.ny.us/parks*

North Woodmere Parks · NC · *750 Hungry Harbor Rd., Valley Stream, NY · 516-571-7800, 7801, 7806* · Features Include: Outdoor Swimming Complex, Olympic-Sized Pool, Diving Pool with Boards, Water Slide, Wading Pool, Training Pool, Interactive Water-Play Area, Spray Pool, Swimming Lessons, Lockers, Dressing Areas, Showers, Concession Stand, Lounge & Deck Chairs, Sun Shelter, Picnic Area with Barbeques, Playground **Hours:** Mon.-Fri.: 11 a.m.-7 p.m., Sat.-Sun.: 10 a.m.-6 p.m., pool open late June-early Sept. **Fee:** Pool: Adults: $7, Kids: $5 with Leisure Pass, Adults: $20, Kids: $15 without Leisure Pass **Directions:** *Belt Pkwy. to Rockaway Blvd., take Rockaway Blvd./Tpke., turn Left onto Peninsula Blvd., turn Left onto Branch Blvd., follow it around to the Right, the park entrance is on the Left* *www.nassaucountyny.gov/agencies/Parks*

Wantagh Park · NC · *Kings Rd. & Canal Pl., Wantagh, NY · 516-571-7460* · Features Include: 111-acre Park on Flat Creek & East Bay, Swimming Complex, Olympic-Sized Pool, Diving Pool, Kiddie Pool, Training Pool, Interactive Water-Play Area, Two 30-ft.Waterslides, 1 & 2-mi. Jogging/Walking/Biking Paths **Hours:** Pool: Mon.-Fri.: 11 a.m.-6:45 p.m., Sat.-Sun.: 10 a.m.-6:45 p.m., pool open late June-early Sept., park open Dawn-Dusk **Fee:** Pool: Adults: $7, Kids: $5 with Leisure Pass, Adults: $20, Kids: $15 without Leisure Pass, Park: Free for residents, Non-Residents Memorial Day-Labor Day: $5 **Directions:** *Southern State Pkwy., take exit 27S. Wantagh Pkwy., take the exit for Sunrise*

Hwy. E., turn Right onto Wantagh Ave., to end, make a Right onto Merrick Rd., at 1ˢᵗ light turn Left into the park

    www.nassaucountyny.gov/agencies/Parks/WhereToGo/active/wantagh.html

Whitney Pond Park · NC · *Northern Blvd., & Community Dr., Manhasset, NY · 516-571-*

8110 · **Features Include:** 24-acre Park, Swimming Pools, Walking Trails **Directions:** *I-495 Long Island Expwy., take exit 33 Community Dr. N., turn onto Community Dr. N., the park is on the Right, just after the police precinct*

YMCA at Glen Cove · *125 Dosoris Ln., Glen Cove, NY* · *516-671-8270* · Features

Include: Aquatic Center, 25-meter Indoor Pool, Aquatic Programs, Swimming Lessons, Outdoor 8-Lane Heated Pool, Playground, Outdoor Kiddie Pool, Picnic Area, Pool House with lockers & shower facilities **Hours:** Building: Mon.-Thurs.: 5:30 a.m.-10 p.m., Fri.: 5:30 a.m.-9 p.m., Sat.: 7 a.m.-5 p.m., Sun.: 7 a.m.-3 p.m., Outdoor Pool: Weekends Only in June: 11 a.m.-5 p.m., Outdoor Pool Summer: Mon.-Fri.: Noon-6 p.m., Sat.-Sun. to Labor Day : 10 a.m.-6 p.m. **Fee:** Program Member: $101, Full Member monthly: $51 **Directions:** *Northern State Pkwy., take the Rte. 107 N. exit, turn Right onto N. Broadway/107 N., 107 becomes Glen Cove Rd., take Glen Cove Rd. to end, turn Right onto Brewster St., becomes Forest Ave., turn Left onto Dosoris Ln., the YMCA will be on the Left*

    http://ymcali.org/gcy/index.aspx · http://ymcali.org · http://ymcali.org

SUFFOLK COUNTY
Brookhaven-Roe YMCA · *155 Buckley Rd., Holtsville, NY · 631-289-4440* · Features

Include: 25-meter Heated Indoor Pool, Swimming Lessons, Aquatic Programs, Men's & Women's Locker Rooms, Dry Heat Sauna, Mini Golf, Preteen & Teen Centers **Hours:** Mon.-Fri.: 6 a.m.-10 p.m., Sat.: 7 a.m.-5 p.m. (Fitness Center & Pool close at 4:30), Sun.: 7 a.m.-5 p.m. (Fitness Center & Pool close at 4:30) **Fee:** Adult Full Membership: $41, Program Membership: $86, Family Membership: $65 full, $190 program membership, per month **Directions:** *I-495 Long Island Expwy., take exit 62 toward Nicolls Rd./Blue Point/Stony Brook, merge onto Expwy. Drive S., turn Right onto Waverly Ave., turn Left at Blue Point Rd., take the 1ˢᵗ Right onto Canine Rd./Dog Ln., turn Right onto Buckley Rd./Peconic Ave., continue to follow Buckley Rd., the YMCA will be on the Left*

    http://ymcali.org/brookroey/index.aspx

Commack YMCA · *74 Hauppauge Rd., Commack, NY · 631-462-9800* · Features

Include: Indoor Swimming Pool, Aquatic Programs, Swimming Lessons, Babysitting Available **Winter Hours:** Mon.-Wed.: 6:30 a.m.-9:45 p.m., Thurs.: 6:30 a.m.-10:15 p.m., Fri.-Sat.: 6:30 a.m.-5:15 p.m., Sun.: 8:30 a.m.-9:15 p.m. **Fee:** Monthly Family Membership: $90 **Directions:** *I-495 Long Island Expwy., take exit 52 N. Commack Rd. N., for 8 lights to Hauppauge Rd., turn Left at the traffic light onto Hauppauge Rd., the Y will be .25 mi. on the Right*   http://ymcali.org

FUN FAMILY

Great South Bay YMCA • *200 West Main St., Bay Shore, NY* • *631-665-4255* • **Features Include:** 75-ft.x42-ft. Heated Indoor Pool, Aquatics Programs, Instructional Swimming, Locker Rooms, Babysitting Available **Building Hours:** Late June -late Aug., Mon.-Fri.: 5:30 a.m.-10 p.m., Sat.: 7 a.m.-6 p.m., pool is closed on Sun. **Fee:** Family Full Membership: $75, Program Membership: $145 **Directions:** *Southern State Pkwy., take the exit onto Robert Moses State Pkwy., take exit RM2E. for New York 27A E. toward Bay Shore, turn Right onto New York 27A E., the YMCA will be on the Right*

http://ymcali.org/gsby/index.aspx

Heckscher • **NYS** • *Heckscher Pkwy., Field 1, East Islip, NY* • *631-581-2100* • *Reservations: 800-456-2267* • **Features Include:** Outdoor Opportunities, Pool Complex, Showers, Swimming on the Great South Bay Beach, Playgrounds, Picnic Areas & Tables **Hours:** Pool: Mon.-Sun.: 10 a.m.-5 p.m., early July-Labor Day, park open Year-Round, 7 days a week, 7 a.m.-Dusk **Fee:** Pool: Adults: $3, Kids Under 12: $1, Park Entry: $10 Memorial Day-Labor Day, Weekends Only until Oct.: $8, Empire Pass Accepted, Free off-season **Directions:** *Southern State Pkwy. E., it ends in the park*

http://nysparks.state.ny.us/parks/info.asp?parkID=153

Huntington YMCA • *60 Main St., Huntington, NY* • *631-421-4242* • **Features Include:** Indoor Pool Complex, Albicocco Pool (25 yds., 6 lanes, barrier free), Norton Pool (25 yds., 4 lanes), Lessons, Youth & Adult Locker Rooms, Men's & Women's Saunas, Babysitting Available **Hours:** Mon.-Thurs.: 5:30 a.m.-10 p.m., Fri.: 5:30.a.m.-9 p.m., Sat.: 6 a.m.-8 p.m., Sun.: 7 a.m.-5 p.m. **Summer Hours:** Late June-Labor Day, Mon. Thurs.: 5:30 a.m.-10 p.m., Fri.: 5:30 a.m.-9 p.m., Sat.: 6 a.m.-6 p.m., Sun.: 7 a.m.-1 p.m., **Babysitting** for kids 6 mos & up: Mon. & Fri.: 8:45 a.m.-2 p.m., Tues. & Thurs.: 5 p.m.-8 p.m., Sat.: 8 a.m.-11 a.m. **Fee:** Membership required **Directions:** *I-495 Long Island Expwy., take exit 42 Northern State Pkwy. toward Hauppauge, take exit 40N. for Rte.110 N. toward Huntington, cross Jericho Tpke., Rte. 110 becomes New York Ave., turn Right onto Main St./25A E. the YMCA will be on the Right, parking in back*

http://ymcali.org/hunty/index.aspx • *http://ymcali.org*

Hidden Pond Park • *660 Terry Rd., Hauppauge, NY* • *631-232-3222* • **Features Include:** Outdoor Swimming Pool **Hours:** Pool: Mon.-Sun.: 10 a.m.-7 p.m., late June-early Sept. **Fee:** Pool: Town of Islip Residents with Rec. Card: $5, Without Rec. Card: $7, Non-Residents: $10 **Directions:** *I-495 Long Island Expwy., take exit 58 N., drive 2 blocks, make a Left onto Terry Rd., turn Left into the park*   *www.therinx.com*

Montauk Downs • **NYS** • *50 South Fairview Ave., Montauk, NY* • *631-668-5000* • *668-3781* • **Features Include:** Outdoor Swimming Pool, Children's Wading Pool,

Showers, Food, Recreation Programs, Clubhouse, Grill Room serving Breakfast & Lunch **Hours:** Pool: Late June-early Sept. **Fee:** Pool: Adults: $5, Kids: $3, Empire Pass Accepted **Directions:** *I-495 Long Island Expwy. E., take exit 68 William Floyd Pkwy. S. toward Shirley, turn Right onto NY-27 E. toward Montauk, turn Left to stay on NY-27 E., turn Left onto Main St., continue onto NY-27 E./Pantigo Rd., follow NY-27 E., turn Right at The Plaza, turn Right onto Edgemere Rd., turn Right onto S. Edin St., turn Left onto Essex St., take the 1ˢᵗ Right onto S. Fairview Ave., the park will be on the Left*

http://nysparks.state.ny.us/sites/info

Patchogue Village YMCA • *Under Construction* • *255 West Main St., Patchogue, NY* • *631-289-4440* • Features **Include:** Olympic Swimming Pool, Swimming Lessons **Directions:** *I-495 Long Island Expwy., exit onto Expwy. Dr. S., turn Right onto County Rd. 83/N. Ocean Ave., turn Right at County Rd. 85/W. Main St., the YMCA will be on the Right* *http://ymcali.org/patchogue/index.html*

YMCA East Hampton RECenter • *2 Gingerbread Ln., East Hampton, NY* • *631-329-6884* • Features **Include:** Indoor Pool Complex, Instructional Swim, Aquatic Program, Canteen Lounge **Building Hours:** Fall/Winter/Spring, Mon.-Thurs.: 6 a.m.-9 p.m., Fri.: 6 a.m.-6:30 p.m., Sat.: 7 a.m.-6 p.m., Sun.: 7 a.m.-4 p.m., Middle School Madness every Fri. night: 7-9 p.m. **Fee:** Family: $55 per month **Directions:** *I-495 Long Island Expwy., take exit 68 William Floyd Pkwy. toward Shirley, merge onto NY-27 E. toward Montauk, turn Left onto Montauk Hwy./NY-27 E., turn Left onto Toilsome Ln., continue onto Gingerbread Ln., the YMCA will be on the Left* *http://ymcali.org/ehy/index.html*

SUGGESTIONS • COMMENTS • ERRORS

Linda.ReidBryce @verizon.net

Thanks

NASSAU COUNTY

Bay Park • NC • *First Ave., East Rockaway, NY • 516-571-7245* • Bay Park borders the East Rockaway Channel & Hewlett Bay. **Features Include:** 96-acre Park, 2 Lighted Tennis Courts **Hours:** Parts of the park are open Year-Round **Fee: Free Directions:** *Southern State Pkwy., take exit 17 Hempstead Ave. S., take Hempstead Ave. to the fork, take Left fork for Ocean Ave., drive through Lynbrook & East Rockaway to Main St., follow park signs, make a Left onto Front St., make a Right onto Althouse Ave., make a Left onto First Ave. & follow to the park* *www.nassaucountyny.gov*

Bethpage State Park • NYS • *99 Quaker Meeting House Rd., Farmingdale, NY • Tennis Courts: 516-777-1358 • Pro Shop: 516-777-4010 • 516-249-0701* • Features Include: Year-Round Tennis, 8 Clay Courts, 4 All-Weather Courts, Junior Programs, Lessons, Workshops, Leagues, Tournaments, Training Programs, Restaurant, Babysitting Available on Weekdays **Hours:** 7 a.m.-10:30 p.m., Year-Round **Court Fees:** Off-Peak 7-11 a.m. or 2-3 p.m.: $21 Hard Court/$25 Clay Court, 7-10 p.m.: $35, Empire Pass Accepted **Directions:** *I-495 Long Island Expwy. E., take exit 44 S. Seaford-Oyster Bay Expwy./ Rte. 135 S., take exit 8 East Powell Ave.* *http://nysparks.state.ny.us*

Cantiague Park • NC • *1 W. John St., Hicksville, NY • 516-571-7058* • *Lessons: 516-572-0210* • Features Include: 5 Lighted Tennis Courts, Tennis Lessons, Free Intro Lesson, New Player Adult & Junior Programs, Seniors 50+ Program, Pro Shop **Hours:** 8 a.m.-10 p.m. **Fee: Free** court usage, Leisure Pass required **Directions:** *I-495 Long Island Expwy., take exit 41 S. Broadway, take fork for 106/107 to West John St., turn Right onto West John St., Cantiague Park entrance is on the Right* *www.tennispoint.com/tennis_court/Cantiague-Park-NY.html*

SUMMER FUN

Cedar Creek Park • *3524 Merrick Rd., Seaford, NY* • *516-571-7470* • The park is on Seaman's Creek & the East Bay. • **Features Include:** 259 acres, 8 Tennis Courts **Fee:** Leisure Pass required for reservations **Directions:** *Northern State Pkwy., exit onto 135-S. Seaford-Oyster Bay Expwy., take exit 1 W. Merrick Rd. W. toward Freeport, merge onto Merrick Rd.*   *www.nassaucountyny.gov/agencies/Parks*

Centennial Park • **NC** • *Centennial Ave., Roosevelt, NY* • *516-571-8695* • **Features Include:** 2 Tennis Courts **Hours:** Dawn-Dusk **Fee: Free**, Non-Residents Memorial Day-Labor Day: $5 **Directions:** *Southern State Pkwy., take exit 21 S. Nassau Rd., to Centennial Ave., the park is on the corner*   *www.nassaucountyny.gov*

Christopher Morley Park • **NC** • *500 Searingtown Rd., Roslyn, NY* • *516-571-8113* • **Features Include:** 98-acre Park, 5 Clay Tennis Courts **Hours:** Dawn-Dusk **Fee: Free** court usage, Leisure Pass required **Directions:** *I-495 Long Island Expwy., take exit 36N., Searingtown Rd., take Searingtown Rd. N., park entrance on the Right, about 200 yds. from the I-495*
www.nassaucountyny.gov/agencies/Parks/WheretoGo/active/morley.html

Cow Meadow Park & Preserve • **NC** • *South Main St., Freeport, NY* • *516-571-8685* • The park is located on Freeport Creek. **Features Include:** 171-acre Park, 6 Lighted Tennis Courts **Hours:** Dawn-Dusk **Fee: Free Directions:** *Southern State Pkwy., take exit 22 S. Meadowbrook Pkwy., exit at M9 W. Merrick Rd., make an immediate Left onto Mill Rd., turn Left onto S. Main St., the entrance is on the Left*   *www.nassaucountyny.gov*

Eisenhower Park • **NC** • *1899 Hempstead Tpke., East Meadow, NY* • *Tennis: 516-572-0348* • *572-0290, 572-0327, 542-0015* • *Recreation Center: 303-692-5650* • **Features Include:** 930-acre Park, 16 Lighted Hard Tennis Courts (Field 2 or 4), Pro Shop, New Player Adult & Junior Programs, Round Robins, Players must sign up for court time **Hours:** April-Oct.: Dawn-9:30 p.m., Park: Open Year-Round, Dawn-Dusk **Court Fee:** $3-$5, Park Entry: **Free** off-season, Non-Residents Memorial Day-Labor Day: $5 **Directions:** *Northern State Pkwy., Meadowbrook Pkwy. S., exit M3 E. Stewart Ave., turn Right onto Stewart Ave. continue to the park*
www.nassaucountyny.gov/agencies/Parks/WhereToGo/active/eisenhower.html

Grant Park • **NC** • *1625 Broadway, Hewlett, NY* • *516-571-7821* • **Features Include:** 35-acre Park, 5 Tennis Courts **Hours:** Dawn-Dusk **Court Fee: Free**, Leisure Pass Required **Directions:** *Southern State Pkwy., take exit 15S. for Corona Ave S., turn Right onto N. Corona Ave., turn slight Left toward Rockaway Pkwy., then slight Right at Rockaway Pkwy., turn Right to stay on Rockaway Ave., turn Right onto Broadway www.nassaucountyny.gov*

FUN FAMILY

Hempstead Lake State Park • NYS • *Eagle Ave. & Lake Dr., West Hempstead, NY • 516-766-1029* • Features Include: 20 Outdoor Clay & Hard Tennis Courts, Open Tennis Tournament in July, Court Usage: First-Come First Serve Sign-Up **Hours:** Open Year-Round, Dawn-Dusk **Fee:** Hard Court: $6 per hr., Clay Court: $8 per hr., Empire Pass Accepted **Directions:** *Southern State Pkwy., take exit 18 Eagle Ave., keep Right at the fork, follow signs for Rockville Centre/Hempstead Lake State Park, turn Right at Eagle Ave.* *www.stateparks.com/hempstead_lake.html*

Inwood Park • NC • *Bayview Ave., Inwood, NY* • 516-571-7894 • The park is surrounded by water. • **Features Include:** 16-acre Park, 2 Tennis Courts, Jogging/Walking Path **Fee:** $4 per car daily from May 25-Sept. 2 **Directions:** *Southern State Pkwy., take exit 19 S., Peninsula Blvd. S. to end, make a Left on Rockerway Tpke. (large intersection), make a Right onto Burnside Ave., curves to the Left & becomes Sheridan Blvd., take Sheridan to Bayview Ave. & turn Right, continue down Bayview into the park* *www.nycgovparks.org/parks/inwoodhillpark*

Nickerson Beach Park • NC • *880 Lido Blvd., Lido Beach, NY* • 516-571-7700 • Features Include: 121-acre Park, .75 mi. on the Atlantic Ocean, 2 Outdoor Concrete Tennis Courts, "Nathan's at Nickerson" Restaurant (open Labor Day-Oct.) **Hours:** Dawn-Dusk **Court Fee: Free** with Leisure Pass, or Nassau County Residents: $8, Non-residents: $20 **Directions:** *Meadowbrook Pkwy., take exit M10 the Loop Pkwy., take to the end, bear Right onto Lido Blvd., continue for 2 lights, make a Left into the park* *www.nassaucountyny.gov/agencies/Parks/WheretoGo/active/nickerson.html*

North Woodmere Park • NC • *750 Hungry Harbor Rd., Valley Stream, NY* • 516-571-7800, 7801 • Features Include: 150-acre Park surrounded by water, 10 Lighted Hard Tennis Courts **Court Hours:** 8 a.m-10 p.m. **Court Fee: Free Directions:** *Belt Pkwy. to Rockaway Blvd., take Rockaway Blvd., make Left onto Peninsula Blvd., make a Left onto Branch Blvd., follow it around to the Right, the park entrance is on the Left* *www.nassaucountyny.gov/agencies/Parks*

Rev. Arthur Mackey Sr. Park • NC • *Lakeside Dr. & Washington Rd., Roosevelt, NY • 516-571-8692* • Features Include: 27-acre Park, 2 Tennis Courts **Court Hours:** 8 a.m.-4 p.m. Summer: 8 a.m.-8:30 p.m. **Court Fee: Free Directions:** *Southern State Pkwy., take exit 23/Meadowbrook Rd. S. (not Meadowbrook Pkwy.), make a Right onto Washington Ave., take over the Pkwy., make a Right onto Lakeside Dr. (across from C.P center), enter the park on the Right* *www.nassaucountyny.gov/agencies/Parks/WheretoGo/active/mackey.html*

Wantagh Park • NC • *Kings Rd. & Canal Pl., Wantagh, NY • 516-571-7460* • Features Include: 111-acre Park on Flat Creek & East Bay, 5 Lighted Outdoor Tennis Courts

Court Hours: Dawn-Dusk, April-Oct. **Court Fee: Free**, Non-Residents Memorial Day-Labor Day: $5 **Directions:** *Southern State Pkwy., take exit 27 S. Wantagh Pkwy., take the exit for Sunrise Hwy. E., make a Right onto Wantagh Ave., to end, make a Right onto Merrick Rd., at 1ˢᵗ light make a Left into the park*   *www.nassaucountyny.gov*

Whitney Pond Park • NC • *Northern Blvd. & Community Dr., Manhasset, NY • 516-869-6311* • Features Include: 24-acre Park, Tennis Courts **Directions:** *I-495 Long Island Expwy., take exit 33 Community Dr. N., make the turn onto Community Dr. N., the park is on the Right, just after the police precinct*

SUFFOLK COUNTY

Abrahams Path Recreation Park • *Abrahms Path, Amagansett, NY • 631-324-2417*
• **Features Include:** 4 Tennis Courts, Restrooms, Attendant on Duty, Reservations Required day of play, sign up in Park Office **Fee: Free Directions:** *I-495 Long Island Expwy., take exit 68 William Floyd Pkwy. toward Shirley, slight Right to merge onto NY-27 E. toward Montauk, turn Left to stay on NY-27 E., turn Left at Main St., continue onto Pantigo Rd., turn Left at Accabonac Rd., turn Right to stay on Accabonac Rd., turn Right onto Town Ln., turn Right at Abrahams Path, the park will be on the Left*

Bridgehampton High School • *Montauk Hwy., Bridgehampton, NY • 631-537-0271*
• **Features Include:** 2 Tennis Courts for public use, First-Come, First-Served, Attendant on Duty **Hours:** Weekdays **Court Fee: Free Directions:** *I-495 Long Island Expwy., take exit 68 to merge onto William Floyd Pkwy. toward Shirley, turn Left onto Montauk Hwy./ NY 27 E., the school will be on the Right*

East Hampton High School • *2 Long Ln., East Hampton NY • 631-329-4130 • 631-329-4143 • Features Include:* 6 Tennis Courts, Attendant on Duty **Hours:** Sign up each morning **Fee: Free Directions:** *I-495 Long Island Expwy., take exit 68 to merge onto William Floyd Pkwy. toward Shirley, turn Right to merge onto NY-27 E. toward Montauk, turn Left at Montauk Hwy./NY-27 E., turn Left at County Rd. 113/Stephen Hands Path, turn Right at Long Ln., the school will be on the Left*

Heckscher Museum & Park, Private • *2 Prime Ave., Huntington, NY• Museum: 631-351-3250 • Town Hall: 631-351-3041* • Features Include: 2 Tennis Courts **Hours:** Dawn-Dusk **Fee: Free Directions:** *I-495 Long Island Expwy., take exit 49 N. Rte. 110 N., follow Rte. 110/Walt Whitman Rd. N. approx. 5 mi., Rte. 110/Walt Whitman Rd. becomes New York Ave., turn Right onto Rte. 25A/Main St. in Huntington Village, Prime Ave. is located along Rte. 25A just 1 traffic light East of the intersection with Rte. 110 in Huntington Village*   *www.heckscher.org*

Herrick Park • *Park Pl., East Hampton, NY* • Features Include: 3 Tennis Courts, Lights for Night Use, Attendant on Duty **Fee: Free Directions:** *Easily accessed from Park Pl. (parking lot behind shops on Main St. & Newtown Ln.)*

FUN FAMILY

Hither Hills Racquet Club • *47 Montauk Hwy., Amagansett, NY* • *P.O. Box 1421* • *631-267-8525* • **Features Include:** Tennis Instruction for Children, Tennis Clinics, Tennis Lessons, Tennis Courts by the hr., Junior Tennis Clinic for Kids 7-12, June-Sept. Beginner & Intermediate levels, 1-hr. Clinic: Mon.-Thurs., Tiny Tots Clinic: 1-hr.Clinic, 4-6, offered June-Sept., Mon.-Thurs. **Court Hours:** Open to the public Memorial Day - Labor Day **Directions:** *I-495 Long Island Expwy., take exit 62 Nicolls Rd. CR-97/Blue Point/Stony Brook, exit onto Expwy. Dr. S., take ramp onto Nicolls Rd. toward Blue Point, take ramp onto Sunrise Hwy./Rte. 27 E., turn Left on Montauk Hwy./Rte. 27, the Racquet Club will be on the Right*

Mashashimuet • *Main St., Sag Harbor, NY* • *631-725-4018* • **Features Include:** 10 Tennis Courts for Public Use, 2 All-Weather Courts, 8 Clay Courts, Attendant on Duty, although this is a membership organization, sometimes courts are available on an hourly basis, & seasonal memberships are reasonable **Directions:** *I-495 Long Island Expwy., take exit 68 to merge onto Suffolk County 46 S./William Floyd Pkwy. toward Shirley, turn Right to merge onto NY-27 E. toward Montauk, turn Left at Montauk Hwy./ NY-27 E., turn Left at Bridgehampton Sag Harbor Tpke., continue onto Main St., sharp Right at old railroad*

Montauk Downs • **NYS** • *50 South Fairview Ave., Montauk, NY* • *631-668-6264* • *668-5000* • **Features Include:** 6 Har-tru Championship Tennis Courts, Attendant on Duty, Food, Catering Facility, Clubhouse, Grill Room Serving Breakfast & Lunch, Restrooms, Showers, Lockers, Restaurants **Hours:** Tennis: mid-May- mid-Sept. **Fee:** Empire Pass Accepted **Directions:** *I-495 Long Island Expwy., take exit 68 William Floyd Pkwy. S. toward Shirley, merge onto William Floyd Pkwy., turn Left at Rte. 27 Sunrise Hwy., turn Left onto S. Fox St., turn Right onto S. Forest St., turn Left onto S. Fulton Dr., turn Right onto S. Fairview Ave.* http://nysparks.state.ny.us/sites/info

Raynor Beach County Park • **SC** • *Ronkonkoma Ave., Lake Ronkonkoma, NY* • *631-854-9699* • **Features Include:** Tennis Courts, Picnic Tables & Walking Trails,**Directions:** *I-495 Long Island Expwy., take exit 60 N. to Ronkonkoma Ave., the entrance is on the Left* www.co.suffolk.ny.us/Home/departments/parks/Parks.aspx

Southampton High School • *141 Narrow Ln., Southampton NY* • *631-591-4600* • **Features Include:** 5 Tennis Courts for Public Use **Court Fee: Free**, first-come, first-served **Directions:** *I-495 Long Island Expwy., take exit 68 William Floyd Pkwy. toward Shirley, turn Right to merge onto NY-27 E. toward Montauk, turn Right onto Hampton Rd., turn Left onto Narrow Ln., the school will be on the Right*

Westhampton Beach High School • *Oneck Ln., Westhampton Beach, NY* • *631-288-3800* • **Features Include:** 8 Tennis Courts for Public Use **Court Fee: Free,**

first-come, first served **Directions:** *I-495 Long Island Expwy., take exit 70 toward Montauk, merge onto County Rd. 111/Port Jefferson-Westhampton Rd., turn Right onto Eastport Manor Rd., turn Left onto County Rd. 71, turn Left onto County Rd. 80 E., turn Right at Lilac Rd., the school will be on the Right*

Directory of community tennis organizations on Long Island:

http://www.ustaonlongisland.com/ctas.htm

Directory of tennis courts on Long Island:

http://www.citidexli.com/2536.htm

SUGGESTIONS • COMMENTS • ERRORS

Linda.ReidBryce@verizon.net

Thanks

Splish Splash • *2549 Middle Country Rd., Calverton, NY • 631-727-3600 •* Features Include: 60-acre Park, 17 Adult Water Slides, 4 Kiddie Pools, Beach, 1,500-ft. Lazy River (tube ride), Mammoth River Ride, Hollywood Stunt Rider "In the Dark" family raft ride, Wave Pool, Kiddie Car Wash, Interactive Play Area, Restaurant, Gift Shop, Changing Room, Lockers **Hours:** Memorial Day Weekends-June, daily from June 14-Sept. 3, call for hrs. **Fee:** Adult: $26.99, Kids Under 48 in.: $19.99, Seniors & Disabled after 4 p.m.: $19.99, Under 48 in.: $15.99, Kids under 3: Free, Parking: $7, Handicap Accessible **Directions:** *I-495 Long Island Expwy., take exit 72 W., turn Left at the 1st, traffic light onto Splish Splash Dr.*   *www.splishsplashlongisland.com*

UP-STATE NEW YORK

The Great Escape & Splashwater Kingdom • *Rte. 9, Lake George, NY • 518-792-3500 •* Features Include: 21 Mild, 14 Moderate, 10 Max Rides, Sasquatch Max Ride (two 19-story towers, shoots you to the top in 3 seconds, then plummets you back to Earth), Festival Area, Storytown, Splashwater Kingdom, Wiggles World, Looney Tunes National Park, Ghost Town, pick up a show schedule at the Guest Relations Desk **Fee:** Kids Under 2: Free **Directions:** *I-87 N., NYS Thruway, to exit 24 toward Albany, continue N. on I-87, take exit 20, travel S. on Rte. 9 approx. .25 mi. & turn Right onto Six Flags Dr.*   *www.lakegeorgenewyork.com/great_escape_splashwater_kingdom.htm*

Six Flags Great Escape Lounge & Indoor Waterpark • *Lake George, NY • 89 Six Flags Dr., Queensbury, NY • 518-824-6000 •* Features Include: White Water Bay Indoor Waterpark, 38,000 sq. ft. **Rides Include:** Tall Timbers Treehouse is a multi-level play structure/water slides with 160 interactive water features, Boogie Bear Surf Sheet Wave for Body Boarding & Surfing, Adventure River Inflatable Tube Ride, Family Raft Ride, 2 Tube-Shaped Water Slides, Activity Play Lagoon with a Basketball Hoop & Cliff -Like Rock Formations, Shallow Activity Pool Area, Adult Water Spa **Height Requirement**: Must be at least 36 in., most rides require 42-54 in. **Directions:** *I-495 Long Island Expwy., take exit 31 N. Cross Island Pkwy., take exit 33 I-295 N. toward New England, merge onto I-95 S. towards New Jersey Tpke., take I-80 State Hwy. 4/Garden State Pkwy., take exit 72A State Hwy. 4 W. toward Paramus, take State Hwy. 17 N. exit toward Garden State Pkwy., merge onto Rte.17 N./New York State Thrwy./I-87 N. exit on the Left toward Albany, take the Right fork to continue toward I-87 N./New York State Thrwy. W., merge onto I-87 N./New York State Thrwy. W., take exit 1N. I-87 N. toward Montreal, take exit 20 toward Whitehall/Fort Ann/State Hwy. 149, turn Right at Six Flags Dr.*

www.sixflagsgreatescapelodge.com

NEW JERSEY

Gillian's Island Water Park • *Plymouth Pl. & Boardwalk, Ocean City, NJ* • *609-399-0483* • Located on the Jersey Shore. **Features Include:** Serpentine Body Slides, Shotgun Falls Slides, Lazy River, Kids' Area, Skypond Journey Slides, Affiliated Theme Park: Gillian's Wonderland Pier, Adventure Golf Course **Hours:** Weekends early Spring: 10 a.m-6 p.m, Memorial Day Weekend: 9 a.m-Midnight, Open: Daily June 21-Labor Day Weekend, 9:30 a.m.-6 p.m., closes the 1st weekend in Sept. **Fee:** Adult: $24, Under 48 in.: $20 **Directions:** *Southern State Pkwy. W., becomes the Belt Pkwy. W., take exit 17 W. onto NY-27 W. toward N. Conduit Ave., turn slight Left onto NY-27 W./Linden Blvd., NY-27 W. becomes Caton Ave., turn Left onto Fort Hamilton Pkwy., becomes 79th St., turn Left onto I-278 W. ramp toward Verrazzano-Narrows Br., merge onto I-278 W./Brooklyn Queens Expwy./Gowanus Expwy. toward Verrazzano Br./Staten Island, keep Right at the fork for I-278 W., take exit 11 toward Bradley Ave., stay straight to go onto N. Gannon Ave., turn Left onto Woolley Ave., becomes Forest Hill Rd., turn Left onto Richmond Ave., turn Right onto Drumgoole Rd. W., take Korean War Veterans Pkwy. S., merge onto NY 440 S. (crossing into New Jersey), take Rte. 35 S. exit, turn slight Right onto NJ 35/Convery Blvd., NJ 35 becomes Chevalier Ave., merge onto Garden State Pkwy. S. via the ramp on the Left, merge onto US 9 S. via exit 123 toward Sayreville Bridge, 34.7 mi., merge onto Garten State Pkwy. S., 54.1-mi., take the Rte. 52 exit, exit 30, toward Somers Point/Ocean City .4 mi., stay straight to go onto W. Laurel Dr./NJ 52, continue to follow NJ 52, pass through 1 roundabout. 3.9-mi., NJ 52 becomes E. 9th St., turn Left onto Ocean Ave. in .2 mi., turn Right onto Plymouth Pl.* *www.gillians.com*

Mountain Creek Water Park • *200 Rte. 94, Vernon, NJ* • *973-827-2000, 973 -864-8444* • **Features Include:** High Anxiety Funnel Ride, Colorado River Family Raft Ride, H2-Oh-No Speed Slide, Tarzan Swings Trapeze Jump, Bombs Away Sheer Drop Slide, the park is built into the side of a mountain, most of the rides use the mountain's natural topography & don't rise above the ground or require climbing towers **Fee:** Over 48 in.: $26.99, Under 48 in. & Seniors: $16.99 **Directions:** *I-495 Long Island Expwy., take the Cross Island Pkwy. N., take exit 31 N., towards the Whitestone Bridge, take exit 33 N. I-295 N. Cross Bronx Expwy., keep Right to take I-95 S., take exit 69 I-80 W. Garden*

State Pkwy./Hackensack, take exit 57 Main St./ toward Paterson, Left on Main St., make a slight Left onto W. Broadway CR 673, becomes Hamburg Tpke./Paterson Hamburg Tpke., turn Left onto Jackson Ave. CR 678, turn Right onto Black Oak Ridge Rd./US 202, turn Left onto Pompton Plains Crossroads/CR 680, becomes Jackson Ave., turn Right onto NJ-23 N., turn Right onto CR 515, Stockholm Vernon Rd., continue to follow CR 515, turn Left onto NJ 94, Mcafee Vernon Rd., end at 202 Rte. 94   *www.mountaincreekwaterpark.com*

Pirate's Cove • **354 Great Meadows Rd., Rte. 611, Hope, NJ** • **908-459-9000** • Land of Make Believe & Pirates Cove is a combination amusement park & water park with 1 price for both parks. **Attractions Included:** Sidewinder Half-Pipe, Blackbeard's River, Buccaneer Pirate Ship Interactive Kids' Area, Pirate's Peak Water Slides, Blackbeard's Lazy River, Pirates Cove Water Slides **Hour:** 10 a.m-6 p.m. **Fee:** Adults: $21, Kids: $23, Parking: Free, Discover Card only, one admission price includes all rides, shows, attractions **Directions:** *I-495 W., take exit 31 N. for Cross Island Pkwy. N. toward Whitestone Br., take the Cross Island Pkwy., take exit 33 to merge onto I-295 N./Throgs Neck Bridge toward Throgs Neck Bridge/Bronx/New England, follow I-295 N., take the exit onto I-95 S. George Washington Bridge Rte. 80 W. exit 12, make 2 Lefts & 1 Right*   *www.lomb.com*

Six Flags Hurricane Harbor • **1 Six Flags Blvd., Jackson, NJ** • **732-928-1821** • Features **Include:** 45-acre Tropical-Themed Waterpark, 1 Million-Gallon Wave Pool, one of the World's Largest Adventure Rivers, 20 Speed Slides, Interactive Kids' Water Play Area, Wave Pool, Tube Slides, Body Slides, Speed Slides, Lazy River Ride, Cannonball Falls & Wahini Falls Speed Slides, Bada Bing, Bada Bang Bada Boom Tube Slides, Blue Lagoon Wave Pool, Discovery Bay, Interactive Water Play Area, the water park is not included in the general admission price at Six Flags Great Adventure, but the park does offer package deals **Fee:** Adults: $34.99, Kids Under 54 in.: $24.99, Under 2: Free, **Directions:** *I-495 Long Island Expwy. W., exit onto Cross Island Pkwy. N., take exit 31N. toward Whitestone Bridge, take exit 33 I-295 N. toward Bronx/New England, I-295 N. becomes I-95 S./Cross Bronx Expwy., keep Right to take I-95 S. toward G.W. Bridge/Lower Level/ Last NY exit, Cross into New Jersey, keep Left to take I-95 Express Ln. S./New Jersey Tpke. S. toward the NJ Tpke. S., take exit 7A, proceed on I-195 East to exit 16A, travel 1 mi. West on Rte. 537 to Six Flags*   *www.sixflags.com*

SUGGESTIONS • COMMENTS • ERRORS

Linda.ReidBryce
@verizon.net

Thanks

MORE FUN

GIANT BUBBLES, SUNSHINE & PAINTING FUN

Bubble Fun

1 gal. Water

2/3 cup Dish washing liquid

3 or 4 Tbsp. Glycerin (purchase at a drugstore)

Pour dish washing liquid & Glycerin into the water and stir well. Storing the mixture in a closed container for 24-hrs. will increase the life of the bubbles.

Alternative Bubble Wands: Coat hangers bent into a shape, Floral Wire can be shaped into any shape, dip the wide end of a funnel into the solution, attach a light rope (tie a loop) to a stick dip it into the bubbles & run with it to create a really big bubble.

Face Painting Fun

Water-based Face Paint (Barnes & Noble sells a nice pallet/Book set)

Q-Tips

Disposable Make-Up Sponges

Mirrors

Container of Water

Small White Plastic Plates

Optional- Tubes of Red, White, & Black Water Based Face Paint

Use Q-Tips as paint brushes, Make-Up Sponges are for covering a full face with a color. Small white plates for mixing colors. Using disposable products prevents the spread of skin and eye conditions between children.

FACE PAINTING FUN

5 IN THIS SECTION

MUSEUM FUN

Let
Fun Flow
Like A
River

MUSEUM FUN

- Scavenger Hunt: Always inquire at the front desk for a scavenger hunt page.
- Sketch Book: Have children sketch + take notes about the things that interest them.
- Outdoor Museums: Give children a disposable camera to photograph things that interest them.

AQUARIUMS

Atlantis Marine World Aquarium • *431 E. Main St., Riverhead, NY* • *631-208-9200*

• **Features Include:** Indoor & Outdoor Exhibits, Snow Monkeys, Koi Pond, Python, Iguana, Poison Dart Frogs, Ancient Reptile Ruins, Sea Lion Show, River Otters, Seals, Penguins, Interactive Exhibits Include: Walk in Salt Marsh (summer only, must be 42.5 in. or taller), Feed & Pet Stingrays, Feed Sharks, Participate in a Fossil Dig, Tour the Peconic River on the Atlantis Explorer Boat (an educational expedition), Cafeteria, Gift Shop **Hours:** 10 a.m.-5 p.m., Year-Round **Fees:** Adults: $21, Kids: $18, Under 2: Free **Directions:** *I-495 Long Island Expwy. E., take exit 71 Rte. 24, turn Right onto Rte. 94/24 E., for 3.5-mi. to the traffic circle, .75 of the way around & make a Right onto Peconic Ave., turn Right onto Main St., Atlantis Marine World is located on the South side of the street, follow signs for parking*   *www.atlantismarineworld.com*

Cold Spring Harbor Fish Hatchery & Aquarium ⑳ • *1660 Rte. 25A, Cold Spring Harbor, NY* • *516-692-6768* • **Features Include:** Feed the Trout, Dock Fishing for Trout, NY Ecosystem Educational Center, New York State Freshwater Reptiles/Fish & Amphibians, Special Events, Educational Programs, Self-Guided Tour Sheets, 8 Outdoor Ponds & Brooks, Brown & Rainbow Trout, the Hatchery Staff is happy to answer questions **Hours:** 10 a.m.–5 p.m. **Fee:** Adults: $5, Kids 3-17: $3 **Directions:** *Northern State Pkwy. or I-495 Long Island Expwy., take Seafood-Oyster Bay Expwy. 135 N. to Jericho Tpke. E., make a Left onto Woodbury Rd. N., make a Left onto Rte. 108 & follow to the end, make a Left & an immediate Right onto Rte. 25A E., the entrance will be on the Left*   *www.cshfha.org*

NEW YORK CITY

New York Aquarium • *Wildlife Conservation Society* • *Surf Ave. & West 8ᵗʰ St., Brooklyn, NY* • *718-265-3454* • **Features Include:** Marine Mammals, Penguins, Jawfish, Moray Eels, Sea Lions, Living Salt Marsh, Hermit Crabs, Horseshoe Crabs, Electric Eel, Corals, Anemones, Jellies, Sharks, Seahorses, Octopus, Walrus, Feedings, Demonstrations, Educational Programs, Endangered Species, William Beebe & Otis Barton's 1934 Diving Vessel, Special Events **Hours:** Mon.-Fri.: 10 a.m.-6 p.m., Weekends: 10 a.m.-7 p.m. **Fee:** Adults: $13, Kids 3–12: $9, Deep Sea 3D: $6, Parking: $8, Nat. Wilflife Fed. Members Park Free **Directions:** *Belt Pkwy. W., take exit 7B Ocean Pkwy., turn Left onto Ocean Pkwy., continue to Surf Ave. to the New York Aquarium*

www.nyaquarium.com

CONNECTICUT

The Maritime Aquarium • *10 North Water St., Norwalk, CT • 202-852-0700* • Features **Include:** Daily Seal Feedings, IMAX Aquatic Movie Adventures, "Adventure Under the Sea Exhibit," Sponges, Crabs, Sea Stars, SpongeBob Squarepants 4D Adventure Ride **Hours:** 10 a.m.-5 p.m., July-Aug.: 10 a.m.-6 p.m., Closed Thanksgiving & Christmas Day **Fee:** Adults: $11, Kids 2-12: $9, Seniors: $10, Kids Under 2: Free **Directions:** *I-495 Long Island Expwy., take exit 31 N. for Cross Island Pkwy. N., take exit 33 to I-295 N. toward the Throgs Neck Bridge, merge onto I-95 N. toward New Haven, take exit 14 toward S. Norwalk, turn Right at Fairfield Ave., continue onto Washington St., turn Left onto N. Water St., the museum will be on the Right* www.maritimeaquarium.org

Mystic Aquarium & Institute for Exploration ⊗ **• *55 Coogan Blvd., Mystic, CT • 860-572-5955* •** Features **Include:** Beluga Whales, Various Marine Life Envioronments, Sea Lion Show, Louisiana's Bayou Experience, Baby Alligators **Hours:** March-Nov.: 9 a.m.-6 p.m. daily, Dec.-Feb.: Mon.-Fri.: 10 a.m.-5 p.m., Sat.-Sun.: 9 a.m.-6 p.m. **Fee:** Adults: $17.50, Kids 3-17: $12.50, Under 2: Free, Seniors: $16.50 **Directions:** *I-495 Long Island Expwy., take exit 31 N. for Cross Island Pkwy N., take exit 33 to I-295 N. toward the Throgs Neck Bridge, merge onto I-95 N. toward New Haven, take exit 90 for CT-27 N., turn Right onto Clara Dr., turn Left onto Coogan Blvd., the aquarium will be on the Left* www.mysticaquarium.org

NEW JERSEY

Adventure Aquarium • *1 Aquarium Dr., on the waterfront • Camden, NJ • 856-365-3300* • Features **Include:** Exotic Sea Life, Hands-On & Interactive Exhibits, 4D Theatre, Swim with the Sharks, Help Feed & Train Sea Turtles, Communicate with Seals, Dive & Feed in an Ocean Realm Exhibit, Swim with Stingrays, 350-lb. Loggerhead Sea Turtle **Hours:** 9:30 a.m.-5 p.m. **Fee:** Adults: $18.95, Kids 2-12: $14.95, Under 2: Free **Directions:** *New Jersey Tpke., take exit 4 onto Rte. 73 N. take Rte. 73 to Rte. 38 W. toward Camden, take Rte. 38 W. & bear Right at overpass to Rte. 30 W., stay on 30 W. approx. 1.6 mi. to the Martin Luther King Blvd./Waterfront Attractions exit on the Right off the ramp, continue straight until the road splits, following the blue "Waterfront/Aquarium" sign stay to the Left onto Martin Luther King Blvd., follow Martin Luther King Blvd approx. 1.1 mi. to 3rd St., turn Right on 3rd St. N., turn Left at the 2nd light onto Market St. W., continue for 3 blocks to its end, turn Left onto Delaware Ave. S., get into the Right lane, parking area entrance is on the Right* www.adventureaquarium.com

New Jersey State Aquarium • *New Jersey Academy for Aquatic Sciences • 1 Riverside Dr., Camden, NJ • 856-365-0352* • Features **Include:** Invertebrates, Sharks, Rays, Fish, Amphibians, Reptiles, Birds, Mammals, 30-min. Electronic Field Trips via Videoconferencing Technology, Research Facility **Hours:** 9:30 a.m-5:30 p.m. **Fee:** Adults: $18.95, Kids 2-12: $14.95 **Directions:** *I-495 Long Island Expwy., take exit I-278 W. toward Brooklyn, take the I-95 S. exit on the Left, merge onto I-95 S./New Jersey Tpke. S., take exit 4 for State*

Hwy. 73 N. toward Camden/Philadelphia, merge onto Rte. 73, take the Rte. 38 W. exit toward Rte. 41 W./Haddonfield, merge onto Rte. 38 E./Rte. 38, turn Left at Kaighns Ave./Rte. 38/Rte. 38, continue to follow Kaighns Ave./Rte. 38, take the ramp to Admiral Wilson Blvd./US-30, keep Left at the fork to continue toward Admiral Wilson Blvd./US-30 & merge onto Admiral Wilson Blvd/US-30, turn Right at S. 17th St., turn Left at Federal St., continue on Market St., turn Left at Delaware Ave., turn Right at Riverside Dr.   *www.njaquarium.org*

ART, CINEMA & CULTURAL ARTS

Cinema Art Center • 423 Park Ave., Huntington, NY • 631-423-7610, 7611 • **Features Include:** Children's Programs, Movies, Festivals, Special Events, Guest Speakers, Discussions, Receptions, Café **Hours:** Check online film & show times **Fee:** Films: $9, Members: $6, Live Shows: $15 **Directions:** *I-495 Long Island Expwy., take exit 49 N Rte. 110, follow Rte. 110/Walt Whitman Rd. N., go 5 mi., Rte. 110/Walt Whitman Rd. becomes New York Ave., turn Right onto Rte. 25A/Main St. in Huntington Village, go 3 traffic lights, turn Right onto Park Ave., 1st driveway on the Right*   *www.cinemaartscentre.org*

Heckscher Museum & Park • Private • 2 Prime Ave., Huntington, NY • 516-351-3250 • **Features Include:** Art Museum, Educational Programs, Historic & Contemporary Masters, Playground, Pond, Free Summer Concerts, Walking Path **Hours:** Tues.-Fri.: 10 a.m.-5 p.m., open until 8:30 p.m. the 1st Friday of each month, Sat.-Sun.: 1-5 p.m. **Fee:** Adults: $8, Students: $5, Under 10: Free, Seniors: $6, Huntington Residents: Adults: $6, Seniors & Students: $4, After 5 p.m.: **Free Directions:** *I-495 Long Island Expwy., take exit 49 N. Rte. 110 N., follow Rte. 110/Walt Whitman Rd. N. for 5 mi., Rte. 110/Walt Whitman Rd. becomes New York Ave., turn Right onto Rte. 25A/Main St. in Huntington Village, Prime Ave. is located along Rte. 25A 1 traffic light East of the Rte. 110*   *www.heckscher.org*

Emily Lowe Gallery • Emily Lowe Hall, South Campus • Hofstra University Museum • 112 Hofstra University, Hempstead, NY • 516-463-5672 • Features Include: Family Performances, Exhibitions, Special Programs, Lectures, Musical Events **Hours:** Tues.-Fri.: 10 a.m.-5 p.m., Sat.-Sun.: 1 p.m.-5 p.m. **Fee: Free**, special events require a small fee **Directions:** *Northern State Pkwy., take the Meadow Brook Pkwy. S., take exit 24 Hempstead Tpke. W., turn Right, the gallery is on the Left side of the campus off the Quad*   *www.hofstra.edu/Community/museum/index.html*

Guild Hall of East Hampton/ John Drew Theater • 158 Main St., East Hampton • 631-324-0806 • Box Office: 631-324-4050 • Features Include: Children's Programs, Art Museum, Paintings, Sculptures, Regional Artists, Exhibitions, Outdoor Stage Performances, Educational Programs, ARTlink (integrates the visual, literary & performing arts) **Hours:** Thurs.-Sun.: 11 a.m.-5 p.m. **Fee:** All: $5, Members: Free **Directions:** *Southern State Pkwy., take exit 40 Robert Moses Cswy. S., take exit RM1E. towards Rte. 27 E./Montauk, turn slight*

Right onto Sunrise Hwy., take the Left ramp & merge onto NY-27 E., turn Left onto NY-27/
Montauk Hwy., turn Left onto Main St./NY-27   www.guildhall.org

Islip Art Museum • *50 Irish Ln., East Islip, NY* • 631-224-5402 • Features Include:

Contemporary Art, New & Emerging Artists, Lectures, Fine Art Classes, Workshops, Tours **Hours:** Wed.-Sat.: 10 a.m.-4 p.m., Sun.: Noon-4 p.m. **Fee:** $3 ea. **Directions:** *I-495 Long Island Expwy., take exit 52 toward CR-4/Commack Rd./Commack/N. Babylon, go onto the S. Service Rd. which becomes Express Dr. S., turn Right onto Crooked Hill Rd./CR-13 S., follow CR-13 S., turn Left onto Candlewood Rd. which becomes Commack Rd. then becomes Nassau Ave., turn Left onto Union Blvd./CR-50, take Union to the 1st traffic light, turn Right onto Irish Ln., the Islip Museum is in the mansion building of Brookwood Hall*   www.islipartmuseum.org

Nassau County Museum of Art ⊗ • *1 Museum Dr., Roslyn Harbor, NY* • 516-484-9338 • Features Include:

200-acre Estate, 10 Galleries, Outdoor Sculpture Garden & Tee Ridder Miniatures Museum (great for children), American & European Artists, Georgian Mansion, Hiking Trails, Educational Programs, Children's Events & Exhibitions, Scavenger Hunts, Children's Performances, Arts & Crafts, Storytelling Events, the museum presents the works of internationally acclaimed artists in the main museum building. The Tee Ridder Miniatures Museum exhibits a collection of miniature rooms & there is a 10-ft. castle that children love looking into. **Hours:** Tues.-Sun.: 11 a.m.-4:45 p.m., Family Tours Sun.: 1 p.m., Family Art Activities Sun.: 1:30 p.m. **Fee:** Adults: $10, Kids: $8 **Directions:** *I-495 Long Island Expwy., take exit 39 Glen Cove Rd. N., turn Left onto Northern Blvd./25A, drive 1.5 blocks & turn Right onto Museum Dr.*   www.nassaumuseum.com

Parrish Art Museum • *25 Job's Ln., Southampton, NY* • 631-283-2118 • Features

Include: 19th-20th Century American Art, Sculpture Garden, Arboretum, Changing Exhibitions, Family & Adult Programs, Lectures, Concerts, School & Youth Programs **Hours:** June 15-Sept. 15, Mon.-Tues. & Thurs.-Sat.: 10 a.m.-5 p.m., Sun.: 1 p.m.-5 p.m. **Fee:** $2 donation appreciated **Directions:** *Southern State Pkwy., take exit 40 Robert Moses Cswy. S., take exit RM1 E. towards Rte. 27 E./Montauk, merge onto Sunrise Hwy. E., take exit 65 S. NY-24 S. toward Hampton Bays, turn Left onto W. Montauk Hwy./CR-80 E., W. Montauk Hwy. becomes Hill St., turn slight Left onto Jobs Ln.*   www.parrishart.org

Pollack-Krasner House • *830 Springs Fireplace Rd., East Hampton, NY* • 631-324-4929 • Features Include:

Abstract Expressionism-Focused House Tour, Jazz Record Collection, Photo Essay of Pollock's Career, Art Studio, Family "Drip Painting!" Workshops (Kids 4-12), Study Center **Hours:** June, July & Aug., Thurs.-Sat.: 1-5 p.m., Tours: Noon, May, Sept., & Oct., Thurs.-Sat.: 11 a.m.-4 p.m., tours occur on the hr., Summer Workshop Sat.: 10-11:30 a.m., Reservations Required **Fee:** Admission: $5, Admission &

Tour: $10 per person, Under 12 & Students: Free **Directions:** *Southern State Pkwy., take exit 40 Robert Moses Cswy. S., take exit RM1 E. towards Rte. 27 E./Montauk, turn Left onto Main St./NY-27, turn slight Left onto N. Main St./CR 40, turn slight Right onto N. Main St. which becomes Springs Rd./Springs Fireplace Rd.*

http://naples.cc.sunysb.edu/CAS/pkhouse.nsf

NEW YORK CITY

MoCCA • *Museum of Comic Book & Cartoonists Art* • *594 Broadway, Ste. 401, NY, NY* • *212-254-3511* • Features Include: Comic Book & Cartoonists Art, the Golden Age of Saturday Morning Cartoons, Animation, Anime, Cartoons, Comic Books, Comic Strips, Gag Cartoons, Humorous Illustrations, Political Illustrations, Editorial Cartoons, Caricatures, Graphic Novels, Sports Cartoons, Computer-Generated Art **Hours:** Tues.-Sat.: Noon-5 p.m. **Fee:** $5 **Directions:** *LIRR to Penn Station, take the B, D, F, or V train to the Broadway/Lafayette St. station* *www.moccany.org*

The Cloisters Museum & Gardens • *99 Margaret Corbin Dr., Fort Tryon Park in northern Manhattan, NY, NY* • *212-923-3700* • Features Include: Medieval Art & Architecture, Garden Tours, Self-Guided Tours, 5 Cloisters, the Trie Garden Café **Hours:** March-Oct.: Tues.-Sun.: 9:30 a.m.-5:15 p.m., Nov.-Feb.: Tues.-Sun.: 9:30 a.m.-4:45 p.m., Closed Mon. **Fee: Free**, donation appreciated **Directions:** *Nothern State Pkwy. W., becomes Grand Central Pkwy., go over the Triborough Bridge, take FDR Dr. Southbound/Downtown, take the 96th St. exit, turn Left onto York Ave., turn Right on 86th St., turn Left onto 5th Ave. & enter museum parking garage at 80th St.* *www.metmuseum.org*

Museum of the Moving Image • *35th Ave. at 37th St., Astoria, NY* • *718-784-0077* • *Administrative Offices: 718-784-4520* • *School Groups: 718-777-6820* • Features Include: Interactive Exhibitions, Holiday Film Programs, Animation Workshops, Film Screenings, Handicap Accessible **Hours:** Tues.-Fri.: 10 a.m.-4 p.m., Sat.-Sun.: Noon-6 p.m., Closed Mon. **Fee: Free**, donations appreciated **Directions:** *Northern State Pkwy. W. to the Grand Central Pkwy., take exit 45, 31st St. (last exit before the Triborough Bridge), get into the Left lane, turn Left onto 31st St. (under the elevated subway) & proceed to 35th Ave., follow signs for the Museum, turn Left onto 35th Ave. & proceed to 37th St.* *www.movingimage.us*

The Metropolitan Museum of Art • *1000 5th Ave. at 82nd St., NY, NY* • *212-535-7710* • *212-570-3828* • Features Include: Monthly Family Art Programs, Printed Family Guides Show Kids How to Hunt for Details, Current Exhibition-Focused Art Projects, Teen Programs **Hours:** Tues.-Thurs.: 9:30 a.m.–5:30 p.m., Fri.-Sat.: 9:30 a.m.-9 p.m., Sun.: 9:30 a.m.–5:30 p.m. **Fee:** Adults: $20, Kids Under 12 & Members: Free, Students: $10, Seniors: $15 **Directions:** *LIRR to Penn Station, take the C local train to 81st St. & transfer to the M79 crosstown bus across Central Park to 5thAve.*

www.metmuseum.org

AVIATION MUSEUMS

American Air Power Museum • *Republic Airport, 1100 New Hwy. Hangar 3, East Farmingdale, NY • 1230 New Hwy., Farmingdale, NY • 631-293-6398 • Office of Public Affairs: 212-843-8010 • Educational Tours: 212-843-8010* • Features Include: Museum Tours given by WWII Veterans, Planes, Stories, Flight Demonstration Events, Vintage Aircrafts Operated (weather permitting), gain a sense of what was required to keep our nation free **Hours:** Thurs.-Sun.: 10:30 a.m.-4 p.m. **Fee:** Adults: $10, Kids 5-13: $5, Seniors: $8 **Directions:** *I-495 Long Island Expwy., take exit 49 S. toward Amityville to Rte. 110 S., make a Left on Conklin St., turn Right onto New Hwy., see the Museum sign on Hangar 3* *www.americanairpowermuseum.com*

Bayport Aerodrome Society Museum • *Cartwright Loop, Bayport • 631-732-6509 • 516-322-2509 P.O. Box 728, Vitamin Dr. off Church St., Bayport, NY • 631-472-2393* • Features Include: Early 20th Century Aviation, 24 Hangar Complex, Antique & Experimental Aircraft, Local Aviation History Exhibit, Aerodrome & Museum Tours, Sport Aviation, Military Trainers, Vintage Airplanes, Weekend Flight Demonstrations, anyone can join & volunteer to assist in projects at the aerodrome. Past Events have Included: May-Hornpoint Flyout, June-Sentimental Journey Flyout, August-Antique Airplane Clubs Annual Fly **Hours:** Sat.-Sun.: Noon-4 p.m., March-Dec., weather permitting, reserve for tours **Fees: Free** Directions: *Sunrise Hwy., take exit 51, take Nicolls Rd. (Rte. 97) South to the 1st traffic light, turn Right onto Church St., make a Left onto Vitamin Dr., turn Left into the Bayport Aerodrome parking lot* *www.bayportaerodrome.org*

Cradle Of Aviation Museum ⊛ • *"Museum Row" • Charles Lindbergh Blvd. • 1 Davis Ave., Garden City, NY • 516-572-4111* • Features Include: Long Island's Aerospace Heritage Exhibits, Hands-On Activities/Projects, IMAX Theatre, Educational & Feature Films **Hours:** Tues.-Sun.: 9:30 a.m.-5 p.m., IMAX is open 7 days **Fee:** Museum: Adults: $9, Kids: $8, IMAX: Adults: $8.50, Kids: $6.50, Hollywood IMAX: Adults: $13.50, Kids: $11.50, Firefighters Museum: Adults: $4, Kids: $3.50 **Directions:** *Northern State Pkwy., to the Meadowbrook Pkwy., take exit M4, follow signs to Museum Row which will put you on Charles Lindbergh Blvd., stay on Charles Lindbergh Blvd. to the 2nd traffic light & turn Right into the parking lot* *www.cradleofaviation.org*

Northrop Grumman History Center • *600 Grumman Rd. W. & South Oyster Bay Rd., Bethpage NY • 516-349-5941* • Features Include: Aviation & Space Pioneer History, circa 1929-1994, US Military Planes, Lunar Module (the 1st spacecraft to land on the moon), Models, Photos, History Center, Staffed by Retired Grumman Employees **Hours:** Mon.-Wed.: 9 a.m-4 p.m. **Directions:** *Northern State Pkwy., exit onto S. Oyster Bay Rd., turn Left onto Grumman Rd W.* *www.bethpagecommunity.com/Grumman*

BOTANICAL & NATURAL

Bayard Cutting Arboretum • *440 Montauk Hwy., Great River, NY* • *631-581-1002* • **Features Include:** Arboretum, Small Hikes, Great Lawn, Connetquot River, Shaded Walks, Flower-Lined Paths, Massive Weeping Trees, Cutting Family Manor House, Concerts, Art Exhibits, Carriage House, Fir, Spruce, Dec. Holiday Decorations, Café with Open Porch **Hours:** Tues.-Sun.: 10 a.m.-5 p.m. **Fee:** Historical house tours: $6 donation, Parking: $6, there are no fees during the winter **Directions:** *Southern State Pkwy., take the exit toward Harwood Ave., turn Right onto Harwood Ave., take the 1st Right onto Co. Rd. 50/Union Blvd., turn Right onto S. Country Rd./NY-27A W., the park will be on the Left* www.bayardcuttingarboretum.com

Planting Fields Arboretum Ⓥ • *Oyster Bay, NY* • *516-922-8600* • **Features Include:** Historic Buildings, Rolling Lawns, Formal Gardens, Specimen Plantings, Greenhouses, Picnicking, Hiking Trails **Hours:** Mon.-Sun.: 9 a.m.-5 p.m. **Fee: Free** off-season, Parking: $6 May 1-Oct. 31, weekends & holidays from Oct. 31-April 30, Empire Pass Accepted, Handicap & Stroller Accessible **Directions:** *Long Island Expwy. to exit 41 N., or Northern State Pkwy. to exit 35 N., proceed North on Rte. 106 toward Oyster Bay, turn Left onto 25A/Northern Blvd., make 1st Right onto Mill River Rd., follow green & white signs to the Arboretum on Planting Fields Rd.* www.plantingfields.org

Sands Point Preserve • *Middle Neck Rd., Sands Point, Port Washington, NY* • *516-571-7900* • **Features Include:** 216-acre Preserve, 6 Marked Walking/Hiking Trails, Trail Maps, Guided Nature Walks, Forests, Meadows, Woodlands, Shoreline Beach (LI Sound), Cliffs, Lawns, Gardens, Freshwater Pond, Woods, Fields, Nature Trails provide access to the preserve & highlight specific points of interest in self-guiding literature **Hours:** 10 a.m.-5 p.m., Year-Round **Fee: Free** Preserve & Trails, Sat.-Sun.: $2, Falaise Tours: $2 **Directions:** *I-495 Long Island Expwy., take exit 36 Searingtown Rd. N, drive for approx. 6 mi., the road becomes Port Washington Blvd. & then Middle Neck Rd., enterance is on the Right 1-mi. past the stone & brick gate of the Sand Point Village Club* www.sandspointpreserve.org/htm/info.htm

BROOKLYN

Brooklyn Botanical Garden • *900 Washington Ave., Brooklyn, NY* • *718-623-7200* • **Features Include:** Children's Programs, Garden Guides, Terrace Café, Visitors Center, Picnicking, Japanese Garden, Conservatory Gallery Exhibits, Gardeners Resource Center, Workshops **Hours:** March-Oct.: Tues.-Fri.: 8 a.m.-6 p.m., Weekends & Holidays: 10 a.m.-6 p.m., closed Mon., Nov.-March: Tues.-Fri.: 8 a.m.-4:30 p.m., Weekends & Holidays: 10 a.m.-4:30 p.m., closed Mon., Handicap Accessable **Fee:** Adults: $8, Students: $4 Kids Under 12: Free **Directions:** *I-495 Long Island Expwy. W., take the BQE W., exit at Kent Ave., follow the service road/Park Ave. alongside & then under the expwy., go 5 blocks, turn Left onto Washington Ave. for 1.75 mi.* www.bbg.org

NEW YORK CITY

The New York Botanical Garden • *200th St. & Kazimiroff Blvd., Bronx, NY • 718-817-8700* • **Features Include:** Children's Adventure Garden, Family Garden, Family Events have included: Puppet Shows, Dance Performances, Garden Music Concerts **Hours:** Sat.: 9:30 p.m.-7 p.m., Sun.: 9 a.m.-6 p.m., Tues.-Fri.: 10 a.m.-6 p.m. **Fee:** Adults: $20, Kids 2-12: $10, Students: $18 **Directions:** *Northern State Pkwy., take the Cross Island Pkwy. N. to the Throgs Neck Bridge, take I-95 New England Thrwy. N., take exit 8C Pelham Pkwy. W. cross Bronx River Pkwy. (Pelham Pkwy. turns into Fordham Rd. after 2 mi., turn Right onto Kazimiroff Blvd. & continue to the Garden entrance on the Right*
www.nybg.org

QUEENS

Queens Botanical Garden • *43-50 Main St., Flushing, NY • 718-886-3800* • **Features Include:** Children's Events, Exhibits, Tours, Seasonal Displays, Children's Garden, Bee Garden, Constructed Wetlands, Craft Beds, Fragrance Walks, Green Roof Plant Collection, Herb Garden, Meadow, Wedding Garden **Hours:** April-Oct.: Tues.-Fri.: 8 a.m.-6 p.m., Sat.-Sun.: 8 a.m.-7 p.m., Nov.-March: Tues.-Sun.: 8 a.m.-4:30 p.m. **Fee: Free**, donation appreciated, Parking: $5, Members: $3 **Directions:** *I-495 Long Island Expwy. W., take exit 23 Main St., make a Right turn on Main St., turn Left on Dahlia Ave. becomes Crommelin St., the parking lot entrance is on the Left*
www.queensbotanical.org

CHILDREN'S MUSEUMS

Long Island Children's Museum ⓥ • *11 Davis Ave., Garden City, NY • 516-224-5800* • **Features Include:** Interactive Exhibits, Music, Investigate Sound, International Instruments, Communications, Broadcast Station, Create Animations, Build Things, Bubbles, 2-Story Climbing Structure, Backyard Sensory Gardens, Pattern Studio, Giant Kaleidoscopes, Construct with Tools, Tot Spot, Weekend Theatre Programs **Hours:** Wed.-Sun.: 10 a.m.-5 p.m., closed Mon. **Fee:** Adults: $9, Kids Under 1& Members: Free, Family Membership: $85
Directions: *Northern State Pkwy., take the Meadowbrook Pkwy. S. to exit M4 (Nassau Coliseum), bear Right (before Hempstead Tpke.) onto Charles Lindbergh Blvd., go to the 1st traffic light (Nassau Coliseum on the Left, Nassau Community College on the Right), proceed through this traffic light & the LICM will be on the Right*
www.licm.org

Children's Museum of the East End • *376 Sag Harbor Tpke., Bridgehampton, NY • 631-537-8250* • **Features Include:** Interactive Displays, Explore LI People/Plants, & Animal Life of the East End, LI Agriculture/Fish & Wildlife, Local Community, World Cultures, Permanent & Rotating Exhibits, Classes, Workshops, Events, Parties **Hours:** Mon., Wed.-Sat.: 10 a.m.-5 p.m., Sun.: 10 a.m.-5:30 p.m., closed Tues. **Directions:** *I-495 Long Island Expwy., take exit 68 S. William Floyd Pkwy./Co. Hwy. 46 S. toward Shirley,* merge onto County Rte. 46/William Floyd Pkwy., turn Left onto Rte. 27 E., make a U-turn, turn Right onto Stephen Hands Path, turn Left onto Rte. 114/Sag Harbor Tpke.

www.cmee.org

NEW YORK CITY
Children's Museum of Manhattan • *212 West 83rd St., NY • 212-721-1223* • Features

Include: Ancient Greece, Gods, Myths & Mortals, Play Works, Block Party, City Splash, Dora the Explorer Exhibit, Youngest Visitors Floor, Art, Science, Math, Language, Imagination, Programs, Children with Disabilities Guide **Hours:** Tues.-Sun.: 10 a.m.-5 p.m. **Fee:** Adults & Kids: $10, Under 12 months & Members: Free, Seniors: $7

Directions: *LIRR to Penn Station, take the 1 train to 79th or 86th St. station, or take the 2 or 3 Express to 72nd or 96th St. station, then transfer to the 1 train, or take the A, B, C, or D train to the 59th St. station, then transfer to the 1 train, or take the B or C train to 81st St. station*

www.cmom.org

BROOKLYN
The Brooklyn Children's Museum • *145 Brooklyn Ave., Brooklyn, NY • 718-735-*

4400 • Features Include: Totally Tots for kids 5 & under, Special Events, Performances, Movies **Hours:** Winter: Sat.-Sun.: 10 a.m.-5 p.m., Wed.: Noon-5 p.m. (Totally Tots opens at 11 a.m.), Thurs.-Fri.: Noon-5 p.m. **Fee:** Free before 11 a.m., $7.50 per person, Kids Under 1 & Members: Free **Directions:** *Northern State Pkwy. W., becomes the Grand Central Pkwy., take the Jackie Robinson Pkwy. (formerly Interboro Pkwy.), take the Bushwick Ave. exit, turn Right on Bushwick., drive for 2 blocks & turn Left onto the Eastern Pkwy. Extension, pass Brooklyn Ave., turn Right on New York Ave., drive 6 blocks, turn Right onto St. Mark's Ave., the museum is 1 block ahead*   *www.bchildmus.org*

CULTURAL HISTORY & COMMUNITY
African American Museum • *110 North Franklin St., Hempstead, NY • 516-572-0730*

• Features Include: 6,000-sq.-ft. Museum, Exhibits, Local & National African-American Art, History & Culture, Black Power Movement, Black History Exhibit Center, Art Instillations, Historical Exhibits, Film Programs, Community Service Events, Educational Programs, African-American Genealogy Society, Genealogy Workshops **Hours:** Tues.-Sat.: 10 a.m.-5 p.m. **Fee:** Free **Directions:** *Northern State Pkwy., take the Meadowbrook Pkwy. S., take exit 31-A Jones Beach, take the W. Old Country Rd. exit, take M1-W. toward Mineola, turn Right onto Old Country Rd., turn Left onto Clinton Rd. (becomes Clinton St.), turn Right onto Fulton Ave./ Hempstead Tpke., turn Right onto N. Franklin St.*   *www.aamoflongisland.org*

The Blydenburgh Historic District • *Smithtown, Veteran's Memorial Hwy., Smithtown, NY • Tours & Programs: 631-360-0753 • 631-854-3713* • Features Include: 1798 New Mill, 1802 Miller's House, Farm Cottage circa 1860, Outbuildings, Blydenburgh Farmhouse

circa 1820, this milling center was established in 1798 by members of the Smith & Blydenburgh families of Smithtown, a period-clothed person offers a historic film & tour in the farmhouse on Saturdays **Hours:** Sat.: Film: 1 p.m., House Tour: 1:30 p.m., **Fee: Free**, donations appreciated **Directions:** *Northern State Pkwy. to end, slight Right onto Rte. 347/454 the main (southern) entrance to the park is on 347, the Historic District is on the North side of the park, take 347, turn Left onto Brooksite Dr. N., next light turn Left onto New Mill Rd., follow to the park entrance at end, walk in to the Right, see the Weld House/Blydenburgh Farmhouse* Ligreenbelt.org

Bayville Historical Museum • *34 School St., Bayville, NY* • *516-628-1720, 2011* • *516-628-5498* • The museum is housed in the only remaining building complex that was part of the Harrison Williams "Oak Point" Estate. **Features Include:** 88-acre Estate, Bayville's History, Shellfish & Asparagus Industries, Country Store, Rotating Exhibitions & Events **Hours:** By appointment only, Summers: Wed. & Sun.: 1 p.m.-4 p.m., **Fee: Free Directions:** *Northern State Pkwy., take exit 35 N. 106 N., turn Left onto Main St., becomes W. Shore Rd., drive over the Bayville Bridge/Ludlam Ave., turn Left onto Bayville Ave., turn Left onto School St./Schoolhouse Rd.*

Colonial Arsenal Museum • *425 Park Ave., Huntington, NY* • *Huntington Town Historian: 631-351-3244* • **Features Include:** Dutch Farm Building circa 1740, Costumed Docent Tours **Hours:** 1-4 p.m., Sun. June-Oct. **Fee: Free**, donations appreciated **Directions:** *Northern State Pkwy., take exit 36B 135 N. toward Syosset, take exit 14E., turn Right onto Jericho Tpke. E. toward Woodbury, turn Left onto Rte. 110 N./ New York Ave., bear Right onto Nassau Rd. (near the Big H Shopping Center), turn Right onto Woodhull Rd., turn Left onto Park Ave., the Arsenal will be on the Left*

Huntington Historical Society Museums • *209 Main St., Huntington, NY* • *631-427-7045* • **Features Include:** Tours of: **Tidemill & Conklin House**, High St. at New York Ave., 18th & 19th Century Period Rooms, Table & Chair used by Washington during his 1790 Long Island Tour, Exhibit, **1795 Kissam House & Barn**, 434 Park Ave., **1905 Sewing & Trade School**, now a Research Center, **1892 Sailors Memorial Building**, 228 Main St., 209 Main St. is one of the country's first vocational schools, **Huntington Visitors Center**, Children's Summer Program for kids 7-12, Lecture Series, Genealogy Workshops, Special Events **Hours:** Mon.-Fri.: 9 a.m.-5 p.m., Kissam House: by appointment only, Conklin House: 1-4 p.m., Thurs.-Fri., Sun., Research Center & Library: 1-4 p.m., Wed. & Thurs.: Year-Round or by appointment **Fees:** Kissam & Conklin House: Adults: $5, Seniors & Students: $3, Under 5 & Members: Free, Research Center: $4 per person **Directions:** *Northern State Pkwy., take exit 135 N., exit Jericho Tpke. toward Woodbury, make a Left onto New York Ave., turn Right onto Main St.* *www.huntingtonhistoricalsociety.org*

MUSEUM FUN

Holocaust Memorial & Tolerance Center of Nassau County • *100 Crescent Beach Rd., Glen Cove, NY* • *516-571-8040* • **Features Include:** Outdoor Children's Garden, Documentary, Narrative Interviews, the museum presents issues of individual creativity & imagination & the destructive nature of prejudice, apathy, bullying & hatred. The museum is on the Welwyn Preserve property. **Hours:** Mon.-Fri.:10 a.m.-4 p.m., Sat.-Sun.: Noon-4 p.m. **Fee: Free**, donations appreciated **Directions:** *Northern State Pkwy., exit onto Glen Cove Rd. N. to end, turn Right onto Brewster St./Forest Ave., travel for 4 lights, turn Left at the 4th Light onto Dosoris Ln., travel 1 mi., turn Left onto New Woods Rd., travel to the stop sign, turn Right onto Crescent Beach Rd., make the 1st right*   *www.holocaust-nassau.org/#pageID=1831*

Lauder Museum • *Amityville Historical Society* • *170 Broadway, Amityville, NY* • *631-598-1486* • **Features Include:** Collection, Preservation & Display of Historical Objects, Historical Facts, Activities, Memorabilia, Materials from Long Island's South Shore in & around Amityville **Hours:** Sun., Tue. & Fri.: 2-4 p.m., Tours & Research Library: by appointment **Fee: Free Directions:** *Southern State Pkwy., take exit 32 S. 110 toward Amityville, turn Right onto Co. Line Rd., turn Right onto Broadway/110 S., the museum will be on the Right*   *www.amityvillehistoricalsociety.org*

LongHouse Reserve • *133 Hands Creek Rd., East Hampton, NY* • *631-329-3568* • **Features Include:** 16-acre Reserve, Nature Art, Houses, Sculpture Gardens, Gallery, Arboretum, Fantasy & Themed Gardens, Yoko Ono's Giant Chess Set, Fly's Eye Dome **Hours:** Wed. & Sat.: 2-5 p.m. **Fee:** Adults: $10, Under 12: Free, Seniors: $8 **Directions:** *I-495 Long Island Expwy., take exit 67, turn Right onto Yaphank Ave., turn Left onto Horseblock Rd., turn Right onto NY-27 E., turn Left onto Stephen Hands Path, turn Right onto Cedar St., make the 2nd Left onto Old Orchard Ln., turn Right onto Hanks Creek Rd., the museum will be on the Right*

The Long Island Museum • *Member of the Smithsonian Institute* • *1208 Rte. 25A, Stony Brook, NY* • *631-751-0066* • **Features Include:** 9-acre Complex, American Art Museum, History Museum, Carriage Museum **Hours:** Fri.-Sat.: 10 a.m.-5 p.m., Sun.: Noon-5 p.m. **Fee:** Adults: $9, Kids: $4, Under 6: Free, Seniors: $7 **Directions:** *I-495 Long Island Expwy., take exit 62 N. onto Nicolls Rd., travel to its end, turn Left onto Rte. 25A, travel to the intersection of 25A & Main St. in Stony Brook, the museum will be on the Left*   *longislandmuseum.org*

Third House/Camp Wikoff • *Montauk Hwy., Montauk, NY* • *631-852-7878* • America's first cattle ranching system was located in 17th century Montauk. The early cattle keepers lived in the historic Third House at Theodore Roosevelt County Park. Third House was also the headquarters for Camp Wikoff in 1898. The Rough Riders, as well as 28,000 soldiers were quarantined at Camp Wikoff. **Features Include:** Spanish-American War Exhibit, Gift Shop, Horseback Riding, Hiking (self-guided nature trail map) **Hours:** Wed.-Sun.:

10 a.m.-5 p.m., exhibit open May-Oct. **Directions:** *Southern State Pkwy., follow Montauk Hwy. E. through Montauk Village, past East Lake Dr., park sign & entrance is on North side of Montauk Hwy.*

www.co.suffolk.ny.us

Old Bethpage Village Restoration Ⓥ • NC • *1303 Round Swamp Rd., Bethpage, NY •*

516-572-8400 • 8301 • **Features Include:** 209-acre Park, mid-19th-Century American Village, Living History Museum, Homes, Farms, Businesses, Educational Programs, Old-Time Baseball Games, the Noon Inn serves pretzels & root beer, Powell Farm, Chickens, Cows, Sheep, Oxen, Pigs **Hours:** Mar -Nov., Tues.-Sun.: 10 a.m.-5 p.m. **Fee:** Adults: $4, Kids: $3, Seniors: $2 **Directions:** *I-495 Long Island Expwy., take exit 48 Round Swamp Rd. toward Old Bethpage/Farmingdale, make a Left onto Round Swamp Rd., turn Left onto Old Country Rd., make a slight Right onto Round Swamp Rd.*

www.nassaucountyny.gov

Polish American Museum • *16 Belleview Ave., Port Washington, NY • 516-883-6542*

• **Features Include:** 30 Rooms, 15 Galleries, Polish Culture, Folk Heritage, Documents, Artifacts, Paintings, Research Library, Archacki Archives, Lecture Hall, Examples of Polish Contributions to Humanity, Gift Shop **Directions:** *I-495 Long Island Expwy., take exit 36 Searingtown Rd./Shelter Rock Rd., turn Right onto Searingtown Rd., continue on Port Washington Blvd., turn Left onto Main St., turn Left onto Belleview Ave., the museum will be on the Right* *http://polishamericanmuseum.org*

Raynham Hall Museum • *20 West Main St., Oyster Bay, NY • 516-922-6808 •* Features

Include: 20-room House/Museum circa 1740, Period Furnishings, Programs & Workshops, Children & Family Events, the Townsends were 1 of the founding families of the Town of Oyster Bay, Raynham Hall was used as British headquarters during the American Revolution, Tours & Educational Programs are available by appointment **Hours:** Tues.-Sun.: 1-5 p.m., July 1-Labor Day: Noon-5 p.m. **Fee:** Adults: $5, Under 6: Free, Students & Seniors: $3, Audio Tours: add $1 to admission **Directions:** *I-495 Long Island Expwy., take exit 41 N., follow Rte. 106 approx. 6 mi. North into the village of Oyster Bay, turn Left onto West Main St., the museum is the 3rd building on the Right (North) side of the street, park in the municipal parking lots, there is 1 directly across the street from Raynham Hall or just West of the museum on the North side of the street* *www.raynhamhallmuseum.org*

St. James General Store • *National Register of Historic Places • 516 Moriches Rd., St. James, NY • 631-854-3740 • 631-862-8333 •* **Features Include:** General Store circa

1857, Local Craftsman-made Jewelry/Scarves/Bags/Music/Children's Games **Fee:** Free **Directions:** *I-495 Long Island Expwy., take exit 56 towards Smithtown, turn Left onto Wheeler Rd./NY111 N., turn Left onto Hauppauge Blvd., continue on New York 25A E./ Nissequogue River Rd., turn Left onto Moriches Rd., the store will be on the Left*

MUSEUM FUN

September 11 Memorial • *Western Waterfront* • *West End Ave., Oyster Bay, NY* • *516- 797-4110* • Features Include: Granite-Clad Semi-Circle Shaped Monument, Steel Beam from the World Trade Center, Meditation Garden, Nautical Mast-Style Flagpole, Benches, View of the World Trade Center Site, View the words "We shall never forget the forty-sixth minute of the eighth hour of the eleventh day of September 11, 2001" **Hours:** Dawn-Dusk **Fee: Free Directions:** *Northern State Pkwy., exit onto 106/107 N., turn Left onto W. Main St., turn Right onto Bayside Ave., take the 3rd Left onto West End Ave., Tobay Beach will be on the Left, the memorial is situated at the Western Waterfront*

Shinnecock Nation Cultural Center • *100 Montauk Hwy., Southampton, NY* • *631-287-4923* • Features Include: Log Building/Museum, Traditional Shinnecock Replica Home, Interactive Exhibits, Hand-Painted Murals, Artifacts, the Shinnecok's were the earliest dwelling people on eastern Long Island **Hours:** Fri.-Sat.: 11 a.m.-4 p.m., Sun.: Noon-4 p.m. **Fee:** Adults: $5, Kids & Seniors: $3, Under 5: Free **Directions:** *I-495 Long Island Expwy., take exit 70 Manorville Rd., turn Right onto Manorville Rd. S., take Sunrise Hwy. Rte. 27 E. to the Southampton College exit, turn Right at exit, cross the railroad tracks to traffic light at Montauk Hwy., turn Right onto W. Gate Rd./Shinnecock Indian Reservation, the museum is on the corner of Montauk Hwy. & W. Gate Rd., turn Left into the parking lot behind the museum* www.shinnecockmuseum.org

Suffolk County Historical Museum • *300 W. Main St., Riverhead, NY* • *631-727-2881* • Features Include: 20,000 Objects on Display, Civil War, Whaling, Transportation, Blacksmiths Shop, Historic Farming, Native Indian Life, Special Events, Library, Gift Shop **Hours:** Tues.-Sat.: 12:30-4:30 p.m., Library: Wed.-Sat. **Fee: Free Directions:** *I-495 Long Island Expwy., take exit 72, follow the signs for Riverhead, proceed East on Rte. 25 (W. Main St.) to Court St., the museum is on the corner of Court St. & W. Main St., will be on the Left* www.suffolkcountyhistoricalsociety.org

Suffolk County Vietnam Veterans Memorial Park • *SC* • *Bald Hill, Farmingville, NY* • *631-854-4949* • Features Include: Veteran's Memorial Pyramid, Bald Hill, Highest Points on Long Island, Panoramic View of Suffolk County **Directions:** *I-495 Long Island Expwy., take exit 63 N., North Ocean Ave./ Rte. 83, follow signs to the memorial parking area* http://www.co.suffolk.ny.us

Village Blacksmith Shop • *319 Main St., Greenport, NY* • *631-477-2100 ext. 206* • *Mitchell Park: 631-477-2200* • Features Include: Replica Blacksmith Shop, 4-acre Mitchell Park, Waterfront Village, Antique Carousel, Observation Deck, Camera Obscura, Ice Rink, Harbor Walk, 60 Slip Marina **Fee: Free Hours:** Sat. Blacksmith Shop Demonstrations: 10 a.m.-4 p.m. **Directions:** *I-495 Long Island Expwy., take exit*

72, follow signs toward Riverhead, follow W. Main St./NY-25 E./Middle Country Rd., turn Right onto Main Rd., turn Left onto Main St., the blacksmith shop is on the East side of Mitchell Park   *www.greenportvillage.com/mitchellpark.html*

Wantagh Museum • *Wantagh Ave., Wantagh, NY* • *516-826-8767* • Features Include: Restored 1904 Train Station, the "Jamaica" Parlor Railroad Car (with Solarium, Cooking Facilities & an Ice-Cooled Air Conditioning System, Wantagh's Original Post Office, Ticket Booth, Turn-of-the-Century Photographs, Historical Memorabilia **Hours:** Sun.: 2-4 p.m., April-Dec. **Fee: Free Directions:** *Southern State Pkwy., take exit 28 S., take Wantagh Ave. S., the museum will be on the Right*   *www.wantagh.li/museum*

Water Mill Museum • *41 Old Mill Rd., Water Mill, NY* • *631 726-4625* • **Features Include:** Water-Powered 1644 Grist Mill, Windmill, Restored Mill & Museum, Grain Grinding Demonstrations, Art Shows, Brunches & Teas throughout the year **Hours:** Thurs.-Mon.: 11 a.m.-5 p.m., Sun.: 1-5 p.m., May-Nov. **Directions:** *Southern State Pkwy., take Sunrise Hwy./Rte. 27 E. (from Southampton), enter the hamlet of Water Mill, Old Mill Rd. is on the Left, just before the Water Mill Square shops*

www.watermillmuseum.org

NEW YORK CITY

Museum of Chinese In America Ⓥ • *211 Centre St., NY, NY* • *212- 619-4785* • **Features Include:** The Chinese American Experience, Hands-On Exhibits, Video Exhibits, Family Programs, Tours, Special Events **Hours:** Mon.:11 a.m.-5 p.m., Thurs.: 11 a.m.-9 p.m., Fri.: 11 a.m.-5 p.m., Sat. & Sun.: 10 a.m.-5 p.m. **Fee:** Adults: $7, Kids Under 12: Free, **Free** admission on Thurs. **Directions:** *I-278 W. toward the Brooklyn/ Queens Expwy., turn Left onto Delancey St., turn Left onto Bowery, turn Right onto Canal St. before turning right at Centre St., MOCA will be on the Left, or LIRR to Penn Station, take the N, R, Q, W, J, M, Z, & 6 train to Canal St., or 1 of the M9, M15, M103 buses www.mocanyc.org*

Museum of American Financial History • *48 Wall St., NY, NY* • *212-908-4110* • **Features Include:** United States Finance History, Oldest Known Photograph of Wall St., Evolution & Development of American Financial Markets, Machinery, Board Games, Memorabilia, Stocks, Bonds, Prints, Engravings, Photographs, Banknotes, Stocks & Bonds Certificates from the Gilded Age including US Steel & Standard Oil, Company Charter Documents, a US Treasury Bond issued to George Washington, $100,000 Bond Issued to Andrew Carnegie in 1901, 90-min. Walking Tour of the Financial District, Archives **Hours:** Tues.-Sat.: 10 a.m.-4 p.m. **Fee:** Adults: $8, Students: $5, Under 6: Free **Directions:** *LIRR to Penn Station, take the 2,3,4,5 train to Wall St., J,M to Broad St., 1,R,W to Rector St.*   *www.moaf.org*

MUSEUM FUN

Museum of Jewish Heritage • *Safra Plaza* • *36 Battery Place, NY, NY* • *646-437-4200* • **Features Include:** A Living Holocaust Memorial, Personal Objects, Photographs, Jewish Heritage Films, Cafe **Hours:** Sun.-Tues., Thurs.: 10 a.m.-5:45 p.m., Wed.: 10 a.m.-8 p.m., Fri.: 10 a.m.-5 p.m. **Fee:** Adults: $12, Students: $7, Under 12: Free, Free every Wed. from 4-8 p.m. **Directions:** *Subway: 4/5 to Bowling Green, walk West along Battery Place, W/R to Whitehall St., walk West along Battery Place, 1 to South Ferry, walk North along Battery Park/State St., turn Left & walk West on Battery Place* *www.mjhnyc.org*

National Museum of the American Indian Ⓖ • *One Bowling Green, NY, NY* • *212-668-6624* • *Groups: 212-514-3705* • **Features Include:** Traditional & Contemporary Native American Art, Beautiful Museum, Galleries Surround a Rotunda **Hours:** 10 a.m.-5 p.m. daily, Thurs.:10 a.m.-8 p.m. **Fee: Free Directions:** *LIRR to Penn Station, take the 4 or 5 train to Bowling Green or N, R to Whitehall St. or 1, 9 to South Ferry, located in the old Customs House across the street from Battery Park* *http://www.si.edu/nmai*

Statue of Liberty • *National Park Services* • *Liberty Island NY, NY* • *Recorded Message: 212-363-3200* • *Crown Reservations: 866-782-8834* • *212-363-7770* • **Features Include:** Museum, Promenade Tour, Observatory Tour, Audio Tour, Climb to the Crown (reservations required), Views From Liberty Island, Restaurant, Allow for ferry transportation time in your schedule. The busiest months are July & Aug., while the least busiest months are are Jan. & Feb. Only people arriving with a crown reservation can enter the monument. **Hours:** Mon.-Sun.: 9:30 a.m.-5 p.m. **Fee: Free** admission, Ferry Ticket to Statue of Liberty & Ellis Island: Adults: $12, Kids 3-17: $5, Seniors: $10 **Directions:** *take the LIRR to Penn Station, take the 1 train to South Ferry, or the 4 or 5 train to Bowling Green, or the R or W train to Whitehall St., Liberty & Ellis Islands are accessible by Statue of Liberty/Ellis Island ferries only 1 round trip ferry ticket includes visits to both islands. Ferries depart from Battery Park in New York* *www.statuecruises.com* • *www.statuereservations.com*

Ellis Island Immigration Museum • *The Statue of Liberty-Ellis Island Foundation, Inc.* • *History Center* • *17 Battery Place #210, NY, NY* • *212-561-4588* • **Features Include:** Ellis Island Museum, Family Genealogy, American Immigration Experience, Time line, Photos, Multimedia Exhibits, Documentaries, Archives, Professional Assistance for Investigating Immigration History, Family Documentation, Genealogical Exploration, the Ellis Island Immigration Museum is part of the Statue of Liberty National Monument & is one of the country's most popular historic sites *www.ellisisland.org*

LANDMARK STRUCTURES

The Long Island Duck • *Flanders Rd., Flanders, NY* • *631-852-8290* • Features

Include: 1930 Duck-Shaped Cement Building, Measurments: 18-ft. x 30-ft., 20-ft. tall, Each year, the first Wed. in Dec., there is an Annual Holiday Lighting of the Big Duck the first Wed. in Dec. Local school children sing "Duck" carols, & warm refreshments including hot chocolate, cookies & doughnuts are served. Visitors join in singing the duck carols while awaiting the arrival of Santa Claus, transported by the Flanders Fire Department. Once Santa arrives, the switch is flipped & the Big Duck lights up for all to see. **Hours:** Memorial-Labor Day: 10 a.m.-5 p.m. (closed for lunch: 1-1:30 p.m.), weekends only through Nov. (call to verify) **Fee: Free Directions:** *I-495 Long Island Expwy., take exit 71, turn Right onto CR-94 E./Edwards Ave./Rte. 24 E. for 4.3 mi. At traffic circle, take the 3rd exit onto Flanders Rd./Rte. 24 E. 2.4 mi. the duck is on the Left* www.roadsideamerica.com/story/2173

Lucy The Elephant • *National Historic Site• 9200 Atlantic Ave., Margate, NJ • 609-823-6473* • **Features Include:** The World's Largest Elephant, 6-story Wooden/ 65-ft. tall, 90 Ton Tin Elephant Building circa 1881, Eyes are Windows, Views of the Ocean, Lucy's Birthday Party is July 20 & includes: Balloons, Birthday Cake, Rides, Games, web site offers coloring pages of Lucy **Hours:** vary dramatically throughout the year **Fee:** Adults: $4, Kids: $3, Under 12: Free **Directions:** *Garden State Pkwy. S., take exit 36 Rte. 563 E. (it's the only direction you can go when exiting) follow Rte. 563 for 2-3 mi., cross over Rte. 9, go about .75 mi. to a 5-point intersection, make an easy Left onto the Margate Bridge Cswy. take the Cswy. into Margate, pay a $1 toll, you will be on Jerome Ave. drive to the 5th traffic light, Ventnor Ave., turn Right on Ventnor Ave. & go 14 blocks to Decatur Ave., turn Left on Decatur Ave. & go to the end (1 block), Lucy will be on your Right, corner of Decatur & Atlantic Ave.*

www.lucytheelephant.org

FARMING

Hallockville Museum Farm • *6038 Sound Ave., Riverhead, NY • 631-298-5292* • **Features Include:** 28-acre Farm Preserve, 18 Historic Houses, Barns & Outbuildings, Museum, Gardens, Tours, Gas Station, Cows, Sheep, Chickens, Eastern Long Island's Agricultural Heritage, Children's Educational Programs **Hours:** Sat.-Sun.: 10 a.m.-4 p.m. **Fee:** Adults: $7, Kids 6-12 & Seniors: $5, Under 6: Free **Directions:** *I-495 Long Island Expwy., take exit 73 Old Country Rd. toward Orient/Greenport/Co. Hwy. 58, Left onto County Rte. 58/Old Country Rd., Left onto Rte. 43/Northville Tpke., turn Right onto Sound Ave.*

www.hallockville.com

Queens County Farm Museum • 73-50 Little Neck Pkwy., Floral Park, NY • *718-347-3276* • **Features Include:** Historic Farmhouse Tours, Hay rides (weather permitting), Feed Sheep & Goats, Gift Shop **Hours:** Mon.-Fri.: 9 a.m.-5 p.m. (outdoor visiting only), Sat.-Sun.: 10 a.m.-5 p.m., Year-Round **Fee: Free** (except on special event days) **Directions:** *Northern State Pkwy. W. into Grand Central Pkwy. W., take exit 24 Little Neck Pkwy., turn Left onto Little Neck Pkwy., drive 3 blocks to museum* www.queensfarm.org

Wyckoff Farmhouse Museum ⓥ • *Pieter Claesen Wyckoff House* • *5816 Clarendon Rd., Brooklyn, NY* • *718-629-5400* • **Features Include:** Living History Museum circa1652, Dutch Colonial Wychkoff Farmhouse, New York City's Oldest Structure **Hours:** Tues-Sun.: 10 a.m.-4 p.m.: April-Oct. **Fee:** Adults: $5, Students & Seniors: $3, Under 10: Free **Directions:** *Southern State Pkwy., Belt Pkwy. W. toward Brooklyn, take exit 14 for Pennsylvania Ave., turn Right onto Granville Payne Ave./Pennsylvania Ave., turn Left onto Flatlands Ave., turn Right onto E. 80ᵗʰ St., slight Right onto Ralph Ave., turn Left onto Clarendon Rd., the farm museum is on the Left* www.wyckoffassociation.org

HISTORIC HOMES & BUILDING MUSEUMS

Clinton Academy Museum • *151 Main St., East Hampton, NY* • *516-324-1850* • **Features Include:** 1-room Schoolhouse circa 1731, 1st School in New York State, Dominy Clock, Interactive Activities for Kids, Write on Slates, Try a Quill Pen, Mock 1860 Class Session **Directions:** *I-495 Long Island Expwy., take exit 67 Yaphank Ave. toward Yaphank/Brookhaven, turn Right onto Yaphank Ave., turn Left onto Horseblock Rd., turn Right onto Rte. 27 E., turn Left onto Main St.* www.easthamptonhistory.org

Old Westbury Gardens • *71 Old Westbury Rd., Old Westbury, NY* • *516-333-0048* • **Features Include:** 160 acres, circa 1906, Children's Programs, Special Events, Family Programs, Exhibits, Special Events, Indoor & Outdoor Classical Concerts, Formal Gardens, Landscaped Grounds, Woodlands, Ponds, Lakes, Decorative Arts, Lectures, Book Signings, Horticultural Demonstrations, Workshops, Tours **Hours:** 10 a.m.-5 p.m., House: 11 a.m.-4 p.m., April-Oct. 31 **Fee:** Adults: $10, Kids 7-12: $5, Under 6: Free, Seniors: $8 **Directions:** *I-495 Long Island Expwy., take exit 39 Glen Cove Rd., follow the East service road for approx.1.1 mi., turn Right onto Old Westbury Rd., continue .4 mi., enterance on the Left* www.oldwestburygardens.org

Sagamore Hill National Historic Site ⓥ • **the National Park Service** • **20 Sagamore Hill Rd., Oyster Bay, NY** • **516-922-4447** • **Features Include:** 1884 Victorian Mansion, Original Film Clips, Narrated Program, Junior Ranger Activities for Children, Children's Scavenger Hunt, Letterboxing, Museum Exhibits, Audio Visual Programs, President Theodore Roosevelt used this as the "Summer White House" from 1901-1909. There is an afternoon concert series on summer weekends. Summer music, storytelling & demonstrations take place from 2-4 p.m. on most weekends. **Hours:** 9:30 a.m-5 p.m. **Fee:** 16-62: $1, Under 15: **Free** **Directions:** *Northern State Pkwy., take exit 35 N. or I-495 Long Island Expwy. to exit 41N., take Rte. 106 N., drive 4 mi., turn Right onto Rte. 25A E., drive 2.5 mi., at the 3ʳᵈ traffic light turn Left onto Cove Rd. & drive for 1.7 mi., turn Right onto Cove Neck Rd. N., 1.5 mi. to Sagamore Hill* www.nps.gov/sahi

The Suffolk County Vanderbilt Museum • *180 Little Neck Rd., Centerport, NY* • *631-*

854-5555 • *631-854-5579* • **Features Include:** 1947 "Gold Coast" Estate, Museum, Planetarium, Dinosaur Exhibit, Egyptian Mummy, Fine & Decorative Arts, Listed on the National Register of Historic Places, Many Special Programs, Light Shows, Historical Artifacts, Marine & Natural History Museum, Park, Astronomical Society Monthly Observing Session on the Wed. evening closest to the New Moon **Hours:** Grounds, Mansion & Exhibits: Mon. 11 a.m.-5 p.m., Tues.: Noon-5 p.m., Sat.: 11 a.m.-5 p.m., Sun.: Noon-5 p.m., Planetarium: Fri. Night: 8, 9, 10 p.m., Sat.: 11 a.m., Noon, 1, 2, 3, 4, 7, 8, 9, 10 p.m., Sun.: Noon, 1, 2, 3, 4 p.m. **Fee:** Adults: $7, Kids: $3, Seniors: $6, Mansion Tour: $5, Planetarium Show: Adults: $7, Under 12: $3, Seniors: $6 **Directions:** *Northern State Pkwy., take exit 42N., Deer Park Ave. N. , turn Left at the fork (at traffic light) onto Park Ave. at 3rd light, make a Right turn onto Broadway, continue for 4-5 mi. until you reach Rte. 25A, cross 25A (to left of Centerport Automotive), Little Neck Rd., the museum is on the Right*
http://www.vanderbiltmuseum.org

Walt Whitman Birthplace Museum • *National Register of Historic Places* • *246 Old Walt Whitman Rd., Huntington Station, NY* • *516-427-5240* • **Features Include:** 1819 Farm House, Museum, Guided Tours, Hiking on Walt Whitman Trail, Picnicking, Gift Shop **Hours:** Wed.-Fri.: 1-4 p.m., Sat.-Sun.: 10 a.m.-4 p.m. **Fee: Free Directions:** *I-495 Long Island Expwy., take exit 49 N., follow the Walt Whitman signs, take Rte.110 N. 1.8 mi., turn Left onto Old Walt Whitman Rd., the museum will be on the Right*
www.waltwhitman.org

INSTRUMENTS

American Guitar Museum • *1810 New Hyde Park Rd., New Hyde Park, NY* • *516-488-5000* • **Features Include:** Special Events, Guitar Resources, Study Resources, Guitar Doctor, Restoration Clinic **Hours:** Tues., Wed., Fri.: 10 a.m.-6 p.m., Thurs.: 10 a.m.-10 p.m., Sat.: 9 a.m.-5 pm., Sun. & Mon.: reserved for group tours **Fee: Free Directions:** *I-495 Long Island Expwy., take exit 34 New Hyde Park Rd. S., the museum will be on the Left, 100 ft. before the Hillside Ave. intersection, turn into the driveway & park in the parking lot behind the museum*
www.americanguitarmuseum.com

MATHEMATICS

Goudreau Museum of Mathematics • *999 Herricks Rd., New Hyde Park, NY* • *516-747-0777* • **Features Include:** Hands-On Learning Experiences, 3D Models, Puzzles, Games, Workshops, Special Events, Exhibitions, Resource Library, Pi Day, Contests, Museum Store, Math Usage in the Arts & Sciences, call ahead to confirm public times of operation **Hours:** Sat.: Noon-3 p.m., open to the public **Fee:** varies depending on events **Directions:** *I-495 Long Island Expwy., take exit 35, Shelter Rock Rd., turn Right onto Shelter Rock Rd. S., drive 1.3 mi., turn Right* *onto Herricks Rd., immediate Right into the parking lot, the museum is in the Herricks Community Center, go upstairs to room 202 in the left side of the building*   *www.mathmuseum.org*

NATURAL HISTORY

Garvies Point Museum & Preserve ⓨ • **NC** • *50 Barry Dr., Glen Cove, NY* • *516-571-8010* • **Features Include:** Long Island Native American Culture, Geology, Archeology, Dioramas, Models, Artifacts, 62 acres of Glacial Moraine Covered by Forests/Thickets & Meadows, 5 mi. of Marked Nature Trails (trail maps available in the museum), Hempstead Harbor Beach (Dinosaur Fossil site), Educational Programs, Guided Tours **Directions:** *Northern State Pkwy, exit 107 N. toward Oyster Bay/Glen Cove, 107 N. becomes Pratt Blvd./Glen Cove Rd., which becomes Glen Cove Ave., turn Right onto Village Square/Brewster St., turn Left onto Mill Hill Rd. which becomes The Place, stay straight to go onto Ellwood St., turn Left onto McLaughlin St., turn Left onto Barry Dr.*   *www.garviespointmuseum.com*

Hicksville Gregory Museum • *1 Heitz Pl., Hicksville, NY* • *516-822-7505* • **Features Include:** Heitz Place Courthouse circa 1895, Long Island's Largest Rock & Mineral Collection, 5,000 Butterfly & Moth Specimens, Plant/Shell & Animal Fossils **Hours:** Tues.-Fri.: 9:30 a.m.-4:30 p.m., Sat.-Sun.: 1-5 p.m. **Fee:** Adults: $5, Kids & Seniors: $3 **Directions:** *Northern State Pkwy., exit onto S. Oyster Bay Rd., turn Right onto Woodbury Rd., turn Left onto Bay Ave., turn Right onto Heitz Pl., the museum will be on the Left*   *www.gregorymuseum.org*

Museum of Long Island Natural Science • **Stony Brook University** • **Earth & Space Science Building** • *1208 Rte. 25A, Stony Brook, NY* • *631-632-8230* • **Features Include:** Children's Programs, Long Island Sea & Wildlife, Native American Artifacts, Live Fish & Snail Display, Native & Invasive Reptiles & Amphibians, New York's Geological History, Local Marine Habitat Ecology, Energy Sources, Consumer Material Composition, Biological/Mechanical & Chemical Recycling Processes, Major Issues Surrounding Human Consumption of Marine Organisms, Biodiversity, Population Biology, Predator-Prey Roles in Marine Ecosystems, Food Web **Hours:** Mon.-Fri.: 9 a.m.-5 p.m., open weekends for special events **Fee:** *Free,* donations appreciated **Directions:** *I-495 Long Island Expwy., take exit 62 & follow Nicolls Rd. N. for 9 mi., turn Left onto the campus at the South Entrance, follow South Dr. to Marburger Dr., turn Right onto Marburger Dr. & go around the rotary, take the 2nd Right & head West onto Circle Rd., turn Right onto Campus Dr., quick Left onto John S. Toll Dr., park in the large parking lot (Red Faculty/Staff) on the Right, the Earth & Space Sciences Building is the 4-story concrete building at the far left corner of the parking lot, pick up a temporary parking permit at the museum office when the university is in session*   *www.geosciences.stonybrook.edu/museum*

The Roosevelt Sanctuary & Audubon Center ⓨ • *134 Cove Rd., Oyster Bay, NY* • *516-922-3200* • **Features Include:** 12-acre Sanctuary, Museum, Flora & Fauna Exhibits, Natural Sciences/Wildlife/Ecology & Native American Programs, Programs for Pre-K-12th grade &

Scouts, After-School Workshops, Special Events, Self-Guiding Nature Trail, Previously Held Events: Animal Forensics, Daring Defenses, Critter Café, Animal Families **Hours:** Mon.-Fri.: 9 a.m.-4 p.m., Sat.-Sun.: 11 a.m.-3 p.m., Grounds: 10 a.m.-4 p.m. **Fee: Free Directions:** *Long Island Expwy., exit 41 N., Rte. 106 N., to the Village of Oyster Bay, turn Right onto E. Main St., proceed 1.5 mi. up E. Main St. (eventually becomes Cove Rd. at Oyster Bay High School), see signs for the T.R. Sanctuary parking lot on the Left* ny.audubon.org/trsac.htm

Theodore Roosevelt Statue • *Corner of Rte. 106 & Berry Hill Rd., Oyster Bay, NY* • Made from the original casting of the famous "Theodore Roosevelt Rough Rider" sculpture created in 1921 by renowned sculptor Alexander Phimister Proctor.

Youngs Memorial Cemetery • *Cove Road, Oyster Bay Cove, NY* • Features Include: 17th century Burial Ground, President Theodore Roosevelt & Wife Edith Kermit Roosevelt, Headstone Bears the Presidential Seal, climb 26 steps signifying the 26th president **Hours:** 9 a.m.-Dusk

Tackapausha Museum & Preserve Ⓒ • **NC** • *Washington Ave., Seaford, NY* • *516-571-7443* • **Features Include:** 3,000-sq.-ft. Museum, Ecology of Long Island, Animal Exhibits, Shows, Children's Interactive Activities, 84-acre Preserve, 77-acre Tract of Glacial Outwash Plain, Varied Natural Long Island Habitats, Educational Programs, Wildlife Sanctuary, Woods, Swamps, Streams, Ponds, 5 mi. of marked trails **Hours:** Tues.-Sat.: 10 a.m.-4 p.m., Sun.: 1-4 p.m. **Fee: $1-$2 Directions:** *I-495 Long Island Expwy., take exit 44 S., Rte. 135 S. Seaford-Oyster Bay Expwy., take exit 1E. Merrick Rd. E., turn Left onto Washington Ave., the museum is on the Right* http://www.nassaucountyny.gov

NEW YORK CITY

American Museum of Natural History • *79ᵗʰ St. & Central Park W., NY, NY* • *212-769-5100* • **Features Include:** Human Origins, Hall of Minerals, Dioramas, Fossils, Dinosaurs, Hall of Planet Earth, Hall of Ocean Life, Many Special Exhibits **Hours:** 10 a.m.-5:45 p.m. **Fee:** Suggested Admission: Adults: $16, Kids 2-12: $9, Seniors: $12 **Directions:** *I-495 Long Island Expwy., to the Midtown Tunnel, turn Right onto 34ᵗʰ St., at the traffic circle turn Right onto 8ᵗʰ Ave., take the 3ʳᵈ exit onto Central Park W., the museum will be on the Left. By Train: Take the LIRR to Penn Station, take the B train (weekdays only) or C train to 81ˢᵗ St., 2 blocks West of the museum, the 1 train stops at Broadway & West 79ᵗʰ St.* www.amnh.org

CONNECTICUT

Dinosaur Park Ⓒ • *Dinosaur State Park* • *400 West St., Rocky Hill, CT* • *860-529-8423* •*FDPA: 860-257-7601* • **Features Include:** Largest Dinosaur Track Sites in North America, 55,000-sq.-ft. Exhibit Space, Exhibit Center-enclosed Tracks, Films & Videos, Track Talks, Narrated Slide Shows, Natural History Walks, Nature Trails, Display Gardens

& Arboretum, Track Casting Area, check the supply list on the web site & plan to cast a Dinosaur Track to take home **Hours:** May 1-Oct. 31: 9 a.m.-4:30 p.m., trails close at 4 p.m., Exhibit Center: Tues.-Sun.: 9 a.m.-4:30 p.m.,Year-Round **Fee:** Adults: $5, Kids 6-12: $2, Under 5: Free, Local Museums of Interest: Yale Peabody Museum of Natural History, Springfield Science Museum, Amherst College Museum of Natural History **Direction:** *I-495 Lond Island Expwy., take exit 31 Cross Island Pkwy. N., take exit 33 I-295 N. Throgs Neck Bridge, merge onto I-95 N., take Left exit 48 to merge onto I-91, take exit 23 Wall St., a few mi. S. of Hartford* www.dinosaurstatepark.org

NAUTICAL THEMES

American Merchant Marine Museum • *Steamboat Rd., Merchant Marine Academy, Kings Point, NY* • *516-773-5515* • Features Include: Merchant Marine & Nautical Artifacts, Art, Ship Models, Learning Center, USA's Seafaring Heritage, Ship's Wheel from the USS Constitution, Navigation Instrument Room, the Japanese Surrender Sword from WW II, National Maritime Hall of Fame, Century-Old Steam Engine, the Restored Nantucket, the Restored Emery Rice **Hours:** Tues- Fri.: 10 a.m.-3 p.m., Sat.-Sun.: 1 p.m.-4:30 p.m., Emery Rice Exhibit: Sat.: 1 p.m.-4:30 p.m. **Fee: Free** Directions: *I-495 Long Island Expwy., take exit 33 Community Dr., turn Right onto Community Dr., follow for 2.5 mi. (street name changes to E. Shore Rd. & later Hicks Ln.), turn Right onto Middle Neck Rd., turn Left onto Steamboat Rd., drive 1 mi. to the Academy's main gate* www.usmma.edu

Cold Spring Harbor Whaling Museum ⓥ • *279 Main St. (Rte. 25A), Cold Spring Harbor, NY* • *631-367-3418* • Features Include: 4-room Museum, Scavenger Hunt, Make Crafts & Puzzles, Memorabilia, 19th Century 30-ft. Whaleboat (1 of a dozen in the world), Harpoons, Scrimshaw, Diorama of the 1850s Whaling Port, Listen to the Song of the Humpback Whale, Hands-On Activity Center, Many Special Events such as: "Ship in a Bottle," "Ocean Discoveries: Sink or Float, Folk Singers & Storytellers **Hours:** 11 a.m.-5 p.m. daily, closed Mon. from Labor Day-Memorial Day **Fee: Free,** Suggested Donation: Adults: $5, Kids 5-18 & Seniors: $4, Families: $15, Military: Free **Directions:** *I-495 Long Island Expwy., take exit 44 N., I-135 N. toward Syosset, exit onto Jericho Tpke. toward Woodbury, turn Right onto Jericho Tpke. E., turn Left onto S. Wood Rd., turn Right onto Cold Spring Rd., turn Right onto 25A E., becomes Main St.* www.cshwhalingmuseum.org

East End Seaport Museum & Marine Foundation • *Third St. • P.O. Box 624 • Greenport, NY • 631-477-2100* • Features Include: Wind Exhibit, Hands-On Sailing Principles, Model Historic Local Sailboats, Photo Exhibit, Museum Tour, Board the "Mary E"-a 1906 Historic 75-ft. Sailing Schooner, Sail around Greenport Harbor, Long Island's Sail-Making Industry Exhibit, Special Events have included: Maritime Knitting, Soap & Ornament Making, 4 Essay-Based Scholarships to win a Summer Sailing Program, Lectures on Sailing **Hours:** Mid-May-June Weekends: 11 a.m.-5 p.m., July & Aug.: Mon., Wed, Thurs., & Fri.: 11 a.m.-5 p.m., Sat. & Sun.: 9:30 a.m.-5 p.m., Sept. Weekends: 11 a.m.-5 p.m., Blacksmith Hours: June-Sept.: Sat.-Sun.: 11 a.m.-5 p.m., closed Oct.-mid-May **Fee:** $2 **Directions:** *I-495 Long Island Expwy., take exit 73 Rte. 58 E. which becomes Rte. 25 E., approx. 25 mi. to Greenport*

www.eastendseaport.org

East Hampton Marine Museum • *301 Bluff Rd., Amagansett, NY* • *631-267-6544*

• **Features Include:** Sea Captains, Water Travel, Hands-On Children's Discovery Room, Whale Harpoons, Cannon, Marine-Themed Books, Puzzles, Wooden Boats, Photographs, Models, Displays, Maritime Life Exhibits, Farmer-Fisherman, Offshore Whaling, Photo Gallery: Lives of the Baymen, Commercial Fishing Methods & Aquaculture, Shipwreck Hall, Garden & Outdoor Exhibit Featuring: the Indian Field Gunning Shanty, a Jungle Gym Trawler, a Wooden Boat Collection including the Dominy Whaleboat, the Gil Smith Catboat, Great for Preschoolers through Teens **Hours:** Sat.: 10 a.m.-5 p.m., Sun.: Noon-5 p.m., Fri. & Mon.: 10 a.m.-5 p.m. (July & Aug.),**Fee:** Adults: $4, Students: $2, Seniors: $3, Members: Free **Directions:** *I-495 Long Island Expwy., take exit 68 S., William Floyd Pkwy. toward Shirley, turn Left onto 27 E. toward Montauk, 27 E. becomes Main St. & Pantigo Rd., turn Right onto Hand Ln., turn Right onto Bluff Rd., the museum will be on the Left* *www.easthamptonhistory.org*

Long Island Maritime Museum ⊗ • *86 West Ave., West Sayville, NY* • *631-447-8679* • **Features Include:** Outdoor Walking Museum, LI's Oyster Industry, Oyster Shucking House, Sail Boat Hulls, Seafaring Life in the 1800s, Gift Shop **Hours:** Mon.-Sat.: 10 a.m.-4 p.m., Sun.: 12-4 p.m. **Fee:** Adults: $4, Kids: $2 **Directions:** *Southern State Pkwy., to Heckscher State Pkwy. S., take exit 45 E. for State Hwy. 27A E., merge onto E. Main St./Rte. 27A, continue on S. Country Rd./County Rte. 85/Main St., turn Right at West Ave., continue to follow County Rte. 85/Main St., the museum will be on the Right* *www.limaritime.org*

NEW YORK CITY
Intrepid Sea, Air & Space Museum ⊗ • *Pier 86, NY, NY* • *212-843-8296* • Features

Include: Intrepid Aircraft Carrier, Period Aircrafts, Soldier Stories, Growler Nuclear Deterrent Submarine, Concorde Airliner (fastest commercial airliner ever built), Children's Interactive Zone, Flight Simulators-Thrill Ride, Guided Tours, Educational Demonstrations, Weekend Band Performances **Hours:** Oct. -Mar. 31, Tues.-Sun.: 10 a.m-5 p.m., April-Sept. 30, Mon.-Fri.: 10 a.m.-5 p.m., Sat.-Sun. & Holidays: 10 a.m.-6 p.m. **Fee:** Adults: $19.50, Kids 6-17: $14.50, Kids 2-5: $7.50, Members: Free **Directions:** *I-495 Long Island Expwy. W., through the Midtown Tunnel, exit tunnel to the Right, northbound, turn Left onto 42nd St. (westbound), turn Right on 12th Ave. (northbound) to 49th St., make a U-turn around barriers heading South to 46th St. & 12th Ave. By Train: LIRR to Penn Station, take the A, C, E, N, Q, R, S, W, 1, 2, or 3, train to 42nd St., then walk or take the M 42 bus West to Hudson River (12th Ave), walk North to Intrepid, enter through the Welcome Center* *www.intrepidmuseum.org*

PLANETARIUMS

The Suffolk County Vanderbilt Museum & Planetarium • *180 Little Neck Rd., Centerport, NY • 631-854-5555 • 631-854-5579* • Features Include: 43-acre Estate, Historical Artifacts, Planetarium Shows, Natural History Exhibits, Ethnographic Artifacts, Fine & Decorative Arts, Special Programs, Children's Workshops, Marine Museum Galleries, Dinosaur Exhibit, Egyptian Mummy, Mansion Tour, Diversity of Life, the Astronomical Society of Long Island holds its monthly observing session at the Vanderbilt Planetarium on the Wed. evening closest to the New Moon **Hours:** Museum: Mon. & Sat.: 11 a.m.-5 p.m., Tues. & Sun.: Noon-5p.m., Planetarium: Fri. Night: 8, 9, 10 p.m., Sat.: 11 a.m-10 p.m., Sun.: Noon-4p.m. on the Hr. **Fee:** Museum: Adults: $7, Kids Under 12: $3, Seniors: $6, Planetarium Shows & Observatory: Adults: $7, Kids: $3.50, Seniors: $6, Laser Shows: Adults: $10, Kids: $8, Seniors: $9 **Directions:** *I-495 Long Island Expwy., take exit 51, or Northern State Pkwy., take exit 42N., or Southern State Pkwy., take exit 39N. Deer Park Ave. N., turn Left onto Park Ave., turn Right onto Broadway, drive 4-5 mi. to Rte. 25A, cross 25A & turn Left at Centerport Automotive onto Little Neck Rd., the museum is 1.5 mi. on the Right*   *http://www.vanderbiltmuseum.org*

NEW JERSEY

The Newark Museum & Dreyfus Planetarium • *49 Washington St., Newark, NJ • 973-596-6550* • Features Include: New Jersey's Largest Museum, Mini Zoo, Planetarium, 80 Galleries of World-Class Collections, American, Asian, African, Classical, Victorian Ballantine House (a National Historic Landmark), Gallery Tours, Café, Shop **Hours:** Museum: Wed.-Fri.: Noon-5 p.m., Oct.-June: Sat.-Sun.: 10 a.m.-5 p.m., July-Sept.: Sat.-Sun.: Noon-5 p.m. **Fee:** Museum: Adults: $10, Kids & Seniors: $6, Planetarium Admission: Adults: $3, Kids & Seniors: $2 **Directions:** *New Jersey Tpke., take exit 15W. to I-280 W., take exit 15A toward Broad St., turn Left onto Broad St., stay to the Right, pass Central Ave., make the next Right onto New St., turn Right onto Washington St. (stay to the Left), pass Central Ave. & quickly turn Left into Museum parking lot*   *www.newarkmuseum.org*

PUBLIC SERVICE

The Brookhaven Volunteer Fireman's Museum • *25 Middle Country Rd., Ridge, NY • 631-924-8114* • Features Include: 1889 Fire House, 2 floors of Fire Memorabilia, 2-Truck Buildings House, 12 Fire Trucks, Photos, Equipment, Patches, Old Toys, Badges, Extinguishers, a 85-ft. Seagrave Ladder from 1956, a 1943 Brush Truck, a Class "C" Racing Rig, Gift Shop **Hours:** Tues. & Thurs.: 10 a.m.-3 p.m., Sat.: 10 a.m-4 p.m., Sun.: Noon-4 p.m., Nov. 1-May 1: Sat.: 10 a.m.-2 p.m. **Fee: Free**, donations appreciated **Directions:** *I-495 Long Island Expwy., take exit 68 N. Rte. 25/Middle Country Rd E., travel Rte. 25 for 1 mi. to Fireman's Memorial Park, the entrance is on the Left, .1 mi. on Firefighters Way, the museum is on the Right*   *www.angelfire.com*

Firefighter's Museum & Education Center • *Charles Lindbergh Blvd.* • *1 Davis Ave., Garden City, NY* • *516-572-4111* • Features Include: 5,000-sq.-ft. Museum within the Cradle of Aviation Museum, Learn Fire Safety, Live Demonstrations, Hands-On-Activities, Exhibits, History of the Nassau County Volunteer Fire Service, Photos, Vintage Fire Trucks, Historical & Modern Fire Equipment, Uniforms, Interactive Educational Facility, Fire Prevention Education **Hours:** Tues.-Sun.: 9:30 a.m.-5 p.m. **Fee:** Adults: $4, Kids: $3 **Directions:** *Northern State Pkwy., to the Meadowbrook Pkwy., take exit M4, follow signs to Museum Row which will put you on Charles Lindbergh Blvd., go to the 2nd traffic light & turn Right into the parking lot*   *www.cradleofaviation.org* • www.ncfiremuseum.org

Firemen's Museum • *Sage & Church St., Sag Harbor NY* • *631-725-0779* • Features Include: NYS's Oldest Volunteer Fire Department circa 1803, Early Forms of Communication, Speaking Trumpet, Alarm Bells, Trophies, Water Pumps, Potbelly Wood Stove, Photographs, Leather Fire Buckets, Hand-Pulled Hose Cart **Hours:** 11 a.m.-4 p.m., July 4th-Labor Day **Fee:** Adults: $1, Kids: .50¢, Under 10: **Free Directions:** *I-495 Long Island Expwy., take exit 68, William Floyd Pkwy. S. toward Shirley, merge onto Montauk Hwy. E., turn Left onto Bridgehampton Sag Harbor Tpke., continue on Main St., turn Right onto Washington St., take the 1st Right onto Church St., the museum is on the corner of Sage St. & Church St.*
www.sagharborfd.com/museum.htm

Nassau County Police Museum • *1490 Franklin Ave., Mineola, NY* • *516-573-7620* • *573-7400* • Features Include: Police History, Vintage Police Station Desk, Switch Board, Vintage Motorcycles, Traffic Safety Town, Crime Scene Unit, Motorcycle, Helicopter, Under Water Search & Rescue Team, Emergency Service Rescue Truck, Bomb Squad Truck, Bomb Retrieval Robot, Police Boat, Rollover Simulator, Vintage Police Cars, Police Helicopter, Uniforms, Weapons **Hours & Fee:** By Appointment Only **Directions:** *Northern State Pkwy., exit 31A towards Rte. 25, turn Right onto Glen Cove Rd., turn Left onto Jericho Tpke./Rte. 25, turn Left onto Mineola Blvd., continue on Franklin Ave.*   *www.policeny.com/ncpdm2005.html*

Verizon Telecom Pioneer Museum • *445 Commack Rd., Commack, NY* • *631-543-1371* • Features Include: History of the Telephone, Interactive Displays, Artifacts **Hours:** 1-4 p.m., the 1st Sun. of each month **Fee:** **Free Directions:** *Northern State Pkwy., take exit 43 N. toward Commack, turn Left onto Vanderbilt Motor Pkwy., turn Left at Commack Rd., the museum will be on the Left*

NEW YORK CITY

New York City Police Museum • *100 Old Slip* • *NY, NY* • *212-480-3100* • Features Include: Transportation Exhibits, Communication Room, Uniforms, Rotating Exhibits, Multimedia Exhibit, Jail Cell, Weapons, Notorious Criminals, 9/11 Exhibit, New

Technology/Intelligence Gathering, Community Outreach, Crime, Terrorism, Valor Medals, Hall of Heroes, Kids Test Sirens, Take "Mug Shots," Police Line-Up, Jail Cell, Forensic Science **Hours:** Mon-Sat.: 10 a.m.-5 p.m. **Fee:** Adults: $7, Kids 6-18 & Seniors: $5 **Directions:** *I-495 Long Island Expwy., exit onto I-278 toward Brooklyn, take exit 29 & merge onto Tillary St. toward the Manhattan Bridge, follow Brooklyn Bridge Blvd., take Pearl St./FDR Dr. exit, turn Right onto Pearl St., continue on Water St., turn Left onto Old Slip, the museum will be on the Right, By Train: LIRR to Penn Station, take the 2, 3 to Wall St., walk South on William St. for 3 blocks* *www.nycpolicemuseum.org*

New York City Fire Museum • *278 Spring St. (SOHO), NY, NY • 212-691-1303 •*

Features Include: Fire Engines, Firefighter Suits, Equipment, Paintings, Photographs, Staffed By Off-Duty Firefighters **Hours:** Tues.-Sun.: 10 a.m.-4 p.m. **Fee:** Adults: $4, Kids Under 12: $1, Seniors/Students: $2 **Directions:** Take *LIRR to penn Station, take the 1 to Houston St., or C, E to Spring St., located in an old firehouse that was converted into a museum* *www.nycfiremuseum.org*

SCIENCE THEME MUSEUMS

Cold Spring Harbor Laboratory • *1 Bungtown Rd., Cold Spring Harbor, NY • 516-367-6895 • 367-8800 •* **Features Include:** Founded in 1890, Research Programs include: Cancer, Neuroscience, Plant Genetics, Genomics, Bioinformatics, Scheduled Outdoor Community Tours, Historic Architecture, the Nobel Legacy, the tour requires a lot of stair-climbing & steep hills, & it is not recommended for people who have difficulty walking **Hours:** vary, open Spring, Summer & Fall **Fee:** $5 per person, Reservations Required **Directions:** *I-495 Long Island Expwy., take exit 41N. toward Rte. 107/106, bear Right to stay on Rte. 106, drive approx. 4 mi. North, turn Right onto Rte. 25A E. for 4 mi., look for the Bungtown Rd. sign before the entrance, turn Left at the traffic light, look for the lighted CSHL sign* *www.cshl.edu*

Dolan DNA Learning Center • *334 Main St., Cold Spring Harbor, NY • 516-367-5170 • 516-367-8398 •* This center is an educational arm of the Cold Spring Harbor Laboratory & the world's 1st science center dedicated to DNA science. **Features Include**: Exhibit Hall, Hands-On Exhibits, Displays, Genome & Shared Ancestry, Summer Biotechnology Workshops: "The Genes We Share," the "Saturday DNA," Science Activities Program (by reservation), Multimedia Presentation: "Long Island Discovery" Check the web site for a complete schedule **Hours:** Mon.-Fri.: 10 a.m.-4 p.m., Sat.: Noon-4 p.m., Long Island Discovery: Mon.-Fri.: 10 a.m., 11 a.m. & 1 p.m., Sat.: 1-3 p.m. **Fee: Free Directions:** *I-495 Long Island Expwy., take exit 44, 135 N. toward Syosset, turn Right onto Jericho Tpke., turn Left at S. Woods Rd., turn Right onto Cold Spring Rd., turn Right onto 25A E., becomes Main St. in Cold Spring Harbor, the center will be on the Right* *www.dnalc.org • www.vector.cshl.org*

The Long Island Science Center ⑤ • *11 W. Main St., Riverhead, NY • 631-208-8000 •*

Features Include: Hands-On Educational Center, Interactive Exhibits, Science, Technology,

Engineering, Math, In-House & Outreach Programs, many Special Science-Themed Events, Scout Programs, Teacher Training, Family Science, Camp Programs, Science Birthday Parties **Hours:** Sun.: 11 a.m.-4 p.m. **Fee:** Adults: **$2**, Kids: **$5 Directions:** *I-495 Long Island Expwy. E., take exit 72 for 25 E., follow signs to Riverhead, pass the Suffolk County Historical Society on your Left, at the 3rd traffic light turn Right (Chase Bank), then make an immediate Right into the bank parking lot, slight Left passing the drive-thru, turn Right into the parking lot, follow around, turn Right into the parking lot adjacent to the museum, entrance faces the parking lot* www.lisciencecenter.org

Science Museum of Long Island • *1526 North Plandome Rd., Manhasset, NY • 516-627-9400* • **Features Include:** Teaching Museum, Science Activity Center, Hands-On Workshops, Electricity, Volcanoes, Summer Camp, Family Events: Family Experiments, Crafts, Demonstrations, Classroom Setting Only, Must Pre-Register **Hours & Fees:** vary **Directions:** *I-495 Long Island Expwy, take exit 36, turn Right onto Searingtown Rd., becomes Port Washington Blvd., turn Left onto Stonytown Rd., turn Right onto Plandome Rd., the museum will be on the Right, located on the Leeds Pond Preserve* http://www.smli.org/

BNL Science Museum • *Brookhaven National Laboratory • William Floyd Pkwy., Upton, NY • Public Affairs Office: 631-344-2345 • 631-344-4495* • The Laboratory staffs 3,000 scientists, engineers, technicians & over 4,000 guest researchers annually. There are special days the museum is open to the public, such as Summer Sundays. You must bring a photo ID to attend. **Features Include:** 3-story Decommissioned Nuclear Reactor, Participatory Exhibits, Audio-Visual Presentations, Historic Collections, Shake Hands with a Skeleton, Whisper Around a Corner, Interactive Exhibits, Science Learning Center Programs for grades K-8 **Hours:** Weekdays by Appointment, Science Sundays: July-Aug. 10-3 p.m., Weekly Learning Center, the Weather Center is a favorite **Fee: Free Directions:** *I-495 Long Island Expwy., take exit 68 William Floyd Pkwy. N., drive approx. 1.25 mi. to BNL's gate on Right at 2nd light* http://www.bnl.gov/education/ • www.bnl.gov/slc

NEW YORK CITY
NY Hall of Science • *47-01 111th St., Queens, NY • 718-699-0005* • **Features Include:** Hands-On Science & Technology Center, 450 Hands-On Exhibits, Explore Biology, Chemistry, Physics, Preschool Place, Science Programs, Crafts, Shows, Magnificent Outdoor Playground on the Roof **Hours:** Sept.-June, Tues.-Thurs.: 9:30 a.m.-2 p.m., Fri.: 9:30-5 p.m., Sat. & Sun.: 10 a.m.-6 p.m., **Free** hours on Fridays: 9:30 a.m.-2 p.m. & Sun.: 10 a.m.-11 a.m. **Fee:** Adults: $11 Kids 2-17: $8, Under 2: Free, Students & Seniors: $8, Rocket Park Mini Golf: $6, Kids: $5, Parking: $10, Members: Free **Directions:** *I-495 Long Island Expwy., take exit 22A Grand Central Pkwy. toward 108th St., take the Horace Harding Expwy. N., keep Right at the fork, follow signs for 108th St. & merge onto Horace Harding Expwy. N., turn Right onto 108th St., turn Right onto 47th Ave., turn onto 111th St.*

www.nyscience.orgwww.nyhallsci.org

MUSEUM FUN

TRANSPORTATION & RAILROAD THEMES

The Long Island Steamers ⑨ • *Southaven County Park* • *175 Gerrard Rd.,*
Brookhaven, NY • *631-345-0499* • Features Include: Miniature Trains Big Enough to
Ride, Ride through the Woods, Steam, Diesel, Electric, Powered by Coal, Oil or Wood,
Stationary & Railroad Related Steam Engines **Hours:** "Run Days"-the 2nd & last Sun. of
the month, May-Oct. 10:30 a.m.-3 p.m. **Fee: Free**, donations appreciated **Directions:**
I-495 Long Island Expwy., take exit 68 S., William Floyd Pkwy. S. (Rte. 46), turn Right on Victory Ave.,
drive 1 mi., make a Right onto Gerrard Rd. N. for about .5 mi., see the Long Island Live Steamers sign
on your Right, make a Left onto the dirt road, park in the parking lot on the Right
www.longislandlivesteamers.org • *http://www.trainweb.org/lils*

The Long Island Museum • *Member of the Smithsonian Institute* • *1208 Rte. 25A,*
Stony Brook, NY • *631-751-0066* • Features Include: 9-acre Complex, Carriage
Museum, American Art Museum, History Museum, Family & School Programs **Hours:**
Fri.-Sat.: 10 a.m.-5 p.m., Sun.: Noon-5 p.m. **Fee:** Adults: $9, Kids 5-17: $4, Seniors: $7, Under
6: Free **Directions:** *I-495 Long Island Expwy., take exit 62 N. Nicolls Rd. to its end, turn Left*
onto Rte. 25A, turn Left onto Main St. *www.longislandmuseum.org*

Oyster Bay Railroad Museum • *102 Audrey Ave., Oyster Bay NY* • *516-558-7036* •
Features Include: Long Island's Railroad History, Model Railroad Layouts, Railroad Life,
Work Life, Passenger Experiences, Historic Railroad Buildings, Rolling Stock, Interactive
Hands-On Exhibits, Audio-Visual Exhibits, Changing Exhibits, View Plans For the
Completion of New Museum, Gift Shop **Hours:** Sat.: Noon-4 p.m. **Fee: Free** Directions:
Northern State Pkwy., take exit 35N. 106/107 toward Oyster Bay, remain on 106N., turn Left
onto Audrey Ave. *www.oysterbayrailroadmuseum.org/home.html*

The Railroad Museum of Long Island • *440 4ᵗʰ St., Greenport, NY* • *631-477-0439* •
Features Include: Guided Tour of the Riverhead & Greenport Sites, Handicap Accessible
Hours: vary seasonally **Fee:** Adults: $5, Kids 5-12: $3, Under 5: Free, admission tickets
are good for both the Riverhead & Greenport sites **Directions:** *I-495 Long Island Expwy.,*
take exit 73, Old Country Rd./Rte. 58 E., drive to the intersection with Rte. 25, take Rte. 25 E./
Main Rd., follow Rte. 25 E. to the Village of Greenport, approx. 23 mi. E. of the end of I-495,
Main Rd. becomes Front St. in Greenport, turn Right onto 4ᵗʰ St. & drive 2 blocks to the railroad
tracks, the museum will be on the Left, adjacent to the LIRR Station

The Railroad Museum of Long Island • *416 Griffing Ave., Riverhead, NY* • Features
Include: Ride World's Fair Miniature Train on a 670-ft. Long Track (Spring, Summer & Fall),
Small Train Displays, 1ˢᵗ Aluminum Double Decker Passenger Car), Baggage Car, 7737 Class
BM-62 Combination Baggage & Mail Car, Bay Window Caboose Number C-68, Inside View
of Working Conditions for Freight Train Crews, Brooklyn Eastern District Terminal No.16,

the Last Steam Engine Operating in NYC, 1928 Class B-62 Baggage, Crossing Shanty Protect Gatemen, Gatemen Operated the Crossing Gates, Engine 39 G-5s Locomotives, Narrow Gauge H.K. Porter Steam Locomotive, RS-3 Number 1556, 85-ft. Turntable, Handicap Accessible **Directions:** *I-495 Long Island Expwy., take exit 72, Rte. 25 E. Main St., follow Rte. 25 approx. 3 mi., turn Left onto Griffing Ave., drive 2 blocks, the museum is on the Right just over the railroad tracks*   *www.rmli.us/Welcome.html*

NEW YORK CITY

New York Transit Museum ⑤ • **Brooklyn Heights, NY • 718-694-3451 • 718-694-1600 •**
Features Include: Housed in a Historic 1936 IND Subway Station, Urban Public Transportation History, New York City's 100 yr-old Subway System, Trolleys & Buses, Subway Cars, Interactive Exhibitions, Educational Tours & Programs, Workshops, Special Events & Exhibitions **Hours:** Tues.-Fri.: 10 a.m.-4 p.m., Sat. & Sun.: Noon-5 p.m., Closed Mon. **Fee:** Adults: $5, Kids 3-17 & Seniors: $3, Wed.: Free for seniors, Members: Free **Directions:** *Take the LIRR to Penn Station, take the 2,3,4,5 train to Borough Hall, or take the A,C to Hoyt-Schermerhorn St., or take the A,C to Jay St./Borough Hall, the museum is an underground subway station & its entrance is at the corner of Boerum Pl. & Schermerhorn St.*   *www.mta.info/mta/museum*

SUGGESTIONS • COMMENTS • ERRORS

Linda.ReidBryce
@verizon.net

Thanks

6 **IN THIS SECTION**

TODDLER SPOTS

Let
Fun Flow
Like A
River

PLAY PLACES

RUNNING, LAUGHTER & PURE ADRENALINE

Active Kidz • *Long Island, 210 Forest Dr., East Hills, NY* • *516-621-6600* • **Features Include:** 8400-sq.-ft. Indoor Play Area, Open Play, Trained Coaches, Sports Equipment, Rock Climbing Room, 3 Rock Walls, Lazer Tag, Traverse & Belay Rock Climbing, Toddler Area, Soft Play Equipment, 3-level Maze with Tunnels, Slides, Web Climbs & Obstacles, Classes & Activities, Birthday Parties **Hours:** 7 days a week **Fee:** Toddler Area: $4, Adventure Maze: $10, Rock Climbing: $15, 1-12 yrs. **Directions:** *Long Island Expwy. to exit 37 Willis/ Mineola Ave., turn Left at the traffic light onto Mineola Ave., travel 1.5 mi. & turn Right onto Northern Blvd. Proceed .5 mi. over viaduct, turn Right onto Forest Dr. & bear Left around the bend to Active Kidz Long Island*   *www.Activekidzlongisland.com*

Broadway Mall ☻ • *Rte. 106/107, Hicksville, NY* • *516-939-0679* • **Features Include:** Soft Play Place, Food Court, Movie Theatre, Tues. is Balloon Day, all kids get a balloon, & the 1st movie of the day is $5 **Fee: Free** play area **Directions:** *I-495 Long Island Expwy., exit 106/107 S., park in the back & use the movie theatre enterance, take the elevator up 1 flight, the play place is at the far end of the food court*   *www.broadwaymall.com*

Bouncers & Slydos • *1835 New Hwy., Farmingdale, NY* • *631 752-2324* • **Features Include:** 11,000-sq.-ft. Indoor Inflatables Playground, Open Play for Kids Under 6, Birthday Parties, Fri. & Sat. Night Camp (includes free play, pizza & a movie), Toddler Time, "Airbots" Inflatable Wrestling Suits **Hours:** Open Play: Mon.-Fri.: 10 a.m.-Noon, Noon-2 p.m. **Fee:** Kids: $12, Parents: **Free Directions:** *Long Island Expwy., take exit exit 49S. Rte. 110, drive 2 mi., turn Left ontp Ruland Rd. (Costco on Corner), 1st Light, turn Right onto Republic which will turn into New Hwy., .5 mi. on Left*   *www.bouncersandslydos.com*

TODDLER SPOTS

Burger King Play Place • Hours: vary per location Fee: *Free*
5141 Sunrise Hwy., Bohemia, NY • 631-567-7495
1131 Wantagh Ave., Wantagh, NY • 516-679-9191
6021 East Jericho Tpke., Commack, NY • 631-499-2052
334 North Broadway, Jericho • 516-822-6486
501 Old Country Rd., Plainview • 516-935-1455
22210 Northern Blvd., Flushing, NY • 718-225-1695
242-02 61ˢᵗ Ave., Douglaston, NY • 718-819-2133

The Children's Safari • *6 Rockaway Ave., Valley Stream, NY • 516-872-2600 •* Features Include: Indoor Play Area, Slides, Mazes, Tunnels, Rock-Climbing Walls, Sand-Pit, Separate "Soft Playground" for toddlers, Animal Theme Classes, Special Events Include: Puppet Shows, Clowns, Concerts, Live Animals, Magic Shows, Kids Bingo **Hours:** Open Play: Mon.-Thurs.:10 a.m.-6 p.m., Fri.: 10 a.m.-4 p.m. **Fee:** $11 **Directions:** *Southern State Pkwy., take exit 15S. Corona Ave. S., turn Right onto N. Corona Ave., slight Left toward Rockaway Pkwy., then slight Right to stay on Rockaway Pkwy.* *www.azchildrenssafari.com*

Chuck E Cheese's • Mornings are fairly empty & a great time to go because it's easy to keep track of children & there is plenty to do. Buy $10 worth of coins & receive double the amount. Save some for next time! **Hours & Fee:** vary per location   *www.chuckecheese.com*
2115 Jericho Tpke., Commack, NY, 631-864-5434
3416 48ᵗʰ St., Long Island City, NY
4818 Northern Blvd., Long Island City, NY
11 Hanover Pl. # 15, Hicksville, NY, 516-433-3343
155 Sunrise Hwy., West Islip, NY, 631-376-1800
162 Fulton Ave., Hempstead, NY, 516-483-3166
121 Sunrise Hwy., Patchogue, NY, 631-654-9373

Fun Craft • Features Include: Open Studio Hours, Plaster Craft Painting, Create Your Own CD, Stuff-a-Pet **Hours & Fee:** vary per location   *www.funcraftparties.net*
800 Northern Blvd., Great Neck, NY • 516-487-0255
497 N. Broadway, Jericho, NY, 516-933-1785,
1740 E. Jericho Tpke., Huntington, NY, 631-462-0576
6333 Jericho Tpke., Commack, NY 631-493-0620,
1234 Merrick Rd., Copiague, NY, 631-789-2733, 516-933-1785

Fun Fridays • *Cold Spring Harbor Fish Hatchery & Aquarium • 1660 Rte. 25A, Cold Spring Harbor, NY • 516-692-6768 •* Features Include: Celebrate the Creature of the Month, Crafts, Games, Snacks **Hours:** 10 a.m.-5 p.m. **Fee:** *Free* **Directions:** *I-495 Long Island Expwy., take exit 44N. onto Rte. 135 toward Syosset, take the exit for Jericho Tpke. E. toward Woodbury, turn Left onto S. Woods Rd., turn Right onto Cold Spring Rd., turn Right onto 25A E., the Hatchery will be on the Right* *www.cshfha.org*

Fun Station USA • *40 Rocklyn Ave., Lynbrook, NY* • *516-599-7757* • Features Include:
Video Games, Lazer Tag, Bumper Cars, Carousel, Multi-Level Play Maze, Safari Jeeps, Full Restaurant, Birthday Parties **Hours:** Thurs.-Sun.: 11 a.m-8 p.m. **Fee:** Bracelet: $11.95 **Directions:** *Southern State Pkwy., take exit 175 for Hempstead Ave. S. toward Malverne, merge onto Hempstead Ave., continue on Ocean Ave., turn Right on Merrick Rd., turn Left toward Rocklyn Ave., turn Right at Rocklyn Ave.*   *www.funstationfun.com*

Fun-4-All • *200 Wilson St., Port Jefferson, NY* • *631-331-9000* • Features Include:
Slides, Towers, Treehouse Play, Tunnels, Preschool Play Areas, Inflatable Bouncers, Indoor Moon Room, Carousel Café, Uniquely Decorated Environment, Half-Acre Indoor, Air-Conditioned, Kids Ages 1-15 **Hours:** 10 a.m.-8 p.m. **Fee:** Kids: $13, no time limit **Directions:** *I-495 Long Island Expwy., take exit 64 N./Rte. 112 N., to the railroad tracks in Port Jefferson Station, turn Left onto Wilson St., 1 block before the railroad tracks to Fun-4-All*   *www.fun4all-ny.com*

Giggles & Grins • *926 Hempstead Tpke., Franklin Square, NY* • *516-354-5800*
• **Features Include:** 2-level Jungle Gym Area, Toddler Matted Area, Open Play Hours, Mommy & Me Classes, Separation Classes, Craft Classes & "Date Night" Drop-Off Events **Hours:** Open Play: Wed.: 10 a.m.-2 p.m. **Fee:** Kids: $6, includes a snack **Directions:** *I-495 Long Island Expwy., take exit 40 W. toward Mineola, turn Left on Denton Ave. S., Denton Ave. becomes Tanners Pond Rd., Tanners Pond Rd. becomes Edgemere Rd., Edgemere Rd. becomes Plain Ct., turn Right on Court House Rd., turn slight Left on New Hyde Park Rd., turn Left on Hempstead Tpke./NY-24*   *www.gigglesandgrinz.com*

Synergy Kidfit USA • *38 Motor Ave., Farmingdale, NY* • *516-777-4374* • Features
Include: Balls, Rings, Play Fitness Games, Kids Ages 6-10 **Hours:** Mon.-Sun: 8 a.m.-Noon, Mon.-Thurs.: 5-9 p.m. **Fees:** Kids: $10 **Directions:** *I-495 Long Island Expwy., take exit 44 S., merge onto Rte. 135 S. toward Seaford, take exit 7E. & merge onto Hempstead Tpke., Rte. 24E. toward Farmingdale, slight Right at Fulton St. onto Rte. 109 E., turn Right on Main St., turn Right on Motor Ave.*   *www.synergyfitclubs.com*

Kangaroo Kids • *1015 Grand Blvd., Deer Park, NY* • *631-871-8762* • Features
Include: Open Play Sessions, Inflatable Party Center **Hours:** Open Play varies, call for possibilities **Fee:** Kids: 1 hr.: $5, 2 hr.: $10 sessions **Directions:** *Northern State Pkwy., take the Sagtikos Pkwy., take exit S3 Pine Aire Dr. toward Deer Park, turn Left onto Pine Aire Dr., continue .6 mi., see the train station, turn Left onto Corbin Ave. & continue .6 mi., turn Right onto Grand Blvd. just past Saf-T-Swim, turn Right onto E. Industry, turn Right into fenced parking area, enter through the Saf-T-Swim breezeway & door*
Facebook: Kangaroo Kids Inflatable Party Center

TODDLER SPOTS

Little Chefs, Ltd. • *33 Jackson Ave., Syosset, NY* • *516-496-0754* • *9 Soundview Market Pl., Port Washington, NY* • *516-767-7633* • Features Include: Cooking Classes, Mommy & Me, Fairytales & Mother Goose, Cooking with Colors, Shapes & Numbers, Cooking & Story-Time, Holiday Classes, Playdates, Scouts Programs, For Ages 2-15, Cooking Birthday Parties **Hours & Fees:** vary **Syosset Directions:** *I-495 Long Island Expwy., take exit 43 N., South Oyster Bay Rd., cross over Jericho Tpke., continue on Jackson Ave., go over railroad tracks, make an immediate Right into train station parking lot, Little Chefs is on the Left* **Port Washington Directions:** *I-495 Long Island Expwy., take exit 36 N. Searingtown Rd./Port Washington Blvd., cross over 25A, turn Left onto Main St., turn Right onto Shore Rd., turn Right into the 2nd shopping center*   *www.littlechefs.com*

Long Island Children's Museum ⊗ • *11 Davis Ave., Garden City, NY* • *516-224-5800* • Features Include: Bubbles, It's Alive, Bricks & Sticks, Climb-It, Music Experience, Pattern Studio, Sandy Island, Tool Box, Tot Spot, Communication Station, Special Events, Monthly Themes **Hours:** 10 a.m.-5 p.m., Closed: Mon. **Fee:** Adults: $9, Under 1 & Members: Free **Directions:** *Northern State Pkwy., take the Meadowbrook Pkwy. S., take exit M4 (Nassau Coliseum), bear Right onto Charles Lindbergh Blvd., go to the 1st traffic light (Nassau Coliseum on your left, Nassau Community College on your Right), proceed through this traffic light & continue on to LICM on the Right side of the road*   *www.licm.org*

McDonald's Play Place • Features & Hours: very per location Fee: **Free**
575 Franklin Ave., Franklin Square, NY • *516-354-4420*
879 Broadway Mall, Rte. 106-107, Hicksville NY • *516-827-1499*
1560 Broadway, NY, NY • *646-823-9961* • The McDonald's next to Times Square is considered 1 of the top themed McD's in the world.
26 Bowery, NY, NY • *212-406-0426* • This McDonald's has very nice chinese decor.
8003 Queens Blvd., Flushing, NY • *718-478-1204*

NY Party Zone • *1270 Broad Hollow Rd., Farmingdale, NY* • *516-694-0079* • *888-538-7586* • Features Include: Open Play, Inflatable Rides & Slides, Interactive Obstacle Course, Crazy Cow Soft Mechanical Bull Ride, 28-ft. Inflatable Volcano, Planned Parties **Hours:** Open Play Times Fri.: 11 a.m-2 p.m., Fri. night: 5:30-8:30 p.m., Sat.: 8 p.m.-11 p.m. **Fee:** Open Play: $10, Fri. & Sat. night: $15 **Directions:** *Northern State Pkwy., take exit 40 S. Rte. 110, the NY Party Zone will be on the Right*   *www.nypartyzone.com*

Once Upon A Tree Top • *151 Dupont St., Plainview, NY* • *516-349-1140* • Features Include: 8200-sq.-ft. Facility, Interactive City, Climbing Gym, Classes, Parties **Hours:** Open Play: Mon.: 10 a.m.-2 p.m., Tues.: 10 a.m.-5 p.m., Wed.: 10 a.m.-5 p.m., Thurs.: 10 a.m.-2 p.m., Fri.: 10 a.m.-2 p.m. **Fee:** Walker: $12, Crawler: $6, feel free to pack a lunch & stay awhile, Snacks & beverages are also available for purchase **Directions:** *Northern*

State Pkwy., take exit 38 Sunnyside Blvd. toward Plainview, turn Left onto Sunnyside Blvd., turn Left onto Fairchild Ave., turn Left onto Dupont St.   *www.onceuponatreetop.com*

WoodKingdom ⊕

111 Milbar Blvd., Farmingdale, NY • 631-845-3804 •
544 Middle Country Rd., Coram, NY • 631-698-0212 •
3060 Rte. 112, Medford, NY • 631-451-2200 •

Features Include: Open Play Sessions, Inflatables, Climbing, complimentary lemonade, cookies & coffee **Hours:** Mon.-Fri.: 10 a.m.-2 p.m. **Fee:** Open Play: $8 **Farmingdale Directions:** *I-495 Long Island Expwy., take exit 49S. toward Rte. 110 S./ Amityville, stay straight to go onto S. Service Rd., turn Right onto Broad Hollow Rd./ NY 110 S., turn Left onto Milbar Blvd.* **Coram Directions:** *Northern State Pkwy., take exit 42 toward Hauppauge, becomes Rte. 347 E., turn Right onto Middle Country Rd./ NY-25/ E. Jericho Tpke. continue to follow Middle Country Rd./ NY-25* **Medford Directions:** *I-495 Long Island Expwy., take Rte.112 to exit 64 toward Port Jefferson/ Patchogue, turn Left onto Express Dr. S./ Expwy. Dr. S., turn Left onto 112/ Medford Rd., continue to follow NY-112*   *www.woodkingdom.com*

Suggestions • Comments • Errors

Linda.ReidBryce
@verizon.net

Thanks

ZOOS & ANIMALS

GRACEFUL BIRDS, A CAMEL & A GNU

Encourage children to observe + draw the wildlife.

NASSAU COUNTY

Old Bethpage Village Restoration 🐾 • **NC** • *1303 Round Swamp Rd., Bethpage, NY • 516-572-8400* • **Features Include:** 209-acre Park, Living History Museum, mid-19th Century Long Island Village, Homes, Farms, Businesses, Educational Programs, Old-Time Baseball Games, the Noon Inn serves Pretzels & Root Beer, Powell Farm, Chickens, Cows, Sheep, Oxen, Pigs, Food CO-OP **Hours:** Mar.-Nov., Tues.-Sun.: 10 a.m.-5 p.m. **Fee:** Adults: $4, Kids: $3, Seniors: $2 **Directions:** *I-495 Long Island Expwy., take exit 48 Round Swamp Rd. toward Old Bethpage/Farmingdale, make a Left onto Round Swamp Rd., turn Left Old Country Rd., slight Right at Round Swamp Rd.*

www.nassaucountyny.gov/agencies/Parks

SUFFOLK COUNTY

Animal Farm Petting Zoo 🐾 • *Wading River Rd., Manorville, NY • 631-878-1785* • **Features Include:** Pony Rides, Turtle Train Ride, "Super Cow Musical Puppet Show," Creatures Encounter Show, Safari Train Tour, Nature Shop, Picnic Area, See, Feed & Pet the Animals, Large Selection of Rare & Unusual Poultry, Monkeys, Llamas, Reptiles & Other Exotic Animals **Hours:** Mon.-Fri.: 10 a.m.-5 p.m., Sat.-Sun.: 10 a.m.-6 p.m. **Fee:** Adult: $13.50, Kids: $11.50 **Directions:** *Long Island Expwy., take exit 69 Wading River Rd. S., drive 2.5 mi., the park will be on the Right* *www.afpz.org*

Benner's Farm • *56 Gnarled Hollow Rd., Setauket, NY • 631-689-8172, 631-689-8172* • **Features Include:** Farm circa 1700, Farm Animals, Nature Trails, Special Events, Public Workshops, Gardens, Fields, Woods, Farm Life Stories, Tractors, Tools,

Vegetables, Herbs, Sheep Sheering, Egg Collecting, 300-yr.-old Oak Tree Swing, Wagon Rides **Hours:** Sat.-Sun.: Noon- 4 p.m. **Fee:** Adults: $6, Kids: $5 **Directions:** *I-495 Long Island Expwy., take exit 62 Nicoll's Rd. N., follow Nicoll's Rd. to the end (cross Rte. 25, Rte. 347 & Stony Brook Univ.), turn Right on Rte. 25A E., at the 5th light turn Right onto Old Town Rd., drive 2.5 blocks to the end, turn Right onto Gnarled Hollow Rd., farm is on the Right, use the 3rd driveway for parking, if there is no parking in lot, park along the street* www.bennersfarm.com

Cold Spring Harbor Fish Hatchery & Aquarium • *1660 Rte. 25A, Cold Spring Harbor, NY* • *516-692-6768* • **Features Include:** Circa 1883, Environmental Education Center, Demonstrations, Fish Hatchery, NY State's Largest Collection of Native Freshwater Fish, Reptiles, Amphibians, Katch & Keep Trout Fishing (poles & bait provided), Feed the Newly Hatched Trout, Turtles **Hours:** Mon.-Sun.: 10 a.m.-5 p.m., Katch & Keep: Fri.-Tues.: 10 a.m.-Noon & 1-3 p.m. **Fee:** Adults: $6, Kids 3-12 & Seniors: $4, Under 2: Free **Fishing Fee:** $5, trout caught is $4 per lb., donation appreciated **Directions:** *Northern State Pkwy., take exit 35 N. Rte. 106/107, OR the I-495 Long Island Expwy., take exit 41 N. Rte. 106/107, drive 1 mi. & take Right fork for Rte. 106 N., drive 3 mi., turn Right onto Rte. 25A E., the Hatchery is 4 mi. on the Right* www.cshfha.org

ECSS Sweetbriar Nature Center Ⓥ • *62 Eckernkamp Dr., Smithtown, NY* • *631-979-6344* • **Volunteers Needed: 631-979-6344** • Through education & examples, ECSS encourages responsible decision making, appreciation & respect for the unique wildlife & ecosystems found on Long Island. **Features Include:** 54-acre Farm, Butterfly & Moth Vivarium, Vulture, Falcon, Bald Eagle, Cockatoo, Canaries, Snakes, Chinchilla, Porcupine, Rabbit, Sweetbriar Nature Center's Rainforest Room, Hike, Picnic Tables, 1920s Farm House, Wetland Habitats, Nissequogue River, Camp & Scout Programs, Birthday Party, Adopt an Animal, Natural Science Education Services, Native Wildlife Rehabilitation Services **Hours:** 10 a.m.-4 p.m., June-Sept. **Fee:** Adults: $3, Kids Under 12 & Seniors: $2 **Directions:** *Northern State Pkwy., Sagtikos Pkwy., Jericho Tpke./25E., pass Caleb State Park, the Smithtown Bull, turn Left onto Edgewood St. (Dunkin Donuts on corner), turn Left onto Landing Ave., cross the river, take the first Left onto Eckernkamp Dr.* www.sweetbriarnc.org

Hallockville Museum Farm • *6038 Sound Ave., Riverhead, NY* • *631-298-5292* • **Features Include:** 28-acre Farm Preserve, 18 Historic Houses, Barns & Outbuildings, Museum/Gardens & Collections Tours, Fields, Gas Station, Cows, Sheep, Chickens, Educational Resource of Eastern Long Island's Agricultural Heritage, Tours, Summer Camp, Children's Educational Programs **Hours:** Sat.-Sun.: 10 a.m.-4 p.m. **Fee:** Adults: $7, Kids 6-12 & Seniors: $5, Under 5: Free **Directions:** *I-495 Long Island Expwy., take*

exit 73 Old Country Rd. toward Orient/Greenport, turn Left onto County Rte. 58/Old Country Rd., turn Left onto Rte. 43/Northville Tpke., turn Right onto Sound Ave.

www.hallockville.com

Holtsville Ecology Site & Animal Preserve, Park & Zoo ⓨ • *Buckley Rd., Holtsville, NY • 631-758-9664* • Features Include: Goats, Sheep, Lions, Bobcats, Bald Eagles, Deer & Petting Zoo. The preserve rescues non-releasable handicapped wild domestic animals. The Brookhaven Wildlife Center donates veterinary care, food & habitats for each animal. **Hours:** Mon.-Sun: 9 a.m.-4 p.m., Year-Round **Fee: Free Directions:** *I-495 Long Island Expwy., take exit 63 S., at the 4th light turn Right onto Woodside Ave., go to the Buckly Rd. exit, make a Right at the stop sign just down the block*   *www.brookhaven.org/things_to_do/ecology.asp*

Long Island Game Farm Ride Park • *638 Chapman Blvd., Manorville, NY • 631-878-6644* • Features Include: A Complete Zoo, Petting Zoo, Wild Bengal Tiger Shows, Bambiland, Spinning Teacup Ride, Antique Carousel, Pony Rides, "Please Touch" motto, Long Island's Largest Zoo & Encounter Park, "Pettable" animals include: Ducks, Rabbits, Ponies & Turtles **Hours:** Mon.-Fri.: 10 a.m.-5 p.m., Sat.-Sun.: 10 a.m.-6 p.m. **Fee:** Off-season (April 23-May 26, Sept. 6-Oct. 9): Adults: $13.95, Kids 3-11: $11.95, Handicapped: $9.95, Seniors: $11.95, Memorial Day-Labor Day: Adults: $16.95, Kids: $14.95, Handicapped: $9.95, Seniors: $14.95 **Directions:** *I-495 Long Island Expwy., take exit 70 Suffolk County Rd. 111 S. /Manorville, if heading eastbound on Expwy., make a Right after you exit hwy., if heading westbound, make a left after exiting, go approx. .5 mi. to traffic light, make a Right onto Chapman Blvd., the farm is approx. 1.5 mi. on the Left*

www.longislandgamefarm.com

Suffolk County Farm & Education Center • *360 Yaphank Ave # 2C, Yaphank, NY • 631-852-4600 • 631-852-5300, 4612* • This is a working production farm. **Features Include:** 300-acre Farm, Public Workshops, Demonstrations, Festivals, Animal Petting & Feeding, Sheep, Goats, Pigs, Beef Cattle **Hours:** Mon.-Sun.: 9 a.m.-3 p.m., Year-Round, some animals are not accessible during winter **Fee: Free**, except for special events **Directions:** *I-495 Long Island Expwy., take exit 67 S. Yapank Ave., farm entrance is on the Right*

White Post Farm • *250 Old Country Rd., Melville, NY• 631-351-9373* • Features Include: Animal Farm, Petting Zoo, Winter Indoor Animal Farm, Outdoor Animals, Goats, Lambs, Pigs, Deer, Alpacas, American Buffalo, Tibetan Yak, Oryx Antelope, Ring-Tailed Lemurs, Southern Madagascar, Ostriches, Grevy Zebras, Nilgai Antelopes, Aoudads, Japanese Koi Pond, Singing Chicken Show, Pony Rides, Farmland Express Train Ride, Outstanding Playground, Giant Pirate Ship Playground, Children's Wooden

Village, Children's Birthday Parties, Mining Village, Farm Market, Download Discount Coupons **Hours:** Fri.-Sun.: 10 a.m.-5 p.m. **Fee:** Adult/Kids: $7, Pony Rides: $5, Feed Cones: $1, Train Ride: $2, Mining: $6.50 **Directions**: *Northern State Pkwy., take exit 40 S. Rte. 110 S., turn Left onto Old Country Rd., .25 mi on the Right*

www.whitepostfarms.com

QUEENS

Green Meadow Farms • *73-50 Little Neck Pkwy., Floral Park, NY* • *718-470-0224* • *800-336-6233* • **Features Include:** Feeding & Petting Zoo, Cows, Sheep, Chickens, Pigs, Rabbits, Ducks, Pony Rides, Milk a Cow, Free Pumpkins in the Fall **Hours:** Sat.-Sun.: 11:30 a.m.-2:30 p.m., open to families Oct.-Nov. & May **Fee:** $9 per person **Directions:** *Northern State Pkwy. to the Grand Central Pkwy., take exit 24 Little Neck Pkwy., turn Left onto Little Neck Pkwy.* *www.visitgreenmeadowsfarm.com*

Queens County Farm Museum • **NC** • *73-50 Little Neck Pkwy., Floral Park, NY* • *718-347-3276* • **Features Include:** Circa 1697, 47-acre Farm, Working Historical Farm, Historic Farm Buildings, Greenhouse Complex, Livestock, Farm Vehicles & Implements, Planting Fields, Orchard, Herb Garden, Hay Rides, Feed Sheep & Goats, Gift Shop **Hours:** Mon.-Sun.: 10 a.m.-5 p.m. (outdoor visiting only), Year-Round **Fee:** Free Directions: *Northern State Pkwy., to the Grand Central Pkwy. W., take exit 24 Little Neck Pkwy., make a Left onto Little Neck Pkwy., drive 3 blocks to museum or Long Island Expwy. W. to exit 32 Little Neck Pkwy., make Left onto Little Neck Pkwy, drive 1.5-mi. to museum*

www.queensfarm.org

Queens Zoo • *53-51 111th St., Flushing, NY* • *718-271-1500* • **Features Include:** Endangered Spectacled Bear, Otis the Celebrity Coyote, Bald Eagle, Flemish Giant Rabbits, Hairy Highland Cows, Cashmere Goats, Ducks, Turkeys, Coyotes, Bison, Antelope, Sea Lion Pool, World's Smallest Deer, Andean Bears, Thick-Billed Parrots, Barnyard Animals, Great Plains Animals, Sandhill Cranes, Trumpeter Swans, Lynx, Puma, Owls, Native Elk **Hours:** Mon.-Sun.: 10 a.m.-4:30 p.m. **Fee:** Adults: $6, Kids 3-12: $2, Seniors: $2.25, Under 2: Free **Directions:** *I-495 Long Island Expwy., exit onto 108th St., turn Right onto 108th St., turn Right onto 52nd Ave., turn Right onto 111th St., proceed to parking lot between 54th & 55th Ave.* *www.queenszoo.com*

NEW YORK CITY

Alley Pond Environmental Center • *228-06 Northern Blvd., Douglaston* • *718-229-4000* • **Features Include:** 150 acres, Animal Care & Education Center, Small Animal Menagerie, Rabbits, Hamsters, Fowl, Doves, Turtles, Fish, Woodlands, Trails, Streams, Ponds, Aquarium, Pre-School Nature Room, Working Windmill **Hours:** Sept.-June, Mon.-Sat.: 9 a.m.-4:30 p.m., Sun.: 9 a.m.-3:30 p.m. Closed Sun. in July & Aug. **Fee:** Free

Directions: *Southern State Pkwy. or Northern State Pkwy. (Grand Central Pkwy.), take the Cross Island Pkwy. N., take exit 31E. onto Northern Blvd., Alley Pond Environmental Center will be on the Right* *www.alleypond.com*

Central Park Zoo • *830 5th Ave., NY, NY* • *212-439-6500* • Features Include: Tisch Children's Zoo, Sea Lion Pool, Polar Bears, Penguins, Puffins, Endangered Snow Leopards, Snow Monkeys, Red Pandas, Barnyard Animals, Sheep, Alpacas, Duck Pond, Tortoises, Hornbills **Hours:** Mon.-Sun.: 10 a.m.-4:30 p.m. **Fee:** Adults: $10, Kids 3-12: $5, Seniors: $4, Under 3: Free, admission includes entry to the Tisch Children's Zoo **Directions**: *I-495 Long Island Expwy., Midtown Tunnel, exit toward 3rd Ave./41st St./38th St./37th St./2nd Ave./35th St./34th St., merge onto E. 37th S., turn Right onto Park Ave., turn Left onto E. 66th St., turn Left onto 5th Ave. Mass Transit: LIRR to Penn Station, take the E, N or R train to the 5th Ave. stop, walk North 4 blocks to 64th St., or take the Lexington Ave. 6 train to 68th St./Hunter College Station, walk West 3 blocks to 5th Ave., then 4 blocks South, located on 64th St. & 5th Ave.*
www.centralparkzoo.com

Prospect Park Zoo • *450 Flatbush Ave., Brooklyn, NY* • *718-399-7339* • Features Include: Animal Lifestyles, Prairie Dogs, Wallabies, Hamadryas, Hamadryas Baboons, Red Pandas, Prairie Dogs, Kangaroos, Barbados Sheep, Pygmy Goats, Alpacas, Ducks, Butterflies, California Sea Lions, Planted Pathways, Lush Gardens, Marshes **Hours:** Mon.-Sun.: 10 a.m.-4:30 p.m. **Fee:** Adults: $6, Kids 3-12: $2, Seniors: $2.25, Under 3: Free

Directions: *Brooklyn-Queens Expwy. to Tillary St. exit, turn Left at the 2nd light onto Flatbush Ave., continue to Grand Army Plaza, go halfway around the traffic circle, continue on Flatbush Ave. to entrance on Right, no parking is available at the zoo itself but, there is street parking on Flatbush Ave.* *www.prospectparkzoo.com*

WESTCHESTER

The Wolf Conservation Center • *P.O. Box 421, South Salem, NY* • *914-763-2373*

Reservations Required • The Wolf Conservation Center is dedicated to teaching the public about wolves & their relationship to the environment. The center is open to the public for educational programs. **Features Include:** Rocky Mountain Wolves, Red Wolves, Mexican Grey Wolves, Wolves for Kids, Wolves of North America, Winter Wolves **Hours:** vary per program **Fee:** Adults: $12, Kids Under 12: $10, prices vary per program **Directions:** *I-495 Long Island Expwy., take exit 31 Cross Island Pkwy. N./ Whitestone Bridge, take exit 33 Throgs Neck Bridge, I-295 N., I-95 S., take exit 69 Garden State Pkwy. N., onto I-80 Express Ln., take exit 62, continue on New York State Thrwy. N., make a U-turn on I-87, take exit 23 Albany/Troy onto I-787 N. toward downtown Albany, continue on Rte. 787 N. for 2.1 mi.* *www.nywolf.org*

BRONX

Bronx Zoo • Wildlife Conservation Society • 2300 Southern Blvd., Bronx, NY • 718-367-1010 • **Features Include:** Largest Metropolitan Zoo in the USA, 265 acres of Parklands & Naturalistic Habitats, over 4,000 Animals, African Plains, Congo Gorilla Forest, Jungle World, Nile Crocodile, Madagascar, Tiger Mountain, Astor Court, Sea Lion Pool, Baboon Reserve, Big Bears, Children's Zoo, Himalayan Highlands, Bug Carousel, Monkey House, Mouse House, Russell B. Aitken Sea Bird Colony & Aquatic Birds, World of Darkness, Reptiles, Birds, Camel Rides **Hours:** Winter: 10 a.m.-4:30 p.m., Summer: Mon.-Fri.: 10 a.m.-5 p.m., Sat-Sun.: 10 a.m.-5:30 p.m. **Fee:** Adults: $15, Kids 3-12: $11, Seniors: $13 **Directions:** *I-495 Long Island Expwy., take exit 31N. Cross Island Pkwy., take exit 33 & merge onto I-295 N. toward New England, exit onto I-95 S., take exit 4B toward Bronx River Pkwy./Rosedale Ave., take the Cross Bronx Expwy., turn Right onto Rosedale Ave., turn Left onto E. Tremont Ave., turn Right onto Southern Blvd., the zoo will be on the Right*   *www.bronxzoo.com*

NEW JERSEY

Six Flags Wild Safari • Jackson, NJ • **Features Include:** 350-acre Wildlife Preserve, 4.5-mi. Auto Trail, Animals Walk up to your Car, Brown Bears, Guided Bus Tour, Giraffes, Elephants, Rhinoceros, Lions, Kangaroos, 1,200 Animals, Hands-On Adventure at the Exploration Station, Educational Shows Featuring Exotic Birds, Snakes & Reptiles, Capuchin Monkey, Kinkajou, Interactive Science Exhibits, Gift Shop, Café **Fee:** Wild Safari: $19, includes the Exploration Station **Directions:** *I-495 Long Island Expwy., take the Cross Island Pkwy. N., take exit 31N. toward the Whitestone Bridge I-295 N. via exit 33 toward Bronx/New England, I-295 N. becomes I-95 S./Cross Bronx Expwy., keep Right to take I-95 S. toward George Washington Bridge to New Jersey Tpke. S., take exit 7A, proceed on I-195 E. to exit 16A, then 1 mi. West on Rte. 537 to Six Flags*   *www.sixflags.com*

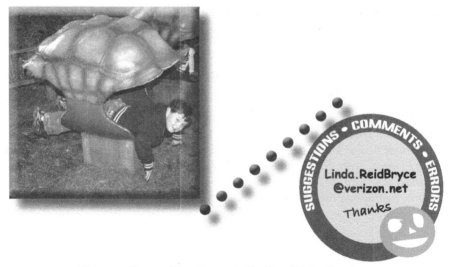

Linda.ReidBryce
@verizon.net

Thanks

NASSAU COUNTY

Bay Park • NC • *First Ave., East Rockaway, NY • 516-571-7245 •* Bay Park borders the East Rockaway Channel & Hewlett Bay. **Features Include:** 96-acre Park, Playground, Spray Pool, Bicycle & Running Paths, Outdoor Roller Rink, Picnic Area Bocce Court, Horseshoe Pit, 2 Lighted Tennis Courts, 2 Lighted Basketball Courts, Fishing Dock, Dog Run (size sensitive), sports fields require permits **Hours:** Parts of the park are open Year-Round **Fee: Free Directions:** *Southern State Pkwy. to exit 17/Hempstead Ave. S., take Hempstead Ave. to fork, take Left fork Ocean Ave. through Lynbrook & E. Rockaway to Main St. (follow park signs), make a Left onto Front St., make a Right onto Althouse Ave., make a Left onto First Ave. & follow to the park* www.nassaucountyny.gov

Bethpage State Park • NYS • *99 Quaker Meeting House Rd., Farmingdale, NY • 516-249-0701 •* **Features Include:** Playground, Biking Trails, Picnic Facilities, Hiking, Nature Trail, Playing Fields, Tennis Courts, Bridle Paths, Bethpage State Park Houses a Restaurant & Catering Facilities, Handicap Accessible **Hours:** Dawn-Dusk, Year Round **Fee: Free** entry off-season, Memorial Day-Labor Day: Sun.-Sat.: $8 Parking, Empire Pass Accepted **Directions:** *I-495 Long Island Expwy. E., take exit 44S. Seaford-Oyster Bay Expwy./Rte. 135 S., take exit 8 E. Powell Ave.* http://nysparks.state.ny.us

Cantiague Park ⊗ • NC • *1 West John St., Hicksville, NY • 516-571-7058 •* **Features Include:** Playground, Picnic Areas, Shuffleboard Courts, Bocce Court, Chess & Checker Table Boards, Miniature Golf, Ice Rink, Indoor Ice Skating Rink, Outdoor Swimming Pool Complex **Hours:** Dawn-Dusk **Fee: Free**, Non-Residents Memorial Day-Labor Day: $5 **Directions:** *I-495 Long Island Expwy., take exit 41 S. Broadway, take fork 106/107 to W. John*

St., turn Right onto West John St., Cantiague Park entrance is on the Right
www.longislandgolfnews.com/Course%20descriptions/cantiague.htm

Cedar Creek Park • *3524 Merrick Rd., Seaford, NY* • *516-571-7470* • The park is on
Seaman's Creek & the East Bay. • **Features Include:** 259-acres, Fenced-in Playground, Large
Play Structures, Outdoor Roller Rink, 2 Family Jogging/Walking Paths (1.5 & 1 mi.), **Fee:**
Free, Non-Residents Memorial Day-Labor Day: $5 **Directions:** *Northern State Pkwy., exit*
onto 135 S. Seaford Oyster-Bay Expwy., take exit 1 W. Merrick Rd. W. toward Freeport, Merge
onto Merrick Rd.
www.nassaucountyny.gov/agencies/Parks

Centennial Park • **NC** • *Centennial Ave., Roosevelt, NY* • *516-571-8695* • **Features**
Include: 2-acre Park, Picnic Tables, Playground, Table Games, Seasonal Water
Sprinklers **Hours:** Dawn-Dusk **Fee: Free Directions:** *Southern State Pkwy., take exit 21*
S. Nassau Rd., to Centennial Ave., the park is on the corner
www.nassaucountyny.gov

Christopher Morley Park • **NC** • *500 Searingtown Rd., Roslyn, NY* • *516-571-8113* •
Features Include: 98-acre Park, Nature Trails, Playground, Horseshoes, Shuffleboard,
Picnic Areas with Barbecue Equipment, 140 by 300-ft. Model Boats Basin, Fitness Trail
Farmer's Market **Hours:** Dawn-Dusk **Fee: Free Directions:** *I-495 Long Island Expwy.,*
take exit 36N., Searingtown Rd., take Searingtown Rd. N. & look for the park entrance on
the Right, about 200 yds. from the I-495
www.nassaucountyny.gov/agencies/Parks/WheretoGo/active/morley.html

Cow Meadow Park & Preserve • **NC** • *S. Main St., Freeport, NY* • *516-571-8685* • The
park is located on Freeport Creek. **Features Include:** 171-acre Park, Playground,
Hiking, Picnic Area with Barbeques, Nature Preserve, Marina, Fishing Pier, Birding
(150 varieties of birds) **Hours:** Dawn-Dusk **Fee: Free Directions:** *Southern State Pkwy.,*
take exit 22 S. Meadowbrook Pkwy., exit at M9 W. Merrick Rd., immediate turn Left onto
Mill Rd., turn Left onto S. Main St., the entrance is on the Left

Eisenhower Park ⊙ • **NC** • *1899 Hempstead Tpke., East Meadow, NY* • *516-572-*
0348, 572-0290, 572-0327, 542-0015 • *Eisenhower Recreation Center: 303-692-*
5650 • This is the largest park in Nassau County. • **Features Include:** 930-acre Park, 3
Playgrounds, Sprinkler Pool (located on the Hempstead Ave. side of the park near
Parking Field No. 2), a 2nd playground is on the Merrick Rd. side by Parking Field No.
1A, & a 3rd by the Park Blvd. side near Hempstead Tpke./Parking Field No. 4 **Hours:**
Dawn-Dusk **Fee: Free**, Non-Residents Memorial Day-Labor Day: $5 **Directions:**
Northern State Pkwy., Meadow Brook Pkwy. S., exit M3 E. Stewart Ave., make a Right
onto Stewart Ave., continue to the park *www.nassaucountyny.gov*

Grant Park • NC • *1625 Broadway, Hewlett, NY • 516-571-7821 •* Features Include: 35-acre Park, 2 Playgrounds, Spray Pool Area, Roller Rink, Ice Skating Rink, Lake Fishing, Jogging/Walking Paths, Bicycling Paths **Hours:** Dawn-Dusk **Fee:** **Free** **Directions:** *Southern State Pkwy., take exit 15S. for Corona Ave S., turn Right onto N. Corona Ave., turn slight Left toward Rockaway Pkwy., then slight Right at Rockaway Pkwy., turn Right to stay on Rockaway Ave., turn Right onto Broadway* www.nassaucountyny.gov

Hempstead Harbor Park • NC • *West Shore Rd., Port Washington, NY • 516-869-6311 •* **Features Include:** 60-acre Park, Playground, .5-mi. Harbor Beach, .5-mi. Promenade, Fishing Pier, Aerodrome for Model Planes (permit), Picnic Area, Open-Air Shelter with Picnic Tables & Grills (reservations required) **Hours:** 11:00 a.m.-Dusk (Lifeguard) **Fee:** **Free** off-season, Memorial Day-Labor Day: Resident: $15, Non-Resident: $20, NC Permit: $40 **Directions:** *Northern State Pkwy., take exit 29, Roslyn Rd. N., to West Shore Rd.*
www.nassaucountyny.gov/agencies/Parks/WhereToGo/active/hempstead.html

Hempstead Lake State Park • NYS • *Eagle Ave. & Lake Dr., W. Hempstead, NY • 516-766-1029 •* This is the largest lake in Nassau County. • **Features Include:** Playgrounds, Picnic Areas & Pavilion, Historic Hand-Carved Wooden Carousel **Hours:** Dawn-Dusk, Year-Round **Fee:** **Free** off-season, April-Oct.: $8, Empire Pass Accepted **Directions:** *Southern State Pkwy., take exit 18 Eagle Ave., keep Right at the fork, follow signs for Rockville Centre/Hempstead Lake State Park, turn Right at Eagle Ave.*
www.stateparks.com/hempstead_lake.html

Inwood Park • NC • *Bayview Ave., Inwood, NY • 516-571-7894 •* The park is surrounded by water. • **Features Include:** 16-acre Park, Playground, Water Slide, Jogging/Walking Path, Picnic Area (fee for reserved areas) **Directions:** *Southern State Pkwy., take exit 19 S., Peninsula Blvd S. to end, make a Left onto Rockerway Tpke. (large intersection), make a Right onto Burnside Ave., curves to the Left & becomes Sheridan Blvd., take Sheridan to Bayview Ave. & turn Right, continue down Bayview into the park*
www.nycgovparks.org/parks/inwoodhillpark

Jones Beach State Park ⓦ **• NYS •** *1 Ocean Pkwy., Wantagh, NY • 516-785-1600 •* **Features Include:** 6.5 mi. of Ocean Beach, Playground, 2 mi. Boardwalk, Deck Games, Miniature Golf, Picnic Tables, Food, Gift Shop, Museum/Visitor Center, **Hours:** Year-Round, Dawn-Dusk **Fee:** **Free** off-season, Memorial Day-Labor Day: $10, Weekends only until Oct.: $8, Empire Pass Accepted **Directions:** *Northern State Pkwy., take Meadowbrook Pkwy. S. or Wantagh Pkwy. S. to the park* www.jonesbeach.com

Nickerson Beach Park • NC • *880 Lido Blvd., Lido Beach, NY • 516-571-7700 •* **Features Include:** 121-acre Park, .75 mi. on the Atlantic Ocean, Fun Zone Area, Playground, Picnic Tables & Grills **Hours:** Dawn-Dusk **Fee:** **Free** off-season, May-Labor Day: Leisure Pass: $40 or Nassau County Residents: $8 per day, Non-Residents: $20 **Directions:** *Meadowbrook Pkwy., take exit M10 the Loop Pkwy., take to the end, bear Right onto Lido Blvd., continue for 2 lights, make a Left into the park* *www.nassaucountyny.gov*

North Woodmere Parks • NC • *750 Hungry Harbor Rd., Valley Stream, NY • 516-571-7800, 7801* • Features Include:
150-acre Park Surrounded by Water, Playground, Spray Pool, Picnic Area with Barbeques, Interactive Water-Play Area, Concession Stand **Hours:** Dawn-Dusk **Fee:** **Free**, Memorial Day-Labor Day Non-Residents: $5 **Directions:** *Belt Pkwy. to Rockaway Blvd., take Rockaway Blvd. (Tpke.), turn Left onto Peninsula Blvd, turn Left onto Branch Blvd., follow it around to the Right, the park entrance is on the Left* *www.nassaucountyny.gov/agencies/Parks*

Rev. Arthur Mackey Sr. Park • NC • *Lakeside Dr. & Washington Rd., Roosevelt, NY • 516-571-8692* • Features Include:
27-acre Park, Playground, Walk/Jog around the Lake, Picnic Area (large group reservations: 516-571-8692) **Hours:** Dawn-Dusk **Fee:** **Free** Directions: *Southern State Pkwy., take exit 23/Meadowbrook Rd. S. (not Meadowbrook Pkwy.), make a Right onto Washington Ave., take over the Pkwy., make a Right onto Lakeside Dr. (across from C.P. center), enter the park on the Right* *www.nassaucountyny.gov/agencies/Parks/WheretoGo/active/mackey.html*

Valley Stream • NYS • *320 Fletcher Ave., Valley Stream, NY • 516-825-4128* •
Features Include: Children's Play Areas, Horseshoes, Volleyball, Bocce Ball Courts, Nature Trails, .5-mi. 15-Station Walking Course, Picnic Areas with Tables, Fireplaces, Grills **Fee:** **Free** off-season, late May-early Sept.: $4 per car, Empire Pass Accepted **Directions:** *Southern State Pkwy., exit 15 A, exits into the park* *http://nysparks.state.ny.us/parks/info.asp?parkID=51*

Wantagh Park ⊗ • NC • *Kings Rd. & Canal Pl., Wantagh, NY • 516-571-7460* •
Features Include: 111-acre Park on Flat Creek & East Bay, Playground, 1 & 2-mi. Jogging/ Walking/Biking Paths, 2-mi. 20-Station Fitness Trail, Picnic Areas with Barbeques & Shelters, Fishing Pier, Boating, Marina, Bocce & Horseshoe Courts, Chess, Checkers **Hours:** Dawn-Dusk **Fee:** **Free**, Non-Residents Memorial Day-Labor Day: $5 **Directions:** *Southern State Pkwy., take exit 27 S. Wantagh Pkwy., take the exit for Sunrise Hwy. E., make a Right onto Wantagh Ave., to end, make a Right onto Merrick Rd., at 1st light make a Left into the park* *www.nassaucountyny.gov/agencies/Parks/WhereToGo/active/wantagh.html*

SUFFOLK COUNTY

Belmont Lake State Park • *625 Belmont Ave., W. Babylon, NY • 631-667-5055* •
This full service park is the headquarters of the Long Island State Park Region.

Features Include: Playgrounds, Boat Rentals, Fishing, Picnicking, Biking, Hiking, Horseshoes, Handicap Accessibile, Food, Nature Trail, Pavilions with Picnic Tables **Hours:** Dawn-Dusk, 7 days a week, Year-Round **Fee:** Free off-season, April-Nov.: $8, Empire Pass Accepted **Directions:** *Southern State Pkwy, exit 37 N., merge onto Belmont Ave.*   *http://nysparks.state.ny.us*

Blydenburgh County Park • SC • *Smithtown, Veteran's Memorial Hwy., Smithtown, NY • 631-854-3713 •* There are forested hills & valleys at the headwaters of the Nissequogue River, rowing & fishing on Stump Pond, casual walks through the Blydenburgh Farm & New Mill Historic District which features a grist mill. **Features Include:** 627-acre Park, Playground, Hiking, Picnicking, Freshwater Fishing, Rowboat Rentals, Rowboat Rentals: mid-May-Labor Day, use the southern (Veteran's Memorial Hwy.) entrance for these activities **Hours:** Dawn-Dusk, Year-Round **Fee:** Free off-season, Green Key Holders: $3, or Memorial Day-Labor Day: $8 **Directions:** *Northern State Pkwy. to end, slight Right onto Rte. 347/454 the main southern entrance to the park is on the North side of Veterans Memorial Hwy., opposite the H. Lee Dennison County Center in Smithtown, the northern entrance can be reached by following Rte. 347 to Brooksite Dr. N., turn Left onto New Mill Rd., follow to the park entrance at end*
www.co.suffolk.ny.us/departments/parks/Blydenburgh County Park.aspx

Captree State Park • *1 Rescue Rd., Babylon, NY• 631-669-0449 •* Captree State Park lies at the eastern tip of Jones Beach Island in the heart of the fishing grounds. Captree is noted for fishing & picnicking. **Features Include:** Playground, Picnic Tables, Fishing, Marina, Food, Family events have included: Aug.-Snapper Derby, Sept.-Fall Harvest & Seafood Festival, Oct.-I Fish New York Salt Water Clinic & South Shore Fishing Classic **Hours:** Year-Round **Fee:** Free off-season, Memorial Day-Labor Day: $10, Weekends Only Until Oct.: $8, Empire Pass Accepted **Directions:** *Southern State Pkwy, exit 40 Robert Moses Cswy. S. to park*   *www.nysparks.com*

Cedar Point County Park • SC • *East Hampton, NY • 631-852-7620 •* **Features Include:** 607-acre Park, Views of Gardiner's Bay, Playground, Rowboat Rentals, Bicycling, Picnicking, Hiking, Nature Trails, Lighthouse, Vehicle Access to the Outer Beach (with permit only), Cedar Point General Store & Snack Bar offers Sat. night family movies on the lawn behind the store & free use of recreational equipment **Hours:** Dawn-Dusk **Fee:** Free **Directions:** *Montauk Hwy. E. to Stephen Hands Path in E. Hampton, turn North, turn Right onto Northwest Rd., bear Left & continue to Alewive Brook Rd., the park entrance is 100 yds. down the road*   *www.co.suffolk.ny.us*

Hecksher Park ☺ **•** *Main St./Rte. 25A, Huntington, NY •* **Feature Include:** 3 Play-Grounds, 2 Sets of Swings, Tennis Courts, Wide-Open Fields, Shaded Picnic Tables, Quarter Mile Loop Walking Trail around the Small Lake, Ducklings, Baby Turtles, Ice

Cream Truck **Hours:** Dawn-Dusk **Fee:** Free **Directions:** *Northern State Pkwy., take exit 40 N. Rte. 110, Rte 110 becomes New York Ave., turn Right onto Prime Ave.*

Heckscher State Park • *Heckscher Pkwy., Field 1, East Islip, NY* • *631-581-2100* • *Reservations: 800-456-2267* • **Features Include:** Playgrounds, Nature Trails, Hiking, Bicycling, Great South Bay Beach Fishing, Picnic Areas & Tables, Food, Recreation Programs **Hours:** Year-Round, 7 days a week, 7 a.m.-Dusk **Fee:** Free off-season, Memorial Day-Labor Day: $10, Weekends Only until Oct.: $8, Empire Pass Accepted **Directions:** *Southern State Pkwy. E., it ends in the park*

http://nysparks.state.ny.us/parks/info.asp?parkID=153

Hither Hills • **NYS** • *50 South Fairview Ave., Montauk, NY* • *631-668-2554* • *Reservations: 800-456-2267* • **Features Include:** Playground, Horseshoe Courts, Volleyball, Tetherball, Ocean Beach, Biking, Picnic Area, Fireplaces, Tables, Hiking, Nature Trail, "Walking Dunes" of Napeague Harbor are located on the eastern boundary of the park **Hours:** Year-Round, Dawn-Dusk, 7 days a week **Fee:** Free off-season, Memorial Day-Labor Day: $10, Weekends Only until Oct.: $8, Empire Pass Accepted **Directions:** *I-495 Long Island Expwy., take exit 68, William Floyd Pkwy. S., take Sunrise Hwy. Rte. 27 E., turn Left onto 27 E., Right turn onto Birch Dr./Oak Ln., Right onto Birch St./Birch Dr., turn Left onto Old Montauk Hwy.*

http://nysparks.state.ny.us/parks/info.asp?parkId=48

Indian Island County Park • **SC** • *Cross River Dr. (Rte. 105), Riverhead, NY* • *631-852-3232* • *Camping Reservations: 631-244-7275* • The "Island" at Indian Island County Park is now connected to the mainland by a causeway composed entirely of white sands. Indian Island County Park is located at the estuarine mouth of the Peconic River. **Features Include:** 275-acre Park, Playground, Finest Picnicking in Suffolk County, Views of Flanders Bay, Picnic Tables & Grills, Hiking, Fishing **Hours:** Year-Round **Fee:** Free off-season, Green Key: $3, Non-Residents Memorial Day-Labor Day: $8 **Directions:** *I-495 Long Island Expwy., take exit 71, Right turn onto Rte. 24 at end of exit ramp, follow Rte. 24 S. through the Riverhead Traffic Circle, continue on Rte. 24 & make a Left turn at the next traffic light onto Rte. 105, follow Rte. 105 to the entrance on Right*

www.co.suffolk.ny.us/Home/departments/parks/Parks.aspx

Lake Ronkonkoma County Park • **SC** • *Smithtown Blvd. @ Lake Shore Rd., Lake Ronkonkoma, NY* • *631-854-9699* • **Features Include:** New Playground on the Shore of Lake Ronkonkoma, Bright Colors, Peaceful Setting, Fishing Pier, Handicap Accessible **Hours:** Dawn-Dusk **Directions:** *I-495 Long Island Expwy., take exit 59 toward Ocean Ave./Ronkonkoma, merge onto Expwy. Dr. S., turn Left onto Ocean Ave., continue onto Rosevale Ave., continue onto Gibbs Pond Rd., turn Right at Margaret Dr., slight Right at Steuben Blvd., take the 1st Left onto Mill Path, take the 1st Left onto Ryder Pl.*

Meschutt Beach County Park • SC • *Canal Rd. & Old North Hwy., Hampton Bays, NY • 631-852-8205* • Features Include: Playground, Picnicking, Food Concession, Stillwater Bathing Beach on the Great Peconic Bay **Directions:** *I-495 Long Island Expwy., take exit 68, William Floyd Pkwy./Co. Hwy. 46 S. toward Shirley, merge onto County Rte. 46/William Floyd Pkwy., take Rte. 27 E. Sunrise Hwy., take exit 66 (1ˢᵗ exit on East side of the Shinnecock Canal), proceed straight through intersection, make a Right turn at the stop sign, make 1ˢᵗ Left, the park entrance will be on the Right*

www.co.suffolk.ny.us • www.thebeachhuts.com

Northport Village Park ⊗ • *Main St. (Rte. 25A), Northport, NY* • Features Include: Newly Rennovated Park, Large Playground, Water Views, Dock Fishing, in Quaint Village of Northport, Picnicking Field, Benches, Tables **Hours:** Dawn-Dusk **Fee:** **Free** **Directions:** *Northern Pkwy., take exit 42 N., merge onto Deer Park Ave., merge onto Jericho Tpke. E., turn Left onto Elwood Rd., continue onto Reservoir Ave., continue onto Church St., turn Left onto Main St., the park is at the end of the street*

Orient Point • NYS • *Rte. 25, Orient Point, NY • 631-323-2440* • Features Include: 45,000 ft. of frontage on Gardiner's Bay, Playground, Beach, Nature Trails, Picnic Tables, Pavilions, Food, Biking, Fishing, Bike Rentals **Hours:** Year-Round, Dawn-Dusk **Fee:** **Free** off-season, Memorial Day-Labor Day: $10, Weekends Only Until Oct.: $8, Empire Pass Accepted **Directions:** *I-495 Long Island Expwy., take exit 73 for Old Country Rd. toward Orient/Greenport/Co. Hwy. 58, slight Left onto County Rte. 58/Old Country Rd., at Roanoke Ave. take the 2ⁿᵈ exit & stay on County Rte. 58/Old Country Rd., slight Left at Main Rd./Middle Country Rd./Rte. 25, continue to follow Main Rd./Rte. 25, turn Left at Love Ln., turn Right at County Rte. 48/Rte. 48, continue to follow County Rte. 48, continue on Main Rd./Rte. 25 E. to the park* *http://nysparks.state.ny.us/sites/info*

Raynor Beach County Park • SC • *Ronkonkoma Ave., Lake Ronkonkoma, NY • 631-854-9699* • Features Include: 2 Playgrounds, Picnic Tables & Walking Trails **Hours:** Dawn-Dusk **Fee:** **Directions:** *I-495 Long Island Expwy., take exit 60 to Ronkonkoma Ave., head North, the entrance is on the Left* *www.co.suffolk.ny.us*

Robert Moses State Park • *Fire Island National Seashore • Box 247, Babylon, NY • 631-669-0470* • Features Include: 5 mi. of Ocean Beach, Playground & Lighthouse at Field 5, Picnic Areas, Picnic Tables, 18-hole Pitch & Putt Golf Course, Food, Recreation Programs **Hours:** Dawn-Dusk, Year-Round **Fee:** **Free** off-season, Memorial Day-Labor Day: $10, Weekends Only Until Oct.: $8, Empire Pass Accepted **Directions:** *Southern State Pkwy. to Robert Moses Cswy., take exit 40 S., the park is at the western end of Fire Island* *http://nysparks.state.ny.us/parks*

FUN FAMILY

Smith Point County Park • SC • *Fire Island, Shirley, NY •* **631-852-1313** • Smith Point is Suffolk County's largest oceanfront park. **Features Include:** Playground, Food Concession, Restaurant, & Special Events in season, protective fencing around the nest sites of endangered shorebirds inhabiting the ocean & bay beaches **Hours:** Sat.-Wed.: 8:30 a.m.-6 p.m., Thurs. & Fri.: 8:30 a.m.-9 p.m. **Fee:** Free off-season, with Green Key: $5, Memorial Day-Sept.: $10 **Directions:** *I-495 Long Island Expwy., exit 68 S. William Floyd Pkwy. to end, it terminates at Fire Island*

www.co.suffolk.ny.us/Home/departments/parks/Parks.aspx

Sunken Meadow State Park ☺ • *Rte. 25A & Sunken Meadow Pkwy., Northport, NY •* **631-269-4333** • **Features Include:** 3 mi. of Beach, Playground, .75-mi. Boardwalk, Picnicking & Picnic Tables, Food, Biking, Hiking, Nature Trails, Children's Summer Theatre programs: Sat. at 2 p.m., Recreation Programs **Hours:** Year-Round, Dawn-Dusk **Fee:** Free off-season, Memorial Day-Labor Day: $10, Weekends Only Until Oct.: $8, Empire Pass Accepted **Directions:** *I-495 Long Island Expwy., take exit 53 Sunken Meadow/Sagtikos Pkwy. to the end*   *http://nysparks.state.ny.us/parks*

West Hills County Park • SC • *Sweet Hollow Rd., Melville, NY •* **Park Office: 631-854-4423** • **Stables: 631-351-9168** • **Starflower Experiences: 516-938-6152** • **Sweet Hollow Hall: 631-854-4422** • **Features Include:** Playground, Hiking, Picnicking, Nature Trails, Historic Walt Whitman Trail to Jayne's Hill (Long Island's highest peak) **Hours:** Dawn-Dusk **Fee:** Free **Directions:** *I-495 Long Island Expwy., exit 48 N. to High Hold Dr., entrance is on the Right, for hiking, take Sweet Hollow Rd. & turn Right into the North entrance*   *www.co.suffolk.ny.us/Home/departments/parks/Parks.aspx*

Wildwood • NYS • *P.O. Box 518, North Wading River Rd., Wading River, NY •* **631-929-4314** • **Reservations: 800-456-2267** • **Features Include:** 600-acre Park, Playground, Biking, Nature Trails, Fishing, Hiking, Picnic Tables, Recreation Programs, Food **Hours:** Year-Round **Fee:** Free off-season, Memorial Day-Labor Day: $10, Weekends Only until Oct.: $8, Empire Pass Accepted **Directions:** *I-495 Long Island Expwy., take exit 68, Rte. 46 N., take Rte. 25A E., turn Left onto Sound Ave., turn Left at traffic light onto Hulse Landing Rd., the park entrance is on the Right*   *http://nysparks.state.ny.us/sites/info*

SUGGESTIONS • COMMENTS • ERRORS

Linda.ReidBryce
@verizon.net

Thanks

TODDLER SPOTS

NASSAU COUNTY

Hempstead Lake State Park • NYS • *Eagle Ave. & Lake Dr., West Hempstead, NY •* ***516-766-1029*** • **Features Include:** Historic Hand-Carved Wooden Carousel Newly Restored to its Original Colors **Hours:** Dawn-Dusk, Year-Round **Fee: Free** park entry off-season, April-Oct.: $8, Empire Pass Accepted **Directions:** *Southern State Pkwy., take exit 18 Eagle Ave., keep Right at the fork, follow signs for Rockville Centre/Hempstead Lake State Park, turn Right at Eagle Ave.* www.stateparks.com/hempstead_lake.html

Roosevelt Field • *Old Country Rd. & Meadowbrook Pkwy., Garden City, NY • 516-742-8000* • **Features Include:** Children's Carousel **Hours:** Mon-Sat.: 10 a.m.-9:30 p.m., Sun: 11 a.m.-7 p.m. **Directions:** *Northern State Pkwy., take exit 31A toward Jones Beach, merge onto Meadowbrook State Pkwy. S., take exit M1E. for Old Country Rd. E. toward Westbury, merge onto Old Country Rd., the mall will be on the Right, enter near JC Penney*

SUFFOLK COUNTY

Antique Carousel • *Mitchell Park & Marina, 115 Front St., Greenport, NY • 631-477-2200* • **Features Include:** 1920s Antique Carousel, Glass Carousel Pavilion, Capture the Brass Ring & Win a Free Ride, Observation Deck, Camera Obscura, Harbor Walk, 60 Slip Marina **Hours:** Summer: 10 a.m.-9 p.m., Off-Season: Weekends & Holidays, weather permitting **Fee: Free** park entrance **Directions:** *I-495 Long Island Expwy., exit onto W. Main St./Middle Country Rd./NY-25 E. toward Riverhead, continue to follow W. Main St./NY 25 E., turn Right onto Main Rd./NY-25 E., continue to follow NY-25 E., turn Right at 3rd St., the park will be on the Left, located at Mitchell Park on Front St.*

Smith Haven Mall · *313 Smith Haven Mall, Lake Grove, NY* · *631-724-1433* · Features Include: Children's Carousel **Hours:** Mon-Sat.: 10 a.m.-9:30 p.m., Sun.: 11 a.m.-6 p.m. **Directions:** *I-495 Long Island Expwy., take exit 42 for Northern Pkwy. E. toward Hauppauge, merge onto Northern State Pkwy., take exit 45 toward Sunken Meadow Park N., merge onto Sagtikos Pkwy., continue onto Sunken Meadow Pkwy., take exit SM3E. for NY-25 E./Jericho Tpke. toward Smithtown, turn Right at Jericho Tpke./NY-25 E., continue to follow NY-25 E., turn Left onto Moriches Rd.*

BROOKLYN

Prospect Park Alliance · *95 Prospect Park W., Brooklyn, NY* · *718-965-8951* · *718-965-8999* · In 1912, master carver Charles Carmel created the sporting horses for Coney Island & in 1952 the carousel was moved near the Willink Entrance of Prospect Park. **Features Include:** Children's Carousel, Wurlitzer Band Organ, Ornamented with Brass & 1,000 Lights, Lefferts Historical House, Prospect Park Zoo, Peddle Boats on the Lake, Nature Trails, Audubon Center Café, Electric Boat Tours, Wollman Ice Skating Rink, Grand Army Plaza, Brooklyn Museum, Vanderbuilt Playground **Hours:** vary by event **Fee:** vary by event, Free parking Year-Round **Directions:** *I-495 Long Island Expwy., take the Brooklyn-Queens Expwy., exit at Tillary St., turn onto Flatbush Ave., (the Brooklyn Public Library will be on your Left & the park on your Right), pass the zoo & Lefferts Historic House on the Right, make a Right at the traffic light onto Ocean Ave., at the next major intersection (Ocean & Parkside Ave.), turn Right into the Park, take Park Dr. to the flashing light, make a Left into the Wollman Rink parking lot, follow signs to the Audubon Center, a 5-min. walk from the parking lot* www.prospectpark.org

NEW YORK CITY

Central Park Carousel · *830 5ᵗʰ Ave., NY, NY* · *212-879-0244*· Features Include: Operating Since 1871, Features the Largest Hand Carved Figures Ever Constructed, Horses are .75 the Size of an Actual Horse, Hand-Painted Horses, a Ruth Sohn Band Organ Playing Wurlitzer 150 Music **Directions:** *LIRR to Penn Station, take A, B, C, D or 1 train to 59ᵗʰ St. & Columbus Circle, walk East along 59ᵗʰ St. (Central Park S.), enter park at 6ᵗʰ Ave. entrance, follow Park Dr. N. for approx. 200 yds., carousel will be located on Left-hand side of the drive* www.centralparkcarousel.com

SUGGESTIONS · COMMENTS · ERRORS
Linda.ReidBryce
@verizon.net
Thanks

● More ● Fun ● Family ● & To Buy This Book ●

NASSAU COUNTY

Bay Park · NC · *First Ave., East Rockaway, NY · 516-571-7245* · Features Include: 96-acre Park, Spray Pool, Playground, Bicycle & Running Paths, Outdoor Roller Rink, Bocce Court, Horseshoe Pit, 9-hole Golf Course, Picnic Area **Hours:** Dawn-Dusk, Year-Round **Directions:** *Southern State Pkwy. to exit 17/Hempstead Ave. S., take Hempstead Ave. to fork Ocean Ave., take Left fork Ocean Ave. to Lynbrook & East Rockaway to Main St., follow park signs, make a Left onto Front St., make a Right onto Althouse Ave., make a Left onto First Ave. & follow to the park* www.nassaucountyny.gov

Centennial Park · NC · *Centennial Ave., Roosevelt, NY · 516-571-8695* · Features **Include:** 2-acre Park, Seasonal Water Sprinklers, Picnic Tables, Playground, Table Games **Hours:** Dawn-Dusk **Directions:** *Southern State Pkwy., take exit 21 S. Nassau Rd., to Centennial Ave., the park is on the corner* www.nassaucountyny.gov

Eisenhower Park · NC · *1899 Hempstead Tpke., East Meadow, NY· 516-572-0348, 572-0290, 572-0327, 542-0015 · Eisenhower Recreation Center: 303-692-5650* · **Features Include:** 930-acre Park, 3 Playgrounds (the largest includes a Sprinkler Pool near Parking Field No. 2), Batting Cage with 9 separate batting areas, 2-mi. Fitness Trail with 20 Fitness Stations, 18-hole Mini Golf Course with Waterfalls, Bocce Court & Tables with Inlaid Chess & Checker Boards, Horseshoe Pits **Hours:** Dawn-Dusk **Fee: Free**, Non-Residents Memorial Day-Labor Day: $5 **Directions:** *Northern State Pkwy., Meadow Brook Pkwy. S., exit M3 E. Stewart Ave., make a Right onto Stewart Ave., continue to the park* www.nassaucountyny.gov/agencies/Parks/WhereToGo/active/eisenhower.html

Grant Park · NC · *1625 Broadway, Hewlett, NY · 516-571-7821* · Features Include: 35-acre Park, 2 Playgrounds, Spray Pool Area, Roller Rink, Ice Skating Rink, Lake Fishing, Jogging/Walking Paths, Bicycling Paths **Hours:** Dawn-Dusk **Fee: Free Directions:** *Southern State Pkwy., take exit 15S. for Corona Ave S., turn Right onto N. Corona Ave., turn slight Left toward Rockaway Pkwy., then slight Right at Rockaway Pkwy., turn Right to stay on Rockaway Ave., turn Right onto Broadway* www.nassaucountyny.gov

North Woodmere Parks · NC · *750 Hungry Harbor Rd., Valley Stream, NY · 516-571-7800, 7801* · Features Include: 150-acre Park Surrounded by Water, Playground, Spray Pool, Picnic Area with Barbeques **Directions:** *Belt Pkwy. to Rockaway Blvd., take Rockaway Blvd., make Left onto Peninsula Blvd., make a Left onto Branch Blvd., follow it around to the Right, the park entrance is on the Left*
www.nassaucountyny.gov/agencies/Parks

Tree House Spray Park · *Tanner Park · Amityville, NY · 631-842-8550* · Features Include: Newly Opened, Large Splash Park **Hours:** Dawn-Dusk **Directions:** *Southern State Pkwy., exit onto Broadway, turn Left at Merrick Rd./27A E., turn Right onto Baylawn Ave., continue to Tanner Park* www.babylonbeacon.com

Water Spray Park · *Venetian Shores Park · Lindenhurst, NY · 631-893-2100* · The Beach Hut: *631-956-0066* · Features Include: Single Entry Splash Park, Raw Bar, Restaurant **Directions:** *Southern State Pkwy., take exit 39S., merge onto 231 S. Deer Park Ave. toward Babylon, turn Right onto W. Main St./27A W., turn Left onto Venetian Blvd., turn Left to stay on Venetian Blvd., go to the southern end of Granada Pkwy.*
www.lindenhurst-village.com

Wantagh Park · NC · *Kings Rd. & Canal Pl., Wantagh, NY · 516-571-7460* · Features Include: Interactive Water Play Area, "Kiddie" Pool, Training Pool, Two 30-ft. Waterslides, Olympic-Sized Main Pool, Diving Pool **Directions:** *Southern State Pkwy., take exit 27 S. Wantagh Pkwy., take the exit for Sunrise Hwy. E., make a Right onto Wantagh Ave., to end, make a Right onto Merrick Rd., at 1st light make a Left into the park*
www.nassaucountyny.gov/agencies/Parks/WhereToGo/active/wantagh.html

SUGGESTIONS · COMMENTS · ERRORS

Linda.ReidBryce
@verizon.net

Thanks

Kids Workshop 🐭 • **Home Depot** • *All Locations* • **Features Include:** How-To-Clinics, Learn New Skills, children make objects that can be used around the home **Hours:** 9 a.m.-Noon, 1ˢᵗ Sat. of each month **Fee: Free**, Kids 5-12 *www.HomeDepo.com*

1550 Old Country Rd., Riverhead , NY • 631- 284-2530
1440 Old Country Rd., Riverhead, NY • 631-369-4297
10 Gateway Blvd., Patchogue, NY • 631-286-4665
399 William Floyd Pkwy., Shirley, NY • 631-395-3764
20 Farber Dr., Bellport, NY • 631-286-0210
1881 Sunrise Hwy., Bay Shore, NY • 631-666-3800
301 South Research Pl., Central Islip , NY • 631-234-2670
475 Commack Rd., Deer Park, NY • 631-242-0215
839 New York Ave., Huntington, NY • 631-424-9170
40 Oser Ave., Hauppauge, NY • 631-478-6101
1101 Sunrise Hwy., Copiague, NY • 631-789-9200
475 Commack Rd., Deer Park, NY • 631-242-0215
1881 Sunrise Hwy., Bay Shore, NY • 631-666-3800
86 Jericho Tpke., Jericho, NY • 516-997-9595
101 Green Acres Rd., Valley Stream, NY • 516-823-0700
160 Sunrise Hwy., Freeport, NY • 516-546-6280
150 Fulton Ave., Hempstead, NY • 516-485-2067
1300-1320 Corporate Dr., Westbury, NY • 516-794-1101
111 Jericho Tpke., Syosset, NY • 516-364-4677
10 Skyline Dr., Plainview, NY • 516-806-2127
86 Jericho Tpke., Jericho, NY • 516-997-9595
172 Fulton Ave., Hempstead, NY • 516-565-3700

Build & Grow Clinics • Lowe's Home Improvement • *All Locations* • Features Include: How-To-Clinics, Learn New Skills, sign up for individual clinics on the Lowes web site. Hours: vary Fee: Free   *www.lowesbuildandgrow.com*

700 Dibblee Dr., Garden City , NY • 516-794-6531
920 South Broadway., Hicksville , NY • 516-733-7840
90 Price Pkwy., Farmingdale, NY • 631-927-3470
800 Sunrise Hwy., Bay Shore, NY • 631-954-9001
2150 Nesconset Hwy., Stony Brook , NY • 631-406-2015
2796 Rte. 112, Medford , NY • 631-207-4541

Michael's Craft Store • *All Locations* • Features Include: Demos & Events, How-To-Clinics, Learn New Skills, check the website for specifics **Hours:** vary **Fee:** many are
Free   *www.michaels.com*

1440 Old Country Rd., Riverhead, NY• 631-284-2201
346 Rte. 25A # 40, Rocky Point, NY • 631-209-2932
28 Maidstone Park Rd., East Hampton, NY • 631-324-0725
2799 Rte. 112, Medford, NY • 631-758-1835
832 Sunrise Hwy., Bay Shore, NY • 631-206-1251
50 Veterans Memorial Hwy., Commack, NY • 631-499-2408
3210 Middle Country Rd., Lake Grove, NY • 631-585-0462
350 Walt Whitman Rd, Huntington Station, NY • 631-423-0381
3675 Hempstead Tpke., Levittown, NY • 516-796-8800
3610 Long Beach Rd., Oceanside, NY • 516-855-0220
25301 Rockaway Blvd., Jamaica, NY • 516-791-1526
1280 Corporate Dr., Westbury, NY • 516-693-0420
1350 Northern Blvd., Manhasset, NY • 516-627-2875

SUGGESTIONS • COMMENTS • ERRORS

Linda.ReidBryce
@verizon.net

Thanks

7 **IN THIS SECTION**

BACK PAGES

Let
Fun Flow
Like A
River

Index

Directory of Public Libraries

The Long Island Library System offers many programs + events, including educational, cultural arts, exhibitions, performances, lecture series, summer reading programs + vacation programs.

Suffolk County Libraries: *http://www.longisland.com/library_suffolk.php*
Nassau County Libraries: *http://www.longisland.com/library_nassau.php*

Ambulance, Fire, Police: *911 (dial "O" for the operator), TTY (speech & hearing impaired) dial 711 (NY Relay)*
Adult Protective Services: *631-853-2236*
Child Abuse & Maltreatment Reporting Center: *Albany 800-342-3720*
Coalition Against Domestic Violence: *516-222-2293*
Community Resource Information: *24/7 (United Way) 211*
Electric Emergency: *800-490-0075*
Emergency Pediatric Doctors: *516-677-5437, Jericho Tpke., Syosset, NY, 5 p.m.-Midnight*
www.pmpediatrics.com
Emergency Phone: *911*
FBI: *631-501-8600*
Gas Emergency: *800-490-0045*
High Risk Individuals Lifelines: *800-345-4571*
NY Domestic Violence Hotline: *800-942-6906, en español: 800-942-6908*
NYS Terrorism Tip Line: *866-SAFE-NYS (866-723-3697)*
Poison Control Center: *800-222-1222*
Rabies Information: *631-853-3000, 631-853-555 (out of hours)*
Rape/Sexual Violence Hotline: *800-656-4673, 24 hrs.*
State Trooper Emergency Information: *112*
Suicide & Crisis Counseling: *631-751-7500*
US Coast Guard: *North Shore: 631-261-6868, South Shore: 631-878-0320*
US Secret Services: *631-293-4028*

Telephone: *All telephone numbers have a 3-digit area code, followed by a 7-digit number*
Directory Assistance: *411*
International Access Code: *011*
Country Code: *1*
Long Island Area Codes: *Nassau County: 516, Suffolk County: 631*
New York City Area Codes: *Manhattan: 212 & 646, Brooklyn, Bronx, Queens County & Staten Island: 718*
Connecticut: *203, 475, 860, & 959*
New Jersey: *201, 551, 609, 732, 848, 856, 862, 908, & 973*

Exchange Rates: *Based on $100,*
www.x-rates.com/calculator.html

Entertainment Resources:
lipulse.com
loreli.com
.com/community/guide/lihistory
gisland.com/calender_list.cfm
ngisland.com

PLEASE EVALUATE OUR BOOK

Our readers are our best helpers, so please take a moment + help us improve this book. Use this form + mail it to: Escapade Publishing, LLC, P.O. Box 361, Woodbury, NY 11797 USA, fill it out online at: www.EscapadePublishing.com, or email your comments to: LindaReidBryce@verizon.net Many thanks for your help.

OVERALL RATING

Hated It   **Loved It**

1   2   3   4   5   6   7   8   9   10

What I liked best about the presentation: _____

_____

_____

This is the chapter or information I found most useful: _____

_____

_____

Here are my suggestions for improvement: _____

_____

_____

This is what I think you should add to your book: _____

_____

_____

Additional comments: _____

_____

_____

_____

_____

_____

_____

_____

Thanks

Escapade Publishing   P.O. Box 361, Woodbury, NY 11797

MAR 2 5 2011

Order Fun Family

ONLINE ORDERS: www.EscapadePublishing.com

MAIL TO:

Escapade Publishing, LLC
P.O. Box 361
Woodbury, NY 11797

Name: _____
please print

Address: _____
please print

City: _____ State: _____ Zip: _____
please print

Tel.: _____

Email: _____
please print

Please make check payable to: Escapade Publishing, LLC

Credit Card: ☐ Visa   ☐ Master Card   ☐ AMEX   ☐ Discover

Credit Card #_____

Expiration Date:_____

Month/Year: _____ Security Code: _____

Name as it appears on your credit card:

_____
please print

Signature:_____

Fun Family, 1,100 things to do with your kids on Long Island & Beyond

Unit Price: $21.95 x Quantity_____ = Total _____

Sales Tax: **8.625%** ($1.89 per book) _____

Shipping & Handling: $3.50 for first book, $2 each additional book _____

Total Amount Due _____

Publishing

P.O. Box 361, Woodbury, NY 11797